For Mark — To commemorate the
big trip "down under" in 1991!

love Keth
Christmas 1991

THE ILLUSTRATED
WISDEN
ANTHOLOGY 1864-1989

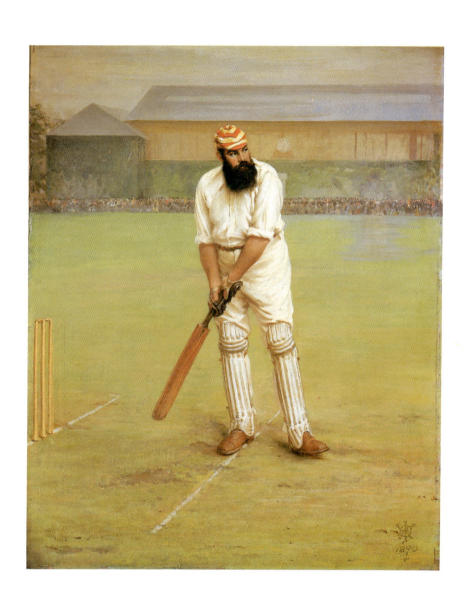

THE ILLUSTRATED
WISDEN
ANTHOLOGY 1864-1989

EDITED BY BENNY GREEN
WITH A FOREWORD BY JOHN ARLOTT

The publishers would like to thank the following collections for allowing us to reproduce their photographs:

BBC HPL: BBC Hulton Picture Library, MCC: Marylebone Cricket Club.

Page 9 MCC; 5, 10, 11, 13, 14 Bridgeman Art Library; 16 BBC HPL; 19 left Roger Mann; 19 right, 20 BBC HPL; 24, 26 Roger Mann; 28 BBC HPL; 30 top left MCC; 30 top right Bridgeman Art Library; 30 below BBC HPL; 31 top MCC; 31 below left & right, 33 Roger Mann; 35 BBC HPL; 36, 37, 40 Roger Mann; 42 MCC; 45, 46 Roger Mann; 48/49 top, 48 below BBC HPL, 49 MCC; 51 BBC HPL; 52 Roger Mann; 53 BBC HPL; 56 Wills; 59, 60 Roger Mann; 61 top Bridgeman Art Library; 61 below Roger Mann; 62 BBC HPL; 68 Wills; 69, 74, 77, 80 Roger Mann; 83 BBC HPL; 86, 90 Roger Mann; 92 MCC; 95, 96 Roger Mann; 96 top right BBC HPL; 96 below Roger Mann; 97 top BBC HPL; 97 below Photo Source; 100, 102 Roger Mann; 103 BBC HPL; 104, 106, 107, 108 Roger Mann; 109, 111 BBC HPL; 114 Roger Mann; 116 left BBC HPL; 116 right MCC; 119, 120, 121, 123, 124, 125, 128 left Roger Mann; 128 right Photo Source; 131 BBC HPL; 133 top Press Association; 133 below, 135, 137 BBC HPL; 139 Roger Mann; 143 Photo Source; 144 top Roger Mann; 144 below Press Association; 145 BBC HPL; 146 left Roger Mann; 146 right Photo Source; 149, 151 BBC HPL; 152 top left & below left Wills; 152 right Roger Mann; 154 Players; 157 top Roger Mann; 157 below, 161, 163 BBC HPL; 165 Associated Press; 166, 169, 170, 172 Roger Mann; 176, 182 left BBC HPL; 182 right, 183 Bridgeman Art Library; 184 BBC HPL; 186, 187 Roger Mann; 189, 191, 194, 195 BBC HPL; 202 Roger Mann; 205 Colorsport; 207 BBC HPL; 209 MCC; 211, 214 top Photo Source; 214 BBC HPL; 215 top Roger Mann; 215 centre Photo Source; 215 below BBC HPL; 219, 220 Roger Mann; 225, 228 BBC HPL; 223 Colorsport; 237 BBC HPL; 242 Patrick Eagar; 245, 247 BBC HPL; 249 News Chronicle; 253, 258, 259 BBC HPL; 264 Photo Source; 266 BBC HPL; 267, 269, 271, 274 Photo Source; 277 left Patrick Eagar; 277 right Photo Source; 278 Patrick Eagar; 281 BBC HPL; 282 Photo Source; 285 Roger Mann; 286 BBC HPL; 288 Photo Source; 292 BBC HPL; 295 Patrick Eagar; 298 Photo Source; 301 left Patrick Eagar; 301 right BBC HPL; 304, 305, 306, 308, 311, 316 left Patrick Eagar; 316 right BBC HPL; 317 Roger Mann; 322, 323 Patrick Eagar; 326 BBC HPL; 328 Patrick Eagar; 332 BBC HPL; 335, 340 Patrick Eagar; 342 BBC HPL; 346, 350, 353 Patrick Eagar; 356 Roger Mann; 358, 360, 363, 365, 367, 370, 372, 376, 377, 379, 383, 384 Patrick Eagar; 387 top left BBC HPL; 387 top right Patrick Eagar; 387 below left Press Association; 387 below right Patrick Eagar.

Senior Art Editor: Philip Lord
Designers: Cooper·Wilson

ANGUS & ROBERTSON PUBLISHERS

Unit 4, Eden Park, 31 Waterloo Road,
North Ryde, NSW, Australia 2113, and
16 Golden Square, London W1R 4BN,
United Kingdom

First published in Australia
by Angus & Robertson Publishers in 1988
Published by arrangement with
Macdonald & Co (Publishers) Ltd
a member of Maxwell Pergamon Publishing Corporation plc

© Macdonald & Co (Publishers) Ltd
Original *Wisden* material © John Wisden & Co Ltd
Additional material © Benny Green 1988

This book is copyright.
Apart from any fair dealing for the purposes of private study, research, criticism or review, as permitted under the Copyright Act, no part may be reproduced by any process without written permission: Inquiries should be addressed to the publishers.

Printed and bound in Great Britain by
Hazell Watson & Viney Limited
Member of BPCC plc
Aylesbury, Bucks, England
ISBN 0-207-16136-4

Contents

Foreword *6*

Introduction *8*

1864 – 1900 THE VICTORIAN AGE *12*

1900 – 1940 THE GOLDEN AGE *58*

1940 – 1963 THE POSTWAR YEARS *182*

1963 – 1988 THE MODERN ERA *274*

CRICKET RECORDS *387*

Index *394*

View of Lord's Pavilion, circa 1874
BARRAUD, HENRY (1811–1874)

FOREWORD

A CRICKET SPECIALIST is by no means automatically, nor even necessarily, the best person to write a book on cricket. For a rounded book, a writer needs a rounded outlook. Indeed, C. L. R. James in one of the best of all books on cricket *Beyond a Boundary* took as his text — "What do they know of cricket who only cricket know?"

So, while Benny Green is basically well equipped to write on the subject, he brings to it a broader vision than that of the technique or statistics of the game. Even the owner of a set of *Wisden* can be grateful for his searches through its 124 years. The late Walter Robins, all-rounder-leg-spinner for England, captain of Middlesex, used to keep *Wisden* always at his bedside and he was on the second circuit when he died. Even he, though, used to complain that he did not retain as much of it as he wished.

Here we have the result not merely of diligent research — Mr. Green has obviously been through *Wisden* critically and thoroughly many times. He also brings to his editorial duties a general experience and appreciation, that of a man who has written on humour — not always present in many writings on cricket — London life, films, television, jazz and studies of characters as widely different as Fred Astaire, P. G. Wodehouse, and George Bernard Shaw. He has, too, as his prefaces show, read widely in history — including, most importantly, social history — and literature, especially poetry. The result is the filtering of a specialist cricket annual — "the cricketer's bible" — through a cultured and literary mind, possessed of a sense of humour and, crucially, a relish of cricket and its humanity.

Cricket brings together many little worlds — those of statistics, technique, and travel among them — to such an extent that it is more than merely a game. To those who would refute that point of view one can only paraphrase C. L. R. James "what do they see of cricket who only cricket see?"

Those who know Mr. Green's four massive volumes of *Wisden Anthology* — running to over 4,000 pages — will recognize that this is an anthology of those anthologies, plus a further six years, with the bonus of generous illustration.

When the Sussex professional bowler, John Wisden, the "Little Wonder", first put together his *Cricketers' Almanack for 1864* he can have had no idea that it would become one of the outstanding sporting reference books of the world with an unbroken run down to the present. In fact, that first issue was something of a ragbag, padded out unconvincingly with the rules of bowls, quoits and knur-and-spell, the dates of the Crusades and the battles of the Wars of the Roses.

He soon found the way past such page-filling manoeuvres but it is doubtful if he saw cricket as Mr. Green does "as a microcosm of the larger life". The innovator, editor and publisher was too busy with his business to concern himself with such notions. So, as a general rule, were his successors in the editorial chair, until relatively recent times. Even the most narrowly cricket-minded of them however, perhaps inadvertently, allowed literature, imagination, even profundity, to creep in to their pages. That material Mr. Green has unearthed and preserved: he is, though, far too wise to forget that this is primarily a cricket book. The solid stuff of the game's history is all here, recorded as it happened.

What we have, in fact, is convincing evidence that cricket, especially in England, has reflected the social life of its people throughout their history ever since the middle of the last century. Thus cricket and the writing about it have been in turn Victorian, Edwardian, inter-war flux, and modern. Even the wars are obliquely recorded, nowhere more movingly than in the terse obituaries of the First World War. Until latterly, sports writing in general has not always been of a high standard but, somehow, *Wisden* has constantly contrived to print the best thinking about the game and much of literary merit — often in extremely thoughtful obituary notices.

Until recently *Wisden* was somewhat thin on illustration and, in that respect, this anthology fills a gap of which the almanack's readers must inevitably have been conscious these many years.

What comes through here is a series of attitudes: Mr. Green's enthusiasm for the game, a feeling for its history, his easy movement through all the years of *Wisden*, his anthologising sensitivity and his immense relish for the task he has carried out so efficiently as to send away his readers delighted and enriched.

JOHN ARLOTT

INTRODUCTION

AT THE END OF the 1863 season, the Sussex and United England bowler John Wisden decided to retire from the field. Now in his thirty-eighth year, he could look back to an illustrious cricketing career which had brought him wide fame as 'The Little Wonder' – a soubriquet bestowed upon him by those who marvelled at both his talents and his dimensions! Standing five feet two inches and weighing just seven stone, Wisden was, and still is, the smallest, frailest fast bowler in the history of the game. Though his batting was generally derided he did score one first-class century and also taught the art of batsmanship for a while to the pupils of Harrow school.

One of that breed of canny professionals who had never been content to strain an elbow raising their cap to the grandees who ran the English game, Wisden, even before he retired, had given ample evidence of his emergent gifts as businessman and entrepreneur. When he and a few friends, weary of the autocratic captaincy and niggardly financial habits of William Clarke, broke away from Clarke's All England to form their own rival touring side, the United England XI, it was Wisden who put the new enterprise on a business footing. And soon after this, in 1855, he went into business with Fred Lillywhite when the pair of them opened a 'cricketing and cigar business' just off Leicester Square. Those who knew their man suspected that once John Wisden retired, he would remain a dominant presence in the world of cricket. However, not even his most fervent admirers could have suspected that Wisden was now on the threshold of achieving immortality.

For some years before his retirement, he had been taking note of the fact that Lillywhite had been doing well out of an annual publication called *Lillywhite's Guide to Cricketers*. Now that he was free of playing's strains and stresses, Wisden decided that he too would produce an annual. There was only one slight drawback: He had not the remotest idea what to put into his publication.

Students of cricket history have never failed to be stupefied by the comical ineptitude of the first issue of *Wisden Cricketers' Almanack*. The year was 1864, and Wisden, never having performed previously in an editorial capacity, must have stared in sudden panic at the 112 virgin pages lying before him. Even after including details of every Gentlemen v Players match ever staged, even after resuscitating ancient scoresheets and match-cards, he found himself with little more than half an almanack. And so, like every editor who has no idea what to put into his publication, Wisden threw in anything and everything, from the results of the Boat Race and the horseracing classics to the length of the main British canals and a list of the more important battles of the Wars of the Roses. He gave the dates of foundation of several scholarly societies whose connections with cricket might best be defined as tenuous and he even paused for a few sentences to consider the constitutional implications of the trial of Charles I. What his small band of readers must have made of his daft gallimaufry has never been recorded, but the enterprise must have balanced its books, because in the following year Wisden triumphantly produced the second edition of his almanack.

INTRODUCTION

To his credit, he learned fast. Hastily dispensing with extraneous material, by 1866 he was including full scores of the previous season's important matches. In 1867 he introduced 'Births and Deaths of Cricketers' and began accepting advertisements. By the 1870 edition he was publishing brief match accounts, and two years later instituted the policy adhered to ever since of introducing the affairs of each county with a summarising essay. By 1884 when John Wisden died, the almanack bearing his name had become an intrinsic part of the English cricket season. Its yellow covers were seen on drawing-room tables and on study shelves all over the nation. Club committee rooms and private libraries purchased it, and cricketers slowly began to realise that the degree of their lasting fame might well depend on what Wisden had to say about them. To this day we can get a fairly clear statistical idea of the English game in any year simply by referring to the appropriate almanack. We can discover the initials of Oxbridge Blues, the date of birth of W. G. Grace's mother, the cost of spending a night at a respectable Turkish Baths in the Edwardian era, the home addresses of all first class umpires, where to buy a smart riding hat – in fact everything about the game of cricket from its fundamentals to its most whimsical items of arcana.

After Wisden died the reporting of matches became the chore of W. H. Knight, whose fulsome style flowered on at least one occasion into epigram, although sadly not in the pages of the almanack. In describing a match in 1877 in which Dr E. M. Grace had carried his bat for 200, with Dr A. Grace 28 not out at the close, Knight achieved profundity with 'A doctor at

John Wisden (1826–1884), Sussex and All England, at 5'2" the smallest fast bowler in history, one of the great professionals of his day and a shrewd businessman. All his considerable cricketing feats pale before his creation of the world-famous almanack which has kept his name before the public for 124 years.

INTRODUCTION

the beginning and a doctor at the end. Such is life'. The remark would no doubt have been applauded by John Wisden, who commanded a fair turn of wit himself, and could reasonably claim to have been one of the few Victorians capable of outshining Oscar Wilde. When Wilde, sent to New York in 1882 as a kind of animated sandwich board for Gilbert and Sullivan, was asked what he thought of the Atlantic Ocean, he replied that he was disappointed. When the same challenge had confronted Wisden on the 1859 American tour, he glanced at the heaving waves and observed, 'What this pitch wants is ten minutes of the heavy roller'. As for Knight, he passed on in 1880, at which point the almanack entered its golden age with the advent of the Pardon brothers.

Charles Pardon took over the editorship in 1876, died four years later and was succeeded by his brother Sydney, who remained at the helm for the next thirty-five years. Apart from being one of the sporting oracles of the age, with an encyclopaedic knowledge of billiards, racing, athletics, rowing and boxing, the younger Pardon often contributed erudite pieces to *The Times* on opera and drama. By the time he died, *Wisden* had long since become established as an indispensable event in the English year. Its arrival on the brink of each new season was – and still is – the signal for thousands of cricketers everywhere to dig out their yellowing flannels, scrape away the mud of last year's battles from their boot-studs, oil their bats and start all over again in the pursuit of cricketing excellence. When *Wisden* blooms, can spring be far behind?

In the beginning there appears to have been no records preserved of print-runs and circulation. We know that in 1936 8,500 soft-cover copies were sold, but there are no statistics for hardbacks. During the Second World War, paper rationing held down circulation but in 1947, the first year after the lifting of wartime printing restrictions, the figure had grown to

The founding of Wisden's Almanack was not the only splendid event of 1864. In the painting by Henry Garland (1854–1890) we see the hero of the Excelsior Club in a famous victory at Islington.

The Australian victory over England in The Oval test of 1882 was the first Australian triumph over a full strength English XI in England. This unparalleled disaster led to the appearance in the Sporting Times *of a mock obituary notice announcing the cremation of the body of English cricket. The Ashes were to be taken to Australia and have been fought over by the two countries ever since.*

14,000 soft-cover and 6,000 hard-back. By 1949 these impressive sales had increased to 21,500 and 10,500 respectively. By the early 1970s sales had crept up to 35,000, and in the last two decades, with the almanack entering the lists with a more competitive attitude, each year more than 40,000 copies of *Wisden* are snapped up. Those pages of the first issue have grown to over 1,200 while the original purchase price of one shilling has crept up over the years to £16.50 for a hard-back edition. Even more impressive is the value placed on a complete run of the almanack since 1864. Occasionally collections come on to the market and are eagerly bid for by Wisdenophiles prepared to fork out £10,000–£12,000 for the prize.

In short, the little annual which John Wisden thought of all those years ago has grown into one of the most prodigious publishing successes ever known. In fact, so extraordinary has its triumph been that even its detractors love it with a passion verging on the effusive. Even that most curmudgeonly of all cricketing writers, the late Roland Bowen, could scarce forbear to cheer when, in grumbling at some omission from one edition of the almanack, he conceded: 'It is always called *Wisden*, and its formal name does not really matter. It is part of cricket's mythology because claims are made for it and beliefs held about it which differ only in degree from those which the fanatical devotees of some religions make for their own revealed books'.

  This astonishing publication, part sporting statistics, part English social history, has somehow contrived to distil within its covers the sunlight of the generations. I invite the reader to now bask in that sunlight, and to seek cricketing enlightment in the absolute conviction that he will find it. For, as a notorious romantic once very nearly said, 'But soft, what light through yonder *Wisden* breaks?'

BENNY GREEN

1864 — 1900 THE VICTORIAN AGE

VICTORIAN CRICKET was very much a gentleman's world. Although by mid-century the game was a trade practised by professionals in every corner of the kingdom, the hired hand had no say in cricket's administration, nor in the formulation of its rules or etiquette. Moreover, as almost every amateur who played the game at first-class level had learned its rudiments at prep and public school, cricket in 1864 was virtually an extension of the recreational side of the more expensive forms of education. The links between classroom and dressing room were so close that many cricketing associations stretched far back into boyhood and even infancy. Reading the surviving annals of the period, we get the impression of a large, boisterous and mutually admiring family blessed by fluke of circumstance with sufficient means to play the game as regularly and seriously as the most dedicated professional.

Inevitably there were certain ideas and beliefs peripheral to public school life which found their way into the traditions of the game. Throughout the later Victorian years there was an ideal called 'manliness' which loomed large in the considerations of every gentleman. Lord Byron, who had cared deeply enough about cricket to tell white lies about his batting average at Harrow, had defined playing cricket as 'manly toil', and when, in a match between Gloucestershire and Lancashire at Old Trafford in 1887, the Gloucestershire player A. C. M. Croome gashed his throat on the pavilion railings while attempting to save a boundary, it was only to be expected that Dr W. G. Grace, exhibiting Olympian composure, should hold the wound together while messengers scoured Stretford to find a surgical needle. It was said that throughout the thirty-minute ordeal, Grace's hand never once shook, a feat possible, as one of his biographers has written, only to a man of iron nerve and fantastic stamina. But then Grace, being an amateur, would have been expected to possess those qualities.

Nowhere is the notion of cricket as a microcosm of the larger life more vividly exemplified than in its relationship with religion during this period. At this time cricket was, to millions of Englishmen, synonymous with Christianity. A century later all that survives of this curious vanity is a handful of moral concepts such as 'playing the game', 'keeping one's end up', 'keeping a straight bat' and of course, 'it's not cricket'. But at the time John Wisden launched his annual, the analogies were much more striking. Historians, being bookish men, have generally tended hopelessly to underestimate the significance of codified team games in the charter of the *Pax Britannica*, and it has been left to Sir Robert Ensor (*The Oxford History of England: Vol. 14*) to remind posterity that the development of organized games on any reckoning may stand among England's leading contributions to world culture. On a more specific level L. C. B. Seaman, not a historian given to reckless romanticism, says of the England inhabited by the Wisdens and the Lillywhites:

'Cricket was associated with religion; just as freemasons referred to God as the Great Architect of the Universe, young cricketers were taught to think of Him as the One Great Scorer, and almost to regard a Straight Bat as second in religious symbolism only to the cross of Jesus'.

Whether, in adhering to these beliefs, the Victorian sportsman was elevating a game to the eminence of a religion, or merely debasing his religion to the level of a game, it is difficult to decide. Certainly no suspicion of any such conflict ever clouded the thought of the Victorian sportsman himself, who took his cricket so seriously as to perceive no hint of blasphemy in the drawing of religious parallels such as that much-quoted of Lord Harris, who likened the cricket field to 'God's classroom'.

And so it was that, season after season the obituary columns of the sporting prints of the period overflowed with prayers of sad devotion to the Venerables and Reverends who had delivered their last sermon and struck their last boundary. There we find them, the sporting gentlemen of the cloth, blissful diocesan butterflies who, through the emergent years of John Wisden's holy book, came fluttering out, white-flannelled and buckskin-booted, from vicarage and deanery, rectory and presbytery, glebe and oratory, to play their eager part in the bizarre and endearing ritual which posterity has since identified as Muscular Christianity.

And although it is true that this marriage between Holy Writ and the Laws of Cricket was solemnised at the public schools through whose gates so many gifted amateur cricketers emerged, it should not be forgotten that

Above: A painting by Dickinson of the Gentlemen v Players match at Lord's in 1895.

Though very real distinctions existed between the gentlemen and professionals in the England team of 1896 this was one occasion (left) on which they enjoyed the same magnificent fare.

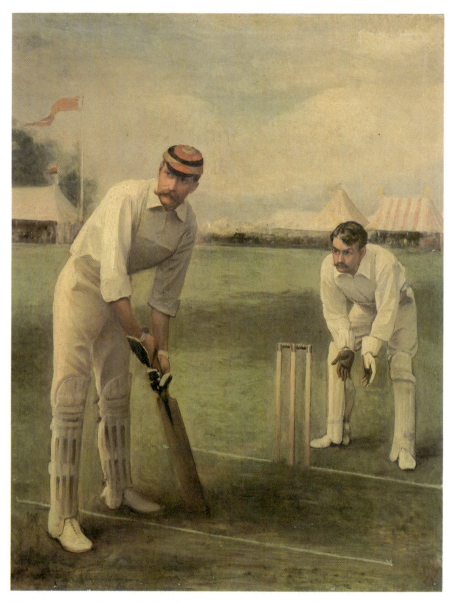

Stoddart and MacGregor — Painting by unknown artist. Two notable all-round sportsmen of the late Victorian era, both played cricket for Middlesex and England and were rugby internationals. MacGregor was capped several times for Scotland and Stoddart for England.

it was a professional, that grandiloquent wordsmith Albert Knight, who on arrival at the crease, would address a few well-chosen words to the One Great Scorer before receiving his first ball; that it was a professional, the spherical Richard Tyldesley, who once defined his scrupulous honesty as a fieldsman, 'Westhaughton Sunday School, tha knows'; that it was a professional, Ted Wainwright who once remarked to Neville Cardus on the batting of Ranjitsinhji, "E never made a Christian stroke in his life'. And if, as dullards sometimes say, Cardus was making it all up, then the religious analogy can be forgiven, for Cardus was a creative artist probing tirelessly for the apt metaphor.

The great hero of the period under discussion was, of course, William Gilbert Grace, whose life's work was a denial, couched in comic terms, of the very canons of good taste which so many non-cricketing historians appear to think was obligatory. If Grace's batting was a monument of classical orthodoxy, his etiquette was not; which is precisely why the British continue to celebrate him. Regarding the morality of Grace, there are political as well as religious overtones to be considered. Posterity would be woefully mistaken to assume that the players of the Victorian age regarded cricket as 'only a game'. But if it was not a game, and yet not quite a religion, what was it? It seems to have been a typically English compromise between a religious manifestation and an instrument of policy. Thus a century later, it remains a whimsical geo-political truth, that all a schoolboy need do to name the component parts of the old Empire is to rattle off the names of the Test-playing nations. Where cricket is today, there was the Empire yesterday; although it is a cruel irony that John Wisden's own labours in the cause of the gospel met with failure. Today cricket in the United States and Canada remains what it has been too long, a lost cause. 'Sport', writes James Morris of the British, 'was their chief spiritual export, and was to prove among their more resilient memorials. They took their cricket to Samoa and the Ionian Islands, and the Samoans and the Ionians took it up with enthusiasm'. They took it also to Australasia and South Africa, to India and the Caribbean, all of which colonial outposts figure in this section.

So both the religious and the empire-building elements of the cricket of the period flourished, and it would be an unenterprising cricket lover who could not, after studying the canon of John Wisden, produce full elevens comprised of gentlemen of the cloth and of those holding the Queen's commission. Reality may have gone a little too far by providing a cricketing parson called Parsons (J. H., of Warwickshire) but not even the wildest satirist would have dared to invent a team of army officers all from one county, even allowing for the extent to which Hampshire County Cricket Club secretaries have benefited over the years from the accidental proximity of the Aldershot garrison.

At the beginning of the period cricket was still emerging from the empirical experiments of the pioneers; by the end the game had taken on both the structure and the appearance instantly familiar to the modern eye. By 1900 Test matches were a convention, six balls an over compulsory, and there was a County Championship involving no fewer than fifteen of the seventeen county clubs known to the later twentieth century. The game, as that gifted cricketer Sir Arthur Conan Doyle (see page 146) would have said, was certainly afoot.

ETON v HARROW
Played at Lord's July 12 and 13, 1872

NEVER BEFORE WAS congregated on Lord's Ground so numerous and brilliant a company as that which on the 12th of last July crushed and crowded on to that famous cricket arena to witness the first day's play in this, "the fashionable match of the season." Every seat in the spacious grand stand had been secured several days prior to the match, and up to the close of the day preceding, applications for "seats in the stand" were continuously arriving. On "the day before the battle commenced," so extensive a use had been made of members' privileges in regard to standing room for their carriages, and so numerous had been the applications from non-members for space for their vehicles, that every available foot of the old ground set apart for carriage standing was secured; so, in order to lessen public disappointment as much as possible, the Committee caused to be inserted in the morning journals of Friday the following:

Notice.
"In consequence of the great number of applications for carriages on the part of the members, the Committee regret that they will be unable to accommodate any more visitors' carriages to-day at Lord's Ground.
By order of the Committee,
Lord's Ground, July 12   R. A. FitzGerald, Secretary, MCC"

The crush at the gates on the first day was great and lasting beyond all precedent, the crowd waiting their turn to pay and pass on to the ground extending in a line some distance up St. John's Wood Road, and for hours the "clack" "clack" of the turnstiles resounded as rapidly and as regularly as the men in the two boxes could take the admission shillings. On the Saturday, the storms that fell at mid-day doubtless deterred hundreds from visiting Lord's; but when all was over, the tell-tales notified that

On the Friday,	and	On the Saturday,
16,450 visitors had paid and passed		11,005 visitors had paid and passed
through the turnstiles		through the turnstiles

The number that paid on the Friday exceeded by nearly 3,000 those that paid on the first day of the match in 1871, and although the number paying on the second day was about 130 fewer than on the second day in '71, the aggregate number that paid on the two days

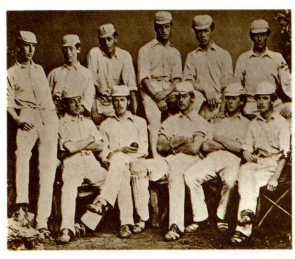

The Eton v Harrow games of the 19th century were played with great intensity and attracted huge crowds. In the 1872 match, the intensity of the game seems to have communicated itself to the crowd, judging from the letter which subsequently appeared in Bell's Life in London.

was considerably greater, and by those best qualified to ascertain, it was computed that – Club members and carriage company included – there were 38,000 visitors on Lord's Ground during the two days of the Eton and Harrow match of 1872.

Friday was a superb day for cricket and other out-door pleasures, and when about 5.30 that afternoon The Prince and Princess of Wales and Prince Arthur came on the ground, the scene at old Lord's was indeed "splendid." Grand stand, pavilion, carriages, and the space between the carriages and ropes set apart for visitors on foot were all as crowded as they possibly could be. The four-in-hand enclosure at the top end of the pavilion was packed with drags, not one of which had room for another outside passenger; and stand, drags, and carriages were all made bright and glorious by a crowd and wealth of brilliantly attired beauteous women, such as can be seen nowhere out of grumbling but glorious Old England. Some disturbance after the conclusion of the match led to the publication of the following letter in Bell's Life in London of July 19th:

"Mr Editor: The committee regret that notwithstanding all their efforts to prevent a scene of confusion at the termination of the Schools match, their efforts were frustrated by the unseemly conduct of some persons on the ground. Such scenes as those witnessed on Saturday would not occur if the partisans of both schools would assist the authorities in checking the immoderate expression of feeling at the conclusion of the match. The committee appeal to the old and young members of the two schools to assist them in future in preventing a repetition of such disorder which must inevitably end in a discontinuance of the match.

By order of the committee,
R. A. FitzGerald, Secretary, MCC"

Etonians do not reckon this match as one of the regular series: Harrovians argue that it should be so reckoned.

YORKSHIRE v NOTTINGHAMSHIRE
Played at Sheffield, May 31 and June 1, 1875

PLEASANT CRICKETING WEATHER favoured this match, wherein 274 overs were bowled for 360 runs from the bat, and nineteen of the thirty-four wickets down were bowled. The first half of the match was played out with curious equality, thus: the Yorkshiremen played a first innings of 89 runs, their highest scorer being Ulyett with 26; then Nottinghamshire played a first of 84 runs, their highest scorer being young Shrewsbury with 26. In the Yorkshiremen's innings six wickets were bowled down. In the Nottinghamshiremen's innings five wickets were bowled down; and when the first day's play ceased each side had played out one innings, the high bowling fame of each Shire having been ably maintained; the result of that day's ball work being 140 overs for 151 runs from the bat. Ulyett's 26 was chronicled as "made without giving a chance", and included three 4s, two of them fine on-drives from McIntyre; Arthur Shrewsbury's 26 included five 4s, and was reported "a fine innings".

The second day's play resulted in some good bowling by Shaw and Morley; an innings of 27 runs by Rowbotham; another 26 by young Shrewsbury; a splendidly hit innings of 61 runs by Wyld, and a very unpleasant incident. Yorkshire had played a second innings of 107 runs, setting Nottinghamshire 113 to score to win. Wyld and William Oscroft commenced to the bowling of Emmett and Hill; they had made 10 runs when the following took place as reported word for word in *Bell's Life*:

"Wyld played one of Hill's to Ullathorne at mid-off. That fielder immediately returned the ball to Pinder, the wicket keeper, who at once transferred it to Hill, the bowler. The latter seeing that Oscroft had not regained his crease, out of which he had been in the act of making ground, put down the wicket and the decision of Coward was against the batsman. Wyld accompanied Oscroft off the ground, and the Yorkshire team, after waiting some time, also made their way to the Pavilion. A delay of half-an-hour occurred during which the spectators got on the ground and gave vent to expressions indicative of a wish for the continuation of play. Of course the whole thing hangs on whether the ball was finally settled in the wicket keeper's hands or not. The Yorkshiremen aver that Pinder received a signal from Hill to shy it over, and he threw the ball with the intention of running him out. However Coward was the only one to judge, and his decision, right or wrong, should have been respected."

Old "Bell" is right, "Umpires decisions should in every case be strictly obeyed", and the two Nottinghamshire batsmen leaving the ground displayed bad taste, bad cricket, and a bad example. However, in thirty minutes Shrewsbury accompanied Wyld back to wickets, and the two hit finely; so finely that they had increased the score from 10 to 85 when Shrewsbury was smartly had at wicket for 26 another good innings. Wyld and Selby then made the score 104 when Hill bowled Wyld for 61, the largest score in the match, and a sample of free, fine, and heavy hitting that included nine 4s (six cuts). Anthony was bowled at 106, and shortly after Nottinghamshire had won by six wickets.

YORKSHIRE

First Innings

J. Hicks *c and b* Alfred Shaw	3
T. Armitage *c* Alfred Shaw *b* McIntyre	12
Andrew Greenwood *lbw b* McIntyre	1
Ephraim Lockwood *b* McIntyre	10
George Ulyett *c* Selby *b* Alfred Shaw	26
Emmett *b* McIntyre	0
R. Clayton *b* McIntyre	3
C Ullathorne *b* Alfred Shaw	14
Rowbotham *b* Alfred Shaw	8
Allen Hill *not out*	3
Pinder *b* Alfred Shaw	0
B 6, l-b 2, w 1	9
	89

Second Innings

b Alfred Shaw	1
c Daft *b* Alfred Shaw	11
c Morley *b* McIntyre	1
b Alfred Shaw	21
c Alfred Shaw *b* McIntyre	5
c Clark *b* Alfred Shaw	8
b Morley	8
hit wkt b Morley	1
b Morley	27
b Morley	0
not out	15
B 5, l-b 3, w 1	9
	107

NOTTINGHAMSHIRE

First Innings

William Oscroft *c* Pinder *b* Hill	9
F. Wyld *b* Emmett	3
Arthur Shrewsbury *b* Hill	26
Richard Daft *lbw b* Hill	6
Martin McIntyre *b* Emmett	1
J. Selby *c* Lockwood *b* Armitage	8
H. Reynolds *b* Armitage	0
Alfred Shaw *c* Pinder *b* Clayton	18
W. Clark *run out*	0
A. Anthony *b* Hill	0
Morley *not out*	0
B 6, l-b 7	13
	84

Second Innings

run out	9
b Hill	61
b Hill	26
not out	9
not out	6
b Hill	0
B 3, n-b 1	4
	115

Nottinghamshire Bowling

	Overs	Mdns	Runs	Wkts	Overs	Mdns	Runs	Wkts
A. Shaw	39	23	33	5	36	24	34	4
M. McIntyre	31	14	44	5	10	2	23	2
Morley	7	6	3	—	34.3	18	40	4
Oscroft					3	2	1	—

Yorkshire Bowling

	Overs	Mdns	Runs	Wkts	Overs	Mdns	Runs	Wkts
Hill	31.1	18	29	4	24	8	45	3
Emmett	20	12	19	2	13.1	4	21	—
Clayton	8	6	5	1	4	1	11	—
Armitage	4	—	18	2	2	—	9	—
Lockwood					5	—	12	—
Ulyett					2	—	13	—

Umpires: C. Coward and W. H. Luck.

George Pinder (1842–1903) of Yorkshire. One of the finest wicket-keepers of the 1870's, he was also a useful tail-end hitter, an occasional lob bowler and had a bizarre taste in collars and ties.

Thomas Box (1808–1876) who kept wicket for Sussex for 24 years without benefit of gloves or pads. This portrait does much to explain why, in the early 19th century, the duties of long-stop were arduous.

MIDDLESEX v NOTTINGHAMSHIRE
At Prince's, July 10, 11, 12, 1876

THIS MATCH WILL long be remembered with a saddening interest, from its connection with the awfully sudden death of poor Tom Box, who literally died in harness, the match being in full play on the third day when Box – engaged on his duties at the score board – fell from his seat and died almost instantaneously. As a Sussex County Player; as one of The Players of England against The Gentlemen; as a South v North Cricketer; as a member of Clarke's All England Eleven; as a Ground Proprietor, and in other capacities, Box had passed a long and honourable life time on the Cricket Grounds of England, taking – and holding, for a long career – front rank as a wicket-keeper and batsman. *Scores and Biographies* tells us Box commenced cricketing when a boy. We all know he continued cricketing until he was an old man, and was "playing his part" when Death, with such fearful suddenness, cut him down.

GLOUCESTERSHIRE v YORKSHIRE

Played on the Cheltenham College Ground, August 17, 18, 19, 1876

"A BEST ON record" was made by Mr W. G. Grace in this match; that is to say his 318 not out is the largest score ever hit in a County v County contest. The match was commenced at 12.30 by Mr W. G. Grace and Dr E. M. Grace starting the Gloucestershire innings to the bowling of Hill and Armitage. Dr Grace left at 29; Mr Gilbert at 160; Mr Townsend at 167; and Mr G. F. Grace at 168. Then Mr Moberley and Mr W. G. Grace stayed and hit so grandly that when "time" was up that day the Gloucestershire score stood in this form:

```
Mr W. G. Grace not out .......................216
Dr E. M. Grace caught out ......................5
Mr W. Gilbert bowled..........................40
Mr F. Townsend stumped ........................0
Mr G. F. Grace bowled..........................0
Mr W. O. Moberley not out ....................73
       Extras..................................19
                                       ─────
                             (4 wkts) 353
```

The 1877 Gloucestershire team who beat England by 5 wickets at The Oval.

On the second day rain fell, preventing play commencing until one o'clock; then the two not outs increased the score to 429 when cover point caught out Mr Moberley for 103, so many as 261 runs having been added to the score since the fall of the preceding wicket. The sixth, seventh, eighth and ninth wickets fell quickly; but Mr J. A. Bush, the last man in, was so troublesome that he and Mr W. Grace hit the score from 466 to 528 before the end came by Ulyett bowling Mr Bush for 32.

Mr W. G. Grace commenced the innings at 12.30 on the Thursday; when the innings finished, at ten minutes to four on the Friday, Mr W. G. Grace was the not out man, having made 318 out of the 528 (504 from the bat) runs scored. He was timed to have been about eight hours batting; he ran 524 times between wickets, and the hits he made were seventy-six singles, thirty 2s, twelve 3s, twenty-eight 4s (112 by fourers), three 5s, two 6s and a 7. One critic described this 318 "a wonderful innings"; and another as "played in his very best style with only one chance, and that was when he had made 201".

Mr Moberley's 103 was also highly praised, and stated to have been made by one 5, ten 4s, one 3, ten 2s and thirty-five singles.

Yorkshire hitting was commenced at 5.20 by Lockwood and Myers; the score was at 39 when Lockwood hit wicket, and play for that day ceased, Myers not out 16. On the third day they resumed play at 11.40, but at two o'clock a thunder and rain storm ended the match the Yorkshiremen having lost seven wickets and scored 127 runs, Myers (first man in) not out 46, made by excellent cricket. Emmett scored 39 by vigorous hitting, that included a cut for 5 and five 4s. The match was drawn, 294 overs having been bowled, and 655 runs scored, for the seventeen wickets down.

GLOUCESTERSHIRE

W. G. Grace Esq. *not out*	318
Dr E. M. Grace *c sub. b Armitage*	5
W. Gilbert Esq. *b Armitage*	40
F. Townsend Esq. *st Pinder b Armitage*	0
G. F. Grace Esq. *b Emmett*	0
W. O. Moberley Esq. *c Myers b Emmett*	103
R. E. Bush Esq. *c Lister b Clayton*	0
C. R. Filgate Esq. *b Clayton*	1
E. J. Taylor Esq. *run out*	1
R. F. Miles Esq. *b Clayton*	4
J. A. Bush Esq. *b Ulyett*	32
B 12, l-b 8, w 4	24
	528

YORKSHIRE

Ephraim Lockwood *hit wkt b W. Grace*	23
Matthew Myers *not out*	46
B. Lister *c J. A. Bush b Miles*	1
D. Eastwood *c W. Grace b Miles*	4
George Ulyett *c Filgate b W. Grace*	4
Emmett *b Gilbert*	39
T. Armitage *c F. Grace b Gilbert*	1
Allen Hill *run out*	6
W 3	3
	127

A. Champion, R. Clayton and Pinder did not bat.

Yorkshire Bowling

	Overs	Mdns	Runs	Wkts
Clayton	57	18	122	3
Emmett	51	18	94	2
Armitage	31	3	100	3
Ulyett	25	7	64	1
Hill	16	2	64	—
Lockwood	14	2	35	—
Eastwood	12	4	21	—
Myers	4	2	4	—

Gloucestershire Bowling

	Overs	Mdns	Runs	Wkts
Mr W. Grace	36	17	48	2
Mr F. Grace	17	7	34	—
Mr Miles	15	8	23	2
Mr Gilbert	8	5	9	2
Mr Townsend	8	—	10	—

Umpires: C. K. Pullin and another.

BATS v BROOMSTICKS

THE ABRUPT AND early termination of the match on August 15, 1877, was the cause of a fill-up-the-time match being arranged for the Gloucestershire Eleven with broomsticks, to play Eleven of Cheltenham with bats. The broomsticks made a first innings of 290 runs; of those runs

Dr E. M. Grace made 103, and Midwinter 58.

The batsmen had lost two wickets and scored 50 runs, when time was up.

CRICKET IN THE WINTER OF 1878-79

ALL ENGLAND WILL remember, with a shiver and a shudder, the long, sad, and severe winter of 1878–'79, commencing, as it did in October '78, and continuing – with more or less severity – up to the middle of May '79; and even then the cold, nipping, bronchitis creating winds seemed loth to leave the land they had so sorely stricken with distress, disease, and death. But there is no black cloud without its silver lining, and one bright spot in this dark winter was its severity and length enabled more cricket matches on the ice to be played than were ever before played in the course of one winter.

LORD HENRY NEVILL'S SIDE v MR WILLIAMS' SIDE
Played on the Ice at Eridge Castle, Kent, February 1, 1879

THE MARQUIS OF Abergavenny, with that considerate courtesy characteristic of his race, had the gates of his park thrown open to all who chose to enter and witness the grand Fete on the frozen water of the great lake at his Lordship's seat – Eridge Castle. The Marquis and a distinguished company were present, and some 2000 other visitors assembled, who appeared to heartily enjoy the jolly games of Hockey, played at one end of the lake, and cricket at the other. As to the cricket match both Captains were (as Captains should be) well in front of their men, Lord Henry Nevill taking the lead with 70, not out – pronounced by the critics "A remarkably good innings, his lordship having been frequently applauded for the dexterity he displayed, and the command he evinced over skates and bat". But Mr Williams ran a close second to his lordship, both as to skill on skates and run getting, for he scored an innings of 68 in good form; and, if it could have been played out to the pleasant end, the game would doubtless have had a most interesting finish, for when the early darkness stopped play Mr Williams' side had two wickets to fall, with only 53 runs to make to win.

LORD H. NEVILL'S SIDE

Ovenden *run out*	2
Stephenson *b* Williams	49
Mr Booty *lbw b* Simpson	27
Pullen *b* Williams	4
Lord Henry Nevill *not out*	70
Lord George Pratt *run out*	4
Mr W. W. Dickinson *run out*	9
Mr Howard *st* Stafford	26
Mr Forty *b* Stafford	0
Mr Biddlestone *st* Stafford	12
Lord G. Nevill *b* Wilson	9
B 8, l-b 2, w 6	16
	228

MR E. S. WILLIAMS' SIDE

Mr E. S. Williams b Booty	68
Mr F. W. Stone run out	24
Mr S. Culran run out	10
Mr Stafford b Booty	4
Mr Wilson run out	26
Mr F. W. Ellis run out	21
Mr A. Simpson run out	1
Mr G. Edwards b Booty	13
W. Knight not out	3
Chapman not out	6
	176

THE ENGLISH ELEVEN v THE NEW SOUTH WALES ELEVEN
Played on the Association Ground, Sydney, February 7, 8, 10, 1879

THE WEATHER WAS splendid. On the first day it was recorded there were 4000 persons present, including Lady Robinson and party. On the second day, a Saturday, and the day of disturbance, it was reported there were fully 10,000 persons present; but on the third day (Monday) there were not more than 1,500 on the ground.

The Englishmen having won choice, commenced the batting on good wickets, with Hornby and Lucas, to the bowling of Spofforth and Evans. They made a truly great stand, for, notwithstanding several bowling changes, the score was hit to 125 before the first wicket fell by Spofforth bowling Lucas for 51 – chronicled in the *The Australasian* as "A fine exhibition of cricket, he did not give a chance all through". When but 7 more runs had been added, Spofforth also bowled Hornby for 61 – stated to have been "A fine innings, with only one possible chance". Ulyett and Lord Harris then made another good stand, as they increased the score from 132 to 217 ere they were separated by Ulyett being magnificently caught out for 55 by Evans close to the pavilion fence. Touching this catch, *The Australasian* remarked, "Ulyett hit a ball from Spofforth towards the pavilion enclosure; Evans running at full speed made a kangaroo-like bound at the flying leather, and secured it with one hand. The performance of course brought down the house". With the score at 234 Evans bowled Lord Harris for "a fine innings of 41 runs". Then came a collapse, for the fifth wickets also fell at 234, the sixth at 235, the seventh at 247, the eighth at 255, the ninth at 262, and the tenth at 267. Soon after the third wicket fell Charles Bannerman had to retire from fielding, consequent on the reopening of a wound on his hand received in a previous match. It may here be stated that Hornby's 67 included seven 4s; Lucas's 51, four 4s; Ulyett's 55, seven 4s; Lord Harris's 41, four 4s; and Penn's 13, two 4s. The NSW innings was commenced by A. Bannerman and Murdoch to the bowling of Lucas and Schultz, who were subsequently relieved by Emmett and Ulyett, and in the latter's first over A. Bannerman was out for 16 (including three 4s), the score standing at 34 for that first wicket. At 37 Thompson was out, whereupon Massie faced Murdoch, and when (in a bad light) the stumps were drawn for that day the Sydney score stood at 53 for two wickets, Murdoch, not out, 28.

On the Saturday the not outs resumed their innings about noon, to the bowling of Lucas and Emmett, the former being subsequently succeeded by Ulyett, and he by Hornby, who, later on, clean bowled Massie for 38 – an innings that included four 4s. The score was at 130 when Massie was bowled. Then Emmett's bowling had a good time, inasmuch as it captured the remaining seven wickets, the innings closing for 177 runs, Murdoch having triumphantly played all through the innings, taking his bat out for 82 – described "a grand innings". Murdoch's hits were eleven 4s, three 3s, nine 2s and eleven singles. Emmett's bowling in that innings summed up 52 overs (less one ball) for 47 runs and eight wickets.

George, Lord Harris, the very model of an ancient Major-General. A dedicated Etonian who became the uncrowned king of Kentish cricket, the autocrat of St. John's Wood, Governor of Bombay and the first great colonial cricketing figure. His Lordship was born in the West Indies.

Being in a minority of 90 runs, the NSW men, in due course, "followed on", Murdoch and A. Bannerman commencing their second innings, 19 runs had been made, 10 of them by Murdoch, when an appeal to Coulthard, the Umpire, resulted in Murdoch being run out, then arose

The Disturbance

that *The Australasian* remarked would "for ever make the match memorable in the annals of New South Wales cricket". It appears that on the decision being given Murdoch (like a true cricketer) retired; whereupon arose cries of "Not Out!" – "Go back, Murdoch!" "Another Umpire!" and so on. The crowds rushed to the wickets, and, stated *The Australasian*, "rowdyism became rampant for the rest of the afternoon". The Eleven Englishmen were surrounded by a rough and excited mob, who prevented further cricket being played that day. Much was said and written on this deplorably disgraceful affair; but it is gratifying to record that all respectable portions of Australian society, and all the leading journals in the Colonies strongly condemned this outrage. *The South Australian Register* stated "The scene was a disgrace to the people", and "profound regret is expressed at the occurrence". *The Sydney Mail* remarked, "The English team soon found themselves in the centre of a surging, gesticulating, and shouting mob, and one rowdy struck Lord Harris across the body with a whip or stick". *The Australasian* stated "His Excellency, Lady Robinson, and party were present, and were pained witnesses of all that occurred", and "The disgraceful affair was the talk of the town"; furthermore, *The Australasian* headed a report with "What will they say in England!" *The South Australian Chronicle* chronicled the remark that "Such a scene had never before been witnessed on a cricket field". And in a subsequent edition, *The Australasian* added "Before the game was resumed on the Monday, Mr R. Driver (President of the Cricket Association), Mr F. H. Dangar, and others, waited upon Lord Harris, and on behalf of the cricketers of Sydney expressed their extreme regret at the disgraceful scene that took place on the Saturday. The Captain of the English team, in reply, said, "he did not place any blame on the Association, or the cricketers of Sydney, but it was an occurrence which it was impossible he could forget'".

The Sydney Morning Herald of February 27, said: – "Our English readers will be glad to learn that steps have been taken to wipe out the disgrace of the discreditable attack on Lord Harris and his cricketers. William Rigney and John Richards were recently charged at the Water Police Court with having participated in the disorder arising in consequence of Murdoch being declared out by the Umpire for the English team. Both men expressed deep regret for what had occurred, and pleaded guilty, and it was in consideration of this rather tardy contrition, and the good character given them by the police that the Bench fined them 40s., and to pay 21s. professional costs, and 5s. costs of Court. Mr Driver, who appeared for the prosecution, stated that inmates of the pavilion who had initiated the disturbance, including a well-known book-maker of Victoria who was at the time ejected, had had their fees of membership returned to them, and they would never again be admitted to the ground. The Bench referring to the kindly hospitable treatment the Australian cricketers received in England, expressed deep regret that Lord Harris and his team should have met such a disagreeable experience".

On Monday, the third day, play was resumed at 12.20. In the interim the wickets had been softened by heavy rainfalls; none made a stand but A. Bannerman who (first man in) was ninth out, the score at 49, his 20 being made by three 4s, one 2 and six singles. The tenth wicket fell with the score unaltered, so the Englishmen won by an innings and 41 runs, Emmett's bowling having taken five wickets for 21 runs, and Ulyett's three for 13 runs.

THE ENGLISH TEAM

A. N. Hornby *b* Spofforth 67
A. P. Lucas *b* Spofforth 51
George Ulyett *c* Evans *b* Spofforth 55
Lord Harris *b* Evans 41
F. Penn *c* Massie *b* Spofforth 13
A. J. Webbe *b* Evans 0
T. Emmett *c* Evans *b* Spofforth 0
V. Royle *c and b* Evans 6
C. A. Absolom *c and b* Evans 6
S. S. Schultz *c and b* Evans 5
L. Hone *not out* 4
       Extras 19
                                                267

THE NEW SOUTH WALES ELEVEN

First Innings

W. Murdoch *not out* 82
A. Bannerman *c* Royle *b* Ulyett 16
N. Thompson *c* Lucas *b* Emmett 3
H. H. Massie *b* Hornby 38
Charles Bannerman *c* F. Penn *b* Emmett 9
E. Evans *b* Emmett 5
D. Gregory *c* Ulyett *b* Emmett 4
E. Sheridan *c* Schultz *b* Emmett 0
F. Spofforth *b* Emmett 0
E. Powell *c* Hone *b* Emmett 5
E. Tindall *lbw b* Emmett 0
       Extras 15
                                               177

Second Innings

run out 10
c A. J. Webb *b* Emmett 20
c F. Penn *b* Emmett 0
b Emmett 8
c Hornby *b* Emmett 4
c Emmett *b* Ulyett 1
c A. J. Webbe *b* Ulyett 0
b Emmett 0
c A. J. Webbe *b* Ulyett 0
not out 0
c F. Penn *b* Emmett 0
       Extras 6
                                 49

The New South Wales Bowling

	Overs	Mdns	Runs	Wkts
Spofforth	44	12	93	5
Evans	38	13	62	5
Tindall	27	6	79	—
Thompson	11	4	14	—

The English Bowling

	Overs	Mdns	Runs	Wkts	Overs	Mdns	Runs	Wkts
Emmett	51.3	27	47	8	28	13	21	6
Hornby	22	13	24	1	5	2	9	—
Ulyett	17	4	44	1	22	15	13	3
Lucas	12	4	20	—				
Schultz	15	5	27	—				

Umpires: Mr E. Barton for NSW and Coulthard for England.

RUGBY v MARLBOROUGH
Played at Lord's, July 28, 29, 1886

THIS PROVED TO be one of the most interesting and well-contested of the public school matches played during the season of 1886, and it was made specially remarkable by a very singular incident which occurred late on the second afternoon. When Kitcat, the Marlborough captain, was disposed of it was discovered that Bengough, the Rugby captain, had by some oversight been allowed to go on twice at each end and in his first over from the pavilion wicket (the second time he had been on at that end) he got Kitcat caught at cover point. A long discussion ensued; but it was decided by the umpires that Kitcat, having been fairly caught, could not go in again. As a result, however, on the objection of the Marlborough captain, Bengough was not allowed to bowl another ball in

S. A. P. Kitcat, the Marlborough captain dismissed by a dastardly ploy on the part of C. W. Bengough, his opposite number in the Rugby eleven. In later years both young men represented Gloucestershire, but their eventual fates made a dramatic contrast. Kitcat died in Esher in 1942; Bengough passed on at the American outpost of Laramie, which was generally considered to be a fate worse than death.

the innings after he had completed his over. The affair gave rise to a great deal of correspondence, and indeed it was not thoroughly settled at the time whether or not the umpires had acted rightly. Of course it was a clear oversight on the part of the umpires that Bengough went on at this wrong end, but the universal opinion afterwards was that Kitcat having been fairly caught, the umpires had no option but to give him out.

On the first day Rugby won the toss and scored 163, G. H. R. Wilson, a very small cricketer, playing in capital form for 36, and W. Bowden-Smith and F. E. Gaddum showing about the best form of the others. This total of 163 was headed by Marlborough by 8 runs, S. B. Prest and F. J. Poynton playing exceedingly well for their respective scores. R. H. Wilson (fast right) bowled remarkably well at the start of the innings but did not last. Bengough, the captain, effected a remarkable catch off his own bowling in dismissing Kitcat. Going in a second time Rugby lost four wickets for 47 runs, so that the chances of the game seemed rather in favour of Marlborough, Rugby being being 39 runs ahead with six wickets to fall.

On the second day the interest in the game was maintained right up to the finish. Thanks mainly to a very finely played innings of 95 by H. Bowden-Smith, and an excellent 48 by H. C. Bradby, the total in the second innings of Rugby reached 240. Bowden-Smith's invaluable 95 included ten 4s, five 3s and six 2s. He and Bradby put on 81 during their partnership. Marlborough wanted 233 runs to win, and though the boys made an admirable and plucky attempt to save the game, their last wicket fell for 195, and so Rugby were left with a most creditable and hard-earned victory by 37 runs. On all hands it was admitted that both teams were above the average. It will be seen that in the second innings of Marlborough no fewer than eight members of the team got into double figures, Poynton's 47 being the best display of cricket on the side.

RUGBY

First Innings

Mr H. C. Bradby c Robertson b Nockolds 2
Mr R. G. Lewis b Robertson 4
Mr F. E. Gaddum c Browning b Nockolds 28
Mr G. H. R. Wilson b Nockolds 36
Mr G. F. Jackson b Sale 5
Mr W. Bowden-Smith *not out* 31
Mr R. H. Wilson b Nockolds 2
Mr C. W. Bengough b Robertson 6
Mr H. Bowden-Smith c Browning b Nockolds 21
Mr B. H. Milne b Nockolds 15
Mr A. W. Dixon b Nockolds 0
B 10, l-b 3 13

163

Second Innings

run out 48
b Nockolds 0
run out 7
b Sale 2
b Nockolds 31
c and b Nockolds 13
c Browning b Sale 3
run out 18
c Browning b Poynton 95
c Robertston b Sale 5
not out 5
B 5, l-b 5, w 3 13

240

MARLBOROUGH

First Innings

Mr F. H. Browning b R. H. Wilson 3
Mr W. L. Rowell b R. H. Wilson 1
Mr F. J. Poynton b R. H. Wilson 30
Mr S. A. P. Kitcat c and b Bengough 12
Mr F. B. Prest c Milne b R. H. Wilson 37
Mr W. W. Sale b R. H. Wilson 0
Mr H. de L. Houseman b Bengough 28
Mr H. M. Barnes *run out* 20
Mr E. M. Dawson-Thomas b Bengough 16
Mr W. H. Robertston b Bengough 7
Mr A. G. Nockolds *run out* 0
B 7, l-b 10 17

171

Second Innings

not out 15
c Milne b R. H. Wilson 20
c W. Bowden-Smith b R. H. Wilson.47
c W. Bowden-Smith b Bengough . . 27
b R. H. Wilson 35
b R. H. Wilson 10
c Bradbury b Lewis 14
b Bengough 16
st Milne b Gaddum 2
c Milne b R. H. Wilson 16
b Lewis 7
B 8, l-b 7, w 1 16

225

Marlborough Bowling

	Overs	Mdns	Runs	Wkts	Overs	Mdns	Runs	Wkts
Robertson	19	7	43	2	10	1	22	0
Nockolds	32.3	16	45	7	42	20	68	3
Dawson-Thomas	21	12	13	0	24	10	43	0
Poynton	14	8	16	0	13.2	2	22	1
Barnes	10	3	21	0	3	0	10	0
Sale	13	8	7	1	19	6	38	3
Kitcat	2	1	5	0	4	0	11	0
Houseman					6	3	13	0

Rugby Bowling

	Overs	Mdns	Runs	Wkts	Overs	Mdns	Runs	Wkts
Bengough	36	18	64	4	42	24	49	2
R. H. Wilson	40	24	50	5	64	41	72	5
Dixon	15	5	26	0	7	3	12	0
Lewis	14	9	14	0	29.1	14	36	2
Gaddum					4	2	10	1

John Briggs, the great Lancashire spin bowler and a more than useful batsman who took over 2,000 wickets with his left-arm deliveries. His career was curtailed in tragic circumstances when he fell victim to an epileptic fit while playing for England against Australia at Leeds in 1899. Although he made a brief comeback a year later, he never recovered and died at the early age of 39 in 1902. Throughout his career Briggs was a special favourite with the Old Trafford crowds.

ENGLISH TEAM v ELEVEN OF SOUTH AFRICA
Played at Cape Town, March 25, 26, 1889

THE LAST MATCH of the tour and a complete triumph for the Englishmen, who out-played their opponents at every point, and won in an innings with 202 runs to spare. It was the second eleven-a-side fixture, and was more decisively won than any other match during the trip. The South African team, with the exception of Mr Tancred could do absolutely nothing against Briggs, batsmen who had scored well in earlier matches failing dismally. The Lancashire bowler met with wonderful success, taking in all fifteen wickets for 28 runs – a worthy finish up to his brilliant exertions during the trip. Abel too, wound up in splendid form, making his third hundred during the tour. He went in first and was out seventh, scoring 120 out of 287.

ENGLISH TEAM
R. Abel b Ashley	120
G. Ulyett b Ashley	22
J. Briggs b Vintcent	6
M. Read c Hutchinson b Ashley	12
F. Hearne b Vintcent	20
H. Wood c Innes b Vintcent	59
Mr M. P. Bowden c Hutchinson b Ashley	25
Mr B. A. F. Grieve c Tancred b Ashley	14
Mr E. J. McMaster c Innes b Ashley	0
Hon. C. J. Coventry not out	1
A. J. Fothergill b Ashley	1
Extras	12
	292

ELEVEN OF SOUTH AFRICA

First Innings		Second Innings	
A. B. Tancred not out	26	b Briggs	3
A. R. Innes lbw b Fothergill	1	run out	0
A. E. Ochse run out	1	b Briggs	3
P. Hutchinson b Briggs	3	b Briggs	0
O. R. Dunell b Briggs	0	b Fothergill	5
W. H. Milton b Briggs	7	b Briggs	4
W. H. Richards c Abel b Fothergill	0	b Briggs	4
C. H. Vintcent b Briggs	4	b Briggs	9
F. Smith b Briggs	0	b Briggs	11
N. Thennissen lbw b Briggs	0	not out	2
W. H. Ashley b Briggs	1	b Briggs	0
Extras	4	Extras	2
	47		43

South African Bowling
	Overs	Mdns	Runs	Wkts
Thennissen	20	5	51	0
Innes	12	3	30	0
Ashley	43.1	18	95	7
Vintcent	42	8	88	3
Milton	6	2	16	0

English Bowling
	Overs	Mdns	Runs	Wkts	Overs	Mdns	Runs	Wkts
Fothergill	24	12	26	2	14	4	30	1
Briggs	19.1	11	17	7	14.2	5	11	8
Ulyett	4	4	0	0				

Top Left: The Rev. E. T. Drake of I. Zingari 1862.
Top Right: William Clarke's All-England XI.
Below: Robert Peel, Yorkshire and England 1857–1941.
Bottom Left: The Australian XI 1878.
Bottom Right: E. M. Grace Gloucestershire and England 1841–1911.
Bottom Far Right: K. S. Ranjitsinhji H. H. Jam Saheb of Nawanagar.

SOUTH AUSTRALIA v VICTORIA
Played at Adelaide, November 7, 9, 10, 11, 1891

VICTORIA DID NOT send by any means a representative team to Adelaide, and the result of the match was a single innings victory for South Australia with 164 runs to spare. This decisive issue was clearly due to the two great South Australian cricketers, George Giffen and J. J. Lyons. George Giffen was batting seven hours for his splendid innings of 271, and afterwards followed up his success by taking sixteen wickets for 166 runs. Including this 271, Giffen has during the past five years scored 921 runs against Victoria in seven innings. Lyons's 104 was a fine display, but he gave a couple of chances.

SOUTH AUSTRALIA
J. J. Lyons c Laver b Phillips	104
A. H. Jarvis b McLeod	2
G. Giffen c McLean b Phillips	271
H. Le Haldane c Harry b Phillips	9
H. Blinman c Harry b Phillips	32
W. F. Giffen *retired hurt*	65
J. Reedman c McLeod b Marshall	11
J. Noel c Harry b Phillips	10
C. W. Hayward lbw b Marshall	27
H. Moore c McLeod b Phillips	0
F. Jarvis *not out*	19
B 8, l-b 4	12
	562

VICTORIA

First Innings		Second Innings	
F. H. Walters b G. Giffen	50	c and b G. Giffen	0
A. N. A. Bowman lbw b G. Giffen	52	b G. Giffen	0
R. McLeod c Noel b G. Giffen	27	b G. Giffen	0
J. Harry c and b Lyons	17	b G. Giffen	19
J. McC. Blackham b G. Giffen	22	b Lyons	31
H. Stuckey b G. Giffen	7	st Haldane b G. Giffen	22
H. McLean b G. Giffen	12	st Haldane b Lyons	33
R. Carlton c Reedman b G. Giffen	16	c and b G. Giffen	16
F. Laver c Reedman b G. Giffen	5	c Scrymgour b Moore	1
J. Phillips c Hayward b G. Giffen	13	*not out*	39
H. Marshall *not out*	5	c Noel b G. Giffen	0
Extras	9	L-b	9
	235		**163**

Victoria Bowling

	Balls	Mdns	Runs	Wkts
McLeod	240	11	116	1
Laver	168	4	64	0
Marshall	225	6	96	2
Phillips	360	7	156	6
Carlton	132	1	72	0
Blackham	12	1	4	0
Harry	78	5	31	0
McLean	24	0	11	—

South Australian Bowling

	Balls	Mdns	Runs	Wkts	Overs	Mdns	Runs	Wkts
F. Jarvis	132	11	30	0	78	3	29	0
Lyons	198	12	59	1	48	0	51	2
G. Giffen	301	12	96	9	155	4	70	7
Noel	96	4	26	0				
Moore	36	2	13	0	24	1	11	1
Reedman	24	1	2	0				

George Giffen, known in his native land as "The Australian W. G. Grace; was notorious as a cricketer whose hunger for the game was at times excessive. Whenever captaining a side, he found it impossible not to put himself on to bowl, and even more impossible to take himself off. Once, when he had bowled a prodigious number of overs and conceded a prodigious number of runs, his teammates suggested it might be time for a bowling change. Giffen agreed, and put himself on at the other end.

CARDINAL MANNING died on January 14, 1892, aged eighty-three. It may seem a little strange to include Cardinal Manning's name in a cricket obituary, but inasmuch as he played for Harrow against Winchester at Lord's in 1825, in the first match that ever took place between the two schools, his claim cannot be disputed.

LEICESTERSHIRE v SURREY
Played at Leicester, August 10, 11, 1893

THE OPENING DAY'S cricket was of a startling character, a thunderstorm overnight having so seriously affected the ground that thirty-one wickets went down for 149 runs. Leicestershire at the drawing of stumps had nine wickets to fall and wanted 48 runs to win. For a little while on the second morning the result was in doubt, as half the side were out for 27 runs. At that point, however, Pougher and Hillyard became partners, and the former, playing very finely, Leicestershire won the game by five wickets. For their highly creditable victory the home side were largely indebted to Pougher's all-round cricket. In the whole match he took eleven wickets for 38 runs and scored 34 for once out. For Surrey, Richardson had a similar bowling record, taking eleven wickets for 35 runs. This was the first occasion since 1888 Leicestershire had beaten Surrey on the Aylestone Road ground.

SURREY

First Innings
R. Abel c Stocks b Woodcock 8
T. Hayward c Whiteside b Pougher 3
A. Street c Pougher b Woodcock 0
C. Baldwin c Whiteside b Woodcock 5
R. Henderson b Pougher 5
W. Brockwell b Woodcock 9
G. W. Ayres c Hillyard b Pougher 1
H. Wood c Woodcock b Pougher 2
J. W. Sharpe c Stocks b Woodcock 0
F. Smith c Finney b Pougher 0
T. Richardson not out 0
    B 1 1
                                                                   34

Second Innings
c Lorrimer b Woodcock 10
b Woodstock 0
b Pougher 4
c Lorrimer b Pougher 12
b Pougher 7
c Lorrimer b Woodcock 0
c and b Pougher 14
c Whiteside b Pougher 4
run out 1
not out 4
c Tomlin b Pougher 0
    B 7, w 1 8
                               64

LEICESTERSHIRE

First Innings
J. Holland c Ayres b Richardson 10
Finney c Smith b Sharpe 5
Chapman b Sharpe 1
W. Tomlin c and b Richardson 0
A. D. Pougher b Richardson 10
Mr D. Lorrimer b Sharpe 0
Mr G. W. Hillyard c Abel b Richardson 0
Mr C. Marriott b Richardson 8
A. Woodcock c Smith b Richardson 1
Mr F. W. Stocks c Smith b Sharpe 2
J. P. Whiteside not out 0
    B 2, l-b 4 6
                                                                  48

Second Innings
c Baldwin b Richardson 4
c Brockwell b Richardson 4
c Brockwell b Richardson 13
not out 24
c Hayward b Richardson 0
not out 9
b Richardson 1
    W 1 1
                                 56

Leicestershire Bowling

	Overs	Mdns	Runs	Wkts	Overs	Mdns	Runs	Wkts
Woodcock	12	7	18	5	19	7	33	3
Pougher	12	6	15	5	19.4	11	23	6
Hillyard					1	1	0	0

Surrey Bowling

	Overs	Mdns	Runs	Wkts	Overs	Mdns	Runs	Wkts
Richardson	11	6	18	6	11	5	17	5
Sharpe	11	3	19	4	9	2	35	0
Brockwell					1.2	0	3	0

CANON CAZENOVE, who died in August, 1893, while playing lawn tennis, performed an extraordinary bowling feat at Oxford on May 5, 6, 1853. Playing for the Undergraduates of Oxford against Oxfordshire, he obtained no fewer than sixteen wickets, securing all the ten in the first innings of the county, and six in the second. Five of the ten wickets were taken in one over, the umpire inadvertently allowing an extra ball. Canon Cazenove was born at Clapton in Middlesex on February 12, 1833, and played for Oxford against Cambridge at Lord's in 1851 and 1852. He was a round-arm bowler of medium pace.

Gloucestershire XI 1893. Top: J. Smith (scorer), F. H. Champain, E. C. Wright, A. G. Richardson, W. S. Brown, H. Wrathall, F. G. Roberts. Bottom: W. M. Hemingway, C. L. Townsend, W. G. Grace, G. L. Jessop, J. Board.

GLOUCESTERSHIRE IN 1893

IN THE LATTER part of the summer a remarkable young player was introduced into the eleven in the person of Mr C. L. Townsend, a son of Mr Frank Townsend, one of the old school of Gloucestershire cricketers. Both he and Mr W. G. Grace, jun. – the eldest son of the champion – while still at Clifton College, made their first appearance in county cricket, in the match against Middlesex on their own school ground, and for Mr Townsend there is unquestionably a future as a bowler. His first experience was not altogether satisfactory, as, on a good wicket and with indifferent support from the field, he met with severe treatment; but in the four games in which he took part he succeeded in taking twenty-one wickets for just over 23 runs each. For one so young – he is only seventeen and looks at least two years younger – he bowls with admirable judgment and is able to make the ball break either way. He, however, relied mainly on his leg break, and this he bowled with quite as much success as could be expected. At first sight this young bowler, with his slight build, gives the impression of being scarcely strong enough to stand the fatigue of a three days' match, but yet in his first outing in the field he sent down no fewer than seventy overs. There is little doubt that in Mr Townsend Gloucestershire have discovered a bowler of considerable natural talent, and his career will be followed with close interest.

Turning to the batting it is pleasant to again find Mr W. G. Grace occupying the post of honour. Though not so successful in county cricket as in 1892, when he scored 802 runs with an average of 36, the champion had a good season, his aggregate being 711, and his average 28. Satisfactory as these figures are, they do not convey an adequate impression of the splendidly consistent batting of the famous cricketer. He had a big share in the victories over Kent and Middlesex, scoring 46 and 42 not out against the former county, and 96 and 8 at Lord's. Against the Surrey bowlers at The Oval he carried his bat through the first innings for 61, and later in the season he played a fine innings of 75 in the return with Sussex, and scored 68 against Middlesex. Outside the county matches Mr Grace was even more successful, the admirable form he displayed in the many encounters with the Australians being quite a feature of a busy season. Playing for the Marylebone Club against Kent he made 128, this being his best score in important cricket in England since 1890. July, with some soft wickets, was a rather bad month for Mr Grace, but while the grounds

C. L. Townsend in 1895, aged 18, took 16 Nottinghamshire wickets in the one match with his enormous leg-breaks.

W. G. Grace Junior, a goodish cricketer who never stepped out of the shadow of his father. He died aged 30 after an appendix operation.

were hard and firm he fully held his own with the best of the younger batsmen. Altogether in first-class cricket Mr Grace scored 1,609 runs with an average of 35.34, a remarkable record for a player who was at the zenith of his fame when most of his present-day rivals were still at school.

With regard to the other Gloucestershire batsmen a few words will suffice. Mr Ferris made a great advance, his aggregate rising from 350 to 687, and his average from 17.19 to 22.5, and he had the distinction of playing the only three-figure innings obtained for the county, scoring 106 against Sussex at Brighton. Mr Kitcat confirmed the good impression he made in the previous year, but Mr Rice was a disappointment. Against Nottinghamshire he scored 34 and 64 not out – an achievement that practically secured for him his Blue at Oxford – but afterwards he failed to maintain the admirable form he displayed in 1892. It may, however, be assumed that in the case of a young batsman with most approved methods, the falling off is merely temporary. A left-handed batsman and excellent field made his appearance in the county ranks in the person of Mr G. S. De Winton, who was seen at his best in an innings of 80 against Somerset at Cheltenham. Mr Radcliffe had a poor season, and Painter, though he played three or four brilliant innings, had to be content with modest results. During the latter part of the season, Mr W. H. Brain, of Oxford, a brother of Mr J. H. Brain, the old Gloucestershire cricketer, kept wicket, and acquitted himself with great credit. There is little further that need be said with regard to Gloucestershire cricket, but it is necessary to remark that the team did not work harmoniously together. It was quite an open secret that a spirit of mutiny prevailed, and matters went so far that at one point a crisis seemed imminent. Happily, however, good counsels prevailed, and the difficulties that had arisen were smoothed over. There is no doubt that, owing to the cause indicated, Gloucestershire suffered last season, and it is to be hoped that in future a better state of affairs will exist. In the latter part of the season. Mr W. G. Grace wrote to the Committee expressing his desire to give up the captaincy of the eleven, but in the autumn he withdrew his resignation.

THE REV. JAMES PYCROFT, who died on March 10, 1895, at Brighton, aged eighty-two, will be remembered for all time as the author of *The Cricket Field*. In the course of his long life he wrote much about the game to which he was devoted, but *The Cricket Field* is emphatically the work upon which his fame will rest. A good cricketer himself in his Oxford days, he played at Lord's in 1836 in the second of the long series of matches between the two Universities, among those who took part in the same game being Lord Bessborough – then the Hon. Frederick Ponsonby – Mr R. Broughton and Mr C. G. Taylor. The University match was first played in 1792, and became an annual fixture in 1838. Knowing cricket thoroughly, Mr Pycroft was certainly one of the best writers on the game. He was, if we may judge from some of his works, a little inclined to think that the great men of the Fuller Pilch and Alfred Mynn era were superior to any of their successors, but this perhaps unconscious prejudice in favour of the cricketers of his young days does not make his pages any the less entertaining. He was for about thirty years on the committee of the Sussex County Club, and retained to the last a lively interest in Sussex cricket.

ENGLISH TEAM v SOUTH AUSTRALIA
Played at Adelaide, March 28, 29, 30, April 1, 2, 1895

THE FINAL MATCH of the tour was a sensational one indeed, the Englishmen running up the huge total of 609 and winning by ten wickets. In face of a score of 397 in South Australia's first innings this was a very fine performance. Albert Ward was batting six hours and three-quarters for his 219 – the second highest score obtained for the English team during their trip. Though not entirely free from luck it was a great innings. Equally good was the performance of young Clement Hill, the South Australian colt, who completed his eighteenth year on the first day of the match. The finish of the game was exciting, Brockwell and Ford just hitting off the runs in time to win. South Australia lost A. H. Jarvis's services after the first day, the famous wicket-keeper being thrown out of a trap and so much hurt that he could not play any more. George Giffen's analysis in the first innings of the Englishmen is probably unprecedented in first-class cricket. He was on nearly all through the innings, and had 309 runs hit from him.

George Giffen, possessor of an unenviable record.
The first Australian bowler ever to concede more than 300 runs in an innings.

SOUTH AUSTRALIA

First Innings

J. J. Lyons c Peel b Richardson	6
A. H. Jarvis b Richardson	5
G. Giffen c MacLaren b Briggs	51
J. Darling b Richardson	15
J. Reedman run out	46
H. Dyer b Briggs	0
H. Blinman c Peel b Richardson	3
C. Hill not out	150
W. F. Giffen b Lockwood	81
F. Jarvis b Richardson	32
E. Jones c Ward b Brockwell	1
L-b 4, n-b 1, w 3	8
	397

Second Innings

c Philipson b Peel	32
absent hurt	0
c Brown b Richardson	27
b Briggs	36
b Peel	1
not out	40
c Philipson b Richardson	17
c Philipson b Richardson	56
c Philipson b Richardson	4
b Briggs	27
b Lockwood	3
B 5, l-b 4, n-b 1, w 2	12
	255

ENGLAND

First Innings

W. Brockwell lbw b G. Giffen	35
A. Ward lbw b G. Giffen	219
J. T. Brown b G. Giffen	101
Mr A. C. MacLaren c and b G. Giffen	18
Mr F. G. J. Ford run out	106
R. Peel b Lyons	57
W. Lockwood run out	23
J. Briggs not out	27
Mr J. H. Gay c Hill b Lyons	1
Mr H. Phillipson c Reedman b G. Giffen	2
T. Richardson c and b Lyons	0
B 9, l-b 4	13
	609

Second Innings

not out	24
not out	18
B 3	3
	45

English Bowling

	Overs	Mdns	Runs	Wkts	Overs	Mdns	Runs	Wkts
Richardson	37	8	148	5	44	17	91	4
Peel	26	7	62	0	29	7	62	2
Briggs	32	6	92	2	17	3	54	2
Lockwood	12	1	43	1	11.5	1	36	1
Brockwell	10.4	3	25	1				
Ford	6	1	19	0				

South Australian Bowling

	Overs	Mdns	Runs	Wkts	Overs	Mdns	Runs	Wkts
Jones	37	10	84	0	2	0	19	0
F. Jarvis	21	2	85	0	1.4	0	10	0
G. Giffen	87	12	309	5	4	0	13	0
Lyons	21.1	6	80	3				
Reedman	15	5	38	0				

SOMERSET v LANCASHIRE
Played at Taunton, July 15, 16, 17, 1895

SEVERE AS HAD been their beating in the previous match, Somerset fared even worse in this engagement, Lancashire defeating them by an innings and 452 runs – one of the most decisive wins on record. The match was made memorable for all time by the wonderful innings of 424 by A. C. MacLaren, who thus surpassed all previous individual scores in first-class matches. The previous highest was, of course, W. G. Grace's 344 in 1876. Only once had MacLaren's score been beaten in any kind of cricket, A. E. Stoddart making 485 for the Hampstead Club in 1886. MacLaren, who went in first and was seventh out at 792, was batting for seven hours and fifty minutes, and only gave two chances, the first at 262. His score comprised one 6, eleven 3s, thirty seven 2s, and sixty three singles. Paul, who played a fine innings of 177, assisted MacLaren to put on 363 runs in three hours and ten minutes for the second wicket – a partnership which has only been surpassed in first-class cricket by the 398 by Shrewsbury and Gunn for Nottinghamshire against Sussex in 1890. Lancashire's innings only lasted eight hours, the total of 801 being the highest ever obtained in a county match.

LANCASHIRE

Mr A. C. MacLaren c Fowler b Gamlin	424
A. Ward c R. Palairet b Tyler	64
A. Paul c Gamlin b L. Palairet	177
A. Hallam c Fowler b L. Palairet	6
Mr C. H. Benton c and b Fowler	43
F. H. Sugg c Wickham b Woods	41
A. Tinsley c Gamlin b Woods	0
G. R. Baker st Wickham b L. Palairet	23
J. Briggs not out	9
C. Smith c Trask b L. Palairet	0
A. Mold c R. Palairet b Gamlin	0
B 9, l-b 4, w 1	14
	801

SOMERSET

First Innings

Mr L. C. H. Palairet b Briggs	30
Mr G. Fowler c sub b Hallam	39
Mr R. C. N. Palairet c Hallam b Mold	2
Mr H. T. Stanley c Smith b Briggs	8
Mr R. B. Porch run out	18
Mr S. M. J. Woods c Smith b Mold	11
Dr J. E. Trask c Ward b Mold	11
Rev. A. P. Wickham b Mold	3
E. J. Tyler not out	15
Mr E. W. Bartlett b Briggs	4
Gamlin st Smith b Briggs	0
L-b 2	2
	143

Second Innings

b Mold	4
c Maclaren b Mold	46
st Smith b Briggs	7
c Smith b Mold	12
c MacLaren b Mold	1
b Briggs	55
c and b Mold	26
not out	0
b Briggs	41
c Mold b Briggs	6
hit wkt b Briggs	0
L-b 8	8
	206

Somerset Bowling

	Overs	Mdns	Runs	Wkts
Tyler	59	5	212	1
Woods	46	5	163	2
L. Palairet	44	10	133	4
Gamlin	26	8	100	2
Fowler	23	5	97	1
R. Palairet	11	3	41	0
Trask	2	0	9	0
Porch	5	3	16	0
Bartlett	6	0	16	0

Lancashire Bowling

	Overs	Mdns	Runs	Wkts	Overs	Mdns	Runs	Wkts
Briggs	37.3	15	59	4	37	17	78	5
Mold	35	15	75	4	33	11	76	5
Hallam	2	1	7	1	8	2	19	0
Baker					5	8	25	0

Umpires: J. Lillywhite and E. Goodyear.

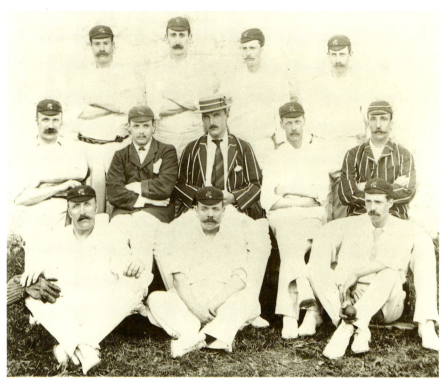

Archie MacLaren, leading from the front in a straw boater. His innings against Somerset in the County Championship caused a sensation throughout the cricket world. Although nearly a century has passed since his great feat, the record score still stands.

NOTTINGHAMSHIRE v GLOUCESTERSHIRE
Played at Nottingham, July 25, 26, 27, 1895

WITH SHREWSBURY KEPT away by an injured hand, the Nottinghamshire eleven were fairly outplayed on a slow wicket, and before half-past three on the third afternoon Gloucestershire won the match in the easiest fashion by 135 runs. This decisive result was clearly brought about by Townsend, who actually took sixteen wickets (eight in each innings) at a cost of only 122 runs. On the slow ground he had the Nottinghamshire batsmen at his mercy. Gunn in particular being quite at fault in trying to play him. Townsend, Hemingway, and Wrathall all batted well on the second day, but the best innings in the match was Jessop's 55, a brilliant display which lasted just thirty-five minutes. Only 61 runs were scored while he was in.

GLOUCESTERSHIRE

First Innings

Mr W. G. Grace c Gregory b Attewell	4
Mr R. W. Rice b Gregory	1
Mr W. McG. Hemingway b Flowers	23
Mr J. J. Ferris c sub b Flowers	13
H. Wrathall b Gregory	15
Mr C. L. Townsend ht wkt b Flowers	6
Mr G. L. Jessop c Gunn b Attewell	55
J. H. Board c and b Attewell	21
Mr S. De Winton c Wilkinson b Gregory	24
Mr F. C. Bracher c Sub b Gregory	3
F. G. Roberts not out	2
B 3, l-b 3	6
	173

Second Innings

c and b Attewell	14
c Flowers b Attewell	6
b Daft	45
c Bagguley b Attewell	2
c Bagguley b Flowers	41
c Lowe b Attewell	41
c and b Flowers	1
lbw b Gregory	16
c Wilkinson b Flowers	5
b Attewell	13
not out	2
B 2	2
	188

NOTTINGHAMSHIRE

First Innings

W. Flowers hit wkt b Townsend	2
R. Bagguley b Townsend	27
W. Gunn c Grace b Townsend	5
Mr J. A. Dixon b Roberts	19
Mr C. W. Wright st Board b Townsend	7
Mr A. C. Jones c Jessop b Townsend	13
W. Attewell c Ferris b Townsend	1
H. B. Daft c Board b Townsend	1
Mr W. H. G. Lowe not out	15
A. Wilkinson st Board b Townsend	12
D. Gregory b Jessop	0
B 11, n-b 7	18
	120

Second Innings

b Ferris	24
b Townsend	11
c Wrathall b Townsend	10
c Grace b Townsend	16
c Board b Townsend	2
b Townsend	0
c Wrathall b Ferris	11
st Board b Townsend	2
b Townsend	14
not out	11
b Townsend	0
B 3, n-b 2	5
	106

Nottinghamshire Bowling

	Overs	Mdns	Runs	Wkts	Overs	Mdns	Runs	Wkts
Attewell	40	18	71	3	13.2	11	63	5
Gregory	15.3	30	48	4	21	3	41	1
Flowers	24	5	48	3	18	2	56	3
Daft					11	4	22	1
Dixon					2	1	1	0
Wilkinson					1	0	3	0

Gloucestershire Bowling

	Overs	Mdns	Runs	Wkts	Overs	Mdns	Runs	Wkts
Townsend	37	12	52	8	21.1	2	70	8
Jessop	14	6	22	1	7	5	6	0
Ferris	4	1	9	0	12	2	25	2
Roberts	19	9	19	1				

Umpires: Hay and Collishaw.

W. G. Grace converses with F. S. Jackson. Jackson had been Churchill's fagmaster at Harrow. From such exalted beginnings he moved on to captain England at cricket, command a West Yorkshire infantry regiment, govern Bengal and chair the Conservative Party.

YORKSHIRE v AN ENGLAND ELEVEN
Played at Scarborough, September 5, 6, 1895

IT HAD BEEN intended that the concluding fixture of the Scarborough Festival should be between elevens of Yorkshire and Lancashire, but the first match at Hastings, by taking some of the Lancashire men away, rendered the arrangement impossible. As an alternative an England team was got together to oppose Yorkshire, and though by no means representative it proved quite strong enough for the task in hand, the county suffering a severe defeat by nine wickets. A very disagreeable incident marred the pleasure of a game that presented few features of interest. Owing to the state of the ground a start could not be made at the ordinary time on the first day, and a section of the crowd indulged in a most unseemly demonstration, such insulting remarks being addressed to Mr H. T. Hewett that that gentleman – who was to have captained the England team – retired from the match after fielding till the luncheon interval. We think he acted unwisely, but he was much provoked.

YORKSHIRE

First Innings

Mr F. S. Jackson *lbw b* Mead	9
J. T. Brown *b* Mead	1
J. W. Tunnicliffe *c* Jones *b* Hearne	35
R. Moorhouse *b* Hearne	8
E. Wainwright *c and b* Mead	6
R. Peel *b* Hearne	1
Lord Hawke *c* Tyler *b* Mead	5
J. Mounsey *run out*	0
G. H. Hirst *b* Mead	4
Haigh *c* MacLaren *b* Hearne	0
D. Hunter *not out*	0
B 11	11
	80

Second Innings

b Spofforth	8
c Mead *b* Spofforth	6
c Tyler *b* Mead	3
b Mead	9
c Spofforth *b* Mead	0
c Woodcock *b* Spofforth	0
c and b Mead	4
b Mead	13
c Baker *b* Mead	9
c Tyler *b* Spofforth	18
not out	7
B 4, l-b 1	5
	82

AN ENGLAND ELEVEN

First Innings

Mr A. C. MacLaren *c and b* Haigh	24
Mr A. O. Jones *c* Tunnicliff *b* Peel	2
A. Hearne *c* Peel *b* Jackson	44
W. G. Quaife *c and b* Jackson	19
Mr G. L. Jessop *st* Hunter *b* Jackson	4
G. R. Baker *c* Tunnicliffe *b* Jackson	0
Mr F. R. Spofforth *c* Tunnicliffe *b* Jackson	1
W. Mead *c* Hunter *b* Wainwright	10
E. J. Tyler *c* Mounsey *b* Jackson	1
Woodcock *c* Tunnicliffe *b* Wainwright	0
J. H. Board *not out*	3
B 13	13
	121

Second Innings

not out	32
not out	6
run out	5
B 1, l-b 1	2
	45

An England Eleven Bowling

	Overs	Mdns	Runs	Wkts	Overs	Mdns	Runs	Wkts
Mead	15.3	3	29	5	16	1	38	6
Tyler	10	0	12	0				
Hearne	13	2	28	4				
Spofforth					17	5	39	4

Yorkshire Bowling

	Overs	Mdns	Runs	Wkts	Overs	Mdns	Runs	Wkts
Peel	10	2	21	1				
Haigh	5	0	29	1	3	0	15	0
Jackson	18.1	9	24	6	6.2	2	20	0
Wainwright	15	3	34	2	3	1	3	0

Umpires: Ulyett and Whatmough.

MIDDLESEX v SUSSEX
Played at Lord's, July 14, 15, 16, 1898

SUSSEX WERE UNABLE to place their full strength in the field, and after having the worst of the game all through, were beaten by 235 runs. Some capital all round cricket was shown on the opening day, when Middlesex after completing an innings of 251 dismissed four of the Sussex batsmen for 117. Fry increased his not out innings of 56 to 104, and moreover carried his bat right through the innings. He batted splendidly but met with poor support. Trott finished off the innings by taking five wickets for 18 runs. Several of the Middlesex batsmen were seen to great advantage at the second attempt, and on Saturday morning Stoddart declared. Fry was bowled first ball in the visitors' second innings and with his dismissal went all chance of saving the game. Trott again bowled with marked success. On the Friday afternoon Fry was no-balled for throwing.

MIDDLESEX

First Innings		Second Innings	
Mr P. F. Warner *run out*	38	*b* Bland	7
Mr H. B. Hayman *b* Bland	20	*c* Fox *b* Bland	59
Mr A. E. Stoddart *c* Fox *b* Bland	60	*c* Bean *b* Killick	25
Mr F. G. J. Ford *b* Bland	5	*b* Bean	78
J. T. Rawlin *b* Bland	45	*run out*	56
Sir T. C. O'Brien *b* Bland	8	*b* Brann	62
A. E. Trott *b* Bland	13	*c and b* Tate	14
Mr R. W. Nicholls *c* Killick *b* Bland	19	*b* Tate	4
Mr F. H. E. Cunliffe *st* Fox *b* Killick	8	*not out*	14
Mr E. H. Bray *c* Tate *b* Killick	22	*c* Killick *b* Brann	23
J. T. Hearne *not out*	0		
B 16, l-b 4	20	B 15, l-b 17, n-b 3	35
	258	(9 wkts dec.)	377

SUSSEX

First Innings		Second Innings	
Mr G. Brann *c* Stoddart *b* Rawlin	1	*c* Stoddart *b* Cunliffe	27
Mr C. B. Fry *not out*	104	*b* Trott	0
Mr W. I. Murdoch *c* O'Brien *b* Rawlin	9	*b* Hearne	42
F. W. Marlow *b* Cunliffe	11	*b* Trott	45
E. H. Killick *lbw b* Cunliffe	20	*b* Hearne	17
J. Vine *b* Hearne	18	*c* Nicholls *b* Trott	11
J. Bean *c* Stoddart *b* Trott	10	*b* Trott	18
G. Cox *lbw b* Trott	0	*c and b* Trott	6
F. W. Tate *b* Trott	3	*c* Bray *b* Trott	3
C. H. G. Bland *b* Trott	0	*b* Hearne	0
Mr R. W. Fox *b* Trott	0	*not out*	0
B 18, l-b 2, n-b 1	21	B 30, l-b 1, n-b 3	34
	197		203

Sussex Bowling

	Overs	Mdns	Runs	Wkts	Overs	Mdns	Runs	Wkts
Tate	19	7	44	—	34	7	117	2
Killick	25.2	7	62	2	12	—	50	1
Cox	19	18	32	—	13	3	26	—
Bland	34	5	100	7	26	4	72	2
Fry					5	—	24	—
Bean					13	2	44	1
Brann					5.2	2	9	2

Middlesex Bowling

	Overs	Mdns	Runs	Wkts	Overs	Mdns	Runs	Wkts
Hearne	27	8	62	1	28	1	56	3
Rawlin	10	2	31	2				
Cunliffe	17	3	47	2	28	8	41	1
Trott	11.3	3	36	5	36	7	72	6

Umpires: W. Hearn and M. Sherwin.

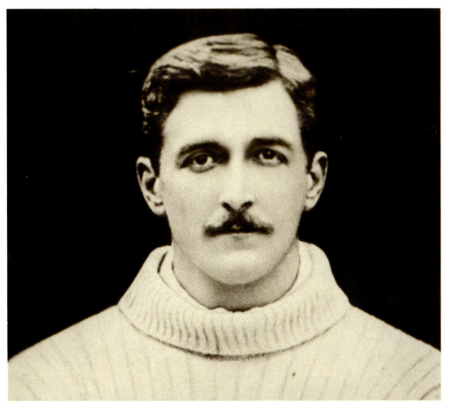

Charles Burgess Fry (1872–1956) always insisted that his bowling action was legal, much to the consternation of umpires, who often disagreed. On one occasion, intent on demonstrating his legality, Fry attempted to employ Socratic methods of proof by suggesting to his captain that he encase his bowling arm in a splint. His captain feebly refused permission.

JOHN PLATTS, the well-known Derbyshire cricketer – one of the best all round players possessed by the county in its early days – died on August 6, 1898. He was in his fiftieth year having been born on December 6, 1848. A tragic interest attached to the start of Platts' career as a cricketer, as it was a ball bowled by him in the MCC and Nottinghamshire match at Lord's in 1870 that caused the death of George Summers. At that time a very fast bowler, Platts afterwards lessened his pace and the catastrophe made such a painful impression upon him, that it is said he never in subsequent years could play, with any pleasure, at Lord's ground. After dropping out of active work in the cricket field he became one of the regular county umpires.

DERBYSHIRE v YORKSHIRE
FOR W. SUGG'S BENEFIT

Played at Chesterfield, August 18, 19, 20, 1898

THIS GAME WILL live long in the memories of those who were fortunate enough to witness it, for Brown and Tunnicliffe, commencing Yorkshire's innings on the Thursday, were not parted for five hours and five minutes, their stand lasting until Friday and producing the unprecedented number of 554. Needless to say this remarkable achievement completely eclipsed all previous records in important cricket, not only for the first, but for any wicket. Tunnicliffe was out first and Brown, having reached his 300, knocked his wicket down. Subsequently the order of batsmen threw away their wickets in the most sportsmanlike fashion in order to give their side time to win, and the innings realised 662. Derbyshire had a somewhat worn pitch to bat on, and were got out for 118 and 157, ultimately suffering an overwhelming defeat by an innings and 387 runs. Brown gave four chances during the five hours and ten minutes he was batting, and hit forty-eight 4s, six 3s and nineteen 2s. Tunnicliffe was five minutes less making his 243, his figures including forty-eight 4s, three 3s and seven 2s. The proceeds of the match amounted to £340.

John Thomas Brown (1869–1904) and John Tunnicliffe (1867–1948) comprised the most renowned opening partnership of the late Victorian age, putting on eighteen century stands together. Their brilliant feat against the hopeless Derbyshire bowlers remained unsurpassed for a generation, until it was finally exceeded by another brace of Yorkshiremen, Herbert Sutcliffe and Percy Holmes.

YORKSHIRE

J. T. Brown *hit wkt* b Storer 300
J. Tunnicliffe *c* F. Davidson *b* Storer 243
Lord Hawke *c* Walker *b* Storer 14
D. Denton *b* F. Davidson 45
G. H. Hirst *c* G. Davidson *b* Walker 0
Mr F. S. Jackson *c* Storer *b* Walker 14
W. Rhodes *c* Storer *b* Walker 6
Mr F. W. Milligan *c* Chatterton *b* F. Davidson 4
Mr Ernest Smith *c* Storer *b* Walker 4
S. Haigh *c* Ashcroft *b* F. Davidson 13
D. Hunter *not out* 0
B 14, l-b 4, n-b 1 19

662

DERBYSHIRE

First Innings

Mr S. H. Evershed *c* Hunter *b* Jackson 18
Mr L. G. Wright *c* Hawke *b* Hirst 0
H. Bagshaw *c* Haigh *b* Jackson 20
W. Storer *c* Denton *b* Milligan 13
W. Chatterton *b* Milligan 6
G. Davidson *b* Jackson 36
Mr E. M. Ashcroft *c* Hunter *b* Jackson 1
W. Sugg *c* Brown *b* Smith....................... 8
F. Davidson *c* Haigh *b* Smith 3
Mr A. Charlesworth *c* Haigh *b* Rhodes 7
Mr G. G. Walker *not out*......................... 0
B 5, l-b 1 6

118

Second Innings

b Smith 12
st Hunter *b* Rhodes 5
b Jackson 2
c Rhodes *b* Jackson 25
c and b Rhodes 54
lbw b Jackson 2
not out 21
b Rhodes 3
retired 5
absent hurt .... –
b Haigh 7
B 15, l-b 6 21

157

Derbyshire Bowling

	Overs	Mdns	Runs	Wkts
G. Davidson	1	—	3	—
Walker	55	11	199	4
F. Davidson	39.3	9	133	3
Sugg	5	—	27	—
Bagshaw	11	1	50	—
Storer	26	1	142	3
Ashcroft	6	1	21	—
Evershed	3	—	13	—
Wright	3	—	24	—
Charlesworth	7	1	31	—

Yorkshire Bowling

	Overs	Mdns	Runs	Wkts	Overs	Mdns	Runs	Wkts
Hirst	10	3	19	1				
Jackson	28	12	52	4	37	22	26	3
Milligan	12	3	36	2	4	2	6	—
Smith	7.1	6	5	2	21	10	35	1
Rhodes	1	1	—	1	29	13	47	3
Brown					4	1	9	—
Haigh					7.1	4	13	1

Umpires: H. Holmes and J. H. Holmes.

*Above: Lord's Cricket Ground during the lunch interval Oxford v Cambridge 1898.
Left: The Lancashire XI 1881.
Right: Tom Richardson, Surrey and Somerset.
Far right: A commemorative plate of W. G. Grace's 100 centuries.*

ENGLISH TEAM v AUSTRALIA

Played at Sydney, December 13, 14, 15, 16, 17, 1898

A VERY UNPLEASANT INCIDENT, which gave rise to almost endless discussion, preceded the first test match, the trustees of the Sydney ground taking it upon themselves to postpone the commencement of the game without consulting the captains of the sides. Heavy rain had fallen, but it was not thought by the players on the Thursday – the match being fixed to start on the following morning – that any postponement would be necessary. As it happened the ground on Saturday, after heavy rain for several hours, was under water, and it thus came about that the anxiously-expected game did not begin till Monday the 13th of December. The delay had one happy result for the Englishmen, Ranjitsinhji, who had been very ill, recovering sufficiently to take his place in the team and playing finer cricket than on any other occasion during the trip. Considering his physical condition – he was quite exhausted after scoring 39, not out, on the first evening – his innings of 175 was a marvellous piece of batting. Before resuming play on the second morning he was in the hands of the doctor. He hit twenty-four 4s, and was batting in all three hours and thirty-five minutes. Scarcely inferior was the cricket shown by MacLaren, who made a third hundred in succession on the Sydney ground. On the second afternoon the Australians in face of a total of 551 lost five wickets for 86, and from these disasters, despite the superb play in the second innings by the two left-handers – Darling and Hill – they never recovered. The Englishmen won the match by nine wickets. With this victory their good fortune in Australia came to an end.

ENGLISH TEAM

First Innings

Mr A. C. MacLaren (capt.) c Kelly b McLeod 109
Mr J. R. Mason b Jones 6
T. Hayward c Trott b Trumble 72
W. Storer c and b Trott 43
Mr N. F. Druce c Gregory b McLeod 20
G. H. Hirst b Jones 62
K. S. Ranjitsinhji c Gregory b McKibbin 175
E. Wainwright b Jones 10
J. T. Hearne c and b McLeod 17
J. Briggs run out 1
T Richardson not out 24
    B 11, w 1 12

                          551

Second Innings

not out 50
b McKibbin 32

not out 8

B 5, n-b 1 6

                          96

AUSTRALIA

First Innings

J. Darling (SA) c Druce b Richardson 7
J. J. Lyons (SA) b Richardson 3
F. A. Iredale (NSW) c Druce b Hearne 25
C. Hill (SA) b Hearne 19
S. E. Gregory (NSW) c Mason b Hearne 46
G. H. S. Trott (V) (capt.) b Briggs 10
J. J. Kelly (NSW) b Richardson 1
H. Trumble (V) c Storer b Mason 70
C. McLeod (V) not out 50
T. R. McKibbin (NSW) b Hearne 0
E. Jones (SA) c Richardson b Hearne 0
    B 1, l-b 1, n-b 4 6

                          237

Second Innings

c Druce b Briggs 101
c Hayward b Hearne 25
b Briggs 19
b Hearne 86
run out 31
b Richardson 27
not out 46
c Druce b Hearne 2
run out 26
b Hearne 6
lbw b Richardson 3
  B 12, l-b 1, w 4, n-b 10 27

                        408

Australian Bowling

	Overs	Mdns	Runs	Wkts	Overs	Mdns	Runs	Wkts
McKibbin	34	5	113	1	5	1	22	1
Jones	50	8	130	3	9	1	28	0
McLeod	28	12	80	3				
Trumble	40	7	138	1	13	4	40	0
Trott	23	2	78	1				

English Bowling

	Overs	Mdns	Runs	Wkts	Overs	Mdns	Runs	Wkts
Richardson	27	8	71	3	41	9	121	2
Hirst	28	7	57	0	13	3	49	0
Hearne	20.1	7	42	5	38	8	99	4
Briggs	20	7	42	1	22	3	86	2
Hayward	3	1	11	0	5	1	16	0
Mason	2	1	8	1	2	0	10	0

Umpires: J. Phillips and C. Bannerman.

A print from The Graphic, *29th January, 1898, showing Stoddart's successful England XI at Sydney Cricket Ground.*

THOMAS LORD died on April 22, 1899.

ESSEX v YORKSHIRE
Played at Leyton, May 25, 26, 1899

IN THIS MATCH, at the end of Whitsun week, the Essex eleven cut a very sorry figure. Indeed, apart from the fine bowling of Walter Mead, there was nothing in the game upon which they could look back with satisfaction. Not one of their batsmen could make headway against Rhodes on a slow wicket, while on the other hand the Yorkshire team – favoured by the fact that the ground was at starting too soft to be difficult – scored uncommonly well. Rhodes gave a very significant suggestion of what sort of a bowler he would be if ever he should he favoured with a wet season by taking fifteen wickets for 56 runs. This is one of the biggest things he has ever done. Yorkshire won the match by 241 runs.

YORKSHIRE

First Innings

J. Tunnicliffe *c and b* Mead	14
J. T. Brown *b* Mead	16
Mr F. S. Jackson *c* Russell *b* Young	28
Mr F. Mitchell *b* Reeves	10
D. Denton *c* Carpenter *b* Mead	33
E. Wainwright *b* Mead	51
G. H. Hirst *lbw b* Mead	6
S. Haigh *c* Reeves *b* Mead	0
Lord Hawke *c* Mead *b* Young	0
W. Rhodes *lbw b* Mead	3
D. Hunter *not out*	0
B 3, l-b 8	11
	172

Second Innings

b Mead	27
b Mead	40
b Mead	23
b Mead	8
b Bull	37
c McGahey *b* Mead	12
c Perrin *b* Young	4
b Mead	30
b Mead	0
b Ayres	8
not out	2
L-b 1	1
	192

Wilfred Rhodes, Yorkshire and England (1877–1973) one of the greatest all-rounders the game has known and, in his roughly-tutored Yorkshire way, a fertile source of aphorisms perhaps his most enduring being, "If batsmen thinks as I'm spinnin' them, then I am".

ESSEX

First Innings

Mr H. G. Owen *b* Rhodes	0
H. Carpenter *b* Rhodes	1
Mr P. Perrin *b* Rhodes	11
Mr C. McGahey *b* Rhodes	8
Mr A. J. Turner *b* Rhodes	0
G. Ayres *c* Wainwright *b* Rhodes	0
T. M. Russell *c* Hirst *b* Rhodes	3
W. Reeves *c* Denton *b* Rhodes	12
W. Mead *b* Jackson	12
Mr F. G. Bull *b* Rhodes	4
H. Young *not out*	3
B 2, l-b 3	5
	59

Second Innings

b Haigh	3
st Hunter *b* Rhodes	17
c and b Haigh	8
b Rhodes	0
b Haigh	12
st Hunter *b* Rhodes	0
b Haigh	0
st Hunter *b* Rhodes	2
b Rhodes	1
c Jackson *b* Rhodes	6
not out	5
B 8, l-b 2	10
	64

Essex Bowling

	Overs	Mdns	Runs	Wkts	Overs	Mdns	Runs	Wkts
Mead	36.1	18	37	7	38.2	11	90	7
Young	22	4	56	2	20	8	55	1
Bull	17	5	43	0	16	3	33	1
Reeves	6	1	21	1	4	2	11	0
Ayres	1	0	4	0	3	1	2	1

Yorkshire Bowling

	Overs	Mdns	Runs	Wkts	Overs	Mdns	Runs	Wkts
Rhodes	15.2	6	28	9	16.3	4	28	6
Jackson	15	5	26	1				
Haigh					16	5	26	4

Umpires: J. J. Tuck and W. Hearn.

TONBRIDGE SCHOOL v DULWICH COLLEGE
Played at Dulwich, June 3, 1899

Tonbridge winning easily by 170 runs

DULWICH COLLEGE

First Innings

C. F. Krabble *b* Marriott	12
F. L. Nightingale *run out*	13
J. C. L. Farquharson *c* Hammill *b* Worthington	12
A. L. Inglis *c* Manser *b* F. V. Hutchings	11
L. A. Whitely *c* Walford *b* F. V. Hutchings	0
G. F. Legg *c* Hammill *b* Worthington	17
D. G. Hurlbatt *b* Worthington	0
H. W. Ripley *run out*	4
N. A. Knox *b* Worthington	0
A. G. Skey *not out*	1
P. G. Wodehouse *c* Worthington *b* Walford	0
B 5, n-b 2	7
	77

Second Innings

c K. Hutchings *b* Worthington	6
b Marriott	0
c K. Hutchings *b* Worthington	8
c Worthington *b* Manser	35
not out	9
b Manser	0
c Hammill *b* Manser	0
B 1	1
	59

TONBRIDGE SCHOOL

F. V. Hutchings b Wodehouse	74
R. M. Manser lbw b Whitely	0
R. H. Marriott lbw b Wodehouse	12
R. F. Worthington b Ripley	23
K. L. Hutchings c Skey b Wodehouse	60
A. Brown b Wodehouse	3
G. S. Cooper b Wodehouse	7
S. S. Hayne b Wodehouse	13
A. T. Millner c Farquharson b Wodehouse	1
A. Hammill b Knox	28
J. A. S. Walford not out	0
B 15, l-b 9, n-b 2	26
	247

HAMPSHIRE IN 1899

President – Lord Aberdare.

Treasurer – Mr H. K. Grierson.

Hon. Secretary – Dr Russell Bencraft, 6, Anglesea Place, Southampton.

Captain – Captain E. G. Wynyard.

WITH A PROGRAMME increased by fixtures with Worcestershire, Hampshire enjoyed a somewhat less disastrous season than in 1898, gaining four victories as against two, while strangely enough the remaining sixteen games were again equally divided into draws and defeats. Such a record does not suggest any exceptional merit in the side and it cannot be claimed that there was any – generally speaking – but the presence of two great players always left an element of doubt as to what might happen when Hampshire took the field. Major Poore and Captain Wynyard had always to be reckoned with when in the eleven, and had they been able to play throughout the summer the county would have undoubtedly held a higher position in the struggle for the Championship. The services of Captain Wynyard were enjoyed fairly regularly after the first three matches and that he was in as good form as ever his average of 49 testifies. Playing consistently well all through, Wynyard enjoyed one great triumph when at Taunton he scored 225. Another brilliant innings was his 108 against Worcestershire. His doings, however, were quite insignificant compared with those of Major Poore whose batting was phenomenal. In the previous summer Poore had proved himself a great acquisition to English cricket and for two months last season he was perhaps the most prominent man playing. Between the 12th of June and the 12th of August he scored 1399 runs in sixteen innings, with an average of 116.58. No one has ever approached such figures as these and it was not only in the matter of average that Major Poore distinguished himself. In his first match – that against Somerset at Portsmouth – he scored 104 and 119 not out and he followed up this rare feat of making two hundreds in a match with 111 against Lancashire at Southampton, adding his name to the list of those who have scored three consecutive hundreds. Nor did his successes end there. On four other occasions he exceeded the hundred and surpassed all his other performances by scoring 304 against Somerset in the same game in which Wynyard played his big innings. Moreover Poore never failed, his lowest score being 11 against Essex. Very naturally Poore's superb batting had its reward in his being included in the Gentlemen and Players' matches at The Oval and Lords. Unfortunately he did not do himself justice on either of the two great London grounds. Had he met with success, he would, no doubt, have had as a concluding triumph the honour of representing England against the Australians.

Robert Montagu Poore (1866–1938) who burst like a comet over the skies of English cricket in 1899. A natural athlete with a Herculean physique, Poore taught himself to bat from a cricket manual, and, by the time he came home from the outposts of the Empire to assist Hampshire, he had already learnt far too much for most of the county bowlers.

HAMPSHIRE v SOMERSET
Played at Portsmouth, June 12, 13, 14, 1899

A HEAVY SCORING MATCH, made famous by Major Poore scoring two innings of over a hundred, was drawn after three day's cricket. Poore's performance was the more remarkable as it was his first appearance of the season in the Hampshire eleven. His 119 not out was a much more vigorous innings than his 104, occupying an hour less and including a five and fifteen 4s. Spens was his most useful assistant on each day their partnerships producing 109 on the Monday and 174 on the Wednesday. Hedley batted admirably for Somerset in each innings.

HAMPSHIRE

First Innings

Mr C. Robson c Cranfield b Gill	24
V. Barton c Cranfield b Woods	58
Major R. M. Poore c Woods b Cranfield	104
Mr E. A. English b Robson	1
Mr E. M. Sprot c Cranfield b Woods	13
Col. J. Spens c Woods b Hedley	74
Mr C. Heseltine b Gill	77
Mr D. A. Steele b Gill	21
H. Baldwin c Woods b Gill	4
E. Tate b Gill	16
T. Sutherland not out	0
B 4, l-b 2, n-b 1	7
	399

Second Innings

c Woods b Cranfield	33
lbw b Cranfield	9
not out	119
c Nichols b Cranfield	0
b Woods	21
c Daniell b Stanley	71
b Stanley	2
not out	0
B 11, l-b 2, n-b 1	14
	(6 wkts dec.) 269

SOMERSET

First Innings

Mr H. T. Stanley c Robson b Baldwin	9
Mr W. Trask run out	41
E. Robson c Tate b Baldwin	52
Capt. W. C. Hedley lbw b Tate	92
Mr S. M. J. Woods c and b Baldwin	12
Mr H. W. Kettlewell c Tate b Baldwin	1
G. B. Nichols run out	28
G. Gill lbw b Heseltine	10
Mr J. Daniell c English b Baldwin	35
B. Cranfield c Heseltine b Sprot	14
Rev. A. P. Wickham not out	4
B 9, l-b 5, w 5	19
	317

Second Innings

b Heseltine	0
c Robson b Heseltine	16
c Poore b Heseltine	14
not out	75
b Steele	26
not out	6
B 1	1
	138

Somerset Bowling

	Overs	Mdns	Runs	Wkts	Overs	Mdns	Runs	Wkts
Cranfield	37	6	96	1	18	7	41	3
Gill	24.2	5	62	5	12	1	50	0
Nichols	21	6	60	0	4	1	11	0
Hedley	19	4	64	1	8	0	30	0
Woods	14	4	55	2	15	2	46	1
Stanley	3	0	18	0	4	1	11	2
Robson	13	3	37	1	13	3	36	0
Kettlewell					8	0	30	0

Hampshire Bowling

	Overs	Mdns	Runs	Wkts	Overs	Mdns	Runs	Wkts
Heseltine	16	6	42	1	20	10	31	3
Baldwin	39	16	71	5	35	18	35	0
Sutherland	13	2	39	0	5	1	19	0
Tate	24	9	36	1	5	4	2	0
Sprot	17	5	45	1	1	1	0	0
Steele	11	2	36	0	12	6	29	1
Spens	3	0	16	0				
English	7	1	13	0	3	2	7	0
Barton					2	0	14	0

Umpires: R. Thomas and J. Lillywhite.

1900 – 1940 THE GOLDEN AGE

AS A MAN grows older, he comes at last to believe that the earliest reminiscences are the sweetest. The further back he drifts, the rosier the vista, whether in cricket or in any other province of experience – which is why the Golden Age is always far behind us. This is normal enough and just as it should be, for, without the perspective of time, very little which has happened seems to make much sense. But, even allowing for the illusions of sentimental hindsight, the period between the end of the Boer War and the outbreak of the Second World War must be regarded, even by the most dispassionate observer, as a golden age of cricket. Indeed, the most perceptive of all its historians, Neville Cardus, has argued the case that between 1900 and 1940 there blossomed not one golden age but two, sundered by the bloodbath of 1914-18. Cardus is surely right, and the only refinement of his argument might be to suggest that the two golden ages each possessed quite distinct personalities; at which point we realise how relentlessly the forces of social history bear down even on an innocuous ball game.

To over-simplify, the period up to 1914 represented the heyday of the amateur, the gentleman/cricketer, who mingled freely enough with the considerable body of professionals, but only on the field of play. The period saw the rise of A. C. Maclaren of the imperious forward play; of Charles Burgess Fry, the renaissance man of English sporting life; of Andrew Stoddart, who took his own life in the despondent anti-climax of retirement; of the Fosters and the Crawfords; of the Maharajah Jam Sahib of Nawanagar, known all over the world as Ranji; and dozens of others, from the Olympic boxing Champion J. W. H. T. Douglas, to the Wodehousean blueblood Sir Timothy O'Brien. No first-class county was without a nucleus of gifted amateurs, and, of course, none would have dreamed of appointing anyone but a gentleman as captain. After all, had not every one of these paragons received expensive instruction at his public school in the art of leadership and the shouldering of responsibility? And if the greatest Gentleman of them all, W. G. Grace, was neither a public school product, nor an Oxbridge graduate, nor even in the strictest sense an amateur, perhaps this can explain his occasional lapses into gamesmanship.

As the new century opens William Gilbert Grace is enjoying the last few seasons of his career. His race is almost run now, but he retains some of the old skill and all of his magisterial authority. He made his debut soon after the death of the Prince Consort, lived through several evolutionary phases in the game's history, and was still at the crease when young Jack Hobbs began his career. But his ponderous Victorian bulk was about to be superseded by a new generation. As though acknowledging subconsciously that, during his lifetime, Britain had become the first nation in the world history to possess more townspeople than country folk, Grace was ending his career not with the Gloucestershire of his birth, but with a new club of his own concoction. This was London County, whose home ground was at Crystal Palace, and whose playing strength depended very much on which of his old comrades the Doctor could rope in for duty. The club disappeared as swiftly as it had arrived, once Grace had given up for good,

Gilbert Laird Jessop (1875–1955) played some of the most amazing innings ever recorded, none more phenomenal than his legendary annihilation of the emergent bowling artists of West Indian cricket. It is said that the victims of Jessop's onslaught were so delighted by the sheer virtuosity of the exhibition that some of their elders, sensibly giving up the task of stemming the tide, rolled over on the grass instead, laughing with hysterical joy. This was always the best reaction to Jessop's art.

but he consoled himself for the loss of one patch of greenery by commandeering another, becoming in old age the founding father of English bowls and first captain of its national side. However before he left the shire of his birth – amid considerable acrimony – Grace endowed it with one of the most glorious jokes in cricket history: A package of heretical devices called Gilbert Jessop, the fastest-scoring batsman of all time and a player whose miraculous exploits passed into the folklore of the game even as he was thrashing the ball to all parts of the ground and frequently out of it.

And yet the picture of English cricket dominated by the Gentlemen Amateur is not quite accurate. The greatest fast bowler of the pre-war period was Tom Richardson of Surrey. Its finest spin bowlers were Wilfred Rhodes of Yorkshire and Colin Blythe of Kent. Its greatest allrounder was George Hirst of Yorkshire. Its most complete batsman was Jack Hobbs of Surrey. All these men were paid professionals. So were Albert Trott, John Tyldesley, Frank Woolley, and dozens of other hired hands who happened also to be virtuosi. These paid players, with the exception of the menacing genius Sydney Barnes, appear to have been perfectly content with their lot, but even had they attempted a palace revolution, it would have been put down swiftly enough by the thoroughly unmodern major-generals who ruled the game.

The most prominent of these was Lord Harris, of Eton, Oxford, the M.C.C. Kent and England; an autocrat so stiffnecked that posterity is inclined less to tremble than to laugh. Having captained his country, Harris was understandably a stickler for form when it came to selecting national sides, and it was his opposition to Ranjitsinhji, ostensibly on the grounds that His Highness had been born in India, which bedevilled Ranji's early international career – Lord Harris, one should add, was born in the West Indies. One of his staunchest allies down there in the last ditch was Lord Hawke, captain of Yorkshire and an even more comic figure than Harris. Hawke, who once prayed to God in public that no professional should even captain England, also decreed that only men born within the county boundaries should ever be allowed to play for Yorkshire: Lord Hawke was born in Lincolnshire.

Among the things which the Great War blasted into history was the assumption of unquestioned authority by the Hawkes and Harris's of the establishment. Lloyd George's death duties, the passing of political power from land to industry, the slaughter of so many sprigs of the aristocracy in the war – these, and other factors, gradually rendered the gentleman/cricketer passé and at last obsolete.

The period between the two wars saw international cricket become a series of wars writ small. It saw the rise of the greatest runmaker in the history of the game, Don Bradman, who thrived both on the plumb pitches of his native Australia and on the sticky dogs of old England. It saw Hobbs pass Grace's record of 126 first-class centuries. It saw that pretty transferring of the baton from one generation to the next as, at the end of the period, Patsy Hendren, Jack Hobbs and Frank Woolley retired and Denis Compton, Len Hutton and Bill Edrich took their places. Most significant of all, it saw the succession of amateur captains of England finally dry up.

At first the old traditions were maintained by Douglas, Tennyson, Chapman, Jardine and Allen. Then, in 1938, with England in sore need of a leader whose status was Simon-Pure and whose cricket was good enough to justify his selection, the Gloucestershire professional Walter Hammond suddenly, magically, and most conveniently, metamorphosed into Mr W. R. Hammond the distinguished gentleman/cricketer.

Frank Reynolds' cartoons from Punch, *1932. A fertile source of cricket humour,* Punch *was carrying on a tradition of caricature that dated back to Victorian times.*

The reader will notice that the intervention of the Great War, while it swelled the *Wisden* obituary section, contributed literally nothing in the way of first-class cricket. This was due to an amazing misapprehension by the forces governing the game that to be seen playing cricket in public while there was a war on somehow hinted at anarchy, disloyalty, cowardice, or whatever else possessed the minds of those who made the decision. This crazy belief, which was blessedly conspicuous by its absence when the Second World War broke out, was based on the notion that in some mysterious way, prowess at ball games implied prowess at war, from which it followed that gifted athletes ought not to be frittering away their virtuosity when there were enemies to be killed. Posterity smiles – until it reads of captains who led their men over the top into the inferno of no-man's-land by punting a rugby football at the enemy and leading the chase to retrieve it. In 1939 the world knew better.

WEST INDIANS v GLOUCESTERSHIRE
Played at Bristol, June 28, 29, 30, 1900

AS GLOUCESTERSHIRE IN meeting the West Indians put a far more representative team into the field than did most of the counties, their overwhelming victory by an innings and 216 runs was in no way surprising. The hitting of the county on the opening day was brilliant in the extreme, 518 runs being scored for the loss of seven wickets. While Jessop was in 201 runs were actually scored in an hour, the great hitter's share of that number being 157.

GLOUCESTERSHIRE

Mr N. O. Tagart c Burton b Mignon	9
Mr W. S. A. Brown c Mignon b Burton	60
J. H. Board c Goodman b Burton	3
Mr H. J. Hodgkins b Burton	0
H. Wrathall c Constantine b Mignon	123
Mr C. L. Townsend b Mignon	140
Mr G. L. Jessop c Hinds b Mignon	157
Mr O. E. Wreford-Brown not out	44
Langdon c Sproston b Burton	50
A. Paish b Burton	0
Mr F. G. Roberts b Mignon	11
B 15, l-b 6, n-b 1	22
	619

Jessop (above) played in the 1900 Gentlemen v Players game along with R. E. Foster (right) a member of a large sporting brotherhood, the seven cricketers whose dominance of the Worcestershire side caused it to be known as "Fostershire". R.E., who died prematurely from diabetes, remains the only man in history to have captained the full England side at both cricket and Association football.

WEST INDIANS
First Innings

Mr S. W. Sproston c Paish b Townsend	1
Mr C. A. Ollivierre c Paish b Roberts	15
Mr G. C. Learmond c Langdon b Townsend	0
Mr P. A. Goodman *run out*	38
Mr F. Hinds *lbw* b Roberts	8
Mr L. Constantine b Roberts	21
W. J. Burton b Roberts	0
Mr W. Browning *not out*	5
Mr A. Warner b Roberts	3
Mr W. H. Mignon b Townsend	1
S. Woods b Townsend	0
B 1, l-b 2, n-b 1	4
	96

Second Innings

c Townsend b Paish	36
run out	42
c Board b Langdon	17
c Paish b Roberts	34
c Board b Roberts	34
c sub. b Brown	65
c sub. b Townsend	11
c Townsend b Langdon	21
lbw b Langdon	24
c Board b Townsend	10
not out	5
B 7, n-b 1	8
	307

West Indians' Bowling

	Overs	Mdns	Runs	Wkts
Ollivierre	23	2	137	—
Burton	25	4	68	5
Woods	33	5	141	—
Mignon	33.3	5	162	5
Hinds	3	—	72	—
Goodman	7	1	17	—

Gloucestershire Bowling

	Overs	Mdns	Runs	Wkts	Overs	Mdns	Runs	Wkts
Townsend	16.3	1	53	4	17.1	1	62	2
Roberts	16	8	39	5	18	4	50	2
Langdon					13	3	57	3
Brown					27	10	67	1
Paish					15	2	63	1

LEICESTERSHIRE v SUSSEX
Played at Leicester, July 12, 13, 14, 1900

SO COMPLETELY DID the bat master the ball throughout this game that not only was it drawn but only 18 wickets fell during three full days, while 1295 runs were scored. Needless to say the pitch could not have been more favourable to batting, and Leicestershire weakened by the absence of Woodcock and Whiteside never had any chance of winning despite their heavy scoring. They declared their innings closed as early as possible, but on Friday evening had only dismissed two of their visitors for 248, while on Saturday their total was exceeded by 77. Wood helped materially in Leicestershire's excellent start, scoring 92 out of 187 in two hours and a half, but the feature of the innings was the partnership of Knight and Whitehead who added 256 in two hours and three quarters. Knight played brilliantly hitting a 5 and twenty 4s during his stay of four hours. Fry reached his hundred on the second evening, and the last day was remarkable for the superb play of Ranjitsinhji, whose 275 runs was his highest score in important cricket. At the wicket five hours and five minutes he was only once at fault, just before getting out, and he hit twenty-nine 4s, eleven 3s and twenty-seven 2s. He and Fry added 194, and Collins helped his captain to put on 138.

LEICESTERSHIRE

Mr C. E. de Trafford b Bland	34
Mr C. J. B. Wood c Butt b Bland	92
J. H. King c Butt b Bland	39
A. E. Knight c Marlow b Fry	182
H. Whitehead c and b Tate	116
S. Coe c Relf b Ranjitsinhji	68
L. Brown c Relf b Fry	21
F. Geeson *not out*	8
Mr G. E. Rudd c Collins b Tate	36
B 5, l-b 2, w 5, n-b 1	13
(8 wkts dec.)	**609**

H. Burgess and T. Marlow did not bat.

SUSSEX

Mr C. B. Fry b Geeson	135
A. E. Relf b Wood	46
E. H. Killick c Coe b Geeson	21
K. S. Ranjitsinhji c Whitehead b Coe	275
F. W. Marlow *run out*	18
Mr G. Brann c Wood b King	7
Mr A. Collins c and b Geeson	98
J. Vine b Geeson	40
H. R. Butt *not out*	8
B 23, l-b 13, w 3, n-b 2	38
(8 wkts)	**686**

F. W. Tate and C. H. G. Bland did not bat.

Sussex Bowling

	Overs	Mdns	Runs	Wkts
Bland	40	5	165	3
Killick	17	1	83	—
Tate	25.4	9	47	2
Fry	21	3	65	2
Collins	9	2	34	—
Relf	6	1	29	—
Ranjitsinhji	27	7	99	1
Brann	13	—	48	—
Vine	1	—	1	—
Butt	4	1	5	—
Marlow	2	—	20	—

Leicestershire Bowling

	Overs	Mdns	Runs	Wkts
Burgess	32	5	116	—
King	43	14	105	1
Wood	21	4	77	1
Rudd	19	—	105	—
Geeson	39.4	8	110	4
Coe	15	4	35	1
Marlow	29	4	91	—
Brown	2	—	—	—

Umpires: A. F. Smith and M. Sherwin.

Whitehead, Knight, Fry. Of the above, Harry Whitehead, in 1906, figured in Leicestershire's first wicket record partnership of 380 with C. J. Wood at Worcester.

THE LORD'S MATCH

GENTLEMEN v PLAYERS
Played at Lord's, July 16, 17, 18, 1900

THE GENTLEMEN v PLAYERS match at Lord's in 1900, was certainly the most remarkable game of the whole season, and in every way worthy of comparison with the memorable match under the same title on the same ground in 1898. It presented two points that were quite without precedent in the long series of Gentlemen v Players matches. R. E. Foster followed up his record innings in the University match by making two separate hundreds, a feat never before performed at Lord's or elsewhere for either Gentlemen or Players, and the Players, though set to make 501 in the last innings, won the game by two wickets. Never before in a match of such importance – and only once indeed in the whole history of first-class cricket – has a total of over five hundred been obtained in the fourth innings. The one previous occasion – also at Lord's ground – was in 1896, when Cambridge were set to make 507 against the MCC and succeeded in accomplishing the task. The performance of the Players was a magnificent one, but they could consider themselves lucky in having sufficient time left them in which to make such a huge score. Under ordinary circumstances the task would have been out of the question. It was in this way that the opportunity of doing an unprecedented thing presented itself. On the second afternoon the Gentlemen already held what was on paper an overwhelming advantage, and Mr Woods, their captain, wishing to have the Players in before the close of the afternoon, instructed his side to play a hitting game, and be out by a certain time. His instructions were loyally obeyed, and though the Gentlemen's score stood at 238 for three wickets when Foster left, the innings was all over for 339. From lunch time till the end of the innings 279 runs were scored in two hours and twenty minutes. No one was disposed to criticise Mr Woods at all severely, some people going so far as to say that if the Gentlemen could not win with a lead of 500 runs they did not deserve to win at all. This was all very well, but the fact remained that there was only one possible way by which the Gentlemen could lose the match, and that their captain adopted it. If he had not been so anxious for his side to be out before the end of the second afternoon he could have made defeat absolutely impossible, and yet have left his side a whole day in which to win. Of course he could not regard it as at all within the range of probability that the Players would make 500 runs in the last innings, but it is a wholesome rule to take nothing for granted at cricket, and to throw nothing away except under stress of absolute necessity. However, though the Gentlemen suffered a defeat to the risk of which they need not have been exposed, the public profited, the cricket on the last day being quite a marvel of sustained interest. Overnight the Players had lost Albert Ward's wicket for 44 runs, so that on Wednesday morning, with nine wickets to go down, they wanted 457 to win. By wonderful batting the task was accomplished, the honours being divided between Brown, Hayward and Abel. Of the three batsmen Abel made the smallest score, but in the opinion of many good judges he played the best cricket. Quite early in the day victory for the Players was seen to be possible, a great stand by Brown and Abel putting them in a flattering position. Abel joined Brown at 81, for two wickets, and when lunch time came the score had reached 242, and the two batsmen were still together. So far Brown had made 106 and Abel 94. On the game being resumed Abel seemed certain of his hundred, but he was a little too anxious, and after getting one boundary hit he attempted a big pull on a short-pitched ball from Jessop, and was easily caught at forward short leg. In this way the third wicket went down at 246, Abel having in a couple of hours scored 98 out of 165. When he left it wanted five minutes to three, and the Players with seven wickets to fall required 255 runs to win. Brown, who had been playing a masterly game all the morning, was then joined by Hayward, and again the good bowling of the Gentlemen was mastered. Hayward had been unwell and away from the ground on the previous day, but having quite shaken off his indisposition, he played superbly. For close upon an hour and a half the two batsmen stayed together, and the total was up to 348 when at last Brown's innings was ended by a catch at cover slip. He had one or two narrow escapes of being bowled and might, with his score at 127, have been caught on the leg-side by Jessop off one of Jephson's lobs, but all the same he played great cricket. He hit one 5 (4 for an overthrow) twenty-nine 4s, two 3s and nine 2s, and was batting for four hours and three-quarters. Brilliant cutting was perhaps the best feature of his game. His 163 is the highest innings ever hit for the Players against the Gentlemen at Lord's, beating by 24 runs the great score made by William Gunn in 1898. When Brown left an interval of a quarter of an hour was taken for tea, the Players with six wickets in hand, wanting 153 to win. A fresh start was made at twenty-five minutes to five, and except that Carpenter failed, things continued to go well for the batting side, victory seeming absolutely certain so long as Hayward and Lilley stayed together. However, Lilley left, sixth wicket down, at 448, and at 469 Hayward's splendid innings was closed by a catch by the wicket-keeper, standing back to Kortright's bowling. In as nearly as possible three hours Hayward had scored 111, his play, though a little unequal in quality, being for the most part admirable. At his dismissal the Players wanted 32 to win with three wickets to fall, and the issue remained in doubt. With 16 added John Gunn was bowled, but on Rhodes joining Trott the end soon came. At half-past six the score stood at a tie, and on Woods taking the ball Rhodes made the winning hit, a wonderful match ending in favour of the Players by two wickets.

We have described the closing stage of the game at considerable length, the cricket being so extraordinary in character. As regards the rest of the match it must suffice to pay proper tribute to the magnificent batting of Foster, and to the excellent services rendered to the Gentlemen in different ways by Fry, Mason, and Jessop. On the second morning Mason and Jessop, with Kortright to help them at the finish, bowled in such capital form that the Players' first innings was finished off for 136, after 66 runs had been scored overnight for two wickets. The performance was the more remarkable as there was nothing the matter with the wicket. Foster's first innings at 102 not out was in many ways a remarkable effort. So keen was he to do well in this, his first Gentlemen and Players' match that, sternly restraining all desire to hit, he was at the wickets nearly half an hour before he made his first run. He was not out 6 at lunch time, but on starting afresh he played a very different game, carrying his score to 102 in less than two hours. As a matter of record, it may be added that he hit fifteen 4s, three 3s, and nine 2s. His second innings was from first to last astonishingly brilliant, but was marred by a palpable chance to John Gunn at mid-on when he had made 40. He completed his first 50 runs in little more than an hour, and then hit away in such tremendous form that when at last Brown caught him in the deep field in front of the pavilion, he had only been at the wickets an hour and three-quarters. In that time he scored 136 out of 195, hitting in his wonderful innings, twenty-four 4s, two 3s, four 2s, and twenty-six singles. Not often, except by such a hitter as Jessop, have first-rate professional bowlers been treated more lightly. Under ordinary circumstances, a batsman who scored 68 and 72 for the Gentlemen at Lord's would stand out very prominently, but Fry on this particular occasion was quite overshadowed by Foster. It should be said for him, however, that in the second innings he played a most unselfish game, caring nothing for his own success when he saw that Foster had a chance of making his second hundred.

GENTLEMEN

First Innings

Mr A. O. Jones c Ward b Trott	9
Mr C. B. Fry b Roberts	68
Mr C. L. Townsend run out	30
Mr R. E. Foster not out	102
Mr J. R. Mason b Trott	2
Mr D. L. A. Jephson lbw b Rhodes	9
Mr G. L. Jessop c Lilley b Rhodes	18
Mr S. M. J. Woods c Lilley b Rhodes	7
Mr E. Smith c Rhodes b Gunn	26
Mr C. J. Kortright b Gunn	4
Mr H. Martyn c Brown b Gunn	3
B 15, l-b 3	19
	297

Second Innings

b Rhodes	5
hit wkt b Ward	72
b Rhodes	22
c Brown b Trott	136
c Lilley b Trott	27
not out	18
b Trott	18
c Carpenter b Ward	0
c Brown b Trott	16
c sub. b Trott	12
c Quaife b Trott	4
B 5, l-b 4	9
	399

PLAYERS

First Innings

R. Abel b Jessop	30
A. Ward c Jones b Mason	16
T. Hayward b Jessop	8
W. G. Quaife c Foster b Jessop	9
J. T. Brown sen. c Foster b Mason	18
H. Carpenter run out	14
A. A. Lilley b Mason	10
A. E. Trott c Foster b Mason	9
J. Gunn c Martyn b Kortright	4
W. Rhodes not out	1
W. Mead b Kortright	4
B 9, l-b 4	13
	136

Second Innings

c Jones b Jessop	98
c Martyn b Jessop	4
c Martyn b Kortright	111
lbw b Jones	29
c Jones b Smith	163
b Woods	9
b Mason	30
not out	22
b Kortright	3
not out	7
B 13, l-b 8, w 1, n-b 4	26
	502

Players' Bowling

	Overs	Mdns	Runs	Wkts	Overs	Mdns	Runs	Wkts
Rhodes	30	4	93	4	15	2	51	2
Trott	27	11	66	2	20.2	—	142	6
Mead	21	5	58	—	14	1	57	—
Gunn	17.3	3	61	3	7	3	23	—
Ward					10	3	39	2
Quaife					1	—	18	—

Gentlemen's Bowling

	Overs	Mdns	Runs	Wkts	Overs	Mdns	Runs	Wkts
Kortright	12.4	4	30	2	18	4	60	2
Jephson	4	—	9	—	14	2	46	—
Mason	17	7	40	4	34	11	92	1
Jessop	14	5	28	3	28	8	74	2
Jones	5	—	16	—	23	4	69	1
Woods					19.5	3	70	1
Smith					18	3	57	1
Townsend					2	—	8	—

Umpires: J. Wheeler and J. Phillips.

SUSSEX v SURREY

Played at Brighton, July 19, 20, 21, 1900

AMONGST MANY BRILLIANT triumphs last season, C. B. Fry had particular reason to remember this return game for he not only succeeded in making his highest score in first-class cricket, but for the second time in his life obtained two separate hundreds in one match. In his first innings he started unsteadily but soon ran into splendid form, while in putting his 229 together he not only gave no chance, but scarcely made a bad stroke. Sussex started by getting 121 for the first wicket, but Richardson and Lockwood afterwards bowled very finely, and Surrey, scoring 94 without loss, left off with a big advantage. Next day they carried their total to 493 for seven wickets. Abel's 110 was not one of his best innings. Miller batted with great judgement, and later in the day Lockwood and Crawford hit splendidly. With Sussex 239 in arrear, Fry and Collins put on 133 for the first wicket, while for the third Ranjitsinhji and Fry added 197 in a hundred minutes, the batting despite the great pace, being scarcely marred by the slightest fault. Fry was fifth out at 408, and with a draw inevitable the game was abandoned half an hour before the usual time.

SUSSEX

First Innings

Mr C. B. Fry *lbw b* Richardson	125
A. E. Relf *b* Richardson	42
E. H. Killick *c and b* Lockwood	12
K. S. Ranjitsinhji *c* Stedman *b* Lockwood	8
Mr A. Collins *b* Richardson	15
J. Vine *b* Richardson	0
F. W. Marlow *b* Lockwood	6
H. R. Butt *not out*	35
C. H. G. Bland *run out*	25
F. W. Tate *b* Jephson	3
W. W. Humphreys *b* Richardson	9
B 8, l-b 9, n-b 3	20
	300

Second Innings

c Jephson *b* Richardson	229
c Richardson	6
c Hayward *b* Richardson	0
c Stedman *b* Richardson	103
c Hayward *b* Richardson	37
b Richardson	3
not out	32
B 1, l-b 1, n-b 5	7
	417

SURREY

R. Abel *b* Collins	110
W. Brockwell *c* Butt *b* Tate	64
Mr N. Miller *c* Collins *b* Humphreys	81
T. Hayward *c* Vine *b* Tate	52
W. Lockwood *c* Butt *b* Ranjitsinhji	85
Mr V. F. S. Crawford *c* Butt *b* Tate	79
W. Lees *b* Tate	12
Mr D. L. A. Jephson *c* Vine *b* Ranjitsinhji	0
Mr E. M. Dowson *not out*	4
T. Richardson *c and b* Tate	38
E. Stedman *c and b* Tate	1
B 7, l-b 4, w 1, n-b 1	13
	539

C. B. Fry captained England at cricket, held the world long jump record, represented England at football, played in an FA Cup Final and only missed a rugby blue through injury.

Ranjitsinjhi (left) played with Fry for Sussex. They were good friends and Ranji when representing India at the League of Nations employed Fry as his speech writer and secretary. Above: A great Yorkshire triumvirate — Schofield Haigh, George Hirst and Wilfred Rhodes. Hirst and Rhodes both came from the village of Kirkheaton and retired to similar positions, Hirst to coach at Eton and Rhodes to coach at Harrow.

Surrey Bowling

	Overs	Mdns	Runs	Wkts	Overs	Mdns	Runs	Wkts
Richardson	18.5	2	76	5	26	2	116	6
Brockwell	5	—	21	—	16	5	58	—
Lees	15	1	43	—	13	3	48	—
Dowson	16	2	72	—				
Lockwood	16	3	52	3	16	3	69	—
Jephson	5	—	16	1	7	2	19	—
Hayward					4	—	26	—
Miller					13	—	74	—

Sussex Bowling

	Overs	Mdns	Runs	Wkts
Bland	28	8	76	—
Humphreys	11	—	72	1
Tate	48.5	16	132	6
Killick	17	2	75	—
Ranjitsinhji	27	7	88	2
Fry	16	3	41	—
Collins	19	3	42	1

Umpires: W. Hearn and H. Pickett.

NOTTINGHAMSHIRE v YORKSHIRE

Played at Nottingham, June 20, 21, 1901

THIS MATCH FURNISHED the sensation of the season at Trent Bridge, the Nottinghamshire eleven finding Rhodes and Haigh unplayable on a sticky wicket, and being got rid of for 13 – the lowest total ever obtained in county cricket, and, with one exception, the lowest on record in first-class matches. One wicket fell for a single run on the Thursday evening, and on the following day, when owing to the state of the pitch cricket did not begin till ten minutes to one, the innings was finished off in fifty-four minutes, the batsmen being absolutely helpless. Counting the few minutes' play overnight, the innings lasted as nearly as possible an hour. A. O. Jones made a leg hit for 4, and Carlin a 2, the other 7 runs being all singles. The innings was so extraordinary in character that it may be of interest to give the fall of the wickets:

1/1 2/3 3/3 4/4 5/8 6/8 7/10 8/10 9/12 10/13

When Nottinghamshire followed on, A. O. Jones and Iremonger scored 82 in an hour before the first wicket fell, but after that Hirst bowled in form just as wonderful as that of Rhodes and Haigh in the first innings, and soon after six o'clock the match came to an end, Yorkshire winning by an innings and 18 runs. Shrewsbury started playing in the match, but split his hand so badly in fielding a ball at point that he had to retire before play had been in progress an hour, his place in the Nottinghamshire team, thanks to Lord Hawke's courtesy, being taken by Harrison. Denton's batting for Yorkshire was exceptionally good.

YORKSHIRE

J. T. Brown c Anthony b Wass	6
J. Tunnicliffe b Dixon	31
D. Denton c W. Gunn b J. Gunn	73
Mr F. Mitchell c and b J. Gunn	22
E. Wainwright b J. Gunn	20
G. H. Hirst c Harrison b J. Gunn	2
L. Whitehead c W. Gunn b Hallam	27
Lord Hawke c and b Wass	1
S. Haigh c Carlin b J. Gunn	5
W. Rhodes c Wass b Hallam	11
D. Hunter not out	3
B 1, n-b 1, w 1	3
	204

NOTTINGHAMSHIRE

First Innings

A. Hallam c Tunnicliffe b Rhodes	1
C. E. Dench c Wainwright b Haigh	0
W. Gunn c Hunter b Rhodes	2
Mr A. O. Jones b Haigh	4
Mr J. A. Dixon c Tunnicliffe b Rhodes	1
J. Carlin c Tunnicliffe b Rhodes	2
J. Gunn c Hawke b Haigh	0
J. Iremonger not out	0
I. Harrison c Haigh b Rhodes	0
G. Anthony b Haigh	2
T. Wass st Hunter b Rhodes	1
	13

Second Innings

b Hirst	0
c Hunter b Hirst	0
c and b Haigh	2
c Mitchell b Wainwright	47
b Rhodes	8
b Wainwright	8
c Hunter b Hirst	35
not out	55
b Hirst	0
b Hirst	5
b Hirst	0
B 13	13
	173

Nottinghamshire Bowling

	Overs	Mdns	Runs	Wkts
Wass	26	3	84	2
Hallam	16.5	6	34	2
J. Gunn	33	15	49	5
Dixon	9	2	23	1
Jones	3	1	11	—

Yorkshire Bowling

	Overs	Mdns	Runs	Wkts	Overs	Mdns	Runs	Wkts
Hirst	1	—	1	—	12.1	2	26	6
Rhodes	7.5	4	4	6	22	4	53	1
Haigh	7	2	8	4	16	3	53	1
Wainwright					13	6	28	2

Umpires: G. Porter and W. Hearn.

SOMERSET v SUSSEX
Played at Taunton, August 8, 9, 10, 1901

SOME REMARKABLE SCORING was witnessed in this match, which was left unfinished, 1,262 runs being scored, and only 19 wickets falling. Apart from an admirable innings by Brann, Sussex quite failed at their first attempt, but when the visitors went in again 324 behind, Charles Fry, Ranjitsinhji and Vine made ample amends. Vine helped Ranjitsinhji to score 174 for the first wicket, and then the two great batsmen added 292 more without being separated. Fry's batting was not worthy of his reputation, but Ranjitsinhji's was magnificent, his score surpassing anything he had previously done in first-class cricket. The Somerset batting was excellent, Palairet and Lewis scoring 258 for the first wicket, while the former and Braund put on 104 for the second partnership. Palairet's innings was without a blemish.

SUSSEX

First Innings

Mr C. B. Fry c Daniell b Braund	20
J. Vine b Cranfield	14
K. S. Ranjitsinhji c Cranfield b Woods	45
E. H. Killick lbw b Braund	8
Mr G. Brann c Palairet b Cranfield	107
Mr A. M. Sullivan st Wickham b Woods	0
A. E. Relf b Woods	6
Mr K. R. B. Fry c Palairet b Braund	15
Mr W. Newham not out	15
F. W. Tate b Braund	1
J. Bean b Braund	0
B 4, l-b 1	5
	236

Second Innings

not out	119
c Braund b Cranfield	49
not out	285
B 2, l-b 1, w 5, n-b 5	13
	466

SOMERSET

Mr L. C. H. Palairet b Bean	194
Lewis c Sullivan b Vine	120
L. C. Braund run out	94
Mr F. A. Phillips b Vine	53
Mr S. M. J. Woods b Ranjitsinhji	50
E. Robson b Relf	14
Mr V. T. Hill b Ranjitsinhji	0
Mr J. Daniell not out	9
G. Gill b Relf	5
B 10, l-b 8, n-b 1, w 2	21
(8 wkts dec.)	560

B. Cranfield and Rev. A. P. Wickham did not bat.

Somerset Bowling

	Overs	Mdns	Runs	Wkts	Overs	Mdns	Runs	Wkts
Cranfield	18	4	63	2	29	5	93	1
Braund	25.3	2	102	5	31	8	106	—
Gill	5	1	20	—	36	6	126	—
Woods	13	3	46	3	4	1	12	—
Hill					1	—	4	—
Palairet					13	2	60	—
Robson					12	1	40	—
Lewis					4	1	12	—

Sussex Bowling

	Overs	Mdns	Runs	Wkts
Relf	29.4	1	71	2
Vine	37	6	141	2
C. B. Fry	15	4	89	—
Killick	25	5	88	—
Tate	11	3	32	—
Bean	35	9	130	1
Brann	3	—	19	—
Ranjitsinhji	8	1	19	2

Umpires: M. Sherwin and C. E. Richardson.

YORKSHIRE v REST OF ENGLAND

Played at Lord's, September 12, 13, 14, 1901

IT WAS ORIGINALLY arranged that the match for the benefit of William Yardley's widow and children should be played under the title of Lord Hawke's Eleven v Mr W. G. Grace's Eleven, but consequent on Yorkshire's brilliant doings it was changed to Yorkshire v The Rest of England. The England team won by an innings and 115 runs, inflicting on Yorkshire the second defeat sustained by the county during the season. C. B. Fry played a beautiful innings – his sixth hundred in succession in first-class matches – but the feature of the game was the astounding batting of Jessop, who has never hit in more wonderful form. At the end of the first afternoon, he was not out 176, and on the following morning he carried his score to 233. His innings – the highest he has ever played in a first-class match – lasted two hours and a half, and comprised two 5s, thirty-three 4s, four 3s, twenty-four 2s, and thirty-one singles. He gave a very sharp chance to Wainwright at slip when he had made 81, and an absurdly easy one off Rhodes's bowling to Tunnicliffe at slip at 155, but considering the pace at which he scored his faulty strokes were few indeed. Yorkshire never looked like avoiding defeat, and soon after lunch time on Saturday the match was over. Trott bowled splendidly. As a benefit, the match satisfied all reasonable expectations, the proceeds, including subscriptions, amounting to about £350.

REST OF ENGLAND
Mr A. O. Jones *c* Tunnicliffe *b* Smith 65
Mr P. F. Warner *c* Wainwright *b* Rhodes 29
Mr G. W. Beldam *c* Tunnicliffe *b* Rhodes 54
Mr C. B. Fry *c* Hirst *b* Rhodes 105
Mr G. L. Jessop *b* Hirst 233
J. Gunn *b* Whitehead 21
Mr J. H. Sinclair *b* Hirst 1
Mr H. D. G. Leveson-Gower *b* Hirst 0
A. E. Trott *b* Hirst 0
Wilson *not out* 4
Mr R. B. Brooks *b* Hirst 4
B 7, l-b 3 10

526

YORKSHIRE

First Innings

J. Tunnicliffe *b* Jones 27
J. T. Brown *st* Brooks *b* Jones 12
D. Denton *lbw b* Trott 12
Mr T. L. Taylor *lbw b* Trott 1
Lord Hawke *b* Trott 28
G. H. Hirst *c* Brooks *b* Sinclair 48
Mr E. Smith *b* Trott 52
W. Rhodes *c and b* Sinclair 26
Lees Whitehead *not out* 14
D. Hunter *c* Warner *b* Trott 1
E. Wainwright *absent hurt* 0
B 6, l-b 2 8

229

Second Innings

b Trott 9
lbw b Trott .41
c Wilson *b* Trott 2
st Brooks *b* Trott 0
lbw b Trott 1
b Trott 5
not out 59
c and b Trott 15
b Wilson 6
c Wilson *b* Trott 2
b Sinclair 30
B 9, l-b 2, w 1 12

182

Having been omitted from the Australian team to tour England in 1896 Albert Trott made his own way over and, joining the Lord's ground staff, soon forced his way into the Middlesex XI. He was a fine all-rounder and was also notable for being the only man ever to strike a ball over the pavilion at Lord's. Since the unlucky victims of this magnificent blow were the touring 1899 Australians it seems that Trott may have successfully registered his displeasure at his earlier non-selection.

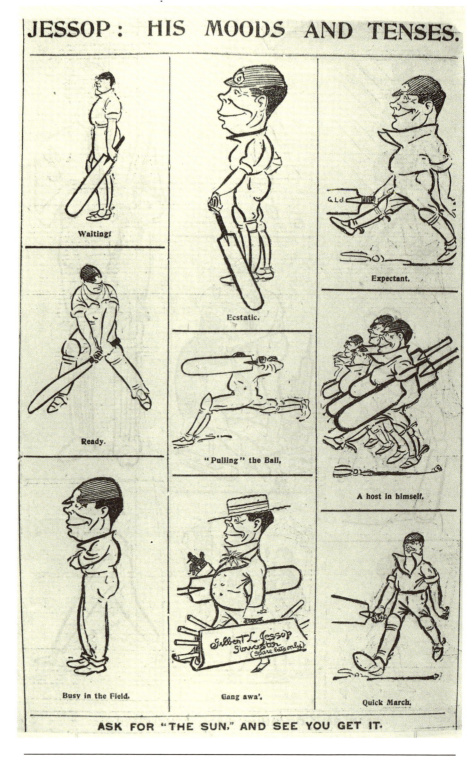

Yorkshire Bowling

	Overs	Mdns	Runs	Wkts
Hirst	26.3	5	92	5
Rhodes	43	6	179	3
Wainwright	9	2	49	—
Brown	9	—	53	—
Smith	19	4	75	1
Whitehead	14	1	68	1

Rest of England Bowling

	Overs	Mdns	Runs	Wkts	Overs	Mdns	Runs	Wkts
Wilson	18	2	50	—	16	5	24	1
Trott	27.5	4	86	5	29.5	8	84	8
Jones	6	1	29	2				
Gunn	6	2	23	—				
Sinclair	10	2	33	2	13	3	62	1

Umpires: V. A. Titchmarsh and W. A. J. West.

ENGLAND v AUSTRALIA
Played at The Oval, August 11, 12, 13, 1902

AUSTRALIA HAVING ALREADY won the rubber, the fifth and last of the Test matches had not at starting the same importance that would under other circumstances have attached to it, but it produced a never-to-be-forgotten struggle and a more exciting finish, if that were possible, than the one at Manchester. In face of great difficulties and disadvantages England won by one wicket after the odds had been fifty to one on Australia. Some truly wonderful hitting by Jessop made victory possible after all hope had seemed gone, and Hirst and Rhodes got their side home at the close. In its moral results the victory was a very important one indeed, as no one interested in English cricket could have felt other than depressed and low spirited if all the Test matches played out to finish had ended in favour of Darling's team. In making up the English side the Selection Committee restored Jessop and Hirst to the places they ought to have filled at Manchester, and for the first time in the series of games gave a place to Hayward, Ranjitsinhji, Tate and Abel being left out. Hayward had done enough to deserve a trial, but, as it happened, he proved a great failure as a batsman and was by no means lively in the field. The Australians of course kept to the team that had been victorious at Sheffield and Old Trafford. The wicket, through a trifle slow from the effects of recent rain, was in very good condition, and the Australians, staying in for the whole of the first day, made the highly satisfactory score of 324. At one time they did not seem likely to do nearly so well as this for, though Trumper and Duff scored 47 for the first partnership, there were four wickets down for 82 and five for 126. The change in the game was brought about by Hirst, who for a time bowled in quite his form of 1901. Duff was out to a marvellous catch by the wicket-keeper standing back, Lilley jumping a yard or more on the leg side and holding a ball that would have gone for 4. Noble and Armstrong by putting on 48 runs considerably improved the Australians' position, but with seven wickets down for 175 the outlook was none too promising. However, all these disasters were so well retrieved that the three remaining wickets added 149 runs, an invaluable partnership by Hopkins and Trumble putting on 81. The batting was very painstaking, but an unlucky mistake by Lilley at the wicket when Trumble had made 9 had, from England's point of view, a deplorable effect on the game.

If the weather had kept fine the Englishmen would not on an Oval wicket have been afraid of facing a score of 324, but the bad luck that had handicapped them at Sheffield and Manchester still pursued them, heavy rain during the early hours of Tuesday morning making a great difference in the pitch. Under the circumstances they did not do at all badly to score 183, but apart from some bright hitting by Tyldesley there was nothing remarkable in the efforts of the early batsmen. At lunch time six wickets were down for 83, and it seemed certain that the side would follow on and be beaten. Braund and Hirst made a great effort, the latter hitting with the utmost freedom, but when he left the total had only reached 137, England still wanting 38 runs to avoid going in again. Thanks, however, to a bad blunder by Hill, who palpably missed Lockwood at long-on when that batsman had made 11, the follow-on was saved, the innings ending for 183 or 141 runs behind. Braund was often beaten by balls that missed the wicket, but in staying in for an hour and a half he did invaluable work for his side. Trumble bowled throughout the innings in splendid form and took eight wickets for just over 8 runs apiece. Possessing such a big lead the Australians looked, when they went in for the second time, to have the match in their hands. They opened their innings with a great misfortune, Trumper throwing away his wicket in attempting a foolish run, and for the rest of the afternoon the batting was marked by such extreme care that at the drawing of stumps the score, with eight men out, had only reached 114, two hours and three-quarters being occupied in getting these runs. The wicket was still rather difficult and Lockwood bowled very finely. Hill was out to a magnificent catch low down in the slips in one hand by MacLaren, and Noble bowled on his pads by a ball that he did not attempt to play with his bat.

On Wednesday morning Lockwood quickly obtained the two outstanding wickets, bringing the Australian innings to a close for 121, and then England went in with 263 wanted to win the match. Tuesday's cricket, while the turf was still soft after rain, had damaged the pitch to no small extent, and up to a certain point the batsmen were so helpless against Saunders and Trumble that the easiest of victories for Australia appeared in prospect. Three wickets fell to Saunders for 10 runs and but for Gregory missing Hayward badly at short-leg there would have been four wickets down for 16. Even as it was half the side were out for 48 and the match looked all over. At this point Jackson, who had gone in third wicket down, was joined by Jessop and a stand was made which completely altered the game. At first, however, Jessop's cricket was far from suggesting the wonderful form he afterwards showed. When he had made 22 Kelly missed stumping him and at 27 he gave a rather awkward chance to Trumper at long-off. At lunch time the two batsmen were still together, Jackson, who had played superb cricket, being 39 and Jessop 29. After the interval Jackson was far indeed from keeping up his previous form, being repeatedly in difficulties and giving a palpable chance to Armstrong at slip. Jessop, on the other hand, settled down at once, and hit as he only can. At one point he scored four 4s and a single off successive balls from Saunders. The partnership had added 109 runs in sixty-five minutes when Jackson was easily caught and bowled. Jessop went on hitting for some little time longer, but at 187 he closed his extraordinary innings by placing a ball gently into short-leg's hands. He scored, in just over an hour and a quarter, 104 runs out of 139, his hits being a 5 in the slips, seventeen 4s, two 3s, four 2s, and seventeen singles. All things considered a more astonishing display has never been seen. What he did would have been scarcely possible under the same circumstances to any other living batsman. The rest of the match was simply one crescendo of excitement. Hirst played a great game and, after Lockwood's dismissal at 214, received such help from Lilley that victory gradually came in sight. The score was advanced to 248, or only 15 to win, and then from a good hard drive Lilley was finely caught at deep mid-off. Rhodes as last man had a trying crisis to face, but his nerve did not fail him. Once, however, he nearly lost his wicket. Armstrong at slip getting a catch in his hand, but, being partly overbalanced, dropping the ball. Hirst went on imperturbably, scoring again and again by means of cleverly placed singles, and at last he had the extreme satisfaction of making the score a tie. Then Rhodes sent a ball from Trumble between the bowler and mid-on, and England won the match by one wicket. Hirst's innings was in its way almost as remarkable as Jessop's. So coolly did he play that of his last fourteen hits that scored thirteen were singles, whereas in the early part of his innings he had hit half-a-dozen 4s. Darling is not often at fault in the management of his bowling, but he leaned too heavily on Saunders and did not make enough use of Noble. Trumble, bowling from the Pavilion end, was never changed during the match.

AUSTRALIANS
First Innings
V. Trumper b Hirst 42
R. A. Duff c Lilley b Hirst 23
C. Hill b Hirst 11
J. Darling c Lilley b Hirst 3
M. A. Noble c and b Jackson 52
S. E. Gregory b Hirst 23
W. W. Armstrong b Jackson....................17
A. Hopkins c MacLaren b Lockwood 40
H. Trumble not out 64
J. J. Kelly c Rhodes b Braund....................39
J. V. Saunders lbw b Braund 0
    B 5, l-b 3, n-b 2 10

                                           324

Second Innings
run out 2
b Lockwood 6
c MacLaren b Hirst 34
c MacLaren b Lockwood 15
b Braund 13
b Braund 9
b Lockwood 21
c Lilley b Lockwood 3
not out 7
lbw b Lockwood 0
c Tyldesley b Rhodes 2
    B 7, l-b 2 9

                         121

ENGLAND
First Innings
Mr A. C. MacLaren c Armstrong b Trumble 10
Mr L. C. H. Palairet b Trumble 20
J. T. Tyldesley b Trumble 33
T. W. Hayward b Trumble 0
Hon. F. S. Jackson c Armstrong b Saunders 2
L. C. Braund c Hill b Trumble 22
Mr G. L. Jessop b Trumble 13
G. H. Hirst c and b Trumble 43
W. H. Lockwood c Noble b Saunders 25
A. A. Lilley c Trumper b Trumble 0
W. Rhodes not out..............................0
    B 13, l-b 2 15

                                           183

Second Innings
b Saunders 2
b Saunders 6
b Saunders 0
c Keely b Saunders 7
c and b Trumble 49
c Kelly b Trumble 2
c Noble b Armstrong 104
not out 58
lbw b Trumble 2
c Darling b Trumble 16
not out 6
    B 5, l-b 6 11

                         263

Jessop's historic century against Australia won a Test match already lost and remained by far the most staggering feat of attacking batsmanship in a Test match until, in 1981, another batsman from the West Country matched him, miracle for miracle.

English Bowling

	Overs	Mdns	Runs	Wkts	Overs	Mdns	Runs	Wkts
Lockwood	24	2	85	1	20	6	45	5
Rhodes	28	9	46	—	22	7	38	1
Hirst	29	5	77	5	5	1	7	1
Braund	16.5	5	29	2	9	1	15	2
Jackson	20	4	66	2	4	3	7	—
Jessop	6	2	11	—				

Australian Bowling

	Overs	Mdns	Runs	Wkts	Overs	Mdns	Runs	Wkts
Trumble	31	13	65	8	33.5	4	108	4
Saunders	23	7	79	2	24	3	105	4
Noble	7	3	24	—	5	—	11	—
Armstrong					4	—	28	1

Umpires: C. E. Richardson and A. A. White.

MR FREDERICK AITKEN LEESTON-SMITH, who had played for Brecknockshire and Somerset, died during 1903. He was a powerful hitter, a middle-paced round-armed bowler, and generally fielded at point. In 1881 he played an innings of 204 for Weston-super-Mare v Clevedon. He was educated at Malvern, but did not obtain a place in the Eleven, leaving there at the age of fourteen. He afterwards went to Christ College, Brecon, where he was in the eleven. He was born in London, May 10, 1854, was 5ft 10½in in height and weighed 12st 4lbs. In 1880 he assumed the name of Leeston. In a match between Weston-super-Mare and Thornbury, he once hit E. M. Grace for four 6s from consecutive balls, a performance which the latter has described as follows: – "F. L. Cole off my first ball, F. A. Leeston-Smith 6 off the second, 6 off third, 6 off fourth, 6 off fifth, when the umpire said, "I am afraid it is over, Doctor." I said, "Shut up, I am going to have another," and on this one he was stumped. Weston-super-Mare had to follow their innings. Leeston-Smith came in first, and the first ball I bowled him he hit for 6. The second also went for 6, but off the third he was stumped again."

ENGLAND v AUSTRALIA

FIRST TEST MATCH

Played at Sydney, December 11, 12, 14, 15, 16, 17, 1903

THE FIRST OF the five Test matches was in many ways the best of the series. Indeed a finer game has rarely been seen in Australia. It lasted into the sixth day, and attracted in all about 95,000 people. The Australians, on winning the toss, lost Trumper, Duff, and Hill for a dozen runs, Trumper being out to a wonderful catch at slip. Thanks to Noble these disasters were retrieved, but when at the end of the day the score stood at 259 for six wickets the Australians did not seem to have done anything out of the common. However, rain in the night made their total look far more formidable. Next day the Australian innings ended for 285 and the Englishmen went in under very anxious conditions, as no one could tell how the wicket would play. Tyldesley, batting with the utmost skill, saved his side from a break-down before lunch, and by four o'clock the wicket had practically recovered. At the drawing of stumps the total had reached 243 for four wickets, Foster being not out 73, and Braund not out 67. Noble was at the wickets four hours and three-quarters for his 133, and hardly made a mistake. The third day was marked by the most brilliant and sensational cricket seen during the tour, R. E. Foster, with a magnificent innings of 287, beating all records in Test matches. Altogether he was batting for seven hours, among his hits being thirty-eight 4s. The latter part of his innings was described on all hands as something never surpassed. Foster and Braund added 192 runs together, Braund playing an admirable innings, but with eight men out the Englishmen were only 47 ahead. Then came the startling play, Relf and Rhodes helping Foster to put on respectively 115 and 130 runs for the ninth and tenth wickets. The last wicket partnership set up a new record in Test games. Foster's triumph was the more remarkable as he had never before played in an England and Australia match. He did not begin his great innings at all well, and ought to have been caught when he had made 51, but his batting on the third day was beyond criticism. Going in against a balance of 292 runs, Australia had scored 17 without loss when stumps were pulled up. Next day they did great things, carrying their score to 367 and only losing five wickets. There was a very regrettable and indeed disgraceful demonstration on the part of a large section of the crowd when Hill was given run out, a storm of hooting and booing going on for a long time. On the fifth day the Australian innings ended for 485, Trumper taking out his bat for a faultless 185. His hits included twenty-five 4s, and during a stay of three hours and fifty minutes he gave no chance. Rhodes bowled with the utmost steadiness on the hard ground, and in writing home Mr Warner said he did not know what the side would have done without him. England wanted 194 to win, and found the task a very heavy one. They won on the sixth day by five wickets, but they would very probably have been beaten if, after four wickets had fallen for 83, Laver at short leg had not missed Hirst before that batsman had scored a run. As it was Hayward and Hirst made a great stand, and almost won the game together. Hayward was batting just over four hours for his beautifully-played 91.

AUSTRALIA

First Innings

R. A. Duff *c* Lilley *b* Arnold 3
V. Trumper *c* Foster *b* Arnold 1
C. Hill *c* Lilley *b* Hirst 5
M. A. Noble *c* Foster *b* Arnold 133
W. W. Armstrong *b* Bosanquet 48
A. J. Hopkins *b* Hirst 39
W. P. Howell *c* Relf *b* Arnold 5
S. Gregory *b* Bosanquet 23
F. Laver *lbw b* Rhodes 4
J. J. Kelly *c* Braund *b* Rhodes 10
J. V. Saunders *not out* 11
       Extras 3

                                             285

Second Innings

c Relf *b* Rhodes 84
not out 185
run out 51
st Lilley *b* Bosanquet 22
c Bosanquet *b* Rhodes 27
c Arnold *b* Rhodes 20
c Lilley *b* Arnold 4
c Lilley *b* Arnold 43
c Relf *b* Rhodes 6
b Arnold 13
run out 2
       Extras 28

                          485

ENGLAND

First Innings

P. F. Warner *c* Kelly *b* Laver 0
T. Hayward *b* Howell 15
J. T. Tyldesley *b* Noble 53
E. Arnold *c* Laver *b* Armstrong 27
R. E. Foster *c* Noble *b* Saunders 287
L. C. Braund *b* Howell 102
G. H. Hirst *b* Howell 0
B. J. T. Bosanquet *c* Howell *b* Noble 2
A. A. Lilley *c* Hill *b* Noble 4
A. E. Relf *c* Armstrong *b* Saunders 31
W. R. Rhodes *not out* 40
       Extras 16

                                             577

Second Innings

b Howell 8
st Kelly *b* Saunders 91
b Noble *b* Saunders 9
st Kelly *b* Armstrong 19
c Noble *b* Howell 0
not out 60
not out 1

       Extras 6

                        194

England Bowling

	Overs	Mdns	Runs	Wkts	Overs	Mdns	Runs	Wkts
Hirst	24	8	47	2	29	1	79	—
Arnold	32	7	76	4	28	3	93	2
Braund	26	9	39	—	12	2	56	—
Bosanquet	13	—	52	2	24	1	100	1
Rhodes	17.2	3	41	2	40.2	10	94	5
Relf	6	1	27	—	13	5	35	—

Australia Bowling

	Overs	Mdns	Runs	Wkts	Overs	Mdns	Runs	Wkts
Saunders	36.2	8	126	2	10.5	3	51	2
Laver	37	12	116	1	16	4	37	—
Howell	31	7	113	3	31	18	35	2
Noble	34	8	99	3	12	2	37	0
Armstrong	23	3	47	1	18	6	28	1
Hopkins	11	1	40	—				
Trumper	7	1	12	—				
Gregory	2	—	8	—				

Above: R. E. Foster's 287 is still the highest score achieved by an Englishman in a Test match in Australia.
Right: B. J. T. Bosanquet, an all-rounder, as the Middlesex v Sussex game demonstrated.

MIDDLESEX v SUSSEX
Played at Lord's, May 25, 26, 27, 1905

PLAYED JUST BEFORE the first of the test games this was emphatically Bosanquet's match. Thanks chiefly to his superb batting and highly effective bowling, Middlesex, after declaring their second innings closed, won by 324 runs. For the second time in his life Bosanquet made two separate hundreds in one match, and in all he took eleven wickets, carrying everything before him in the last innings. He hit up his 103 in an hour and three-quarters and his 100 not out in seventy-five minutes. Field played fine cricket of a far more careful kind and Warner and George Beldam were also seen at their best. Fry was kept out of the Sussex team by a damaged finger and his absence clearly dispirited the Sussex team.

MIDDLESEX

First Innings

Mr P. F. Warner c Goldie b Tate	49
Mr E. A. Beldam b Tate	26
Mr G. W. Beldam c Butt b Goldie	3
Mr E. Field not out	107
Mr B. J. T. Bosanquet b Goldie	103
Mr G. MacGregor b Goldie	0
Mr J. H. Hunt b Goldie	1
Mr E. S. Littlejohn b Vine	3
Mr H. D. Wyatt c Butt b Cox	13
A. E. Trott c Cox b Goldie	20
J. T. Hearne c Butt b Relf	17
B 4, l-b 11, w 2	17
	369

Second Innings

b Leach	86
lbw b Relf	10
c Butt b Cox	94
not out	100
not out	5
B 15, l-b 1, w 4, n-b 1	21
(3 wks dec.)	316

SUSSEX

First Innings

Mr K. O. Goldie b G. W. Beldam	19
J. Vine c Bosanquet b Hunt	4
E. H. Killick c Hearne b Hunt	32
A. E. Relf c Trott b Hunt	2
Mr A. L. Gorringe b Hearne	16
G. Cox c MacGregor b Trott	38
Mr H. P. Chaplin c G. Beldam b Bosanquet	42
Mr C. L. A. Smith b Bosanquet	41
G. Leach c Field b Hearne	35
H. R. Butt not out	7
F. W. Tate c sub. b Bosanquet	4
B 13, l-b 6	19
	259

Second Innings

c and b Hunt	9
st MacGregor b Bosanquet	31
c and b Bosanquet	9
st MacGregor b Bosanquet	5
b Hunt	0
b Bosanquet	8
lbw b Bosanquet	0
b Bosanquet	12
b Bosanquet	5
c and b Bosanquet	0
not out	16
B 4, l-b 2, w 1	7
	102

Sussex Bowling

	Overs	Mdns	Runs	Wkts	Overs	Mdns	Runs	Wkts
Relf	20	4	53	1	17	3	49	1
Cox	27	9	60	1	14	5	32	1
Goldie	33	10	80	5	10	—	50	—
Tate	25	5	81	2	11	2	46	—
Vine	15	4	54	1	10	—	42	—
Killick	6	3	24	—	11	1	43	—
Leach					8	—	33	1

Middlesex Bowling

	Overs	Mdns	Runs	Wkts	Overs	Mdns	Runs	Wkts
G. W. Baldam	8	1	29	1				
Hunt	19	3	63	3	14	5	42	2
Bosanquet	24.3	2	75	3	13.2	1	53	8
Hearne	18	5	38	2				
Trott	13	3	35	1				

Umpires: W. A. J. West and C. E. Richardson.

ENGLAND v AUSTRALIA

FIRST TEST MATCH

Played at Nottingham, May 29, 30, 31, 1905

IN CHOOSING THE England Eleven for the first of the five Test matches the selectors could not secure quite the side they wanted. At this period of the season George Hirst's leg was giving him a great deal of trouble, and as it would have been absurd to play an unsound man in such a game, he was not even included in the thirteen players from among whom the final choice had to be made. In the previous week, C. B. Fry, already in great form, damaged one of his fingers rather badly in practice at Brighton. and though present at Trent Bridge he did not play, the other man who stood down being Walter Lees. Of the eleven that took the field Bosanquet, John Gunn, and Arnold appeared for the first time in a Test match in England. The Australians had their strongest side, and the wicket being hard and the weather fine the match began under conditions that could scarcely have been better. In the end England won by 213 runs, but only after some truly sensational cricket was this result arrived at.

When England won the toss a total of over 300 was regarded as almost a certainty, but to the consternation of the crowd Hayward, A. O. Jones, MacLaren, and Jackson, were so quickly got rid of that four wickets were down for 47 runs. Tyldesley and Bosanquet, and later in the innings Lilley and Rhodes did something to make up for this disastrous start, but by a quarter to four the innings was all over for 196, the advantage of winning the toss being entirely discounted. There was a little moisture in the ground before lunch, but the chief cause of the failure could be found in the demoralising effect of Cotter's bowling. Pitching little more than half-way at a terrific pace he made the ball get up more than shoulder high, and there can be no doubt that the fear of being hit on the head upset the batsmen considerably. Laver, following up some splended work during the previous fortnight, took seven wickets for 64 runs. He kept an irreproachable length, and varied his pace with the nicest skill, but finely as he bowled he would not have met with so much success if the batsmen had not had their confidence shaken at the other end.

Going in against a total of 196 the Australians started their innings with a couple of misfortunes. Duff was caught very low down at short leg in the second over, and Trumper strained his back so badly that after getting three boundary hits and a single he retired from the field, and, as events turned out, played no more cricket for a fortnight. Of course, it was not known at the time that the injury would prove so serious. For these early troubles Hill and Noble made ample amends, and when the hundred went up with only one man out the Australians stood in a most flattering position. It was just after this that Jackson bowled his now famous over. Noble was out to the first ball, Hill to the fourth, and Darling to the last, the game undergoing a change that can only be described as astonishing. Still the Australians left off for the day with much the best of the game, their score standing at 158 for four wickets. Hill and Noble put on 106 runs, playing masterly cricket together for an hour and three-quarters. The attendance all told numbered quite 15,000. It should be mentioned that the wicket had been prepared in a simple way, without any special use of marl.

The second day brought with it an extraordinary change in the fortunes of the match, the Englishmen playing up in a fashion not unworthy of comparison with their never-to-be-forgotten effort on the second day at Manchester three years before. For a little while the Australians got on remarkably well, and when without further loss their over-night score had been carried to 200, they had every reason to feel satisfied, though they knew that Trumper would not be able to bat. There was such a sudden collapse, however, that the last five wickets fell in less than forty minutes, the innings being finished off for 221. The English fielding while these wickets were going down was amazingly brilliant. Indeed, nothing better could be imagined. The best piece of individual work was done by A. O. Jones, who, in getting rid of Laver, brought on a marvellous catch in the slips, throwing himself forward and taking the ball with the left hand close to the ground. It was a catch

Bosanquet, the conjurer whose family included a famous metaphysician, whose specialities included the contradiction between Appearance and Reality. As this contradiction embodies the very soul of the Googly, it will be understood why some researchers have playfully suggested that the cricketer and the metaphysician were one and the same man.

that recalled George Lohmann's greatest feats. All through the innings Jessop's fielding on the on-side was beyond praise. He stopped everything that came within reasonable distance of him, and such was the moral effect of his presence that a short run was never attempted when the ball went in his direction.

Standing in a far better position than they could possibly have expected after their paltry first innings, the Englishmen went in for the second time before half-past twelve, and at the drawing of stumps they had scored 318 for five wickets. Under ordinary circumstances they would in the same space of time have made a bigger score, but at about three o'clock Armstrong was put on to keep down the runs. He took the ball at 110 and was not changed till the total had reached 301, delivering thirty-five overs for 50 runs. It was something quite new to see the Australians on the second afternoon of a Test Match playing for a draw rather than a win, and the innovation gave rise to endless discussion. In doing so well the Englishmen were mainly indebted to MacLaren and Hayward, who in two hours and a half scored 145 for the first wicket, thus giving their side a splended start. Armstrong's method of keeping the ball wide of the leg stump for over after over irritated the crowd who, quite forgetting their manners, became rather noisy. MacLaren was out second at 222, being finely caught low down at mid-off from a hard drive. His innings of 140, which lasted three hours and forty minutes, was for the most part magnificent. Just after lunch he was inclined to be reckless, but luckily for him the ball always fell out of harm's way, and he soon returned to safer methods. He scarcely cut at all, but he drove and pulled with tremendous power, and nothing could have been more skilful than the way in which he turned the ball on the leg side. Tyldesley played a fine innings, being far more successful than anyone else in scoring from Armstrong, and Jones hit hard at a time when rapid scoring was essential. At the close Jackson and Rhodes were the not-outs. On the following morning these two batsmen gave a splendid display, staying together until a quarter to one, and without being parted carrying the score to 426, Jackson then declaring the innings closed. Altogether he and Rhodes put on 113 runs. Jackson was batting two hours and twenty minutes for his 82 not out. He was not quite happy in the fading light on the second afternoon, but his play in the morning was without a flaw.

The Australians wanted 402 to win, and when they went in at one o'clock four hours and a half remained for cricket. It was not to be supposed, especially with Trumper disabled, that the runs could be obtained, and the only question was whether the Australians would be able to avoid defeat. In the end, as everyone knows, Bosanquet beat them. Darling opened the innings himself with Duff, and at lunch time the score stood at 21 without loss. Everything pointed to a draw when the total reached 60 with the two batsmen still together, but at 62 Duff was easily caught and bowled, and this as it happened proved the turning point. Forty minutes later there were four wickets down, Noble, Darling, and Hill being got rid of. Hill was out to a remarkable catch. He hit a ball back to Bosanquet so high that only a man standing fully six feet could have got near it. Bosanquet jumped up, got the ball with one hand then kept hold of it, though he stumbled backwards and fell to the ground. It was a great change from 62 for no wicket to 93 for four, and a little later Armstrong was easily caught at cover-point, the Englishmen then looking to have the match in their hands. Bosanquet had taken all the five wickets. Gregory and Cotter added 39 runs together, but at the tea interval seven wickets had fallen for 173. The players were only away ten minutes but during that time the light became very faulty. Gregory, who had played splendid cricket for an hour, was out at 175 – caught at mid-on at the third attempt, and Kelly joined McLeod. With Trumper unable to bat these were the last two men. The light grew worse and worse with every sign of on-coming rain, and the Englishmen had reason to fear that all their efforts would be thrown away and the match left drawn. For a quarter of an hour play went on in deep gloom, and then McLeod was out leg-before-wicket, England winning a memorable game by 213 runs. In bringing off the victory that MacLaren's hitting had first made possible, the Englishmen owed everything to Bosanquet. He took eight of the nine wickets that fell, completely demoralising the batsmen with his leg-breaks. He gained nothing from the condition of the ground, the pitch remaining firm and true to the end. In the first flush of his triumph his place in the England team seemed secure for the whole season, but he never reproduced his form, and dropped out of the eleven after the match at Leeds. In the course of the three days at Trent Bridge 31,622 people paid for admission.

ENGLAND

First Innings

Mr A. O. Jones *b* Laver 4
T. Hayward *b* Cotter 5
J. T. Tyldesley *c* Duff *b* Laver 56
Mr A. C. MacLaren *c* Kelly *b* Laver 2
Hon. F. S. Jackson *b* Cotter 0
Mr B. J. T. Bosanquet *b* Laver 27
J. Gunn *b* Cotter 8
Mr G. L. Jessop *b* Laver 0
A. A. Lilley *c and b* Laver 37
W. Rhodes *c* Noble *b* Laver 29
E. Arnold *not out* 2
B 21, l-b 5 26
                                                 ———
                                                  196

Second Innings

b Duff 30
c Darling *b* Armstrong 47
c and b Duff 61
c Duff *b* Laver 140
not out 82
b Cotter 6

not out 39
B 11, l-b 9, w 1 21
                              ———
                (5 wkts dec.) 426

AUSTRALIA

First Innings

R. A. Duff c Hayward b Gunn	1
V. T. Trumper retired hurt	13
C. Hill b Jackson	54
M. A. Noble c Lilley b Jackson	50
W. W. Armstrong st Lilley b Rhodes	27
J. Darling c Bosanquet b Jackson	0
A. Cotter c and b Jessop	45
S. E. Gregory c Jones b Jackson	2
C. E. McLeod b Arnold	4
F. Laver c Jones b Jackson	5
J. J. Kelly not out	1
B 16, l-b 2, w 1	19
	221

Second Innings

c and b Bosanquet	25
absent hurt	0
c and b Bosanquet	8
st Lilley b Bosanquet	7
c Jackson b Bosanquet	6
b Bosanquet	40
b Rhodes	18
c Arnold b Bosanquet	51
lbw b Bosanquet	13
st Lilley b Bosanquet	5
not out	6
B 4, l-b 3, w 2	9
	188

Australian Bowling

	Overs	Mdns	Runs	Wkts	Overs	Mdns	Runs	Wkts
Cotter	23	2	64	3	17	1	59	1
Laver	31.3	14	64	7	34	7	121	1
McLeod	8	2	19	—	28	9	84	—
Armstrong	6	3	4	—	52	24	67	1
Noble	3	—	19	—	7	1	31	—
Duff					15	2	43	2

England Bowling

	Overs	Mdns	Runs	Wkts	Overs	Mdns	Runs	Wkts
Arnold	11	2	39	1	4	2	7	—
J. Gunn	6	2	27	1				
Jessop	7	2	18	1	1	—	1	—
Bosanquet	7	—	29	—	32.4	2	107	8
Rhodes	18	6	37	1	30	8	58	1
Jackson	14.5	2	52	5	5	3	6	—

Umpires: J. Phillips and J. Carlin.

MR GEORGE EDWARD HEMINGWAY, a brother of Messrs. W. M'G. and R. E. Hemingway, died at Rangoon on March 11, 1907. He was born at Macclesfield in 1872, was in the Uppingham Eleven in 1888, and in 1898 appeared for Gloucestershire against Yorkshire at Sheffield. He was a free batsman and in the field generally stood mid-off or cover-point, but business and weak sight handicapped his play considerably. On one occasion, when playing a single-wicket match against his two brothers, he hit the ball into a bed of nettles; the fieldsmen quarrelled as to who should recover it, and during the argument the batsman ran about 250.

MIDDLESEX v SOMERSET
Played at Lord's, May 20, 21, 22, 1907

ALBERT TROTT RENDERED his benefit match memorable by an extraordinary bowling performance in the second innings of Somerset, dismissing Lewis, Poyntz, Woods, and Robson with successive balls, and later on disposing of Mordaunt, Wickham, and Bailey, also with successive balls. Thus he accomplished the unprecedented feat of performing the "hat trick" twice in an innings. Thanks to Trott's bowling, Middlesex won by 166 runs. Rain seriously interfered with cricket on the opening day, the whole time available being occupied by the home team's first innings. Middlesex blundered in the field on Tuesday, but thanks to Tarrant secured a useful lead. Litteljohn followed up his success against Hampshire with two capital displays of batting.

MIDDLESEX

First Innings

Mr P. F. Warner b Mordaunt	46
F. A. Tarrant c Lee b Lewis	52
Mr G. W. Beldam lbw b Mordaunt	12
Mr B. J. T. Bosanquet c Johnson b Mordaunt	32
Mr E. S. Litteljohn c Braund b Lewis	44
A. E. Trott b Lewis	1
Mr H. A. Milton b Lewis	3
Mr G. MacGregor c Woods b Bailey	39
H. R. Murrell b Robson	33
J. T. Hearne not out	3
E. Mignon b Bailey	1
B 15, l-b 4, n-b 1	20
	286

Second Innings

b Lewis	11
c Palairet b Mordaunt	28
lbw b Lewis	0
b Bailey	29
b Mordaunt	52
c Wickham b Robson	35
b Mordaunt	0
c Poyntz b Robson	39
c and b Braund	9
not out	4
c Wickham b Braund	0
B 3, l-b 2, n-b 1	6
	213

Above: George Dennett who took 15 wickets for Gloucester against Northants in 1907. A professional cricketer, he served in the Great War and rose to the rank of Captain. Promotion, however, is more difficult to come by in cricket than in war, and on the playing field Dennett never captained anybody.

Right: Whit Monday 1907 witnessed Albert Trott's final magnificent flourish. From then on his career fell into irreversible decline as shortly afterwards did his health. He died tragically by his own hand on July 30, 1914.

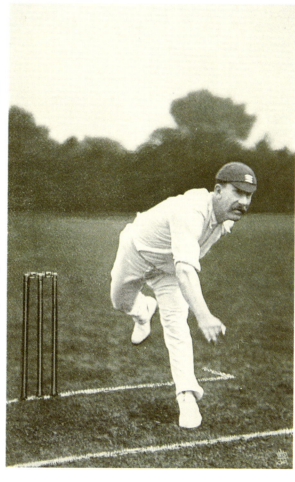

SOMERSET

First Innings

Mr L. C. H. Palairet c MacGregor b Mignon	6
L. C. Braund c MacGregor b Bosanquet	59
Mr P. R. Johnson b Tarrant	57
A. E. Lewis c Tarrant b Mignon	31
Mr E. S. M. Poyntz *lbw b* Tarrant	9
Mr S. M. J. Woods c Bosanquet b Tarrant	17
E. Robson *not out*	20
Mr F. M. Lee b Hearne	18
Mr O. C. Mordaunt c Beldam b Tarrant	1
Rev. A. P. Wickham c Trott b Tarrant	0
A. E. Bailey c Littlejohn b Tarrant	3
L-b 14, w 1	15
	236

Second Innings

c Bosanquet b Tarrant	35
not out	28
c Trott b Tarrant	14
lbw b Trott	1
b Trott	0
b Trott	0
b Trott	0
c Trott b Tarrant	7
c Mignon b Trott	4
b Trott	0
c Mignon b Trott	0
B 4, l-b 4	8
	97

Somerset Bowling

	Overs	Mdns	Runs	Wkts	Overs	Mdns	Runs	Wkts
Lewis	32	14	88	4	7	2	17	2
Bailey	16	5	33	2	16	3	58	1
Braund	13	1	33	—	13.4	1	55	2
Mordaunt	30	6	97	3	15	1	47	3
Robson	7	1	15	1	6	2	30	2

Middlesex Bowling

	Overs	Mdns	Runs	Wkts	Overs	Mdns	Runs	Wkts
Beldam	4	1	15	—	3	1	10	—
Mignon	24	6	88	2	5	1	24	—
Trott	5	1	10	—	8	2	20	7
Hearne	8	1	22	1				
Bosanquet	8	—	39	1				
Tarrant	15	4	47	6	14	4	35	3

Umpires: F. W. Marlow and S. Brown.

GLOUCESTERSHIRE v NORTHAMPTONSHIRE
Played at Gloucester, June 10, 11, 12, 1907

IN THIS GAME a fresh record was made by Dennett and Jessop in dismissing Northamptonshire for 12 runs. This is the smallest total for a first-class inter county match, the previous lowest being 13 by Nottinghamshire against Yorkshire at Trent Bridge, in 1901. Play on the first day was restricted to fifty minutes, Gloucestershire losing four wickets for 20 runs, and, despite some hitting by Jessop, being all out next day for 60. The first innings of Northamptonshire only lasted forty minutes, Dennett, who made the ball turn in a remarkable manner, being practically unplayable. Dennett accomplished the "hat trick," in dismissing Hawtin, Beasley and Buswell with successive balls, and should have had four wickets in as many balls, Wrathall dropping a catch offered by East. In Gloucestershire's second innings Jessop and Mackenzie were the only batsmen to overcome the difficulties of the wicket, but Northamptonshire were set 136 to get to win. At their second attempt the visitors again failed before Dennett, who in the course of the day took fifteen wickets for 21 runs. Northamptonshire finished up on the second day in practically a hopeless position, wanting 97 runs to win with only three wickets left, but rain came to their rescue. Not a ball could be bowled on the Wednesday, the game having to be abandoned as a draw.

GLOUCESTERSHIRE

First Innings

H. Wrathall b Thompson	4
Mr E. Barnett lbw b Thompson	3
J. H. Board b Thompson	3
Mr M. G. Salter c Buswell b East	3
Mr G. L. Jessop b East	22
Mr R. T. H. Mackenzie b East	0
T. Langdon b East	4
J. H. Huggins c Crosse b East	8
E. Spry lbw b Thompson	6
Parker not out	2
G. Dennett c Pool b Thompson	0
B 2, l-b 3	5
	60

Second Innings

b Thompson	7
b East	0
lbw b Thompson	5
c and b East	3
c Hawtin b East	24
c King b East	21
lbw b Thompson	4
c Buswell b East	3
b East	4
not out	8
b East	0
B 9	9
	88

NORTHAMPTONSHIRE

First Innings

Mr E. M. Crosse c Board b Dennett	4
M. Cox lbw b Dennett	2
Mr C. J. T. Pool c Spry b Dennett	4
W. A. Buswell st Board b Dennett	1
Mr L. T. Driffield b Dennett	0
G. J. Thompson b Dennett	0
Mr R. W. R. Hawtin lbw b Dennett	0
W. East st Board b Dennett	0
Mr R. N. Beasley b Jessop	1
Mr S. King not out	0
W. Wells c Parker b Jessop	0
	12

Second Innings

c and b Dennett	0
c Barnett b Dennett	12
st Board b Dennett	9
c Langdon b Dennett	0
not out	5
lbw b Dennett	8
lbw b Dennett	2
b Dennett	0
not out	1
B 2, l-b 1	3
	40

Northamptonshire Bowling

	Overs	Mdns	Runs	Wkts	Overs	Mdns	Runs	Wkts
Thompson	16.5	7	29	5	15	2	43	3
East	16	5	26	5	14.2	4	36	7

Gloucestershire Bowling

	Overs	Mdns	Runs	Wkts	Overs	Mdns	Runs	Wkts
Dennett	6	1	9	8	15	8	12	7
Jessop	5.3	4	3	2	10	3	20	—
Parker					5	2	5	—

Umpires: A. Millward and J. E. West.

ENGLAND v SOUTH AFRICA

SECOND TEST MATCH
Played at Leeds, July 29, 30, 31, 1907

THE SECOND TEST Match was the only one of the three that had a definite result, England winning in the end by 53 runs. A less satisfactory Test game has seldom been played. The wicket was soft before the start, and on the second day especially cricket had to be carried on with extreme difficulty between the showers. On the whole the Englishmen had no great reason to congratulate themselves on their victory. They certainly had the best of the luck as regards the ground and, though this is a point on which we would not venture to express an opinion, it was freely stated that the umpiring told against the South Africans in the last innings. With the ground as it was, it was clearly a mistake to play Knox for England in preference to J. N. Crawford. The fast bowler was no more than a passenger on the side, only bowling four overs in the match. There was no particular advantage in winning the toss, but when at lunch time on Monday, 34 runs had been scored in forty minutes for the loss of Fry's wicket, England seemed to have opened well. However, a dismal collapse followed, nine wickets going down after the interval in less than an hour and a quarter for an addition of 42 runs. Faulkner enjoyed his greatest success during the tour. Disguising his break with the utmost skill, he made the ball turn so much both ways that the batsmen were almost hopeless against him, the result being that he took seven wickets in eleven overs at a cost of only 17 runs. Hirst alone showed any capacity to cope with him on the slow pitch. In comparison with most of the batsmen Hayward played exceedingly well. On paper it was not much for him to score 24, but he showed very skilful defence, stopping among other good balls a tremendous break-back from Vogler. Out for such a paltry score as 76 England had of course an uphill task for the rest of the day. Everything depended on Blythe, none of the other bowlers being able to take advantage of the state of the ground. Still if all the catches had been held there would not have been much to choose on the first innings. Four chances were allowed to escape, and though none of them had any serious consequences the blunders naturally proved somewhat demoralizing. As events turned out the South Africans stopped in till ten minutes to six for a total of 110, thus leading on the first innings by 34 runs. They were only twenty behind with half their wickets in hand but when the seventh wicket fell they were still 17 runs behind the England total. Happily for the Englishmen Blythe did not fail them. He was not quite so accurate in length as he might have been, but he made the ball do a good deal and though two catches were missed off him he took eight wickets for 59 runs. But for him the match might have been irretrievably lost on the first day.

Twenty-five minutes remained for play and R. E. Foster felt much concerned as to what he should do. However, after some consideration, he determined to keep to the previous order and sent in Fry and Hayward. This policy answered admirably, the two batsmen playing with great skill and scoring 25 runs without loss before the call of time. Cricket on the second day was carried on under extreme difficulties. Four times between eleven o'clock and half-past one rain drove the players from the field, but between the showers England's score was carried to 110 for four wickets. After lunch the weather was so bad that nothing further could be done. At half-past two the umpires announced that even in the most favourable circumstances play would be impossible until late in the day and eventually a brief but heavy storm caused stumps to be drawn at ten minutes to five. So far as it went the cricket was full of interest. The South African bowlers were much handicapped by having to use a wet ball, but they triumphed over this disadvantage in a remarkable way, not only keeping their length surprisingly well but getting on a lot of spin. Fry played superbly, his innings of 54 going far to secure England's ultimate victory. He made his 54 out of 100 and was batting altogether for an hour and a quarter. Running no undue risks but seizing every fair opportunity, he made a number of good drives, always picking on the right balls to hit. He gave no chance, but he had a lucky escape on the Monday evening, playing a ball from Faulkner on to his wicket without removing the bails. Tyldesley, though not by any means up to Fry's form, scored an invaluable 30.

So much rain had fallen, the wicket being under water at six o'clock on Tuesday, that everyone thought the start of play would be delayed on the third morning. Thanks, however, to a fine night and a bright windy morning, play was quite practicable at eleven o'clock. Run-getting proved a very hard matter and with the game twice stopped by rain England only increased their overnight score to 162, the innings being all over by a quarter to one. Gordon White and Faulkner bowled uncommonly well, getting on any amount of leg break. Foster made a great effort for his side, his score of 22 being of far more value than it looks on paper. In second wicket down on Tuesday he was out ninth after batting for seventy minutes.

The South Africans wanted 129 to win and the task seemed by no means impossible. However, they made a bad start, losing two wickets for 10 runs before rain came on at twenty past one and stopped play till after luncheon. A third wicket should have fallen, Braund missing Hathorn at slip. Play was not resumed till five minutes to three and then the South Africans soon found themselves in an almost hopeless position, Nourse, Hathorn, and White, being so speedily got rid of that five wickets were down for 18. Sinclair raised the hopes of his side by punishing Blythe for a dozen runs in one over, but at 38 he was caught at slip. After this Faulkner and Snooke made a determined effort to save the game, but though they showed strong defence they could not get the ball away. Faulkner, after exercising the sternest self-restraint for an hour, was tempted at last to hit out at Blythe, and skied the ball to forward point where Foster caught him. From the moment he left the result was never in doubt, the last four wickets falling in less than half-an-hour and the innings ending at a quarter to five for a total of 75. Tyldesley caught Vogler at long off in a wonderful way. He had to run some distance for the catch and fell over, but contrived to keep the ball off the ground. Blythe, who bowled himself almost to a standstill, clearly won the game, taking seven wickets for 40 runs. Altogether he took fifteen wickets, a feat that has only once been equalled in Test matches – by Rhodes for the MCC's England team in Melbourne in 1904.

Colin Blythe (1879–1917) was the gentlest soul who ever rose to cricketing heights. A Cockney from Deptford whose left-arm bowling was one of the most beautiful sights of the Golden Age, his temperament was so finely attuned that his nervous disposition caused him to retire from the strains of international cricket. His destruction of the South African side at Leeds was only one triumph among dozens; when Wisden *published his obituary, his bowling feats filled several pages. His memorial may be found at the county ground in Canterbury.*

ENGLAND

First Innings

T. Hayward st Sherwell b Faulkner 24
Mr C. B. Fry b Vogler 2
J. T. Tyldesley b Faulkner 12
Mr R. E. Foster b Sinclair 0
L. C. Braund lbw b Faulkner 1
G. H. Hirst c Hathorn b Sinclair 17
Mr G. L. Jessop c Sherwell b Faulkner 0
E. Arnold b Faulkner 0
A. A. Lilley c Schwarz b Faulkner 3
C. Blythe not out 5
Mr N. A. Knox c Faulkner b Sinclair 8
    B 1, l-b 2, n-b 1 4

                                    76

Second Innings

st Sherwell b Vogler 15
lbw b White 54
c Snooke b Schwarz 30
lbw b Faulkner 22
c Schwarz b White 0
b White 2
c Hathorn b Faulkner 10
c Schwarz b Faulkner 12
lbw b White 0
not out 4
run out 5
    B 7, l-b 1 8

                                      162

SOUTH AFRICA

First Innings

Mr P. W. Sherwell lbw b Blythe 26
Mr L. J. Tancred st Lilley b Blythe 0
Mr M. Hathorn c Lilley b Hirst 0
Mr A. D. Nourse c Arnold b Blythe 18
Mr G. C. White c Hirst b Blythe 3
Mr J. H. Sinclair st Lilley b Blythe 2
Mr G. A. Faulkner c Braund b Blythe 6
Mr S. J. Snooke c Lilley b Knox 13
Mr W. A. Shalders c Fry b Blythe 21
Mr A. E. Vogler c Hayward b Blythe 11
Mr R. O. Schwarz not out 5
    B 3, l-b 1, n-b 1 5

                                      110

Second Innings

c Foster b Blythe 1
run out 0
b Arnold 7
lbw b Blythe 2
c Arnold b Blythe 7
c Braund b Blythe 15
c Foster b Blythe 11
c Hirst b Blythe 14
lbw b Hirst 5
c Tyldesley b Blythe 9
not out 0
    B 3, n-b 1 4

                                       75

South African Bowling

	Overs	Mdns	Runs	Wkts	Overs	Mdns	Runs	Wkts
Vogler	8	3	14	1	4	—	18	1
Schwarz	7	—	18	—	5.4	—	18	1
Faulkner	11	4	17	6	20	3	58	3
Sinclair	10.3	2	23	3	4	—	13	—
White					16	3	47	4

England Bowling

	Overs	Mdns	Runs	Wkts	Overs	Mdns	Runs	Wkts
Hirst	9	3	22	1	9	2	21	1
Blythe	15.5	1	59	8	22.4	9	40	7
Arnold	4	1	11	—	13	7	10	1
Knox	4	—	13	1				

Umpires: J. Moss and J. Carlin.

HENRY PICKETT, once so well known as a fast bowler for Essex and the MCC, came to a sad end. He disappeared on the 27th of September, 1907, and his body was discovered on the beach at Aberavon on the 3rd of October. Not till the end of December, however, was his fate known, some articles found in his clothes proving his identity. Born on the 26th March, 1862, he was in his 46th year. For several seasons he was a valuable member of the Essex team. His best piece of work for the county was done in a match against Leicestershire at Leyton in 1895 – the year in which Essex took part for the first time in the championship. At a cost of 32 runs he took all ten wickets in Leicestershire's first innings. Despite his fine performance, however, Essex lost the game by 75 runs. After he retired from first-class cricket he was for some time coach at Clifton College.

MR EDWARD BANKS, JP, one of the oldest Kent cricketers, died at Sholden Lodge, near Deal, on January 12, 1910, aged 89. He was born in South Wales on August 12, 1820, but moved into Kent before completing his second year. Ill-health limited his appearances in county cricket to ten matches between 1842 and 1846. In the last-mentioned year he appeared for the Gentlemen against the Players at Canterbury, and fielded at Lord's for Alfred Mynn in the first of his single wicket matches with Felix. *Scores and Biographies* (iii – 159) says of him, "Batted in a good free style, and was a most excellent field." Fuller Pilch recalled that "I found him down Sandwich way, where his property lay. He and his youngest brother, Mr William, were the quickest between the wickets I ever did see, and Mr Edward was one of the smartest in the long-field. He was like a thorough-bred horse, for no matter how far the ball was off he would try; and when I sang out "Go to her, Mr Edward! Go to her!' he would outrun himself almost, and, as sure as ever he got his hands to her, the ball was like a rat in a trap." His younger brother, the late Mr W. J. Banks, played occasionally for Kent in 1846 and 1848. The deceased, who was a grandson of Sir Edward Banks, the builder of London Bridge, rode a tricycle as recently as three months before his death.

"The Croucher"
This photograph demonstrates more effectively than any words why Jessop was so often referred to by this nickname. He did not so much strike the ball as launch himself into it, and the crouching stance must have made his job a little easier.

WORCESTERSHIRE v GLOUCESTERSHIRE
Played at Stourbridge, July 7, 8, 1910

THANKS ALMOST ENTIRELY to a magnificent display of batting by G. L. Jessop, Gloucestershire gained a victory over Worcestershire by 94 runs. Up to a point, Worcestershire had the best of the game, and on going in a second time 52 behind Gloucestershire lost three wickets for 45. From this point, however, Jessop by his wonderful hitting brought about a complete change in the fortunes of the match. He scored his 100 in an hour and at the drawing of stumps was not out 106. Gloucestershire were then 126 on with seven wickets in hand – a vivid illustration of how a hard hitter can sometimes transform a match. On the following day Jessop continued to play brilliant cricket, carrying his score to 165. He obtained his runs in two hours out of 215, his superb innings including six 6s and twenty 4s. He hit with characteristic certainty and power in all directions. After Jessop left the last five Gloucestershire wickets fell for 11 runs. Worcestershire were left with 210 to get to win, and on damaged pitch they did not at any time look like accomplishing the task against the fine bowling of Dennett and Parker.

GLOUCESTERSHIRE

First Innings		Second Innings	
J. H. Board b Burrows	0	b Burrows	24
T. Langdon b Cuffe	19	c Foster b Burrows	2
P. Mills c Bale b Taylor	1	b Burrows	35
A. Nott c Turner b Taylor	6	c Cuffe b Burrows	4
Mr G. L. Jessop c Turner b Burrows	6	c Taylor b Arnold	165
Mr D. L. Priestley b Arnold	13	c Turner b Arnold	7
Mr H. J. Merrick b Cuffe	4	c Bale b Burrows	0
Mr S. Levy b Cuffe	0	b Burrows	0
J. H. Huggins c Foster b Cuffe	10	b Burrows	0
C. Parker c Burrows b Arnold	0	not out	5
G. Dennett not out	0	b Arnold	5
B 1, l-b 2, w 1	4	B 10, l-b 3, n-b 1	14
	63		261

WORCESTERSHIRE

First Innings		Second Innings	
F. Bowley c Parker b Mills	6	lbw b Dennett	6
F. Pearson lbw b Dennett	27	c Langdon b Huggins	5
E. Arnold c Merrick b Dennett	6	st Board b Dennett	17
Mr G. N. Foster b Parker	6	b Parker	46
J. A. Cuffe c and b Parker	16	b Dennett	11
R. E. Turner st Board b Parker	16	lbw b Dennett	0
Mr G. H. Simpson-Hayward c Jessop b Parker	13	c Jessop b Parker	5
R. Burrows c Merrick b Dennett	0	c Dennett b Parker	7
C. G. A. Collier b Dennett	14	run out	0
Mr W. H. Taylor not out	7	not out	6
E. Bale c Mills b Dennett	0	b Dennett	7
B 3, n-b 1	4	B 2, l-b 3	5
	115		115

Worcestershire Bowling

	Overs	Mdns	Runs	Wkts	Overs	Mdns	Runs	Wkts
Burrows	6	1	27	2	26	1	111	7
Taylor	11	4	16	2	8	1	44	—
Cuffe	7.5	2	12	4	18	3	69	—
Arnold	2	—	4	2	4.2	2	6	3
Pearson					5	—	17	—

Gloucestershire Bowling

	Overs	Mdns	Runs	Wkts	Overs	Mdns	Runs	Wkts
Dennett	20.3	10	48	5	20.5	7	55	5
Mills	8	2	11	1				
Parker	12	1	52	4	11	3	33	3
Huggins					9	2	22	1

Umpires: W. Flowers and Guttridge.

ETON v HARROW
Played at Lord's, July 8, 9, 1910

ETON AND HARROW have been meeting on the cricket field for over a hundred years, but they have never played a match quite so remarkable as that of 1910. Indeed in the whole history of cricket there has been nothing more sensational. After following their innings Eton were only four ahead with nine wickets down, and yet in the end they won the game by 9 runs. The nearest parallel to this finish that one can recall was one between Lancashire and Oxford University in 1888. On that occasion the county followed-on, and managed to win although when their eighth wicket fell they were still 17 runs behind. The struggle between the two public schools last season will be known for all time as Fowler's match. Never has a school cricketer risen to the occasion in more astonishing fashion. When Harrow went in with only 55 to get, Fowler took command of the game, secured eight wickets – five of them bowled down – for 23 runs and brought off what might fairly be described as a forty to one chance.

Until the second afternoon was far advanced the match proved one-sided to a degree. On the first day Harrow going in on a soft, but by no means difficult pitch, ran up a total of 232, and when bad light caused stumps to be drawn, five of Eton's best wickets had fallen for 40 runs. By far the best batting for Harrow was shown in different styles by Wilson and Hillyard. In first and out fifth wicket down at 133 Wilson took two hours and a quarter to get his 53, his play all the time being very patient and watchful. Hillyard, more vigorous in his methods, scored 62 in an hour and three-quarters, among his hits being a six to square leg and half-a-dozen 4s. On Saturday morning. Eton's first innings was soon finished off for 67, and a follow-on against a balance of 165 was involved. At first things went so badly that half the wickets were down for 65, no one being able to get the ball away on the slow pitch. The first change in the game came with the partnership between Fowler, and Wigan, 42 runs being added for the sixth wicket in fifty minutes. When Wigan left, Boswell, who had been last man in the first innings, joined Fowler and another good start was made, three-quarters of an hour's play producing 57 runs. Still despite Fowler's heroic efforts – his 64 was the highest innings in the match – the position was reached of Eton being only 4 runs ahead with a wicket to fall. Then began the cricket which will for ever make the match memorable. Kaye joined Manners, and so finely and fearlessly did Manners hit that in less than twenty-five minutes 50 runs were put on, the total being carried from 169 to 219. A remarkable catch in the slips at last brought the innings to an end, Hopley just reaching the ball and turning it to Jameson, who held it a few inches from the ground. There can be no doubt that Earle, the Harrow captain, who had made many changes in the early part of the innings, was at fault in keeping himself and Hillyard on too long. In the case of any ordinary match the ground would have been half empty before the Eton innings closed, but an Eton and Harrow crowd is a law to itself and when Harrow went in with 55 to get about 10,000 people watched the cricket. Whatever their feelings, they must have been glad they stayed as they may never see such a finish again. Probably Harrow made a mistake in having the heavy roller on. At any rate Fowler was able at once to bowl his off-break with deadly effect. He bowled Wilson in the first over; at eight he bowled Hopley; and at the same total, Turnbull, the left-handed hitter was caught in the long field. Earle seemed likely to win the match easily enough for

Harrow, but after he had hit up 13 runs, a catch at slip sent him back at 21. Without the addition of a run, Monckton was bowled and Hillyard well caught low down at short mid-on. In this way, as the result of half an hour's cricket, six wickets were down for 21, Fowler having taken them all. Blount was caught and bowled at 26 by Steel, who had just gone on for Kaye, and then Jameson, who had been batting for nearly forty minutes without getting a run, was so badly hurt that for a few minutes the game had to be delayed. With victory in sight, the Eton team played the keenest possible cricket, nothing being thrown away in the field. A yorker bowled Straker at 29, and, after Graham had hit a three, Jameson was bowled by Fowler. It was not to be expected that Graham and Alexander would get the 23 runs still required, but they made a desperate effort, carrying the score to 45 or only 10 to win. Then a catch low down in the slips got rid of Alexander and a wonderful match was over. The scene of enthusiasm at the finish was quite indescribable. From the time he went on at 21, Steel with his leg breaks gave Fowler excellent support and the Eton fielding all round was magnificent.

Robert St. Leger Fowler (seated centre) holds an exalted place in the pantheon of public school heroes. In winning virtually single-handed the Eton–Harrow match of 1910, Fowler's achievement outstripped the bounds of fictional propriety. Later he enjoyed great success in Army cricket, won the Military Cross in the Great War, and in the 1920s played a few times for Hampshire.

HARROW

First Innings

Mr T. O. Jameson c Lubbock b Fowler	5
Mr T. B. Wilson b Kaye	53
Mr G. W. V. Hopley b Fowler	35
Mr T. L. G. Turnbull lbw b Fowler	2
Mr G. F. Earle c Wigan b Steel	20
Mr W. T. Monckton c Lubbock b Stock	20
Mr J. M. Hillyard st Lubbock b Fowler	62
Mr C. H. B. Blount c Holland b Steel	4
Mr A. C. Straker c Holland b Steel	2
Mr O. B. Graham c and b Steel	6
Hon. R. H. I. G. Alexander *not out*	2
B 18, l-b 2, n-b 1	21
	232

Second Innings

b Fowler	2
b Fowler	0
b Fowler	8
c Boswell b Fowler	0
c Wigan b Fowler	13
b Fowler	0
c Kaye b Fowler	0
c and b Steel	5
b Fowler	1
not out	7
c Holland b Steel	8
B	1
	45

Continued on P. 98

Left: Jessop in an unfamiliar pose.
Below: Colin Blythe.
Bottom left: Sussex 1909.
Top right: 1912 MCC XI.
Top row: Smith, Woolley, Barnes, Iremonger, Mead, Vine, Strudwick. Middle row: Rhodes, Douglas, Warner, Foster, Gawley (Manager), Hobbs, Gunn. Bottom row: Hitch, Hearn.
Bottom right: Jack Hobbs employs the sweep.

ETON

First Innings
Mr R. H. Lubbock *lbw b* Earle	9
Mr C. W. Tafnell *b* Hillyard	5
Mr W. T. Birchenough *c* Hopley *b* Graham	5
Mr W. T. Holland *c* Hopley *b* Hillyard	2
Mr R. St. L. Fowler *c* Graham *b* Jameson	21
Mr A. I. Steel *b* Graham	0
Mr D. G. Wigan *c* Turnbull *b* Jameson	8
Mr A. B. Stock *lbw b* Alexander	2
Hon. J. N. Manners *c* Graham *b* Alexander	4
Mr K. Lister Kaye *c* Straker *b* Alexander	0
Mr W. G. K. Boswell *not out*	0
B 10, w 1	11
	67

Second Innings
c Straker *b* Hillyard	9
lbw b Alexander	7
c Turnball *b* Jameson	22
st Monckton *b* Alexander	5
c Earle *b* Hillyard	64
c Hopley *b* Hillyard	6
b Graham	16
lbw b Earle	0
not out	40
c Jameson *b* Earle	13
b Earle	32
B 2, w 3	5
	219

Eton Bowling

	Overs	Mdns	Runs	Wkts	Overs	Mdns	Runs	Wkts
Fowler	37.3	9	90	4	10	2	23	8
Steel	31	11	69	4	6.4	1	12	2
Kaye	12	5	23	1	3	—	9	—
Stock	7	2	12	1				
Boswell	8	4	17	—				

Harrow Bowling

	Overs	Mdns	Runs	Wkts	Overs	Mdns	Runs	Wkts
Earle	12	9	4	1	17.3	3	57	3
Hillyard	19	9	28	2	23	7	65	2
Graham	9	7	13	2	8	2	33	1
Jameson	4	1	4	2	9	1	26	1
Alexander	4.1	1	7	3	14	4	33	2
Wilson					2	2	—	—

Umpires: J. Moss and J. P. Whiteside.

JOSEPH WELLS, who played for Kent in 1862 and 1863, died at Liss, in Hampshire, on October 20, 1910. He was born at Redleal, Penshurst, in Kent, on July 14, 1828, and was therefore in his eighty-third year at the time of his death. *Scores and Biographies* (vii – 243) says of him: – "Height 5ft 8½ins, and weight about 10st 7lbs (or 11 st). Bowls very Fast round-armed, with a low delivery; but did not appear for his county till he was about thirty-four years of age.... As a bat he does not excel, and fields generally at short-slip." He will always be remembered for his great feat in the match between Kent and Sussex on Box's ground at Brighton in June, 1862, when, in the first innings of Sussex he bowled down the wickets of Dean, Mr S. Austin Leigh, Ellis and Eillery with consecutive balls. In 1856 he was responsible for the revival of the Bromley CC, whilst from 1857 to 1869 he was engaged at Chislehurst by the West Kent Club, from 1870 to 1872 by Bickley Park, and afterwards by Norwich Grammar School. He was the father of H. G. Wells, the famous novelist, and a nephew of Timothy Duke, the noted bat and ball maker of Penshurst.

SUSSEX v NOTTINGHAMSHIRE
Played at Brighton, May 18, 19, 20, 1911

A PHENOMENAL DISPLAY OF driving on the part of Edward Alletson rendered this match memorable. Alletson went in when Nottinghamshire in their second innings, with seven men out, were only 9 runs ahead. Before lunch, he took fifty minutes to make 47, but on resuming hit away with such extraordinary power and freedom that he added 142 out of 152 for the last wicket in forty minutes, actually scoring his last 89 runs in fifteen minutes. Twice he sent the ball over the stand, and on six other occasions cleared the ring, while in one over from Killick that included two no-balls, he hit three 6s and four 4s – 34 runs in all. His glorious innings was made up by eight 6s, twenty-three 4s, four 3s, ten 2s and seventeen singles. Sussex, instead of gaining the easy victory which appeared assured before Alletson's tremendous hitting, had 237 to make in three hours and a quarter. Robert Relf and Vine scored 112 in seventy-five minutes, but six men were out for 148 and the eighth wicket fell ten minutes before time.

NOTTINGHAMSHIRE

First Innings

Mr A. O. Jones *b* Cox 57
J. Iremonger *c and b* A. E. Relf 0
G. Gunn *st* Butt *b* Cox 90
J. Hardstaff *b* Cox 8
J. Gunn *c* R. Relf *b* Killick 33
W. Payton *c* Heygate *b* Killick 20
W. Whysall *b* Killick 1
G. M. Lee *c and b* Killick 10
E. Alletson *c* Killick *b* A. E. Relf 7
T. Oates *not out* 3
W. Riley *c* Smith *b* Killick 3
B 5, n-b 1 6

238

Second Innings

b Leach 0
c Tudor *b* Killick 83
st Butt *b* R. Relf 66
c Butt *b* A. E. Relf 7
b R. Relf 19
lbw b A. E. Relf 0
c Butt *b* A. E. Relf 3
c Cox *b* Leach 26
c Smith *b* Cox 189
b Leach 1
not out 10
B 3, l-b 2, w 2, n-b 1 8

412

SUSSEX

First Innings

R. Relf *b* Jones 42
J. Vine *b* Jones 77
Mr R. R. Heygate *c* Lee *b* Iremonger 32
G. Cox *c* Alletson *b* Riley 37
A. E. Relf *c and b* Jones 4
Mr C. L. Tudor *c* Oates *b* Riley 23
E. H. Killick *c* Hardstaff *b* Lee 81
G. Leach *b* Lee 52
Mr C. L. A. Smith *not out* 33
J. H. Vincett *c* Iremonger *b* Lee 9
H. R. Butt *b* Riley 13
B 4, l-b 3, w 1, n-b 3 11

414

Second Innings

c Oates *b* Jones 71
c Payton *b* Riley 54
b J. Gunn 13
st Oates *b* Riley 5
c Oates *b* Riley 0
b J. Gunn 4
c Lee *b* Riley 21
b J. Gunn 31
not out 12
not out 1

N-b 1 1

213

Sussex Bowling

	Overs	Mdns	Runs	Wkts	Overs	Mdns	Runs	Wkts
A. E. Relf	19	5	40	2	33	13	92	3
Leach	11	2	53	—	19	2	91	3
Vincett	4	—	31	—	3	1	25	—
R. Relf	11	—	36	—	19	6	39	2
Cox	25	4	58	3	9.4	2	27	1
Killick	10.2	4	14	5	20	2	130	1

Nottinghamshire Bowling

	Overs	Mdns	Runs	Wkts	Overs	Mdns	Runs	Wkts
Iremonger	34	7	97	1	14	2	34	—
Riley	29.4	5	102	3	33	9	82	4
J. Gunn	29	2	87	—	25	9	41	3
Jones	22	2	69	3	5	1	24	1
Alletson	1	—	3	—				
Lee	14	1	45	3	4	—	31	—

Umpires: H. Wood and A. A. White.

Above: E. B. Alletson (1884–1963) has retained for more than seventy years his status as one of the most freakish cricketers who ever lived. A moderate bowler who had some difficulty retaining his place in the county side, Alletson knew just one afternoon in an otherwise unremarkable life when he reached heights of godhead unparalleled. That such a feat should have been achieved by someone who was never to score a century again makes the 1911 Brighton fixture between Nottinghamshire and Sussex one of the great melodramas of cricket history. In the same year, C. B. Fry (right) made his highest score in first-class cricket.

HAMPSHIRE v GLOUCESTERSHIRE
Played at Southampton, August 10, 11, 12, 1911

IN ANOTHER MATCH at Southampton, drawn through high scoring, some brilliant batting was seen, Jessop making two hundreds in a game for the fourth time in his career, and Fry playing his third three-figure innings of the week. Both men played in characteristic style. Jessop scored his 153 out of 221 in an hour and fifty minutes, hitting two 6s and twenty-four 4s. He took only an hour and forty minutes over his 123, which included twenty-two 4s. Dipper also batted very well, his sound play being of great value in helping the visitors to avoid defeat. Fry showed such consummate skill that he gave no chance until 220, and, in putting together his highest score in important cricket, he was at the wicket five hours and a quarter. Powerful driving, clever placing to leg, and accurate cutting marked his innings, which included one 5, and thirty-four 4s. The famous batsman exercised considerable caution. Brown obtained 126 in three hours out of 246, the batting during this partnership being perfect.

GLOUCESTERSHIRE

First Innings

J. H. Board *run out*	37
A. G. Dipper *lbw b Brown*	8
Mr A. W. Roberts *c Stone b Brown*	2
Mr P. H. Bell *lbw b McDonell*	10
Mr G. L. Jessop *c Sprot b McDonell*	153
Mr F. B. Roberts *b Newman*	17
T. Langdon *c McDonell b Newman*	21
Mr W. S. A. Brown *run out*	21
Mr W. M. Brownlee *c and b McDonell*	0
G. Dennett *c McDonell b Newman*	0
C. Parker *not out*	19
B 12, l-b 7, w 10	29
	317

Second Innings

c Bowell b McDonell	32
b Mead	119
c Forster b Newman	51
not out	123
not out	21
c Mead b McDonell	22
c McDonell b Brown	16
B 8, l-b 7, w 2, n-b 2	19
	403

HAMPSHIRE

C. P. Mead *lbw b Dennett*	34
A. Bowell *b Dipper*	33
A. Stone *b Dipper*	16
Mr C. B. Fry *not out*	258
G. Brown *c Dipper b Parker*	126
Mr E. M. Sprot *b F. B. Roberts*	28
Mr H. C. McDonell *c Parker b F. B. Roberts*	68
J. Moore *not out*	25
L-b 3, n-b 3	6
(6 wkts dec.)	594

J. Newman, Mr W. Moorcroft and Col.-Sergt H. Forster did not bat.

Hampshire Bowling

	Overs	Mdns	Runs	Wkts	Overs	Mdns	Runs	Wkts
Brown	14	2	67	2	16	3	58	1
Newman	20	—	79	3	21	5	72	1
McDonell	17.5	1	113	3	31	4	110	2
Moorcroft	6	—	17	—	13	1	51	—
Bowell	1	—	3	—	1	—	6	—
Forster	3	1	9	—	9	3	18	—
Mead					8	4	32	1
Moore					6	—	37	—

Gloucestershire Bowling

	Overs	Mdns	Runs	Wkts
Brownlee	9	1	32	—
Parker	32	4	107	1
Dipper	33	6	126	2
Dennett	31	5	134	1
A. W. Roberts	2	—	20	—
F. B. Roberts	27	3	110	2
Brown	7	—	49	—
Langdon	5	—	10	—

Umpires: W. Vining and J. Blake.

ENGLAND v AUSTRALIA

FOURTH TEST MATCH
Played at Melbourne, February 9, 10, 12, 13, 1912

IN THE FOURTH Test match the Englishmen put the seal on their reputation, giving a most brilliant and convincing display of all-round cricket, and winning by an innings and 225 runs. As they had already won two matches out of three, the victory gave them the rubber. The first day's play went far towards determining the result. Heavy rain had made the ground soft, and Douglas, on winning the toss, put Australia in. At first his policy did not seem likely to answer, the score reaching 53 before the first wicket fell, but Barnes and Foster afterwards bowled splendidly and, despite Minnett's hitting, the innings ended for 191. Hobbs and Rhodes were not out with 30 and 23 respectively at the close of the first day, and on Saturday they set up a test match record, scoring 323 for the first wicket. They were together for just upon four hours and a half. Hobbs, who was first to leave, hit twenty-two 4s in his superb 178. At the drawing of stumps, the total was 370 for one wicket. On Monday, the Englishmen took their total to 589. Rhodes beat Hobbs's score by a single run, and was then caught at the wicket. Though not by any means free from fault, his innings, which lasted nearly seven hours, was a remarkable display of careful batting. The Australians went in for a few minutes at the end of the afternoon, and on Tuesday they failed, being all out just after the tea interval for 173. Douglas bowled in great form. At one point he had sent down fifteen overs for 21 runs and four wickets.

The progress of Jack Hobbs (left) had been magisterial when in 1912 he shared in one of the famous opening partnerships in Test history. But the identity of his partner represents one of the great romances of English cricket. Wilfred Rhodes (right), who at the turn of the century was acknowledged as the world's canniest slow bowler, had been a number eleven who, by the application of a shrewd cricketing brain, steadily transformed himself into a batsman of international class.

Pictured (above) England play Australia later in the year at The Oval. Hobbs is shown scoring the first run of the match.

AUSTRALIA

First Innings

C. Kelleway c Hearne b Woolley 29
H. V. Hordern b Barnes 19
W. Bardsley b Foster 0
V. T. Trumper b Foster 17
C. Hill c Hearne b Barnes 22
W. W. Armstrong b Barnes 7
R. B. Minnett c Rhodes b Foster 56
V. S. Ransford c Rhodes b Foster 4
T. J. Matthews c Gunn b Barnes 3
A. Cotter b Barnes 15
H. Carter not out 6
    B 1, l-b 5, n-b 7 13
                                                           191

Second Innings

c Smith b Barnes 5
c Foster b Douglas 5
b Foster 3
b Barnes 28
b Douglas 11
b Douglas 11
c Douglas 7
not out 29
b Foster 10
c Mead b Foster 8
c Hearne b Douglas 38
  B 9, l-b 2, n-b 7 18
                                  173

ENGLAND

J. B. Hobbs c Carter b Hordern 178
W. Rhodes c Carter b Minnett 179
G. Gunn c Hill b Armstrong 75
J. W. Hearne c Armstrong b Minnett 0
Mr F. R. Foster c Hordern b Armstrong 50
Mr J. W. H. T. Douglas c Bardsley b Armstrong 0
F. E. Woolley c Kelleway b Minnett 56
C. P. Mead b Hordern 21
J. Vine not out 4
E. J. Smith c Matthews b Kelleway 7
S. F. Barnes c Hill b Hordern 0
    Extras 19
                                               589

England Bowling

	Overs	Mdns	Runs	Wkts	Overs	Mdns	Runs	Wkts
Foster	22	2	77	4	19	3	38	3
Barnes	29.1	4	74	5	20	6	47	2
Woolley	11	3	22	1	2	—	7	—
Rhodes	2	1	1	—				
Hearn	1	—	4	—	3	—	17	—
Douglas					17.5	6	46	5

Australia Bowling

	Overs	Mdns	Runs	Wkts
Cotter	37	5	125	—
Kelleway	26	2	80	1
Armstrong	36	12	93	3
Matthews	22	1	68	—
Minnett	20	5	59	3
Ransford	2	1	8	—
Hordern	47.5	5	137	3

GEORGE JOHN BONNOR, born at Orange (NSW), February 25, 1855; died at Orange (NSW), June 27, 1912. Though he was last seen on an English cricket ground more than twenty years ago, George Bonnor had not in one sense outlived his fame, his doings being constantly recalled and talked about. He was, indeed, far too striking a personality to be forgotten in less than a generation. Australia has sent to England many finer batsmen, but no other hitter of such extraordinary power. During his five visits to this country – he came here with the Australian teams of 1880, 1882, 1884, 1886, and 1888 – Bonnor earned a reputation akin to that of our own C. I. Thornton, the question being often discussed as to which of the two men could make the bigger drives. Whether Bonnor ever equalled Thornton's longest hit at Brighton, or his famous drive over the old racquet court at The Oval, is a moot point, but, be this as it may, the Australian in his own particular line had only one rival. Bonnor was a splendid specimen of manhood. He stood about 6ft 5in, but he was so finely proportioned that there was nothing ungainly in his figure or carriage. His presence contributed almost as much as his wonderful hitting to the fame that he enjoyed wherever he played. He was not content to be a hitter pure and simple, setting himself at times to play quite an orthodox game. These efforts at steadiness afforded him some satisfaction, but they made his colleagues in various Australian elevens furious. They argued that his business was to hit, and that when he failed to fulfil his proper mission he was no use. Bonnor never met with much success as a batsman in Test matches in England, but in games only less important he played many a fine innings. One remembers in particular his 74 against the Gentlemen of England at The Oval in 1882. In the same season he gave a remarkable display against I Zingari at Scarborough. Nothing in Bonnor's career is more often recalled than the catch with which George Ulyett got him out in the England and Australia match at Lord's in 1884. Bonnor hit a half-volley back with all his force; Ulyett put up his right hand, and the ball stuck. Probably no harder hit was ever caught. Members of the England eleven gathered round Ulyett in wonderment at what he had done. All the bowler said was that if the ball had hit fingers he should have had no more cricket that season. Another famous catch – of quite a different kind – to which Bonnor was out was in the England and Australia match at The Oval in 1880 – the first Test match in England. The ball was hit to such a tremendous height that the batsmen had turned for the third run when Fred Grace caught it. That great cricketer, who died a fortnight after the match, said he was sure his heart stopped beating while he was waiting for the ball to drop. In first-class matches Bonnor scored 4,989 runs with an average of 20.70.

MCC TEAM v SOUTH AFRICA

SECOND TEST MATCH
Played at Johannesburg, December, 26, 27, 29, 30, 1913

FOR THE SECOND Test match South Africa made four changes from the team beaten at Durban, Zulch, Beaumont, Tancred, and Newberry taking the places of Tapscott, Lewis, Cooper, and Baumgartner. The result was not quite so overwhelming as before, but the Englishmen won by an innings and 12 runs. It was Barnes's match. On no occasion during the tour was the great bowler seen to quite such advantage. He took seventeen wickets – eight for 56 and nine for 103 – proving quite irresistible on the last morning. The English batting fell away strangely after a splendid start. Rhodes was too cautious to please the crowd, but his steadiness was invaluable to his side. Batting five hours and ten minutes for his 152, he hit twenty-one 4s. Managing, at last, to get a hundred in a Test match, Mead played extremely well for something over three hours and a half.

SOUTH AFRICA

First Innings

H. W. Taylor b Barnes 29
J. W. Zulch c Woolley b Barnes..................14
P. A. M. Hands c Rhodes b Barnes 0
R. Beaumont c Strudwick b Barnes 0
A. D. Nourse b Barnes..........................17
L. J. Tancred st Strudwick b Barnes 13
G. P. D. Hartigan c Smith b Rhodes 51
T. A. Ward b Woolley 19
C. J. Newberry st Strudwick b Barnes 1
J. M. Blanckenberg not out 0
J. L. Cox c Strudwick b Barnes 0
    B 10, l-b 4, n-b 2 16

                        160

Second Innings

c Rhodes b Barnes 40
c Relf b Barnes 34
c Rhodes b Barnes 40
c Strudwick b Relf 5
c Strudwick b Barnes 56
b Barnes 20
lbw b Barnes 2
b Barnes 0
st Strudwick b Barnes 5
not out 12
b Barnes 0
    B 9, l-b 6, n-b 2 17

                        231

MCC TEAM

A. E. Relf b Blanckenberg 63
W. Rhodes c and b Blanckenberg 152
J. B. Hobbs lbw b Newberry 23
C. P. Mead c Beaumont b Blanckenberg 102
Hon. L. H. Tennyson lbw b Cox 13
Mr J. W. H. T. Douglas c Taylor b Blanckenberg 3
F. E. Woolley b Newberry 0
Mr M. C. Bird c Ward b Newberry 1
E. J. Smith lbw b Cox 9
H. Strudwick c Cox b Blanckenberg 14
S. F. Barnes not out 0
    B 22, w 1 23
                                          403

MCC Team Bowling

	Overs	Mdns	Runs	Wkts	Overs	Mdns	Runs	Wkts
Douglas	2	—	11	—	6	—	27	—
Barnes	26.5	9	56	8	38.4	7	103	9
Relf	14	1	24	—	9	3	19	1
Woolley	3	1	5	1	21	5	45	—
Rhodes	13	5	23	1	9	2	20	—
Bird	4	1	15	—				

South African Bowling

	Overs	Mdns	Runs	Wkts
Cox	30	8	74	2
Nourse	21	2	62	—
Blanckenberg	38	13	83	5
Newberry	26	2	93	3
Hartigan	5	—	24	—
Taylor	6	—	17	—
Hinds	8	—	27	—
Beaumont	1	1	—	—

This England touring side could have had no faint inkling of its position in the historical scheme of things, for it was destined to be the last party of England cricketers to set out on a tour before the outbreak of the First World War.

When on trial for Lancashire Sydney Barnes (above) struck A. C. MacLaren several times with balls rising from a length. Barnes apologised and was met with the response, "Don't be sorry Barnes. You're coming to Australia with me."

THE REV. A. H. C. FARGUS. He was not lost, as stated in the Press, in Admiral Cradock's flagship, the *Monmouth*, on November 1, 1914. Missing a train, he was prevented from re-joining the ship just before it left for the Pacific and was appointed to another.

LIEUT ARTHUR EDWARD JEUNE COLLINS, of the Royal Engineers, who was killed in action on November 11, 1914, came suddenly into note by scoring 628 not out for Clarke's House v North Town, in a Junior house match at Clifton College, in June, 1899, when only thirteen years old. During the six hours and fifty minutes he was in he hit a 6, four 5s, thirty-one 4s, thirty-three 3s, and 146 2s, carrying his bat through the innings, and Clarke's, who scored 836, won by an innings and 688 runs. Collins also obtained eleven wickets in the match, seven in the first innings and four in the second, and in partnership with Redfern (13) put on as many as 183 for the last wicket. In 1901 and 1902 he was in the College XI, in the former year scoring 342 runs with an average of 38.00, his highest innings being 112 against Old Cliftonians. He was a free-hitting batsman, but his military duties prevented him from taking cricket seriously: still he made many good scores in Army matches, and for Old Cliftonians v Trojans at Southampton in August, 1913, he and F. G. Robinson made 141 without being parted for the first wicket in thirty-eight minutes, Collins scoring 63 and his partner 77. His best performance at Lord's was to make 58 and 36 for RE v RA in 1913. He was born in India in 1885, gazetted second Lieutenant in 1904 and promoted Lieutenant in 1907.

ANDREW ERNEST STODDART, one of the greatest of batsmen, died by his own hand on Saturday, the 3rd of April, 1915, shooting himself through the head. A brilliant career thus came to the saddest of ends. Mr Stoddart was born at South Shields on March 11, 1863, and had thus completed his 52nd year. Curiously enough, considering the great fame he won, he did not take to cricket seriously until 22 years of age, when he became associated with the Hampstead Club, and showed such form, scoring no fewer than five separate hundreds for that team, that before the end of the season of 1885 he had been tried for Middlesex. From 1886 to 1898, except for the summer of 1888, when he was engaged playing rugby football in Australia and New Zealand, Mr Stoddart proved a tower of strength to Middlesex in batting, keeping up his skill so well that in 1898 – his last full season in county cricket – he averaged 52. He soon became a popular idol at Lord's, his batting, in conjunction with that of T. C. O'Brien, making the Middlesex matches far more attractive than they had ever been before his day.

He turned out only once for Middlesex in 1899, and twice in the following year, but in his last match for the county – against Somerset at Lord's – he put together a score of 221, the highest of his career in first-class cricket. Among his most famous innings were 215 not out against Lancashire at Manchester in 1891 and 151 for England against the MCC at Lord's in 1887, when he and Arthur Shrewsbury raised the total to 266 for the first wicket. In 1886, for Hampstead against the Stoics, he played an innings of 485 – at that time the highest individual score on record.

On four occasions Mr Stoddart paid visits to Australia, first in 1887, as a member of G.F. Vernon's team, when he averaged 32. Four years later he formed one of the side taken out by Lord Sheffield, his average then amounting to 37. In 1894–95, and again in 1897–98, he himself took a team out to Australia. The first of these undertakings resulted in England winning the rubber after two victories had been gained by each country, but the second proved a big disappointment, no fewer than four of the five Test matches ending in favour of Australia. Still, in the two tours associated with his leadership, Mr Stoddart came out well with averages of 51 and 34. In the fifth match in the tour of 1894–95, which decided the rubber in England's favour, J. T. Brown played a memorable innings of 140, and Albert Ward scored 91. As a Test match player in this country, Mr Stoddart achieved no special distinction. He took no part in those games in 1890, and although he played in all three matches three years later, making 83 at The Oval, his only other appearances for England at home were at Lord's and Manchester in 1896.

A splendid batsman to watch, Mr Stoddart had all strokes at his command, but was especially strong in driving and hitting on the leg side. Again and again he proved his greatness by his ability to make runs under conditions which found other batsmen at fault, his play, both on fiery and on soft wickets, being quite exceptional. As a special instance of his power on fiery wickets one recalls a superb innings of 91 for Middlesex against Surrey at The Oval in 1892. The Oval was not in good order that year, and Lockwood's bowling needed some facing. Stoddart, however, did not mind a bit. Two or three times he hit to the boundary balls that got up as high as his head. Almost equally good was his batting, when in with W. G. Grace, against Richardson and Mold in the Gentlemen and Players match at Lord's in 1895. In the early part of his career he proved a useful change bowler, and anywhere in the field he was both brilliant and safe. In his early seasons for Middlesex he had onerous work to do on the off-side when George Burton was bowling, but he was never known to flinch.

Mr Stoddart was one of the very few men who have represented their country at rugby football as well as at cricket. Between 1886 and 1893 he took part in ten international rugby matches, and would have certainly have played in more but for the fact that in two of the intermediate seasons England, owing to a dispute with the other Unions, had no international matches. He appeared twice against Scotland, three times against Ireland, and four times against Wales, while in 1889 he played against the Maories. A splendid runner, with plenty of pace and dodging ability and not above jumping over an opponent on occasion, he was a great three-quarter – possessed of a very fine pair of hands – a brilliant kick, and a player full of resource.

It was a memorable drop-kick against a gale of wind he made that, giving Middlesex victory over Yorkshire by a goal to four tries, led to the rules of the game being altered. At that time a goal counted more than any number of tries. Mr Stoddart captained England against Wales in 1890, when, on a muddy swamp at Dewsbury, Wales, scoring a try to nothing, gained their first victory over England. Another famous match in which he took part that at Cardiff in 1893, when, after England had established a commanding lead, Wales finished in great form, and, under the method of scoring then in vogue, succeeded in snatching a win by one point. It may be questioned whether any two players ever enjoyed a better understanding than Alan Rotherham, at half, and Andrew Stoddart at three-quarter. Certainly the combination of these two men formed one of the brightest features of the rugby game in the "eighties." C. S. C.

WILLIAM GILBERT GRACE, was born at Downend near Bristol on July 18, 1848 and died at his home, Fairmount, Eltham, Kent on October 23, 1915. In no branch of sport has anyone ever enjoyed such an unquestioned supremacy as that of W. G. Grace in the cricket field. In his great days he stood alone, without a rival. Not even George Fordham and Fred Archer as jockeys, or John Roberts as a billiard player, had such a marked superiority over the men who were nearest to them in point of ability. Whatever may be in store for the game of cricket in the future it seems safe to say that such a player will never be seen again. A rare combination of qualities went to the making of W. G. Grace. Blessed with great physical advantages, he united to a strength of constitution that defied fatigue a devotion to the game which time was powerless to affect. When he was in his prime no sun was too hot and no day too long for him. It is on record that when, for a cricketer, he was no longer young, he spent the whole night by the bedside of a patient, and on the following day stepped on to the Clifton College ground and scored over 200 runs.

Mr Grace's career in the cricket field – almost unexampled in point of length – can be sharply divided into two portions. His early fame as a batsman culminated in the season of 1876, when in the month of August he scored in three successive innings, 344 against Kent at Canterbury, 177 against Nottinghamshire at Clifton, and 318 not out against Yorkshire at Cheltenham. Soon after that, having passed his examination at Edinburgh as a surgeon, he thought of gradually retiring from cricket and settling down, like his elder brothers, to the busy life of a general practitioner. As a matter of fact, he did for many years hold a parish appointment at Bristol, a locum tenens doing his work in the summer months. There can be little doubt that his change of plans was mainly due to the appearance in England in 1878 of the first Australian eleven. Those whose memories go back to that now somewhat distant time will remember the tremendous sensation caused by the victories of that eleven, and in particular by

Spofforth's bowling, and Blackham's wicket-keeping. Englishmen realised, with an excusable shock of surprise, that in the cricket field there were serious rivals to be faced.

Mr Grace had never been in such poor batting form as he was in 1878, and on the few occasions that he met the Australian bowlers he did nothing in the least degree worthy of his reputation. I have no exact knowledge on the point, but I feel tolerably certain that the success of the Australians revived Mr Grace's ambition. At any rate, the fact remains that, though the most brilliant part of his career had ended before the invasion of 1878, the Australians found him for the best part of twenty years the most formidable of their opponents. This second part of his career as a batsman began towards the end of the season of 1880. Following some fine performances for Gloucestershire he played, as everyone will remember, a great innings of 152 at The Oval in the first match in this country between England and Australia. Even then, however, though only in his 33rd year, he laboured under one serious disadvantage. In the four years following his triumphs of 1876, he had put on a lot of weight and was very heavy for so young a man.

He said himself at the time that he was never in better form than in those closing weeks of the season of 1880, and that, but for lack of condition, he would have made many more runs. Against increasing bulk he had to battle for the rest of his cricket life. For a long time he retained his activity to a surprising extent, but as the years went on his once splendid fielding gradually left him. He kept up his batting, however, in a marvellous way, the success of what one may call his second period in the cricket field reaching its climax when in 1895 he scored a thousand runs in first-class cricket in the month of May. His batting at that time has never been approached by a man of the same age; he was nearly 47. In 1896 he was still very good, but after that the years began to tell on him, and in 1899, when he moved from Bristol to the Crystal Palace, he played at Trent Bridge his last match for England against Australia. Still, though he had now done with Test matches, he went on playing first-class cricket for several seasons, his career practically ending with the Gentlemen and Players' match at The Oval in 1906. The finish was worthy of him as, on his 58th birthday, he scored 74, batting up to a certain point with much of the vigour of his younger days.

Of Mr Grace's cricket from the time of his first appearance at Lord's in July, 1864, for the South Wales Club against the MCC down to the end of 1876, columns could be written without exhausting the subject. He was picked for the Gentlemen, as a lad of 17, both at Lord's and The Oval in 1865, the honour being conferred upon him quite as much for his medium-pace bowling as for his batting. A year later, however, he proved himself, beyond all question, the best batsman in England, two wonderful innings at The Oval establishing his fame. He scored 224 not out for England against Surrey and 173 not out for Gentlemen of the South against Players of the South. An attack of scarlet fever interfered with his cricket in 1867, but after that he never looked back. His best seasons as a batsman were, I fancy, 1871, 1873, and 1876. His play in 1871 far surpassed anything that had ever been done before.

In his whole career he scored in Gentlemen and Players' matches 6,008 runs with an average of 42 and took 271 wickets for a trifle under 19 runs each. He made seven hundreds for the Gentlemen at Lord's, four at The Oval, and one each at Brighton, Prince's, Scarborough, and Hastings. The first of his seven hundreds at Lord's was obtained in 1868, and the last, after an interval of twenty-seven years, in 1895. Of these seven innings the first was, perhaps. the most remarkable. Going in first wicket down for a very strong side he took out his bat for 134, the total only reaching 201. As Lord Harris has pointed out the wickets at Lord's in those far-off days were by no means so true and easy as careful attention made them in later years. A score of a hundred at Lord's in the '60's, against the best bowling was an incomparably bigger feat than it is at the present time.

No mention has yet been made of Mr Grace's connection with Gloucestershire cricket. With his two brothers, E.M. and G.F., and other fine, though less gifted, players to help him, he built up a team of remarkable strength in batting and fielding. The county club was established in 1871, and in 1876 and 1877 the eleven stood ahead of all rivals. Until beaten at Clifton by the first Australian Eleven in 1878 the team never lost a match at home. After G. F. Grace's death in 1880, Gloucestershire never seemed quite the same as before, but in 1885, and again in 1898, there was, thanks to W.G.'s batting and C. L. Townsend's bowling, a brief revival of old glories. The Gloucestershire matches at Clifton and Cheltenham in the old days were delightful, the Gloucestershire eleven being quite a family party. Like other families they had their little differences of opinion, but there was a great feeling of comradeship among them, and they played cricket with tremendous zest.

Mr Grace's venture in connection with the London County at the Crystal Palace did not add to his fame. He was in his 51st year when he left Bristol, the experiment being made far too late. Many pleasant matches were played at the Palace, but they were carried through in too leisurely a spirit to appeal to a public brought up on cricket of a much sterner character. If tried fifteen years earlier the project might have proved a success. As it was the London County faded out when Mr Grace's contract with the Crystal Palace Company came to an end.

With Mr Grace's characteristics as a batsman I must deal rather briefly. He was, in the main, quite orthodox in style, his bat being as perfectly straight as Fuller Pilch's, but he greatly enlarged the domain of orthodoxy, playing a far more aggressive and punishing game than any of the classic batsmen who came before him. It should be explained here that E. M. Grace, who first made the family name famous, played a game of his own and was a little outside comparisons. W.G. developed the art of batting to an extraordinary degree, but he was not, like E.M., a revolutionist. There is his own authority for stating that he did not indulge in the pull till he was forty. A splendid all-round hitter, he excelled all his predecessors in his power of placing the ball on the on-side. A story is told of a cricketer who had regarded Fuller Pilch as the last word in batting, being taken in his old age to see Mr Grace bat for the first time. He watched the great man for a quarter of an hour or so and then broke out into expressions of boundless delight. "Why," he said, "this man scores continually from balls that old Fuller would have been thankful to stop." The words conveyed everything. Mr Grace when he went out at the ball did so for the purpose of getting runs. Pilch and his imitators, on the other hand, constantly used forward play for defence alone.

When the wicket was difficult and the ball turning, Mr Grace trusted for defence to that strong back play which, even in his boyhood, convinced his people at home that he would be a greater batsman than his brother, E.M. Mr Grace's batting from 1868 onwards quite overshadowed his bowling, and yet during his career he took many hundreds of wickets. Indeed, old Bob Thoms, the umpire, always contended that if he had not been such a wonderful batsman he would have been the best slow bowler in England. Even as it was he held his own very well with such masters as Alfred Shaw and Southerton. He bowled medium pace with a purely round arm action in his young days, but slackened his speed about 1872.

His superb strength and health enabled him to stand any amount of cricket, but in his best two years as a bowler – 1875 and 1877 – his batting fell off fifty per cent. He did not rely much on break, only turning in a little from leg, but he had great command over his length and very seldom indeed pitched short. His chief strength lay in head work. No one was quicker to find out the weak points of a batsman or more certain to lure an impetuous hitter to his doom. In Gloucestershire's great days he was much helped by brilliant fielding. Fred Grace in particular, at deep square leg, being invaluable to him. When he first appeared for the Gentlemen, Mr Grace was a splendid outfield, capable of throwing the ball a hundred yards, but as time went on he took to fielding near the wicket and for many years he had no superior at point except his brother E.M.

Personally, W.G. struck me as the most natural and unspoiled of men. Whenever and wherever one met him he was always the same. There was not the smallest trace of affectation about him. If anything annoyed him he was quick to show anger, but his little outbursts were soon over. One word I will add. No man who ever won such world-wide fame could have been more modest in speaking of his own doings. Mr Grace was married in 1873 to Miss Agnes Day. His domestic life was unclouded except by the death of his only daughter in 1899 and of his eldest son in 1905. Mrs Grace and two sons – Captain H. E. Grace, RN, and Captain C. B. Grace, KFRE – survive him.

S. H. P.

LEICESTERSHIRE v SURREY
Played at Leicester, June 9, 10, 1920

AN EASY VICTORY by an innings and 105 runs was gained by Surrey on the second afternoon. The match was remarkable for the fact that five men were unable to play on the Thursday. Salmon, Mounteney, and Benskin were injured by severe blows when batting on the previous day; Rushby strained his side when bowling, and Fender, called away on urgent business, did not return until the match was over. Hobbs captained Surrey during the home side's second innings. Hobbs played a wonderful innings of 134. Getting his runs in ninety-five minutes without a mistake, he hit a 6 and nineteen 4s, his cutting, driving, and pulling being equally brilliant. Sandham helped in a first partnership of 177

Two of the five men unable to play on the Thursday, were P. G. H. Fender (left) and A. Mounteney (right) the Leicestershire No 4. What 'urgent business' it was that dictated Fender's sudden departure it would be interesting to know. Whatever the reason, his absence does not seem to have embarrassed his colleagues who remained far better equipped than the decimated Leicestershire side which lost by an innings and 105 runs.

runs, and Hitch and Harrison put on 58 in twenty-five minutes. Rushby took five wickets at the start of Leicestershire's innings, and when he had to retire, Reay proved almost as effective. Coe once more batted resolutely, but in the unfortunate circumstances Leicestershire made nothing of a fight against their powerful visitors.

SURREY

J. B. Hobbs *c* Shingler *b* Mounteney	134
A. Sandham *c* Sidwel *b* Benskin	49
A. Ducat *c* Shingler *b* Mounteney	11
T. Shepherd *c* Sidwell *b* Benskin	8
H. A. Peach *c* Whitehead *b* Benskin	1
H. S. Harrison *c and b* Astill	34
Mr P. G. H. Fender *c* Whitehead *b* Benskin	17
W. Hitch *b* Astill	41
Mr G. M. Reay *lbw b* Shipman	0
H. Strudwick *c and b* Simpson	5
T. Rushby *not out*	3
B 1, l-b 5	6
	309

LEICESTERSHIRE

First Innings

Mr C. J. B. Wood *b* Rushby	1
H. Whitehead *b* Rushby	33
W. E. Astill *c* Strudwick *b* Rushby	0
A. Mounteney *c* Harrison *b* Rushby	3
S. Coe *b* Rushby	21
Mr G. H. Salmon *retired hurt*	13
G. Shingler *b* Fender	13
A. Shipman *not out*	10
F. Bale *b* Rushby	2
W. E. Benskin *b* Rushby	0
T. E. Sidwell *c* Ducat *b* Hitch	5
B 13, l-b 3	16
	117

Second Innings

c Shepherd *b* Hitch	17
c Ducat	19
b Reay	1
absent hurt	0
b Shepherd	40
absent hurt	0
b Reay	4
b Reay	0
b Reay	0
absent hurt	0
not out	1
B 5	5
	87

Leicestershire Bowling

	Overs	Mdns	Runs	Wkts
Benskin	20	3	83	4
Astill	13	1	56	2
Shipman	10.5	—	60	2
Bale	5	—	37	—
Shingler	4	—	28	—
Mounteney	11	3	39	2

Surrey Bowling

	Overs	Mdns	Runs	Wkts	Overs	Mdns	Runs	Wkts
Hitch	16.1	4	34	1	9	1	25	1
Rushby	21	9	32	7	2	1	6	—
Reay	5	1	13	—	9	2	32	4
Fender	8	1	22	1				
Ducat					5	—	16	1
Shepherd					2	—	3	1

Umpires: G. P. Harrison and J. Moss.

Left: Jack Hobbs whose dismissal for low scores in both innings helped Middlesex win the 1920 County Championship.
Above: Pelham Warner, the Middlesex captain, was carried off the field shoulder high when his team won with ten minutes to spare. Warner, after a lifetimes involvement in cricket at various levels, was to have a stand named after him at Lord's and his ashes scattered on the out-field close to the spot where he had hit his first boundary for Rugby v Marlborough in 1889.

MIDDLESEX v SURREY
Played at Lord's, August 28, 30, 31, 1920

THIS WAS THE match of the season. Middlesex and Lancashire were running neck and neck for the Championship, and as Lancashire on the same days had the simplest of tasks against Worcestershire, Middlesex knew that nothing less than an actual victory would be of real value to them. Never before has a county match proved such an attraction at Lord's. On the Saturday there must have been nearly 25,000 people on the ground, 20,700 paying for admission at the gates. A great fight was looked forward to, and as it happened all expectations were exceeded. It was a game never to be forgotten. Middlesex in the end winning by 55 runs, and so securing the Championship. Winning the toss Middlesex had the advantage of batting first on a hard wicket, but nothing could have been less promising than their start. For once Lee and Hearne failed them, and in less than an hour three wickets were down for 35 runs. After these disasters nothing was risked, and at the end of the afternoon the Middlesex score with eight men out had only reached 253.

Warner was blamed in some quarters for over-caution, but he saved his side. In getting 79 he was batting for nearly four hours and a half. On the Monday there was again an enormous attendance, the number paying at the gates this time being 20,021. Owing nearly everything to Sandham, Surrey had the best of the day's cricket. Sandham had some luck – a chance of stumping at 40 and a chance at slip at 77 – but for the most part he played superbly, combining an ever-watchful defence with his clean hitting. For his 167 not out he was batting four hours and twenty minutes, his figures including seventeen 4s. With the object of getting Middlesex in before the end of the afternoon Fender declared with nine wickets down, but his policy met with no reward, Skeet and Lee batting for forty minutes and taking the score to 27. For sustained excitement the third day beat everything seen in London last season. Skeet and Lee made victory for Middlesex possible, staying in until after lunch and sending up 208 for the first wicket. Lee was splendid, and Skeet, though not so certain in timing the ball, played better than he had ever played before in a first-class match. Warner declared at twenty minutes to four, leaving Surrey to get 244 in a trifle over three hours. The downfall of Hobbs – caught in the slips at 22 – was discouraging, but Surrey went for the runs and, with Sandham playing even more finely than on the previous day, the 100 was up in an hour and a quarter for two wickets. However, Hendren got rid of Shepherd by means of a wonderful catch in the deep field just in front of the screen with his hands above his head – this being really the turning-point of the game. Surrey's great hope departed when Sandham – the sixth man out – was caught and bowled from a full pitch. In the end Middlesex won with ten minutes to spare. Warner was carried off the field shoulder high, and before the crowd dispersed he and Fender had to make speeches.

MIDDLESEX

First Innings

Mr C. H. L. Skeet c Ducat b Rushby	2
H. W. Lee c Hitch b Fender	12
J. W. Hearne c and b Hitch	15
E. Hendren b Reay	41
Mr P. F. Warner b Rushby	79
Mr F. T. Mann c and b Fender	12
Mr N. Haig b Reay	18
Mr G. T. S. Stevens b Fender	53
Mr H. K. Longman b Fender	0
H. R. Murrell c Ducat b Hitch	9
T. J. Durston not out	0
B 12, l-b 12, n-b 3	27
	268

Second Innings

c Fender b Hitch	106
b Hitch	108
lbw b Rushby	26
c Sandham b Rushby	5
not out	14
c Peach b Fender	22
b Rushby	1
not out	21
b Reay	0
B 8, n-b 4, w 1	13
(7 wkts dec.)	316

SURREY

First Innings

J. B. Hobbs c Mann b Hearne	24
A. Sandham not out	167
Mr M. Howell c Murrell b Durston	7
T. Shepherd c Murrell b Durston	0
H. A. Peach hit wkt b Stevens	18
A. Ducat st Murrell b Lee	49
Mr P. G. H. Fender c Haig b Durston	30
W. Hitch b Durston	1
Mr G. M. Reay c Haig b Lee	6
H. Strudwick b Hearne	9
T. Rushby not out	6
B 17, l-b 5, n-b 2	25
(9 wkts dec.)	341

Second Innings

c Lee b Haig	10
c and b Hearne	68
st Murrell b Stevens	25
c Hendren b Stevens	26
b Stevens	11
lbw b Hearne	7
b Durston	1
b Stevens	6
b Hearne	5
b Stevens	10
not out	7
B 11, l-b 1	12
	188

Surrey Bowling

	Overs	Mdns	Runs	Wkts	Overs	Mdns	Runs	Wkts
Hitch	32.1	10	66	2	20	5	71	2
Rushby	23	9	48	2	22	7	73	3
Fender	28	4	76	4	16.5	2	70	1
Reay	26	17	31	2	18	1	61	1
Ducat	3	1	10	—	3	—	12	—
Shepherd	6	3	10	—	4	—	16	—

Middlesex Bowling

	Overs	Mdns	Runs	Wkts	Overs	Mdns	Runs	Wkts
Durston	30	9	97	4	14	1	42	1
Haig	10	4	25	—	8	—	19	1
Stevens	16	—	72	1	13.4	—	61	5
Hearne	24	8	57	2	11	—	37	3
Lee	15	2	66	2	4	—	17	—

Umpires: J. Blake and G. P. Harrison.

AN ENGLAND XI v AUSTRALIANS
Played at Eastbourne, August 27, 29, 30, 1921

THIS WAS THE match that produced the sensation of the season. Unbeaten up to the closing days of August, it seemed certain that the Australians, surpassing the records of all the previous teams, would go through their tour without suffering defeat, but, as events turned out, the side selected by MacLaren won the game after a tremendous struggle by 28 runs. MacLaren all through the summer had maintained that he could pick a side good enough to overcome the Australians, but all hope of victory seemed gone when on winning the toss, and taking first innings on a perfect wicket, the Englishmen went down in an hour and a quarter for a score of 43. Probably the strong wind that was blowing accounted in some measure for the failure, but be that as it may, McDonald and Armstrong were irresistible. Gregory started the bowling with McDonald, but he hurt the thumb of his bowling hand after sending down two overs and had to retire. With the match to all appearance in their hands the Australians possibly regarded their task too lightly. Thanks to Bardsley and Macartney the score was up to 80 with only one man out, but the last eight wickets went down for 91 runs, Falcon bowling finely. Still, though the total only reached 174 there did not seem the least cause for apprehension, especially as the Englishmen lost a wicket for 8 runs before the drawing of stumps. Bardsley played a beautiful innings, making 70 in two hours without giving a chance. On the Monday Faulkner and Hubert Ashton brought about a marvellous change in the game. Becoming partners with the score at 60 for four wickets, they put on 154 runs together, both playing superbly. Ashton was out lbw at 214, and Faulkner left, eighth wicket down, at 307. Not since the first match of the Triangular Tournament in 1912 had Faulkner played such an innings as his 153. He hit a 6 and twenty 4s, and was at the wicket for three hours and a half without making a mistake. Ashton did not hit so hard, but his innings was also flawless. The Australians were left with only 196 to get, and at the close of play they had scored 21 for the loss of Collin's wicket. Most people took it for granted that the Australians would win readily enough, nothing in their record suggesting failure in the last innings. If what happened could in any way have been foreseen the Eastbourne ground would hardly have accommodated the crowd. Bardsley was bowled at 52, and at the same total Carter was caught at point. Then at 73 a fine ball clean bowled Macartney, this being perhaps the turning point of the game. Andrews and Pellew added 30 runs together, but at lunch time the Australians had five wickets down, and still required 87 runs to win. For some little time after resuming things went well for them, Andrews and Ryder taking the score to 143 before Ryder left. Gregory, who followed, was out leg-before-wicket to the second ball he received, and the chances veered round. Andrews was out at 153, and amidst intense excitement Armstrong was lbw. Mailey, the last man, joined McDonald with 42 runs still wanted. Thirteen runs were added, and then Gibson clean bowled Mailey and won the match. When it was all over there was a scene of wild enthusiasm, MacLaren, in particular, coming in for endless congratulations. For once last season the English fielding was magnificent, and it was said that Gibson, in taking six wickets for 64 runs, scarcely sent down a bad length ball. So fine was the fielding of both sides that no catch which went to hand was dropped.

AN ENGLAND XI

First Innings

Mr G. N. Foster c Gregory b McDonald 5
Mr G. A. Faulkner b Armstrong 3
Mr G. Ashton lbw b Armstrong 6
Mr H. Ashton b McDonald 0
Mr A. P. F. Chapman b McDonald 16
Mr C. T. Ashton c Ryder b Armstrong 1
Mr M. Falcon b McDonald 8
Mr G. E. C. Wood lbw b Armstrong 1
Mr A. C. MacLaren b McDonald 0
Mr C. H. Gibson not out 1
Mr W. Brearley b Armstrong 1
N-b 1 1

43

Second Innings

c and b McDonald 11
c Mailey b Armstrong 153
lbw b Armstrong 36
lbw b Armstrong 75
b McDonald 11
b McDonald 0
c and b McDonald 17
b McDonald 2
b McDonald 5
not out 0
run out 0
B 10, l-b 1, n-b 5 16

326

The undefeated Australians at the end of their tour were beaten by a scratch side captained by the ageing Archie MacLaren. He had insisted that he could pick a team to defeat the tourists. The vindication of his boast proved to be one of the greatest upsets in cricket history.

AUSTRALIANS

First Innings
H. L. Collins b Falcon 19
W. Bardsley lbw b Faulkner 70
C. G. Macartney b Faulkner 24
T. J. E. Andrews b Faulkner 0
C. E. Pellew c H. Ashton b Falcon 1
J. Ryder b Falcon 10
W. W. Armstrong b Falcon 13
H. Carter c H. Ashton b Faulkner 10
J. M. Gregory not out 16
E. A. McDonald b Falcon 4
A. A. Mailey b Falcon 4
    B 1, l-b 2 3
                                                           174

Second Innings
c H. Ashton b Gibson 12
b Gibson 22
b Falcon 14
b Faulkner 31
c H. Ashton b Gibson 16
c G. Ashton b Gibson 28
lbw b Faulkner 11
c C. T. Ashton b Falcon 16
lbw b Gibson 0
not out 9
b Gibson 0
    L-b 3, n-b 5 8
                                                           167

Australian Bowling

	Overs	Mdns	Runs	Wkts	Overs	Mdns	Runs	Wkts
Gregory	2	—	6	—	9	—	51	—
McDonald	10	2	21	5	31	3	98	6
Armstrong	8.1	4	15	5	24.5	6	74	3
Ryder					5	1	11	—
Mailey					22	3	76	—

An England XI's Bowling

	Overs	Mdns	Runs	Wkts	Overs	Mdns	Runs	Wkts
Falcon	18.4	2	67	6	18	2	82	2
Gibson	14	2	54	—	22.4	6	64	6
Faulkner	16	1	50	4	5	1	13	2

Umpires: H. Butt and J. P. Whiteside.

MR CHARLES WILLIAM BEAL, who died at Randwick, Sydney, on February 5, 1921, aged 65, was manager of the Australian teams of 1882 and 1888. He was captain of the eleven whilst at Sydney Grammar School, and nephew of Mr J. Beal who played in 1856, in the first of the long series of matches between New South Wales and Victoria. Mr Beal made many friends during his two trips to England, being genial and sociable to a degree. He was extremely proud of being associated with the great team of 1882. As manager in 1888 he had to face a very awkward crisis. It was largely due to his tact that the nature of S. P. Jones's illness was so carefully kept secret. Had it become known that Jones was suffering from small-pox the tour might have been nearly ruined.

William George Quaife (1872–1951) and William Bestwick (1876–1938), of Warwickshire and Derbyshire respectively, each had the immense satisfaction of seeing their sons follow them into the county side. As if this was not remarkable enough, in the match between the two counties played at Derby in June 1922, they met in a clash of the two generations.

DERBYSHIRE v WARWICKSHIRE
Played at Derby, June 3, 5, 1922

WEAK BATTING AGAIN brought about Derbyshire's defeat, Warwickshire winning easily on the second afternoon by ten wickets. Cadman and G. R. Jackson made the one stand in the first innings and Bowden alone stayed long on the Monday until Elliott helped him in a partnership which had most to do with clearing off the arrears, the eighth wicket adding 41 runs. A blow on the arm from Howell's bowling compelled Bowden to retire and rest fifty minutes before completing his innings. Warwickshire lost four men for 84 on the Saturday but W. G. Quaife mastered the bowling on Monday and was the one batsman in the match to be seen to much advantage. At the wicket four and a half hours he did not make a mistake until after completing his hundred. At one time the two Quaifes were opposed by the two Bestwicks. For father and son to be batting against bowlers similarly related was a remarkable incident – regarded as unique in county cricket.

DERBYSHIRE

First Innings

H. Storer *b* Calthorpe	6
J. Bowden *b* Howell	6
J. M. Hutchinson *b* Partridge	2
S. Cadman *b* W. G. Quaife	42
Mr G. R. Jackson *st* Smith *b* W. G. Quaife	34
Mr G. Curgenven *c* C Smart *b* Howell	1
Mr A. H. M. Jackson *c* Smith *b* Howell	10
J. Fisher *b* Howell	3
H. Elliott *not out*	6
R. Bestwick *b* W. G. Quaife	2
W. Bestwick *c* C. Smart *b* Howell	6
B 4, l-b 7, n-b 1	12
	130

Second Innings

c Santall *b* Calthorpe	1
c Smith *b* Calthorpe	45
c Venn *b* Calthorpe	4
b Howell	5
c C. Smart *b* Howell	7
c Santall *b* Howell	2
c and b W. G. Quaife	9
b Partridge	4
c C. Smart *b* Calthorpe	30
b Howell	10
not out	1
B 2, l-b 1, n-b 1	4
	122

WARWICKSHIRE

First Innings

Mr H. Venn *c* Elliott *b* W. Bestwick	8
Mr F. R. Santall *run out*	1
L. A. Bates *c* Elliott *b* Cadman	11
W. G. Quaife *b* R. Bestwick	107
Hon. F. S. G. Calthorpe *b* Storer	14
E. J. Smith *c* Elliott *b* W. Bestwick	22
Mr B. W. Quaife *b* A. H. M. Jackson	20
Mr N. E. Partridge *c* A. H. M. Jackson *b* R. Bestwick	31
J. Smart *c* Storer *b* W. Bestwick	0
C. Smart *b* W. Bestwick	1
H. Howell *not out*	1
B 11, l-b 9, n-b 3	23
	239

Second Innings

not out	10
not out	4
	14

Warwickshire Bowling

	Overs	Mdns	Runs	Wkts	Overs	Mdns	Runs	Wkts
Howell	26.2	8	60	5	20	2	50	4
Partridge	9	3	12	1	6	—	16	1
Calthorpe	12	4	17	1	18.5	6	31	4
W. G. Quaife	9	2	29	3	8	—	21	1

Derbyshire Bowling

	Overs	Mdns	Runs	Wkts	Overs	Mdns	Runs	Wkts
W. Bestwick	41	7	66	4				
R. Bestwick	24.4	4	47	2				
Cadman	21	7	36	1				
Storer	15	5	37	1				
Fisher	5	1	15	—				
A. H. M. Jackson	7	1	15	1	1	—	2	—
Hutchinson					1.2	—	12	—

Umpires: A. J. Atfield and J. Moss.

Left: George Brown and (*above*) W. Livsey who, batting at numbers six and ten respectively for Hampshire, at first saved and then won a famous game against Warwickshire. Outside cricket Livsey was employed as Lord Tennyson's valet.

WARWICKSHIRE v HAMPSHIRE
Played at Birmingham, June 14, 15, 16, 1922

THIS WAS THE sensational match of the whole season, at Birmingham or anywhere else, Hampshire actually winning by 155 runs after being out for a total of 15. That their astounding failure in the first innings was just one of the accidents of cricket, and not due in any way to the condition of the ground, was proved by their getting 521 when they followed on. The victory, taken as a whole, must surely be without precedent in first-class cricket. Hampshire looked in a hopeless position when the sixth wicket in their second innings went down at 186, but Shirley helped Brown to put on 85 runs, and then, with Livsey in after McIntyre had failed, the score was carried to 451. Brown batted splendidly for four hours and three-quarters and Livsey made his first hundred without a mistake.

WARWICKSHIRE

First Innings		Second Innings	
L. A. Bates c Shirley b Newman	3	c Mead b Kennedy	1
E. J. Smith c Mead b Newman	24	c Shirley b Kennedy	41
Mr F. R. Santall c McIntyre b Boyes	84	b Newman	0
W. G. Quaife b Newman	1	not out	40
Hon. F. S. G. Calthorpe c Boyes b Kennedy	70	b Newman	30
Rev. E. F. Waddy c Mead b Boyes	0	b Newman	0
Mr B. W. Quaife b Boyes	0	c and b Kennedy	7
J. Fox b Kennedy	4	b Kennedy	0
J. Smart b Newman	14	c and b Boyes	15
H. Howell not out	1	c Kennedy b Newman	11
L-b 2	2	B 6, l-b 4	10
	223		158

HAMPSHIRE

First Innings
A. Bowell b Howell 0
A. Kennedy c Smith b Calthorpe 0
Mr H. L. V. Day b Calthorpe 0
C. P. Mead not out 6
Hon. L. H. Tennyson c Calthorpe b Howell 4
G. Brown b Howell 0
J. Newman c C. Smart b Howell 0
Mr W. R. Shirley c J. Smart b Calthorpe 1
Mr A. S. McIntyre lbw b Calthorpe 0
W. H. Livsey b Howell 0
G. S. Boyes lbw b Howell 0
B 4 4

                                                 15

Second Innings
c Howell b W. G. Quaife 45
b Calthorpe 7
c Bates b W. G. Quaife 15
b Howell 24
c C. Smart b Calthorpe 45
b C. Smart 172
c and b W. G. Quaife 12
lbw b Fox 30
lbw b Howell 5
not out 110
b Howell 29
B 14, l-b 11, w 1, n-b 1 27

                              521

Hampshire Bowling

	Overs	Mdns	Runs	Wkts	Overs	Mdns	Runs	Wkts
Kennedy	24	7	74	2	26	12	47	4
Newman	12.3	—	70	4	26.3	12	53	5
Boyes	16	5	56	4	11	4	34	1
Shirley	3	—	21	—				
Brown					5	—	14	—

Warwickshire Bowling

	Overs	Mdns	Runs	Wkts	Overs	Mdns	Runs	Wkts
Howell	4.5	2	7	6	63	10	156	3
Calthorpe	4	3	4	4	33	7	97	2
W. G. Quaife					49	8	154	3
Fox					7	—	30	1
J. Smart					13	2	37	—
Santall					5	—	15	—
C. Smart					1	—	5	1

A. J. Atfield and B. Brown.

H. Howell (right) and the Hon. F. S. G. Calthorpe (far right), the two Warwickshire bowlers whose first innings figures bore little relation to their second.

A. P. "Tich" Freeman, a tiny man with a huge gift for taking wickets, Freeman broke all records in the English domestic game, and remains the only bowler ever to have taken 300 wickets in an English season. His international career, however, proved to be curiously inglorious. Although he took 3776 wickets in his career, he played for England only twelve times without ever duplicating the mastery he so often displayed at county level. He remains one of the great leg-spinners of all time.

SUSSEX v KENT
Played at Brighton, August 30, 31, September 1, 1922

SUSSEX WOUND UP their season in dismal fashion, Kent beating them in an innings with 23 runs to spare. Beyond everything else the bowling of Freeman stood out by itself. In the whole match he took seventeen wickets for 67 runs – an astounding performance, much as rain had affected the pitch. His nine wickets for 11 runs in the first innings was altogether out of the common even among the many feats of bowlers getting rid of nine or ten men in one innings. Kent had four men out for 69 dismissing Sussex in seventy minutes, but Hardinge and G. J. Bryan added 81 in seventy minutes. Hardinge batted two hours while Bryan hit seven 4s in a splendid display lasting ninety minutes. Kent gained a lead of 149 runs and declaring first thing on Friday again got rid of Sussex cheaply. Roberts hit freely and Bowley showed good form before being bowled by a googly he made no attempt to play. On the first day due to rain there was little more than fifty minutes cricket.

SUSSEX

First Innings

J. Vine c Collins b Freeman	4
E. H. Bowley c G. J. Bryan b Freeman	24
Mr R. A. Young st Hubble b Freeman	0
Mr V. W. C. Jupp c J. L. Bryan b Freeman	2
T. Cook c Troughton b Freeman	0
H. E. Roberts c Hedges b Freeman	9
G. Cox c Ashdown b Freeman	4
M. W. Tate b Freeman	0
Mr A. E. R. Gilligan c Hedges b Freeman	3
G. Street c Ashdown b Woolley	0
Mr A. H. H. Gilligan *not out*	0
N-b 1	1
	47

Second Innings

c G. J. Bryan b Freeman	0
b Freeman	31
c J. L. Bryan b Freeman	8
c Ashdown b Woolley	0
c Seymour b Freeman	4
c G. J. Bryan b Freeman	31
c Troughton b Hardinge	4
b Freeman	0
b Freeman	10
c Ashdown b Freeman	21
not out	12
B 1, l-b 4	5
	126

KENT

Mr J. L. Bryan c Street b Bowley	0
H. T. W. Hardinge c Young b Cox	44
J. Seymour b Cox	23
F. E. Woolley b Jupp	14
Mr L. P. Hedges b Cox	20
Mr G. J. Bryan c Roberts b Cox	64
W. Ashdown st Street b Cox	0
G. C. Collins *run out*	5
J. C. Hubble *not out*	6
Mr L. H. W. Troughton b Jupp	11
B 5, l-b 3, w 1	9
(9 wkts dec.)	196

A. P. Freeman did not bat.

Kent Bowling

	Overs	Mdns	Runs	Wkts	Overs	Mdns	Runs	Wkts
Collins	1	—	6	—				
Woolley	10.1	3	29	1	20	5	61	1
Freeman	10	4	11	9	23.5	6	56	8
Hardinge					4	3	4	1

Sussex Bowling

	Overs	Mdns	Runs	Wkts
Bowley	19	3	46	1
Tate	8	2	26	—
Cox	19	2	42	5
Jupp	11.1	—	58	2
A. H. H. Gilligan	4	1	14	—

Umpires: T. Flowers and F. Chester.

STAFFORDSHIRE IN 1924

Joint Hon. Secretaries – Mr J. S. Heath, "Ryecroft", Wolstanton, Stoke-on-Trent, and Mr G. A. F. Bagguley, Newcastle, Staffordshire

Easily the outstanding feature of Staffordshire cricket last summer was the splendid bowling of Sidney Barnes. Taking as many as seventy-three wickets, the England bowler, at the age of forty-eight, wound up with the truly remarkable average of 7.17. A. Lockett fell away considerably but Sedgwick was deadly at times and altogether Staffordshire possessed a formidable attack. As regards the batting, however, there was a sad weakness. In the home games with Cheshire and Norfolk, the side went down for very small scores and there was another failure against Lancashire's Second Eleven. Although not playing very often, H. W. Homer and W. H. Fitchford were fairly consistent bats and the latter had one brilliant innings of 100 not out. Playing ten games, Staffordshire won the first two – against Lincolnshire and Nottinghamshire Second Eleven – and also succeeded in the return engagements with these counties. An unusual happening was that three times during the season Staffordshire's opponents saved the follow-on by 1 run.

GLOUCESTERSHIRE v ESSEX
Played at Gloucester, July 25, 27, 28, 1925

WON BY GLOUCESTERSHIRE by an innings and 109 runs the match proved a veritable triumph for Parker, who in the two innings had the astounding record of seventeen wickets for 56 runs – a very remarkable performance. He took every wicket that fell to the bowlers when Essex, having been put in after losing the toss, were disposed of soon after lunch on the opening day. So well did Gloucestershire follow this up that when stumps were drawn they held a lead of five runs with only two men out. There was no play on the Monday so Gloucestershire forced matters on Tuesday and, declaring with a lead of 172 shortly before three o'clock, finished off the match in dramatic fashion. Parker's eight wickets for 12 runs represented deadly bowling. He was almost unplayable on the treacherous pitch. Dipper carried off the batting honours, being in for three hours and forty minutes. He scarcely made a bad stroke. Hammond helped him to add 83 runs in forty-five minutes.

ESSEX

First Innings

Mr L. C. Eastman c Robinson b Parker	16
J. Freeman c Hammond b Parker	18
J. O'Connor b Parker	18
A. C. Russell *run out*	0
Mr P. Perrin c Hammond b Parker	2
Mr C. T. Ashton *lbw* b Parker	0
J. A. Cutmore *lbw* b Parker	14
Mr R. C. Joy st Smith b Parker	4
Mr H. M. Morris *not out*	21
A. B. Hipkin c Dennett b Parker	9
M. S. Nichols b Parker	11
B 1, l-b 1	2
	115

Second Innings

c Hammond b Parker	11
lbw b Parker	2
b Parker	21
c Hammond b Parker	0
c Hammond b Parker	2
b Parker	0
b Dennett	0
b Dennett	17
c Hammond b Parker	5
b Parker	2
not out	0
B 2, l-b 1	3
	63

GLOUCESTERSHIRE

Lt-Col D. C. Robinson c Russell b Hipkin	22
A. G. Dipper b Russell	107
H. Smith c O'Connor b Eastman	16
R. A. Sinfield c Morris b Eastman	23
W. R. Hammond st Freeman b Eastman	40
B. S. Bloodworth *not out*	35
Mr R. G. W. Melsome c Joy b Hipkin	25
Mr G. A. Wedel *not out*	5
B 7, l-b 7	14
(6 wkts dec.)	287

Gloucestershire Bowling

	Overs	Mdns	Runs	Wkts	Overs	Mdns	Runs	Wkts
Parker	31.3	13	44	9	17	10	12	8
Dennett	27	8	58	—	17	5	48	2
Wedel	4	1	11	—				

Essex Bowling

	Overs	Mdns	Runs	Wkts
Nichols	10	4	26	—
Eastman	28	5	77	3
Hipkin	29	8	66	2
O'Connor	9	1	27	—
Ashton	12	2	43	—
Russell	15	2	32	1
Joy	2	1	2	—

Umpires: A. E. Street and H. Chidgey.

Above: Charlie Parker whose slow left arm bowling brought him 17 wickets for 56 against Essex.
Right: Jack Hobbs brings up his 126th century at Taunton in 1925.

SOMERSET v SURREY
Played at Taunton, August 15, 17, 18, 1925

THIS WAS THE match rendered for ever memorable by the triumph of Hobbs who, playing innings of 101 and 101 not out, equalled on the Monday morning W. G. Grace's aggregate of 126 centuries in first-class cricket, and on the Tuesday afternoon beat the "Grand Old Man's" record. Circumstances generally combined to invest the occasion with exceptional excitement. During the early part of the season Hobbs had been so phenomenally successful that by July 20, when he completed a score of 105 at Blackheath, there were a dozen hundreds standing to his credit and the three-figure innings of his career numbered 125. There, as it happened, his extraordinary run of triumphs temporarily ended. He made many substantial scores but in match after match the century needed to bring his total up to that of W. G. Grace eluded his efforts. Thus it came about that when Surrey entered upon their contest with Somerset on August 15, Hobbs was still one short of the coveted number of hundreds. That the Taunton ground, with its rather short boundaries, might furnish Hobbs with the opportunity he wanted, was very generally expected and a big crowd gathered in the hope of assisting at his triumph. No such gratification was vouchsafed for those present on the Saturday, but the play was of absorbing interest, Hobbs batting for two hours and twenty minutes and leaving off not out 91. Those spectators who did not hear "no ball" called had an anxious moment when in the first over Hobbs gave a catch to cover point, and there came another thrill shortly afterwards, the famous batsman with his score at seven making on the leg-side a stroke which might have brought about his dismissal, had MacBryan moved more smartly. Thenceforward he played masterly cricket, exercising great care when facing White, but making a number of fine drives and leg hits off Bridges and Robertson-Glasgow. Towards the close, however, he was content to score mainly by singles. Wanting only nine for his hundred on Monday morning Hobbs did not keep the large company long in suspense. Three singles, a four off a no-ball and another single brought him to 99, and then placing a ball from Bridges to square leg for a further single, he attained the object of his great ambition, the total then standing at 167. Tremendous cheering, of course, greeted the accomplishment of the feat; indeed so pronounced was the enthusiasm that the progress of the game was delayed some minutes while at the end of the over all the players in the field shook hands with Hobbs, and the Surrey captain brought out a drink for the hero of the occasion, who raised the glass high and bowed to the crowd before partaking of the refreshment. The memorable innings – put together exactly four weeks after Hobbs' 105 at Blackheath – came to an end shortly afterwards through a catch at the wicket. The total at that point was 177 and Hobbs, batting two hours and thirty-five minutes, had hit nine 4's.

Fortunately for Hobbs, Somerset played up so well at the second attempt that Surrey were set a task substantial enough to furnish that batsman with the chance of making a second hundred. Of that opportunity he duly availed himself, and so less than thirty hours after equalling W. G. Grace's record, he surpassed it. Surrey had 183 to make to win and Hobbs and Sandham obtained that number in two hours and twenty-five minutes without being separated. Hobbs, who reached three figures with the total at 174, hit fourteen 4s and gave no chance. As in the first innings he treated White with great respect, but otherwise played a game as bold as it was skilful and attractive. In putting together this further hundred, Hobbs not only beat Grace's record but, bringing his three-figure innings for 1925 up to fourteen, he created a new record, the previous largest number of centuries in a season having been thirteen – made by C. B. Fry in 1901, Tom Hayward in 1906 and Hendren in 1923. On two previous occasions Hobbs had obtained two separate hundreds in the same match.

Somerset made a most disastrous start on Saturday, but were saved from complete failure by Young and Johnson. As it was, with Sandham afterwards helping Hobbs to bring the score to 50 and Knight sharing in a partnership of 100, Surrey left off only 16 behind with seven wickets in hand. On Monday after Hobbs' dismissal, Jardine and Holmes put on 51 and Fender, let off when seven, hit up 59 in less than an hour, Surrey, although batting one short, establishing a lead of 192. In Somerset's second innings MacBryan batted in splendid form, scoring 109 out of 184 in two hours and a quarter with sixteen 4s as his chief strokes. Young was also seen to advantage but gave two chances. The home side entered upon the third day's cricket 64 ahead with seven wickets in hand, but there was little in their batting except some hard hitting by Hunt. Still, when Surrey went in to knock off the runs the home team fielded admirably. Sandham played truly admirable and most unselfish cricket for his 74 not out.

SOMERSET
First Innings
Mr J. C. W. MacBryan b Holmes	6
A. Young c Sadler b Lockton	58
Mr T. E. S. Francis b Sadler	0
Mr J. C. White b Sadler	1
Mr P. R. Johnson c and b Lockton	30
Mr E. F. Longrigg b Sadler	5
Mr R. A. Ingle b Fender	22
G. Hunt b Lockton	4
Mr R. C. Robertson-Glasgow c Jardine b Lockton	4
Mr J. J. Bridges c and b Shepherd	25
Mr M. L. Hill not out	0
L-b 8, w 4	12
	167

Second Innings
b Fender	109
c Strudwick b Sadler	71
c Strudwick b Lockton	12
c Strudwick b Sadler	30
c Peach b Fender	16
run out	4
c Shepherd b Peach	23
b Fender	59
c Sadler b Fender	5
b Fender	26
not out	1
B 9, l-b 5, n-b 4	18
	374

SURREY
First Innings
J. B. Hobbs c Hill b Bridges	101
A. Sandham c Longrigg b Bridges	13
Mr D. J. Knight run out	34
T. Shepherd b White	0
Mr D. R. Jardine run out	47
Mr E. R. T. Holmes c Hill b R-Glasgow	24
Mr P. G. H. Fender st Hill b Young	59
H. A. Peach b Young	20
W. Sadler c Johnson b Young	25
H. Strudwick not out	10
Mr J. H. Lockton absent	0
B 15, l-b 8, n-b 3	26
	359

Second Innings
not out	101
not out	74
B 6, l-b 1, n-b 1	8
	183

Surrey Bowling
	Overs	Mdns	Runs	Wkts	Overs	Mdns	Runs	Wkts
Sadler	16	4	28	3	21	5	59	2
Holmes	6	2	12	1	17	—	56	—
Fender	13	3	39	1	35.5	8	120	5
Lockton	16	4	36	4	9	2	15	1
Peach	9	2	21	—	20	7	46	1
Shepherd	6.3	1	19	1	21	5	60	—

Somerset Bowling
	Overs	Mdns	Runs	Wkts	Overs	Mdns	Runs	Wkts
Robertson-Glasgow	26	1	144	1	6	—	42	—
Bridges	37	5	115	2	11	3	27	—
White	29	13	51	1	14	6	34	—
Hunt	4	1	14	—	8	4	15	—
Young	5.3	1	9	3	15.5	1	39	—
Longrigg					3	—	18	—

Umpires: H. Draper and H. Young.

MR FREDERICK ROBERT SPOFFORTH, one of the most remarkable players the game has ever known, was born at Balmain, Sydney, on September 9, 1853, and died at Ditton Hill Lodge, Ditton Hill, Surbiton, Surrey, on June 4, 1926, aged 72. As in another part of the *Almanack*, Lord Harris, Lord Darnley, and Mr C. I. Thornton have given their recollections of Mr Spofforth and his wonderful bowling, it will suffice here to deal with the chief facts of a memorable career. From his earliest days cricket had the greatest possible fascination for him, and whilst still quite a small boy at Eglington College, Sydney, he determined, through seeing the success met with by George Tarrant, of Cambridge, to become as fast a bowler as possible. Later he studied the methods of Southerton and Alfred Shaw, and resolved, if possible, to combine the styles of all three men. He had played with success in good class matches before he ever bowled a ball in England, but his great days may be said to date from May 27, 1878, when he had so much to do with the wonderful victory gained, in the course of a single day, by D. W. Gregory's team over a very strong MCC side at Lord's. From that day forward, Spofforth was always regarded as a man to be feared, even by the strongest teams. He probably never did anything better than to take fourteen wickets for 90 runs in the Test match at The Oval in 1882, when Australia gained their first success – by 7 runs – in an international game on English soil. It is to be regretted that when he came over with the teams of 1878 and 1880 so few eleven a side matches were played, for he was presumably then at about his best, and his energies were expended for the most part in mowing down wickets in games against odds. For the former side he obtained 764 wickets at a cost of 6.08 runs each, and for the latter 763 for 5.49 apiece. These figures include his doings in the colonies and (in 1878) in America.

MIDDLESEX v SURREY

Played at Lord's, August 28, 30, 31, 1926

HOBBS SEIZED UPON this occasion to make what was at once the highest score of his wonderful career, and the highest ever made at Lord's, beating his own 266, not out, for Players against Gentlemen at Scarborough in 1925, and Holmes' 315, not out, for Yorkshire against Middlesex – also put together in the previous summer. The great batsman, who obtained his runs mainly on the on side, placed the ball with marvellous skill and did not appear to give a chance. He was at the wickets six hours and fifty-five minutes, scoring forty-one 4s, six 3s, twenty 2s, and ninety-four singles. Sandham helped to raise the total to 115 – the two Surrey men's thirty-sixth three-figure first wicket stand. Ducat shared in the partnership of 101, and Jardine in one of 270. Hendren, in the first innings of Middlesex, withstood the Surrey attack for three hours and a half, and put together his seventh hundred of the season, but the home side had to follow on 304 in arrears, and Surrey, fielding brilliantly, won the match by an innings and 63 runs.

SURREY

J. B. Hobbs *not out*	316
A. Sandham *c* Hendren *b* Haig	58
A. Ducat *b* Durston	41
T. Shepherd *c and b* Stevens	15
Mr D. R. Jardine *c and b* Powell	103
Mr A. Jeacocke *run out*	26
Mr P. G. H. Fender *not out*	1
B 12, l-b 7	19

(5 wkts dec.) 579

Mr E. R. T. Holmes, H. A. Peach, H. Strudwick and S. Fenley did not bat.

MIDDLESEX

First Innings

Mr G. T. S. Stevens *c* Strudwick *b* Holmes	2
Mr H. L. Dales *b* Jardine	52
Mr G. O. Allen *c* Shepherd *b* Peach	21
E. Hendren *not out*	101
Mr H.J. Enthoven *run out*	1
Mr F.T. Mann *c* Peach *b* Jardine	3
Mr N. Haig *c* Strudwick *b* Fender	12
H. W. Lee *run out*	42
B. R. Murrell *c* Peach *b* Fenley	20
T.J. Durston *b* Fender	0
J. A. Powell *c and b* Fender	0
B 15, l-b 6	21

275

Second Innings

c Fender *b* Peach	63
c Fender *b* Holmes	4
c Jardine *b* Fenley	17
c Fenley *b* Jardine	37
b Fenley	5
not out	37
c Shepherd *b* Fender	18
c Strudwick *b* Holmes	31
c Fenley *b* Peach	7
b Holmes	1
c Strudwick *b* Holmes	4
B 11, l-b 3, w 2, n-b 1	17

241

Middlesex Bowling

	Overs	Mdns	Runs	Wkts
Haig	37	7	118	1
Durston	31	12	69	1
Allen	19	3	88	—
Stevens	22.3	1	95	1
Lee	8	1	44	—
Powell	27	4	109	1
Enthoven	10	1	37	—

Surrey Bowling

	Overs	Mdns	Runs	Wkts	Overs	Mdns	Runs	Wkts
Holmes	14	2	41	1	15.4	2	49	4
Peach	18	7	26	1	23	5	41	2
Fenley	24	4	76	1	23	4	66	2
Fender	23	5	76	3	14	2	38	1
Shepherd	9	5	22	—	8	3	12	—
Jardine	8	2	13	2	6	1	18	1

Umpires: R. D. Burrows and H. Chidgey.

The great batsman obliging an idolatrous schoolboy with an autograph. Hobbs was the perfect hero, modest, polite and generous. A teetotaller, a man for the family hearth, and a player who believed that cricket sides should always be led by gentlemen, he was also the greatest English batsman of the twentieth century, and his record score at Lord's in 1926 still stands.

STAFFORDSHIRE IN 1926

Hon. Secretary – Mr G. A. F. Bagguley, Newcastle-under Lyme, Staffordshire

Bad weather spoiled several of Staffordshire's matches, but despite this misfortune the county made some progress. The feature of the seasons's work was the wonderful success of Barnes, who, heading the bowling averages once again, despite his 50 years, brought his total of wickets in the course of fourteen seasons to 1,050 for 7.98 runs each. His best performance was in taking fourteen wickets for 31 runs in the second match with Lincolnshire. Without Barnes the side must have been in a sad plight, for only A. Lockett and Sedgwick of the other bowlers rendered anything like valuable help. While, however the attack was more effective than before, the batting frequently disappointed. The main trouble lay in the inability of the county to find a really capable opening pair – a difficulty in no way lessened by the fact that no fewer than twenty-five players were called upon during the season. Most of the regular members of the side met with little success, but H. W. Homer was consistently good, with an average of 27 for ten innings.

MIDDLESEX v WEST INDIES
Played at Lord's, June 9, 11, 12, 1928

A SPLENDID ALL-ROUND performance on the part of Constantine enabled West Indies to gain a memorable victory by three wickets. When that player went in on Monday the tourists, as the result of more than two hours' laborious batting, had lost half their wickets for 79, and stood in no small danger of having to follow on. In such a brilliant manner did he deal with the situation that, driving with great power, and pulling in daring fashion, he made 86 out of 107 in less than an hour. Despite this fine effort, the visitors fell 122 short of the total at which, with six men out, Middlesex had declared, but in the county's second innings, Constantine, hitting the stumps five times, proceeded to take seven wickets for little more than 8 runs apiece. On going on to bowl for the second time, Constantine sent down six overs and three balls for 11 runs and six wickets. Even after this deadly piece of bowling, West Indies – set 259 to win and losing five batsmen for 121 – looked sure to be beaten. Coming once again to the rescue of his side, however, Constantine crowned a wonderful display by hitting up 103 out of 133 in an hour, with two 6s and twelve 4s as his chief strokes. Martin shared in his success on Monday, and in the further triumph, Fernandes was his partner. Haig, whom Hearne assisted to add 153, settled down after a moderate start to the making of a capital 100, and Hendren, who also reached three figures, was seen to advantage. In stopping a drive from Constantine, Hearne had a finger so badly damaged that he could play no more cricket last season.

MIDDLESEX

First Innings
Mr N. Haig *b* Small 119
H. W. Lee *c* Martin *b* Constantine 7
J. W. Hearne *c* Nunes *b* Roach 75
E. Hendren *not out* 100
Mr E. T. Killick *b* Francis 6
Mr G. O. Allen *run out* 4
Mr F. T. Mann *b* Francis 32
Mr I. A. R. Peebles *not out* 0
T. J. Durston (*did not bat*)
W. F. Price (*did not bat*)
J. A. Powell (*did not bat*)
B 2, l-b 4, n-b 3 9

(6 wkts dec.) 352

Second Innings
b Constantine 5
b Constantine 15
lbw b Small 28
c Francis *b* Constantine 52
c Francis *b* Constantine 4
c and b Francis 7
b Small 4
b Constantine 0
not out 9
b Constantine 3
b Constantine 1
B 3, l-b 2, n-b 3 8

136

WEST INDIES

First Innings
G. Challenor *c* Hendren *b* Durston 23
C. A. Roach *c* Lee *b* Durston 0
M. P. Fernandes *c* Hearne *b* Allen 29
W. H. St Hill *c* Hendren *b* Peebles 5
E. L. Bartlett *st* Price *b* Powell 13
F. R. Martin *not out* 26
L. N. Constantine *b* Peebles 86
J. A. Small *c* Hendren *b* Haig 7
R. K. Nunes *b* Durston 17
C. R. Browne *c* Allen *b* Durston 0
G. N. Francis *lbw b* Haig 1
B 18, l-b 3, n-b 2 23

230

Second Innings
b Haig 33
run out 10
c Allen *b* Haig 54
b Durston 5
lbw b Hearne 26
not out 1
c Haig *b* Lee 103
c and b Peebles 5
not out 4

3 B 18 18

259

West Indies Bowling

	Overs	Mdns	Runs	Wkts	Overs	Mdns	Runs	Wkts
Francis	35.5	4	107	2	10	3	30	1
Constantine	20	1	77	1	14.3	1	57	7
Browne	11	2	21	—				
Small	29	5	72	1	11	3	36	2
Martin	13	—	30	—	3	—	5	—
Roach	7	—	36	1				

Middlesex Bowling

	Overs	Mdns	Runs	Wkts	Overs	Mdns	Runs	Wkts
Durston	21	10	16	4	15	3	32	1
Haig	24.4	7	32	2	22	5	80	2
Hearne	11	4	25	—	15	3	51	1
Peebles	18	2	51	2	11	2	45	1
Allen	8	2	43	1				
Powell	7	1	40	1	1	—	6	—
Lee					4.4	—	27	1

Umpires: J. W. Day and W. R. Parry.

Learie Constantine (1901–1971), flanked by Small and Bartlett, was a fast bowler with a beautiful action, great pace and control. He was also a mercurial batsman who could turn the fortunes of a game in a few overs.

GLOUCESTERSHIRE v SURREY
Played at Cheltenham, August 15, 16, 17, 1928

BEATING SURREY BY 189 runs Gloucestershire owed almost everything to the magnificent work of Hammond and Parker. Hammond gave a memorable display of all-round cricket. Not only did he perform – for the second time against Surrey – the feat of scoring two separate hundreds in a match, but in the two Surrey innings he brought off ten catches. In this latter way he rendered splendid help to Parker, whose skilful bowling – pronounced spin combined with great accuracy of length – produced a record of thirteen wickets in the match for 197 runs. Hobbs, on Thursday played masterly cricket, but his dismissal and also that of Sandham on the last afternoon for 13 rendered Surrey's task of getting 357 runs practically hopeless. Hammond scored 139 out of 199 in two hours and forty minutes, his second three-figure innings lasting forty-five minutes longer.

GLOUCESTERSHIRE

First Innings

A. E. Dipper c and b G-Wells	7
R. A. Sinfield b Peach	0
W. R. Hammond c Shepherd b Peach	139
Mr B. H. Lyon c and b Fender	6
Mr F. J. Seabrook c Gregory b Fender	0
Mr W. L. Neale c Ducat b G-Wells	10
H. Smith c Fender b Shepherd	56
Mr C. J. Barnett c G-Wells b Peach	0
Capt. M. A. Green c Sandham b Fenley	37
C. Parker c Brooks b Fender	19
P. Mills not out	7
B 12, l-b 10, n-b 1	23
	304

Second Innings

c and b Peach	41
lbw b Shepherd	22
c Gregory b Fenley	143
c Hobbs b Shepherd	27
b Fender	5
b Shepherd	0
c Ducat b Fenley	45
not out	21
c Shepherd b Fenley	11
b Shepherd	2
B 2	2
	(9 wkts dec.) 319

SURREY

First Innings

J. B. Hobbs c Seabrook b Hammond	96
A. Sandham c Smith b Sinfield	0
A. Ducat c Dipper b Parker	6
T. Shepherd c Barnett b Parker	52
T. H. Barling c Hammond b Parker	4
R. J. Gregory c Hammond b Parker	7
Mr P. G. H. Fender c Hammond b Sinfield	55
Mr H. M. Garland-Wells c Hammond b Parker	6
H. A. Peach b Mills	5
E. W. Brooks lbw b Parker	2
S. Fenley not out	0
B 27, l-b 7	34
	267

Second Innings

c Smith b Parker	2
c Hammond b Sinfield	10
c Hammond b Parker	55
c Hammond b Parker	17
c Hammond b Parker	2
c Hammond b Parker	3
c Hammond b Parker	20
st Smith b Sinfield	49
c Smith b Parker	1
run out	0
not out	0
B 1, l-b 7	8
	167

Surrey Bowling

	Overs	Mdns	Runs	Wkts	Overs	Mdns	Runs	Wkts
Fender	24.3	10	57	3	25	6	55	1
Peach	27	6	68	3	26	9	71	1
Fenley	12	2	44	1	18	2	83	3
Shepherd	15	4	43	1	32.4	5	74	4
Garland-Wells	22	5	65	2	14	3	34	—
Gregory	2	—	4	—				

Gloucestershire Bowling

	Overs	Mdns	Runs	Wkts	Overs	Mdns	Runs	Wkts
Hammond	22	3	71	1				
Sinfield	9	4	10	2	27	9	59	2
Parker	38.4	6	117	6	32	10	80	7
Mills	24	11	35	1	6	—	20	—

Umpires: W. Bestwick and H. Young.

Walter Hammond (1903–1965) here seen as a young man, was one of the dominant figures in English cricket for twenty years. He is remembered primarily for his batting, and especially for a princely off-drive and the concentration to build long innings, but in the 1920s his bowling and fielding were also of a remarkably high standard. He was the finest slip fieldsman of his day, and a worthy successor in the Gloucestershire county annals to W. G. Grace as a master cricketer.

GLOUCESTERSHIRE v WORCESTERSHIRE
Played at Cheltenham, August 18, 20, 1928

HAMMOND, ENJOYING ANOTHER personal triumph almost as great as, if of a different description from, that in the Surrey game, Gloucestershire overplayed Worcestershire so completely that they won in two days by an innings and 168 runs. On this occasion bowling brought honours to the famous all-rounder who, proving more effective with the ball than ever before, secured nine Worcestershire wickets in the first innings for 23 runs. As he caught the other batsman on Parker's bowling, he had a hand in disposing of the whole of the side. On a pitch recovering from heavy dew Hammond made the ball turn appreciably as well as swerve through the air and against his deadly attack Worcestershire offered most feeble resistance, their total of 35 being the smallest of the season in county cricket. When Worcestershire faced arrears of 335, Hammond again accomplished fine work with the ball. In the whole match he took fifteen wickets for 128 runs. Parker, too, gave the batsmen a lot of trouble, his left hand slows providing a telling contrast to Hammond's quick right-hand bowling. Worcestershire in their second innings displayed some stubbornness in defence. Higgins remaining until the total reached 73 and Quaife staying an hour. Batting of a very high quality came from Gloucestershire. Dipper and Sinfield showed to advantage in an opening partnership of 116 and Hammond and Lyon added 108 in first-rate style. Gloucestershire finished the first day leading by 246 with five wickets in hand.

WORCESTERSHIRE

First Innings

Mr J. B. Higgins *b* Hammond	2
L. Wright *st* Smith *b* Hammond	8
Mr B. W. Quaife *c* Hammond *b* Parker	2
W. V. Fox *c* Lyon *b* Hammond	1
H. H. Gibbons *c* Stephens *b* Hammond	4
F. Root *c* Seabrook *b* Hammond	0
C. V. Tarbox *b* Hammond	6
J. W. King *not out*	0
J. J. Bowles *c* Lyon *b* Hammond	4
Capt. D. V. Hill *c* Parker *b* Hammond	0
F. T. Summers *b* Hammond	0
B 5, l-b 3	8
	35

Second Innings

c Lyon *b* Parker	35
b Parker	1
c Seabrook *b* Hammond	19
c Lyon *b* Hammond	1
c Lyon *b* Parker	9
lbw b Hammond	1
c Barnett *b* Hammond	29
c Seabrook *b* Hammond	4
hit wkt b Parker	20
st Smith *b* Hammond	17
not out	0
B 21, l-b 10	31
	167

GLOUCESTERSHIRE

A. E. Dipper *c* Qualife *b* Wright	77
R. A. Sinfield *c* Hill *b* Wright	30
W. R. Hammond *c* Summers *b* Wright	80
Mr B. H. Lyon *b* Tarbox	38
Mr F. J. Seabrook *b* Hill	29
H. Smith *lbw b* Hill	6
Mr W.L. Neale *not out*	51
Mr C. J. Barnett *not out*	34
B 15, l-b 9, n-b 1	25
(6 wkts dec.)	370

P. H. Stephens, C. Parker and P. Mills did not bat.

Gloucestershire Bowling

	Overs	Mdns	Runs	Wkts	Overs	Mdns	Runs	Wkts
Hammond	10.2	2	23	9	33.3	5	105	6
Sinfield	2	1	3	—				
Parker	8	7	1	1	33	22	31	4

Worcestershire Bowling

	Overs	Mdns	Runs	Wkts
Root	37	10	82	—
Hill	20	1	71	2
Bowles	17	3	49	—
Tarbox	30	5	88	1
Wright	20	4	55	3

Umpires: W. Bestwick and H. Young.

MR CHARLES INGLIS THORNTON, born at Llanwarne, Herefordshire, on March 20, 1850, died suddenly in London on December 10, 1929, aged 79. With his death there passed a great personality in the history of cricket. He had long given up active participation in the game, but in his day he was one of the biggest – if not actually the mightiest of all time – of hitters. To the present generation he was only a name, but in the memories of those who, like Lord Harris and Mr A. J. Webbe, were his contemporaries, his famous deeds must remain firmly implanted. He went to Eton in 1861, to the Rev. G. R. Dupuis's house, and was in the eleven in 1866, 1867, and 1868, being captain in his last year. He also played in Oppidan and Mixed Wall and Field XI's, won the school fives and was keeper in 1867 and 1868, and won the double rackets and putting the weight in 1868, and throwing the cricket ball in 1867. Going up to Trinity College, Cambridge, he played in the eleven four times from 1869, being captain in 1872, the year that Cambridge, thanks to a fine innings of 130 by W. Yardley and some effective bowling of W. N. Powys, beat Oxford in an innings. Thornton was on the winning side for Cambridge three times out of four. The year that Oxford won was in 1871, when S. E. Butler took all ten wickets in the first innings of Cambridge. Thornton also played from 1867 onwards for Kent, and a little for Middlesex in the middle seventies. To him more than to anybody else was due the success of the annual Scarborough festival. He was largely instrumental in starting it, and although he had long given up cricket he never lost his interest in the famous week, even until last season. To mark the esteem in which he was held and to recognise his services to the Scarborough festival, which had then been in existence a quarter of a century, he was, in 1894, presented with a silver loving-cup subscribed for by the members of the Scarborough Cricket Club. He received another presentation in 1921 and was also given the Freedom of the borough.

Like many others of his day, Thornton always regarded cricket more as a game than as a serious business. Adventurous by nature, he felt that in cricket he could indulge this spirit to the full. Whenever he was captain he liked going in first. Individual in style, he jumped quickly to the ball in making his magnificent drives, and in this respect differed from the famous Australian hitters, Bonnor, McDonnell and Lyons, all of whom were fast-footed. In his brilliant career he put together many scores of a hundred in remarkable time, and the length of some of his drives was enormous. It is on record, for instance, that in the North v South match at Canterbury in 1871, he hit a ball from W. M. Rose a strictly measured 152 yards, while at the practice nets at Hove the same year he sent it 168 yards 2 feet and 162 yards. Playing against Harrow at Lord's in 1868, he drove the ball over the old pavilion, and at The Oval he accomplished the same feat, while it is noted that at Canterbury he hit V. E. Walker out of the ground each ball of an over. The over then consisted of four balls.

A good story is told of him when, visiting the neighbourhood of Oakham school and going to the cricket ground, he was asked to play as a substitute. Nobody at the time knew who he was, but they had reason to before the day was out, for in the second innings he scored 188 out of 216 in two hours, sending the ball out of the ground thirteen times. Hitting the ball out of the ground was a feat he always took a delight in accomplishing. On one occasion at Scarborough, on the bowling of A. G. Steel, he drove a ball over a four-storeyed house into the adjoining street, called Trafalgar Square.

To slow bowlers Thornton was a terror, and on James Southerton, in particular, he was generally very severe. He often threatened to hit Southerton out of The Oval, and at length succeeded. As the ball sailed over the fence Thornton dropped his bat, put his hands on his hips, and laughed uproariously, saying, "I told you I would do it, Jim." Southerton shook his head, and replied, "Quite right, Mr Thornton, but I shall get you out." And get him out he did. As a matter of fact he hit Southerton twice over the pavilion, once over the scoring-box, and also for a 2 in a four ball over, and, altogether, he hit out of three sides of The Oval. Once, in a match between Kent and Nottinghamshire, Thornton hit a ball back to Shaw, who, although knocked off his feet, held it and thus brought off a marvellous catch. In the power and consistency of his driving, Thornton was by himself, constantly bringing off hits that have become more or less historic in the game. As showing the difference between cricket in his days and now, he took part, in six seasons for Kent, in only eighteen matches. Still, in 34 innings he got three hundreds. Probably his finest exhibitions in the latter part of his career were a couple of hundreds at Scarborough for the Gentlemen of England against 1 Zingari. In the game of 1866, he made 107 out of 133 in seventy minutes in 29 hits – eight 6s, twelve 4s, two 2s and seven singles. A. G. Steel was among the bowlers on that occasion. Thornton stood 6ft and had rather sloping shoulders, so that he was admirably proportioned for the batting style he loved.

In business Thornton was in the timber trade for 35 years, and retired in 1912. A keen motorist, he was also extremely fond of travelling, having been all through Japan, Siberia, and Russia. When the war broke out he was in Berlin, and was very nearly caught. In his book, *East and West and Home Again*, he described a trip round the world. He had been a member of the MCC and of the Orleans Club for fifty years. He married Fanny, daughter of Mr Charles Dowell, of Croydon, but left no children.

NEW SOUTH WALES v QUEENSLAND
Played at Sydney, January 3, 4, 6, 7, 1930

EVERYTHING ELSE IN this game paled before the phenomenal performance of Bradman, who, in scoring 452 not out – a feat that occupied him 415 minutes – played the highest individual innings recorded in first-class cricket. That splendid exhibition led the way to a victory for New South Wales by 685 runs. Displaying a wider range of strokes than usual. Bradman batted without a trace of error during his long stay and hit no fewer than 49 4's. His prolific scoring followed upon comparatively low totals in the first innings of each side. Against Hurwood, who kept an admirable length, New South Wales found run getting hard and Queensland fared no better, only Bensted and Goodwin appearing to advantage. New South Wales going in again eight runs ahead, gained a complete mastery over the bowling. Bradman, batting with such brilliancy, made matters easy for his colleagues. Kippax put together a hundred, and McCabe and Allsopp also scored readily. Faced with the appalling task of getting 770 runs, Queensland offered scarcely any resistance. Half the wickets actually fell for 23, and on the last morning Everett finished off the innings. In the two spells of bowling he disposed of six batsmen at a cost of less than four runs each.

NEW SOUTH WALES

First Innings

C. Andrews *st* Leeson *b* Burwood	56
D. G. Bradman *c* Leeson *b* Hurwood	3
A. Marks *c* Hurwood *b* Thurlow	40
A. F. Kippax *lbw b* Thurlow	15
S. McCabe *c* Leeson *b* Thurlow	15
A. Allsopp *c* Thurlow *b* Hurwood	9
A. Fairfax *b* Brew	20
S. C. Everett *c* Bensted *b* Brew	41
H. L. Davidson *lbw b* Hurwood	14
S. Burt *b* Thurlow	10
H. Chilvers *not out*	6
B 3, l-b 3	6
	235

Second Innings

c Levy *b* Hurwood	16
not out	452
c Bensted *b* Hurwood	5
lbw b Rowe	115
c Leeson *b* Hurwood	60
b Hurwood	66
st Leeson *b* Hurwood	10
c Goodwin *b* Hurwood	4
c and b Goodwin	22
B 6, l-b 1, w 2, n-b 2	11
(8 wkts dec.)	761

In scoring 452 not out against Queensland, then the highest ever score in first class cricket, Bradman was merely warming up for his first tour of England later that year. In that first tour the 5' 7" genius was to make 2,960 runs at an average of 98.66.

QUEENSLAND

First Innings

R. M. Levy c Everett b Fairfax	6
L. P. O'Connor c Andrews b Fairfax	21
P. C. Thompson lbw b Chilvers	1
W. Rose b McCabe	11
F. J. Gough c Marks b McCabe	14
E. C. Bensted c Davidson b McCabe	51
V. Goodwin c Marks b Fairfax	67
A. Hurwood b Chilvers	4
F. M. Brew b McCabe	20
H. Leeson c Davidson b McCabe	14
H. M. Thurlow not out	3
B 9, l-b 3, n-b 3	15
	227

Second Innings

b Everett	0
b McCabe	17
lbw b Everett	0
c Bradman b Chilvers	1
c Allsopp b Chilvers	20
b Everett	5
run out	4
b Everett	6
c Davidson b Everett	26
not out	2
b Everett	0
B 1, l-b 1, w 1, n-b 2	5
	84

Queensland Bowling

	Overs	Mdns	Runs	Wkts	Overs	Mdns	Runs	Wkts
Thurlow	18.1	—	83	4	25	—	147	—
Hurwood	22	6	57	4	34	1	179	6
Bensted	6	—	39	—	12	—	70	—
Brew	8	—	50	2	6	—	61	—
Rowe					19	—	143	1
Thompson					15	—	90	—
Gough					4	—	40	—
Levy					2	—	20	—
Goodwin					0.1	—	—	1

New South Wales Bowling

	Overs	Mdns	Runs	Wkts	Overs	Mdns	Runs	Wkts
Everett	10	1	46	—	8.5	1	23	6
Fairfax	15	1	53	3	7	3	12	—
Chilvers	20	5	52	2	8	—	22	2
McCabe	15.1	5	36	5	5	3	15	1
Burt	8	1	25	—	2	—	7	—

Umpires: G. Borwick and E. J. Shaw.

SUSSEX v NORTHAMPTONSHIRE
Played at Brighton, May 7, 8, 9, 1930

TO DULEEPSINHJI THIS match brought the great distinction of beating the Sussex record made by his uncle, K. S. Ranjitsinhji, at Taunton in 1901. Going in with one run on the board, Duleepsinhji scored 333 out of 520 and, when seventh out was taking many risks. Batting for five hours and a half, he hit a 6 and thirty-four 4s, his stroke play all round the wicket being magnificent. Three steady partners helped him to master the bowling and then Tate, chiefly by powerful drives and pulls, hit up 111 out of 255 in an hour and three-quarters. Gilligan having declared first thing on the second morning, Wensley, on a pitch which, slow and easy on the first day, proved rather treacherous as it became faster, bowled swingers cleverly. Tate in the follow-on took four of the first five wickets for 22 runs. Bellamy did not concede a bye and he showed the soundest defence for the visitors, who in the end had to admit defeat by an innings and 209 runs.

SUSSEX

E. H. Bowley c Bellamy b Thomas 1
J. Parks c Liddell b Thomas 9
K. S. Duleepsinhji st Bellamy b Matthews 333
T. Cook c Liddell b Clark 19
James Langridge b Cox 17
H. Parks b Clark 11
M. W. Tate b Partridge 111
Mr A. H. H. Gilligan not out 8
A. F. Wensley not out 0
    L-b 6, n-b 6 12

                                        (7 wkts dec.) 521

R. A. Hollingdale and W. Cornford did not bat.

NORTHAMPTONSHIRE

First Innings

C. N. Woolley b Wensley 18
A. H. Bakewell lbw b J. Parks 12
J. E. Timms c J. Parks b Langridge 19
Mr V. W. C. Jupp c Duleepsinhji b Wensley 0
B. Bellamy b Wensley 21
A. D. Matthews lbw b J. Parks 13
A. G. Liddell c Gilligan b Bowley 18
A. L. Cox lbw b Tate 40
A. E. Thomas lbw b Wensley 29
R. J. Partridge not out 3
E. C. Clark b Tate 1
    B 9, l-b 4 13

                                                  187

Second Innings

c Duleepsinhji b Wensley 4
b Tate 7
lbw b Tate 20
lbw b Tate 11
c Cornford b Tate 35
c Duleepsinhji b Tate 0
c Cook b Tate 28
c Cornford b Cook 4
b Hollingdale 11
b Tate 2
not out 0
    B 2, l-b 1 3

                                 125

K. S. Duleepsinhji, seen here batting for England against Australia in the third Test of 1930, followed his uncle, the great Ranji, into the Sussex and England sides. Against Northants he passed his uncle's record score of 285 for Sussex.

Continued on P. 146

Right: A. C. MacLaren, captain of England and Lancashire. An imperious right-handed batsman and a rigid and authoritarian leader. Below: Maurice Tate in action against Australia in 1926 helping to regain the Ashes. Top right: Arthur Fagg acknowledging the crowd after scoring his 2000th run of the 1938 season. Bottom right: "Tich" Freeman, leading his own eleven out at Gravesend, illustrates the reason for his nickname.

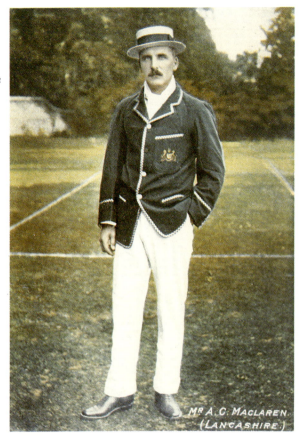

Northamptonshire Bowling

	Overs	Mdns	Runs	Wkts
Clark	27	1	75	2
Thomas	29	11	69	2
Partridge	12	—	80	1
Matthews	22	2	101	1
Jupp	20	3	92	—
Cox	11	2	50	1
Liddell	2	—	16	—
Timms	3	—	26	—

Sussex Bowling

	Overs	Mdns	Runs	Wkts	Overs	Mdns	Runs	Wkts
Tate	9.5	1	18	2	20.2	3	45	7
Wensley	28	10	45	4	14	5	41	1
J. Parks	22	11	37	2	2	—	12	—
Langridge	14	7	21	1				
Hollingdale	10	2	21	—	8	3	14	1
Bowley	13	2	32	1	4	2	6	—
Cook					1	—	4	1

Umpires: P. Toone and F. Chester.

SIR ARTHUR CONAN DOYLE, MD (Edin.), the well-known author, born at Edinburgh on May 22, 1859, died at Crowborough, Sussex on July 7, 1930, aged 71. Although never a famous cricketer, he could hit hard and bowl slows with a puzzling flight. For MCC v Cambridgeshire at Lord's, in 1899, he took seven wickets for 61 runs, and on the same ground two years later carried out his bat for 32 against Leicestershire, who had Woodcock, Geeson and King to bowl for them. In *The Times* of October 27, 1915, he was the author of an article on "The Greatest of Cricketers. An Appreciation of Dr Grace". (It is said that Shacklock, the former Nottinghamshire player, inspired him with the Christian name of his famous character, Sherlock Holmes, and that of the latter's brother Mycroft was suggested by the Derbyshire cricketers.)

ENGLAND v AUSTRALIA

THIRD TEST MATCH
Played at Leeds, July 11, 12, 14, 15, 1930

THE THIRD TEST match, while it afforded that remarkable young batsman, Bradman, the opportunity of leaving all individual batting records in representative matches far behind, was in many respects an unsatisfactory affair. England had the worst of it from start to finish but escaped with a draw, a heavy storm on Sunday night, followed by further rain on the Monday restricting the third day's play to forty-five minutes while, on the Tuesday, further delay occurred owing to defective light.

The game will go down to history on account of the wonderful batting performance accomplished by Bradman who, with an innings of 334, beat the previous highest – 287 by R. E. Foster for England at Sydney – which had stood since December, 1903. In the course of this, Bradman achieved fame in other directions. Like C. G. Macartney on the same ground four years previously, he reached three-figures before lunch-time on the first day. Not out 309 at the close he had then exceeded a total of a thousand runs in Test cricket and reached an aggregate of exactly 2,000 runs for the season. In playing two consecutive innings of over 200 in Test Matches he equalled the performance of Hammond during the previous tour in Australia. He also equalled Macartney's performance of 1926 in scoring three separate hundreds in successive Test matches. Truly could it be called "Bradman's

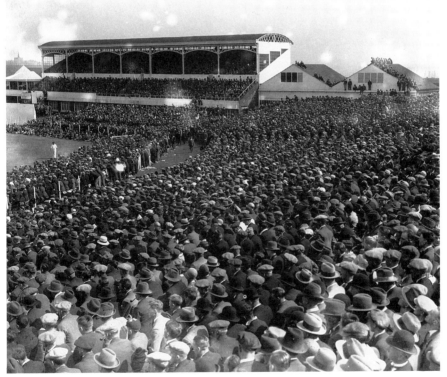

In 1930 English crowds saw for the first time the art of infallible batsmanship on a good wicket raised to unprecedented heights by the mastery of the young Bradman. His astonishing achievements seem even more impressive in retrospect, taking into account the great strength of the English bowling resources against which he was obliged to play.

Match". Bigger though it was and characterised by splendid stroke play, Bradman's innings did not quite approach his 254 at Lord's in freedom from fault but as to its extraordinary merit there could be no two opinions. As usual, he rarely lifted the ball and when making two or more consecutive scoring strokes seldom sent it in the same direction. His footwork was admirable as was the manner in which he played his defensive strokes to balls just short of a length.

Australia, who had played the same eleven in the previous two games, had to make two changes. Suffering from gastritis, Ponsford stood down and Fairfax had not completely recovered from an operation he had had to undergo at Nottingham. Jackson and A'Beckett, therefore, played in their first Test match in England.

England also had alterations. Woolley, Hendren, Allen, Robins and White were all dropped, Sutcliffe, Larwood and Richard Tyldesley coming back and Leyland and Geary being included. As events proved, some of these changes might just as well have not been made. For one thing, the English fielding compared most unfavourably with that in the earlier matches. Tyldesley, avowedly brought in with the idea of keeping the Australian batsmen quiet, again failed in his mission. Geary's bowling had no terrors at all while Larwood, still looking very drawn as the result of his illness, had not the stamina to bowl at his full pace and was terribly expensive. Tate, as usual, bore the brunt of the attack and bowled as pluckily as ever but, taken all round, the Englishmen lacked the attributes of a great side and Hammond alone made over fifty runs.

This time, Woodfull won the toss and Australia led off so brilliantly that, when the first day's play ended, they had 458 runs on the board with only three wickets down. The pitch, like those at Nottingham and Lord's, was, on the first day at any rate, lacking in life and pace and all in favour of batsmen. Opening the innings with Woodfull, Jackson off the fifth ball of the second over was caught at forward short leg but England had to wait until five minutes past three before they took another wicket, Woodfull and Bradman, in the meantime, putting on 192 runs in two hours and thirty-five minutes. This was very largely the work of Bradman who, quick to settle down, completed 102 out of the first 127 in ninety-five minutes. All the same, Woodfull, by another great display of defensive cricket, rendered his side invaluable assistance. After Woodfull left, bowled in trying to hook a shortish ball, Bradman found another admirable partner in Kippax who, if overshadowed by his colleague, played uncommonly well in helping to add 229 in rather less than two and three-quarter hours. The next day McCabe, who had batted twenty minutes overnight, stayed until 63 runs had been put on but nothing of any consequence was accomplished by the rest, the last seven wickets falling in a hundred minutes for 108 runs. Bradman, sixth out at 508, obtained his 334 in six hours and a quarter, his score being made up of forty-six 4s, six 3s, twenty-six 2s, and eighty singles. When he had made 141 he put up a ball towards mid wicket and at 202 he skied a ball over Tate's head at mid-on. Indeed, a man a little quicker on his feet than Tate might have made a catch of it. Actually, Bradman gave only one chance, being missed at the wicket off Geary at 273 when the total was 385. He hit very hard in front of the wicket, scored splendidly on the leg side and very often cut in dazzling fashion. Nobody could have had a better reception than that accorded to Bradman on his return to the pavilion.

Before lunch Hobbs and Sutcliffe scored 17 runs for England but the total was only 53 when Hobbs was out in a manner which provoked considerable discussion. A'Beckett, fielding very close in on the on-side to Grimmett's bowling, took the ball from a gentle stroke very low down, turning a complete somersault but retaining possession. Hobbs was about to walk away but stepped back into his crease on overhearing a remark by Oldfield and an appeal from other members of the side. An appeal having been made, Hobbs was perfectly justified in waiting for the decision. Oates, the umpire at the bowler's end, was unable to give one. A'Beckett in falling over obscuring his view, so he referred to Bestwick standing at square leg. Unhappily, Bestwick hesitated before holding up his finger, and the great majority of the crowd took the view that A'Beckett had not properly made the catch.

Soon afterwards Sutcliffe was out but Hammond and Duleepsinhji added 59 and then Leyland helped to put on 83, Hammond, when 52, having just previously been missed by

Oldfield standing back to Wall. Geary was run out at 206 and England at the close of play, with five wickets down for 212, found themselves 354 behind and requiring 205 to save the follow-on. On the Monday the weather following a storm in the night, which resulted in water lying in patches on the ground, was very bad. So long a delay occurred that not until half past five was play proceeded with. From the manner in which the pitch rolled out it was quite obvious that cricket would have been possible at least an hour earlier. 30 runs were scored before an appeal against the light at a quarter past six was upheld.

On Tuesday morning Duckworth, who had gone in for ten minutes on Saturday evening, batted so well that the score was up to 289 before he was caught at the wicket, 83 runs having been added in rather more than two hours. Hammond stayed until the score was 319, after resisting the bowling for five hours and twenty minutes. He hit only fourteen 4s but gave a splendid display of skilful batting, neglecting very few opportunities of scoring off anything in the nature of a punishable ball. Chapman, hitting hard, put on 51 runs with Tate but England were all out at a quarter to three for 391, their innings lasting nearly eight hours. The last three wickets fell in half an hour for 36 runs.

England followed on 179 behind and, as over three hours remained for cricket, there was always a possibility of them losing. Hobbs and Sutcliffe opened the innings in a very poor light. After a quarter of an hour, they appealed against it and the players went in. For some extraordinary reason the crowd took this in very bad part, booing the batsmen and cheering the Australians, while on the game being resumed there was a continuance of this

Above McCabe, shown here bowled by Larwood in the third Test match at Leeds in 1934. Left: The 22 year old Don Bradman bound for England in April 1930. He was soon to introduce himself to English crowds and cricketers in the most emphatic way.

unseemly behaviour. With 24 scored, Hobbs was brilliantly thrown out by Bradman from deep mid-off but Sutcliffe and Hammond stayed nearly an hour to add 50. After Duleepsinhji had been caught at point off a ball which he afterwards confessed he did not see, another appeal against the light was made at ten minutes to six and no further cricket took place.

The total attendance reached 77,500, and the gate receipts £8,597.

AUSTRALIA

W. M. Woodfull b Hammond 50
A. Jackson c Larwood b Tate 1
D. G. Bradman c Duckworth b Tate 334
A. F. Kippax c Chapman b Tate 77
S. McCabe b Larwood 30
V. Y. Richardson c Larwood b Tate 1
E. L. A'Beckett c Chapman b Geary 29
W. A. Oldfield c Hobbs b Tate 2
C. V. Grimmett c Duckworth b Tyldesley 24
T. W. Wall b Tyldesley 3
P. M. Hornibrook not out 1
B 5, l-b 8, w 1 14

566

ENGLAND

First Innings

J. B. Hobbs c A'Beckett b Grimmett 29
H. Sutcliffe c Hornibrook b Grimmett..............32
W. R. Hammond c Oldfield b McCabe 113
K. S. Duleepsinhji b Hornibrook 35
M. Leyland c Kippax b Wall 44
G. Geary run out 0
G. Duckworth c Oldfield b A'Beckett 33
Mr A. P. F. Chapman b Grimmett 45
M. W. Tate c Jackson b Grimmett 22
H. Larwood not out 10
R. Tyldesley c Hornibrook b Grimmett 6
B 9, l-b 10, n-b 3 22

391

Second Innings

run out 13
not out 28
c Oldfield b Grimmett 35
c Grimmett b Hornibrook 10
not out 1

L-b 8 8

95

England Bowling

	Overs	Mdns	Runs	Wkts
Larwood	33	3	139	1
Tate	39	9	124	5
Geary	35	10	95	1
Tyldesley	33	5	104	2
Hammond	17	3	46	1
Leyland	11	—	44	—

Australia Bowling

	Overs	Mdns	Runs	Wkts	Overs	Mdns	Runs	Wkts
Wall	40	12	70	1	10	3	20	—
A'Beckett	28	8	47	1	11	4	19	—
Grimmett	56.2	16	135	5	17	3	33	1
Hornibrook	41	7	94	1	11.5	5	14	1
McCabe	10	4	23	1	2	1	1	—

Umpires: W. Bestwick and T. Oates.

ESSEX v YORKSHIRE
Played at Leyton, June 15, 16, 17, 1932

HOLMES AND SUTCLIFFE, Yorkshire's famous opening batsmen, made this match memorable by creating a world's record first wicket stand of 555. They surpassed an achievement that had stood unequalled for 34 years – that of two other Yorkshiremen, J. T. Brown and John Tunnicliffe, who scored 554 together for the first wicket against Derbyshire at Chesterfield in 1898. The partnership between Holmes and Sutcliffe was the seventieth of three-figures in which those two men had participated and their 65th for Yorkshire.

While every credit can be given to the two batsmen for their performance, the fact must not be overlooked that Holmes, almost directly he went in, experienced a great piece of luck. He had indeed scored merely three runs when he was missed behind the wicket, low down on the off side where Sheffield got both hands to the ball but failed to hold it. That fault apart, the batting during the big partnership proved wonderfully sound and confident. Rather unusually, Holmes scored more slowly than his colleague but the pair put a hundred runs on the board in an hour and three-quarters and proceeded to maintain their mastery over the bowling for nearly seven hours and a half. The following times indicate the progress of the batsmen:

>100 in an hour and forty-five minutes.
>200 in three hours twenty minutes.
>300 in four hours thirty-five minutes.
>400 in five hours twenty-five minutes.
>500 in six hours fifty-five minutes.
>555 in seven hours twenty-five minutes.

Herbert Sutcliffe and Percy Holmes comprised one of the most consistent opening partnerships of all time, Yorkshire's answer to the equally effective pairing in the Surrey side of Hobbs and Sandham. In any other era, both Holmes and Sandham would have been automatic choices for England. As it was, their fate was to play second fiddle to two of the greatest opening batsman of all time.

A curious incident occurred immediately after the new record had been made. Sutcliffe – very naturally, since it was obviously Yorkshire's policy to declare as soon as possible – threw away his wicket, playing on with a rather casual stroke, and all the players at once left the field. Then, to everyone's amazement, the total on the score board was altered to read 554. For the moment there seemed reason to fear that the chance of beating the record had been missed but eventually it was discovered that a no ball had not been counted in the total.

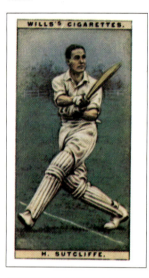

Holmes and Sutcliffe in all made 18 stands exceeding 250, and 69 exceeding 100.

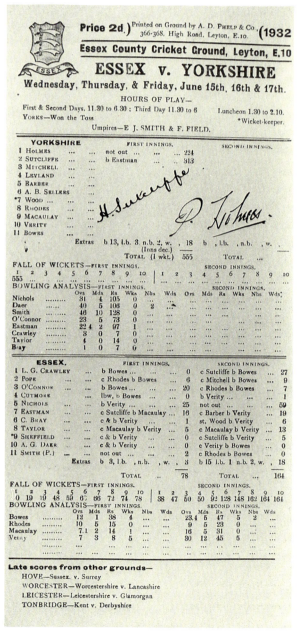

Holmes and Sutcliffe, on a perfect Leyton wicket, made their runs in admirable style. They ran singles skilfully and, if neither man took many risks, runs came at an average rate of scoring. Playing the highest innings of his career, Sutcliffe cut, drove and hit to leg with sound judgment. His straight drives, perfectly timed, were particularly good to watch. Holmes, too, showed a lot of skill when off-driving and cutting but in this innings did not properly reveal his strength on the leg side. He hit nineteen 4's while Sutcliffe among his figures had a 6 and thirty-three 4s. The partnership was a magnificent feat in every way and especially of endurance.

The contrast of the Yorkshiremen's batting with that which followed proved truly remarkable. Bowes, with pace off the pitch, and Verity, by cleverly flighted bowling, developed such a mastery that inside two hours Essex were all out for 78. A fourth wicket stand of 29 between O'Connor and Nichols represented the best of the innings. The last five wickets fell for 19 runs, Verity having the striking figures of five wickets in seven overs for eight runs.

From this pronounced collapse, Essex did not recover, and shortly after one o'clock on Friday Yorkshire emerged from an historic match winners by and innings and 313 runs. In the follow-on, with Essex 477 in arrears, Bowes again made the ball get up awkwardly and, although Crawley brought off some powerful drives, Nichols was the only man who really checked Yorkshire's progress towards victory. By the close of play on Thursday Essex had five wickets down for 92. Nichols, who had gone in third wicket down at 50, batted with rare pluck and skill and remained to carry out his bat. He withstood the attack for two hours and a half and hit a 6 and six 4s.

Verity, particularly deadly towards the close of the innings, took five wickets for 45 – a performance which gave him a record for the match of ten for 53. Bowes brought his figures for the two innings to nine for 85.

YORKSHIRE

P. Holmes *not out* 224
H. Sutcliffe *b* Eastman 313
B 13, l-b 2, n-b 2 18

(1 wkt dec.) 555

A. Mitchell, M. Leyland, W. Barber, Mr. A. B. Sellers, A. Wood, A. C. Rhodes, G. G. Macaulay, H. Verity and W. E. Bowes did not bat.

ESSEX

First Innings

Mr L. G. Crawley *b* Bowes	0
D. F. Pope *c* Rhodes *b* Bowes	6
J. O'Connor *b* Bowes	20
J. A. Cutmore lbw *b* Bowes	0
M. S. Nichols *b* Verity	25
L. C. Eastman *c* Sutcliffe *b* Macaulay	16
Mr C. Bray *c and b* Verity	1
R. H. Taylor *c* Macaulay *b* Verity	5
J. R. Sheffield *c and b* Verity	0
Mr A. G. Daer *c and b* Verity	0
P. Smith *not out*	2
B 3	3
	78

Second Innings

c Sutcliffe *b* Bowes	27
c Mitchell *b* Bowes	9
c Rhodes *b* Bowes	7
b Verity	1
not out	59
c Barber *b* Verity	19
st Wood *b* Verity	6
c Macaulay *b* Verity	13
c Sutcliffe *b* Verity	5
c Mitchell *b* Bowes	0
c Rhodes *b* Bowes	0
B 15, l-b 1, n-b 2	18
	164

Essex Bowling

	Overs	Mdns	Runs	Wkts
Nichols	31	4	105	—
Daer	40	5	106	—
Smith	46	10	128	—
O'Connor	23	5	73	—
Eastman	22.4	2	97	1
Crawley	3	—	7	—
Taylor	4	—	14	—
Bray	1	—	7	—

Yorkshire Bowling

	Overs	Mdns	Runs	Wkts	Overs	Mdns	Runs	Wkts
Bowes	12	1	38	4	23.4	5	47	5
Rhodes	10	5	15	—	9	5	23	—
Macaulay	7.1	2	14	1	16	5	31	—
Verity	7	3	8	5	30	12	45	5

Umpires: E. J. Smith and F. Field.

Hedley Verity, gentle, modest, left-arm spin virtuoso, whose career was to end in such tragic circumstances. A master of flight, Verity was a worthy successor to the crown once worn by such Yorkshiremen before him as Peel and Rhodes. The modern age will always be impressed by Cardus's description of him sailing on the boat to Australia, passing the longueur of the seemingly interminable journey by reading the seemingly interminable Seven Pillars of Wisdom.

YORKSHIRE v NOTTINGHAMSHIRE
Played at Leeds, July 9, 11, 12, 1932

VERITY IN THIS match took – for the second time in his career – all ten wickets in an innings. Prior to lunch on the last day Nottinghamshire scored 38 without loss but on resuming, their ten wickets went down for 29 runs. Verity not only performed the "hat trick" in sending back Walker, Harris and Gunn, but got rid of Arthur Staples and Larwood with the last two balls of his next over and then, disposing of Voce and Sam Staples with the third and fourth balls of his following over, brought the innings to a close. This splendid bowling feat Sutcliffe and Holmes followed up by hitting off in about an hour and a half the 139 runs required for victory. Thus, Yorkshire gained a glorious win by ten wickets although, when on Monday afternoon a thunderstorm burst over the ground, they had stood 71 behind with only one wicket to fall.

NOTTINGHAMSHIRE

First Innings
W. W. Keeton *b* Rhodes 9
F. W. Shipston *b* Macaulay 8
W. Walker *c* Barber *b* Bowes .36
Mr A. W. Carr *c* Barber *b* Verity 0
A. Staples *b* Macaulay 3
C. B. Harris *lbw b* Leyland 35
G. V. Gunn *b* Verity 31
B. Lilley *not out* 46
H. Larwood *b* Leyland 48
W. Voce *b* Leyland 0
S. J. Staples *b* Leyland 0
    B 8, l-b 6, w 2, n-b 2 18

                                    234

Second Innings
c Macaulay *b* Verity 21
c Wood *b* Verity 21
c Macaulay *b* Verity 11
c Barber *b* Verity 0
c Macaulay *b* Verity 7
c Holmes *b* Verity 0
lbw b Verity 0
not out 3
c Sutcliffe *b* Verity 0
c Holmes *b* Verity 0
st Wood *b* Verity 0
    B 3, n-b 1 4

                            67

YORKSHIRE

First Innings
P. Holmes *b* Larwood 65
H. Sutcliffe *c* Voce *b* Larwood 0
A. Mitchell *run out* 24
M. Leyland *b* Voce 5
W. Barber *c and b* Larwood 34
Mr A. B. Sellers *b* A. Staples 0
A. Wood *b* Larwood 1
A. C. Rhodes *c* A. Staples *b* Voce 3
H. Verity *b* Larwood 12
G. G. Macaulay *not out* 8
W. E. Bowes *not out* 1
    B 5, l-b 5 10

                 (9 wkts dec.) 163

Second Innings
not out 77
not out 54

    B 4, l-b 4 8

                           139

Yorkshire Bowling

	Overs	Mdns	Runs	Wkts	Overs	Mdns	Runs	Wkts
Bowes	31	9	55	1	5	—	19	—
Rhodes	28	8	49	1				
Verity	41	13	64	2	19.4	16	10	10
Macaulay	24	10	34	2	23	9	34	—
Leyland	8.2	3	14	4				

Nottinghamshire Bowling

	Overs	Mdns	Runs	Wkts	Overs	Mdns	Runs	Wkts
Larwood	22	4	73	5	3	—	14	—
Voce	22	2	52	2	10	—	43	—
S. J. Staples	7	2	8	—	18.4	5	37	—
A. Staples	11	3	20	1	6	1	25	—
Harris					3	—	12	—

Umpires: H. G. Baldwin and W. Reeves.

ENGLAND v AUSTRALIA

THIRD TEST MATCH
Played at Adelaide, January 13, 14, 16, 17, 18, 19, 1933

THE THIRD TEST match of the tour, in which England – well on top when an innings had been completed on each side – were victorious by no fewer than 338 runs, will go down in history as probably the most unpleasant ever played. So hostile was the feeling of the Australian public against Jardine that on the days before the game started people were excluded from the ground when the Englishmen were practising. As Jardine won the toss and England batted first nothing out of the common occurred to begin with, but later on, when Australia went in and Woodfull was hit over the heart again while Oldfield had to retire owing to a blow he received on the head, the majority of the spectators completely lost all hold on their feelings. Insulting remarks were hurled at Jardine, and when Larwood started to bowl his leg-theory he came in for his share of the storm of abuse. Not to put too fine a point on it, pandemonium reigned. A passage of words between P. F. Warner and Woodfull in the dressing-room increased the bitter feeling prevalent in the crowd, and the dispatch of the cablegram protesting against "body-line" bowling served no purpose in whatever endeavours were made to appease tempers already badly frayed by the various happenings.

Altogether the whole atmosphere was a disgrace to cricket. One must pay a tribute to Jardine. He did not shrink from the line of action he had taken up; he showed great pluck in often fielding near to the boundary where he became an easy target for offensive and sometimes filthy remarks; and above all he captained his team in this particular match like a genius. Much as they disliked the method of attack he controlled, all the leading Australian critics were unanimous in their praise of his skill as a leader.

England made a dreadful start, four wickets going down in an hour for 30 runs and the score being 37 at lunch, but then came a stand which turned the course of the game and put England on the road to ultimate success. Leyland and Wyatt, if enjoying a certain amount of luck, batted, in the circumstances, uncommonly well while adding 156 in about two and a half hours. Leyland, who in the end played on, hit thirteen 4s, in an innings which included many fine off-drives. Wyatt, whose hitting to square-leg brought him two or three 6s, left soon afterwards, but Paynter – included in the side for Pataudi – and Allen added a useful 32 runs, so that at the end of the day England had 236 on the board with seven men out. On the next morning Paynter continued to bat marvellously well, and Verity, who took Bowes's place in the England team, defended so manfully that the stand for the eighth wicket realised 96 runs in about two and a quarter hours. Paynter pulled and drove well, while his cutting and leg-glancing were almost as good. England were all out soon after three o'clock for 341 and followed this up by getting down the first four Australian wickets for 51. It was during this time that Woodfull, ducking to avoid what he thought would be a rising ball, was hit on the body. Later, Ponsford and Richardson added 58 in the last seventy minutes, but Australia wound up 232 behind with six wickets to fall. Ponsford played a fine fighting innings, cutting very well and meeting the leg-theory form

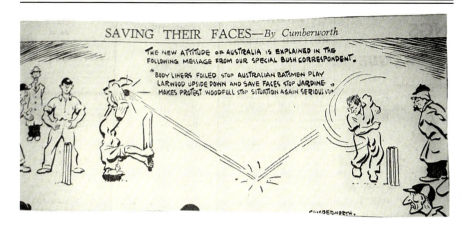

In the litany of cricket history, no phrase sounds more ominous than "Voce and Larwood". The Nottinghamshire opening fast-bowling pair were deputed by persons unknown (because too cowardly to confess) to use their speed not to win matches against Australia but to intimidate the Australian batsmen, especially Bradman, with the fear of physical injury. The plan worked like a dream, or rather a nightmare, the casualty being Larwood himself (pictured right), whose international career terminated abruptly. The Bodyline series, as it became known, seemed likely, at the height of the acrimony, to imperil the Empire itself.

of attack in able style. He and Richardson put on 80 runs and Oldfield stayed for just over two hours when his active participation in the match was closed by a blow on the head by a ball from Larwood. Australia finished their innings 119 behind, and although with one wicket down for 85 England lost Sutcliffe cheaply they stood, at the close of play, 204 runs ahead. On the fourth day, England placed themselves in such a position that they could not very well lose, and realising that their team was going to be beaten the Adelaide public who went to the ground were not nearly so noisy and insulting. Both Leyland and Wyatt again made useful scores; Verity supplemented his 45 in the first innings with 40, while Jardine, Hammond and Ames by first-rate cricket all played important parts in carrying England towards victory. England wound up with six men out for 296 and were thus 415 runs ahead.

As the wicket showed definite signs of wear, the outlook for Australia was very gloomy. Jardine batted four hours and a quarter and did great work in wearing down the bowling.

Hammond and Leyland accomplished some bright and fearless hitting, and altogether it was a very good day for the Englishmen. Ames and Verity adding 98 runs in just over two hours England in the end put together a total of 412 so that Australia were left to get 532 to win. Before the fifth day's play ended, the home side lost four of their best batsmen for 120 runs and to all intents and purposes the game was as good as over. Australia in their last innings had Fingleton and Ponsford out with only 12 runs on the board, but then came an excellent stand by Woodfall and Bradman, 88 being put on in an hour and a quarter. Bradman was in first-rate form, hitting a six and ten 4s, but just when he was becoming dangerous Verity caught him from a hard return. On the last day of the match Richardson and Woodfull defended stubbornly for a time, but they were separated at 171, and then Allen and Larwood quickly finished off the innings for 193. The greatest praise is due to Woodfull who for the second time in his career in a Test match carried his bat through the innings. He was in for nearly four hours, making most of his runs from strokes on the leg-side. Throughout the match the Englishmen fielded well, while Allen bowled splendidly.

ENGLAND

First Innings

H. Sutcliffe c Wall b O'Reilly	9
Mr D. R. Jardine b Wall	3
W. R. Hammond c Oldfield b Wall	2
L. E. G. Ames b Ironmonger	3
M. Leyland b O'Reilly	83
Mr R. E. S. Wyatt c Richardson b Grimmett	78
E. Paynter c Fingleton b Wall	77
Mr G. O. Allen lbw b Grimmett	15
H. Verity c Richardson b Wall	45
W. Voce b Wall	8
H. Larwood not out	3
B 1, l-b 7, n-b 7	15
	341

Second Innings

c sub. b Wall	7
lbw b Ironmonger	56
b Bradman	85
b O'Reilly	69
c Wall b Ironmonger	42
c Wall b O'Reilly	49
not out	1
lbw b Grimmett	15
lbw b O'Reilly	40
b O'Reilly	8
c Bradman b Ironmonger	8
B 17, l-b 11, n-b 4	32
	412

AUSTRALIA

First Innings

J. H. Fingleton c Ames b Allen	0
W. M. Woodfull b Allen	22
D. G. Bradman c Allen b Larwood	8
S. J. McCabe c Jardine b Larwood	8
W. H. Ponsford b Voce	85
V. Y. Richardson b Allen	28
W. A. Oldfield retired hurt	41
C. V. Grimmett c Voce b Allen	10
T. W. Wall b Hammond	6
W. J. O'Reilly b Larwood	0
H. Ironmonger not out	0
B 2, l-b 11, n-b 1	14
	222

Second Innings

b Larwood	0
not out	73
c and b Verity	66
c Leyland b Allen	7
c Jardine b Larwood	3
c Allen b Larwood	21
absent hurt	0
b Allen	6
b Allen	0
b Larwood	5
b Allen	0
B 4, l-b 2, w 1, n-b 5	12
	193

Australia Bowling

	Overs	Mdns	Runs	Wkts	Overs	Mdns	Runs	Wkts
Wall	34.1	10	72	5	29	6	75	1
O'Reilly	50	19	82	2	50.3	21	79	4
Ironmonger	20	6	50	1	57	21	87	3
Grimmett	28	6	94	2	35	9	74	1
McCabe	14	3	28	—	16	—	42	—
Bradman					4	—	23	1

England Bowling

	Overs	Mdns	Runs	Wkts	Overs	Mdns	Runs	Wkts
Larwood	25	6	55	3	19	3	71	4
Allen	23	4	71	4	17.2	5	50	4
Hammond	17.4	4	30	1	9	3	27	—
Voce	14	5	21	1	4	1	7	—
Verity	16	7	31	—	20	12	26	1

Umpires: G. Hele and G. Borwick.

THE SECOND-CLASS COUNTIES IN 1933

AN UNFORTUNATE OVERSIGHT in the notification of the result of the match between Yorkshire Second Eleven and Staffordshire in the Minor Counties' competition of 1933 led to a serious blunder coming to light. As originally made up, the final table of results showed that Norfolk, with a percentage of 72.00, and Yorkshire Second Eleven, with a percentage of 71.66 finished first and second in the competition. Exercising their right to participate in a challenge match with the leaders, Yorkshire Second Eleven duly met Norfolk and defeated them. Some seven weeks later, when the table was being checked for insertion in *Wisden's Cricketers' Almanack*, it was discovered that certain of the columns of figures did not agree. Closer investigation, followed by correspondence with Maj. R. C. Campbell, the Hon. Secretary of the Minor Counties' Cricket Association, elicited the fact that mistakes had occurred in calculating the points of Yorkshire Second Eleven and Staffordshire.

It was then found that, as the outcome of the match between these elevens at Sheffield in July when cricket did not take place on the second day, Yorkshire, owing to a late and ambiguous report being sent to the secretary of the Minor Counties, had been credited with points for a win in a one-day match instead of points for a win on the first innings. This revelation meant that Yorkshire's percentage was reduced from 71.66 to 68.33, and that in consequence, their position in the table was third, Wiltshire being second with a percentage of 70.00.

An extraordinary situation was thus created. Yorkshire had played Norfolk in the challenge match when actually they possessed no right to an honour which should have fallen to Wiltshire but, the cricket season being closed (it was then towards the end of October), no opportunity presented itself, should Wiltshire have claimed to play the leaders, for a meeting between Norfolk and Wiltshire in a challenge match. Yorkshire Second Eleven obviously had no standing in the matter and could not be regarded as champions of the Minor Counties' competition because their position as third in the list precluded then from taking part in a challenge match. Meanwhile, Major Campbell placed his resignation as Hon. Secretary in the hands of the committee, but at the Annual Meeting of the Minor Counties' Cricket Association at Lord's on December 5th, he withdrew this and was re-elected, a resolution exonerating him from all blame in connection with the incorrect table of percentages being passed unanimously. It was also agreed to regard the Championship of 1933 as "not decided" and to ignore the so-called challenge match between Yorkshire Second Eleven and Norfolk. As the match took place, the batting and bowling figures are included in the averages of the counties concerned.

ENGLAND v AUSTRALIA

FOURTH TEST MATCH
Played at Leeds, July 20, 21, 23, 24, 1934

JUST AS AT Lord's rain came to damage the wicket and ruin Australia's chance of making an even fight of it, so in the fourth Test match on the Headingley ground at Leeds did one of the shortest but heaviest rainstorms seen at a cricket match for years arrive just in time to rob Australia of victory and enable England to draw a game in which they were completely outplayed. Escaping defeat in the luckiest manner possible, the England team accomplished nothing in the match on which they could congratulate themselves. In their unavailing efforts to get together a side which "balanced" the selectors made further changes from those who had represented England at Manchester. A strained leg compelled Sutcliffe to stand down, Keeton of Nottinghamshire thus getting the opportunity of making his first appearance for his country; G. O. Allen and Clark were left out and Bowes and Mitchell of Derbyshire reintroduced. James Langridge and Nichols attended and it was decided not to include Langridge and to make Nichols – for the third time – twelfth man.

His good fortune in the matter of winning the toss again attended Wyatt and for the third consecutive game England enjoyed the advantage of batting first. Wyatt himself described the wicket as being "like a feather-bed", whatever that may have meant. The assumption at the time was that it would be slow and easy. There was nothing in the way it played during the first day to suggest that it was otherwise, yet England, giving one of the worst displays of batting probably ever seen under similar conditions were all dismissed between twenty-five minutes to twelve and twenty-five minutes past five for a paltry total of 200. It can be said that O'Reilly, Grimmett and Chipperfield bowled very well, but nothing they accomplished with the ball was quite sufficient to account for the shocking exhibition of weak and hesitant batting given by the Englishmen. Even Walters, who with 44 made top score, did not, after Wall had been taken off at 30, show anything of the brilliance that characterised many of his strokes at Lord's and Manchester. Keeton made two good cuts and a square drive in scoring 25 out of 43 in fifty minutes and although, after Walters' dismissal at 85, Hammond and Hendren put on 50 in an hour none of the rest, equally with those who had gone before, played in form worthy of the occasion.

Before cricket ended, however, further surprises were in store for the crowd. Bowes and Hammond started the bowling for England and both Ponsford and Brown played them so easily that there seemed no reason to expect any pronounced success for the England attack up to half-past six. Bowes, however, changed ends and, coming on again at 37 from the pavilion wicket, bowled Brown at 37 and two runs later sent back Oldfield and Woodfull in one over. Stumps were then pulled up, Bowes having sent down ten balls from the pavilion end and dismissed three batsmen without conceding a run. Australia, therefore, finished the day 161 runs behind with seven men to be disposed of and the situation had thus completely changed. Those, however, were the last crumbs of comfort England were destined to enjoy in this disastrous match. Bradman joined Ponsford the next morning and not until ten minutes to six on Saturday evening did another wicket fall. Giving a great display of batting, the two famous Australian run-getters beat all previous partnership records in Test matches. They carried the score in five and a half hours to 427 before Ponsford, hooking a short ball from Verity, trod on his wicket, knocked the leg bail off and was out. Altogether their stand realised no fewer than 388 runs. They always scored at a good rate but, as usual with Australians, unless the bowling is exceptionally steady, pushed along very quickly after tea when, in an hour, 98 runs were put on. Up to lunch time they scored 129 in two hours and twenty-five minutes and between lunch and tea 161 in two hours and five minutes.

Ponsford's innings was very good indeed. In the course of the partnership each batsman gave a chance, for Ponsford when 70 should have been caught by Mitchell at cover-point while Bradman at 71 was let off by Hopwood. Ponsford obtained many of his runs by late cuts and turning the ball to leg and all through his innings, which lasted six and a quarter hours and included nineteen 4s, he hit the ball hard and placed it well when scoring in front of the wicket. Moreover, his defence was rocklike in its steadiness and accuracy. For the greater part of the day Bradman, who unlike Ponsford obtained most of his runs in front of the stumps batted with the utmost certainty but during the last thirty-five minutes when he and McCabe were raising the score to 494 he played in a more light-hearted spirit. Twice he lifted the ball over the ring for six, and hit Hopwood for 15 runs in one over.

Australia, therefore, began the third day in a most comfortable position being 294 runs on with six wickets to fall and altogether Bradman and McCabe added 90 in an hour before McCabe was out. Thanks to some most effective bowling by Bowes Australia's innings was finished off in a hundred minutes, the last six wickets falling on Monday morning for 90 runs. Bradman, sixth out at 550, made his 304 in six hours and fifty-five minutes. Going in third wicket down, he took the leading part in adding 51 runs while as many more wickets fell. Not out on Saturday with 271 he was perhaps lucky in reaching 300 because when 280 he was missed at third slip by Verity. He did not play so well during the fifty minutes he was in on Monday morning as he had done previously but all the same his innings was a masterly affair. He hit the ball very hard and placed his strokes beautifully while until joined by McCabe on Saturday evening he rarely sent the ball into the air. He hit two 6s, forty-three 4s, one 3, fifteen 2s and eighty-seven singles.

Bowes was responsible for the Australian innings being wound up so quickly and in the end he came out with what was a really good record of six wickets for 142 runs. Yet on the Saturday when Ponsford and Bradman were scoring so readily Bowes, like the rest of the England bowlers, looked quite innocuous. His analysis was interesting enough to bear dissection. After going on at 37 on Friday, he took three wickets for no runs. On Saturday he bowled over twenty-eight overs, did not take a wicket and had 81 runs hit from him while up to the time he dismissed Darling at 551 he took three wickets on Monday morning in nine overs and four balls for 25 runs. Verity was the only other man to get a wicket but his three cost him 113.

England went in again at one o'clock 384 runs behind so that the most they could hope for was a draw. Keeton fell just before lunch at 28 and afterwards Hammond played better than in any other Test match during the season. He was seeing the ball well, hitting it hard and accurately and seemed likely to put together an innings in his best style. With the total up to 70, however, a dreadful disaster occurred, for Hammond, responding to the call of Walters for a foolish run and then checking himself, lost his wicket. From that blow England did not recover. Walters left at 87 but by dint of very hard work and much

In 1934, in the wake of the Bodyline series, the Australians agreed to tour England provided intimidating bowling were conspicuous only by its absence. With Larwood no longer in the England line-up, Bradman was once again free to demonstrate his genius against ordinary mortals.

watchful batting Hendren and Wyatt added 65 in rather less than two hours. During this stand Bradman, trying to stop the ball in the long field with his foot, strained his leg and had to retire. Hendren and Leyland, both entirely on the defensive, stayed together for the last fifty-five minutes and added 36, Hendren having been in for three hours and a quarter when stumps were pulled up. Coupled with the rain which fell on Tuesday this stand saved England but they began the last day with only 188 on the board and still wanting 196 to save the innings defeat. Heavy rain fell in the night and the wicket was very wet, while a further shower caused a delay soon after cricket had been resumed. Then Hendren was out at 190 and when Ames left at 213 the end seemed very near. Just before one o'clock a thunderstorm broke over the ground and, although it lasted only ten minutes, the downpour was so severe that no further cricket was possible. Not until six o'clock, however, was the decision to abandon the match arrived at. Not only the pitch but parts of the outfield and especially that in front of the pavilion was, even then, far too wet for cricket to be proceeded with.

ENGLAND

First Innings

Mr C. F. Walters *c and b* Chipperfield 44
W. W. Keeton *c* Oldfield *b* O'Reilly 25
W. R. Hammond *b* Wall 37
E. Hendren *b* Chipperfield 29
Mr R. E. S. Wyatt *st* Oldfield *b* Grimmett 19
M. Leyland *lbw b* O'Reilly 16
L. E. G. Ames *c* Oldfield *b* Grimmett 9
J. L. Hopwood *lbw b* O'Reilly 8
H. Verity *not out* 2
T. B. Mitchell *st* Oldfield *b* Grimmett 9
W. E. Bowes *c* Ponsford *b* Grimmett 0
 L-b 2 2

1/43 2/85 3/135 4/135 5/168 6/170   200
7/189 8/189 9/200

Second Innings

b O'Reilly 45
b Grimmett 12
run out 20
lbw b O'Reilly 42
b Grimmett 44
not out 49
c Brown *b* Grimmett 8
not out 2

 B 1, l-b 6 7

1/28 2/70 3/87 4/152   229
5/190 6/213

AUSTRALIA

W. A. Brown *b* Bowes 15
W. H. Ponsford *hit wkt b* Verity 181
W. A. Oldfield *c* Ames *b* Bowes 0
W. M. Woodfull *b* Bowes 0
D. G. Bradman *b* Bowes 304
S. J. McCabe *b* Bowes 27
L. S. Darling *b* Bowes 12
A. G. Chipperfield *c* Wyatt *b* Verity 1
C. V. Grimmett *run out* 15
W. J. O'Reilly *not out* 11
T. W. Wall *lbw b* Verity 1
 B 8, l-b 9 17

1/37 2/39 3/39 4/427 5/517   584
6/550 7/551 8/557 9/574

Australia Bowling

	Overs	Mdns	Runs	Wkts	Overs	Mdns	Runs	Wkts
Wall	18	1	57	1	14	5	36	—
McCabe	4	2	3	—	5	4	5	—
Grimmett	30.4	11	57	4	56.5	24	72	3
O'Reilly	35	16	46	3	51	25	88	2
Chipperfield	18	6	35	2	9	2	21	—

While Bradman (above) laid the English bowling to waste, the most deadly bowler in history was approaching retirement in the backwaters of the Second-Class Counties. Even as an old man, Sydney Barnes, irascible, forbidding, unsentimental, had returned astonishing analyses.

England Bowling

	Overs	Mdns	Runs	Wkts
Bowes	59	13	142	6
Hammond	29	5	82	—
Mitchell	23	1	117	—
Verity	46.5	15	113	3
Hopwood	30	7	93	—
Leyland	5	—	20	—

Umpires: J. Hardstaff and A. Dolphin.

STAFFORDSHIRE IN 1934

Hon. Secretary – Mr L. W. Hancock, 4 Kingsland Avenue, Oakhill, Stoke-on-Trent

DUE LARGELY TO their inability to place in the field a regular eleven – 34 players were called upon in eight matches – Staffordshire, as in 1933, fared very moderately. In addition, several batsmen of experience often failed unaccountably while Sydney Barnes, the famous bowler, concluded his career with the county after the first two matches. A. Smith, E. Perry, E. Mayer, S. Crump, Lockett and Backhouse did most of the run-getting, but unfortunately neither Smith nor Perry was able to play regularly. The bulk of the attack fell upon Lockett, Backhouse and Crump, and they were splendidly supported in the field. A feature of the season was the high standard of wicket-keeping shown by C. C. Goodway. In twenty-two seasons covering a period of 31 years with Staffordshire, his native county, Barnes had the following figures:

Overs	Maidens	Runs	Wickets	Average
5367.1	1,629	11,500	1,432	8.03

GLOUCESTERSHIRE v NOTTINGHAMSHIRE

T. W. GODDARD'S BENEFIT MATCH
Played at Gloucester, August 29, 31, September 1, 1936

GLOUCESTERSHIRE WON BY an innings and 70 runs. Thanks to Hammond the county finished the season in great style. He was in really wonderful form and putting together an innings of 317 beat his previous best score in England and surpassed the aggregate of 1,278 runs in August set up by W. G. Grace. Hammond's mastery of the Nottinghamshire bowlers and his phenomenal powers of endurance were shown by the fact that after batting five hours for his first two hundred runs he hit the third hundred in just over seventy minutes. In this last stage he cast aside all restraint and exploited his superb off-drive in devastating fashion. Altogether, Hammond batted close on six and a half hours and in all that time made one false stroke. That occurred at 111 when he almost played on. He hit three 6s and thirty-four 4s. Neale, Crapp and Hopkins aided him admirably in stands of 164, 83 and 133 respectively. Staples proved Nottinghamshire's best batsman. Hardstaff in the first innings supported him in a partnership of 76, and Harris and Staples scored 71 together on the last day when Hammond, owing to a badly bruised instep, could not play. The second day's attendance of 7,000 was the largest ever seen on the ground.

NOTTINGHAMSHIRE

First Innings

W. W. Keeton *b* Stephens	35
C. B. Harris *b* Hammond	6
W. Walker *c* Barnett *b* Goddard	6
J. Hardstaff *c* Hopkins *b* Stephens	46
G. V. Gunn *b* Goddard	5
A. Staples *c* Goddard *b* Cranfield	58
Mr G. F. Heane *c* Page *b* Cranfield	11
W. Voce *b* Cranfield	25
F. G. Woodhead *not out*	6
A. B. Wheat *c* Stephens *b* Goddard	1
H. J. Butler *lbw b* Goddard	0
L-b 1	1
	200

Second Innings

lbw b Cranfield	20
c sub *b* Stephens	50
b Cranfield	9
b Cranfield	0
b Goddard	12
c Allen *b* Cranfield	52
c Barnett *b* Stephens	18
b Barnett	23
c Stephens *b* Barnett	0
c Page *b* Barnett	24
not out	3
B 3, l-b 1	4
	215

GLOUCESTERSHIRE

C. J. Barnett *b* Voce	2
R. W. Haynes *c* Staples *b* Voce	18
Mr B. O. Allen *c* Staples *b* Butler	18
W. R. Hammond *b* Woodhead	317
W. L. Neale *c* Heane *b* Butler	66
J. F. Crapp *c* Woodhead *b* Gunn	22
Mr D. A. C. Page *lbw b* Heane	8
E. J. Stephens *b* Voce	0
T. W. Goddard *b* Heane	1
V. J. Hopkins *not out*	25
M. Cranfield *c* Wheat *b* Staples	0
B 6, l-b 1, n-b 1	8
	485

Gloucestershire Bowling

	Overs	Mdns	Runs	Wkts	Overs	Mdns	Runs	Wkts
Hammond	7	—	21	1				
Barnett	13	3	51	—	11.3	2	25	3
Goddard	28.1	9	49	4	25	6	71	1
Stephens	11	—	27	2	8	1	32	2
Cranfield	23	6	51	3	33	11	71	4
Haynes					6	1	12	—

Nottinghamshire Bowling

	Overs	Mdns	Runs	Wkts
Voce	31	2	117	3
Butler	31	5	79	2
Woodhead	24	3	86	1
Staples	17.4	2	69	1
Gunn	19	3	53	1
Heane	28	5	73	2

Umpires: W. A. Buswell and G. Brown.

Capable of amassing huge scores in the very highest company, Hammond often ran riot against the counties. The treble century was scored against a moderate attack sadly lacking the fire of Larwood.

MR DONALD ELIGON, died at Port of Spain, Trinidad, on June 4, 1937, aged 28. After playing for Shannon Cricket Club he joined the Trinidad inter-colonial team in 1934 and quickly became one of the outstanding bowlers in West Indies. Last season he took seven wickets for 63 runs in the second innings against British Guiana, and five for 39 against Grenada. His death was due to blood poisoning caused by a nail in his cricket boot.

WORCESTERSHIRE v LANCASHIRE
Played at Dudley, June 22, 23, 24, 1938

DRAWN. FOR THE first time in their history Worcestershire fielded an entirely professional eleven. A strange incident occurred on the first day. Phillipson, foolishly going for a short run off a no-ball, collided with Jackson, who was trying to throw down the wicket. Phillipson dislocated his left collar-bone and Jackson hurt his back; neither took further part in the match. Hopwood and Iddon batted well in a stand of 113 but Nutter was missed three times off Perks. Lister helped to add 81. Although six men reached double figures, Worcestershire had to follow on 207 behind. Then King and Cooper made 84 together while Gibbons, the acting captain, played at the top of his form in a stand which turned a deficit of 102 into a lead of 105. Gibbons cut and drove beautifully, and Cooper maintained a sound defence for four hours and forty minutes. Wilkinson took five wickets for 27 in his last twelve overs. Rain came soon after Worcestershire's declaration.

In the early history of cricket there is recorded an incident in which two batsmen collided so violently while attempting a short run that one of them subsequently died from his injuries. Although the tragedy has never since been repeated, the Lancashire player Phillipson (right) and his opponent, Jackson, seem to have come peculiarly close.

LANCASHIRE

First Innings

J. L. Hopwood c Jackson b Martin	67
C. Washbrook b Perks	4
J. Iddon c and b Martin	60
N. Oldfield c Howorth b Perks	1
A. Nutter not out	89
Mr D. M. Matthews c Gibbons b Jackson	22
Mr W. H. L. Lister lbw b Howorth	46
W. E. Phillipson retired hurt	15
W. Farrimond c Gibbons b Martin	0
R. Pollard b Martin	1
L. L. Wilkinson b Perks	0
L-b 2	2
	307

Second Innings

not out	18
not out	16
L-b 1, w 1	2
	26

WORCESTERSHIRE

First Innings

C. H. Bull lbw b Nutter	0
B. P. King c Wilkinson b Pollard	0
E. Cooper c Farrimond b Pollard	13
H. H. Gibbons b Pollard	11
S. H. Martin c Farrimond b Pollard	5
F. Warne b Nutter	17
J. Horton not out	15
S. Buller c Nutter b Wilkinson	15
R. Howorth c and b Wilkinson	16
R. T. D. Perks st Farrimond b Wilkinson	4
P. F. Jackson absent hurt	0
L-b 3, n-b 1	4
	100

Second Innings

c Farrimond b Pollard	17
b Pollard	56
c Farimond b Wilkinson	111
lbw b Wilkinson	123
not out	42
b Pollard	6
b Wilkinson	9
c Nutter b Wilkinson	0
c Pollard b Wilkinson	0
not out	1
L-b 6, n-b 1	7
(8 wkts dec.)	372

Worcestershire Bowling

	Overs	Mdns	Runs	Wkts	Overs	Mdns	Runs	Wkts
Perks	30.2	4	91	3				
Martin	32	6	90	4				
Howorth	13	3	47	1				
Jackson	10	1	36	1				
Warne	12	—	41	—	3	—	7	—
Horton					4	—	17	—

Lancashire Bowling

	Overs	Mdns	Runs	Wkts	Overs	Mdns	Runs	Wkts
Pollard	19	6	42	4	28	5	79	3
Nutter	10	4	12	3	32	7	71	—
Wilkinson	18.2	2	42	3	37	4	118	5
Iddon					31	7	85	—
Hopwood					3	—	12	—

Umpires: T. Oates and H. G. Baldwin.

ESSEX v KENT

Played at Colchester, July 13, 14, 15, 1938

DRAWN. THE MATCH was notable for the world-record feat achieved by Fagg, of Kent, in scoring two double-hundreds. Essex were without their regular bowlers, engaged in the Gentlemen and Players game at Lord's, but Fagg's performance, nevertheless, was extraordinary. In the first innings he made 244 out of 386 in five hours, and in the second innings he batted two hours and fifty minutes for 202 not out, before Chalk declared. Vigorous on-drives and powerful strokes to leg were his chief means of scoring and he hit thirty-one 4s in the first innings and twenty-seven in the other. On the opening day, Kent kept Essex in the field until six o'clock. Todd helped Fagg in a stand of 133 and Chalk assisted in a partnership of 137. Wright, who in one spell took four wickets for six runs, worried Essex with slow leg-break bowling but Pearce and Smith put on 131 for the ninth wicket. Pearce gave a splendid display of driving and glancing. When Kent batted again leading by 79, Fagg played brilliant cricket. He so dominated the proceedings that he reached three figures out of 134 in 69 minutes, and when stumps were drawn Kent, with three wickets left, led by 221. Play on the last morning was rendered memorable by the completion of Fagg's exploit, and spectators and players alike applauded him all the way to the pavilion. Essex, needing 393 to win, started badly, but rain intervened and prevented a finish.

KENT

First Innings

A. Fagg *lbw b* Taylor	244
P. R. Sunnucks *c* Wade *b* Smith	3
Mr W. H. V. Levett *c* Wilcox *b* Daer	0
L. J. Todd *b* Smith	39
T. Spencer *c* Taylor *b* Vigar	14
Mr F. G. H. Chalk *c* Lavers *b* Eastman	61
F. G. Foy *c and b* Taylor	25
N. W. Harding *st* Wade *b* Vigar	9
D. V. P. Wright *c* Wade *b* Taylor	2
A. E. Watt *not out*	24
C. Lewis *c* Vigar *b* Taylor	5
L-b 3	3
	429

Second Innings

not out	202
run out	82
not out	24
B 2, l-b 2, n-b 1	5
(1 wkt dec.)	313

ESSEX

First Innings

Mr D. R. Wilcox *c* Harding *b* Todd	5
L. C. Eastman *lbw b* Todd	44
R. M. Taylor *b* Lewis	37
J. O'Connor *c* Lewis *b* Wright	63
A. V. Avery *b* Wright	1
Mr T. N. Pearce *not out*	137
Mr A. B. Lavers *lbw b* Wright	1
T. H. Wade *b* Wright	4
F. Vigar *lbw b* Wright	0
R. Smith *c* Fagg *b* Wright	37
H. Daer *lbw b* Wright	4
B 5, l-b 6, n-b 6	17
	350

Second Innings

b Watt	1
c Wright *b* Todd	0
not out	7
not out	0
	8

Essex Bowling

	Overs	Mdns	Runs	Wkts	Overs	Mdns	Runs	Wkts
Smith	22	4	96	2	10	3	46	—
Daer	10	3	51	1	9	—	46	—
Eastman	40	15	68	1	17	2	52	—
Lavers	9	1	30	—				
Vigar	19	3	91	2	13	—	75	—
O'Connor	2	—	6	—	5	—	23	—
Pearce	10	—	43	—				
Taylor	10.1	1	41	4	10	—	46	—
Wilcox					4	—	20	—

Kent Bowling

	Overs	Mdns	Runs	Wkts	Overs	Mdns	Runs	Wkts
Todd	19	6	46	2	2	—	6	1
Watt	22	3	63	—	1.3	—	2	1
Harding	5	1	34	—				
Wright	31.3	7	107	7				
Lewis	26	7	83	1				

Umpires: J. Newman and C. W. L. Parker.

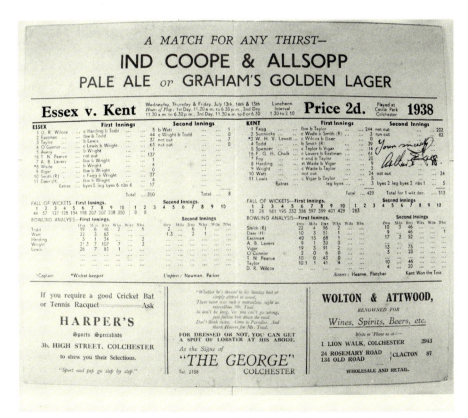

In the winter preceding this match at Colchester, Arthur Fagg had travelled to Australia with G. O. Allen's side. The only man ever to score two double hundreds in the same match, Fagg went on to become one of the best-known and most resolute of international umpires.

BRIGADIER-GENERAL ROBERT MONTAGU POORE, who during one season was the most prolific scorer in England, died on July 14, 1938, aged 72. He used to relate that he did not take seriously to cricket before going to India as a lieutenant in the 7th Hussars. Then he studied text books on the game while playing in Army matches. From 1892 to 1895 when ADC to Lord Harris, then Governor of Bombay, he averaged 80 for Government House. Going to South Africa, better opportunities came for finding his true ability when facing the formidable bowlers under the command of Lord Hawke. He hit up 112 at Pietermaritzburg and at Durban, when fifteen of Natal were set to get 228, he scored 107, being mainly responsible for the local side winning by five wickets; these were the only hundreds scored against the touring team of 1895–96. He also appeared for South Africa in the three Test matches without distinguishing himself more than did some others in badly beaten elevens.

In the course of a few months in Natal he scored 1,600 runs, including nine separate hundreds, so that when returning to England in 1898 at the age of 32, Major Poore was ready for first-class cricket. On a soft wicket at Lord's he scored 51 and helped appreciably in an innings victory for MCC over Lancashire. He averaged 34 for eleven Hampshire matches and next season he became the most sensational batsman in the country, his doings being described as phenomenal. Making a late start he scored in two months – June 12 to August 12 – 1,399 runs for Hampshire with an average of 1 16.58. Major Poore hit seven centuries, two against Somerset at Portsmouth, and in his next innings another off the Lancashire bowlers at Southampton; he also scored exactly 100 runs in two innings against the Australians. In 21 first-class innings he made 1,551 runs, average 91.23 – a figure not exceeded until Herbert Sutcliffe averaged 96.96 in 1931. The return with Somerset at Taunton was specially noteworthy, Major Poore scoring 304 and with Captain E. G. Wynyard (225) adding 411 in four hours twenty minutes – the English record for the sixth wicket. Chosen for the Gentlemen against the Players at both The Oval and Lord's, Poore did little. Military duty took him back to South Africa before the end of the season, and after occasional appearances his county cricket ceased in 1906, but so well did he retain his form and activity that in 1923, when 57 years old, he hit three consecutive centuries during a tour of MCC in the west country. His 304 stood as a Hampshire record for 38 years, being surpassed in 1937 by R. H. Moore with 316 against Warwickshire at Bournemouth.

Six feet four inches in height, of massive frame with powerful limbs, Major Poore when at the top of his form used his long reach with great effect in driving, his strokes between the bowler and cover point going with such speed over the turf that fieldsmen, no matter how placed, could not prevent him from scoring freely. Before becoming accustomed to English wickets, he played forward more in defence for smothering the ball than as a hitter, but his drive ripened to one of the most powerful ever known.

A versatile sportsman, Major Poore was one of the finest swordsmen in the Army, taking the highest honours at the military tournament. A first-rate polo player he also twice won the West of India lawn tennis championship, a feat he repeated in Matabeleland and was in his regimental shooting team. His exceptional physical powers were demonstrated in his wonderful 1899 season; during a fortnight in June he played in the winning team of the inter-regimental polo tournament, won the best-man-at-arms mounted event at the Royal naval and military tournament and scored three consecutive centuries for Hampshire, 104 and 119 not out against Somerset and 111 against Lancashire.

ENGLAND v AUSTRALIA

FIFTH TEST MATCH
Played at The Oval, August 20, 22, 23, 24, 1938

ENGLAND WON BY an innings and 579 runs and each country having gained one victory the rubber was drawn. No more remarkable exhibition of concentration and endurance has ever been seen on the cricket field than that of Leonard Hutton, the Yorkshire opening batsman, in a match which culminated in the defeat of Australia by a margin more substantial than any associated with the series of matches between the two countries. Record after record went by the board as Hutton mastered the bowling in calm, methodical fashion for the best part of two and a half days. At the end of an innings which extended over thirteen hours twenty minutes, this batsman of only 22 years had placed the highest score in Test cricket to his name, and shared in two partnerships which surpassed previous figures. Adding 382 with Leyland, he took part in a stand which was a record not only for England's second wicket but for any wicket for England, and his stand of 215 with Hardstaff established a new record for England's sixth wicket. As a boy of fourteen, Hutton, at Leeds in 1930, had seen Bradman hit 334 – the record individual score in Test matches between England and Australia. Now on his third appearance in the series the Yorkshireman left that figure behind by playing an innings of 364.

This Test will always be remembered as "Hutton's Match", and also for the calamity which befell Australia while their opponents were putting together a mammoth total of 903. First of all Fingleton strained a muscle and Bradman injured his ankle so badly that he retired from the match and did not play again during the tour. Before this accident, England had established a supremacy which left little doubt about the result; indeed, Hammond probably would not have closed the innings during the tea interval on the third day but for the mishap to the opposing captain.

The moral effect of the loss of Bradman and Fingleton upon the other Australians was, of course, very great. After fielding out an innings lasting fifteen hours and a quarter, several of them batted – to all appearances – with very poor heart but Brown, going in first, was last man out before a follow-on 702 runs in arrears. He played an heroic innings under the shadow of impending defeat and Barnes, in his first Test match, well justified his choice, but from a depressing start in each innings there was no real recovery. This came as an anti-climax after the batting mastery which obtained until the tea interval on Monday. It was not a case of England driving home the advantage but rather of Australia losing inspiration to make a braver struggle to put a better face on defeat.

Hammond's fourth consecutive success in the toss was, of course, one factor influencing the result. Another was the way in which the Australian team was chosen. The risks taken by Bradman in going into the match with only O'Reilly, Fleetwood-Smith and Waite to bowl seemed to be inviting trouble. Neuritis was given as the reason for the omission of McCormick, who in any case had done nothing to suggest he was likely to trouble England's batsmen on a good Oval wicket. It came to a question of choosing either White or Ward, or omitting both those bowlers and so making the batting as strong as possible. Whether Bradman, as was suggested, gambled upon winning the toss after three failures and so being in a position to call upon his spin bowlers when the pitch had become worn will probably never be known. Although deprived through injuries of both Ames and Wright, England, with more all-round strength, were able to include six players who were recognised bowlers. The inclusion once again of Leyland was a move which yielded splendid results. As Wood, in his fortieth year, at last gained the honour of keeping wicket for England, there were five Yorkshiremen in England's eleven, and every one of them excelled. Between them they scored 612 of the runs and took ten of the sixteen wickets that fell, and Wood held three catches.

Compared with the England side beaten at Leeds, there were three changes, Hutton, Wood and Leyland replacing Barnett, Price and Wright; the last-named together with Ames, met with injury after being selected. The first day's cricket brought about the overwhelming success of batsmen which, with the wicket easy-paced and true, it was natural to expect. Waite and McCabe, the opening pair of bowlers, were innocuous and

On a Saturday afternoon in 1938 the entire nation crowded round its wireless sets waiting for Len Hutton to deprive Don Bradman of at least one record, the highest innings in an England–Australia Test match. The Yorkshireman passed Bradman's 334 after batting for thirteen hours and scored another 30 runs before being dismissed. Among the first to congratulate him were Bradman himself, and the England batsman at the other end, Joe Hardstaff.

although O'Reilly, soon after he went on, got rid of Edrich and so took his 100th wicket in Tests against England, that was the one success for Australia before stumps were drawn with 347 runs scored. Coming together at 29, Hutton and Leyland settled down to a partnership which surpassed all previous records for England. Each of them enjoyed one escape. Hutton, when 40, jumping in to hit an off-break from Fleetwood-Smith, missed the ball which, with the batsman well out of his ground, Barnett failed to gather. Leyland, having scored 140, would have been run out had not Waite, the bowler, after a fast throw-in by Badcock, knocked the bails off before the ball was in his hands.

With few bowlers of class at his call, Bradman had to conserve the energies of O'Reilly as much as possible. The field was set carefully for the saving of runs and although both the England batsmen scored numerous singles on the off side Australia gave a superb display in the field, Bradman inspiring the team with his fast running and clean picking-up. If the bowling lacked venom it was mainly accurate in length, particularly before lunch-time when 89 runs were scored. In a match with no time limit, Hutton and Leyland very wisely refused to take risks until after the interval; Hutton, in fact, never altered his cautious game. That the scoring rate quickened was due mainly to the powerful driving and neat cutting of Leyland. Hutton used similar types of strokes in correct and fluent style and all the time his defence never faltered. At the close on Saturday, Hutton had scored 160 and Leyland 156 – the former having batted nearly six hours and Leyland fifty minutes less time. A curiosity of the day's cricket was that four times a no-ball led either to the wicket being hit or the ball being caught.

A heavy shower which fell shortly before Monday's play was due to begin caused twenty-five minutes' delay but this improved rather than spoiled the wicket. The first event of note was the passing of the record stand against Australia made by Hobbs and Rhodes, who in 1911–12 at Melbourne shared a first-wicket partnership of 323. Following the same steady lines as before, Hutton and Leyland carried on this magnificent batting until England had 411 runs up when the stand ended through a wonderful piece of fielding. Hutton drove a ball from O'Reilly hard to the off side and Hassett fumbled it. Then he slung in a very fast return to the bowler's end and Bradman sizing up the situation in an instant, dashed towards the wicket from mid-on, caught the throw-in and broke the wicket before Leyland could complete a second run. Out for 187 – his highest of seven three-figure innings against Australia – Leyland batted nearly six and a half hours and hit seventeen 4s.

Hammond was at the wicket to see his personal record of highest score for England in a home Test match surpassed by Hutton. It was a remarkable feature of the season's Test games that the 182 not out by Philip Mead at The Oval in 1921 which stood as the record for England against Australia in any home Test was beaten four times during the current series. At Nottingham Paynter made 216 not out, at Lord's Hammond exceeded this with 240, Leyland followed with 187 and Hutton not only eclipsed these achievements but surpassed all individual records in Test cricket. Hammond stayed two hours twenty minutes and helped to add 135 for the third wicket. He was much more defensive than usual, and although taking 12 off one over by Fleetwood-Smith, hit no more than one boundary stroke during his last two hours at the wicket. Paynter's dismissal with one more run scored after Hammond left was a surprise. Misjudgment of a leg-break was the reason. Rain extended the tea interval to half an hour and Compton left immediately afterwards. By this time Hutton had entered upon the tenth hour of his innings and he remained full of confidence even if becoming a little monotonous by reason of his grim, determined dominance of the bowling. Hardstaff, no. 7 in the order, batted very surely and after an ovation to Hutton when he passed the 287 made at Sydney in 1903–4 by R. E. Foster – before this match the highest innings hit against Australia – an appeal against the light led to stumps being drawn early. England at the end of two days had put together a total of 634 and only half their wickets had fallen.

Hutton claimed exactly 300 of the runs scored at this point and the 30,000 people who assembled at The Oval on Tuesday saw fresh cricket history made. The bowling and fielding of Australia looked more formidable than at any other time in the game and as

Hutton carried his score nearer to the record Test innings, Bradman, the holder of it, brought several fieldsmen close in to the wicket for O'Reilly's bowling. Every run had to be fought for. As might be supposed, Hutton showed an occasional sign of strain and he completely missed the ball when with his total 331 he had an opportunity of beating the record by hitting a no-ball from O'Reilly. However, with a perfect cut off Fleetwood-Smith, Hutton duly reached his objective and the scene at the ground, with the whole assembly rising to its feet, and every Australian player, as well as Hardstaff, congratulating Hutton will be remembered for a long time by those who saw it. Hutton took nearly twice as long as Bradman did over as many runs eight years previously, but the Australian's big innings came during a Test limited in duration whereas Hutton played his innings on an occasion when time did not matter.

Before this memorable incident, Hardstaff hit with judgment without departing from the policy of all his predecessors in avoiding risks. The whole of the batting seemed to be inspired by a desire to build up a stupendous total. Hardstaff reached three figures in three hours ten minutes and a little later Hutton lifted a stroke towards cover and Hassett held the ball easily low down. So a phenomenal innings, lasting from half-past eleven on the Saturday until half-past two on the Tuesday – the longest ever played in first-class cricket – came to an end. Only A. C. MacLaren, who hit 424 for Lancashire v Somerset at Taunton in 1895, has made a higher individual score in England. In addition to thirty-five 4s, Hutton hit fifteen 3s, eighteen 2s and 143 singles.

England's total had reached 770 for the loss of six wickets and some spirited hitting by Wood came as a refreshing contrast to the stern batting which had gone before. Another three-figure stand resulted, Wood adding 106 in an hour and a half with Hardstaff, and shortly after these batsmen were separated there occurred the tragic accident to Bradman, who when bowling caught his foot in a worn foot-hole, fell prone and was carried off the field by two of his colleagues. During the tea interval, England's innings, which was the longest on record and produced the highest total for any Test match innings and the highest for any first-class match in England, was declared closed. It was said that O'Reilly, who bowled 85 overs, wore the skin off a finger in imparting spin to the ball.

Before Australia scored a run, Badcock fell to a catch at short leg and McCabe left at 19. Hassett made some excellent strokes on the leg side; afterwards Barnes and Brown raised the total from 70 to 117 before stumps were drawn and altogether added 75. Bowes on Wednesday twice took two wickets in an over but neither pace nor spin bowling could disturb the equanimity of Brown. An unusual incident happened during the eighth and last stand in which Fleetwood-Smith participated. When Brown cut the last ball of an over, intending to run a single, Hutton, with the idea of trying to give the less experienced batsmen the strike, kicked the ball to the boundary.

Instructions to umpires, however, provide for four runs to be added to the runs already made should a fieldsman wilfully cause the ball to reach the boundary, and as this meant the award to Brown of five runs, he kept the bowling. In the end, Brown missed the distinction of carrying his bat, for Hammond, running from slip, knocked up the ball and caught it at the second attempt, so disposing of Brown and bringing Australia's first innings to a close.

Brown was in for two and three-quarter hours and in the follow-on, when he was fourth out, he again revealed better defence than any of his colleagues. In the most satisfactory batting of this second innings, Barnes and Barnett made some capital strokes while putting on 74. Verity took the wickets of Barnes and Waite with the last two balls of an over and although Barnett stayed for an hour and hooked and drove Farnes with power and certainty Australia were out for 123. They were actually dismissed twice in four and three-quarter hours' cricket. On the fourth day, the proceedings were so one-sided as to be almost farcical. The fact that Australia batted only nine men removed some of the honour and glory from England's triumph but there was nothing in the condition of the wicket to excuse the poor resistance of so many Test batsmen. Bowes, by sustained pace and skilful swerve, made himself England's best bowler and in the two innings he took seven wickets for 74.

The number of people who saw the game was 94,212, including 81,336 who paid for admission. The takings of £ 19,176 3s. 0d. are a record for a Test match at The Oval.

ENGLAND

L. Hutton c Hassett b O'Reilly	364
W. J. Edrich c Hassett b O'Reilly	12
M. Leyland *run out*	187
Mr W. R. Hammond (Capt.) *lbw b* Fleetwood-Smith	59
E. Paynter *lbw b* O'Reilly	0
D. Compton *b* Waite	1
J. Hardstaff *not out*	169
A. Wood *c and b* Barnes	53
H. Verity *not out*	8
B 22, l-b 19, w 1, n-b 8	50

1/29 2/411 3/546 4/547   (7 wkts dec.) 903
5/555 6/770 7/876

Mr K. Farnes and W. E. Bowes did not bat.

AUSTRALIA

First Innings

C. L. Badcock c Hardstaff b Bowes	0
W. A. Brown c Hammond b Leyland	69
S. J. McCabe c Edrich b Farnes	14
A. L. Hassett c Compton b Edrich	42
S. Barnes b Bowes	41
B. A. Barnett c Wood b Bowes	2
M. G. Waite b Bowes	8
W. J. O'Reilly c Wood b Bowes	0
L. O'B. Fleetwood-Smith *not out*	16
D. G. Bradman (Capt.) *absent hurt*	0
J. H. Fingleton *absent hurt*	0
B 4, l-b 2, n-b 3	9

1/0 2/19 3/70 4/145 5/147 201
6/160 7/160 8/201

Second Innings

b Bowes	9
c Edrich b Farnes	15
c Wood b Farnes	2
lbw b Bowes	10
lbw b Verity	33
b Farnes	46
c Edrich b Verity	0
not out	7
c Leyland b Farnes	0
absent hurt	0
absent hurt	0
B 1	1

1/15 2/18 3/35 4/41 123
5/115 6/115 7/117 8/123

Australia Bowling

	Overs	Mdns	Runs	Wkts
Waite	72	16	150	1
McCabe	38	8	85	—
O'Reilly	85	26	178	3
Fleetwood-Smith	87	11	298	1
Barnes	38	3	84	1
Hassett	13	2	52	—
Bradman	3	2	6	—

England Bowling

	Overs	Mdns	Runs	Wkts	Overs	Mdns	Runs	Wkts
Farnes	13	2	54	1	12.1	1	63	4
Bowes	19	3	49	5	10	3	25	2
Edrich	10	2	55	1				
Verity	5	1	15	—	7	3	15	2
Leyland	3.1	—	11	1	5	—	19	—
Hammond	2	—	8	—				

Umpires: F. Chester and F. Walden.

SOUTH AFRICA v ENGLAND

FIFTH TEST MATCH
Played at Durban, March 3, 4, 6, 7, 8, 9, 10, 11, 13, 14, 1939

DRAWN. UNPARALLELED IN the history of the game this was in many ways an extraordinary match, emphasising that there are no limits to the possibilities of what may occur in cricket: but it ended farcically, for insufficient time remained to finish the "time-less" Test. Although undecided, the final Test left the rubber with England after a magnificent and unequalled performance by W. R. Hammond and his men. Stopped by rain on the tenth day, the longest match ever played produced amazing records and brought personal triumph to Edrich who, after most heart-breaking experiences in Test cricket, established his reputation by hitting a double century at a time when England needed an almost superhuman effort to avoid disaster.

South Africa set England to make 696 to win and few people imagined the team had a ghost of a chance of averting defeat, much less of scoring such a colossal total. Instead of going in with their tails down the batsmen set about their task in a magnificent manner and proved what can be done when the wicket remains unimpaired. It was an astonishing achievement to get within 42 runs of their objective with five wickets in hand, but, like The Oval Test between England and Australia the previous August, the game developed into a test of endurance. For one thing the pitch was much too good and many batsmen discarded their natural methods and adopted unnecessary caution.

When heavy rain prevented any more cricket after tea on the tenth day the South African Board of Control and the two captains went into conference before issuing a statement that the game had been abandoned because the England team had to catch the five minutes past eight train that night (Tuesday) from Durban in order to reach Cape Town in time to make the necessary arrangements for their departure on the *Athlone Castle* on Friday. The date of sailing for England could not be postponed.

W. J. Edrich finally confirmed his status as an England player with a double century against South Africa. This was the only Test in history which was terminated because the batting side had to catch a boat home.

Records

During the course of the match the following cricket records were established. (1) The match lasted until tea time on the tenth day and was the longest ever played in first-class cricket. (2) Biggest aggregate of runs in any first-class match, 1,981. (3) England's 654 for five wickets, the highest fourth innings score in a first-class match. (4) South Africa's first innings total of 530 was their highest in Test cricket, and the longest in England v South Africa Tests, lasting 13 hours. (5) Verity bowled 766 balls in the two South African innings – 17 more than J. C. White against Australia at Adelaide in 1929. (6) P. A. Gibb and Paynter, in putting on 280 for the second wicket, set up a record partnership for any wicket in England v South Africa Tests. (7) On eight consecutive days when cricket took place stumps were drawn before time – on seven occasions through bad light and once through rain. (8) A. D. Nourse's 103 in six hours four minutes was the slowest hundred scored for South Africa in Test cricket. (9) P. G. Van der Byl's innings was the longest played by a South African in a Test. It occupied seven hours eighteen minutes. (10) R. E. Grieveson's 75 was the highest first innings in Test cricket by a player chosen to keep wicket. (11) P. G. Van der Byl was the first South African to score a hundred and a ninety in the same Test. Only P. A. Gibb had previously accomplished the feat – in the first Test of the same series. (12) A South African Test record of nine fifties was set up in the two innings. No previous Test had ever produced as many – sixteen fifties by both teams. (13) Each side in the Test scored over 900 runs – South Africa 1,011, England 970. (14) P. A. Gibb's 100 in seven hours thirty-one minutes – the slowest Test century scored for England, rate being 15.96 runs per hour. (15) In the match a record number of balls was bowled – 5,463. (16) W. R. Hammond hit his twenty-first hundred in Test cricket, equalling the record of D. G. Bradman.

First Day (Friday)

After Hammond had won the toss for England eight consecutive times his luck changed, and Melville gained first innings for South Africa. Whereas England made two changes compared with the fourth Test, Perks and Wright replacing Goddard and Wilkinson, South Africa chose the team which shaped so well at Johannesburg. The opening batsmen gave their side a splendid start by scoring 131 together in three hours ten minutes. Against the fast bowling of Farnes and Perks, who frequently made the ball rise awkwardly, they exercised much caution and the total reached only 49 at lunch. Van der Byl spent forty-five minutes before opening his score and three hours elapsed before he hit a boundary. Melville, who brought off some attractive strokes, was more restrained than usual and the innings had lasted two hours ten minutes before he claimed the first boundary by hooking a no-ball. He batted faultlessly until, playing back to Wright, he stepped on his wicket. Van der Byl offered a very hard catch when 71 to Wright, otherwise he did not take the slightest risk though he astonished everyone when he punished Wright for twenty-two in one over, including five boundaries. Next he pulled a ball into the grand stand for 6; Rowan stayed while 88 were added and the total reached 229 for two wickets at the end of the day, Van der Byl being 105 not out after batting four hours forty-seven minutes.

Second Day (Saturday)

Encouraged by their success on the opening day, South Africa went on "Digging for Victory" and another spell of dour cricket was witnessed. Van der Byl was several times hit on the body by the bowling of Farnes but he maintained his unperturbed attitude. Mitchell was bowled off his pads at 236 and, with Nourse and Van der Byl together, the scoring became so slow that the first hour produced only 17 runs. Van der Byl, who hit one 6 and eight 4s, was disposed of after a stay of seven hours eighteen minutes when he was bowled by a ball which swung late. It was his first century in a Test. His dismissal occurred shortly after lunch and with the addition of 4 runs Viljoen also lost his wicket. Another valuable stand for South Africa followed, as Dalton played beautiful cricket while helping Nourse to add 90 for the sixth wicket. Nourse displayed unlimited patience, taking three and a half hours to make 50 and at the close of play South Africa's total was 423 for six wickets.

Third Day (Monday)

Rain on Sunday did not affect the pitch adversely and Nourse and Grieveson carried their unfinished stand of 55 to 107 before Nourse, after batting six hours, was yorked by Perks. He hit six 4s. When Grieveson punished Verity for 4 and sent up 500, it was the first boundary hit off the Yorkshireman since the opening day. At length, Grieveson, having played soundly for three and a half hours, was bowled middle stump, and the innings ended with Langton being caught at long-off. The English bowling analysis made sorry reading, though Perks could be satisfied with his first Test effort in taking five wickets for 100. By his perfect length, Verity kept the runs down, but he did not meet with success until he accounted for Newson and Langton in the final over. England followed their opponents' methods and opened cautiously, making only 10 runs in three-quarters of an hour, and when heavy rain ended play for the day shortly after tea the total stood at 35 for the loss of Gibb.

Fourth Day (Tuesday)

On this day South Africa appeared to gain a real mastery, as accurate bowling, supported by brilliant fielding – only one chance was missed – left them well on top. Misfortune soon overtook England; a misunderstanding with Paynter led to Hutton being run out. Hammond survived a shaky start against Gordon, but at 125 was well stumped trying to drive. Meanwhile, Paynter was completely tied down, and when dismissed he had batted four hours twenty minutes and hit only three 4s. As Edrich promptly fell to an easy catch at short leg, half the side were out for 171. Then the Kent pair, Ames and Valentine, introduced some enterprise to the batting, each driving splendidly until Dalton broke the partnership by getting Valentine stumped. All day the sun never shone and the light became inferior. Dalton bowled Verity at 245 but Ames, joined by another county colleague, Wright, maintained his grand form, the total being raised to 268, with Ames 82 not out and Wright 5 not out, before an appeal against the light was upheld.

Fifth Day (Wednesday)

England suffered an early set-back, as with 8 more scored Ames fell to a smart running catch by Dalton after Melville had tried to hold the ball. Ames made his 84, including seven 4s, in two hours fifty-two minutes. Wright and Farnes each hit vigorously but England were all out for 316, the innings having lasted seven hours thirty-eight minutes. South Africa enjoyed a lead of 214 runs but probably did not consider enforcing the follow-on, and, so well did they drive home the advantage that their opening pair, Mitchell and Van der Byl, were not separated until the score realised 191 in three and three quarter hours. Then Mitchell hit his wicket and England recovered some ground, for, in the same over Rowan was magnificently caught by Edrich, while in the following over – the last of the day – Van der Byl gave an easy catch to short leg. In this way South Africa lost their first three wickets at the same total, and Nourse might have left immediately, but Hammond at mid-off could not hold a very hard drive. At the close South Africa were 193 for three wickets – 407 ahead. Van der Byl failed by only 3 runs to become the first South African to score a hundred in each innings of a Test against England.

Sixth Day (Thursday)

On a pitch that improved, following showers during the night, South Africa took their second innings score to 481. First thing, Nourse and Viljoen showed the utmost confidence but at 242 Nourse mistimed a hook and fell to a good running catch. Although never really aggressive Melville and Viljoen relentlessly strengthened their side's strong position, and the stand produced 124 before Viljoen played on. Batting just over three hours he made some strong forcing strokes, hitting seven 4s. Dalton decided to attack the bowling and punished Wright for a 6 and three 4s. The Kent bowler, however, had revenge by taking a grand return catch. An injured thigh prevented Melville opening the innings, but now, despite lameness, he displayed his best form, making many delightful strokes in front of the wicket. Grieveson, who batted forty minutes before getting a run, gave his captain excellent support, but having completed his first Test century in three hours nineteen minutes, Melville was bowled. His 103 contained ten 4s. A characteristic slip catch by Hammond in his best manner disposed of Langton; Wright bowled Newson and Grieveson was the last to leave. Until the tea interval when the score was 387 for six, Ames kept wicket magnificently, having conceded only six byes while 917 runs were scored altogether, but after the interval Gibb went behind the stumps. England faced the tremendous task of scoring 696 to win and the newspapers everywhere were practically unanimous that it was hopeless. The light was extremely poor when Hutton and Gibb began the last innings and only one ball was bowled before stumps were pulled up on appeal.

Seventh Day (Friday)

After being out-played England at last asserted themselves. Hutton and Gibb were never at fault until, by a timing error, Hutton, after driving and hitting to leg freely, played the ball on to his wicket at 78. Here Hammond revealed a masterly stroke of leadership in promoting Edrich to first wicket down. The young Middlesex batsman lost no time in seizing this opportunity to silence his critics and, hitting cleanly, he claimed eight 4s in his first 50. Gibb pursued his usual placid game and, though handicapped by slight intermittent rain which smeared his spectacles, he offered an impregnable defence. There was a remarkable scene when Edrich completed his first Test hundred (twelve boundaries). The crowd gave him an ovation, the South Africans congratulated him and high up on the balcony shouts of triumph came from his comrades. He and Gibb remained together until bad light stopped cricket ten minutes before time. England's total stood at 253 for one wicket, Gibb 78 and Edrich 107.

Eighth Day (Saturday)

Not a ball could be bowled owing to rain.

Ninth Day (Monday)

The wicket rolled out well after the week-end rain and Edrich and Gibb were still together at lunch time when the score was 331. Altogether the stand produced 280 before Gibb, whose innings lasted nine hours, was bowled. He hit only two 4s. Then Hammond joined Edrich and the score was taken to 447 before Edrich was third out. Very strong on the leg side and driving magnificently, he hit twenty-five 4s, making his 219 in seven hours forty minutes. Hammond and Paynter then took command until again poor light put an early end to the day's play when England were 496 for three wickets, with Hammond 58 and Paynter 24.

Tenth Day (Tuesday)

South Africa put forth a great effort to check the flow of runs and keen fielding, coupled with particularly accurate bowling by Gordon, who aimed at the leg stump, tied England down to 39 runs in the first hour. By this time rain threatened to stop play. Hammond and Paynter, realising that they were now engaged in a race against the weather and the clock, attacked the bowling. A smart catch near the ground by the wicket-keeper off Gordon ended the partnership, which put on 164, at 611. Paynter batted three and a half hours but had to be satisfied with five 4s. Soon two interruptions occurred through rain and Hammond, when endeavouring to force the pace, was stumped. The England captain, in one of the finest innings of his career, excelled with masterly drives and powerful leg hits. His stay lasted six hours, yet his 4s numbered only seven. No sooner had Valentine joined Ames than the threatened downpour broke out over the ground and nothing more could be done.

N. P.

SOUTH AFRICA

First Innings
P. G. Van der Byl *b* Perks	125
A. Melville *hit wkt b* Wright	78
E. A. Rowan *lbw b* Perks	33
B. Mitchell *b* Wright	11
A. D. Nourse *b* Perks	103
K. Viljoen *c* Ames *b* Perks	0
E. L. Dalton *c* Ames *b* Farnes	57
R. E. Grieveson *b* Perks	75
A. B. C. Langton *c* Paynter *b* Verity	27
E. S. Newson *c and b* Verity	1
N. Gordon *not out*	0
B 2, l-b 12, n-b 6	20
	530

Second Innings
c Paynter *b* Wright	97
b Farnes	103
c Edrich *b* Verity	0
hit wkt b Verity	89
c Hutton *b* Farnes	25
b Perks	74
c and b Wright	21
b Farnes	39
c Hammond *b* Farnes	6
b Wright	3
not out	7
B 5, l-b 8, n-b 4	17
	481

ENGLAND

First Innings
L. Hutton *run out*	38
Mr P. A. Gibb *c* Grieveson *b* Newson	4
E. Paynter *lbw b* Langton	62
Mr W. R. Hammond *st* Grieveson *b* Dalton	24
L. E. G. Ames *c* Dalton *b* Langton	84
W. J. Edrich *c* Rowan *b* Langton	1
Mr B. H. Valentine *c* Grieveson *b* Dalton	26
H. Verity *b* Dalton	3
D. V. P. Wright *c* Langton *b* Dalton	26
Mr K. Farnes *b* Newson	20
R. T. D. Perks *not out*	2
B 7, l-b 17, w 1, n-b 1	26
	316

Second Innings
b Mitchell	55
b Dalton	120
c Grieveson *b* Gordon	75
st Grieveson *b* Dalton	140
not out	17
c Gordon *b* Langton	219
not out	4
B 8, l-b 12, w 1, n-b 3	24
	654

England Bowling
	Overs	Mdns	Runs	Wkts	Overs	Mdns	Runs	Wkts
Farnes	46	9	108	1	22.1	2	74	4
Perks	41	5	100	5	32	6	99	1
Wright	37	6	142	2	32	7	146	3
Verity	55.6	14	97	2	40	9	87	2
Hammond	14	4	34	—	9	1	30	—
Edrich	9	2	29	—	6	1	18	—
Hutton					1	—	10	—

South Africa Bowling
	Overs	Mdns	Runs	Wkts	Overs	Mdns	Runs	Wkts
Newson	25.6	5	58	2	43	4	91	—
Langton	35	12	71	3	56	12	132	1
Gordon	37	7	82	—	55.2	10	174	1
Mitchell	7	—	20	—	37	4	133	1
Dalton	13	1	59	4	27	3	100	2

GLOUCESTERSHIRE v KENT
Played at Bristol, July 1, 3, 1939

GLOUCESTERSHIRE WON BY an innings and 40 runs in a match of individual triumphs. Goddard equalled a world record by taking 17 wickets in a day, a feat previously performed only by the left-handers, Verity (Yorkshire) against Essex in 1933 and Blythe (Kent) against Northamptonshire in 1907. Counting the previous match at Bristol, against Yorkshire, Goddard claimed 30 wickets for 205 runs within six days. Even this magnificent achievement did not monopolise the honours for in the Gloucestershire innings Wright dismissed nine men for little over five runs each, finishing with a hat-trick. Hammond scored more than half the total. After a partnership of 125 with Barnett, he shielded his partners from Wright and took out his bat, having hit a 6 and nineteen 4s. He also won the toss for the thirteenth time.

GLOUCESTERSHIRE

C. J. Barnett lbw b Wright	66
R. A. Sinfield c and b Longfield	15
V. Hopkins c and b Wright	2
Mr W. R. Hammond not out	153
J. F. Crapp c Levett b Wright	4
G. M. Emmett lbw b Wright	0
W. L. Neale lbw b Wright	0
E. A. Wilson b Wright	10
R. W. Haynes b Wright	16
G. Lambert b Wright	0
T. W. Goddard lbw b Wright	0
B 7, l-b 10, n-b 1	18
	284

KENT

First Innings

A. Fagg b Goddard	8
Mr F. G. H. Chalk c Neale b Goddard	40
L. E. G. Ames lbw b Lambert	12
Mr B. H. Valentine c Crapp b Goddard	14
L. J. Todd b Goddard	15
T. Spencer b Goddard	0
Mr T. C. Longfield b Goddard	0
D. V. P. Wright b Goddard	0
N. W. Harding not out	19
Mr W. H. V. Levett b Goddard	8
C. Lewis b Goddard	0
B 2, l-b 2	4
	120

Second Innings

c Hammond b Goddard	33
lbw b Sinfield	21
c Haynes b Goddard	16
c Hopkins b Sinfield	0
c Barnett b Goddard	2
lbw b Goddard	15
c Emmett b Goddard	14
st Wilson b Goddard	2
c Emmett b Goddard	13
not out	3
c Haynes b Goddard	5
	124

Kent Bowling

	Overs	Mdns	Runs	Wkts
Harding	12	3	39	—
Todd	25	2	111	—
Longfield	14	3	40	1
Wright	21.5	8	47	9
Lewis	8	—	29	—

Gloucestershire Bowling

	Overs	Mdns	Runs	Wkts	Overs	Mdns	Runs	Wkts
Barnett	2	—	9	—	1	—	6	—
Lambert	8	1	40	1	6	1	19	—
Goddard	15.4	2	38	9	16.2	1	68	8
Sinfield	9	2	29	—	12	3	31	2

Umpires: H. G. Baldwin and H. Cruice.

1940 – 1963 THE POSTWAR YEARS

WITH A GRIM SENSE of timing, the Second World War began just as the 1939 cricket season was drawing to its inevitable close: Yorkshire champions, Middlesex second, with Northants and Leicester in the reverse positions at the bottom of the table. Though there was subsequently no official county cricket played for the duration of the war, the 1914-18 mistake of banning all first class games was not repeated. Portmanteau teams like the British Empire XI and London Counties were raised; Lord's on a Saturday was the scene of many a stirring one-day match and, as the war proceeded, longer games were introduced. Most of the players who starred in these games were old favourites like Hammond,

A wicket-keeper batsman right out of the top drawer. Les Ames (above) played in 47 Test matches for England and scored 102 centuries in first class cricket.
Right: The Long Room at Lord's in a drawing by Dennis Flanders.

Compton, Edrich, Hutton, Ames and Wright, and by the end of the war English cricket had very nearly worked up to a peacetime tempo – except for the fact that two of its greatest bowlers, Hedley Verity and Kenneth Farnes, were sadly dead and gone.

At first English cricket seemed to be in remarkably good health. Crowds were sizeable and enthusiastic. In 1947 attendances rose to an all-time high at county grounds, and the whole cricketing world thrilled to the record-breaking feats of Denis Compton. In 1948 Bradman led the Australian tourists for the last time. Again public interest was enormous. But the attendances of 1947 represented a peak never to be reached again. Crowds started to dwindle as a new, restructured post-war Britain emerged. There were more rival attractions to cricket then ever before and television began its reduction of the live audiences in every spectator sport.

Hedley Verity, the great Yorkshire left-arm spinner pictured in 1934. Below: four other Yorkshire Test players of a different vintage, Watson, Trueman, Wardle and Hutton leave London in 1953 for England's tour of the West Indies.

On the field the supply of cricketing geniuses seemed never-ending, but the English test team no longer enjoyed the easy mastery of years gone by. The Australians had always proved to be difficult opponents but in 1950 it was the West Indies who came over and created the most delightful havoc with a mystery spinner called Ramadhin. His wiles proved altogether too much for most of the local batsmen, just as the three W's, Worrell, Weekes and Walcott, seemed unbowlable. Then, in 1953, England regained the Ashes from Australia after twenty years, and people began to wonder if, after all, our cricketing lives were to proceed as they always had, from one peaceful season to the next.

But even though there was increasing concern at the steady fall in crowds, at the equally steady advance of nations which had always been considered of 'not quite world class'; and at the ominous fall in the number of overs being bowled in an average day's play, nobody seriously believed that this institution, which seemed always to have existed, could ever fade away. In fact, English county cricket, with its championship, its carefully structured social balance between amateurs and professionals, its six balls an over, its regular Test matches, was little more than fifty years old. Moreover, it had evolved to its present stage of sophistication in another world, in the tail-end of the Victorian era, when paternalism, imperialism, the Great Outdoors, Fair Play, Christianity, large cities, cheap transport and a reasonable climate had all been factors in the exotic growth of a national game which had become very nearly worldwide.

Now, after two World Wars, this England had disappeared and county after county found itself struggling to balance the books. Appeals became commonplace. Committees sat to compile reports on how to improve things. Nothing was done. I remember going to Lord's one weekday afternoon to witness a brief passage in the symphony of a county match. I caught the slow movement as usual, and was much struck by the fact that the number of supernumaries and attendants on duty easily outnumbered the audience. It was a situation that would have been unthinkable before the war and it depressed me greatly. A championship match was in progress in the greatest city in the world and nobody was interested.

This is not to say that cricket as a pastime was losing ground. At club and village level many thousands continued to enjoy the game. It was English first-class cricket which appeared to be dying on its feet. In India and Pakistan, in the West Indies and New Zealand, spectacular advances were being made. National sides which had once been used to playing what was virtually an England reserve side, now demanded the very best elevens we could muster, and still seemed likely to beat us. Not only was the master being over-taken by the pupil, but he seemed in danger of disappearing altogether.

Of course, the day-to-day news seemed exciting enough. A venerable tradition was finally broken in the 1950's when Len Hutton, a professional, became a highly successful captain of England, even though the Yorkshire committee, still happily paddling away in the stagnant pools of the nineteenth century, refused to allow a hired hand like Hutton to lead the county. England discovered a new generation of genuinely fast bowlers in Trueman, Statham and Tyson. The arts of the Surrey off-spinner Jim Laker flowered into genius in 1956. Great individual feats continued to be performed. Even so, it was clear that something had to be done.

At the end of the period covered in this section, that *something* was indeed done. The whole shape of English cricket began to change. Its personality altered. Its structure was partly dismantled. Its financial arrangements were modernised. Its administrative style became unrecognisable. At the price of partly disfiguring itself, English cricket survived into a new age of opulence, crisis, ballyhoo, once undreamed-of financial resources, cosmopolitanism, rowdyism and the gradual surrender of autonomy to the forces of television.

But this was still just around the corner as the 1960's opened. The two decades since the resumption of normal activities after the end of the war had turned out after all, not to be a return to normal, but a lull before the most violent storms in English cricket history.

BARTHOLOMEW, MR ARTHUR CHURCHILL, of Oxford, the oldest cricket Blue, passed away on March 29, 1940 some five weeks after completing his 94th year. Born on February 21. 1846, at Lympstone, Devon, he was more than a year senior to the Rev. E. E. Harrison Ward, the oldest Cambridge Blue, who died on Easter Monday, five days earlier. The passing of Mr Bartholomew, Oxford, and Mr Ward within this brief space of time left Mr F. A. MacKinnon, Chief of the Scottish Clan, the senior living Blue of either University. He and Mr Ward both played for Cambridge in the "Cobden" match to which further reference will be found in the biography of Mr Harrison Ward.

It is of interest to add here that Mr MacKinnon, now aged 92, who went to Australia in 1878 with the team captained by Lord Harris, is the oldest living cricketer who has represented England. H. C. Maul, another member of that touring side, died early in the year; Mr A. J. Webbe, Middlesex president for so many years, who reached the age of 86 in January, five weeks before his death, played in the only "test" of that tour.

A. C. Bartholomew went to Marlborough and appeared at Lord's against Rugby in 1865, when he was described as "a good bat with patient defence". Going to Trinity College, Oxford, he headed the University averages in 1867, but did not play against Cambridge until the following season, when, in a match of small totals, he scored 7 and 11 not out. He was regarded as one of the best cover points of the day and a contemporary described "his quick returns straight to the wicket, after running hard to the ball, as a pleasure to see".

For some years failing eyesight prevented him reading, but Mr. Bartholomew retained such a keen interest in the game that as recently as the summer of 1939 he listened eagerly while his daughter read the scores and descriptions of matches. He greatly prized the disc from a blotter presented to him when a master at Durham School. It is inscribed "To A. C. B., Durham School, for his score of 166 against Northumberland at Newcastle-upon-Tyne, June 3, 1871." At one time he played for his native county, Devon, and he organised a cricket week at Reading, where he owned a private school, and coached E. H. Bray, L. P. Collins and J. F. Ireland before they gained their Blues. He founded a cricket eleven and called them "Guinea-pigs" – because, he said, "they had no tail". One of his scholars was Major-General Sir Walter Kirke, Inspector-General of the Home Forces. His son, Major-General A. W. Bartholomew, was appointed Lieutenant of the Tower of London in March 1939.

MR COLE, FREDERICK LIVESAY, an occasional wicket-keeper for Gloucestershire from 1879, when he first appeared at Lord's, died at Sheffield on July 1, 1941. While he would be a useful cricketer to pass muster with W. G. Grace as captain, a more interesting point than his prowess behind the stumps concerns his age. In *Scores and Biographies* the date of his birth is given as October 4, 1856. This tallied with *Wisden* until 1934, when the year was altered to 1842 – a possible misprint due to re-setting "Births and Deaths". Yorkshire papers described how "he joined the Federal Army when 19 and served four years under Generals McClellan and Phil Sheridan": also that during the Franco-Prussian war he was in the siege of Paris and that he was with Sir Archibald Forbes, the war correspondent, in the Russo-Turkish war before being invalided home in 1876. Inquiries at the Bristol Grammar School, where he was said to have been educated, failed to trace him, neither can any mention of his name between 1837 and 1887 be found in the Registers of the Yeovil district, though his birthplace was recorded as Ilminster, together with the date, at the time of his first match at Lord's.

In response to a question in the *Bristol Evening Post*, Mr Harry Wookey wrote that he played "with Fred Cole for Schoolmasters against Bath Association in 1880, when I was only 17 years of age. Fred Cole was born on October 4, 1856". Another Bristol cricketer confirmed that opinion. Yet it was asserted in the Yorkshire papers that "he had three centenarian brothers all living" and that he was 90 when he retired from the Sheffield Gas Company, though no one knew his exact age and thought he was 60 "George", one of the "centenarian" brothers, could not be traced in Bristol.

Fred Cole made plenty of runs in club cricket, and H. E. Roslyn, of the Gloucestershire County Committee, recalls that "Fred Cole scored the first hundred ever made on our county ground and I kept wicket while he did so" – that was the year before the formal opening in 1889.

DEATHS IN THE WAR

FARNES, PILOT OFFICER KENNETH, RAF, the Cambridge, Essex and England fast bowler, was killed during the night of October 20, 1941, when the plane in which he was pilot crashed. His death at the age of 30 come as a great shock to countless friends and the whole world of cricket. After training in Canada he desired to become a night-flying pilot, and within four weeks of his return to England he met his disastrous end.

Discovered when 19 years of age by Mr Percy Perrin in an Essex Club and Ground match against Gidea Park in 1930, Kenneth Farnes took five Kent wickets for 36 runs in his second county match and was welcome in the Essex team whenever available. After three years in the Cambridge eleven, he went as a master to Worksop College, and consequently his appearances in first-class cricket were limited. His university experiences brought continuous improvement. In 1933 his work for Cambridge showed 41 wickets at 17.39 runs apiece, and he was by far the most effective amateur bowler in the country with a record of 113 wickets at 18.38 each. In a drawn match with Oxford seven wickets fell to him at a cost of 71 runs. His best performance that season – 11 wickets for 114 runs, 7 for 21 in the second innings – enabled Essex to beat Surrey by 345 runs at Southend, their first success against these opponents since 1914. In ten matches for the county, Farnes claimed 67 wickets at an average cost of 16.07, and this form brought him the honour of representing England in the first Test against Australia in 1934. Despite his fine performance – ten wickets for 179 runs – England lost by 238 runs. Strangely enough, when England won by an innings and 38 runs at Lord's Farnes did not meet with any reward, Verity taking the honours. Farnes was not called upon again in that series, but in 1938 he took most wickets in Tests against Australia – 17 at 34.17 each.

In 1934 he was largely responsible for the first victory of Essex over Yorkshire since 1911 by taking 11 wickets for 131, Southend again proving a favourable ground for him. Thanks to Farnes dismissing seven men for 59 in the final stage, Essex brought about a great triumph by an innings and 46 runs. After a tour in West Indies knee trouble prevented Farnes from playing in 1935, but next season, for the Gentlemen at Lord's, he created a sensation by bowling Gimblett, Hammond and Hardstaff in quick succession, a stump being sent flying in each case. With four men out for 33, the Players were in danger of defeat, but, after the complete loss of Wednesday owing to rain, there was not time to reach a finish in two days. This fine work influenced the choice of Farnes to tour Australia with the team captained by G. O. Allen in the winter of 1936. Never did he bowl better than in the last Test, when he took six wickets for 96 runs in a total of 604; Australia won by an innings and 200 – a result that decided the rubber.

Farnes bowled well in Test trials at Lord's. In 1938 he gave special proof of being in great form by dismissing eight Players for 43 runs in the first innings and three in the second for 60, so doing a lot towards the Gentlemen winning by 133 runs – their second victory in this encounter since the last war. In the following winter he went with the England touring team to South Africa, where he was second in Test bowling to Verity. His 16 wickets cost 32.43 each, while in the whole tour 44 wickets fell to him at 27.43 apiece. He did the best bowling of the third Test, the only one brought to a definite finish, which gave W. R. Hammond's side the rubber. With four wickets for 29, Farnes was mainly instrumental in making South Africa follow on, and he dismissed three men for 80 in their second innings of 353, which left England still 13 runs to the good after a declaration with only four men out. Paynter, 243 – a South African record – and Hammond, 120, were the great batsmen on that occasion; their stand realised 242.

Farnes made his first appearance of the season in 1939 for the Gentlemen, and showed his fondness for Lord's by disposing of the last three Players in the course of six balls. This final effort by Farnes at headquarters recalls how well he bowled in university matches; but in 1932 he disfigured an analysis of five wickets for 98 runs by being "called" 21 times. The discipline then brought to bear was effective in correcting a faulty approach to the crease. Nearly six feet five inches tall, Farnes, taking a comparatively short and easy run, brought the ball down from a great height with the inevitable effect of sharp lift, which made him extremely difficult to time when retaining a good length. Altogether in first-class cricket Farnes took 720 wickets at an average of 20.55 each.

A very good field near the wicket, Farnes reached many catches that would have been impossible for a man of medium height. He had no pretensions as a batsman, but in 1936, at Taunton, hit up 97 not out in two hours, Wade helping to add 149 for the last wicket; dismissing six men in the match. Farnes was largely responsible for Essex winning by an innings and 66 runs. He laughed at just failing to get a century – the ambition of every batsman.

Farnes wrote a very interesting book – *Tours and Tests*, published in 1940; among his hobbies were painting and music.

SURREY HOME GUARD v SUSSEX HOME GUARD
Played at Lord's, July 23, 1942

ABANDONED. THIS MATCH was given up in tragic circumstances after Andrew Ducat, the Surrey and England cricketer and international footballer, collapsed and died at the wicket. The Surrey side having been sent in to bat, Ducat began his innings before lunch and was 17 at the interval. On resuming he scored steadily, carrying his score to 29. Then he hit a ball from Eaton to mid-on. The ball was returned to the bowler, who was about to send down the next delivery when Ducat fell forward and apparently died immediately though he was moved to the pavilion and quickly taken by ambulance to a nearby hospital. The score of the match as officially recorded by MCC was:

SURREY HOME GUARD
Pte B. Moss *b* Eaton 32
Pte H. E. Wood *b* Bartlett 8
Pte P. Cowan *c and b* Eaton 26
Lt D. A. M. Rome *lbw b* Eaton 30
Pte A. Ducat *not out* 29
Lt R. H. Attwell *not out* 1
B 4, l-b 2 6

(4 wkts) 132

Pte J. C. Johnston, Pte R. A. Levermore. Pte R. A. Eede, Pte A. Jeffery and Lt Col T. C. D. Hassall did not bat.

SUSSEX HOME GUARD
Pte H. S. Mather, Pte J. V. Eaton, Pte V. C. Humphrey, Pte C. Steele, Lt N. C. Fuente, Pte T. Bartlett, Pte D. V. Smith, Lt A. C. Somerset, Lt Col W. E. Grace, Pte H. R. Sexton, Major E. H. Firth.

Sussex Home Guard Bowling

	Overs	Mdns	Runs	Wkts
Eaton	18.2	7	34	3
Smith	12	2	35	—
Bartlett	8	—	47	1
Fuente	5	1	10	—

Umpires: T. W. Natcham and Pte J. Moyer.

Andrew Ducat, one of the elite who represented his county at football and cricket, died in circumstances undeniably tragic and yet perhaps more blessed than any other, in mid-innings, apparently unconscious of the fate awaiting him. In this photograph, the bespectacled Ducat walks out to umpire a charity match with his old Surrey teammate Herbert Strudwick. It is June 1939, and the two veterans are enjoying the very last of the sunshine of peace.

GAINFORD, LORD, who died at Headlam Hall, near Darlington, on February 15, 1943, aged 83, captained Durham County Club from 1886 to 1891, and continued playing cricket until he was 74, when, as he wrote to Mr Bulmer, secretary of Durham County C.C., "Inability to take a quick run forced me to give up the game". His last innings was 9 not out. Joseph Albert Pease, known as "Jack", joined the county club on its formation in 1882 and was the oldest member. He played for the county until 1892, having a batting average of nearly 19, and he kept wicket. In 1878 he went to Cambridge, captained Trinity College cricket eleven, played in the polo team, was master of the drag hounds, and sometimes played Rugby for the University without getting his Blue. One of the proudest moments of his life, he used to relate, was when "I took a catch in the outfield off W. G. Grace, who shook me by the hand". That was in a match for MCC, of which he was a member for many years.

During thirty-four years in the House of Commons he became Postmaster-General, President of the Board of Education, Chancellor of the Duchy of Lancaster, and Chief Liberal Whip. He was raised to the Peerage in 1916 and took an active part in House of Lords debates. Shortly before his death he recalled an occasion in the Commons some fifty years ago when a fray arose over the Home Rule for Ireland Bill, and he used the Rugby tackle to keep Dr Tanner out of the "maul" until John Burns separated the combatants.

GANDAR-DOWER, MR KENNETH CECIL, was lost at sea through Japanese action in February 1944 at the age of 36. He played for Harrow against Winchester in 1927, but not in the Eton match. At Cambridge he did well in the Freshmen's Match and was a Crusader, but his time was mainly given up to tennis, at which he captained the University team. One of the most versatile players of games of any period, he was amateur squash champion in 1938, won amateur championships at fives, and played lawn tennis for Great Britain. In all, he represented Cambridge at six forms of sport: tennis, lawn tennis, Rugby fives, Eton fives, squash rackets and billiards. In fact, time hardly sufficed for their rival calls. He probably created a record when he played simultaneously in the Freshmen's Match and Freshmen's Tournament, with the connivance of the tennis but not the cricket authorities; he disappeared to play off a round during the early part of his sides's innings, with relays of cyclist friends to keep him informed as to the fall of wickets! He flew a private aeroplane to India. In spite of other demands he continued to find time for cricket, making some ten appearances for the Frogs each season almost to the outbreak of war, and got many runs and wickets.

Famous as a big game shot, and extensive traveller, he introduced a team of cheetahs from the Kenya jungle to London and on greyhound tracks they set up speed records. A writer of articles and books, he acted as war correspondent in various theatres of operations up to the time of his death.

MATCHES AT LORD'S IN 1944

UNTIL THE FLYING-BOMBS arrived in London in the middle of June there was every indication that the 1944 cricket season at Lord's would break all war-time records in the matter of crowds and gate receipts. As it was, the raising of the flat-rate admission charge of sixpence to one shilling resulted in more money than ever being given to charity. The sum, £4,117, was allocated as follows: Duke of Gloucester's Red Cross and St John Fund £2,568, Army Cricket Association £352, Colonial Comforts Fund £313, RAAF Welfare Fund £242, King George's Fund for Sailors £220, and RAF War

Emergency Committee £167. Altogether the total paid to charities during the war reached £11,557. Despite various difficulties 167,429 people paid for admission, against 232,390 in 1943. Bad weather accounted partly for this reduction and the flying-bomb menace caused some fixtures to be cancelled – including three big school matches, Clifton v Tonbridge, Rugby v Marlborough, and Cheltenham v Haileybury. These were re-arranged and the descriptions and scores will be found in the Public Schools section. Altogether 41 matches took place at Lord's during the summer, and again, the cricket at headquarters gave enjoyment to everyone concerned.

ENGLAND v AUSTRALIA

(FIRST VICTORY MATCH)
Played at Lord's, May 19, 21, 22, 1945

AUSTRALIA WON BY six wickets. In a dynamic finish, true to the exhortation expressed in the post-war cricket plans, Pepper made the winning hit off the fourth ball of the last possible over just at seven o'clock. To the majority of the 18,000 people who saw the cricket this really fine climax gave intense pleasure and the Australian batsmen reached the pavilion amidst enthusiastic applause. The England team deserved equal praise for the splendid sportsmanship in doing their part in the speediest manner, changing positions quickly and starting each over without a suggestion of delay when the waste of seconds might have meant a drab draw.

While giving Australia hearty congratulations for their triumph, it must be indicated clearly that the prevailing conditions favoured them. After heavy rain overnight England batted on a green pitch with the outfield slow. The immediate loss of Hutton from a poor stroke gave Robertson the opportunity to prove his worth, and for 85 minutes he mastered the well-varied attack. He and Washbrook added 53, Hammond showed his form until after lunch a fast ball took his off stump, Ames and Edrich put on 75, but Stephenson alone of the remainder caused trouble, the last three wickets falling at 267.

Australia made 82 for two wickets before the close, and on Whit-Monday, when some 30,000 watched the game, they found the pitch – completely covered during the week-end and so protected from much rain – after being mown in the morning according to custom, quite favourable to scoring. Also better reward came for scoring strokes. Hassett increased his 27 by 50 before hitting over a yorker. Batting in quiet, resolute fashion, with hooks and cuts his most effective strokes, Hassett maintained his reputation. An interruption by rain

The promises of peace meant the promise of international cricket. On the morning of May 19, 1945, the queues, consisting largely of schoolboys and the middle-aged, form in anticipation of a great contest. The lamp post still carries its black-out strips, cloth caps still crown the hoi polloi, St John's Wood Road is still countrified, as ancient motorcars chug along on rationed petrol.

did not help the fielding side and the bowling was mastered, Miller and Stanford making 99 runs together while Pepper gave an idea of his power in a stand for 73.

Miller accounted largely for Australia gaining the upper hand, his elegant, emphatic style fully meriting the hundred he earned before his first lifted stroke gave Ames a catch at deep mid-off. Batting three and a half hours, Miller hit only six 4s, but he was always getting runs with the soundness characteristic of most Australians. Williams and Price forced the pace with such effect that 88 runs came in fifty minutes for the ninth partnership, Williams, last out to a catch at the wicket, hit eleven 4s in his 53. A repatriated prisoner of war, Williams hit hard in front of the wicket and cut cleanly.

Rain fell as play ceased shortly before half-past six, and in the morning England, 188 behind, batted on turf drying in sunshine. Pepper used his height and strong finger spin and, with the ball keeping low, he dismissed Hutton at 52 and Washbrook at 75, but Robertson, in another admirable display, stayed two hours forty minutes, hitting two 6s to the on and five 4s before Sismey, standing back, caught him off the first delivery by Cheetham, coming on with the new ball. Edrich and Robins further improved matters for England in a stand for 68, but, through haste for runs when victory was out of the question, both left at 286, and the remaining three wickets went for eight runs.

Wanting 107 runs with seventy minutes at their disposal, Australia soon lost Whitington and Miller – dismissed when starting for an impossible second run. Then Pepper joined Hassett and Hammond spread his field out so as to prevent fours, but singles came very frequently and often the boundary could not be saved. Fielding at deep mid-off, Hammond, running across behind the bowler, caught Hassett cleverly, and Cheetham lost his wicket when Pepper refused a sharp run. Then Price came in with twelve minutes left and 31 runs wanted. Hammond did not use the opportunity afforded by these wickets falling to change his bowling. He kept the onus of attack with his two fast bowlers, who stuck heroically to their work, but the effect of such unusual toil was shown when Stephenson, whose first match this was since 1941, got both hands to a high catch at short slip but could not hold the ball.

So Pepper escaped after a cut for four, and in the next over there came four singles and a six from a mighty on-drive into one of the grand-stand boxes. With the clock almost at seven, Price scored one from the second ball by Gover; Pepper followed with a couple of two's to leg, and the terrific strain was over: Australia victorious over a side lacking a left-handed batsman or bowler and generally unfortunate in all the circumstances of the match, hastily extended to three days as a cricket celebration of "V" Day. About 17,000 people saw the finish, while altogether 67,660 paid the shilling admission during the three days, the proceeds of £1,935 3s. 6d. going to Red Cross and Australian charities. Entertainment tax absorbed £957 10s. 10d.

ENGLAND

First Innings

L. Hutton c Sismey b Williams	1
Flt Sgt C. Washbrook st Sismey b Ellis	28
Capt. J. D. Robertson lbw b Ellis	53
W. R. Hammond b Williams	29
Sq Ldr L. E. G. Ames c Price b Cheetham	57
Sq Ldr W. J. Edrich b Miller	45
Sq Ldr R. W. V. Robins b Cheetham	5
Lt Col J. W. A. Stephenson c Sismey b Price	31
Lt Col S. C. Griffith c Sismey b Cheetham	9
Lt D. V. P. Wright b Price	0
A. R. Gover not out	0
B 1, l-b 6, w 1, n-b 1	9
	267

1/1 2/54 3/97 4/130 5/205
6/213 7/233 8/267 9/267

Second Innings

b Pepper	21
lbw b Pepper	32
c Sismey b Cheetham	84
lbw b Ellis	33
b Ellis	7
c Workman b Price	50
c Hassett b Pepper	33
b Price	1
not out	4
run out	1
st Sismey b Pepper	1
B 18, l-b 8, n-b 1	27
	294

1/52 2/75 3/149 4/175 5/218
6/286 7/286 8/289 9/292

AUSTRALIA

First Innings

Flt Sgt J. A. Workman b Gover	1
Capt. R. S. Whitington c Griffith b Wright	36
W/O A. L. Hassett b Stephenson	77
Sq Ldr S. G. Sismey c Wright b Edrich	37
P/O K. R. Miller c Ames b Stephenson	105
F/O R. M. Stanford st Griffith b Stephenson	49
Sgt C. G. Pepper c Griffith b Stephenson	40
Capt. A. G. Cheetham c Hammond b Wright	0
W/O R. G. Williams c Griffith b Wright	53
Sgt C. F. Price c Robertson b Stephenson	35
F/O R. S. Ellis not out	1
B 9, l-b 10, n-b 2	21

1/11 2/52 3/136 4/171 5/270 455
6/357 7/358 8/366 9/454

Second Innings

lbw b Stephenson	0
c Hammond b Gover	37
run out	1
not out	54
run out	0
not out	10
B 4, l-b 1	5

1/9 2/11 3/63 4/76   (4 wkts) 107

Australia Bowling

	Overs	Mdns	Runs	Wkts	Overs	Mdns	Runs	Wkts
Cheetham	13.1	1	49	3	17	2	44	1
Williams	19	2	56	2	21	7	47	—
Pepper	19	2	59	—	32.4	7	80	4
Ellis	31	8	59	2	17	3	33	2
Miller	9	2	11	1	9	1	23	—
Price	9	1	24	2	19	3	40	2

England Bowling

	Overs	Mdns	Runs	Wkts	Overs	Mdns	Runs	Wkts
Gover	25	3	90	1	11.4	1	51	1
Stephenson	36	4	116	5	11	—	51	1
Edrich	17	2	61	1				
Wright	37.3	9	122	3				
Robins	10	—	45	—				

Umpires: G. Beet and A. Fowler.

SURREY v INDIA

Played at Kennington Oval, May 11, 13, 14, 1946

INDIA WON BY nine wickets. A record-breaking last-wicket stand between Sarwate and Banerjee featured in India's first victory of the tour. Although Merchant and Gul Mahomed put on 111 for the third wicket, nine men were out for 205 when the last pair came together. They were not separated for three hours ten minutes, their partnership of 249 being the highest ever recorded for the last wicket in England. Never before in history had Nos. 10 and 11 in the batting order each scored a century in the same innings. Both Sarwate and Banerjee gave masterly displays and neither at any time appeared in difficulties. Fishlock drove well for Surrey, who collapsed badly before the Indian spin bowlers. Nayudu, dismissing Fishlock, Bennett and A. V. Bedser, performed the hat-trick. Following on 319 behind Surrey made a better fight. Fishlock, again in good form, and Gregory opened with a stand of 144, but next day the slow bowlers were again on top. Sarwate followed his fine batting by clever variation of spin, and India were left to get only 20 runs for victory. Gregory batted just short of three hours. Surrey were handicapped by an injury to Gover, who could not bowl again in the match after straining a tendon in his heel before lunch on the first day.

"Banerjee and Sarwate", the phrase which for a brief hour in 1946, raised as many smiles as Laurel and Hardy, Abbot and Costello or Flanagan and Allen. No more spectacular fight can be found in cricket than two no-hope batsmen, relegated to the ignominy of No. 10 and No. 11, outfacing the enemy beyond the call of duty.

INDIA

First Innings

V. M. Merchant *b* Squires	53
V. S. Hazare *lbw b* A. V. Bedser	0
R. S. Modi *b* A. V. Bedser	0
Gul Mahomed *b* A. V. Bedser	89
R. B. Nimbalkar *c* Mobey *b* Parker	18
Mushtaq Ali *lbw b* Parker	6
S. W. Sohoni *lbw b* Watts	6
V. Mankad *c* Mobey *b* A. V. Bedser	16
C. S. Nayudu *c* Bennett *b* A. V. Bedser	9
C. T. Sarwate *not out*	124
S. Banerjee *b* Parker	121
B 7, l-b 4, n-b 1	12
	454

Second Innings

not out	15
not out	4
c Watts *b* A. V. Bedser	1
	(1 wkt) 20

SURREY

First Innings

R. J. Gregory *lbw b* Sohoni	16
L. B. Fishlock *hit wkt b* Nayudu	62
H. S. Squires *c* Nimbalkar *b* Hazare	4
T. H. Barling *b* Hazare	8
J. F. Parker *c* Merchant *b* Banerjee	20
E. A. Bedser *lbw b* Mankad	6
E. A. Watts *b* Mankad	2
N. H. Bennett *c* Mushtaq Ali *b* Nayudu	0
A. V. Bedser *b* Nayudu	0
A. R. Gover *lbw b* Banerjee	7
G. S. Mobey *not out*	6
B 1, l-b 1, n-b 2	4
	135

Second Innings

lbw b Mankad	100
c Merchant *b* Hazare	83
st Nimbalkar *b* Nayudu	21
b Mankad	16
b Sarwate	20
lbw b Sarwate	21
st Nimbalkar *b* Sarwate	2
c Mankad *b* Sarwate	24
not out	31
lbw b Sarwate	0
lbw b Mankad	5
B 5, l-b 9, w 1	15
	338

Surrey Bowling

	Overs	Mdns	Runs	Wkts	Overs	Mdns	Runs	Wkts
Gover	7	2	18	—				
A. V. Bedser	47	8	135	5	3	—	14	1
Watts	38	7	122	1	2.5	—	6	—
Parker	27.2	7	64	3				
Squires	12	1	36	1				
E. A. Bedser	8	—	25	—				
Gregory	5	1	23	—				
Fishlock	3	—	19	—				

India Bowling

	Overs	Mdns	Runs	Wkts	Overs	Mdns	Runs	Wkts
Hazare	16	9	20	2	16	5	36	1
Sohoni	9	1	31	1	6	—	15	—
Banerjee	9	—	42	2	11	1	45	—
Nayudu	12	3	30	3	25	4	93	1
Mankad	5	1	8	2	25	7	80	3
Sarwate					16	5	54	5

SURREY v OLD ENGLAND
Played at The Oval, May 23, 1946

DRAWN. THE KING and some 15,000 enthusiasts attended the one-day match arranged to celebrate the Centenary of the Surrey County Club and of Kennington Oval as a cricket ground. Surrey faced a side comprising ten old England players and Brooks, former Surrey wicket-keeper, the one member of the eleven without the honour of Test match experience. Altogether the caps gained by the ten players and the umpires, Hobbs and Strudwick, numbered 370. On one of the finest days of the summer the cricket proved full of interest. Runs always came fast and there were three stands of over a hundred. Gregory and Squires put on 111 for Surrey; Woolley and Hendren hit up 102, and Hendren and Jardine 108 for Old England in a splendid effort to hit off the runs after Bennett, the new Surrey captain, declared. Fender was prominent in the field, making a neat catch and taking two wickets with successive balls. The most exhilarating cricket came after the fall of Sandham and Sutcliffe for two runs. Woolley, at the age of 59, drove with the same ease that delighted crowds before and after the 1914–18 war. Hendren

The handsome, ever-youthful Frank Woolley, seen here with his Kent colleague C. Wright, was still capable of putting bowlers to the sword at an age when most cricketers have retired to the armchair. Woolley lived on to remarry as an octogenarian and to retire to Canada where his supreme eminence as an athlete can have been hardly appreciated.

showed all his old cheery forcing play until just before time he lifted a catch off Surrey's most famous recruit – A. V. Bedser, already marked for England honours. To stay two and three-quarter hours and hit eight 4s at the age of 57 was a great feat by Hendren. D. R. Jardine, wearing his Oxford Harlequin cap, was as polished as ever in academic skill.

The King, Patron of Surrey, accompanied by officials of the club, went on the ground, where all concerned in the game were introduced to him with the happiest of greetings. The band of the East Surrey Regiment was in attendance, and after the game a dance in the pavilion long room completed the festive occasion.

SURREY

R. J. Gregory b Fender 62
L. B. Fishlock c Fender b Freeman 25
H. S. Squires b Holmes 68
T. H. Barling lbw b Fender 0
J. F. Parker c and b Allom 12
A. J. McIntyre not out 39
E. A. Bedser c Brooks b Allom 23
E. A. Watts not out 13
B 5, l-b 1 6

(6 wkts dec.) 248

N. H. Bennett, G. J. Whittaker and G. S. Mobey did not bat.

OLD ENGLAND

H. Sutcliffe lbw b Watts 1
A. Sandham c A. V. Bedser b Watts 1
F. E. Woolley c McIntyre b A. V. Bedser 62
E. Hendren c Barling b A. V. Bedser 94
D. R. Jardine b Parker 54
P. G. H. Fender not out 12
D. J. Knight not out 2
B 3, l-b 2, n-b 1 6

(5 wkts) 232

M. W. Tate, E. R. T. Holmes, M. J. C. Allom and E. W. J. Brooks did not bat.

Old England Bowling

	Overs	Mdns	Runs	Wkts
Tate	8	1	26	—
Allom	17	2	76	2
Freeman	15	3	58	1
Holmes	8	1	36	1
Fender	8	—	46	2

Surrey Bowling

	Overs	Mdns	Runs	Wkts
A. V. Bedser	21	3	45	2
Watts	18	3	83	2
Parker	15	—	51	1
Squires	7	—	29	—
E. A. Bedser	4	2	3	—
McIntyre	2	—	11	—
Gregory	1	—	4	—

Umpires: J. B. Hobbs and H. Strudwick.

Right: Andy Sandham (pictured here in 1925) was in his late fifties by the time of the Old England v Surrey game. Overshadowed by Jack Hobbs at Surrey he was, nevertheless, a fine batsman and the first ever to make a triple century in a Test, 325 for England against the West Indies at Kingston in the 1929/30 series.

CLIFTON v TONBRIDGE
Played at Lord's, July 29, 30, 1946

TONBRIDGE WON BY two runs. Reputed to be the youngest player to appear in a match at Lord's, 13 year-old Michael Cowdrey, in his first match for Tonbridge, contributed largely to the success of his side. When Tonbridge were sent in to bat on a drying pitch, Cowdrey scored one more than the runs made by his colleagues and in the second innings raised his aggregate to 119. A right-arm spin bowler, mainly with leg break, he proved deadly in the Clifton second innings and with Kirch, medium, supported by smart fielding, dismissed the last five Clifton batsmen for 33 runs, so snatching a victory. Exton, with length and spin, excelled as a bowler, taking 14 wickets for 125.

TONBRIDGE

First Innings

D. S. Kemp lbw b Exton	25
G. Bowler b Exton	28
M. C. Cowdrey c Lindsay b Exton	75
D. K. Horton c Green b Penny	3
J. Wrightson c Lindsay b Penny	0
G. McNicol c Penny b Exton	0
A. J. Turk b Penny	0
M. J. Bickmore c Lindsay b Penny	16
J. D. Bickmore c Bishop b Exton	1
J. F. MacMillan b Exton	1
P. N. Kirch not out	0
B 2, l-b 2, w 3	7
	156

Second Innings

st Lindsay b Exton	44
b Exton	0
c Lindsay b Exton	44
st Lindsay b Bird	51
c Ritchie b Exton	1
c Lindsay b Ritchie	6
c Bishop b Exton	8
b Exton	0
not out	10
b Exton	2
b Exton	1
B 5, l-b 3	8
	175

CLIFTON

First Innings

T. S. Penny c Cowdrey b MacMillan	25
P. M. Crawford c MacMillan b M. J. Bickmore	57
M. L. Green c Wrightson b Cowdrey	56
R. N. Exton b M. J. Bickmore	9
M. F. Bishop not out	44
R. K. Green c Turk b Cowdrey	0
D. B. Bird b Cowdrey	5
D. C. Dickinson b Kirch	8
R. A. M. Whyte b Kirch	0
J. V. Ritchie b Kirch	0
R. T. M. Lindsay b Kirch	0
B 7, l-b 1, w 2	10
	214

Second Innings

absent	0
st Wrightson b Cowdrey	17
st Wrightson b Cowdrey	6
st Wrightson b Cowdrey	28
not out	45
b M. J. Bickmore	1
lbw b Cowdrey	2
b Kirch	8
b Kirch	0
c Horton b Cowdrey	0
b Kirch	0
B 6, w 2	8
	115

Clifton Bowling. – Ritchie 0 for 14 and 1 for 36; Exton 6 for 64 and 8 for 61; Dickinson 0 for 21 and 0 for 39; Bird 0 for 18 and 1 for 15; Penny 4 for 32 and 0 for 16.

Tonbridge Bowling. – Kirch 4 for 20 and 3 for 21; MacMillan 1 for 41 and 0 for 7; M. J. Bickmore 2 for 26 and 1 for 20; Cowdrey 3 for 58 and 5 for 59; Bowler 0 for 33; McNichol 0 for 26.

ENGLAND v AUSTRALIA

FOURTH TEST MATCH

Played at Adelaide, January 31, February 1, 3, 4, 5, 6, 1947

DRAWN. THERE WERE four extraordinary features about this Test. It was played in perpetual heat and dense humidity, with the temperature sometimes 105; Lindwall finished the England first innings by taking three wickets, all bowled, in four balls; and both Compton and Morris achieved the rare feat of hitting two separate hundreds. This was the first time for an Australian to accomplish this in his own country. The South Australian Cricket Association marked these performances by presenting a watch to each of the three players. England put up another brave struggle, but once again Hammond accomplished little with the bat and the bowling was not good enough. England introduced Hardstaff instead of Voce, and, with Barnes unfit, Australia played M. Harvey of Victoria. In both innings Hutton and Washbrook gave England a splendid send-off with a three-figure stand, but after tea on the opening day Edrich, Hutton and Hammond were dismissed in a disastrous thirty-five minutes before Compton and Hardstaff played out the final three-quarters of an hour. Again England were upset by the slower bowlers, and it was not surprising that Bradman did not take the new ball at 200. Third out, Hutton batted without mistake for four hours.

The second day provided plenty of thrills. Hardstaff remained with Compton until after lunch and then, trying to hook a bouncing delivery from Miller, he played-on, the stand having put on 118 in two hours thirty-five minutes. Ikin stayed while 61 were added, and, with Compton in complete control, Yardley saw 74 runs put on for the seventh wicket before the Middlesex player's great innings ended. Lindwall, after a rest and still using the old ball, held a sharp return catch from his first delivery. This was Compton's finest display so far during the tour; at the wicket four and three-quarter hours, he did not offer any kind of chance. His main scoring strokes were fifteen 4s and the feature of his play was powerful driving. Lindwall then took the new ball, and in his next over bowled both Bedser and Evans off-stump with successive deliveries; the next just missed the wicket and the fourth bowled Wright. So Lindwall captured the last four wickets in two overs while conceding only two runs. Twenty-five minutes remained, and Bedser served England splendidly by causing Harvey to play-on and then producing an almost unplayable ball that bowled Bradman for nought. Consequently Australia finished the day 24 for two wickets.

During the third day Australia made a complete recovery by adding 269 while losing only Morris – who hit his second Test century – and Hassett, who helped to put on 189 for the third partnership in nearly four hours. Bedser alone bowled well this day, as Wright, uncertain in his run, delivered many no-balls. Showing more freedom than in previous Tests, Morris drove delightfully and hit two 6s and twelve 4s. Altogether his innings lasted four and a half hours. Miller and Johnson carried the score to 293 for four wickets before the close.

The heat was again almost overwhelming on the fourth day, when Miller and Johnson carried their fifth-wicket stand to 150 before Johnson was leg-before. The high temperature was too much for Bedser, who had to rest for a period in the pavilion. Again Yardley bowled his leg theory splendidly and quietened the batsmen, but Miller became the seventh Australian to hit a century in this series. When Lindwall left, Australia, with two wickets remaining, were 37 behind, and at this point Bedser returned; but without further loss Australia went ahead. The innings closed when Edrich brilliantly ran out Toshack. Miller, who offered three chances after passing three figures, remained unbeaten, having batted attractively for four and a half hours. He hit one 6 and nine 4s. No sooner had Hutton and Washbrook opened England's second innings than a sharp thunderstorm accompanied by vivid flashes of lightning held up the game for twenty-three minutes. Lindwall and Miller each bounced the ball freely, but Hutton and Washbrook seldom missed a scoring opportunity. Their praiseworthy stand reached 96 at the close.

On the fifth day, off the first three deliveries by Lindwall, Hutton and Washbrook got four runs needed to complete their second three-figure opening stand of the match, having batted eighty-seven minutes; then disaster occurred. Tallon, standing well back, held a snick from Washbrook. Some people thought the ball was scooped off the ground. For a time Edrich shaped well, but Johnson bowled Hutton, and Toshack caused such a collapse that by 5.15 p.m. eight England wickets were down for 255. Compton alone of the recognised batsmen remained, and, shielding Evans from the bowling, he defied all Bradman's devices to remove him. At the close England were 274 for eight; Evans had not scored.

Evans again produced a splendid defence on the rare occasions Compton could not face the bowling, but within a quarter of an hour of the resumption, when Compton was 60 and the total 282, Tallon failed to stump Evans off Dooland. Had this chance been accepted, Australia must have won, but, instead England made such an excellent recovery that Hammond was able to declare. Evans was at the wicket ninety-five minutes before he got his first runs by placing Lindwall to leg for two at 309. With the last scoring stroke before lunch Compton hit Dooland through the covers for four, so completing his second hundred. He batted four hours forty minutes, hitting ten 4s, and his gallant stand with Evans realised 85 in two and a quarter hours. Of 98 balls received, Evans scored off only seven.

When one ball had been sent down after lunch Hammond applied the closure, setting Australia to make 314 in three and a quarter hours. Considering England's poor bowling resources and the experienced hitters at Australia's command, this was not an impossible task, but from the outset Bradman declined to accept the challenge. Up to a point Morris was enterprising, but Harvey, in his first Test, naturally was disinclined to take risks. He stayed one hundred minutes while helping Morris to make Australia's first three-figure opening stand of the series. Then Morris and Bradman calmly played out time, and Morris became the second Australian to hit two centuries in a Test against England, the first being W. Bardsley, another left-hander, at Kennington Oval in 1909.

Never before had two players each hit two separate hundreds in a Test; Compton earned the distinction of completing four hundreds in consecutive innings in first-class cricket. This drawn game gave Australia the rubber. The full attendance was 135,980 and the receipts £18,117.

ENGLAND

First Innings

L. Hutton *lbw b* McCool	94
C. Washbrook *c* Tallon *b* Dooland	65
W. J. Edrich *c and b* Dooland	17
W. R. Hammond *b* Toshack	18
D. Compton *c and b* Lindwall	147
J. Hardstaff *b* Miller	67
J. T. Ikin *c* Toshack *b* Dooland	21
N. W. D. Yardley *not out*	18
A. V. Bedser *b* Lindwall	2
T. G. Evans *b* Lindwall	0
D. V. P. Wright *b* Lindwall	0
B 4, l-b 5, w 2	11

1/137 2/173 3/196 4/202 5/320   460
6/381 7/455 8/460 9/460

Second Innings

b Johnson	76
c Tallon *b* Lindwall	39
c Bradman *b* Toshack	46
c Lindwall *b* Toshack	22
not out	103
b Toshack	9
lbw b Toshack	1
c Tallon *b* Lindwall	18
c Tallon *b* Miller	3
not out	10
B 5, l-b 3, w 2, n-b 3	13

1/100 2/137 3/178 (8 wkts dec.) 340
4/188 5/207 6/215 7/250 8/255

AUSTRALIA

First Innings

M. Harvey *b* Bedser	12
A. Morris *c* Evans *b* Bedser	122
D. G. Bradman *b* Bedser	0
A. R. Hassett *c* Hammond *b* Wright	78
K. R. Miller *not out*	141
I. W. Johnson *lbw b* Wright	52
C. McCool *c* Bedser *b* Yardley	2
D. Tallon *b* Wright	3
R. Lindwall *c* Evans *b* Yardley	20
B. Dooland *c* Bedser *b* Yardley	29
E. Toshack *run out*	0
B 16, l-b 6, w 2, n-b 4	28

1/18 2/18 3/207 4/222 5/372   487
6/389 7/396 8/423 9/486

Second Innings

b Yardley	31
not out	124
not out	56
B 2, n-b 2	4

1/116   (1 wkt) 215

Australia Bowling

	Overs	Mdns	Runs	Wkts	Overs	Mdns	Runs	Wkts
Lindwall	23	5	52	4	17.1	4	60	2
Miller	16	—	45	1	11	—	34	1
Toshack	30	12	59	1	36	6	76	4
McCool	29	1	91	1	19	3	41	—
Johnson	22	3	69	—	25	8	51	1
Dooland	33	1	133	3	17	2	65	—

England Bowling

	Overs	Mdns	Runs	Wkts	Overs	Mdns	Runs	Wkts
Bedser	30	6	97	3	15	1	68	—
Edrich	20	3	88	—	7	2	25	—
Wright	32.4	1	152	3	9	—	49	—
Yardley	31	7	101	3	13	—	69	1
Ikin	2	—	9	—				
Compton	3	—	12	—				

Umpires: J. D. Scott and G. Borwick.

ENGLAND v SOUTH AFRICA

SECOND TEST MATCH
Played at Lord's, June 21, 23, 24, 25, 1947

ENGLAND WON BY ten wickets. From first to last this was a delightful match. South Africa put up a brave fight and were by no means as inferior as the result would suggest. Their bowlers again provided an object lesson in length, direction and bowling to a field, and, in spite of a trying ordeal, their fielding remained at a superlatively high standard of efficiency and keenness. Moreover, Melville, Mitchell and Nourse once more proved their worth as batsmen of contrasting characters. Yet these factors were outweighed by the advantage England gained in winning the toss, the greatness of Edrich and Compton, who established a new world record in Test Matches with a third-wicket stand of 370, the shock bowling and slip catching of Edrich, and the consistently fine work of Wright on his first appearance of the season against the touring side.

Through their excellent performance in the First Test, the South Africans attracted big crowds to Lord's, and the gates were closed half an hour before the start on the first day, when the attendance was officially given as 30,600. The thousands of people turned away missed extremely interesting cricket. Except for an occasional ball which lifted in the early stages, conditions favoured batsmen, and England received a sound start from Hutton and Washbrook, who achieved their first objective of staying together for the ninety minutes before lunch. Yet Hutton never found his true form. He batted an hour and fifty minutes for 18 out of 75 before playing outside an off-break. Hutton made only fourteen scoring strokes – twelve singles, a 4 and a 2 – from the 121 balls delivered to him. By comparison, Washbrook found gaps in the field with grand off and cover-drives, but he profited little from his favourite square-cut, for Melville cleverly blocked the stroke with two fieldsmen at third man, one deep and square, the other short and slightly backward. Washbrook looked set for a big score until, with the new ball just in use and the total 96, he flashed at a rising ball outside the off stump. A conjuring catch at second slip, where Tuckett held the ball at the third attempt, ended this attractive display. In view of the obviously long tail, no little responsibility rested on Edrich and Compton, and an enthralling struggle developed between them and a determined attack, splendidly supported in the field, before the two Middlesex batsmen assumed mastery. Then followed a sparkling exhibition of fluent stroke-play, and South Africa conceded 370 runs before the partnership ended. Compton used everything in his complete repertoire, including the brilliant leg-sweep off a slow bowler, and Edrich specially excelled in on-side play. He hooked Rowan for one glorious 6 and frequently brought off a powerful lofted pulled-drive. In three hours ten minutes to the close the stand produced 216 runs, Edrich reaching his first Test century in England and Compton his second in successive Test innings against South Africa. Taking into account the slow start and the twenty-five minutes lost through rain, England's average scoring rate was satisfactory. The day was marred by an unfortunate accident to Melville. Shortly before the close a throw-in from the deep struck him over the right eye. Melville sank to the ground, but, after attention, was able to resume, though during the week-end his eye turned black and became almost completely closed.

Compton and Edrich thrilled another 30,000 crowd on the second day. Both were supremely confident, and by swift and sure running took full value for every stroke. No relief, in fact, came to South Africa until twenty minutes after lunch, when Edrich at last relaxed his concentration and was bowled. He gave a difficult stumping chance when 47, but that was his only blemish. He hit a 6 and twenty-six 4s in 189 out of 391, in five minutes under six hours. The partnership beat by 51 the 319 made by Melville and Nourse in the Nottingham Test and fell only 12 short of the highest for England by any wicket – 382 by Hutton and Leyland against Australia at The Oval in 1938. Compton, dismissed at 515, obtained twenty boundaries in his 208 out of 419 in five hours fifty minutes. His first Test double century brought his total to 436 in three Test innings against South Africa. Barnett led the way in care-free hitting by the following batsmen, so that England after

England v South Africa 1947 usually meant Edrich and Compton versus the rest. Never has any batsman dominated a touring side's bowling as Compton did South Africa's in 1947. Not even Bradman outdid the Middlesex player, who, abetted by his friend Edrich, piled up huge scores in match after match, much to the bewilderment of the South African bowlers, the consternation of statisticians and the unalloyed rapture of spectators.

lunch obtained 111 in sixty-five minutes for six wickets before Yardley declared. Tuckett maintained pace and hostility to the end. In his last spell he dismissed five men for 20 in seven overs, and at all times looked a better fast bowler than anyone England possessed.

At first everything went well for South Africa in their reply. Mitchell and Melville made runs surprisingly fast and easily against a constantly changed attack, and not until Compton joined in was the stand broken at 95, when Mitchell fell to a swift stumping by Evans. With only nine added, Viljoen played on to Wright's faster ball, but Nourse stayed with Melville to the end of the day. Third ball on Tuesday morning provided Melville with the opportunity of obtaining the four runs which completed his fourth successive Test century against England, the only comparable feat to which in Test cricket is that of J. H. Fingleton (Australia), who in 1936 made three against South Africa and one against England. Melville and Nourse saw their side safely through the first vital hour, and their third-wicket stand added 118 before Melville played a tired-looking stroke at a long hop and gave backward short-leg an easy catch. Melville offered a return chance to Wright when 40 and an awkward one at the wicket when 93, but he played another great innings for his side. His easy, elegant strokes charmed the purist – and brought him thirteen 4s. Eight runs later Nourse hit too soon when trying to hook. A fifth-wicket stand of 60 by Dawson and Harris gave South Africa fresh hope, but their separation at 290 was the beginning of the end. In one particularly successful spell of 22 balls Wright bowled Rowan, Tuckett and Mann with fizzing leg-breaks. His figures did him less than justice, for Melville alone played him with complete confidence. South Africa followed-on 227 behind, and, with 15 scored, play was held up for twenty minutes while the cricketers were presented to the King and Queen and the Princesses, Elizabeth and Margaret. Upon the resumption Edrich bowled at a tremendous pace. His second ball flattened Melville's middle stump, and two overs later he sent Viljoen's middle stump flying. These dramatic events caused Mitchell to concentrate almost solely on defence, and he and the more aggressive Nourse remained together during the last one hundred minutes, adding 92 runs.

So South Africa, with eight wickets to fall, began the last day needing 107 to make England bat again, a position similar to England's at Nottingham. Obviously such a recovery could not again be expected, but South Africa received a nasty shock when, with the first ball of the day, Edrich shattered Nourse's wicket. From that point the main question became the margin of England's victory, though Mitchell and Dawson added 72 for the fourth partnership and Rowan made some good hits. Mitchell defended dourly for four hours fifteen minutes before an acrobatic slip catch brought his dismissal. Edrich flung himself full length sideways and grasped with one hand a ball going away from him. His catch off Dawson was nearly as good, and Yardley also distinguished himself with two fine efforts. Again Wright was England's best bowler. True, seven of his ten wickets in the match were those of batsmen in the lower part of the order, but his improved length, direction, sharp spin and lift made him always dangerous. Edrich and Compton gave good bowling support; Bedser would have taken several wickets with normal fortune, for at least four chances off him went to ground, but Pope's inclusion was not a success. In England's brief second innings Hutton appeared more like his former self. R.J.H.

ENGLAND

First Innings

L. Hutton *b* Rowan 18
C. Washbrook *c* Tuckett *b* Dawson 65
W. J. Edrich *b* Mann 189
D. C. S. Compton *c* Rowan *b* Tuckett 208
C. J. Barnett *b* Tuckett 33
N. W. D. Yardley *c* Rowan *b* Tuckett 5
T. G. Evans *b* Tuckett 16
G. H. Pope *not out* 8
A. V. Bedser *b* Tuckett 0
B 2, l-b 10 12

1/75 2/96 3/466 4/515 (8wkts dec.) 554
5/526 6/541 7/554 8/554

Second Innings

not out 13
not out 13

(No wkt) 26

D. V. P. Wright and W. E. Hollies did not bat.

SOUTH AFRICA

First Innings

A. Melville *c* Bedser *b* Hollies 117
B. Mitchell *st* Evans *b* Compton 46
K. G. Viljoen *b* Wright 1
A. D. Nourse *lbw b* Wright 61
O. C Dawson *c* Barnett *b* Hollies 36
T. A. Harris *st* Evans *b* Compton 30
A. M. B. Rowan *b* Wright 8
L. Tuckett *b* Wright 5
N. B. F. Mann *b* Wright 4
J. D. Lindsay *not out* 7
V. I. Smith *c* Edrich *b* Pope 11
L-b 1 1

1/95 2/104 3/222 4/230 5/290   327
6/300 7/302 8/308 9/309

Second Innings

b Edrich 8
c Edrich *b* Wright 80
b Edrich 6
b Edrich 58
c Edrich *b* Compton 33
c Yardley *b* Compton 3
not out 38
b Wright 9
b Wright 5
c Yardley *b* Wright 5
c Edrich *b* Wright 0
B 3, l-b 4 7

1/16 2/28 3/120 4/192 5/192   252
6/201 7/224 8/236 9/252

South Africa Bowling

	Overs	Mdns	Runs	Wkts	Overs	Mdns	Runs	Wkts
Tuckett	47	7	115	5	3	—	4	—
Dawson	33	11	81	1	6	2	6	—
Mann	53	16	99	1	3.1	1	16	—
Rowan	65	11	174	1				
Smith	17	2	73	—				

England Bowling

	Overs	Mdns	Runs	Wkts	Overs	Mdns	Runs	Wkts
Edrich	9	1	22	—	13	5	31	3
Bedser	26	1	76	—	14	6	20	—
Pope	39.2	5	49	1	17	7	36	—
Wright	29	10	95	5	32.2	6	80	5
Hollies	28	10	52	2	20	7	32	—
Compton	21	11	32	2	31	10	46	2

Umpires: H. G. Baldwin and D. Davies.

SURREY v MIDDLESEX
Played at The Oval, August 9, 11, 12, 1947

MIDDLESEX WON BY an innings and 11 runs after giving a display worthy of potential Champions. Denis Compton achieved the best all-round performance of his career by hitting 137 not out and taking twelve wickets for 174 runs. The only regret on the opening day, when Middlesex scored their 537, was that Brown should be bowled for 98 after helping Robertson in an opening stand of 211. Both men batted faultlessly, paving the way for Edrich and Compton to add 287 in two and three-quarter hours without being separated. The Surrey bowling was never loose, and Compton was content with nine 4s compared with eighteen by Edrich. Torn tendons in the right arm, damaged when bowling in the previous match, prevented Edrich fielding on the second day when before tea Surrey scored freely. Squires, Holmes and McIntyre all played brilliantly. Then came a collapse before the slow left-arm unorthodox over-the-wicket bowling of Denis Compton which brought Middlesex victory before lunch on the third day. Both wicket-keepers, L. Compton and McIntyre, bowled. Altogether 54,000 people, of whom 47,000 paid, saw this match. The gates were closed by three o'clock on Saturday when 30,000 were present.

MIDDLESEX

S. M. Brown *b* Surridge 98
J. D. Robertson *c and b* E. Bedser 127
W. J. Edrich *not out* 157
D. C. S. Compton *not out* 137
B 8, l-b 4, n-b 6 18

(2 wkts dec.) 537

F. G. Mann, R. W. V. Robins, A. Thompson. L. Compton. J. Sims. L. Gray and J. Young did not bat.

SURREY

First Innings

L. B. Fishlock *c* L. Compton *b* Gray 16
D. G. W. Fletcher *lbw b* D. Compton 42
H. S. Squires *st* L. Compton *b* D. Compton 98
T. H. Barling *c* L. Compton *b* Sims 16
J. F. Parker *c and b* D. Compton 15
E. R. T. Holmes *b* Sims 61
A. J. McIntyre *c* Robins *b* D. Compton 51
E. A. Bedser *c* Robertson *b* Sims 16
W. S. Surridge *c* Mann *b* D. Compton 1
A. V. Bedser *not out* 3
A. R. Gover *c* Mann *b* D. Compton 4
B 4, l-b 5, w 2 11

334

Second Innings

c L. Compton *b* D. Compton 44
b Young 8
b Robins 20
b D. Compton 44
run out 12
b D. Compton 2
c and b D. Compton 0
lbw b Compton 10
c D. Compton *b* Robins 23
c and b D. Compton 14
not out 5
B 6, l-b 4 10

192

Surrey Bowling

	Overs	Mdns	Runs	Wkts
Gover	17	—	84	—
A. V. Bedser	20	3	67	—
Surridge	18	2	77	1
Parker	21	3	83	—
Squires	17	—	95	—
E. A. Bedser	19	—	82	1
Holmes	3	—	13	—
McIntyre	3	—	18	—

Middlesex Bowling

	Overs	Mdns	Runs	Wkts	Overs	Mdns	Runs	Wkts
Gray	20	4	55	1	8	2	14	—
L. Compton	8	1	32	—				
Sims	27	5	100	3	17	2	47	—
D. Compton	27.3	4	94	6	24.5	6	80	6
Robins	3	—	11	—	8	1	18	2
Young	15	4	31	—	7	2	23	1

Umpires: J. Smart and C. N. Woolley.

MIDDLESEX v KENT
Played at Lord's, August 13, 14, 15, 1947

KENT WON BY 75 runs. They triumphed five minutes from the end of extra time after one of the most exciting struggles of the season. Kent scored so freely when holding a first innings lead of 72 that they were able to set Middlesex the task of getting 397 to win at more than 90 an hour. When four wickets fell for 135 an easy victory for Kent seemed in sight, particularly as Wright was bowling in superb form. Then Denis Compton found a good partner in Mann, and in ninety-seven minutes the score raced along by 161 before Wright broke the threatening stand. During the partnership most of the Kent fieldsmen were placed on the boundary. Compton hit nineteen 4s in his thirteenth century of the season. He played one of his finest innings. Upon Compton's dismissal, when he

1947 was Compton's year. In all first class matches he scored 3,816 runs, including 18 centuries, both of which statistics represented records for a first-class season. Compton was one of the first stars to engage an agent and his good looks, charm and athletic prowess soon provided the agency with a flourishing business.

attempted another big hit, Kent again set an attacking field for Wright and Davies, who accounted for the last five wickets in thirty-seven minutes for 25 runs. In each innings Wright kept a remarkably accurate length and troubled most of the batsmen with variations of leg-breaks and googlies, which brought him eleven wickets for 194 runs. Robertson hit his fifth century in successive matches for Middlesex in the first innings, when Edrich was next highest scorer with 28. All through Kent batted much more consistently. Their biggest stand was 157 by Ames and Valentine for the third wicket in the second innings.

KENT

First Innings

L. J. Todd *b* Sims	62
A. E. Fagg *b* Young	66
L. E. G. Ames *c* L. Compton *b* Sims	8
B. H. Valentine *b* Gray	61
J. G. W. Davies *c* L. Compton *b* Sims	4
G. F. Anson *lbw b* Sims	25
T. G. E. Evans *lbw b* D. Compton	18
R. R. Dovey *run out*	7
D. V. P. Wright *b* Hever	36
F. Ridgway *b* D. Compton	0
N. Harding *not out*	5
B 5, l-b 4	9
	301

Second Innings

b Hever	17
c L. Compton *b* Gray	6
c D. Compton *b* Young	69
c Gray *b* D. Compton	92
lbw b Young	11
c Mann *b* Young	51
c Robertson *b* D. Compton	56
not out	10
c Edrich *b* Young	11
B 5, l-b 6	11
(8 wkts dec.)	324

MIDDLESEX

First Innings

S. M. Brown *c* Valentine *b* Harding	0
J. D. Robertson *c* Evans *b* Wright	110
W. J. Edrich *b* Dovey	28
D. C. S. Compton *b* Wright	16
R. W. V. Robins *c* Harding *b* Wright	24
F. C. Mann *c* Fagg *b* Wright	1
L. H. Compton *c* Harding *b* Wright	6
J. Sims *b* Dovey	7
L. Gray *c* Todd *b* Wright	7
J. A. Young *c* Fagg *b* Wright	17
N. G. Hever *not out*	8
L-b 2, w 2, n-b 1	5
	229

Second Innings

b Harding	5
lbw b Harding	12
c and b Wright	31
c Davies *b* Wright	168
b Davies	21
b Wright	57
st Evans *b* Wright	7
b Davies	7
not out	4
c Evans *b* Davies	0
b Davies	2
L-b 4, n-b 3	7
	321

Middlesex Bowling

	Overs	Mdns	Runs	Wkts	Overs	Mdns	Runs	Wkts
Gray	17	3	44	1	19	3	70	1
Hever	10.1	2	32	1	15	3	37	1
Robertson	3	1	12	—				
Young	16	8	24	1	38.2	12	65	4
D. Compton	24	2	87	2	31	10	86	2
Robins	2	—	6	—	3	—	18	—
Sims	19	—	87	4	12	1	37	—

Sidney Barnes, the Australian opening batsman, about to clip the ball away. Barnes was one of the jokers of the Australian side, a buffoon who combined masterly batting technique with something less than a reverential attitude towards his captain, Bradman.

Kent Bowling

	Overs	Mdns	Runs	Wkts	Overs	Mdns	Runs	Wkts
Harding	5	1	22	1	13	—	56	2
Wright	33.2	5	92	7	24	3	102	4
Dovey	28	5	59	2	20	2	69	—
Ridgway	13	1	46	—	5	—	29	—
Davies	2	—	5	—	19	3	58	4

Umpires: H. G. Baldwin and A. R. Coleman.

ESSEX v AUSTRALIANS

Played at Southend, May 15, 17, 1948

AUSTRALIANS WON BY an innings and 451 runs. In light-hearted vein, they made history by putting together the highest total scored in a day of six hours in first-class cricket. Bradman led the run-getting revel on the Saturday. Complete master of the Essex bowlers on a fast pitch, he scored 187 in two hours five minutes, and by a wide variety of orthodox and unorthodox strokes hit thirty-two 4s and a 5. Brown's 153 occupied three hours and contained seventeen 4s. Loxton (fourteen 4s and a 6) and Saggers (nine 4s) also scored centuries. The biggest partnerships were 219 in ninety minutes between Brown and Bradman for the second wicket, 166 in sixty-five minutes by Loxton and Saggers for the sixth, and 145 in ninety-five minutes between Barnes and Brown for the first. Bailey dismissed Brown and Miller with successive balls, but generally the bowlers failed to stem the scoring. Because of injury Bailey did not bat in either innings. Essex, dismissed twice on Monday, first failed against the pace of Miller and the cleverly varied left-arm deliveries of Toshack; then in the follow-on – apart from Pearce and P. Smith, who made a stand of 133 – they broke down in the face of Johnson's off-spinners. The attendance and receipts – 32,000 and £3,482 – were ground records.

AUSTRALIANS

S. G. Barnes *hit wkt b* R. Smith 79
W. A. Brown *c* Horsfall *b* Bailey 153
D. G. Bradman *b* P. Smith 187
K. R. Miller *b* Bailey 0
R. A. Hamence *c* P. Smith *b* R. Smith 46
S. J. Loxton *c* Rist *b* Vigar 120
R. A. Saggers *not out* 104
I. W. Johnson *st* Rist *b* P. Smith 9
D. Ring *c* Vigar *b* P. Smith 1
W. A. Johnston *b* Vigar 9
E. R. H. Toshack *c* Vigar *b* P. Smith 4
    B 7, n-b 2 9

                                               721

ESSEX

First Innings

T. C. Dodds *c* Ring *b* Miller 0
S. J. Cray *b* Miller 5
A. V. Avery *b* Johnston 10
F. H. Vigar *c* Saggers *b* Miller 0
R. Horsfall *b* Toshack 11
T. N. Pearce *c* Miller *b* Toshack 8
R. Smith *c* Barnes *b* Toshack 25
T. P. B. Smith *b* Toshack 3
F. Rist *c* Barnes *b* Toshack 8
E. Price *not out* 4
T. E. Bailey *absent hurt* .... −
    B 2, l-b 6, n-b 1 9

                                         83

Second Innings

b Toshack 16
b Johnson 15
c Brown *b* Johnson 3
c Johnson *b* Toshack 0
b Johnson 8
c and b Johnson 71
c Ring *b* Johnson 0
lbw b Barnes 54
b Johnson 1
not out 4
absent hurt .... −
    B 6, l-b 3, n-b 6 15

                             187

Essex Bowling

	Overs	Mdns	Runs	Wkts
Bailey	21	1	128	2
R. Smith	37	2	169	2
P. Smith	38	—	193	4
Price	20	—	156	—
Vigar	13	1	66	2

Australian Bowling

	Overs	Mdns	Runs	Wkts	Overs	Mdns	Runs	Wkts
Miller	8	3	14	3	2	1	4	—
Johnston	7	1	10	1	10	4	26	—
Toshack	10.5	—	31	5	17	2	50	2
Ring	11	4	19	—	7	3	16	—
Loxton					12	3	28	—
Johnson					21	6	37	6
Barnes					9.4	5	11	1

Umpires: W. H. Ashdown and D. Hendren.

Edrich and Compton. When the 1948 season opened, people wondered if the Middlesex Twins were to resume where they had left off at the end of the "annus mirabilis" of 1947. The answer was not long in coming, in mid-May in the match against Somerset. In the famous photograph of the two batsmen walking out to bat at Lord's, their purposefulness is plain to see. They are two men boldly striding into history.

MIDDLESEX v SOMERSET
Played at Lord's, May 19, 20, 21, 1948

MIDDLESEX WON BY ten wickets. The match was memorable for a stand of 424 between W. J. Edrich and Denis Compton, which beat all third wicket records in first-class cricket except the 445 by W. N. Carson and P. E. Whitelaw for Auckland v Otago at Dunedin, New Zealand, in January 1937. They stayed together four hours until Mann declared with fifty minutes of the first day still to be played. Steady bowling and keen fielding kept both batsmen comparatively quiet in the early stages of their association, but after tea 209 runs came in seventy minutes. Compton making 139. In his highest first-class innings to date Compton hit three 6s and thirty-seven 4s. Edrich hit one 6 and eighteen 4s. Somerset scored freely, but lost wickets steadily on the second day, when Middlesex claimed an extra half-hour without finishing the match, and forty-five minutes play became necessary on the final day.

MIDDLESEX

First Innings

J. D. Robertson c Hazell b Buse	21
S. M. Brown c Mitchell-Innes b Buse	31
W. J. Edrich *not out*	168
D. Compton *not out*	252
L. Compton (*did not bat*)	
B 4, w 2	6
	(2 wkts dec.) 478

Second Innings

not out	22
not out	7
	(No wkt) 29

F. G. Mann, R. W. V. Robins. H. Sharp, J. Sims, J. A. Young and L. Gray did not bat.

SOMERSET

First Innings

H. Gimblett b Gray	6
E. Hill c L. Compton b Gray	3
M. Coope c L. Compton b Sims	31
N. S. Mitchell-Innes b D. Compton	65
G. E. S. Woodhouse lbw b D. Compton	15
H. T. F. Buse c D. Compton b Young	7
M. F. Tremlett c Robins b Gray	40
W. T. Luckes c Sharp b Young	0
A. W. Wellard c and b Edrich	3
H. Hazell not out	4
P. A. O. Graham b Gray	12
B 4, l-b 4	8
	194

Second Innings

b Gray	29
st L. Compton b D. Compton	69
lbw b Sims	59
lbw b Sims	8
c Edrich b D. Compton	8
c L. Compton b Young	59
c Edrich b Robins	20
c Edrich b Sims	27
c Brown b Robins	14
lbw b Robins	5
not out	4
B 5, l-b 3	8
	310

Somerset Bowling

	Overs	Mdns	Runs	Wkts	Overs	Mdns	Runs	Wkts
Wellard	39	4	158	—				
Tremlett	15	2	50	—	3	—	9	—
Graham	8	—	40	—	2.2	—	20	—
Buse	33	9	107	2				
Hazell	19	4	56	—				
Coope	6	—	61	—				

Middlesex Bowling

	Overs	Mdns	Runs	Wkts	Overs	Mdns	Runs	Wkts
Gray	14	3	27	4	14	5	25	1
Young	13	8	14	2	19	7	41	1
Sims	19	2	61	1	29.4	9	78	3
Edrich	9	2	29	1	3	—	20	—
D. Compton	15	4	55	2	19	3	69	2
Robins					17	2	69	3

Umpires: H. Elliott and P. T. Mills.

ENGLAND v AUSTRALIA

FIRST TEST MATCH

Played at Nottingham, June 10, 11, 12, 14, 15, 1948

AUSTRALIA WON BY eight wickets. Bravely as England fought back, the result became nearly a foregone conclusion by the end of the first day after their disastrous batting against a fast attack of exceptionally high standard. Until the last moment considerable doubt existed about the composition of the England side. As Wright was doubtful through lumbago the selectors sent for Pope (Derbyshire) on the eve of the match, but neither played, Wright being omitted through unfitness. Simpson (Nottinghamshire) was twelfth man. Although only twenty minutes' play was possible before lunch on Thursday, Miller struck a vital blow by clean bowling Hutton with an extra-fast ball and, on a pitch affected sufficiently by a heavy downpour during the interval to make the ball skid through, England lost eight wickets before tea for 74. True, the light never became good and the bowling reached a high level, but England played poorly and there could be no criticism of Yardley's decision to bat first. Washbrook hooked a short-rising ball to long-leg where Brown took a good running catch, Compton trying a leg sweep,

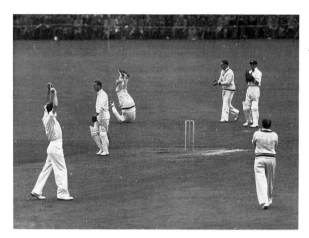

The victim is Joe Hardstaff, caught off the bowling of Johnston by Keith Miller, apparently under the illusion that he is still in Australia.

missed a straight ball and Edrich was late with his stroke. Johnston, in the fifth over of his first Test against England, achieved the splendid feat of dismissing Edrich and Hardstaff, out second ball, and he continued to bowl left-arm medium-fast deliveries of sustained hostility – accurate in length, varied in pace and swing.

When Laker and Bedser came together, Australia were so much on top that there seemed every likelihood that England would be out for less than the lowest score made before in a Test at Nottingham – 112 by England in 1921 – but the two Surrey all-rounders batted so confidently that they more than doubled the total by adding 89 runs in seventy-three minutes. Laker hooked firmly and made many fine off-drives during a stay of ninety minutes, and Bedser mixed good defence with clean driving. A dazzling slip catch by Miller set the keynote on Australia's excellent fielding, but Australia suffered a handicap when Lindwall pulled a groin muscle midway through the innings and could not bowl again in the match. Johnston's full analysis was 25–11–36–5. Less than quarter of an hour remained for Australia to bat and neither Barnes nor Morris took a risk. Barnes made an unsuccessful appeal against the light after the first delivery of the innings – a wide by Edrich.

Although a good spell by Laker gave England great encouragement at one period on the second day Australia recovered and pressed home their advantage, but on a perfect pitch and in ideal weather conditions England deserved equal praise for limiting the batsmen to 276 runs in six hours. For the most part Yardley set a defensive field and, though lacking penetration, his bowlers performed their allotted tasks in concentrating on and just outside the leg stump. At one period Laker's off-breaks put the Australians into a position where they struggled for runs, Laker broke the opening stand of 73 and when he dismissed Barnes and Miller at 121 his analysis read: 12.4–5–22–3. Laker owed a great deal to Evans for disposing of Barnes who cut a ball hard on to the wicket-keeper's thigh whence it bounced into the air; Evans whirled round and diving full length held the ball with one hand inches from the ground. Miller played for an off-break, but the ball went with Laker's arm and resulted in an easy catch at slip. Then Yardley caused surprise by taking off Laker in order to use the new ball against Brown, normally an opening batsman accustomed to swing. The change in bowling provided Bradman with an opportunity to hit his first 4 after eighty-three minutes, but again he relapsed into long periods of defence and, as Brown followed suit, scoring became very slow with Australia fighting to restore their early superiority. They passed England's total without further loss, but at 184 Yardley went on for the first time in the innings and once again he showed his usefulness as a change bowler in Tests by getting Brown leg-before with his fourth delivery. England met with no other success on Friday; an unbroken stand of 108 between Bradman and Hassett left Australia 128 ahead. Seldom had Bradman been so subdued in a big innings as he was over the 28th Test century of his career. He did not welcome Yardley's tactics in asking his bowlers to work to a packed leg-side field, and he spent over three hours and a half in reaching his 100, the last 29 runs taking seventy minutes.

When play began on the Saturday Bradman needed only two runs to become the first player to complete 1,000 for the season. These he obtained, but in the third over Hutton at short fine-leg held the first of his series of catches given by Bradman off Bedser's late in-swinger. Bradman's unusually subdued innings lasted four hours and three-quarters. For the most part he allowed himself no liberty. On Bradman's departure Hassett became the big problem. Johnson fell to Laker's fifth ball and Young took a brilliant return catch from Tallon during a remarkable spell of bowling, before Hassett found an able partner in the hard-driving Lindwall, who did not require a runner in spite of his groin trouble. In one period of over an hour Young sent down eleven overs without conceding a run and his figures for a complete spell of two hours and a half were: 26–16–14–1. In the innings Young gave away only 79 runs in 60 overs. The eighth-wicket stand added 107 before Bedser knocked Hassett's off-stump, so taking his 50th wicket in Test cricket. Four runs later Evans caught Lindwall smartly on the leg side. Though Hassett pursued his policy of defence for five hours and fifty minutes he hit hard whenever the opportunity arose and his strokes included a 6 and twenty 4s. A last-wicket partnership of 33 emphasised England's difficulties which were increased immediately they began the second innings, 344 behind. Once more Australia gained the incentive of a fine start, when in Miller's second over Washbrook attempted to hook a bumper and edged a catch to the wicket-keeper. Misjudgement in cutting a ball outside the off stump cost Edrich his wicket at 39, but Hutton showed sparkling form and Compton overcame an anxious start against Johnson. In a delightful display of stroke-making Hutton reached 50 with two successive 4s off Miller in an over which produced 14 runs. At this period Miller bowled medium-paced off-breaks, but he turned again to fast deliveries and incurred the noisy displeasure of sections of the crowd when he bowled five bumpers to Hutton in his last eight balls, one of which struck the batsman high on the left arm. By the most attractive batting so far in the match Hutton and Compton scored 82 together in the last seventy minutes.

Before play began on Monday the Nottinghamshire Secretary, Mr H. A. Brown, broadcast an appeal to the crowd to leave the conduct of the game to the umpires and he deplored the barracking of Miller on Saturday. The not-out batsmen continued their good work, but the light became even worse than in the first innings. After an unsuccessful appeal play was held up when the ground caught the edge of a thunderstorm. Almost immediately on the resumption Miller produced a fast break-back which beat Hutton completely in the still gathering gloom. Bad light interrupted the game soon afterwards and though the stoppage was brief conditions became so bad again that the players retired a second time. On this occasion Compton wanted only three runs for his century. After fifty-five minutes the umpires thought the light good enough to continue, but it was still bad. Indeed, rarely can a Test Match have been played under such appalling conditions as on this day. Great credit was due to Compton and Hardstaff, even in the absence of Lindwall, for their resolution. Although Hardstaff went at 243 and Barnett did not settle down Compton batted in masterly fashion when continuing his third century in successive Tests at Trent Bridge, and Yardley gave sound aid till Johnston took a return catch smartly. England faced an almost hopeless task at the beginning of the last day when they stood only one run ahead with four wickets left, but hope remained as long as Compton was undefeated. He found another fine partner in Evans and in spite of two short breaks for rain they held out till ten minutes before lunch when Miller released a lightning bumper at Compton. The ball reared shoulder-high, Compton shaped to hook then changed his mind and tried to get his head out of the way. As he ducked Compton lost his balance on the muddy turf and tumbled into his wicket.

This tragic end to one of the best innings of Compton's career and his highest in Test cricket against Australia sealed England's fate. No praise could be too high for the manner in which Compton carried the side's responsibilities and defied a first-class attack in such trying circumstances. He held out for six hours fifty minutes and hit nineteen 4s.

Evans completed a gallant 50, which included eight boundary strokes, but the end of the innings soon came and Australia wanted only 98 to win. Miller, who accounted for England's two best batsmen, Hutton and Compton, in each innings, and Johnston shared chief bowling honours. Australia fielded grandly, in contrast to England, and no one was better than the twelfth man. Harvey, substituting for Lindwall, whose absence threw much extra work on the other bowlers.

Bedser added interest to the last stages by bowling Morris at 38 and dismissing Bradman for his first "duck" in a Test in England, caught in exactly the same manner as in – the first innings; but Barnes and Hassett quickly hit off the runs, Barnes showing tremendous power in square-cutting. The match ended humorously. After making a – boundary stroke Barnes thought the game was over when the scores were level, and he snatched a stump before racing towards the pavilion. Barnes was halfway up the pavilion steps when the shouts of the crowd made him realise the error and he returned to the crease. When Hassett did make the winning hit another scramble for souvenirs took place; and in this Barnes was unlucky. R.J.H.

ENGLAND

First Innings

L. Hutton b Miller	3
C. Washbrook c Brown b Lindwall	6
W. J. Edrich b Johnston	18
D. C. S. Compton b Miller	19
J. Hardstaff c Miller b Johnston	0
C. J. Barnett b Johnston	8
N. W. D. Yardley lbw b Toshack	3
T. G. Evans c Morris b Johnston	12
J. C. Laker c Tallon b Miller	63
A. V. Bedser c Brown b Johnston	22
J. A. Young not out	1
B 5, l-b 5	10

1/9 2/15 3/46 4/46 5/48   165
6/60 7/74 8/74 9/163

Second Innings

b Miller	74
c Tallon b Miller	1
c Tallon b Johnson	13
hit wkt b Miller	184
c Hassett b Toshack	43
c Miller b Johnston	6
c and b Johnston	22
c Tallon b Johnston	50
b Miller	4
not out	3
b Johnston	9
B 12, l-b 17, n-b 3	32

1/5 2/39 3/150 4/243 5/264   441
6/321 7/405 8/413 9/423

AUSTRALIA

First Innings

S. G. Barnes c Evans b Laker	62
A. R. Morris b Laker	31
D. G. Bradman c Hutton b Bedser	138
K. R. Miller c Edrich b Laker	0
W. A. Brown lbw b Yardley	17
A. L. Hassett b Bedser	137
I. W. Johnson b Laker	21
D. Tallon c and b Young	10
R. R. Lindwall c Evans b Yardley	42
W. A. Johnston not out	17
E. R. H. Toshack lbw b Bedser	19
B 9, l-b 4, w 1, n-b 1	15

1/73 2/121 3/121 4/185 5/305   509
6/338 7/365 8/472 9/476

Second Innings

not out	64
b Bedser	9
c Hutton b Bedser	0
not out	21
L-b 2, w 1, n-b 1	4

1/38 2/48   (2 wkts) 98

Continued on P. 216

Above left: Members of the Old England side take to the field at The Oval 1946.
Below far left: Vijay Merchant, India's first outstanding Test batsman.
Centre: Denis Compton and Jack Robertson, Middlesex and England.
Top right: Denis Compton (*centre*) and Leslie Compton (*second from right*).
Above: The 1948 Australians.
Opposite: Patsy Hendren, coaching Sussex juniors.

Australia Bowling

	Overs	Mdns	Runs	Wkts	Overs	Mdns	Runs	Wkts
Lindwall	13	5	30	1				
Miller	19	8	38	3	44	10	125	4
Johnston	25	11	36	5	59	12	147	4
Toshack	14	8	28	1	33	14	60	1
Johnson	5	1	19	—	42	15	66	1
Morris	3	1	4	—				
Barnes					5	2	11	—

England Bowling

	Overs	Mdns	Runs	Wkts	Overs	Mdns	Runs	Wkts
Edrich	18	1	72	—	4	—	20	—
Bedser	44.2	12	113	3	14.3	4	46	2
Barnett	17	5	36	—				
Young	60	28	79	1	10	3	28	—
Laker	55	14	138	4				
Compton	5	—	24	—				
Yardley	17	6	32	2				

Umpires: F. Chester and E. Cooke.

SUSSEX v SOMERSET
Played at Eastbourne, August 18, 19, 20, 1948

DRAWN. AN INNINGS of real merit by Gimblett, who hit his highest score in first-class cricket and set up a record for a Somerset batsman with 310 runs, overshadowed all else in a game that yielded 1,097 runs for 19 wickets. Gimblett, who offered difficult chances when 45 and 115, drove with great power on an easy-paced pitch, and in his stay of nearly seven hours and three-quarters he hit two 6s and thirty-seven 4s. Walford shared with him in an opening stand of 180, and Coope helped him in a fifth wicket partnership realising 210 in two hours and a half. These runs came after Sussex had found run-getting easy. John Langridge and Parks put up 87, and James Langridge (eleven 4s) made 100 in three hours of skilful all-round scoring. Oakes helped him add 89, and Sussex declared at lunch-time on the second day, but, thanks to Gimblett, Somerset easily gained first-innings points.

SUSSEX

First Innings

John Langridge b Tremlett	78
H. W. Parks c Woodhouse b Hazell	46
G. H. G. Doggart c Luckes b Wellard	32
C. Oakes c Walford b Hazell	58
James Langridge c Tremlett b Hazell	100
S. C. Griffith c Luckes b Hazell	36
G. Cox b Hazell	28
P. D. S. Blake b Wellard	16
H. T. Bartlett not out	18
J. Wood c Luckes b Buse	5
J. Cornford not out	1
B 11, l-b 5	16

(9 wkts dec.) 434

Second Innings

c Wellard b Coope	21
c Wellard b Woodhouse	1
not out	14
not out	42
W 1	1

(2 wkts) 79

SOMERSET

H. Gimblett c Wood b Cox	310
M. M. Walford c John Langridge b Wood	71
H. E. Watts b Cornford	11
H. T. Buse c Griffith b James Langridge	7
G. E. S. Woodhouse b Doggart	19
M. Coope b James Langridge	89
M. F. Tremlett *run out*	29
A. W. Wellard c Parks b Cox	24
J. Lawrence *not out*	0
B 12, l-b 11, w 1	24
(8 wkts dec.)	584

W. T. Luckes and H. L. Hazell did not bat.

Somerset Bowling

	Overs	Mdns	Runs	Wkts	Overs	Mdns	Runs	Wkts
Wellard	31	3	109	2				
Tremlett	28	4	89	1				
Buse	28	7	65	—				
Lawrence	26	5	73	—				
Hazell	29	6	82	5				
Gimblett					4	—	18	—
Woodhouse					4	—	8	1
Coope					6	1	25	1
Walford					3	—	12	—
Watts					3	—	15	—

Sussex Bowling

	Overs	Mdns	Runs	Wkts
Wood	37	11	104	1
Cornford	32	10	75	1
Cox	15	2	46	2
Oakes	31	3	121	—
James Langridge	50	10	136	2
John Langridge	8	1	26	—
Bartlett	2	—	12	—
Doggart	8	1	40	1

Umpires: D. Hendren and P. T. Mills.

MIDDLESEX (CHAMPION COUNTY) v REST OF ENGLAND
Played at The Oval, September 13, 15, 16, 17, 1948

MIDDLESEX WON BY nine wickets. For only the third time were the Champion County successful over Rest of England. Yorkshire were winners in 1905 and 1935, the last occasion on which the game took place. The match provided further personal triumphs for Compton and Edrich, who concluded their remarkable season in superb style. Compton, despite a heavily strapped knee which restricted his freedom, played his highest innings in England and was only three short of the 249 he made for Holkar against Bombay in the Indian Championship final of 1944–45. Edrich followed Compton in beating Hayward's record aggregate. Middlesex began by losing three wickets for 53, but Compton and Edrich added 138 before Compton retired through a recurrence of his knee trouble. He resumed on Monday and in all he and Edrich put on 210 and made 426 between them out of the Middlesex total of 543. Compton hit thirty 4s, Edrich a 6 and twenty-one 4s. The Rest lost Washbrook first ball and Place also failed to score. Steady batting by Emmett and a bright display from Evans failed to save the follow-on. Emmett again showed good form, but only Washbrook and Yardley of the others did much and Middlesex were set a simple task. Only fifty minutes' play was necessary on the last day.

MIDDLESEX

First Innings

S. M. Brown c Evans b A. V. Bedser 4
J. D. Robertson c Evans b A. V. Bedser 3
W. J. Edrich st Evans b Goddard 180
F. G. Mann st Evans b Wright 33
D. C. S. Compton st Evans b Goddard 246
R. W. V. Robins c Butler b Goddard 33
A. Thompson c Cranston b Howorth 1
W. F. Price c A. V. Bedser b Goddard 3
J. Sims run out 17
J. Young not out 9
    B 6, l-b 4, n-b 4 14

                    (9 wkts dec.) 543

L. Gray did not bat.

Second Innings

not out 8
lbw b Wright 0
not out 13

                    (1 wkt) 21

REST OF ENGLAND

First Innings

C. Washbrook c Robins b Gray 0
W. Place lbw b Gray 0
R. Howorth st Price b D. Compton 30
G. M. Emmett c Price b Gray 89
N. W. D. Yardley b D. Compton 0
K. Cranston c Price b Gray 18
T. G. Evans lbw b Young 70
A. V. Bedser not out 13
D. V. P. Wright lbw b Young 0
T. W. Goddard st Price b D. Compton 8
H. J. Butler b D. Compton 0
    B 12, l-b 6 18

                    246

Second Innings

b Sims 61
run out 3
c Robertson b Gray 3
b D. Compton 43
lbw b Young 71
b Robins 22
c Thompson b D. Compton 15
b Young 23
c Sims b Gray 29
c and b Gray 14
not out 2
    B 21, l-b 9, w 1 31

                    317

Rest of England Bowling

	Overs	Mdns	Runs	Wkts	Overs	Mdns	Runs	Wkts
Butler	24	4	54	—				
A. V. Bedser	37	10	93	2				
Wright	23	2	97	1	4.2	2	9	1
Goddard	46.3	6	179	4				
Howorth	37	7	106	1				
Cranston					5	1	12	—

Middlesex Bowling

	Overs	Mdns	Runs	Wkts	Overs	Mdns	Runs	Wkts
Gray	18	6	47	4	17.3	4	36	3
Young	29	6	71	2	27	5	77	2
Sims	7	1	29	—	10	—	41	1
Robins	8	1	24	—	5	—	21	1
D. Compton	18.4	2	57	4	16	1	84	2
Thompson					9	1	27	—

Umpires: F. Chester and H. G. Baldwin.

The England touring party leaves for South Africa led by F. G. Mann, standing modestly at the front of his men, waistcoated and with arms behind his back in the hope of giving his opponents a chance. To his left stands Len Hutton, and, on the far left, studying something out of the picture, is the hero of Benoni.

MCC TEAM v NORTH-EASTERN TRANSVAAL
Played at Benoni, December 3, 4, 1948

MCC WON BY an innings and 203 runs. By hitting 300 out of 399 in 181 minutes in his fourth century in five innings, Compton surpassed all his previous fast-scoring achievements. Such power and freedom did he bring into his batting that his strokes included five 6s and forty-two 4s – 198 runs from boundary hits. Compton made his first hundred in sixty-six minutes, his second in seventy-eight and his third in thirty-seven. Often he walked down the pitch before the bowler released the ball and he mixed orthodoxy with a bewildering assortment of unclassified strokes which went from the middle of the bat at lightning speed. He whipped balls pitched outside his off stump to the mid-wicket boundary and he stepped away in order to cut leg-breaks pitched outside the wicket. His was the highest score made by a visiting cricketer to South Africa, his own best to that period and only six short of the record in South African first-class cricket. Much credit was due to Simpson, who gave Compton every opportunity to take the bowling in a stand of 399, second only for an English third wicket to the Compton-Edrich partnership of 424 in May 1948. When taking the last four wickets in five balls in the North-Eastern first innings, Gladwin accomplished the only hat-trick of the tour. In the second innings Jenkins did chief damage. His match-figures were eleven for 137.

NORTH-EAST TRANSVAAL

First Innings

J. Seccombe *c and b* Young	47
T. Louw *c* Griffith *b* Tremlett	5
A. Steyn *c* Compton *b* Jenkins	4
K. Funston *c and b* Jenkins	65
L. Waller *lbw b* Jenkins	0
R. Edwards *c* Mann *b* Jenkins	5
J. Waites *c* Watkins *b* Gladwin	38
H. Patterson *b* Gladwin	2
J. Lindsay *not out*	0
J. Waller *b* Gladwin	0
J. Hayward *b* Gladwin	0
L-b 2	2
	168

Second Innings

c Compton *b* Tremlett	0
c Tremlett *b* Jenkins	14
c Griffith *b* Tremlett	2
b Jenkins	13
lbw b Jenkins	29
c Griffith *b* Jenkins	15
c Compton *b* Jenkins	3
not out	21
b Gladwin	0
st Griffith *b* Jenkins	0
c Griffith *b* Jenkins	11
B 3, l-b 2	5
	113

MCC

C. Washbrook *st* Lindsay *b* J. Waller 38
R. T. Simpson *not out* 130
C. H. Palmer *lbw b* J. Waller 0
D. C. S. Compton *c* Hayward *b* Funston 300
M. F. Tremlett *c* Hayward *b* Funston 7
S. C. Griffith *not out* 9

(4 wkts dec.) 484

F. G. Mann, A. Watkins, R. O. Jenkins, C. Gladwin and J. A. Young did not bat.

MCC Bowling

	Overs	Mdns	Runs	Wkts	Overs	Mdns	Runs	Wkts
Gladwin	15.3	7	27	4	12	5	16	1
Tremlett	10	2	26	1	5	2	7	2
Jenkins	15	1	82	4	13.2	1	55	7
Young	10	2	15	1	10	5	18	—
Compton	4	—	16	—	3	—	12	—

North-Eastern Transvaal Bowling

	Overs	Mdns	Runs	Wkts
Waites	2	—	9	—
Hayward	30	—	175	—
J. Waller	23	—	171	2
Patterson	11	—	94	—
L. Waller	1	—	3	—
Funston	4	—	32	2

SMITH, SIR CHARLES AUBREY, CBE, famous in the world of cricket before making a name on the stage and becoming a universal favourite on the films in comparatively recent years, died on December 20, 1948, aged 85, at Beverly Hills, California. Born in London on July 21, 1863, the son of a doctor, C. A. Smith went to

Charterhouse School and bowled with such success that it came as no surprise that he gained his Blue at Cambridge when a Freshman in 1882. Four times he played at Lord's against Oxford and, by a remarkable series of coincidences, all of these matches ended with a decisive margin of seven wickets, Cambridge winning three of these interesting encounters. In the 1884 match which Oxford won, C. A. Smith was not out 0 in each innings and took two wickets for 65 runs, but in the other three games he showed his worth. In 1883 he helped C. T. Studd dismiss Oxford for 55 and in the second innings he took six wickets for 78 and Oxford just equalled the Cambridge total 215. He made four catches in the match. His last effort for the Light Blues brought six wickets for 81. His captains were the three brothers Studd and the Hon. M. B. Hawke.

He played for Sussex from 1882 until 1896, with varying regularity, and was captain from 1887 to 1889. For Gentlemen at Lord's in 1888 he and S. M. J. Woods dismissed the last four players for one run scored after A. G. Steel handed the ball to Smith. Each of the Cambridge fast bowlers took two of these wickets and Gentlemen won by five runs. In the match Woods took ten wickets for 76 and C. A. Smith five for 36.

In the previous winter he went to Australia, captaining the side organised by Shaw and Shrewsbury, and in 1888–89 he captained the first English side which went to South Africa, Major R. G. Wharton, the Australian, was manager. All the matches were against "odds" except two engagements called "English Team v Eleven of South Africa", but some years afterwards given the description "Tests". During the tour C. A. Smith took 134 wickets at 7.61 each, a modest achievement compared with the 290 wickets at 5.62 credited to John Briggs, the Lancashire left-hander. Smith stayed in South Africa for a time in partnership with M. P. Bowden, of Surrey, a member of the team, as stockbrokers. During this period he captained Transvaal against Kimberley in the first Currie Cup match in April 1890, so initiating a competition which has done much to raise the standard of cricket in South Africa.

Among C. A. Smith's best bowling performances were five wickets for eight runs for Sussex against The University at Cambridge in 1885, and seven for 16 against MCC at Lord's in 1890. A hard-hitting batsman, he scored 142 for Sussex at Hove against Hampshire in 1888.

Over six feet tall, he made an unusual run-up to deliver the ball and so became known as "Round The Corner" Smith. Sometimes he started from a deep mid-off position, at others from behind the umpire, and, as described by W. G. Grace, "it is rather startling when he suddenly appears at the bowling crease".

He maintained his love for cricket to the end. Until a few years ago he captained the Hollywood side and visited England for the Test matches, the last time as recently as 1947, when South Africa were here.

He was knighted in 1944 in recognition of his support of Anglo-American friendship.

A very good Association outside-right, he played for Old Carthusians and Corinthians.
H.P.

WORCESTERSHIRE v MIDDLESEX
Played at Worcester, July 23, 25, 26, 1949

MIDDLESEX WON BY an innings and 54 runs. Robertson, by hitting the highest score of his career, the highest individual score for Middlesex and the largest individual total recorded in England since 1938, put Middlesex in an unassailable position in this match which had an important bearing on the County Championship. Never at fault, Robertson showed excellent judgment in going out to punish the slow bowlers, and his two 6s and thirty-nine 4s were the result of well-timed drives and wristy cuts. He figured in huge stands with Allen, Dewes, Mann and Robins, Middlesex scoring at nearly 100 an hour. Splendid leg-break bowling by Sims and Robins put Middlesex within sight of victory by the end of the second day, and although Cooper, Palmer, Outschoorn, Howorth and Yarnold all provided spirited resistance when Worcestershire followed-on 435 runs behind, they only delayed the inevitable.

MIDDLESEX

J. D. Robertson *not out*	331
S. M. Brown *b* Palmer	3
J. G. Dewes *b* Perks	45
F. G. Mann *c* Bird *b* Palmer	65
G. O. Allen *b* Palmer	98
R. W. V. Robins *c* Cooper *b* Bird	59
B 14, l-b 5, n-b 3	22
(5 wkts dec.)	623

H. Sharp, L. Compton, J. Sims, J. A. Young and L. Gray did not bat.

WORCESTERSHIRE

First Innings

D. Kenyon *c* Robertson *b* Sims	32
E. Cooper *c* Robins *b* Allen	10
C. H. Palmer *st* Compton *b* Young	13
R. E. Bird *not out*	44
R. O. Jenkins *lbw b* Robins	8
R. Howorth *c and b* Robins	0
L. Outschoorn *st* Compton *b* Robins	0
A. F. T. White *b* Sims	9
H. Yarnold *st* Compton *b* Sims	21
R. T. D. Perks *c* Robins *b* Sims	28
P. F. Jackson *c* Mann *b* Sims	14
B 5, l-b 2, w 2	9
	188

Second Innings

hit wkt b Robins	23
b Young	68
lbw b Young	40
b Sharp	4
c Compton *b* Sims	27
c Compton *b* Gray	23
not out	94
b Sims	18
b Young	61
lbw b Gray	0
c Robins *b* Gray	1
B 10, l-b 5, w 6, n-b 1	22
	381

Worcestershire Bowling

	Overs	Mdns	Runs	Wkts
Perks	24	7	92	1
Palmer	30	8	119	3
Jenkins	30	4	153	—
Howorth	24	5	99	—
Jackson	23	1	104	—
Bird	4.3	—	34	1

Middlesex Bowling

	Overs	Mdns	Runs	Wkts	Overs	Mdns	Runs	Wkts
Allen	7	—	26	1	11	1	34	—
Gray	4	—	15	—	13.1	1	26	3
Young	12	4	48	1	56	26	75	3
Sims	19.4	3	54	5	39	5	128	2
Robins	11	1	36	3	26	2	85	1
Sharp					11	5	11	1

Umpires: B. Flint and A. E. Pothecary.

ENGLAND v THE REST

(TEST TRIAL)
Played at Bradford, May 31, June 1, 1950

ENGLAND WON BY an innings and 89 runs. One of the most remarkable representative matches on record finished before lunch on the second day. Such was the mastery of the bowlers on drying turf that in seven hours and fifty minutes of playing time thirty wickets fell for 369 runs, of which Hutton made nearly one-quarter. Although the desperate struggle for runs provided keen interest for spectators, the selectors could have learned little not already known to them. Yardley put in The Rest on winning the toss, and the off-breaks of Laker caused so complete a rout that in 110 minutes they were all out for the lowest total in a match of representative class. The previous smallest score was 30, made by South Africa against England at Port Elizabeth in 1896 and at Edgbaston 1924. On the ground, five miles from his birthplace on which he had enjoyed many League triumphs for Saltaire, Laker dominated the scene. He took two wickets in his first over and a third before conceding a run; in his fifth over he dismissed four more men before being edged for a second single, and he brilliantly caught and bowled the last man. His full analysis was: 14 overs, 12 maidens, 2 runs, 8 wickets. He spun the ball skilfully, his length was immaculate and his direction perfect. The young batsmen opposed to Laker did not possess the ripe experience needed to cope with his skill under conditions so suited to his bowling. England obtained a lead of 202, chiefly through superlative batting by Hutton, ably assisted by Edrich, against bowling of moderate quality apart from that of Berry, the left-hander, and Jenkins with leg spin. Berry did not lose accuracy even when Hutton used every possible means to knock him off his length. Hutton, who made 85 out of 155 in two hours, gave a dazzling display of batsmanship on a difficult pitch. Laker again met with early success in The Rest second innings; but Hollies caused chief damage. He turned the ball sharply and varied flight and pace well. Eric Bedser and Spooner made 42 in the only stand. On the sporting Bradford turf the Australians in 1948 and the West Indies earlier in 1950 also were made to look very ordinary.

THE REST

First Innings

D. J. Kenyon c Evans b Laker 7
D. S. Sheppard lbw b Bailey 4
G. H. G. Doggart c Bailey b Laker 2
P. B. H. May c Hutton b Laker 0
D. B. Carr c Bailey b Laker 0
E. A. Bedser lbw b Laker 3
R. T. Spooner b Laker 0
R. O. Jenkins not out 0
R. Berry b Laker 0
F. S. Trueman st Evans b Bedser 1
L. Jackson c and b Laker 5
B 3, l-b 1, w 1 5

27

Second Innings

lbw b Hollies 9
b Laker 3
st Evans b Hollies 12
b Laker 2
st Evans b Hollies 2
c Evans b Hollies 30
c Yardley b Bedser 22
c Bedser b Hollies 3
c Yardley b Bedser 16
not out 0
st Evans b Hollies 1
B 4, l-b 6, n-b 3 13

113

ENGLAND

L. Hutton b Trueman	85
R. T. Simpson st Spooner b Berry	26
W. J. Edrich lbw b Jenkins	46
J. D. Robertson c Sheppard b Berry	0
J. G. Dewes c Doggart b Berry	34
N. W. D. Yardley c Trueman b Jenkins	13
T. E. Bailey c Spooner b Berry	7
T. G. Evans *run out*	1
J. C. Laker *not out*	6
A. V. Bedser c Jackson b Jenkins	5
W. E. Hollies st Spooner b Berry	4
L-b 1, n-b 1	2
	229

England Bowling

	Overs	Mdns	Runs	Wkts	Overs	Mdns	Runs	Wkts
Bailey	6	4	3	1	5	2	6	—
Bedser	9	3	12	1	9	2	22	2
Laker	14	12	2	8	18	4	44	2
Hollies	7	5	5	—	22.4	13	28	6

The Rest Bowling

	Overs	Mdns	Runs	Wkts
Jackson	12	3	38	—
Bedser	13	—	60	—
Jenkins	10	—	38	3
Berry	32	10	73	5
Trueman	9	3	18	1

Umpires: W. H. Ashdown and H. Elliott.

ENGLAND v WEST INDIES

SECOND TEST MATCH
Played at Lord's, June 24, 26, 27, 28, 29, 1950

WEST INDIES WON by 326 runs. They fully merited their first Test victory in England, which, to their undisguised delight, was gained at the headquarters of cricket. In batting, bowling and fielding they were clearly the superior side, with Ramadhin this time the more successful of the two 20-year-old spin bowlers who during the 1950 summer wrought such destruction among English batsmen. In the match Ramadhin took eleven and Valentine seven wickets.

England, already without Compton, suffered further setbacks before the game began by the withdrawal through injury of Simpson and Bailey. In view of heavy rain on Friday, the selectors gambled on the pitch being helpful to spin by choosing Wardle, left-arm slow, to replace Bailey, but instead the turf played easily from the start, and Yardley found himself with three slow bowlers who turned the ball from leg; he would have wished to bowl all of them from the same end. The teams were presented to the King just before the start when 30,500 were inside the ground, the gates having been closed.

Although Wardle took a wicket with his first ball in Test cricket in England by getting rid of Stollmeyer at 37, West Indies were so much on top that shortly after four o'clock the total stood at 233 for two. Brilliant stroke-play came from Worrell, who drove delightfully and made some astonishing late cuts, and Weekes, whose 63 in ninety minutes contained

Ramadhin (pictured left) and Valentine were two spin bowlers produced by the West Indies just when their fast bowling batteries were silent. The spinning twins did better than all the pace bowlers in the world, reducing English batsmen to ineptitude, Valentine with his orthodox left-arm spin, Ramadhin with right-arm deliveries so difficult to read because of the concealment of the hand till the last moment. The West Indian triumph, popularising calypso as well as cricket, came at just the moment when thousands of emigrants from the Caribbean were making their homes in the great English cities.

ten 4s, but Rae, in much less spectacular manner, performed even more important work for West Indies.

A fine ball by Bedser which swung away and broke back after pitching shattered the wicket of Weekes at 233, and from that point England fought back splendidly. Clever slow bowling by Jenkins, in particular, raised England hopes after tea. In a twenty-minute spell of seven overs he sent back Walcott, Rae and Gomez. Rae, who was badly missed in the gully off Bedser when 79, made no other mistake during a patient innings lasting four hours forty minutes, in which he scored 106 out of 273. At times he appeared content to continue a passive defensive policy, but occasionally he would abandon these tactics, as when in one over he hit Jenkins for three of his fifteen 4s. Largely through the inspiration of Yardley, England atoned for earlier catching errors by first-class ground fielding, and in view of the nature of the pitch they could feel satisfied with their performance of taking seven wickets for 320 runs on the opening day. Bedser was the most consistent and reliable bowler, but luck went against him, especially when he saw two catches missed off him during a fine spell of 22 overs for 17 runs with the new ball.

No more than ten minutes were required to finish the innings on Monday, but England's reply was disappointing in the extreme. Neither Hutton nor Washbrook was in his best form, but both played well enough to take the score to 62 before Hutton dashed down the pitch and was stumped yards out. This began a rout which was checked only by spirited hitting by Wardle, who punched six 4s and took part with Berry in the second highest stand of the innings, 29 for the last wicket.

No blame could be attached to the pitch. It gave slow bowlers a little help, but only to those who used real finger spin as did Ramadhin and Valentine. Ramadhin bowled with the guile of a veteran. He pitched a tantalising length, bowled straight at the wicket and spun enough to beat the bat. No English batsman showed evidence of having mastered the problems of deciding which way Ramadhin would spin and he was too quick through the air for any but the most nimble-footed to go down to meet him on the half-volley with any consistency. Valentine lent able support, but the English batsmen might, with profit, have tackled him more boldly. England's score was their lowest for a completed innings in a home Test against West Indies.

Thanks to a remarkably sustained spell of bowling by Jenkins, England prevented West Indies in their second innings from placing themselves in an impregnable position until the association of Walcott and Gomez. Previously Weekes, Worrell and Stollmeyer gave another exhibition of masterly stroke-play, but with only a twenty-minute rest Jenkins kept one end going from the start until tea, and deserved the reward of the four wickets which fell to him.

Unfortunately for England a second series of fielding blunders played into the hands of West Indies at a time when a slight prospect of victory seemed to exist. The most expensive of these occurred when Walcott had scored nine. He was missed at slip off Edrich, who bowled with plenty of life in using the new ball. Before England met with another success Walcott and Gomez put on 211, beating the record for the sixth wicket in England v West Indies Tests established a few weeks earlier at Manchester by Evans and T. E. Bailey. Walcott and Gomez also set up a record Test stand for any West Indies wicket in England. When Goddard declared, setting England 601 to get to win with nearly two days to play, Walcott, the six-foot-two wicket-keeper-batsman, was only one short of the highest score by a West Indies player in Test cricket in England, 169 not out by G. Headley in 1933. As usual, Walcott scored the majority of his runs by drives, even against the good-length or shorter ball, and leg sweeps. He hit twenty-four 4s. Gomez did not put such force into his strokes, but he provided an admirable and valuable foil.

Two batsmen distinguished themselves in England's second innings. For five hours and a half Washbrook withstood the attack, and his only mistake occurred when, at 93, he gave a hard chance to mid-on. Otherwise he batted excellently; although for the most part refusing to take a risk he hit one 6 and fourteen 4s.

The only other success was Parkhouse, who signalised his first Test with a very good innings, in which he showed encouraging confidence and a variety of strokes until he hit a full toss straight to silly mid-off in the last over of the fourth day when wanting only two runs for 50. This mistake came at a time when thoughts were raised that Washbrook might be capable of saving the match if someone could stay with him. Hutton again was dismissed curiously. He made no stroke at a ball which came with Valentine's arm and hit the middle stump.

England started the last day with six wickets left and 383 runs required to win, but when Ramadhin yorked Washbrook, who did not add to his score, the end was in sight and nothing happened to check the inevitable defeat. Ramadhin and Valentine were again the chief executioners. During the five days the full attendance was 112,000.

R.J.H.

WEST INDIES

First Innings

A. F. Rae c and b Jenkins	106
J. B. Stollmeyer lbw b Wardle	20
F. M. Worrell b Bedser	52
E. Weekes b Bedser	63
C. L. Walcott st Evans b Jenkins	14
G. E. Gomez st Evans b Jenkins	1
R. J. Christiani b Bedser	33
J. D. Goddard b Wardle	14
P. E. Jones c Evans b Jenkins	0
S. Ramadhin not out	1
A. L. Valentine c Hutton b Jenkins	5
B 10, l-b 5, w 1, n-b 1	17

1/37 2/128 3/233 4/262 5/273 326
6/274 7/320 8/320 9/320

Second Innings

b Jenkins	24
b Jenkins	30
c Doggart b Jenkins	45
run out	63
not out	168
c Edrich b Bedser	70
not out	5
c Evans b Jenkins	11
L-b 8, n-b 1	9

1/48 2/75 3/108 (6 wkts dec.) 425
4/146 5/199 6/410

ENGLAND

First Innings
L. Hutton st Walcott b Valentine	35
C. Washbrook st Walcott b Ramadhin	36
W. J. Edrich c Walcott b Ramadhin	8
G. H. G. Doggart lbw b Ramadhin	0
W. G. A. Parkhouse b Valentine	0
N. W. D. Yardley b Valentine	16
T. G. Evans b Ramadhin	8
R. O. Jenkins c Walcott b Valentine	4
J. H. Wardle not out	33
A. V. Bedser b Ramadhin	5
R. Berry c Goddard b Jones	2
B 2, l-b 1, w 1	4
	151

1/62 2/74 3/74 4/75 5/86
6/102 7/110 8/113 9/122

Second Innings
b Valentine	10
b Ramadhin	114
c Jones b Ramadhin	8
b Ramadhin	25
c Goddard b Valentine	48
c Weekes b Valentine	19
c Rae b Ramadhin	2
b Ramadhin	4
lbw b Worrell	21
b Ramadhin	0
not out	0
B 16, l-b 7	23
	274

1/28 2/57 3/140 4/218 5/228
6/238 7/245 8/258 9/258

England Bowling

	Overs	Mdns	Runs	Wkts	Overs	Mdns	Runs	Wkts
Bedser	40	14	60	3	44	16	80	1
Edrich	16	4	30	—	13	2	37	—
Jenkins	35.2	6	116	5	59	13	174	4
Wardle	17	6	46	2	30	10	58	—
Berry	19	7	45	—	32	15	67	—
Yardley	4	1	12	—				

West Indies Bowling

	Overs	Mdns	Runs	Wkts	Overs	Mdns	Runs	Wkts
Jones	8.4	2	13	1	7	1	22	—
Worrell	10	4	20	—	22.3	9	39	1
Valentine	45	28	48	4	71	47	79	3
Ramadhin	43	27	66	5	72	43	86	6
Gomez					13	1	25	—
Goddard					6	6	—	—

Umpires: D. Davies and F. S. Lee.

ENGLAND v AUSTRALIA

FIFTH TEST MATCH
Played at The Oval, August 15, 17, 18, 19, 1953

ENGLAND WON BY eight wickets and so won the Ashes for the first time since 1932–33. It was a most welcome victory in Coronation year and a triumph for Len Hutton, the first modern professional to be entrusted with the captaincy of England. Moreover, he led his team to success on the ground on which he made the world record Test score of 364 in 1938 – the last previous occasion England beat Australia in this country. This was the first time England had won the rubber at home since A. P. F. Chapman's team finished 289 runs ahead on the fourth day on this very ground in 1926.

There was something unique in the victory of Hutton's men as far as England and Australia were concerned. Hutton was the only captain who had lost the toss in all five Tests and yet won the series. In 1905, when Sir Stanley Jackson won the toss in the five Tests, England were victorious in the only two matches that were decided. In 1909, when M. A. Noble equalled Jackson's feat, Australia carried home the Ashes by two matches to one. John Goddard, of the West Indies, was similarly successful in India in 1948–49, and

The Oval crowd wishes to engulf the not-out England batsmen Edrich and Compton, after the Middlesex pair have knocked off the runs required to win the 1953 series against the Australians, and bring back the Ashes to England after a period of twenty years.

the only parallel to the failure of Hassett's team occurred in South Africa in 1928–29. Then H. G. Deane successfully spun the coin five times, but England won by two clear victories.

The absence of a genuine spin bowler proved a severe handicap to Australia. The issue was virtually decided on the third afternoon when Australia, 31 behind on the first innings, lost half their side to Laker and Lock for 61.

Compared with the fourth Test, England brought in May and Trueman for Watson and Simpson, and made Wardle twelfth man. For the first time in the series England possessed a properly balanced attack. The introduction of Trueman, who faced Australia for the first time, proved a wise decision. As Johnston had recovered from his knee injury, Australia preferred him to Benaud.

As in 1926, stories of long all-night queues frightened away many would-be spectators on the first day when the ground was comfortable with 26,300 people present. The news that Hassett had again won the toss was received gloomily by most England supporters, but by mid-afternoon, when seven Australian wickets were down for 160, pessimism changed to optimism.

At first the cricket took the expected course. With six days at their disposal, there was no need for Australia to hurry, but like true cricketers they never ignored the loose ball. For example, the second ball of the day, a full toss from Bedser, was hit truly by Hassett to the long-leg boundary.

Trueman was given a great welcome. He set a normal field for an easy-paced pitch: two slips, a gully and two short legs. He began with a lively over. The fifth ball Morris tried to sweep, and as it landed in Evans's gloves Trueman appealed for a catch. The last ball nearly earned a wicket, Compton at short fine leg just failing to reach a very hard chance.

Clearly neither bowler intended to allow Australia any complacency. It was all-out attack with both sides striving for the mastery. Trueman, taking one of the longest runs known in cricket, covered a distance of at least 25 yards in fifteen long strides and required forty-five minutes to complete his first spell of five overs which cost 12 runs.

Then came Bailey, but the initiative appeared to be with Australia. Towards the end of an hour Bedser broke the opening stand in his eighth over when his swerve deceived Morris, who, offering no stroke, turned his back and was leg-before. The Surrey giant had now dismissed Morris five times in nine Tests innings in this series and altogether eighteen times in twenty Tests. This success gave England timely encouragement, and within ten minutes Bailey claimed the dangerous Miller, who, padding up, was also lbw. Hutton used Trueman in short spells, and at lunch the total was 98 for two wickets – Hassett 51, Harvey 29.

Light rain during the interval seemed to enliven the pitch, and suddenly Bedser and Trueman drilled a big hole in the Australia batting. A fine stand of 66 between Hassett and Harvey was terminated when Hassett, playing forward, gave a catch to Evans. In the following over Harvey mistimed a hook and Hutton, running with his back to the pitch from short square leg, brought off a grand catch.

Another shower held up the game for ten minutes, and then de Courcy, having already flashed at Trueman, repeated his error and Evans held another catch – wide of the off stump. That made half the side out in only two and a half hours for 118, but while Archer defended Hole played a splendid innings. Hole declined to be subdued, and though he narrowly escaped when Lock dived in Bedser's leg-trap, he pulled and drove until Trueman beat him by pace and Evans seized his third catch. Without addition, Archer, having stayed nearly an hour, lifted the first ball on Bedser's return to the attack back to the bowler. This turned out to be Bedser's final wicket in the series, but it was an historic one. It gave him his 39th of the 1953 Tests and so he beat M. W. Tate's 38 of 1924–25, the previous best in England-Australia matches.

Now came Lindwall, and with only three wickets to fall he launched a hot attack, ably assisted by the left-handed Davidson. For an hour and fifty minutes Lindwall indulged in a magnificent display of clean hitting. His off and cover drives were of the highest class. The new ball at 210 did not halt him and he hit eight sparkling boundaries before he was last out to the fourth catch of the innings by Evans. By adding 157 the last five wickets more than doubled the score, and in the circumstances no one could deny that Australia had made an excellent recovery.

Although there had been some fine catching, England's fielding again left room for much criticism, for Davidson, Lindwall and Johnston were missed by Edrich, Graveney and Bedser respectively. Still, England had every reason to be satisfied in dismissing Australia for 275. Trueman fully justified his selection. Always hostile, he made good use of the occasional bouncer and he looked the part.

Before bad light stopped the struggle at 6. 17 p.m. there was time for Lindwall and Miller each to send down one over, and England might well have lost Hutton in Lindwall's tearaway effort. The fourth and fifth balls were bouncers. The fifth flew off the handle of Hutton's bat and five slips surged forward for the catch which unexpectedly never arrived. The ball dropped short because it lost its pace in transit through striking Hutton's cap, which it removed. The cap just missed the stumps or Hutton might have been out hit wicket.

If Saturday belonged to England, Monday went to Australia, for the close of play found England 235 for seven – 40 behind with only three wickets left. The gates were closed long before play was resumed at 11.30 a.m. and thousands failed to gain admission. Upon England's batting this day everyone felt that the destination of the Ashes depended, but after a promising beginning the initiative passed to Australia.

The conditions were not in their favour, but they bowled and fielded as if their very lives were at stake. They dropped only one catch compared with five by England on Saturday and they tied England down to a scoring rate of less than 40 runs an hour. For a time England prospered. An early setback occurred when Edrich, having batted splendidly, left at 37, but there followed a grand partnership of 100 between Hutton and May, who were together two hours twenty minutes. When that was broken England went through a very bad time, chiefly because of the uncertainty of Compton.

Previously Hutton had been master of the situation, but when joined by Compton he added only six in the next half hour before being bowled by a well-pitched-up ball from Johnston which moved from leg and hit the middle stump. Third out at 154, Hutton made his 82 in three hours forty minutes and hit eight 4s. The departure of Hutton was a serious setback for England. The new ball was due, but Johnston was so dominant with cleverly flighted left-arm slows that Hassett was able to save Lindwall and Miller for an all-out assault after tea.

When the interval arrived with the total 165 for three, Compton had spent an hour over 16 and Graveney half an hour for two. On a day made for batting, the bowling figures read: Johnston 10–5–14–2; Hole 7–4–8–0. Lindwall and Miller were only warming up after tea with the old ball when Compton's disappointing exhibition ended in a spectacular flying catch by Langley well wide of the leg stump.

Not until the 78th over did Australia take the new ball, and it brought immediate success. The second ball was enough for Graveney, who fell to a brilliant first slip catch, Miller holding a catch at ankle height. That meant half the England wickets down for 170. Miller had five slips, but Evans did not allow anything to worry him. Soon he was hitting cleanly, and in an over which cost Lindwall 10 were two smashing hooks. England had stopped the slump, but the position was still precarious, particularly when Davidson at square leg cut off a vicious stroke by Evans from Johnston. Evans slipped on being sent back and Langley swept a lightning return into the stumps.

Meanwhile Bailey had begun with 15 in thirty-five minutes, but on being joined by Laker he changed his methods and brilliant strokes to the off gave him 11 in an over from Johnston. Laker soon went, but Lock closed an end for the last forty minutes of a dramatic day, England finishing at 235 for seven wickets – Bailey 35, Lock 4.

The way England pulled the game round on the third day was scarcely believable. Light rain at 6 a.m. and the heavy roller left the pitch easy paced. Again Bailey foiled the Australian bowlers, but they gained an early success. The first ball of Lindwall's second over lifted and Lock was caught off his glove in the leg trap. More dazzling fielding, notably by de Courcy, saved many runs, but not even the odd bouncer troubled Bailey, and he and Trueman put on 25, so that only 13 runs separated the totals when the last man, Bedser, walked to the crease.

England took twenty minutes to get those runs. Every ball seemed vital until Bedser lifted one from Johnston over mid-off and the batsmen ran four. Miller misjudged its pace and delayed chasing it. Now Australia became concerned mainly in preventing scoring strokes and Hassett widened the field, but Bailey, to whom Miller bowled round the wicket, drove and hooked beautifully until, going forward to Archer, he was bowled on the stroke of lunch time by a fine ball which hit the top of the stumps. Hitting seven 4s and never offering a chance, Bailey withstood the bowling for three and three-quarter hours, his final stand with Bedser yielding 44. Johnston bowled his left-arm slows with rare skill and Lindwall and Miller never spared themselves.

To Hutton must be given the credit for bringing about Australia's subsequent collapse. He realised by the way Morris slammed Bedser past cover and Trueman to leg that the batsmen would thrive on pace bowling on this somewhat lifeless pitch for which Hassett had ordered the heavy roller. Hutton allowed Trueman only two overs and Bedser three before at 19 he introduced the Surrey spinners, Laker (right-arm off-breaks) and Lock (left-arm slow). That was the move that brought home the Ashes. The Australian batsmen had not settled down before they were confronted by spin, and their vulnerability to the turning ball as well as their fear of it led to their undoing. Suddenly a day which began so gloomily for England swung completely Hutton's way.

Laker started the Australian procession. Bowling round the wicket, he twice beat Hassett, and then with the last ball of his first over he got the Australian captain leg-before as he retreated into his wicket. One hour later half the Australia team were back in the pavilion for 61.

In one astonishing spell of fourteen minutes four wickets fell while only two runs were scored. Lock went over the wicket to the left-handed batsmen, but Hole threatened danger with free hitting at the expense of Laker. Again Hutton countered. He placed a deep extra cover as well as a long-on, and Laker with his very next ball got Hole lbw.

Lock never erred in length or direction from the pavilion end, and as Harvey shaped to drive he knocked back his off stump. In the next over Trueman at short square leg hugged a sharp catch from Miller, and then Morris, playing back and trying to force Lock away, was leg-before. So on this gloriously sunny afternoon Australia found themselves confronted with impending defeat. With half their wickets down they were no more than 30 runs ahead.

Hassett saw that the only possible escape was a repetition of Lindwall's method. Young Archer began the offensive by helping himself to 11 in an over from Laker, but at 85 de Courcy was brilliantly run out by Bailey who at mid-wicket swooped on a stroke by Archer. De Courcy tried to get back but Lock broke the wicket at his leisure.

When Archer on-drove Lock magnificently for 6, Hutton placed May on the pavilion rails and Trueman at deep extra cover, but Archer and Davidson still hit at will. A boundary to long leg and then a hook for 6 gave Davidson 10 in two balls from Laker, so that at tea Australia were 131 for six – Archer 44, Davidson 21.

The break gave England a chance to review the position. Clearly they needed to plan to avoid more heavy punishment. Next Laker exploited leg-theory with only three off fielders and Lock off-theory with only three leg fielders. This sensible arrangement plus two steady spells by Bedser resulted in the four remaining wickets being taken for 31 more runs. Archer, who besides his 6 hit seven 4s, batted an hour for his thrilling 49. Lindwall hooked Lock for 6, received a life at slip from the same bowler, and then, essaying another six, was caught on the pavilion fence by Compton.

England, having dismissed Australia in two hours forty-five minutes for 162, needed 132 to win with ample time at their disposal. They owed much to Lock. The pitch gave him little help, yet such was his finger spin allied to skilful flighting and change of pace that he took five wickets for 45. Laker, too, played a valuable part. He did not approach Lock in accuracy, but he accounted for the dangerous right-handed hitters, Hassett, Miller, Hole and Lindwall. Lock removed three left-handers, Morris, Harvey and Davidson, as well as Archer and Langley.

Fifty minutes remained on Tuesday when Hutton and Edrich began England's final task. Both produced some excellent strokes, but at 24 Hutton brought about his own dismissal. He hit Miller firmly to square leg and took the obvious single, but when de Courcy fumbled he tried to steal a second run and failed to get home. Hutton looked terribly disappointed as he walked slowly back to the pavilion. May stayed with Edrich for the last quarter of an hour and England finished at 38 for one wicket.

They now needed 94, and only rain and a sticky pitch were likely to deprive them of the victory so near their grasp. How those Australians fought to hold the Ashes! Johnston bowled tantalising slows from the Vauxhall end without relief and little help from the slightly worn pitch from 11.30 a.m. till 2.45 p.m., when, with only nine more runs wanted, Hassett ended the struggle by going on with Morris. Lindwall bowled for seventy-five minutes in his first spell, returned for the last ten minutes before lunch, and continued for another half hour. Here is their analysis for the fourth day: Johnston 23–12–36–0; Lindwall 19–5–38–0.

At first Edrich and May made very slow progress: 14 in the first half hour and 24 in the hour. Harvey, Davidson and Lindwall excelled in the field. The attack was always directed at the stumps. Only rarely did Lindwall risk a bumper; runs were too precious to be given away. Slowly the score crept to 88, and then Miller, having dispensed with his slips – five men were on the leg side for his off-spin – got May caught at short fine leg. The stand produced 64 in one hour fifty minutes.

Earlier Edrich magnificently hooked two successive bumpers from Lindwall. Now he was joined by his Middlesex colleague, Compton, and they took England to victory. Compton made the winning hit at seven minutes to three when he swept Morris to the boundary.

At once the crowd swarmed across the ground while Edrich, who batted three and a half hours and hit six 4s, fought his way to the pavilion with Compton and the Australian team. In a memorable scene both captains addressed the crowd, stressing the excellent spirit in which all the matches had been contested both on and off the field.

The attendance for the Test reached 115,000 and the receipts amounted to £37,000.

N.P.

AUSTRALIA

First Innings

A. L. Hassett c Evans b Bedser	53
A. R. Morris lbw b Bedser	16
K. R. Miller lbw b Bailey	1
R. N. Harvey c Hutton b Trueman	36
G. B. Hole c Evans b Trueman	37
J. H. de Courcy c Evans b Trueman	5
R. G. Archer c and b Bedser	10
A. K. Davidson c Edrich b Laker	22
R. R. Lindwall c Evans b Trueman	62
G. R. Langley c Edrich b Lock	18
W. A. Johnston not out	9
B 4, n-b 2	6
	275

1/38 2/41 3/107 4/107 5/118
6/160 7/160 8/207 9/245

Second Innings

lbw b Laker	10
lbw b Lock	26
c Trueman b Laker	0
b Lock	1
lbw b Laker	17
run out	4
c Edrich b Lock	49
b Lock	21
c Compton b Laker	12
c Trueman b Lock	2
not out	6
B 11, l-b 3	14
	162

1/23 2/59 3/60 4/61 5/61
6/85 7/135 8/140 9/144

ENGLAND

First Innings

L. Hutton b Johnston	82
W. J. Edrich lbw b Lindwall	21
P. B. H. May c Archer b Johnston	39
D. C. S. Compton c Langley b Lindwall	16
T. W. Graveney c Miller b Lindwall	4
T. E. Bailey b Archer	64
T. G. Evans run out	28
J. C. Laker c Langley b Miller	1
G. A. R. Lock c Davidson b Lindwall	4
F. S. Trueman b Johnston	10
A. V. Bedser not out	22
B 9, l-b 5, w 1	15
	306

1/37 2/137 3/154 4/167 5/170
6/210 7/225 8/237 9/262

Second Innings

run out	17
not out	55
c Davidson b Miller	37
not out	22
L-b 1	1
(2 wkts)	132

1/24 2/88

England Bowling

	Overs	Mdns	Runs	Wkts	Overs	Mdns	Runs	Wkts
Bedser	29	3	88	3	11	2	24	—
Trueman	24.3	3	86	4	2	1	4	—
Bailey	14	3	42	1				
Lock	9	2	19	1	21	9	45	5
Laker	5	—	34	1	16.5	2	75	4

Australia Bowling

	Overs	Mdns	Runs	Wkts	Overs	Mdns	Runs	Wkts
Lindwall	32	7	70	4	21	5	46	—
Miller	34	12	65	1	11	3	24	1
Johnston	45	16	94	3	29	14	52	—
Davidson	10	1	26	—				
Archer	10.3	2	25	1	1	1	—	—
Hole	11	6	11	—				
Hassett					1	—	4	—
Morris					0.5	—	5	—

Umpires: F. S. Lee and D. Davies.

YORKSHIRE v SUSSEX
Played at Hull, June 2, 3, 5, 1954

YORKSHIRE WON BY an innings and 20 runs. The all-round skill of Wardle served Yorkshire well. Going on in the first innings with Sussex 30 for one, Wardle in the next two and a half hours took the remaining nine wickets. Had all chances been held, his figures would have been even better. Lowson, Wilson and Watson batted soundly enough for Yorkshire to finish the first day on terms with eight wickets left, and next day, with Wardle (eleven 4s) hitting hard and then revelling in a crumbling pitch, they pressed home their advantage. The last morning's cricket consisted of two overs, Wardle finishing with match figures of 16 wickets for 112.

Johnny Wardle, amateur cartoonist and professional left-arm spin bowler, whose sense of humour and general irreverence ended inevitably with his departure from first-class cricket, due to the odd sense of justice displayed by the Yorkshire County club.

SUSSEX

First Innings

J. Langridge *b* Wardle	33
D. V. Smith *c* Hutton *b* Trueman	4
G. H. G. Doggart *c* Lowson *b* Wardle	28
J. M. Parks *c* Watson *b* Wardle	2
K. G. Suttle *b* Wardle	17
A. S. Oakman *c* Wilson *b* Wardle	45
N. I. Thomson *st* Booth *b* Wardle	4
A. E. James *lbw b* Wardle	0
R. G. Marlar *b* Wardle	14
R. T. Webb *not out*	0
D. J. Wood *b* Wardle	0
B 2, l-b 5	7

1/8 2/67 3/69 4/74 5/111   154
6/123 7/129 8/150 9/154

Second Innings

lbw b Trueman	5
c Hutton *b* Wardle	6
b Appleyard	5
lbw b Wardle	35
b Wardle	2
lbw b Trueman	40
b Wardle	1
st Booth *b* Wardle	39
b Wardle	17
c Illingworth *b* Wardle	8
not out	9
B 2, l-b 8, n-b 1	11

1/11 2/15 3/21 4/24 5/99   178
6/99 7/100 8/132 9/163

YORKSHIRE

L. Hutton *b* Wood	1
F. A. Lowson *lbw b* Oakman	33
J. V. Wilson *c* James *b* Marlar	75
W. Watson *run out*	48
N. W. D. Yardley *b* Marlar	35
D. B. Close *c* Webb *b* Thomson	34
R. Illingworth *b* Thomson	9
J. H. Wardle *not out*	66
R. Booth *c* James *b* Wood	23
F. S. Trueman *run out*	1
R. Appleyard *not out*	10
B 11, l-b 6	17

1/2 2/75 3/148 4/195 5/206   (9 wkts dec.) 352
6/241 7/252 8/325 9/332

Yorkshire Bowling

	Overs	Mdns	Runs	Wkts	Overs	Mdns	Runs	Wkts
Trueman	20	6	45	1	13	1	26	2
Appleyard	15	5	33	—	32	4	59	1
Yardley	3	1	7	—				
Wardle	25.4	11	48	9	25	13	64	7
Close	4	1	14	—	4	—	18	—

Sussex Bowling

	Overs	Mdns	Runs	Wkts
Wood	19	1	57	2
Thomson	27	9	64	2
James	16	4	45	—
Marlar	32	8	90	2
Oakman	37	12	79	1

Umpires: W. F. Price and W. T. Jones.

ENGLAND v PAKISTAN

SECOND TEST MATCH
Played at Nottingham, July 1, 2, 3, 5, 1954

ENGLAND WON BY an innings and 129 runs. Pakistan, still striving to acclimatise themselves to cold, wet weather and to adjust their cricket to soft pitches, offered moderate opposition to a side which, although lacking Hutton, who was unfit, showed superiority in all phases. England achieved their first victory at Trent Bridge since 1930, with over ten hours to spare.

When Pakistan began batting on a true pitch, Hanif and Alim-ud-Din faced the England opening attack confidently enough and, despite the dismissal of Alim-ud-Din, neither team could claim appreciable advantage in the first hour. Then Sheppard, deputy to Hutton as captain and opening batsman, called upon Appleyard for his first bowl in Test cricket. No one could have wished for a better start than made by the 30-year-old Yorkshireman, who resumed big cricket that season after two years' illness.

Hanif was leg-before to Appleyard's second ball; Maqsood snicked a catch to the wicket-keeper in his third over; the first ball of the next hit Waqar's middle stump and the second of his fifth sent the off stump of Imtiaz flying. In this dramatic spell of 26 balls, during which the Pakistan total changed from 37 for one to 55 for five, Appleyard took four wickets for six runs. His mixture of in-swingers, off-spinners and leg-cutters, his variation of pace and flight, bore the stamp of a high-skilled craftsman. That exciting period broke the back of the innings and, although Kardar led a commendable rally, Pakistan were all out before tea. On turf so favourable to batsmen, the need for improvement in forward play was clearly revealed.

By contrast, Simpson at once settled into his most pleasing game, driving and hooking with full power and timing his glances admirably. By the close England stood 36 behind with eight wickets left. The one batting failure was May, who, attempting to force a ball well outside his off-stump, pulled it into his wicket.

The sureness of Simpson and Compton's batting next morning carried ominous signs for Pakistan, whose best bowler, Fazal Mahmood, was handicapped by a pulled leg muscle which forced him to shorten his run. Soon after England went in front, however, Compton (20) gave a sharp chance off Fazal. That turned out to be a most expensive miss. Immediately after reaching a handsome century, Simpson picked the wrong ball to hit, but Pakistan's troubles were only in their infancy. First came a fourth-wicket stand of 154 in eighty-five minutes. Well as Compton batted, Graveney played even better. Some of his punishing drives left the bat with the sound of a pistol shot. So did the stroke from which Maqsood courageously, or in self-preservation, caught him at mid-off. England held a formidable position when Bailey joined Compton. This became further strengthened by a partnership of 192 in an hour and three-quarters. Compton scored all but 27 of the runs, yet he owed much to Bailey, who, recognising his partner's form and mood, did all he could to give him the bowling. Making full use of further escapes when 120 and 171, Compton sent the bowling to all parts of the field with a torrent of strokes, orthodox and improvised, crashing and delicate, against which Kardar could not set a field and the bowlers knew not where to pitch. By methods reminiscent of his former glories, Compton raced through his second hundred in eighty minutes and he made his highest score in his 100 innings for England in four hours fifty minutes before missing a leg-break from Khalid Hassan who, at 16, was the youngest cricketer to be chosen for a Test Match. In the record Test innings played in Nottingham, Compton hit a 6 and thirty-three 4s. Until Sheppard declared, the rest of the England innings came as anti-climax.

Pakistan faced an hour's batting before the close, as well as arrears of 401, but so spiritedly did Hanif and Alim-ud-Din tackle the situation that they made 43 in the first half hour and stayed together to the end. A day on which **496** runs were scored for four wickets remained a triumph for Compton, but the memory of Hanif's fierce hooks and cuts lingered nearly as much.

Next day Hanif resumed his aggressiveness until, having crisply made all but eleven of his runs in boundaries, he fell to the alertness of Evans behind the wicket. Rain limited play to three-quarters of an hour before lunch and cricket was then held up until after tea. For a short time afterwards the ball lifted nastily. One delivery which kicked from a length brought Statham the wicket of Waqar, but soon the turf eased, so that Pakistan's closing score of 189 for six was again disappointing. The best and most adventurous batting was that of Maqsood, who hit two 6s and eight 4s. Unfortunately for Pakistan he did not show discretion in trying for another six off Appleyard, Statham confidently atoning for a previous fielding mistake. Off the previous ball May had held a mighty hit just over the square-leg boundary. Much rain fell during the week-end, but the game began promptly on Monday, when, notwithstanding solid work by Fazal, Sheppard brought it to a close by catching Aslam a quarter of an hour before lunch. R.J.H.

PAKISTAN

First Innings

Hanif Mohammad lbw b Appleyard 19
Alim-ud-Din b Statham 4
Waqar Hassan b Appleyard 7
Maqsood Ahmed c Evans b Appleyard 6
Imtiaz Ahmed b Appleyard 11
A. H. Kadar c Compton b Bedser 28
Fazal Mahmood c Sheppard b Bedser 14
M. E. Z. Ghazali b Statham 18
Mohammad Aslam b Wardle 16
Khalid Hassan c May b Appleyard 10
Khan Mohammad not out 13
    B 9, l-b 1, n-b 1 11

1/26 2/37 3/43 4/50 5/55   157
6/86 7/111 8/121 9/138

Second Innings

c Evans b Bedser 51
b Statham 18
c Evans b Statham 7
c Statham b Appleyard 69
lbw b Wardle 33
c Graveney b Wardle 4
b Statham 36
c Statham b Bedser 14
c Sheppard b Appleyard 18
not out 7
c Compton b Wardle 8
    B 4, l-b 3 7

1/69 2/70 3/95 4/164   272
5/168 6/189 7/216 8/242 9/254

ENGLAND

D. S. Sheppard c Imtiaz b Khan 37
R. T. Simpson b Khalid Hassan 101
P. B. H. May b Khan 0
D. C. S. Compton b Khalid Hassan 278
T. W. Graveney c Maqsood b Kardar 84
T. E. Bailey not out 36
T. G. Evans b Khan 4
J. H. Wardle not out 14
    B 2, l-b 1, n-b 1 4

1/98 2/102 3/185   (6 wkts dec.) 558
4/339 5/531 6/536

A. V. Bedser, J. B. Statham and R. Appleyard did not bat.

England Bowling

	Overs	Mdns	Runs	Wkts	Overs	Mdns	Runs	Wkts
Bedser	21	8	30	2	30	11	83	2
Statham	18	3	38	2	20	3	66	3
Appleyard	17	5	51	5	30.4	8	72	2
Bailey	3	—	18	—				
Wardle	6	3	9	1	32	17	44	3

Pakistan Bowling

	Overs	Mdns	Runs	Wkts
Fazal Mahmood	47	7	148	—
Khan Mohammad	40	3	155	3
Kardar	28	4	110	1
Khalid Hassan	21	1	116	2
Maqsood Ahmed	3	—	25	—

Umpires: F. Chester and T. Spencer.

ENGLAND v AUSTRALIA

THIRD TEST MATCH

Played at Melbourne, December 31, 1954, January 1, 3, 4, 5, 1955

ENGLAND WON BY 128 runs at nineteen minutes past one on the fifth day with a day to spare. As in the previous Test, the combined speed of Tyson and Statham proved too much for Australia and again the two young amateur batsmen, Cowdrey (102) and May (91), carried the England batting on a sporting pitch which was said to have been "doctored" on the Sunday. Certainly large cracks were evident on Saturday yet on Monday these had closed and for a time the surface behaved more kindly to batsmen. The Victorian Cricket Association and the Melbourne Cricket Club held an inquiry into a report published in *The Age* alleging watering and issued the following statement:

"After a searching inquiry it is emphatically denied that the pitch or any part of the cricket ground has been watered since the commencement of the third Test match on Friday, December 31."

With Compton fit England had their strongest side (Bedser again being omitted) and Australia welcomed back Ian Johnson, their captain, and Miller, but Langley, the wicket-keeper, stood down through injury which gave Maddocks his opportunity to make his début in Test cricket.

This time Hutton, winning the toss, decided to bat, but apart from Cowdrey, Evans and Bailey, England made a sorry show. Cowdrey went in when Edrich and May had fallen for 21 and soon he saw Hutton and Compton follow, these four wickets going down in less than an hour for 41.

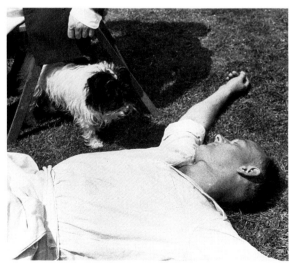

When the England side left for Australia in 1954–55, it included two talking points. The captain of England was a professional, Len Hutton, who was never considered worthy of being appointed to a similar position of authority by his county. The second surprise was the omission from the party of Fred Trueman. Instead, the selectors chose Frank Tyson of Northamptonshire, seen here in a dead faint after hearing of his preferment. Tyson went on to win the series for England.

Then another defiant amateur, Bailey, joined Cowdrey and they checked the Australian bowlers for two hours, adding 74, following which there came a Kent partnership by Cowdrey and Evans that produced 54, before the last four wickets fell for 22. For four hours Cowdrey batted without mistake, getting his body and bat behind short rising balls which Lindwall and Miller were able to bowl off this pitch almost at will. Cowdrey specialised in perfectly-timed drives, both straight and to cover, and he forced the ball skilfully off his legs.

Miller bowled magnificently throughout the ninety minutes before lunch when his figures were 9 overs, 8 maidens, 5 runs, 3 wickets. There were only two scoring strokes against him, a cover drive for 3 by Compton and one for 2 by Cowdrey. As Miller's knee was still suspect Johnson later preferred to conserve his energy for batting. Hutton, troubled by a heavy cold, decided only at the last minute to play.

So England faced the second day knowing that yet again the bowlers must rescue them from a crisis, and thanks to Tyson and Statham ably assisted by Bailey and Appleyard the first eight Australian wickets fell for 151. Hutton used his bowlers in short spells, for the heat was stifling. As Compton could not field, having bruised his thumb when he fell to a bouncer, Wilson acted as substitute, excelling in the leg trap.

Maddocks, who had kept wicket neatly and efficiently, rallied Australia. Arriving when six men had gone for 115 he saw the total to 188 for eight at the close, having made 36 in two and a quarter hours. Maddocks batted another half-hour making top score, 47. He and Johnson added 54 and with Johnson lasting altogether two hours Australia gained a lead of 40, their last four wickets adding 116 against England's 22.

It was essential that the early England batsmen did not let down their side a second time and the arrears were cleared before a turning ball across the wicket took Edrich's off stump. So at eight minutes to three May joined Hutton and proceeded to play masterly cricket in which the straight drive predominated. There was always the possibility that he might be trapped by a "creeper", but May watched the ball intently. At 96 he saw Hutton fall to one which moved fast and low from outside the off stump. The captain had served his side well by remaining nearly two and a half hours and giving a fine example of watchfulness and concentration. With May in such form, Cowdrey preferred to take the defensive, but soon he played on, England being 159 for three at the close; May 83, Compton 10.

On the fourth day May soon left having batted three hours twenty minutes and hit eight 4s. Bailey defended for two and three-quarter hours but Evans and Wardle hit gaily, Wardle taking 16 in one over from Johnston and 14 from the next by Johnson. Actually Wardle hit 38 out of 46 in forty minutes, but this time the rest of the tail failed so that Australia were left to make 240 to win.

A superb right-hand catch by Cowdrey at forward short-leg when he disposed of Morris brought England their first success at 23, but in order to keep Miller fresh, Benaud came next and both he and Favell exercised great care until Appleyard yorked Favell. Nearly half an hour remained that day and Benaud (19) and Harvey (9) raised the total to 79 for two.

This meant that Australia still required 165, a task that seemed far from impossible. The pitch was worn and the experts predicted that England must look to Appleyard, pointing out that the conditions were made for his off spin, and probably they were right, but Tyson and Statham saw England home without Hutton having to look elsewhere for any bowling.

Sheer speed through the air coupled with the chance of a shooter at any moment left the Australian batsmen nonplussed. Tyson blazed through them like a bush fire. In seventy-nine minutes the match was all over, the eight remaining wickets crashing for 36 runs. Here are the bowling figures:

        Tyson   6.3 overs, 0 maidens, 16 runs, 6 wickets.
        Statham 6   overs, 1 maiden, 19 runs, 2 wickets.

A wonderful leg-side catch by Evans when Harvey glanced the seventh ball of the day heralded the collapse. The loss of Harvey was a terrible blow to Australia and with Benaud hooking too soon and Edrich catching Miller at slip from a ball which lifted, Tyson claimed three wickets in 21 balls in the first half-hour.

Then Statham accounted for Hole, who flashed; Maddocks played on to Tyson and in the same over Lindwall went to drive a half-volley which shot under his bat. Next Statham bowled Archer with a fast full toss and finally Evans took his third catch, this time from Johnston high with the left hand, Australia being all out in three hours and five minutes.

The full attendance for the match was 300,270. The receipts, £A47,933, were a record for any Australian match.

ENGLAND

First Innings

L. Hutton c Hole b Miller	12
W. J. Edrich c Lindwall b Miller	4
P. B. H. May c Benaud b Lindwall	0
M. C. Cowdrey b Johnson	102
D. C. S. Compton c Barvey b Miller	4
T. E. Bailey c Maddocks b Johnston	30
T. G. Evans lbw b Archer	20
J. H. Wardle b Archer	0
F. H. Tyson b Archer	6
J. B. Statham b Archer	3
R. Appleyard not out	1
B 9	9

1/14 2/21 3/29 4/41 5/115   191
6/169 7/181 8/181 9/190

Second Innings

lbw b Archer	42
b Johnston	13
b Johnston	91
b Benaud	7
c Maddocks b Archer	23
not out	24
c Maddocks b Miller	22
b Johnson	38
c Harvey b Johnston	6
c Favell b Johnston	0
b Johnston	6
B 2, l-b 4, w 1	7

1/40 2/96 3/128 4/173 5/185   279
6/211 7/257 8/273 9/273

AUSTRALIA

First Innings

L. Favell lbw b Statham	25
A. R. Morris lbw b Tyson	3
K. R. Miller c Evans b Statham	7
R. N. Harvey b Appleyard	31
G. B. Hole b Tyson	11
R. Benaud c sub b Appleyard	15
R. G. Archer b Wardle	23
L. Maddocks c Evans b Statham	47
R. R. Lindwall b Statham	13
I. W. Johnson not out	33
W. A. Johnston b Statham	11
B 7, l-b 3, n-b 2	12

1/15 2/38 3/43 4/65 5/92   231
6/115 7/134 8/151 9/205

Second Innings

b Appleyard	30
c Cowdrey b Tyson	4
c Edrich b Tyson	6
c Evans b Tyson	11
c Evans b Statham	5
b Tyson	22
b Statham	15
b Tyson	0
lbw b Tyson	0
not out	4
c Evans b Tyson	0
B 1, l-b 13	14

1/23 2/57 3/77 4/86 5/87   111
6/97 7/98 8/98 9/110

Australia Bowling

	Overs	Mdns	Runs	Wkts	Overs	Mdns	Runs	Wkts
Lindwall	13	—	59	1	18	3	52	—
Miller	11	8	14	3	18	6	35	1
Archer	13.6	4	33	4	24	7	50	2
Benaud	7	—	30	—	8	2	25	1
Johnston	12	6	26	1	24.5	2	85	5
Johnson	11	3	20	1	8	2	25	1

England Bowling

	Overs	Mdns	Runs	Wkts	Overs	Mdns	Runs	Wkts
Tyson	21	2	68	2	12.3	1	27	7
Statham	16.3	—	60	5	11	1	38	2
Bailey	9	1	33	—	3	—	14	—
Appleyard	11	3	38	2	4	1	17	1
Wardle	6	—	20	1	1	—	1	—

Umpires: M. J. McInnes and C. Hoy.

RICE, FATHER WILLIAM IGNATIUS, O.S.B., M.A., who died at Douai Abbey on April 22, 1955, aged 72, was Headmaster of Douai School from 1915 to 1952. In his younger days he played for Warwickshire during the summer holidays and for some years enjoyed the distinction of being the only monk whose cricket performances were chronicled in *Wisden*.

JESSOP, MR GILBERT LAIRD, who died at St. George's Vicarage, Dorchester, on May 11, 1955, aged 80, was famed as the most remarkable hitter cricket has ever produced. He had lived with the Rev. Gilbert Jessop, his only child, from 1936 till his death.

Born at Cheltenham on May 19, 1874, he enjoyed a memorable career in first-class cricket which, dating from 1894 to the start of the First World War, extended over twenty years. There have been batsmen who hit the ball even harder than Jessop, notably C. 1. Thornton and the two Australians, George Bonnor and Jack Lyons, but no one who did so more often or who, in match after match, scored as rapidly. Where Jessop surpassed all other hitters was in the all-round nature of his scoring. At his best, he could make runs from any ball, however good it might be. Although only 5 ft 7 ins. in height, he bent low as he shaped to play, a method which earned him the sobriquet of "The Croucher". Extraordinary quick on his feet, he was ready to hit firm-footed if the ball were pitched well up and equally, when it was of shorter length, to dash down the pitch and drive. When executing leg-side strokes, he almost lay down and swept round with the bat practically horizontal, putting great power behind the ball as, thanks to strong, supple wrists, he also did when bringing off the square cut. Lightness of foot allied to wonderful sight made it possible for him to run out to the fastest bowlers of his time – Richardson and Mold – and at the peak of his form pull or straight-drive them with almost unerring certainty. No one ever approached him in this particular feat; indeed, nobody else could have attempted it with reasonable hope of success.

At times Jessop sacrificed his wicket through trying to hit before he got a true sight of the ball or judged the pace of the turf and, not unnaturally in view of the liberties he took with good length bowling, the ball which kept low often dismissed him. A batsman with such marvellous gifts that in half an hour he might win a game seemingly lost, he was a wonderful personality on the field and the idol of spectators who always love a fearless batsman.

Jessop's claims to distinction were not limited to the brilliancy of his run-getting. For a number of years he ranked high as a fast bowler and for a man of his pace he showed surprising stamina. Far more remarkable than his bowling, however, was his fielding, which might fairly be termed as phenomenal as his hitting and which was a matter of great pride to him. No hit proved too hard for him to stop and his gathering and returning of the ball approached perfection. In his early days he fielded at cover-point; later he specialised in the position of extra mid-off, standing so deep that with almost anyone else a run would have been a certainty. Jessop's presence deterred the boldest of batsmen from making any attempt. In short, such a fine bowler and such a superb fieldsman was he that, even without his batting ability, he would have been worth a place in almost any team. A man of engaging manners, he was a charming companion and, like most truly great men, modest to a degree.

First tried for Gloucestershire in 1894, Jessop established his reputation a year later when, among other performances, he hit 63 out of 65 in less than half an hour from the Yorkshire bowling at Cheltenham. He continued to assist Gloucestershire till the end of his first-class career and for thirteen years from 1900 he captained the side. By 1897 he had become one of the great players of the day, making 1,219 runs in first-class matches and taking 116 wickets for less than 18 runs each. In that summer he hit two particularly noteworthy innings – 140 for Cambridge University against the Philadelphians in 95 minutes and 101 out of 118 in 40 minutes against Yorkshire at Harrogate. In the course of the latter display he hit the ball six times out of the ground and some dozen times over the ropes. Until 1907 a hit over the ropes counted four; only a hit out of the ground earned six. Except in 1898 he regularly made over 1,000 runs every season until 1909, when a bad back injury sustained while fielding in the Test Match at Leeds in early July kept him out of the game for the rest of the year. In 1900 he scored 2,210 runs and took 104 wickets and next summer his aggregate amounted to 2,323, including 157 out of 201 in an hour against West Indies at Bristol.

Among his 53 centuries were five of more than 200: 286 out of 335 in 175 minutes for Gloucestershire against Sussex at Brighton, 1903 (he and J. H. Board adding 320 for the sixth wicket); 240 out of 337 in 200 minutes for Gloucestershire v Sussex at Bristol, 1907; 234 out of 346 in 155 minutes for Gloucestershire v Somerset at Bristol, 1905; 233 out of 318 in 150 minutes for An England XI v Yorkshire at Lord's 1901; and 206 out of 317 in 150 minutes for Gloucestershire v Nottinghamshire at Trent Bridge, 1904.

Four times for Gloucestershire he reached three figures in each innings of a match: 104 and 139 v Yorkshire at Bradford, 1900, when the newspapers stated that, in the two innings he cleared the ropes more than twenty times; 143 and 133 not out v Somerset at Bath, 1908; 161 and 129 v Hampshire at Bristol, 1909; and 153 and 123 not out v Hampshire at Southampton, 1911 He achieved the feat on another occasion, against Somerset in a friendly game organised for the opening of a new club pavilion. S. M. J. Woods termed this a remarkable performance on a pitch far from true and against professional bowling. Altogether in first-class cricket he hit 26,058 runs, average 32.60.

His bowling successes included eight wickets for 34 runs v Hampshire, 1898; five for 13 v Lancashire, 1895; eight for 54 v Lancashire, 1898; eight for 29 v Essex, 1900; eight for 58 v Middlesex, 1902. All these were achieved for Gloucestershire except that against Hampshire, on which occasion he was playing for Cambridge. His wickets in first-class cricket totalled 851, average 22.9 1.

Jessop took part in eighteen Test matches between 1899 and 1909, thirteen against Australia and five against South Africa, and would probably have appeared in others but for the back strain he suffered in 1909. He disappointed in Australia except for his fielding, and in most of the contests in England met with moderate success; but he earned undying fame in The Oval Test of 1902. There, under conditions considerably helpful to bowlers, England, set 273 to make to win, lost their first five wickets for 48. Australia looked to have the match in hand, but Jessop joined F. S. Jackson and in marvellous fashion hit 104 out of 139 in an hour and a quarter, paving the way to victory by one wicket for England. Twice he sent the ball on to the roof of the Pavilion and from another big hit was caught on the Players' Balcony by H. K. Foster.

Jessop went to Cambridge in 1896 and played for the University for four seasons, being captain in 1899. He accomplished little of note against Oxford in the way of batting, two innings of over 40 being his best scores on the big occasion, but he bowled to good purpose in two of the games, taking six wickets for 65 in the first innings in 1897 and six for 126 in the first innings a year later.

Besides his cricketing ability, Jessop was an all-round athlete of note. He got his Blue as a hockey goalkeeper, but fell ill and could not play in the University match; came near getting an Association football Blue and played for The Casuals as half-back or goalkeeper. He also appeared as a wing three quarter for Gloucester RFC. He would have played billiards for Cambridge against Oxford, but was "gated" and could not take part. In one week he made two breaks of over 150. He could run the 100 yards in 10.2 seconds and frequently entered for sports meetings. A scratch golfer, he took part in the Amateur Championship in 1914, was Secretary of the Cricketers' Golfing Society and for some years Secretary of the Edgware Club.

In addition to the visit he paid to Australia in 1901–2 under A. C. MacLaren, he went to America with the team captained by P. F. Warner in 1897, and again in 1899 when K. S. Ranjitsinhji led the side.

For Beccles School in 1895, when a master there, Jessop scored 1,058 runs, average 132, and took 100 wickets at a cost of less than two and a half runs apiece.

He served as a captain in the Manchester Regiment during the First World War from 1914 till he was invalided out with a damaged heart in 1918. Married in October 1902, he first met his bride a few months earlier during his visit to Australia. She died in 1953.

Tributes paid to Jessop include:

Sir Pelham Warner: "He was a wonderful cricketer. It was a great pleasure to play with or against him. It has been said that he was unorthodox, but no one watched the ball more closely."

Sir John Hobbs: "He was undoubtedly the most consistently fast scorer I have seen. He was a big hitter, too, and it was difficult to bowl a ball from which he could not score. He made me glad that I was not a bowler. Gilbert Jessop certainly drew the crowds, too, even more than Bradman, I should say."

SOMERSET v HAMPSHIRE
Played at Weston-super-Mare, August 17, 18, 1955

HAMPSHIRE WON BY 264 runs. Remarkable bowling by Shackleton gave them their decisive victory. He accomplished one of the best performances in the history of the game in taking eight wickets for four runs in 11.1 overs in the first innings and he followed with six for 25 when Somerset batted again. Rain before the start and during lunch restricted the first day's play when Hampshire did fairly well until the spin took effect. Then Hilton did the hat-trick for the first time, dismissing Harrison, Shackleton and Burden. The pitch was extremely awkward and the Somerset batsmen were helpless. They were all out in 74 minutes and Hampshire, leading by 117, scored readily. Rayment made his only hundred of the season and Horton and Harrison helped in good stands. Somerset, needing 363, again failed dismally, only Stephenson offering resistance with a hard-hit 52.

HAMPSHIRE

First Innings

J. R. Gray c Lawrence b Hilton	43
R. E. Marshall c Stephenson b Yawar Saeed	5
H. Horton b Lawrence b Hilton	43
A. W. H. Rayment c Lawrence b McMahon	12
N. H. Rogers c Williams b Hilton	2
H. M. Barnard b McMahon	19
L. Harrison c Williams b Hilton	9
P. J. Sainsbury not out	13
D. Shackleton st Stephenson b Hilton	0
M. D. Burden b Hilton	0
V. H. D. Cannings c Hilton b McMahon	0
B 8	8
	154

1/11 2/78 3/91 4/94 5/126
6/136 7/149 8/149 9/149

Second Innings

b McMahon	4
c Lobb b Yawar Saeed	12
b Tordoff	59
c Tordoff b McMahon	104
c Williams b Tordon	10
b McMahon	5
not out	35
b Hilton	4
B 7, l-b 5	12
	(7 wkts dec.) **245**

1/12 2/16 3/107
4/127 5/136 6/239 7/245

SOMERSET

First Innings

G. G. Tordoff b Shackleton	0
G. L. Williams c Rogers b Shackleton	2
J. Lawrence lbw b Shackleton	0
M. F. Tremlett c Gray b Shackleton	8
P. B. Wright c Marshall b Shackleton	2
J. G. Lomax c Rogers b Sainsbury	0
H. W. Stephenson not out	18
Yawar Saeed c Barnard b Shackleton	0
J. Hilton b Shackleton	0
J. W. McMahon run out	1
B. Lobb c Rayment b Shackleton	0
L-b 6	6
	37

1/0 2/0 3/3 4/10 5/10 6/20
7/20 8/26 9/27

Second Innings

c Marshall b Shackleton	0
c Burden b Shackleton	2
c Gray b Sainsbury	4
b Shackleton	0
c and b Burden	10
c Rayment b Shackleton	20
c Horton b Sainsbury	52
c Barnard b Shackleton	0
b Shackleton	0
not out	9
c Burden b Sainsbury	0
L-b 1	1
	98

1/0 2/3 3/4 4/16 5/16
6/81 7/81 8/81 9/89

Derek Shackleton who, on more than one occasion, bowled unchanged through an innings and often ran through the opposition virtually without conceding a run. He was at his best in English conditions and never quite confirmed his mastery in Test cricket.

Somerset Bowling

	Overs	Mdns	Runs	Wkts	Overs	Mdns	Runs	Wkts
Lobb	11	4	23	—	6	1	12	—
Yawar Saeed	7	2	16	1	5	—	14	1
Hilton	24	7	49	6	12.2	—	50	1
McMahon	27.3	10	58	3	32	2	122	3
Lomax					2	1	2	—
Tordoff					11	1	33	2

Hampshire Bowling

	Overs	Mdns	Runs	Wkts	Overs	Mdns	Runs	Wkts
Shackleton	11.1	7	4	8	16	7	25	6
Cannings	4	2	5	—	4	2	3	—
Sainsbury	7	2	22	1	13.4	—	63	3
Burden					2	—	6	1

Umpires: A. Skelding and J. S. Buller.

HARGREAVES, MR TOM KNIGHT, who died in hospital at Rotherham on November 19, 1955, aged 61, was a prominent all-rounder in Yorkshire Council cricket from 1921 till 1951. He played for Wath till he was 57, scoring many runs and proving successful as a slow bowler. A forcing batsman, he scored 191 in ninety minutes against Brampton in 1935. He brought off one of the biggest hits in cricket on one occasion when playing at the Wath Athletic Ground. A mighty six sent the ball soaring out of the ground and into a wagon of a goods-train on the nearby railway line. The ball was carried on to Scunthorpe.

SURREY v AUSTRALIANS

Played at The Oval, May 16, 17, 18, 1956

SURREY WON BY ten wickets, so becoming the first county for forty-four years to triumph over an Australian team. There could be no doubt about their superiority in a sensational match, and Johnson, in presenting his cap to the Surrey captain, Surridge, admitted it freely.

To Laker belonged the great distinction of taking all ten wickets. Not since 1878, when E. Barratt, another Surrey man, did so for the Players, also at The Oval, had a bowler taken all ten wickets against an Australian side, and Laker was given the ball and a cheque for £50 by the Surrey Committee. He and, in the second innings, the left-handed Lock, fully exposed the weakness of the Australian batsmen against the turning ball.

Winning the toss appeared to have given the Australians a considerable advantage, and Burke and McDonald emphasised this view while scoring 62 in ninety-five minutes. McDonald, though enjoying two "lives", brought off many good strokes during a stay of three hours thirty-five minutes and he fell only 11 runs short of his second century in successive innings. When he was taken at the wicket the total stood at 151 for four wickets, but Laker brought about such a series of disasters that five more batsmen were dismissed while the total rose by 48. Of these runs 12, including a drive for 6, were hit by Davidson in one over from Laker and 16 came in three strokes by Crawford at the expense of the same bowler. Fortunately for the Australians, Miller, getting as much of the bowling as possible, scored briskly after a careful start, and he and Wilson put on 42 for the last wicket. Even so Laker, maintaining a splendid length in a spell of four hours and a quarter broken only by the lunch and tea intervals, exploited off spin on the dry pitch so skilfully that he came out with this analysis:

Overs	Maidens	Runs	Wickets
46	18	88	10

In the hope that he might achieve similar success, Johnson kept himself on for most of the Surrey first innings, but though he flighted the ball well, his off-breaks caused nothing like the same trouble. Apart from three overs by the fast bowlers, the Australian attack remained in the hands of spin bowlers throughout, a policy which not only failed to bring the desired results, but came in for much criticism.

Still, Surrey did not for a long time find run-getting an easy matter, though Fletcher (six 4s) drove hard during an opening stand with Clark which realised 53. Waiting for the ball to punish and then putting plenty of power into strokes all round, Clark stayed till another 59 were added and then became the second victim of Maddocks at the wicket. Giving no chance during two hours and ten minutes, he hit eight 4s.

Constable, cautious at first, gradually developed more freedom, but wickets fell steadily and six were down for 221. Then Laker attacked the bowling. He helped himself to 16, including a drive for 6 and two 4s, in an over from Johnson, and altogether hit 43 out of 57 added by the seventh partnership in thirty-nine minutes, taking Surrey ahead.

Constable's long stay ended with a return catch when he had batted for four hours thirty-five minutes. Without making a serious mistake, he hit seven 4s, chiefly by on-side strokes, in a most valuable innings. Surridge and Loader put on 34 for the last wicket, and so Surrey gained a lead of 88.

Three overs by the opening Surrey bowlers at the end of the second day did not yield a run, and next morning Surridge reverted to an all-spin attack. For a time matters went

The Australians arrived in England for the 1956 series with memories of Frank Tyson's blistering pace still fresh in their minds. They had not been here long before they were routed by quite a different style of bowling. By taking all ten Australian wickets in the first innings, Jim Laker confirmed his position as the world's best off-spinner. As for the Australians, they could at least take consolation in the fact that Laker's feat had not been performed in a Test match, and that it was extremely unlikely that lightning would strike in the same place twice.

well enough with the Australians and an opening stand of 56 in ninety-five minutes by Burke and McDonald seemed to have made them reasonably safe from defeat.

Then the course of the game changed completely, for Lock, able by now to make the ball turn quickly and occasionally get up awkwardly from a dusty pitch, caused such a breakdown that in a further ninety-five minutes the innings was all over for another 51 runs. Lock, who took the first six wickets at a cost of 40 runs, finished with an analysis of seven for 49 – a marked contrast to his 0 for 100 in the first innings! Actually he achieved all his success from the Pavilion end – that from which Laker bowled in the first innings – in a spell of 23.1 overs, 6 maidens, for 36 runs. He owed something to smart fielding, the catch by which May at slip disposed of Davidson being first-rate. Surrey required only 20 runs to win, but Lindwall and Crawford bowled so fast and accurately that they took fifty-five minutes to accomplish the task.

AUSTRALIANS

First Innings

J. W. Burke lbw b Laker 28
C. C. McDonald c Swetman b Laker 89
K. Mackay c Surridge b Laker 4
R. N. Harvey c Constable b Laker 13
K. R. Miller not out 57
L. Maddocks b Laker 12
R. R. Lindwall b Laker 0
I. W. Johnson c Swetman b Laker 0
A. K. Davidson c May b Laker 21
P. Crawford b Laker 16
J. Wilson c Swetman b Laker 4
    B 4, l-b 8, n-b 3 15

1/62 2/93 3/124 4/151 5/173   259
6/173 7/175 8/199 9/217

Second Innings

c and b Lock 20
c Laker b Lock 45
lbw b Laker 4
c May b Lock 10
c Swetman b Lock 2
c Laker b Lock 0
c Constable b Lock 4
run out 5
c May b Laker 7
not out 5
st Swetman b Lock 1
    L-b 4 4

1/56 2/73 3/83 4/85 5/85   107
6/89 7/92 8/101 9/104

SURREY

First Innings

D. G. W. Fletcher c Maddocks b Johnson 29
T. H. Clark c Maddocks b Burke 58
B. Constable c and b Johnson 109
P. B. H. May st Maddocks b Johnson 27
K. Barrington c Miller b Johnson 4
R. Swetman st Maddocks b Davidson 0
D. F. Cox b Davidson 13
J. C. Laker c McDonald b Johnson 43
W. S. Surridge c Harvey b Johnson 38
G. A. R. Lock b Davidson 0
P. J. Loader not out 12
    B 10, l-b 3, w 1 14

1/53 2/112 3/147 4/192 5/195   347
6/221 7/278 8/302 9/313

Second Innings

not out 9
not out 8

    B 1, l-b 1, n-b 1 3

(No wkt) 20

Surrey Bowling

	Overs	Mdns	Runs	Wkts	Overs	Mdns	Runs	Wkts
Loader	15	4	30	—	2	2	—	—
Surridge	8	2	8	—	1	1	—	—
Laker	46	18	88	10	25	10	42	2
Lock	33	12	100	—	31.1	9	49	7
Cox	5	—	18	—				
Clark					8	4	12	—

Australians Bowling

	Overs	Mdns	Runs	Wkts	Overs	Mdns	Runs	Wkts
Lindwall	2	1	10	—	8	4	8	—
Crawford	1	—	4	—	7	3	9	—
Johnson	60.3	12	168	6				
Davidson	44	14	101	3				
Wilson	19	9	34	—				
Burke	7	2	16	1				

Umpires: K. McCanlis and L. H. Gray.

Laker was only one half of Surrey's spin equation. The other half was the left-arm bowler Tony Lock, who also had days when he monopolised the wicket-taking. Later on, Lock, whose quicker delivery was thought to be illegal by some, emigrated to Australia and became a highly successful captain of Western Australia.

KENT v SURREY
Played at Blackheath, July 7, 9, 10, 1956

SURREY WON BY an innings and 173 runs. Kent were completely outplayed by Surrey for the second time in a week, the match being notable chiefly for the bowling of Lock and the batting of Clark and May. In excellent conditions, Clark batted masterfully on the first day in hitting the biggest score of his career. Most of his twenty-nine 4s came from crisp off-drives. May, who helped to add 174 in two hours, batted far more convincingly than when scoring a century against Kent a week earlier, much of his stroke-play being superb. Week-end rain added to Kent's plight. On the Monday, when Surridge declared first thing, Lock received enough help from the turf to shatter Kent's moderate batting. Only Cowdrey and to a lesser extent Phebey could counter his biting leg-spin and when Kent followed-on even these two succumbed quickly. By the close Lock was in sight of all ten wickets for the first time and this he achieved the following morning by dismissing the last four batsmen without conceding a run. His sixteen wickets in the match for 83 runs made his figures for the two games with Kent twenty-six for 143.

SURREY

T. H. Clark b Ridgway 191
M. J. Stewart c Fagg b Wright 13
K. Barrington c Ridgway b Wright 32
P. B. H. May not out 128
P. C. E. Pratt c Phebey b Page 21
E. A. Bedser not out......................................11
    L-b 8 8

1/47 2/145 3/319 4/360   (4 wkts dec.) 404

R. Swetman, W. S. Surridge, G. A. R. Lock, A. V. Bedser and P. J. Loader did not bat.

KENT

First Innings

A. H. Phebey b Lock 22
M. C. Cowdrey c Swetman b A. Bedser 49
R. C. Wilson c Barrington b Lock 2
T. G. Evans b Loader 1
A. E. Fagg c Stewart b Lock 2
A. L. Dixon c May b Lock 13
D. G. Ufton b Lock 0
F. Ridgway c Surridge b Lock 6
D. J. Halfyard c Pratt b A. Bedser 1
J. C. T. Page not out 1
D. V. P. Wright c Loader b A. Bedser 2
    L-b 2 2

                101

1/55 2/63 3/64 4/67 5/91
6/91 7/91 8/96 9/98

Second Innings

b Lock 12
lbw b Lock 8
b Lock 32
c and b Lock 19
c A. Bedser b Lock 21
b Lock 2
not out 17
c Stewart b Lock 7
c Barrington b Lock 0
b Lock 0
b Lock 0
    B 6, l-b 5, n-b 1 12

                130

1/20 2/29 3/60 4/84 5/101
6/104 7/130 8/130 9/130

Kent Bowling

	Overs	Mdns	Runs	Wkts
Ridgway	15	3	53	1
Halfyard	28	4	104	—
Wright	25	3	85	2
Page	25	2	107	1
Dixon	9	—	44	—
Cowdrey	1	—	3	—

Surrey Bowling

	Overs	Mdns	Runs	Wkts	Overs	Mdns	Runs	Wkts
Loader	16	6	38	1	8	3	7	—
A. Bedser	11	—	28	3	16	5	41	—
Lock	21	12	29	6	29.1	18	54	10
E. Bedser	3	2	4	—	18	10	16	—

Umpires: Harry Elliott (Derbyshire) and W. F. Price.

ENGLAND v AUSTRALIA

FOURTH TEST MATCH
Played at Manchester, July 26, 27, 28, 30, 31, 1956

ENGLAND WON BY an innings and 170 runs, with just over an hour to spare and so retained the "Ashes". This memorable game will always be known as "Laker's Match" because of the remarkable performance by the Surrey off-break bowler in taking nine

wickets for 37 runs in the first innings and ten wickets for 53 in the second. Laker broke all the more important bowling records in the history of cricket. His achievements were:
1. Nineteen wickets in a match, the most in any first-class game. The previous best was 17, achieved twenty times. The most in a Test Match was 17 for 159 by S. F. Barnes for England against South Africa at Johannesburg in 1913–14.
2. Ten wickets in an innings for the first time in Test cricket. The previous best for England against Australia was eight for 35 by G. Lohmann of Surrey in 1886–87. The best for England in any Test innings nine for 28 by G. Lohmann against South Africa in 1895–96.
3. Ten wickets in an innings twice in one season for the first time. Laker previously took ten for 88 for Surrey, also against the Australians at The Oval in May.
4. Thirty-nine wickets in four Test Matches, equalling the record of A. V. Bedser as the highest number in an England-Australia series, with one match to play.
5. Fifty-one wickets in five matches against the Australians to date in the season.

Apart from Laker's personal records, other noteworthy points about the match were:

1. It was the first definite result in a Test Match between England and Australia at Manchester since 1905.
2. For the first time since 1905 England won two matches in a home series against Australia.
3. For the first time since five Test Matches were played in a series regularly from 1897–98 England held the "Ashes" for three series.

Those are bare facts, interesting in themselves, but they fail to capture the drama of one of the most exciting and controversial matches for a long time. The excitement came towards the last day, first when England were trying hard to make up for the time lost by rain to gain the victory which would settle the destination of the "Ashes", and later as Laker drew nearer and nearer his ten wickets in the innings. The controversy arose over

In the fourth test Jim Laker set up records which can never conceivably be equalled. Unplayable from start to finish, he gave a display which was aesthetically moving as well as statistically miraculous.

the preparation of the pitch and for days cricketers, officials, critics and the general public could talk of little else.

The England selectors sprang a surprise when they named Rev. D. S. Sheppard among the twelve from whom the team would be chosen. Sheppard, who had given up regular cricket to take up Holy Orders had played only four innings for Sussex during the season, when selected. One of these was 97 against the Australians at Hove. His previous Test appearance was two years earlier when he captained England against Pakistan. Like nearly every move the Selection Committee made during the season, this one proved fully justified.

Graveney, originally in the twelve, dropped out because of a bruised hand and Oakman, who played at Leeds, was added to the party. The selectors continued their policy of relying on a four-man attack and Trueman was omitted. This meant two changes from the side which won at Leeds, Sheppard and Statham replacing Insole and Trueman. The Australians, with their injured men fit, were able to choose from all seventeen members of their party for the first time since the first Test. They omitted Burge and gave Craig his first chance in a Test against England. Langley, the wicket-keeper, was intended to play, but an unusual mishap kept him out. During the night he slept on his hand and damaged it.

May won the toss for the third time in the series and he gave England a big advantage. The pitch was completely useless to fast and fast-medium bowlers and Richardson and Cowdrey, as at Nottingham, gave delightful displays. They took command from the first over and in three hours ten minutes scored 174 for the opening stand. This was England's best start against Australia since 1938 when L. Hutton and C. J. Barnett began with 219 at Trent Bridge. Both batsmen went all out for their strokes and their perfect understanding in running enabled them to offset the value of Australia's defensive field.

Cowdrey, strong in driving, was first to leave, but Richardson did not survive much longer, batting three hours forty minutes for 104, his first Test century. Most of eleven 4s, the same number as Cowdrey, came from well-timed leg-side strokes, but he also brought off some good cover drives, notably two in an over from Lindwall which were models of execution.

Sheppard and May continued the mastery of the Australian attack, but towards tea time, puffs of dust became noticeable when the ball landed and it seemed that the pitch was breaking up unusually early. Johnson and Benaud, the Australian spin bowlers, were unable to exploit the conditions and England finished the first day with a total of 307 for three. Towards the close May was caught off a quickly spun and lifting leg-break after helping Sheppard add 93. A curiosity was that the first five England batsmen were all amateurs, something that had last happened against Australia in 1899 when C. B. Fry, A. C. MacLaren, K. S. Ranjitsinhji, C. L. Townsend and F. S. Jackson were the men concerned.

Mutterings about the pitch could be heard that evening, but they rose to full fury next day. The Australians still could not get the ball to bite as much as they ought to have done and England went gaily on, adding 152 in two hours eleven minutes before being all out for the highest total against Australia since 1948. Sheppard, 59 overnight, completed a chanceless century and batted five minutes under five hours for 113 which included one 6 and fifteen 4s. He drove delightfully and gave not the slightest suggestion of lack of match practice.

Evans, revelling in the situation, hit lustily and scored 47 out of 62 in twenty-nine minutes. England made their 459 runs in 491 minutes, an unusually rapid rate for Test cricket in recent years.

Australia began their reply just after half-past two and before play ended on the second day they had lost eleven wickets. McDonald and Burke began steadily with a stand of 48, but they had to fight hard against the spin of Laker and Lock, who were brought on early. Laker did not start his devastating work until switched to the Stretford end, from where he took each of his nineteen wickets. McDonald and Harvey fell at the same total and after tea, taken at 62 for two, the last eight wickets went in thirty-five minutes for 22 runs. Lock took his only wicket with the first ball after the interval and Laker did the rest, his after tea spell being seven wickets for eight runs in 22 balls. While admitting that Laker spun his off-breaks appreciably, the Australian batsmen gave a sorry display and appeared to give up too easily.

Following on 375 behind, Australia were unfortunate to lose McDonald, who retired with a knee injury after scoring 11. Harvey replaced him and was out first ball, hitting a full toss into the hands of short mid-on. Harvey failed to score in either innings. Australia finished the day with one wicket down for 51 and the controversial storm broke that night.

Accusations were made that the pitch had been prepared specially for England's spin bowlers and these were denied by the Lancashire authorities. The Australians were said to be extremely bitter over the condition of the pitch, but their captain, Johnson, declined to comment on the subject. The arguments continued over the week-end and not until Laker's wonderful bowling on the last day overshadowed everything did they abate.

The weather changed completely on Saturday, when rain allowed only three-quarters of an hour's cricket between ten minutes past two and five minutes to three. In that brief period Australia added six runs and lost the wicket of Burke. Sunday was an atrocious day and Monday was almost as bad. In two spells of forty-five minutes and fifteen minutes Australia took their score to 84 without further loss. Conditions were terrible for cricket, a fierce wind making batting and bowling extremely difficult. Lignum bails were used and were most successful, not once being blown off.

England looked like being robbed of victory by the weather but it improved considerably on the last day and play began only ten minutes late. The soaking the pitch received left it slow and easy-paced and by fighting, determined cricket, McDonald and Craig remained together until lunch time when the score was 112 for two with four hours left.

Shortly before the interval the sun appeared and almost immediately the ball began to spin quickly. Afterwards Laker began another devastating spell, sending back Craig, Mackay, Miller and Archer in nine overs for three runs. Craig, who helped McDonald add 59, gave a fine, courageous display for four hours twenty minutes; the other three failed to score, Mackay, like his fellow left-hander, Harvey, for the second time in the match. Benaud stayed with McDonald for an hour and a quarter to tea when, with an hour and fifty-five minutes left, England needed to capture four wickets. Occasionally Laker changed ends, but only when he returned to the Stretford end did he continue his success. After tea the ball spun quicker than at any time in the match and Australia's last hope vanished when McDonald fell to the second ball. His 89, made in five hours thirty-seven minutes, showed that the bowling could be played by determined concentration and he deserved the highest praise for his great effort.

The tension mounted as Laker captured his eighth and ninth wickets. There was never a question of giving Laker his tenth wicket for England's only thought was victory. Lock repeatedly beat the bat, but it was not his match and at twenty-seven minutes past five a great cheer went up as Laker successfully appealed to the umpire, Lee, for lbw against Maddocks. The match was over and Laker had taken all ten wickets.

He earned his triumph by remarkable control of length and spin and it is doubtful whether he bowled more than six bad length balls throughout the match. As Johnson said afterwards: "When the controversy and side issues of the match are forgotten, Laker's wonderful bowling will remain."

That night the rain returned and the following day not a ball could be bowled in any of the first-class matches, so it can be seen how close was England's time margin, and how the greatest bowling feat of all time nearly did not happen. L.S.

ENGLAND

P. E. Richardson c Maddocks b Benaud 104
M. C. Cowdrey c Maddocks b Lindwall 80
Rev. D. S. Sheppard b Archer 113
P. B. H. May c Archer b Benaud 43
T. E. Bailey b Johnson 20
C. Washbrook lbw b Johnson 6
A. S. M. Oakman c Archer b Johnson 10
T. G. Evans st Maddocks b Johnson 47
J. C. Laker run out 3
G. A. R. Lock not out 25
J. B. Statham c Maddocks b Lindwall 0
B 2, l-b 5, w 1 8

1/174 2/195 3/288 4/321 5/327   459
6/339 7/401 8/417 9/458

AUSTRALIA

First Innings

C. C. McDonald c Lock b Laker 32
J. W. Burke c Cowdrey b Lock 22
R. N. Harvey b Laker 0
I. D. Craig lbw b Laker 8
K. R. Miller c Oakman b Laker 6
K. Mackay c Oakman b Laker 0
R. G. Archer st Evans b Laker 6
R. Benaud c Statham b Laker 0
R. R. Lindwall not out 6
L. Maddocks b Laker 4
I. W. Johnson b Laker 0

1/48 2/48 3/62 4/62 5/62   84
6/73 7/73 8/78 9/84

Second Innings

c Oakman b Laker 89
c Lock b Laker 33
c Cowdrey b Laker 0
lbw b Laker 38
b Laker 0
c Oakman b Laker 0
c Oakman b Laker 0
b Laker 18
c Lock b Laker 8
lbw b Laker 2
not out 1
B 12, l-b 4 16

1/28 2/55 3/114 4/124 5/130   205
6/130 7/181 8/198 9/203

Australia Bowling

	Overs	Mdns	Runs	Wkts
Lindwall	21.3	6	63	2
Miller	21	6	41	—
Archer	22	6	73	1
Johnson	47	10	151	4
Benaud	47	17	123	2

England Bowling

	Overs	Mdns	Runs	Wkts	Overs	Mdns	Runs	Wkts
Statham	6	3	6	—	16	9	15	—
Bailey	4	3	4	—	20	8	31	—
Laker	16.4	4	37	9	51.2	23	53	10
Lock	14	3	37	1	55	30	69	—
Oakman					8	3	21	—

Umpires: F. S. Lee and E. Davies.

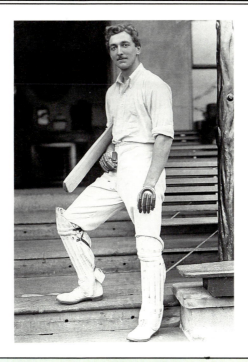

C B FRY
By Neville Cardus

CHARLES FRY was born into a Sussex family on April 25, 1872, at Croydon, and was known first as an England cricketer and footballer, also as a great all-round athlete who for a while held the long-jump record, a hunter and a fisher, and as an inexhaustible virtuoso at the best of all indoor games, conversation.

He was at Repton when a boy, where at cricket he joined the remarkable and enduring roll of superb young players emanating from the school – Fry, Palairet, Ford, J. N. Crawford, to name a few. At Oxford he won first-class honours in Classical Moderations at Wadham, and it is a tribute to his calibre as a scholar and personal force that most of the obituary articles written after the death of Viscount Simon named Fry in a Wadham trinity with Birkenhead. Not the least doughty and idealistic of his many-sided achievements was as a Liberal candidate for Brighton, where he actually polled 20,000 votes long after he had ceased to live in Sussex and dominate the cricket field.

With all his versatility of mind and sinew Fry himself wished that he might be remembered, as much as for anything else, by his work in command of the training-ship *Mercury*. For forty years he and his wife directed the *Mercury* at Hamble, educating youth with a classical sense of values. He once invited the present writer to visit Hamble and see his boys play cricket and perform extracts from "Parsifal"! Hitler sent for him for advice during the building-up of the "Youth Movement" in Germany. He was a deputy for the Indian delegation to the first, third, and fourth Assemblies of the League of Nations, edited his own monthly magazine more than half a century ago, and was indeed a pioneer in the school of intelligent and analytical criticism of sport. He wrote several books, including an autobiography, and a *Key to the League of Nations*, and one called *Batsmanship*, which might conceivably have come from the pen of Aristotle had Aristotle lived nowadays and played cricket.

Fry must be counted among the most fully developed and representative Englishmen of his period; and the question arises whether, had fortune allowed him to concentrate on the things of the mind, not distracted by the lure of cricket, a lure intensified by his increasing mastery over the game, he would not have reached a high altitude in politics or critical literature. But he belonged – and it was his glory – to an age not obsessed by specialism; he was one of the last of the English tradition of the amateur, the connoisseur, and, in the most delightful sense of the word, the dilettante.

As a batsman, of course, he was thoroughly grounded in first principles. He added to his stature, in fact, by taking much thought. As a youth he did not use a bat with much natural freedom, and even in his period of pomp he was never playing as handsomely as his magnificent physical appearance seemed to suggest and deserve. He was, of course, seen often in contrast with Ranjitsinhji, who would have made all batsmen of the present day, Hutton included, look like so many plebeians toiling under the sun. Yet in his prime Fry was a noble straight-driver. He once said to me: "I had only one stroke maybe; but it went to ten different parts of the field." But in 1905, when the Australians decided that Fry could make runs only in front of the wicket, mainly to the on, and set the field for him accordingly, he scored 144 in an innings sparkling with cuts.

In his career as cricketer, he scored some 30,000 runs, averaging 50, in an era of natural wickets, mainly against bowlers of great speed or of varied and subtle spin and accuracy. From Yorkshire bowling alone he scored nearly 2,500 runs in all his matches against the county during its most powerful days, averaging 70, in the teeth of the attack of Hirst, Rhodes, Haigh, Wainwright, and, occasionally, F. S. Jackson. In 1903 he made 234 against Yorkshire at Bradford. Next summer he made 177 against Yorkshire at Sheffield, and 229 at Brighton, in successive innings. Ranjitsinhji's performances against Yorkshire were almost as remarkable as Fry's; for he scored well over 1,500 runs against them, averaging more than sixty an innings. In 1901 Fry scored six centuries in six consecutive innings, an achievement equalled by Bradman, but on Australian wickets and spread over a season. Fry's six hundreds, two of them on bowler's wickets, came one on top of the other within little more than a fortnight.

The conjunction at the creases of C. B. Fry and K. S. Ranjitsinhji was a sight and an appeal to the imagination not likely ever to be repeated: Fry, nineteenth-century rationalist, batting according to first principles with a sort of moral grandeur, observing patience and abstinence. At the other end of the wicket, "Ranji" turned a cricket bat into a wand of conjuration. Fry was of the Occident, "Ranji" told of the Orient.

Cricket can scarcely hope again to witness two styles as fascinatingly contrasted and as racially representative as Fry's and Ranjitsinhji's. Between them they evolved a doctrine that caused a fundamental change in the tactics of batsmanship, "Play back or drive". "Watch the ball well, then make a stroke at the ball itself and not at a point in space where you hope the ball will presently be." At the time that Fry was making a name in cricket most batsmen played forward almost automatically on good fast pitches, frequently lunging out full stretch. If a ball can be reached only by excessive elongation of arms and body, obviously the pitch of it has been badly gauged. Fry and Ranjitsinhji, following after Arthur Shrewsbury, developed mobile footwork.

It is a pungent comment on the strength of the reserves of English cricket half a century ago that Fry and "Ranji" were both dropped from the England team at the height of their fame. In 1901 Fry scored 3,147 runs, average 78.67: in 1903 he scored 2,683 runs, average 81.30. In 1900 Ranjitsinhji scored 3,065, average 87.57. Yet because of one or two lapses in 1902, both these great players were asked to stand down and give way to other aspirants to Test cricket.

As we consider Fry's enormous aggregates of runs summer by summer, we should not forget that he took part, during all the extent of his career, in only one Test match lasting more than three days, and that he never visited Australia as a cricketer. For one reason and another Fry appeared not more than eighteen times against Australia in forty-three Test matches played between 1899, when he began the England innings with W. G. Grace, and 1912, in which wet season he was England's captain against Australia and South Africa in the ill-fated triangular tournament. By that time he had severed his illustrious connection with Sussex and was opening the innings for Hampshire. The general notion is that Fry was not successful as an England batsman; and it is true that in Test matches he did not remain on his habitual peaks. None the less, his batting average for Test cricket is much the same as that of Victor Trumper, M. A. Noble, and J. T. Tyldesley. The currency had not been debased yet.

Until he was no-balled for throwing by Phillips – who also "called" Mold at Old Trafford – Fry was a good fast bowler who took six wickets for 78 in the University match, opened the Gentlemen's bowling against the Players at The Oval, and took five wickets. Twice he performed the hat-trick at Lord's.

He played Association football for his university, for the Corinthians, Southampton, and for England.

In his retirement he changed his methods as a writer on cricket and indulged a brisk impressionistic "columnist" style, to suit the running commentary needed by an evening paper: "Ah, here comes the Don. Walking slowly to the wicket. Deliberately. Menacingly. I don't like the look of him. He has begun with a savage hook. He is evidently in form. Dangerously so. Ah, but he is out. . . ." Essentially he was an analyst by mind, if rather at the mercy of an impulsive, highly strung temperament. He sometimes, in his heyday, got on the wrong side of the crowd by his complete absorption in himself, which was mistaken for posing or egoism. He would stand classically poised after making an on-drive, contemplating the direction and grandeur of it. The cricket field has seen no sight more Grecian than the one presented by C. B. Fry in the pride and handsomeness of his young manhood.

After he had passed his seventieth birthday, he one day entered his club, saw his friend Denzil Batchelor, and said he had done most things but was now sighing for a new world to conquer, and proposed to interest himself in racing, attach himself to a stable, and then set up "on his own". And Batchelor summed up his genius in a flash of wit: "What as, Charles? Trainer, jockey, or horse?"

It is remarkable that he was not knighted for his services to cricket, and that no honours came his way for the sterling, devoted work he did with the training-ship *Mercury*.

Mr Hubert Preston writes: Charles Fry secured a place in the Repton XI in 1888 and retained it for the next three years, being captain in 1890 and 1891. In his last season at school his average reached nearly 50.

When he went up to Oxford, Fry was captain of the cricket and Association football XIs and president of the athletic club, acting as first string in the 100 yards and the long-jump.

He also played a good deal of Rugby football, and his friends insisted that but for an unfortunate injury he would have added a Rugger "Blue" to his other honours. Charles Fry was also a fine boxer, a passable golfer, swimmer, sculler, tennis player and javelin thrower. But it was on the cricket field that he achieved his greatest triumphs. He represented three counties – Sussex, Hampshire and Surrey – scoring altogether 30,886 runs in first-class matches, average 50.22. His total of centuries reached 94 and five times he scored two separate hundreds in a match.

Fry's best season was 1901 when his aggregate reached 3,147, average 78.67. In that summer he scored 13 hundreds and made six in successive innings – a feat equalled only by Sir Donald Bradman. In 1899, 1901, and 1903, Charles Fry hit a century for the Gentlemen against the Players at Lord's, his 232 not out in 1903 remaining the highest individual score for the Gentlemen at Headquarters.

His one three-figure Test innings against Australia was 144 at The Oval in 1905, when the rubber had already been decided. Two years later he made his only other hundred for England, 129 against the South Africans, also at The Oval. Fry shared with Vine (J.) in thirty-three opening partnerships of 100 for Sussex.

Considering the very high rank he attained among batsmen, Fry, at the outset, was a stiff ungainly performer and was still somewhat laboured in stroke-production when he went up to Oxford. But from the time he began playing for Sussex with "Ranji" his game improved. He was a natural on-side batsman with a powerful straight drive and many useful leg-side strokes.

The records contain very few details of Fry's achievements as a bowler. Yet he figured in a somewhat heated controversy in the 'nineties about "unfair deliveries". Cricket writers generally regarded him as a "thrower". Fry was equally insistent that all his deliveries were scrupulously fair.

In his writings, Fry recalled how Jim Phillips, an Australian heavy-weight slow bowler turned umpire, was sent to Hove specially to "no-ball" him.

"A bright move", commented Fry, "because, of course, I rolled up my sleeve above my elbow and bowled with my arm as rigidly straight as a poker. The great Jim, sighting himself as a strong umpire, was not deterred. Large as an elephant, he bluffly no-balled me nine times running. It was a farce and the Sussex authorities and players were very angry.

"However, I bowled often afterwards unscathed, even in Gentlemen v Players' at Lord's and in a Test match."

Outside sport, Fry's greatest work was accomplished as director of the training ship *Mercury*, which he saved from extinction and to which he devoted forty-two years of unsparing effort entirely without remuneration. He was assisted by his wife, formerly Miss Beatrice Holme-Sumner, who died in 1941. In recognition of their work, Charles Fry was given the honorary rank of Captain in the R.N.R. and Mrs Fry was awarded the O.B.E.

In his absorbing autobiography, *Life Worth Living*, published in 1939, Fry told of how he "very nearly became the King of Albania". His association with Ranjitsinhji led him to occupy the position of substitute delegate for India at the Assemblies of the League of Nations at Geneva, where he composed a speech delivered by Ranji which "turned Mussolini out of Corfu".

The Albanians sent a delegation and appointed a Bishop, who bore a striking resemblance to W. G. Grace, to find "an English country gentlemen with £10,000 a year" for their King. Fry had the first qualification but not the second; but Ranji certainly could have provided the money. "If I had really pressed Ranji to promote me," said Fry, "it is quite on the cards that I should have been King of Albania yesterday, if not today."

In collaboration with his wife, he wrote the novel *A Mother's Son* which was published in 1907.

ENGLAND v WEST INDIES

FIRST TEST MATCH
Played at Birmingham, May 30, 31, June 1, 3, 4, 1957

DRAWN. THE RETURN of Test cricket to Edgbaston after an interval of 28 years produced one of the most remarkable matches of all time. Blessed with fine weather throughout, although the last day turned cold, the contest was notable for some excellent personal performances and a wonderful recovery by England who seemed on the brink of defeat when they began their second innings 288 behind. In the end, West Indies had their backs to the wall and had to fight strenuously to ward off disaster.

Among the records set, the following were most notable:

(1) May and Cowdrey put on 411 together, a Test record for the fourth wicket: the highest stand ever made for England and the third highest for any side in the history of Test cricket. It fell 40 short of the highest – 451 by Bradman and Ponsford for the Australian second wicket against England at The Oval in 1934. Roy and Mankad made an opening stand of 413 for India against New Zealand at Madras in 1955–56.

(2) May's 285 not out was the best score by an England captain, surpassing Hammond's 240 against Australia at Lord's in 1938. England's best against West Indies is 325 by Sandham at Kingston in 1930.

(3) May's 285 not out was his highest in first-class cricket and the highest individual score in all post-war Test cricket, beating Compton's 278 v Pakistan at Nottingham in 1954.

(4) Cowdrey's 154 was his highest score in Test cricket and his first Test century in England.

(5) Ramadhin, in his marathon performance, bowled 774 balls, the most delivered by a bowler in a Test, beating Verity's 766 against South Africa at Durban in 1939. He also bowled most balls (588) in any single first-class innings, including Tests, beating his colleague Valentine who sent down 552 balls in the second innings against England at Nottingham in 1950. The highest number of balls ever bowled by one man in a first-class match was 917 by C. S. Nayudu for Holkar v Bombay in 1944–45.

(6) O. G. Smith gained the distinction of hitting a century on his first appearance against England, a feat he had previously accomplished on his first appearance against Australia at Kingston, Jamaica, in 1954–55. Denis Compton hit hundreds on début against Australia, South Africa and West Indies.

England were fortunate when May won the toss for the twelfth time in sixteen matches. From the original thirteen players selected, they left out Graveney and Wardle and West Indies omitted Valentine.

Seldom can England have given such a disappointing exhibition on a perfect pitch. In four hours the whole side were dismissed for 186 and Ramadhin, with seven wickets for 49, had achieved his best performance in Test cricket.

Ramadhin kept his opponents guessing by his peculiar flick of the right wrist. None could tell his intention, whether he was attempting off spin or leg spin. As usual, he kept his shirt sleeves buttoned at the wrists and it was difficult to see how the ball left his right hand. He acquired very little spin and the majority of his wickets were taken with straight balls.

Gilchrist, a wiry, long-armed fast bowler, provided a contrast to Ramadhin. After lunch he bowled without relief for an hour and fifty minutes, maintaining a fiery pace for seventeen overs.

West Indies lost Pairaudeau to a yorker in Trueman's second over, but Rohan Kanhai and Walcott took command and saw the total to 83 for one wicket by the close of the first day. Early the next day, Walcott, stealing a single, pulled a leg muscle so severely that he collapsed and fainted. Soon he was compelled to have Pairaudeau as a runner and later in the innings Pairaudeau also acted as runner for Worrell. Further ill-luck overtook West Indies at another stage when Gilchrist went lame so that neither he nor Worrell could take part in the attack.

The second day produced an unfinished stand of 119 by O. G. Smith and Worrell. When Statham removed Kanhai with the first ball of the day, and later Walcott went for 90 and Sobers for 53, England were holding their own.

A wonderful slip catch by Bailey, who flung himself to his left and held with both hands a vicious cut, dismissed Sobers. Walcott showed much patience in an innings of four hours twenty minutes, but his punishing powers were revealed in the shape of eleven 4s. By mid-

Top left: Maurice Tate, landlord of the King's Arms, Rotherfield, Sussex.
Below far left: Alf Valentine.
Below, centre: P. B. H. May in June 1955.
Top right: Ken Barrington pulls Preston (Essex) to the boundary.
Top far right: Keith Miller, Australia, June 1956.
Bottom right: Sid Buller and Charlie Elliott.

afternoon half the West Indies wickets had gone for 197. They were no more than 11 ahead and Trueman and Statham had the new ball. Here began the long stand by Smith and Worrell. Often each was beaten by the two pace bowlers, but they survived, taking the score to 316 for five wickets.

A record attendance for Edgbaston of 32,000 people saw the cricket on Saturday and still West Indies held the mastery. Indeed, the England bowlers toiled from 3.20 p.m. on Friday until 1.30 p.m. on Saturday before they managed to break the Smith-Worrell partnership of 190 made in five hours.

Pairaudeau occupied an abnormal amount of time in the middle for a man who scored only a single. He spent three and a quarter hours as runner for Walcott and then five hours for Worrell.

Even after Statham bowled Worrell with the last ball before lunch England had to wait another eighty-five minutes for their success. Altogether Smith stayed six hours and fifty-two minutes for his 161, being eighth out at 469. He hit one 6 and eighteen 4s and scored quite quickly after completing his hundred.

When England batted a second time, West Indies had Hall and Asgarali as substitutes for Walcott and Worrell; later Alexander appeared for Gilchrist, who began the bowling with Atkinson. Ninety minutes elapsed before Ramadhin caused more consternation by deceiving Richardson and then bowling Insole in the next over.

Fortunately for England, Close, despite a blow on the left hand, defended resolutely and he and May raised the score to 102 for two wickets at the close of the third day.

Monday was memorable for the feat of May in batting all day and, excepting the first twenty minutes, Cowdrey was with him the whole time. It was a tremendous struggle. Both found the answer to Ramadhin by playing forward to him. His analysis for the day read: 48 overs, 20 maidens, 74 runs, 0 wickets. At the close England were 378 for three wickets; May 193, Cowdrey 78. While May took four hours ten minutes to reach three figures, Cowdrey, avoiding all risks, completed 50 out of 160 in three hours forty minutes.

As the wonderful partnership ripened on the last day many new cricket records were established. With the position still critical, defence remained the prime objective. Just after one o'clock Cowdrey completed his century in seven and three-quarter hours and thereupon he changed his tactics, driving and cutting powerfully so that his third fifty came in fifty-five minutes.

At length, Asgarali caught Cowdrey at long on. The stand had lasted eight hours twenty minutes, Cowdrey having hit sixteen 4s and 63 singles. In the next half-hour May and Evans put on 59 more runs before May declared. Beginning his match-saving effort at 5.40 p.m. on Saturday, May batted till 3.20 p.m. on Tuesday, and helped to change the total from 65 for two wickets to 583 for four. No man could have done more for England than the captain, whose record innings of 285 not out lasted five minutes short of ten hours. May hit two 6s, twenty-five 4s and 111 singles. The perfect stylist and excelling with the cover drive, he made very few false strokes for such a long stay.

Both Ramadhin and Atkinson bowled tirelessly. West Indies used only two balls throughout the innings, the first being changed after 96 overs so that 162 overs were bowled with the second.

After their gruelling time in the field, West Indies. set to make 296 in two hours twenty minutes, lost Kanhai and Pairaudeau to Trueman for only nine runs. Then with the fielders clustered round the batsmen, Laker and Lock ran riot, seven wickets going for 68 runs, but Goddard, the captain, defended solidly for forty minutes, constantly putting his pads to the ball, and Atkinson was there for the final seven minutes.

No doubt May could have declared when Cowdrey left, but having seen his side out of trouble he was not prepared to give West Indies the slightest chance of success. Attendance 64,968; receipts £29,496. N.P.

ENGLAND

First Innings

P. E. Richardson c Walcott b Ramadhin	47
D. B. Close c Rohan Kanhai b Gilchrist	15
D. J. Insole b Ramadhin	20
P. B. H. May c Weekes b Ramadhin	30
M. C. Cowdrey c Gilchrist b Ramadhin	4
T. E. Bailey b Ramadhin	1
G. A. R. Lock b Ramadhin	0
T. G. Evans b Gilchrist	14
J. C. Laker b Ramadhin	7
F. S. Trueman not out	29
J. B. Statham b Atkinson	13
B 3, l-b 3	6
	186

1/32 2/61 3/104 4/115 5/116
6/118 7/121 8/130 9/150

Second Innings

c sub b Ramadhin	34
c Weekes b Gilchrist	42
b Ramadhin	0
not out	285
c sub b Smith	154
not out	29
B 23, l-b 16	39
(4 wkts dec.)	**583**

1/63 2/65
3/113 4/524

WEST INDIES

First Innings

Rohan Kanhai lbw b Statham	42
B. H. Pairaudeau b Trueman	1
C. L. Walcott c Evans b Laker	90
E. D. Weekes b Trueman	9
G. Sobers c Bailey b Statham	53
O. G. Smith lbw b Laker	161
F. M. Worrell b Statham	81
J. D. Goddard c Lock b Laker	24
D. Atkinson c Statham b Laker	1
S. Ramadhin not out	5
R. Gilchrist run out	0
B 1, l-b 6	7
	474

1/4 2/83 3/120 4/183 5/197
6/387 7/466 8/469 9/474

Second Innings

c Close b Trueman	1
b Trueman	7
c Lock b Laker	1
c Trueman b Lock	33
c Cowdrey b Lock	14
lbw b Laker	5
c May b Lock	0
not out	0
not out	4
B 7	7
(7 wkts)	**72**

1/1 2/9 3/25
4/27 5/43 6/66 7/68

West Indies Bowling

	Overs	Mdns	Runs	Wkts	Overs	Mdns	Runs	Wkts
Worrell	9	1	27	—				
Gilchrist	27	4	74	2	26	2	67	1
Ramadhin	31	16	49	7	98	35	179	2
Atkinson	12.4	3	30	1	72	29	137	—
Sobers					30	4	77	—
Smith					26	4	72	1
Goddard					6	2	12	—

England Bowling

	Overs	Mdns	Runs	Wkts	Overs	Mdns	Runs	Wkts
Statham	39	4	114	3	2	—	6	—
Trueman	30	4	99	2	5	3	7	2
Bailey	34	11	80	—				
Laker	54	17	119	4	24	20	13	2
Lock	34.4	15	55	—	27	19	31	3
Close					2	1	8	—

Umpires: E. Davies and C. S. Elliott.

WEST INDIES v PAKISTAN

THIRD TEST MATCH
Played at Kingston, February 26, 27, 28. March 1, 3, 4, 1958

WEST INDIES WON by an innings and 174 runs. All else in this crushing defeat for Pakistan was overshadowed by the feat of Garfield Sobers, the West Indies 21-year-old left-hander, in beating the Test record individual score by Sir Leonard Hutton, made for England against Australia at The Oval nearly twenty years previously. Sobers passed that by one run and was still unbeaten when West Indies declared at the vast total of 790 for three. So elated were the crowd of 20,000 at Sabina Park that they swarmed over the field and the pitch became so damaged that the umpires ordered repairs and the last fifty-five minutes of the fourth day could not be played.

Sobers' monumental innings was his first century in Test cricket. On a perfect pitch he made strokes freely throughout, hitting thirty-eight 4s and batting for ten hours eight minutes, compared with thirteen hours twenty minutes by Hutton. Two factors greatly helped Sobers, the sadly depleted nature of the Pakistan attack. and the splendid support of Hunte, who helped him in a second-wicket stand of 446. This, the second highest stand in Test cricket, fell only five runs short of the record for any wicket, 451 by Sir Donald Bradman and W. H. Ponsford for Australia against England at The Oval in 1934.

Kardar, Pakistan's captain, went into the match with a broken finger on his left hand, yet he bowled 37 overs of his left-arm spinners against doctor's orders. Mahmood Hussain pulled a thigh muscle after only five balls in the first over of the innings, and did not bowl again; Nasimul Ghani, another left-arm bowler, fractured a thumb quite early in the long West Indies' innings. So Fazal Mahmood, who sent down a phenomenal number of overs for a bowler of his pace, and Khan Mohammad were left as the only two fit regular bowlers. Sound batting by Imtiaz Ahmed, Saeed Ahmed and Wallis Mathias gave Pakistan a good start on the first day, but a shower next day helped the seam bowlers E. Atkinson and Dewdney, who brought about a collapse. Wazir Mohammad batted gallantly in a bid to stave off defeat in the second innings, but with Mahmood Hussain and Nasimul Ghani unable to bat West Indies secured victory after only forty minutes' play on the last day.

PAKISTAN

First Innings
Hanif Mohammad c Alexander b Gilchrist 3
Imtiaz Ahmed c Alexander b Gilchrist 122
Saeed Ahmed c Weekes b Smith 52
Wallis Mathias b Dewdney 77
Alim-un-Din c Alexander b Atkinson 15
A. H. Kardar c Sobers b Atkinson 15
Wazir Mohammad c Walcott b Dewdney 2
Fazal Mahmood c Alexander b Atkinson 6
Nasimul Ghani b Atkinson 5
Mahmood Hussain b Atkinson 20
Khan Mohammad not out 3
    B 2, l-b 5, n-b 1 8

1/4 2/122 3/223 4/249 5/287   328
6/291 7/299 8/301 9/317

Second Innings
b Gilchrist 13
lbw b Dewdney 0
c Gilchrist b Gibbs 44
c Alexander b Atkinson 19
b Gibbs 30
lbw b Dewdney 57
lbw b Atkinson 106
c Alexander b Atkinson 0
absent hurt 0
absent hurt 0
not out 0
    B 16, l-b 3 19

1/8 2/20 3/57 4/105 5/120   288
6/286 7/286 8/288

WEST INDIES

C. Hunte *run out* 260
R. Kanhai *c Imtiaz b Fazal* 25
G. Sobers *not out* 365
E. D. Weekes *c Hanif b Fazal* 39
C. L. Walcott *not out* 88
B 1, l-b 8, w 4 13

1/87   2/533   3/602   (3 wkts dec.) 790

O. G. Smith. E. Atkinson, L. Gibbs. F. C. M. Alexander. T. Dewdney and R. Gilchrist did not bat.

West Indies Bowling

	Overs	Mdns	Runs	Wkts	Overs	Mdns	Runs	Wkts
Gilchrist	25	3	106	2	12	3	65	1
Dewdney	26	4	88	2	19.3	2	51	2
Atkinson	21	7	42	5	18	6	36	3
Gibbs	7	—	32	—	21	6	46	2
Smith	18	3	39	1	8	2	20	—
Sobers	5	1	13	—	15	4	41	—
Weekes					3	1	10	—

Pakistan Bowling

	Overs	Mdns	Runs	Wkts
Mahmood	0.5	—	2	—
Fazal	85.2	20	247	2
Khan	54	5	259	—
Nasimul	14	3	39	—
Kardar	37	2	141	—
Mathias	4	—	20	—
Alim	4	—	34	—
Hanif	2	—	11	—
Saeed	6	—	24	—

NOTES BY THE EDITOR, 1959
SOBERS MAKES HIGHEST TEST SCORE

GARFIELD SOBERS, THE tall 22-year-old West Indies left-hander, also distinguished himself by scoring 365 not out in the third Test against Pakistan at Kingston on March 1, 1958 and surpassing Hutton's world record Test innings of 364 for England against Australia at The Oval in 1938. He followed with a century in each innings in the next Test and continued his Bradman-like consistency when touring India, scoring centuries in his first three Tests there. His remarkable sequence brought him 1,115 runs in six successive Tests – ten innings, four times not out.

SURREY v NORTHAMPTONSHIRE
Played at The Oval, June 4, 5, 6, 1958

DRAWN. NORTHAMPTONSHIRE TAKING two points, the first points of the season conceded by Surrey. A long struggle for first innings lead was a story of records but little entertainment. The match had lasted fifteen and three-quarter hours when Northamptonshire, who occupied nine hours of the time, went ahead. Stewart, with his first century of the season, and Constable batted particularly well for Surrey and at the close of the first day the score was 324 for four. McIntyre, captain in the absence of May,

Raman Subba Row, one of only a handful of post-war batsmen to score a treble century in a county match, here seen in the moment of dismissal by the South African bowler Griffin. The occasion was the first Test of the 1960 series.

who, like Loader, Lock and Laker, was playing for England, chose to bat on for three-quarters of an hour next day on an excellent pitch, presumably in the hope of forcing a follow-on. With Northamptonshire 18 for three and then 95 for five, such an eventuality seemed likely but Surrey had to wait another six and three-quarter hours and 376 runs before breaking the sixth-wicket stand. That partnership, between the former Surrey player Subba Row, leading his side at The Oval for the first time, and Lightfoot, created a record for any Northamptonshire wicket. Subba Row's 300 was the highest individual score for the county, as well as equal to the previous highest made against Surrey, and Lightfoot reached his maiden century, which took six hours twenty-three minutes and contained fourteen 4s. In all, Subba Row batted for nine hours twenty-six minutes and hit forty-two 4s. This is the only instance of an individual hitting a treble century against Surrey at The Oval.

SURREY

```
T. H. Clark c Reynolds b Manning ................71
M. J. Stewart b Lightfoot ........................118
D. G. W. Fletcher c and b Lightfoot ..............0
B. Constable c Brookes b Lightfoot ..............73
K. F. Barrington not out .........................62
E. A. Bedser c Tyson b Lightfoot .................27
A. J. McIntyre not out ...........................18
        L-b 4, n-b 5 ..............................9
                                               ─────
1/144  2/156                       (5 wkts dec.) 378
3/218  4/280  5/328
```

R. C. E. Pratt, R. Swetman, D. Gibson and D. A. D. Sydenham did not bat.

NORTHAMPTONSHIRE

D. Brookes lbw b Sydenham 4
P. Arnold b Sydenham 6
B. L. Reynolds b Sydenham 6
D. W. Barrick c Barrington b Gibson 44
R. Subba Row b Clark 300
G. E. Tribe c Constable b Gibson 5
A. Lightfoot c Swetman b Clark 119
J. S. Manning c Barrington b Clark 7
K. V. Andrew c and b Barrington 8
F. H. Tyson not out 14
M. H. J. Allen not out 1
    B 9, l-b 1, w 3, n-b 2 15

1/7 2/15 3/18 4/89   (9 wkts) 529
5/95 6/471 7/492 8/507 9/520

Northamptonshire Bowling

	Overs	Mdns	Runs	Wkts
Tyson	32	8	93	—
Lightfoot	35	9	96	4
Tribe	26	5	78	—
Allen	19	7	40	—
Manning	25	9	62	1

Surrey Bowling

	Overs	Mdns	Runs	Wkts
Gibson	51	12	152	2
Sydenham	36	7	109	3
Bedser	60	39	65	—
Pratt	35	11	77	—
Barrington	22	6	63	1
Clark	10	—	48	3

Umpires: T. W. Spencer and E. Davies.

THE RECORD INDIVIDUAL INNINGS

HANIF'S 499 AT KARACHI

HANIF MOHAMMAD, PAKISTAN'S 24-year-old opening batsman, made 499, the world's highest individual score in first-class cricket, for Karachi against Bahawalpur in the semi-final of the Quaid-e-Azam Trophy at the Karachi Parsi Institute ground on January 8, 9, 11, 12, 1959. This beat the 452 not out by Sir Donald Bradman for New South Wales against Queensland at Sydney in 1929–30.

On a coir matting pitch, Hanif scored 25 in forty minutes on the first evening, 230 in five hours on the second day and 244 in four hours fifty-five minutes on the third day. He was run out when going for his 500 off the last ball of the day. Altogether he batted ten hours thirty-five minutes and hit sixty-four 4s. Hanif played superbly, rarely putting the ball in the air, he did not offer a chance and was beaten only once, and then off the pitch.

Hanif shared a stand of 259 with Wallis Mathias for the second wicket. Hanif is one of four brothers all playing in first-class cricket. Three appeared for Karachi in this match; Wazir was captain and the other was Mushtaq.

The Mohammad dynasty has proved to be one of the most prolific brotherhoods in all cricket. Sadiq played for Gloucestershire and Mushtaq captained Northamptonshire Neither quite matched the stupendous run-getting feats of Hanif, seen here with yet another Mohammad, Wazir, standing on the left of the picture. To be run out within a single run of the first quintuple century in history seems almost too cruel.

BAHAWALPUR

First Innings

Ijaz Hussain *run out*	24
Zulfiqar Ahmed *c* Aziz *b* Mahmood	0
Mohammad Iqbal *b* Ikram	20
Mohammad Ramzan *c* Wallis *b* Ikram	64
Ghiasuddin *b* Ikram	4
Jamil Khalid *run out*	12
Farrukh Salim *c* Aziz *b* Mahmood	3
Riaz Mahmood *b* Mahmood	4
Asad Bhatti *st* Aziz *b* Mushtaq	21
Tanvir Hussan *not out*	16
Aziz Ahmed *b* Ikram	8
Extras	9
	185

Second Innings

c Waqar *b* Mahmood	32
c Aziz *b* Mahmood	8
c Aziz *b* Munaf	0
lbw b Munaf	5
c Wazir *b* Ikram	12
b D'Souza	4
b Ikram	4
lbw b Mushtaq	10
b Ikram	4
c Aziz *b* D'Souza	7
not out	5
Extras	17
	108

KARACHI

Hanif Mohammad *run out*	499
Alim-ud-din *c* Zulfiqar *b* Aziz	32
Waqar Hassan *c* Tanvir *b* Iqbal	37
Wazir Mohammad *st* Tanvir *b* Jamil	31
Wallis Mathias *run out*	103
Mushtaq Mohammad *lbw b* Aziz	21
Abdul Munaf *b* Iqbal	18
Abdul Aziz *not out*	9
Extras	22
(7 wkts dec.)	772

Ikram Elahi, Mahmood Hussain and Antao D'Souza did not bat.

Karachi Bowling

	Overs	Mdns	Runs	Wkts	Overs	Mdns	Runs	Wkts
Mahmood	18	4	38	3	10	2	27	2
Ikram	17	3	48	4	8	2	10	3
Munaf	8	1	23	—	9	1	29	2
D'Souza	11	2	42	—	11	3	17	2
Mushtaq	4	—	19	1	3	—	8	1
Hanif	1	—	6	—				

Bahawalpur Bowling

	Overs	Mdns	Runs	Wkts
Zulfiqar	34	5	95	—
Ramzan	19	—	83	—
Aziz	50	4	208	2
Riaz	9	—	44	—
Ghias	37	3	139	—
Jamil	23	1	93	1
Iqbal	25	3	81	2
Tanvir	3	—	7	—

Umpires: Idris Beg and Daud Khan.

In the final, a few days later, Abdul Aziz, the Karachi wicket-keeper, died while batting against Combined Services. He was struck on the heart by a slow off-break from Dildar Awan and fell. He died fifteen minutes later on the way to hospital. Play was postponed for a day.

SUSSEX v MIDDLESEX
Played at Hove, July 30, August 1, 2, 1960

SUSSEX WON BY 202 runs. The game, which was a personal triumph for Dexter – who scored 183 and took seven wickets – had a remarkable conclusion. Middlesex, set to make 329 to win in five hours, were 121 for six when a storm held up play. Cricket was recommenced with an hour remaining and Dexter, who had taken three wickets for a single just before the stoppage, sent back two more of his rivals with consecutive balls at the same score. Then Warr, suffering from a strained groin, Hooker and Moss, with runs not mattering to them, played dead bats to Dexter, Thomson and Bates and altogether 82 deliveries were sent down without a run coming before Hooker pushed Thomson to cover for a single. When Dexter had Warr brilliantly caught at backward short leg, his spell figures were six for one in eight overs and Sussex won with thirteen minutes to spare. Dexter's 157 in the first innings was a sound yet attractive effort lasting five hours and including nineteen 4s. Like Smith, his partner in a fifth-wicket stand of 181, the Sussex captain drove with power and grace. A pulled muscle prevented Moss bowling in the second innings.

Ted Dexter, of Radley, Cambridge, Sussex and England. The possessor of a lordly straight drive and all the grace of the natural athlete, he also had his days as an effective change bowler.

SUSSEX

First Innings

A. S. M. Oakman c Murray b Bennett 13
L. J. Lenham b Warr 4
*E. R. Dexter b Drybrough 157
†J. M. Parks b Bennett 0
K. G. Suttle c Parfitt b Hooker 9
D. V. Smith c Parfitt b Bennett 80
G. H. G. Doggart not out 39
Nawab of Pataudi not out 18
    B 2, 1-b 5, w 1 8

1/6 2/26 3/27 4/42   (6 wkts dec.) 328
5/223 6/294

Second Innings

c White b Hooker 13
c Murray b Hooker 5
b Titmus 26
c Murray b Bennett 21
c White b Hooker 21
not out 65
not out 20

  L-b 9, w 1 10

1/18 2/19 3/67   (5 wkts dec.) 181
4/67 5/136

N. I. Thomson, R. V. Bell and D. L. Bates did not bat.

MIDDLESEX

First Innings

W. E. Russell c Dexter b Bates 5
R. A. Gale run out 14
R. A. White c Dexter b Thomson 3
R. W. Hooker c Doggart b Thomson 15
P. H. Parfitt c Parks b Thomson 49
F. J. Titmus run out 56
D. Bennett c Suttle b Smith 4
†J. T. Murray b Bates 16
C. D. Drybrough c Bell b Smith 0
*J. J. Warr c Bates b Thomson 12
A. E. Moss not out 6
    N-b 1 1

1/17 2/23 3/26 4/45 5/136   181
6/147 7/150 8/150 9/175

Second Innings

c Bell b Dexter 11
b Bates 33
lbw b Dexter 27
not out 5
b Bates 13
c Bates b Dexter 27
b Dexter 0
c Parks b Dexter 1
c Parks b Dexter 0
c Bell b Dexter 0
c Parks b Thomson 0
  B 5, 1-b 3, n-b 1 9

1/27 2/52 3/68 4/119 5/120   126
6/120 7/121 8/121 9/121

Middlesex Bowling

	Overs	Mdns	Runs	Wkts	Overs	Mdns	Runs	Wkts
Moss	10	1	31	—				
Warr	20	5	49	1				
Bennett	21	2	58	3	20	2	65	1
Hooker	19	4	58	1	20	7	70	3
Titmus	20	3	48	—	10	4	23	1
Drybrough	16	1	65	1	4	2	2	—
Gale	3	—	11	—	1	—	11	—

Sussex Bowling

	Overs	Mdns	Runs	Wkts	Overs	Mdns	Runs	Wkts
Thomson	26.1	11	50	4	22.1	13	26	1
Bates	24	6	57	2	13	4	50	2
Dexter	7	—	24	—	18	11	24	7
Suttle	1	1	—	—	3	2	6	—
Smith	9	1	27	2	5	1	11	—
Bell	8	2	22	—				

Umpires: W. E. Phillipson and Harry Elliott.

One of the several unforgettable features of the famous tied Test of 1960 between Richie Benaud's Australians and Frank Worrell's West Indians was the all-round cricket of Garfield Sobers, who scored a dazzling century and sent down 40 overs of bowling which ranged from genuine fast to assorted spin. One of the finest all-rounders who ever lived, Sobers went on to captain his country and also to lead Nottinghamshire in the county championship.

AUSTRALIA v WEST INDIES

FIRST TEST MATCH
Played at Brisbane, December 9, 10, 12, 13, 14, 1960

A TIE. QUITE APART from gaining a niche in cricket history as the first Test to end in a tie this match will always be remembered with enthusiasm because of its excellent cricket. It was played in a most sporting spirit, with the climax coming in a tremendously exciting finish as three wickets fell in the final over.

Australia, set to score 233 runs at a rate of 45 an hour for victory, crumbled before the fiery, sustained pace of Hall, and lost five wickets for 57. The sixth fell at 92. Then the drama began to build up as Davidson, the Australian all-rounder who enjoyed a magnificent match, was joined by Benaud, in a stand which added 134. They were still together half an hour before time, with 27 needed, when Hall took the new ball – a crucial stage.

In the event, however, the West Indies fieldsmen, often at fault during the match, rose to the occasion so that three of the last four batsmen to fall were run out in the desperate race against time. The first run-out came when Benaud called for a sharp single, but Solomon hit the stumps from mid-wicket to dismiss Davidson. Grout came in and took a single off Sobers, so that when the last momentous over from Hall began, six runs were needed with three wickets left.

The first ball hit Grout on the thigh and a leg-bye resulted: from the second Benaud gave a catch at the wicket as he swung mightily. Meckiff played the third ball back to the bowler, but when the fourth went through to the wicket-keeper, the batsmen scampered a run, Hall missing a chance to run out Meckiff as the wicket-keeper threw the ball to him. Grout hit the fifth ball high in the air, Hall attempted to take the catch himself, but the ball bounced out, and another run had been gained. Meckiff hit the sixth ball hard and high to leg, but Hunte cut it off on the boundary as the batsmen turned for the third run, which would have given Australia victory. Hunte threw in superbly, low and fast, and Grout was run out by a foot. So Kline came in to face the last two balls with the scores level. He played the seventh ball of the over towards square leg and Meckiff, backing up well, raced down the wicket, only to be out when Solomon again threw down the wicket with only the width of a stump as his target. So ended a match in which both sides had striven throughout for victory, with no thought of safety first.

West Indies attacked the bowling from the start of the match only to lose three men for 65 before Sobers, who hit a masterly century in just over two hours, including fifteen 4s, and Worrell mastered the bowling. Solomon, Alexander and Hall added valuable contributions to an innings which yielded 4.5 runs an over, despite much excellent pace bowling by Davidson. Australia succeeded in establishing a lead of 52, largely through the determination of Simpson and O'Neill, who made his highest Test score without reaching his very best form.

Indeed, West Indies missed several chances at vital times. More fine bowling by Davidson caused West Indies to battle hard for runs in their second innings, and they owed much to some high-class batting from Worrell for their respectable total, swelled usefully on the final morning by a last-wicket stand of 31 between Hall and Valentine.

WEST INDIES

First Innings

C. C. Hunte *c* Benaud *b* Davidson 24
C. Smith *c* Grout *b* Davidson 7
R. Kanhai *c* Grout *b* Davidson 15
G. Sobers *c* Kline *b* Meckiff 132
*F. M. Worrell *c* Grout *b* Davidson 65
J. Solomon *hit wkt b* Simpson 65
P. Lashley *c* Grout *b* Kline 19
†F. C. M. Alexander *c* Davidson *b* Kline 60
S. Ramadhin *c* Harvey *b* Davidson 12
W. Hall *st* Grout *b* Kline 50
A. L. Valentine *not out* 0
Extras 4

1/23 2/42 3/65 4/239 5/243   453
6/283 7/347 8/366 9/452

Second Innings

c Simpson *b* Mackay 39
c O'Neill *b* Davidson 6
c Grout *b* Davidson 54
b Davidson 14
c Grout *b* Davidson 65
lbw b Simpson 47
b Davidson 0
b Benaud 5
c Harvey *b* Simpson 6
b Davidson 18
not out 7
Extras 23

1/13 2/28 3/114 4/127 5/210   284
6/210 7/241 8/250 9/253

AUSTRALIA

First Innings
C. C. McDonald c Hunte b Sobers	57
R. B. Simpson b Ramadhin	92
R. N. Harvey b Valentine	15
N. C. O'Neill c Valentine b Hall	181
L. Favell run out	45
K. D. Mackay b Sobers	35
A. K. Davidson c Alexander b Hall	44
*R. B. Benaud lbw b Hall	10
†A. W. T. Grout lbw b Hall	4
I. Meckiff run out	4
L. F. Kline not out	3
Extras	15
	505

1/84 2/138 3/194 4/278 5/381
6/469 7/484 8/489 9/496

Second Innings
b Worrell	16
c sub b Hall	0
c Sobers b Hall	5
c Alexander b Hall	26
c Solomon b Hall	7
b Ramadhin	28
run out	80
c Alexander b Hall	52
run out	2
run out	2
not out	0
Extras	14
	232

1/1 2/7 3/49 4/49 5/57
6/92 7/226 8/228 9/232

Australia Bowling

	Overs	Mdns	Runs	Wkts	Overs	Mdns	Runs	Wkts
Davidson	30	2	135	5	24.6	4	87	6
Meckiff	18	—	129	1	4	1	19	—
Mackay	3	—	15	—	21	7	52	1
Benaud	24	3	93	—	31	6	69	1
Simpson	8	—	25	1	7	2	18	2
Kline	17.6	6	52	3	4	—	14	—
O'Neill					1	—	2	—

West Indies Bowling

	Overs	Mdns	Runs	Wkts	Overs	Mdns	Runs	Wkts
Hall	29.3	1	140	4	17.7	3	63	5
Worrell	30	—	93	—	16	3	41	1
Sobers	32	—	115	2	8	—	30	—
Valentine	24	6	82	1	10	4	27	—
Ramadhin	15	1	60	1	17	3	57	1

Umpires: C. Hoy and C. J. Egar.

Gary Sobers out for 14 in the second innings, comprehensively bowled by the Australian all-rounder Alan Davidson. In this Test the rugged "Davo" became the first player to score 100 runs and take ten wickets in a Test.

HENDREN, ELIAS, who died in a London hospital on October 4, 1962, aged 73, was one of the most famous batsmen to play for Middlesex and England. Only one cricketer, Sir John Hobbs, in the whole history of the first-class game hit more centuries than Hendren's 170; only two, Hobbs and F. E. Woolley, exceeded his aggregate of runs, 57,610 scored at an average of 50.80 per innings.

"Patsy", as because of his Irish ancestry, he was affectionately known the world over, joined the Lord's ground-staff in 1905 and from his first appearance for Middlesex in 1909 he played regularly till 1937. Not always orthodox in style, this short, stockily-built batsman was celebrated for the power with which he invested his driving, for his cutting and for his courage in hooking fast bowlers. On pitches helpful to bowlers, he used his feet with consummate skill. His ability as a deep fieldsman is illustrated to some extent by the number of catches he brought off, 725, but the number of runs he saved cannot be gauged.

Apart from his achievements, "Patsy" was a "character" of a type sadly lacking in modern cricket. No game in which he was engaged could be altogether dull. If it looked like becoming so, Hendren could be relied upon at one time or another to produce some antic which would bring an appreciative chuckle from the onlookers. Furthermore, he was a first-rate mimic and wit, qualities which made him an admirable member of teams on tours, of which he took part in six – three in Australia, one in South Africa and two in the West Indies. Altogether he played in 51 Test matches, 28 of them against Australia, scoring 3,525 runs.

Of his seven centuries in Tests the highest was 205 not out against the West Indies at Port of Spain in 1930, when he and L. E. G. Ames (105) shared a fourth wicket stand of 237. "Patsy's" aggregate of 1,766, average 126.14, in that tour remains a record for a season in the West Indies. His highest innings in first-class cricket was 301 not out from the Worcestershire bowling at Dudley in 1933; on four occasions he put together a hundred in each innings of a match and he reached three-figures for Middlesex against every other first-class county. His best season was that of 1928 when he hit 3,311 runs, including 13 centuries, at an average of 70.44. In three summers he exceeded 3,000 runs; in twelve he made more than 2,000 and in ten over 1,000. Among many big partnerships with his great friend and county colleague, J. W. Hearne, that of 375 against Hampshire at Southampton in 1923 was at the time a world's record for the third wicket.

In 1933 Hendren caused something of a sensation at Lord's when he batted against the West Indies' fast bowlers wearing a special cap. Fashioned by his wife, this cap had three peaks, two of which covered the ears and temples, and was lined with sponge rubber. Hendren explained that he needed protection after being struck on the head two years earlier by the new-fashioned persistent short-pitched bouncers.

Following his retirement from the field, he succeeded Wilfred Rhodes as coach at Harrow School and for four years held a similar post with Sussex. He was elected a life member of MCC in 1949 and also served on the Middlesex Committee. In 1952 he became scorer for Middlesex, continuing till ill-health compelled him to give up in 1960. In his younger days he was a fine Association football wing forward, playing in turn for Brentford, Queen's Park Rangers, Manchester City and Coventry City, and he appeared in a "Victory" International for England in 1919.

SOUTH AUSTRALIA v MCC
Played at Adelaide, December 23, 24, 26, 27, 1962

DRAWN. COWDREY RETURNED to form with a vengeance, scoring 307, the highest innings ever played by a touring player in Australia. In temperature of almost 100 degrees, MCC made 474 for four on the first day, Cowdrey finishing with 244. He was missed when 43 and 91, but otherwise batted faultlessly. Next day he and Graveney carried their fifth wicket stand to 344 in just under four hours, the second highest partnership for MCC in Australia. Cowdrey batted six and a half hours and hit four 6s and twenty-nine 4s, his driving being superb. Favell replied with a brisk century for South Australia, scoring 120 in two hours, fifty-four minutes and bright displays also came from Sobers, McLachlan and Dansie. The temperature dropped by over 30 degrees on the Monday. Leading by 136, MCC lost three for 23, but declared a second time and set South Australia to score 304 in four hours. After the fall of two wickets for 16, Sobers gave a great display of hitting. Rain held up play for fifty-five minutes and also ended the game an hour early. Sobers obtained twelve 4s in scoring 75 not out in sixty-three minutes and a fine finish might have occurred but for the weather.

MCC

First Innings

P. H. Parfitt b Brooks 2
Rev. D. S. Sheppard b Sobers 81
*E. R. Dexter c Chappell b Sobers 16
M. C. Cowdrey c Chappell b Dansie 307
K. F. Barrington run out 52
T. W. Graveney not out 122
F. J. Titmus (did not bat)..............................
†J. T. Murray (did not bat) ....
        B 1, l-b 3, w 2 6

1/2 2/39 3/144 4/242   (5 wkts dec.) 586
5/586

D. A. Allen, L. J. Coldwell and J. D. F. Larter did not bat.

Second Innings

c Jarman b Brooks 7
b Sobers 5
c Chappell b Sangster 37
c McLachlan b Sobers 2
not out 52
b Sincock 35
c Lill b Dansie 4
not out 24
        L-b 1 1

1/82 2/12 3/23   (6 wkts dec.) 167
4/62 5/108 6/121

BOWLING: **First Innings**—Brooks 18-0-74 - 1; Sobers 25-2-124-2; Sincock 26-1-153-0; Sangster 10-0-75-0; Chappell 9-1-49-0; Dansie 10.2-1-59-1; Cunningham 2-0-28-0; McLachlan 3-0-14-0; Favell 1-0-4-0. **Second Innings**—Brooks 8-0-30-1; Sobers 9-1-44-2; Sangster 3-0-23-1; Sincock 10-0-55-1; Dansie 5-1-14-1.

SOUTH AUSTRALIA

First Innings

*L. Favell c Dexter b Allen 120
K. Cunningham c Sheppard b Coldwell 15
J. Lill c Dexter b Titmus 55
G. Sobers c Allen b Barrington 89
I. McLachlan b Allen 62
N. Dansie c and b Barrington 64
I. Chappell run out 2
J. Sangster c Parfitt b Barrington 19
†B. N. Jarman c Barrington b Titmus 11
D. Sincock c Graveney b Titmus..................0
G. Brooks not out 2
        B 2, l-b 4, n-b 5 11

1/27 2/165 3/215 4/343 5/357   450
6/375 7/425 8/442 9/445

Second Innings

c Cowdrey b Coldwell 3
hit wkt b Larter 29
b Coldwell 2
not out 75
b Larter 2
not out 0

        L-b 1, w 1 2

1/8 2/16 3/89 4/97   (4 wkts) 113

BOWLING: **First Innings**—Coldwell 19-3-69-1; Larter 22-1-113-0; Dexter 15-1-60-0; Titmus 21.1-1-88-3. Allen 21-4-54-2; Barrington 18-2-55-3. **Second Innings**—Coldwell 8.7-0-65-2; Larter 5-0-23-2; Dexter 1-0-15-0; Allen 2-0-8-0.

Umpires: C. Egar and R. Joseph.

1963 – 1988 THE MODERN ERA

AS THE 1960's opened, the unthinkable had very nearly come about. English cricket was on the brink of bankruptcy. Virtually every county in the championship was running at a loss which was increasing year by year as the upward spiral of inflation began to run away with the national economy. Since the peak season of 1947, when over two million customers had been tempted inside county grounds, paying for admission to matches which seemed to them well worth the investment, the crowds had dwindled away until, with attendances standing at less than half the post-war record, the first-class game hovered on the brink of liquidation. Although the county game had hardly ever been solvent throughout the history of the championship, there had always been the benefaction of patronage to come to the rescue. The monied aristocracy had always played its part in supporting the game through legacies, bequests and handouts of all sorts: but two world wars and experiments in the redistribution of wealth by successive parliaments had decimated the ranks of prospective patrons. Cricket had, for the first time in its life, to become self-supporting, ironically at the very moment when running costs and wage bills were rising fast. Drastic measures were required and were duly taken amid a chorus of wailing and lamentation.

England win the fifth and final Test against Australia in 1968 as Derek Underwood traps Inverarity LBW. An aggressive field placing features all ten England fielders around the bat.

This parlous situation was not entirely due to social conditions which were beyond the game's influence. Cricket between the counties had become an endless, pointless war of attrition. The number of overs bowled per day had fallen steadily, until at last the cricketers were in effect charging the spectator for a full day's play and then giving him only three quarters of what he had paid for. Drawn matches were by far the most common outcome in the championship. Batting seemed to have grown less enterprising and more negative, so that run scoring fell just as drastically as the rate of overs. And yet an England team which boasted, in the mid-1950s, such stars as Denis Compton, Colin Cowdrey and Peter May could hardly be described as unattractive. Moreover, in Laker of Surrey, the English had found one of the greatest off-break bowlers of all time, while Alec Bedser at fast-medium, and Fred Trueman and Brian Statham as genuine fast bowlers, should have contributed something to the pleasure of watching cricket. It is an indication of the depth of English cricket talent that in the Australian tour of 1954-55 neither Laker, Trueman nor Lock was selected, and yet the Ashes were retained. It was the county championship and not the international scene which was dying on its feet. Indeed, public interest in Test matches increased steadily, until at last, stimulated by the most sophisticated televised ball-by-ball coverage, cricket became a national obsession in countries which not so many years before had been hard put to find a national side capable of offering the home country serious opposition.

But if the county system failed, there could be no continuing supply of Test players. Something had to be done, and this something took the form of radical innovation. One of the most historic fixtures of the century was surely between Lancashire and Leicestershire at Old Trafford on Sunday, 1st May, 1963. Note the brevity of the time allotted to the fixture: one day. In its attempt to save itself, cricket was at last adopting two principles abhorrent to the generations of the old guard who had run the game for two centuries. First, it was attempting to win back the lost votaries by resorting to the slam-bang, hit-or-miss attractions of one-day cricket, complete with sudden-death climax. And second, it was embracing the serpent of 'sponsorship'. That match between Lancashire and Leicestershire was stimulated by the money of the Gillette Razor Company, who were subsidising the first one-day competition of all time, and it must be accounted one of the more priceless ironies of English life that this heretical one-day fixture should, because of the perversities of the local climate, have taken two days to complete. But there is no question that the one-day game, for all its crudities, saved the day. Crowds streamed back in their tens of thousands; books began to balance once more.

But at a price. Cup finals at Lord's gradually became associated with boisterousness; this imperceptibly modulated into drunkenness, which then began to erupt into the occasional fracas. On the field of play too, there was a price to pay for the new-found solvency. In the one-day game it is far more important not to give away runs than to take wickets, more praiseworthy to slog a quick thirty than to play a balanced innings lasting an hour. There were instances of batsmen who actually batted too long to do any good, their tenure of the crease and their rate of scoring combining to become an advantage to the fielding side. Spin bowlers, who in the three or five-day game are perfectly content to spend some runs in the hope of buying a wicket, tended to become a rarity in one-day cricket, and, apart from the first two or three batsmen in the order, it was never possible for a man to enjoy the luxury of playing himself in. Inevitably the superficial manufactured excitement of the one-day game drew a new semi-informed audience which wanted thrills first and cricket only second. The certainty of a finish leaving one side or the other victorious debased the currency of the drama so that eventually half the one-day matches in the world seemed to be decided on the last delivery of the day. And because of the box-office, the tendency was for the administrators to arrange more and more international one-day contests. And, just as inevitable, in countries like India and Pakistan which boasted huge crowds, the one-day game so utterly eclipsed the five-day Test that by the end of the '80s, the situation has become highly alarming.

But more far-reaching than these technical innovations has been the intrusion of the outside world into cricketing affairs. The old dictum of Neville Cardus, that societies get the cricket they deserve was born out in the 1960s as cricket was squeezed out of the cocoon it had occupied for so long. In a land committed to the egalitarian ideal, or at any rate committed to paying lip-service to that ideal, the abolition of the distinction between Gentlemen and Players was inevitable. So was the steady decline in the number of public schools fixtures at Lord's, and the gradual slipping away from authentic first-class status of the Oxford and Cambridge sides. But not even these changes seem in retrospect to have been as significant as two crises of the period which not only convulsed the entire cricketing world, but which spilled over onto those front pages usually preoccupied with the drunken dance of world politics. In the first of these crises cricket was at the mercy of parliamentary heavyweights who do not seem to have provided very wise counsel. In the second crisis cricket once again was swept aside by forces beyond its control, this time those of the media. And the extent to which the game by now had graduated albeit unwillingly on to the world stage is reflected by the fact that each of these crises was rooted in the soil of other lands, other cultures.

In 1969 the England all-rounder Basil D'Oliveira was selected to tour South Africa with the national side. Sending D'Oliveira, who had emigrated from South Africa some years before, was seen by the South African government as a deliberate provocation, and there followed one of the great absurdities in the history of codified team games when the South African government, in a fit of diplomatic dementia, insisted on its right to select its opponent's eleven. D'Oliveira, announced the South African Prime Minister, must not tour. Nor did he. Nor did anyone else. During the debate English cricket grounds were the scene of demonstrations and sit-ins which wrecked the delicate balance of civilised forces which are essential for the continuance of play. South Africa's expulsion from the brotherhood of Test-playing nations, was one more step towards its complete sporting ostracism.

South Africa's lamentable lack of political acumen during the D'Oliveira affair had its commercial parallel in the Packer case in the 1970s, in which an Australian TV and Press entrepreneur opened a campaign to win Australian television rights for Test matches. The battle spilled over into

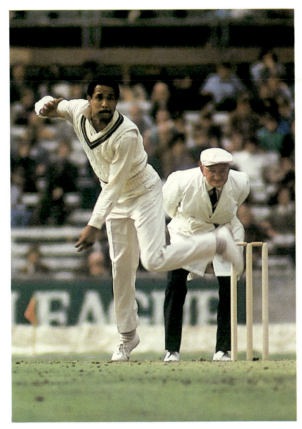

Left: Gary Sobers bowling at The Oval in 1973. Tom Spencer is umpiring.
Above: John Edrich, having just been bowled by Peter Pollock, quizzically surveys the wreckage.

England, where the captain of the national side performed one of the most spectacular *volte faces* in the history of sport when he revealed himself as an agent for the renegades, recruiting star English players at exorbitant financial rates for the new televised cricket circus of the future.

The upshot was a succession of rogue elevens flying false national colours, the wrecking of several distinguished playing careers, a substantial improvement of monies paid to professionals and scenes of acrimony in the courts from which the only beneficiaries were, as usual, the lawyers. There was moreover a pathetic debasement of the game seen on Australian television, which now dressed its heroes in multi-coloured suits of pyjamas and, for the benefit of the less informed viewer, used a cartoon sketch of a duck to denote the dismissal of a player without scoring. Cricket was never the same after the Packer Affair, but then, as cynics were quick to point out, it had never been the same before.

These years have also seen the rise of great individual heroes who probably deserve a place alongside any of the giants of cricket history, notably the West Indians Gary Sobers, Clive Lloyd and Vivian Richards, the South Africans Graeme Pollock and Barry Richards, the Indian Sunil Gavaskar and the Australian Dennis Lillee. In England the Yorkshire batsman Geoffrey Boycott consistently scored centuries and just as consistently inspired rancour and controversy, while Ted Dexter proved to be the very last in the long line

Sunil Gavaskar, who scored 188 in the first innings, follows through on a classic cover drive during the MCC Bicentenary game at Lord's in 1987.

of patrician dazzlers to captain his country. Towards the end of the period there came the rise and extraordinary success as a master-strategist of one of the most successful Test captains of the age, the Middlesex intellectual Michael Brearley.

None of these outstanding cricketers, though, made the impact on world opinion achieved by the Somerset all-rounder Ian Botham, one of the most extraordinary players ever seen. It could be said of Botham as it was once said of Marc Antony, that nobody knew what he would do next and neither did he. One of the most prolific wicket takers in the history of international cricket, the most spectacular hitter of sixes in living memory, Botham will be remembered for a great many extra-cricketing incidents, ranging from the magnificent to the banal. Above all he will be celebrated as the man who, in the Test series against Australia in 1981, dragged the game out of the realms of the feasible into those of pure fantasy. To turn a Test match around singlehanded by scoring a century of dazzling wit and defiance was perhaps not unprecedented. There had been a few instances before, notably Gilbert Jessop's in the 1902 series. But Jessop had only done it once. Botham proceeded to repeat the miracle two Tests later, with an innings so death-defying that the sobriety of *The Times* correspondent collapsed in impassioned euphoria as he described it as 'perhaps the greatest innings of all time'. Nobody had ever approached these feats, and yet Botham went further. In the Test separating his two historic centuries, he turned the game around yet again, although this time with different skills. When Australia looked to be battling successfully towards victory Botham came in for a late burst, took five wickets for one run and dashed off the field with yet another Test triumph in his pocket.

When we remind ourselves that Botham was a Somerset man, and that among his county team-mates were the two great West Indians Vivian Richards and Joel Garner, it is no wonder that Somerset were by far the most attractive club side of the 1980s. Connoisseurs of the arcane may care to note that for the first, and surely the last time in cricket history, there was a Test between England and the West Indies during this period when both sides were led by players from the same English county, neither of whom were captains of the county side in question, yet that captain also took part in the match. This riddle is resolved by the names of Richards and Botham as captains of their respective countries, while the England side also included the Somerset captain, Brian Rose.

From the spectator's point of view this period has been in some respects a golden age, owing to the sudden influx into the county championship of all the great overseas players. Every county except Yorkshire has boasted its imported stars, but Notts in particular with Gary Sobers, Gloucestershire with the South African Mike Proctor and the Pakistani Zaheer Abbas, and Lancashire with Clive Lloyd, were among the clubs responsible for introducing sheer genius to the cricket grounds of England. The overseas player was thought by some to be a threat to the development of local talent. And yet without these stars, would the crowds have remained faithful?

By the end of the 1980s, the dominant factor in cricket has become the one-day game, exalted through financial expediency. Test Matches are now played to relentless tour schedules and in front of dwindling audiences. Dissent on the field and rowdyism off it is becoming commonplace. One international player in this era dropped a brick by flinging one into the crowd. In 1987 the Marylebone Cricket Club celebrated its two hundredth birthday amid a world threatening to split its cricket between those players who consorted with South Africa and those who did not.

But if this vision of the game's future seems bleak, there is one straw in the wind which offers considerable reassurance. The annual sales of *Wisden Cricketers' Almanack* continue to rise.

KENT v MIDDLESEX
Played at Tunbridge Wells, June 15, 17, 18, 1963

DRAWN. THE LATE arrival on Monday morning of nine of the Middlesex team, including Drybrough, the captain, provided a situation without parallel in the history of first-class cricket. At the close on Saturday, Middlesex, having dismissed Kent for 150, were 121 for three wickets with White 43 not out, Hooker 13 not out. The team had stayed at a local hotel on Friday night and arranged to do the same on Monday night, but they returned to their London homes at the week-end.

Three players arrived at the ground with plenty of time to spare. They were White and S. E. Russell, who had already been dismissed, and Clark, the twelfth man. White put on his pads and gloves and waited on the boundary, hoping his partner would be in time while the umpires and the Kent players went to the middle. After a wait of a liberal two minutes, the umpires led the players off the field and it was officially stated that the umpires had closed the Middlesex innings.

It was decided that Kent should begin their second innings within ten minutes and Cowdrey agreed that Clark could keep wicket while if necessary White and S. E. Russell shared the bowling, Kent providing sufficient substitute fielders to make up eleven in the field for Middlesex. Actually, Underwood, Catt, Prodger, Brown and Dye assisted their opponents, but within three overs the whole Middlesex side were present and fielding. Thus, Kent recovered from a desperate situation and thanks to bold hitting by Richardson they were able to set Middlesex to get 371 to win in six and a half hours. An unsatisfactory match was completely spoiled on the last day when rain permitted very little cricket. MCC ruled that the umpires ordered Middlesex to close their first innings.

KENT

First Innings

P. E. Richardson b Hooker	35
B. W. Luckhurst c Murray b Hooker	26
D. Nicholls c Parfitt b Titmus	15
*M. C. Cowdrey c and b Hooker	8
S. E. Leary c Moss b Hooker	6
J. Prodger c Hooker b Titmus	30
†A. W. Catt c Moss b Titmus	19
A. L. Dixon c Titmus b Drybrough	0
D. Underwood not out	4
A. Brown b Drybrough	0
J. Dye lbw b Titmus	1
B 4, l-b 2	6

Second Innings

c Murray b Titmus	95
c sub b Bennett	4
lbw b Bennett	16
c Hooker b Moss	23
not out	92
c Drybrough b Hooker	74
c Hooker b Price	25
c Moss b Price	5
not out	6
B1	1

1/53 2/70 3/79 4/90 5/91 6/144   150
7/145 8/148 9/145

1/5 2/75 3/120   (7 wkts dec.) 341
4/150 5/270 6/307
7/317

BOWLING: **First Innings**—Moss 8-2-12-0; Price 6-1-25-0; Hooker 21-6-57-4; Titmus 29.1-14-39-4; Drybrough 10-4-11-2. **Second Innings**—Bennett 9-1-48-2; Price 11-0-81-2; Moss 22-7-48-1; Titmus 28-6-82-1; Drybrough 19-7-50-0; Hooker 80-0-31-1.

The 1963 Test at Lord's between England and West Indies remains legendary because of the assorted heroics of the participants, from Cowdrey, who came in to bat with a broken arm, to Brian Close, who outfaced the West Indies pace attack with such disdain for his own safety that after his innings of 70 he carried a mass of bruises.

MIDDLESEX

First Innings

W. E. Russell b Dixon	4
S. E. Russell c Cowdrey b Brown	3
P. H. Parfitt run out	54
R. A. White not out	43
R. W. Hooker not out	13
L-b 4	4

1/5 2/9 3/106   (3 wkts dec.) 121

Second Innings

lbw b Dixon	4
c Leary b Dixon	28
c Prodger b Brown	27
not out	19
not out	2
N-b 2	2

1/5 2/51 3/73   (3 wkts) 82

F. J. Titmus, D. Bennett, †J. T. Murray, *C. D. Drybrough, J. S. E. Price, A. E. Moss, did not bat.

BOWLING: **First Innings**—Brown 16-2-34-1; Dixon 18-7-26-1; Dye 2-0-10-0; Underwood 9-3-33-0; Leary 7-2-14-0. **Second Innings**—Brown 11-3-33-1; Dixon 8-4-15-2; Underwood 3.3-1-21-0; Dye 2-0-11-0.

Umpires: O. W. Herman and A. E. Rhodes.

ENGLAND v WEST INDIES

SECOND TEST MATCH
Played at Lord's, June 20, 21, 22, 24, 25, 1963

DRAWN. ONE OF the most dramatic Test matches ever to be played in England attracted large crowds and aroused tremendous interest throughout the country. All through the cricket had been keen and thrilling, but the climax was remarkable, Cowdrey having to go in with a broken bone in his arm. About 300 people rushed the ground at the end of the match seeking souvenirs and patting the players on the back. The West Indies

Brian Close fails to hold on to a hard chance offered by Worrell off Statham. Close was one of several dedicated Yorkshire cricketers of post-war years who, for unfathomable reasons, were not considered by the Yorkshire County Committee to be worthy of representing the county. Close moved to Somerset, where he continued as one of the best county captains on the circuit.

supporters called for Worrell and Hall, who appeared on the balcony, sending them home happy.

When the final over arrived any one of four results could have occurred – a win for England, victory for West Indies, a tie or a draw. The match was drawn with England six runs short of success and West Indies needing one more wicket. Most people felt happy about the result, for it would have been a pity if either side had lost after playing so well.

The England selectors sprang a surprise by recalling Shackleton, aged thirty-eight, after a gap of more than eleven years. His form at the time plus the fact that he had a fine record at Lord's, influenced them. He replaced Statham, and to strengthen the batting Parks came in for Andrew as wicket-keeper. West Indies preferred McMorris as opening batsman to Carew.

Worrell won the toss for West Indies, and after rain had delayed the start for twenty-three minutes the game began on a high note with Hunte taking 4s off the first three balls of the match, bowled by Trueman. Shackleton frequently worried Hunte, who offered two sharp chances off him. The scoring dropped right back, and at lunch the total was only 47. The first wicket fell at 51 and the next at 64. Then Sobers and Kanhai, in an entertaining stand lasting sixty-five minutes, added 63. A fifth wicket partnership of 74 between Kanhai and Solomon put West Indies in a useful position, but with Worrell failing to score England were well in the picture. At the close West Indies were 245 for six, and they carried the total to 301.

Shackleton failed to take a wicket on the first day, but he terminated the innings with three in four balls, dismissing Solomon, Griffith and Gibbs. Trueman bowled well for long spells and claimed six for 100.

Edrich fell to the first ball he received, and with Stewart also going early England were 20 for two at lunch. Afterwards Dexter gave a thrilling display of powerful driving, hooking and cutting. He took only forty-eight minutes to reach 52, and when leg-before he had made 70 in eighty-one minutes on 73 balls received. His hits included ten 4s, and the way he stood up and punished the fiery fast bowling of Hall and Griffith was exciting to see. Barrington played a minor role in helping Dexter add 82 in sixty-two minutes but later took over command.

Cowdrey again disappointed, but Parks shared a sixth wicket partnership of 55 in an hour. Barrington, still searching for his first Test century in England, drove a catch to cover after batting three hours, ten minutes for 80. England finished with 244 for seven. On the Saturday, when the gates were closed ten minutes before the start, Titmus played a sound innings and England finished within four of the West Indies total. Griffith took five for 91, always being awkward to play.

When West Indies lost their opening pair for 15 the issue was wide open. Cowdrey, at slip, held his third successive catch to dismiss Kanhai, and with Sobers and Solomon going cheaply, West Indies were 104 for five with England apparently on top. Then came a complete swing, Butcher, showing excellent form and hitting the bad ball hard, checked the slide and with Worrell carried the score to 214 for five by the close. West Indies then led by 218 and were well placed only to lose ground again in a remarkable twenty-five minutes on Monday morning when the last five wickets went for 15 in six overs.

Butcher, ninth out for 133 (two 6s and seventeen 4s) batted splendidly for nearly four and a half hours. He and Worrell put on 110. Trueman, with five for 52, claimed eleven for 152 in the match, one of his best performances for England. Shackleton supported him well with seven for 165 in the two innings.

So England went in to get 234 to win. Their hopes sank when Edrich, Stewart and Dexter were out for 31, but Barrington again rose to the occasion. He and Cowdrey had to withstand some fierce bowling from Hall, who often pitched short and struck the batsmen on the body and fingers. Eventually Cowdrey received such a blow that a bone just above the left wrist was broken and he had to retire, having shown his best form of the series and helping to carry the score to 72. Close took his place and the England fight back continued, Barrington hitting Gibbs over mid-wicket for two 6s in an over. Bad light handicapped the batsmen, and there were two stoppages before the game was given up for the day at 4.45 p.m. with England 116 for three, needing another 118.

To add to the tenseness of the situation, rain and poor light delayed the resumption next day until 2.20 p.m. Hall and Griffith, bowling at their best on a pitch which had remained lively throughout the match, made the batsmen fight desperately for every run. Barrington added only five in fifty-five minutes, and the first hour brought no more than 18 runs.

Close and Parks took the score to 158, and Titmus also fought well. At tea, it was still anyone's game with England 171 for five, Cowdrey injured and 63 needed in eighty-five minutes. With West Indies averaging only 14 overs an hour, this was a harder task than it looked on paper. The game moved back in West Indies favour when Titmus and Trueman fell to successive balls. Close, who had defended with rare courage despite being hit often on the body and finishing with a mass of bruises, decided the time had come to change his methods. He began moving down the pitch to Hall and Griffith to upset their length. He succeeded for a time, but eventually he just touched the ball when trying a big swing and was caught at the wicket. Worrell said afterwards that while not wishing to detract from a very fine innings, he thought Close's changed tactics were wrong. Others paid high tribute to what they termed a magnificent and courageous innings which lasted three hours, fifty minutes. He made 70, easily his highest score for England.

Shackleton joined Allen with nineteen minutes left and 15 runs required. They fell further behind the clock and when Hall began his last dramatic over eight were needed. Singles came off the second and third balls, but Shackleton was run out off the fourth when

Worrell raced from short-leg with the ball and beat the batsman to the bowler's end. That meant Cowdrey had to come in with two balls left and six wanted. He did not have to face a ball, Allen playing out the last two. If he had to shape up, Cowdrey intended to turn round and bat left-handed to protect his left arm. Hall, in particular, and Griffith, showed remarkable stamina.

Hall bowled throughout the three hours, twenty minutes play was in progress on the last day, never losing his speed and always being menacing. He took four for 93 off forty overs in the innings. Griffith bowled all but five overs on the last day.

The game which attracted 110,287 paying spectators and approximately £25,000 all told, gave cricket a fine boost which was reflected immediately in improved bookings for the third Test at Edgbaston. The receipts were £56,300, not far short of the record for any match. Those who saw it, and the millions who followed the game's progress over television and radio, were kept in a constant state of excitement. It was a game to remember.

WEST INDIES

First Innings

C. C. Hunte c Close b Trueman 44
E. D. McMorris lbw b Trueman 16
G. S. Sobers c Cowdrey b Allen 42
R. B. Kanhai c Edrich b Trueman 73
B. F. Butcher c Barrington b Trueman 14
J. S. Solomon lbw b Shackleton 56
*F. M. Worrell b Trueman 0
†D. L. Murray c Cowdrey b Trueman 20
W. W. Hall not out 25
C. C. Griffith c Cowdrey b Shackleton 0
L. R. Gibbs c Stewart b Shackleton 0
    B 10, l-b 1 11

1/51 2/64 3/127 4/145 5/219   301
6/219 7/263 8/297 9/297

Second Innings

c Cowdrey b Shackleton 7
c Cowdrey b Trueman 8
c Parks b Trueman 8
c Cowdrey b Shackleton 21
lbw b Shackleton 133
c Stewart b Allen 5
c Stewart b Trueman 33
c Parks b Trueman 2
c Parks b Trueman 2
b Shackleton 1
not out 1
    B 5, l-b 2, n-b 1 8

1/15 2/15 3/64 4/84 5/104   229
6/214 7/224 8/226 9/228

BOWLING: **First Innings**—Trueman 44–16–100–6; Shackleton 50.2–22–93–3; Dexter 20–6–41–0; Close 9–3–21–0; Allen 10–3–35–1. **Second Innings**—Trueman 26–9–52–5; Shackleton 34–14–72–4; Titmus 17–3–47–0; Allen 21–7–50–1.

ENGLAND

First Innings

M. J. Stewart c Kanhai b Griffith 2
J. H. Edrich c Murray b Griffith 0
*E. R. Dexter lbw b Sobers 70
K. F. Barrington c Sobers b Worrell 80
M. C. Cowdrey b Gibbs 4
D. B. Close c Murray b Griffith 9
†J. M. Parks b Worrell 35
F. J. Titmus not out 52
F. S. Trueman b Hall 10
D. A. Allen lbw b Griffith 2
D. Shackleton b Griffith 8
    B 8, l-b 8, n-b 9 25

1/2 2/20 3/102 4/115 5/151   297
6/206 7/235 8/271 9/274

Second Innings

c Solomon b Hall 17
c Murray b Hall 8
b Gibbs 2
c Murray b Griffith 60
not out 19
c Murray b Griffith 70
lbw b Griffith 17
c McMorris b Hall 11
c Murray b Hall 0
not out 4
run out 4
    B 5, l-b 8, n-b 3 16

1/15 2/27 3/31 4/130   (9 wkts) 228
5/158 6/203 7/203 8/219 9/228

BOWLING: **First Innings**—Hall 18–2–65–1; Griffith 26–6–91–5; Sobers 18–4–45–1; Gibbs 27–9–59–1; Worrell 13–6–12–2. **Second Innings**—Hall 40–9–93–4; Griffith 30–7–59–3; Gibbs 17–7–56–1; Sobers 4–1–4–0.

Umpires: J. S. Buller and W. E. Phillipson.

ALLETSON EDWARD B., who died on July 5, 1963, aged 79, was celebrated as the batsman who hit more runs in a single over than any other player in the history of the first-class game. That was for Nottinghamshire against Sussex at Hove in 1911, when he punished E. H. Killick for 34, comprising three 6s and four 4s, in an over which included two no-balls. Alletson scored 189 out of 227 in ninety minutes. Beginning quietly, he spent an hour over 50, but, by terrific driving, doubled his score in fifteen minutes and added another 89 in quarter of an hour. From seven overs he obtained 115 out of 120 and in all he hit eight 6s, twenty-three 4s, four 3s, ten 2s and seventeen singles.

While he never achieved another quite such punishing performance, he played fourteen hard-hit innings of 50 or more for his county during a professional career extending from 1906 to 1914 in which he scored 3,217 runs, average 18.47. His most successful season was that of 1913 when he made 634 runs, average 21.13, and hit Wilfred Rhodes, the Yorkshire and England left-arm slow bowler, for three 6s from following deliveries in the game at Dewsbury. He was also a useful fast bowler, as he showed when, with six wickets for 43 in the match with Kent at Trent Bridge in 1913, he helped to bring about the defeat of the eventual champions. His total of wickets was 33 at 18.90 runs each and he brought off 68 catches.

ONE-DAY CRICKET

THE GILLETTE CUP KNOCK-OUT COMPETITION

THE NEW KNOCK-OUT competition aroused enormous interest. Very large crowds, especially in the later rounds, flocked to the matches and 25,000 spectators watched the final at Lord's where Sussex narrowly defeated Worcestershire by 14 runs in a thoroughly exciting match. It says much for this type of cricket that tremendous feeling was stirred-up among the spectators as well as the cricketers with numerous ties being decided in the closest fashion. At Lord's, supporters wore favours and banners were also in evidence, the whole scene resembling an Association Football Cup Final more than the game of cricket and many thousands invaded the pitch at the finish to cheer Dexter, the Sussex captain, as he received the Gillette Trophy from the MCC President, Lord Nugent.

Sussex emphasized their superiority in the one-day game when they beat the West Indies by four wickets in a Challenge match at Hove on September 12.

There were two points which invite criticism. Firstly, the majority of counties were loath to include even one slow bowler in their sides and relied mainly on pace and secondly the placing of the entire field around the boundary to prevent rapid scoring – Dexter used this tactic in the Final – became fairly common. The success of the spinners at Lord's may have exploded the first theory.

There is no doubt that provided the Competition is conducted wisely it will attract great support in the future and benefit the game accordingly.

LANCASHIRE v LEICESTERSHIRE

THE KNOCK-OUT COMPETITION
Played at Manchester, May 1, 2, 1963

LANCASHIRE WON BY 101 runs. Rain held up the start of this opening match in the new competition, between the two bottom counties of the previous season's Championship. After a delay of three hours the Leicestershire captain, Hallam, put Lancashire in to bat, but the decision did not pay. Without undue recklessness Lancashire averaged 4.67 runs per over for the 65 overs, Grieves and Marner adding 136 for the fourth wicket. Although Hallam, like Marner, made a hard-hit century, Leicestershire found their task too heavy against the accurate pace of Statham and steady medium pace of Marner who won £50 and a gold medal as the "Man of the Match".

Ken Higgs, fast-medium bowler and a loyal servant of Lancashire between 1958 and 1969. He later moved to Leicestershire where he figured in a record last wicket partnership of 228 with Illingworth against Northants. He also figured, in 1966, in a memorable last wicket stand of 128 for England with John Snow against the West Indies.

LANCASHIRE

B. Booth b Pratt	50
R. Entwistle *hit wkt* b Pratt	18
J. D. Bond *lbw* b Pratt	7
*K. Grieves c Wharton b Savage	57
P. Marner c Spencer b Savage	121
G. Houlton c Spencer b Savage	1
J. Dyson b Van Geloven	6
†G. Clayton b Savage	28
J. B. Statham b Boshier	0
K. Higgs *not out*	7
C. Hilton *not out*	3
L-b 4, n-b 2	6

(9 wkts) after 65 overs   304
1/42 2/62 3/82 4/218 5/225 6/264
7/266 8/280 9/299

BOWLING: Spencer 15-1-48-0; Boshier 12-1-58-1; Pratt 15-2-75-3; Van Geloven 15-2-63-1; Savage 8-0-54-4.

LEICESTERSHIRE

*M. R. Hallam c and b Marner	106
H. D. Bird b Statham	7
A. Wharton c Clayton b Statham	0
S. Jayasinghe c Clayton b Statham	1
C. Inman c Entwistle b Higgs	26
J. Van Geloven b Higgs	26
R. L. Pratt c Bond b Marner	25
C. T. Spencer b Statham	1
†R. Julian b Statham	4
J. S. Savage b Marner	2
B. S. Boshier *not out*	0
L-b 5	5

1/21 2/21 3/23 4/72 5/164   203
6/183 7/191 8/201 9/203

BOWLING: Statham 12-2-28-5; Higgs 15-2-48-2; Hilton 15-1-73-0; Marner 11.3-0-49-3.

Umpires: R. Aspinall and H. Yarnold.

ENGLAND v AUSTRALIA

FOURTH TEST MATCH
Played at Old Trafford, July 23, 24, 25, 27, 28, 1964

FOR ALL THE remarkable personal achievements in the match, a bad taste was left in the mouth of the cricket enthusiasts who saw Australia retain the Ashes. Simpson's strategy, with his team one up and two to play, was to make certain that Australia did not lose. Dexter, with England kept in the field until the third morning was well advanced, had no hope of winning and so a boring situation resulted in which twenty-eight and a quarter hours of play were needed to produce a decision on the first innings! Both sides were to blame for frequent periods of needlessly tiresome batting on a perfectly-made closely-cut firm pitch of placid pace which gave neither quick nor spin bowlers the slightest help. The intention to win was never once apparent after Simpson, for the first

The Australian tourists of 1964 set sail from Fremantle. Their captain Bobby Simpson, who was to score a treble century in the Manchester Test, is seen on the extreme right of the picture.

time in the series, won the toss, and only rarely were the justifiable expectations of the spectators for entertainment realized.

The match yielded these records:

Lawry and Simpson made 201 for the first wicket – an Australian record against England. The previous best was 180 by W. Bardsley and S. E. Gregory in the Fifth Test at The Oval, 1909.

Simpson's score of 311 was the highest ever made at Old Trafford.

His innings, lasting twelve and three-quarter hours, was the longest ever played against England. It beat F. M. Worrell's 197 not out in eleven hours and twenty minutes in the First Test at Bridgetown, Barbados, January, 1960.

Australia's total of 656 for eight declared and England's 611 were their highest at Old Trafford.

Barrington's score of 256 was England's highest at Old Trafford.

Other notable performances were:

Simpson scored his first Test century in 30 matches.

Barrington made his first Test century in England after hitting nine abroad.

McKenzie took seven wickets for 153 in a total of 611.

Veivers bowled 95.1 overs, only 17 balls short of the record number of 588 balls bowled in an innings by S. Ramadhin for West Indies against England, at Birmingham, in 1957.

Australia made one change from their victorious Third Test team, bringing back O'Neill in place of Cowper, and England, who had to win to retain a chance of recovering the Ashes, took the drastic step of omitting Trueman and Cowdrey. The Selectors picked three seam bowlers – Cartwright and Rumsey were new to Test cricket – and two off-spin bowlers, and eventually left out M. J. K. Smith from the chosen twelve. Price played in his first Test in England.

What would have happened had Dexter won the toss can only be conjectured, for McKenzie, following a severe stomach upset a few days earlier, was not at his fittest. On the easy-paced turf Australia, setting themselves to build a formidable total to stop England winning, scored 253 for two wickets on the first day. There was no encouragement to bowlers from the opening delivery sent down by Rumsey to his rival left-hander Lawry, and although Cartwright, by control of length at medium-pace with some movement off the pitch occasionally worried the batsmen – he had Simpson when 33 missed at the wicket on the leg side – the attack posed no real danger. Lawry adept in hooking, took a 6 apiece off Price, Cartwright and Rumsey before hitting his first four with his score at 64, but the stroke-play generally was far from forceful.

Methodically, the batsmen wore down the toiling bowlers in sunshine. Titmus had a long bowl, but Dexter who set largely defensive fields did not employ Mortimore until twenty past three with the score 173 and Lawry, with a cover-drive off the Gloucestershire bowler, reached his third hundred against England out of 179 in five minutes under four hours. His sound, but unenterprising innings, ended three-quarters of an hour later when, for the third time in Tests in the current series, and for the fifth time in the season, he was run out when Mortimore, the bowler, made a brilliant stop. The partnership produced 201, and Lawry included five 4s besides the three 6s, in his 106.

Dexter, for the first time, crowded the batsmen when Redpath arrived, but Simpson, after five and a half hours at the crease with only six 4s among his neat but far from strong strokes, completed his century out of 232. Cartwright gained reward for his steadiness when beating Redpath off the pitch for leg-before at 233. At the close Australia were 253 for two with Simpson 109, and O'Neill 10.

On the second day, Simpson and his colleagues maintained their dominance yet seldom became free-scoring. Simpson again batted in subdued, if almost faultless, fashion and was barracked before displaying some of his characteristic cuts and drives. O'Neill had given promise of brightening proceedings before a ball which swung across knocked back his leg-stump at 318. Burge did not settle down before Price smartly caught him at backward square leg at 382. From that point, at ten minutes to three, the England bowlers strove without compensation.

In company with Booth, Simpson, who had reached 160 at rather less than 20 an hour since he began, at last decided to open his shoulders. He took 11 in an over off Price with the new ball, but soon reverted to his sedate mood. When 203, Simpson could have been run out backing-up if Titmus, about to bowl, had not been chivalrously inclined, and the Middlesex bowler inappropriately suffered when the Australian captain, bestirring himself again, hit 14 off him in one over. At the end of another hot day, Simpson had been in twelve hours for 265 out of a score of 570 for four, and Booth, who had scored with firm strokes, was 82 in an unfinished partnership of 188. Cartwright, England's best bowler, had sent down 77 overs for 118 runs and two wickets.

Simpson continued Australia's and his own innings next morning and in the light of subsequent events his policy, however, unpalatable it was to cricket lovers, proved correct. Had he declared the previous evening and managed to snatch a couple of wickets a way to victory might have been open to him, but that again is mere surmise. In the event, Simpson made sure that Australia would not lose by extending his team's innings for another hour and raising the total to 656 for eight before declaring. In that time, the batting, for the first time in the match, was consistently entertaining, bringing 86 runs for four wickets.

Simpson had a chance of passing the world record Test score of 365 not out by G. S. Sobers, but this did not affect his attitude. He made no attempt to play safe for the purpose and after straight-driving Mortimore for 6 and hitting four more 4s he fell at the wicket paying the penalty for a slashed stroke played off Price with rather reckless abandon. The crowd, having overlooked the dull spells of his batting, generously gave him an ovation for his score of 311 out of 646 for six. He defied England for three minutes under twelve and three-quarter hours, and in addition to his 6 he hit twenty-three 4s. His stand with Booth, fifth to leave, well caught off a stiff return at 601, added 219 in just over three and a half hours. Booth, who missed a hundred by two, hit one 6 and ten 4s. The innings lasted thirteen hours. Price took three for 183. He, like his team-mates, had his edge blunted by the unresponsive pitch. Barrington, with his leg-breaks, was never tried, a tactical shortcoming by Dexter.

When England began batting at twenty to one on Saturday, there seemed little hope of them making 457 to avoid following-on, and what optimism did exist soon received a check when Edrich edged the now full-recovered fast-medium McKenzie to second slip with the score 15. Then came a renewal of hope with Boycott and Dexter driving and cutting excellently. Simpson unavailingly challenged Dexter with spin and flight and the second wicket brought 111 before Boycott, having stayed three hours, played too soon at a slower ball from McKenzie and was bowled.

A shaky start sent Barrington into his shell and Dexter, too, became so restrained that slow handclapping broke out. At one stage Barrington's disinclination to make a forcing stroke encouraged Simpson to employ four short-legs, for Veivers. With the score carried to 162 for two, Dexter 71 and Barrington 20, bad light stopped play fifty minutes early – a disappointing end to the day for a crowd of 30,000.

Wanting 295 more to make Australia bat again, England had by far their best day on Monday when Dexter carried his score to 174 and Barrington reached 153 not out. Dexter, who hit his eighth Test hundred, was missed twice by McKenzie at backward short leg when 74 and 97, and narrowly escaped being given out at 108 when Burge said he did not really know whether he had made a catch low down at cover, but the later part of Dexter's innings provided much pleasure for the onlookers. From lunch, taken at 247 for two, the batsmen were masters. In turn they forced the game with drives, square-cuts, late-cuts and full-blooded leg-side strokes which punished quick and slow bowlers alike. Poor fielding swelled the scoring and Barrington was fortunate, when 99, that McKenzie, at short-slip failed to hold a cut.

Barrington had played 44 Test innings in England without making more than 87. In one spell of ten overs, Simpson conceded 38 runs and the partnership passed 200 in ten minutes over four hours. Dexter, with a majestic cover-drive off Veivers, exceeded K. S. Ranjitsinhji's 154 not out for England at Old Trafford in 1896, and at tea, with 111 runs having come since lunch, England wanted 99 more to save the follow-on.

Afterwards, England's rising hopes received an unexpected setback in the dismissal of Dexter, third out, at 372. Hawke and Veivers, doing sufficient to keep the batsmen watchful, made runs scarce enough to set impatient onlookers slow handclapping, and whether or not Dexter had his concentration disturbed he eventually played across, in somewhat casual style, at a ball pitched well up to him and was bowled. He, too, was given an ovation for his fine innings, including twenty-two 4s, for which he had kept the Australians at bay for eight hours. The stand of 246 in five hours and twenty-five minutes fell 16 short of the record England third-wicket partnership against Australia of 262 by W. R. Hammond and D. R. Jardine at Adelaide in 1928–29.

Barrington suffered a painful blow on his left shoulder from a bouncer by Corling, but recovered after treatment on the field and he remained unbeaten, with fifteen 4s to his credit, at the close when England, 411 for three, needed 46 more to make Australia go in again.

The fifth and last day proved the most disappointing for England supporters, for lack of enterprise by the batsmen when conditions were all in their favour threw away a golden chance of passing the massive Australian total. Dexter's example counted for nothing. Barrington pushed and deflected when he could have driven powerfully and the opportunity to encourage his partners and thoroughly discourage his rivals was lost. Parks hit only three 4s in his 60 which occupied three hours and twenty minutes, Titmus made nine runs in almost an hour and when Barrington was lbw, seventh to go, at 594 he had been at the crease for eleven hours and twenty-five minutes. He hit twenty-six 4s in his 256.

With McKenzie enlivened and Veivers still pitching a length, the issue was soon settled after Barrington's departure on the stroke of tea, and England, though having kept Australia in the field over two hours longer than the tourists had kept them, finished 45 behind. McKenzie's late successes, achieved by change of pace and deceptive movement, gave him a fine analysis in such a huge total, but the endurance of Veivers, who sent down 46.1 overs unchanged on the last day, was just as remarkable.

The Australians had to bat a second time for the closing five minutes, and it was a suitable ending, seeing what indecisive cricket had gone before, that Simpson and Lawry were bowled to by Barrington and Titmus using an old ball. Simpson, who square-cut

Barrington for the four runs obtained, was on the field for all but a quarter of an hour of the match which, over the five days, was watched by an estimated attendance of 108,000 who paid £36,340 3s. 6d. On the second afternoon, Mr Harold Wilson, Leader of the Opposition, was present and next evening Sir Alec Douglas Home, the Prime Minister, saw some cricket. No interruption occurred through rain during the match which took place in almost unbroken sunny weather.

AUSTRALIA

First Innings

W. M. Lawry *run out* 106
*R. B. Simpson *c* Parks *b* Price 311
I. R. Redpath *lbw b* Cartwright 19
N. C. O'Neill *b* Price 47
P. J. Burge *c* Price *b* Cartwright 34
B. C. Booth *c and b* Price 98
T. R. Veivers *c* Edrich *b* Rumsey 22
*A. T. W. Grout *c* Dexter *b* Rumsey 0
G. D. McKenzie *not out* 0
B 1, l-b 9, n-b 9 19

Second Innings

not out 0
not out 4

1/201 2/233 3/318 4/382   (8 wkts dec.) 656   (no wkt) 4
5/601 6/646 7/652 8/656

N. J. N. Hawke and G. E. Corling did not bat.

BOWLING: **First Innings**—Rumsey 35.5-4-99-2; Price 45-4-183-3; Cartwright 77-32-118-2; Titmus 44-14-100-0; Dexter 4-0-12-0; Mortimore 49-13-122-0; Boycott 1-0-3-0. **Second Innings**—Barrington 1-0-4-0; Titmus 1-1-0-0.

ENGLAND

G. Boycott *b* McKenzie 58
J. H. Edrich *c* Redpath *b* McKenzie 6
*E. R. Dexter *b* Veivers 174
K. F. Barrington *lbw b* McKenzie 256
P. H. Parfitt *c* Grout *b* McKenzie 12
†J. M. Parks *c* Hawke *b* Veivers 60
F. J. Titmus *c* Simpson *b* McKenzie 9
J. B. Mortimore *c* Burge *b* McKenzie 12
T. W. Cartwright *b* McKenzie 4
J. S. E. Price *b* Veivers 1
F. E. Rumsey *not out* 3
B 5, l-b 11 16

1/15 2/126 3/372 4/417 5/560   611
6/589 7/594 8/602 9/607

BOWLING: McKenzie 60-15-153-7; Corling 46-11-96-0; Hawke 63-28-95-0; Simpson 19-4-59-0; Veivers 95.1-36-155-3; O'Neill 10-0-37-0.

Umpires: J. S. Buller and W. F. Price.

KING, JOHN BARTON, who died in a Philadelphia nursing home on October 17, 1965, aged 92, was beyond question the greatest all-round cricketer produced by America. When he toured England with The Philadelphians in 1897, 1903 and 1908, Sir Pelham Warner described him as one of the finest bowlers of all time. Very fast and powerfully built, King made the ball swerve late from leg, demonstrating that what could be done with the ball by a pitcher at baseball, at which he was expert, could also be achieved with a ball half an ounce heavier. In 1897 he took 72 wickets, average 24.20, and hit 441 runs, average 20.10. His best analysis that season was seven wickets for 13 runs at Hove where, on a good pitch, he bowled K. S. Ranjitsinhji first ball for 0 and Sussex were disposed of for 46. Six years later "Bah" King dismissed 93 batsmen for 14.91 runs each and scored 653 runs, average 28.29. At The Oval, where the Philadelphians defeated Surrey by 110 runs, he distinguished himself by scoring 98 and 113 not out and taking six wickets. Against Lancashire at Old Trafford, he followed an analysis of five wickets for 46 in the first innings by sending back nine men in the second – eight of them bowled – for 62, the remaining batsman being run out. In 1908 his record was 87 wickets in first-class games for 11.01 runs each, the best average in England that year, and he scored 290 runs, average 16.11. When Kent made a short tour of America in 1903, King played innings of 39 and 41 for Philadelphia against them and in the first county innings took seven wickets for 39 runs. He played eleven times for the USA against Canada from 1892, rarely being on the losing side, and in 1902, 1904, 1908 and 1911 held the Childs Cups for the best batting and bowling in Philadelphia cricket.

McCABE, STANLEY JOSEPH, who died on August 25, 1968, aged 58, following a fall from a cliff at his home in Sydney, was one of Australia's greatest and most enterprising batsmen. In 62 Test innings between 1930 and 1938 he scored 2,748 runs, including six centuries, for an average of 48.21. During a first-class career lasting from 1928 to 1942, he obtained 11,951 runs, average 49.39, reaching three figures on 29 occasions. Short and stockily-built, with strong arms, flexible wrists and excellent footwork, he was at his best when facing bowlers of pace. Though he scored most of his runs by strokes in front of the wicket, with the drive his speciality, he also hooked splendidly. In addition, he was a useful change bowler above medium pace, with the ability to send down the occasional ball which came back from the off at disconcerting speed, and an energetic and accurate fielder.

He displayed an early aptitude for cricket when, after a month in the second team at St Joseph's College, Hunter Hill, Sydney, he gained a place in the first eleven as an all-rounder at the age of 14 and held it for three years. After leaving school, he assisted Grenfell Juniors, a country district club, and in 1928 made the first of many appearances for New South Wales. His form for the State was such that he earned a place in W. M. Woodfull's team which visited England in 1930 when, having taken some time to become accustomed to unfamiliar conditions, he averaged 35 in the five Test matches and in all first-class fixtures reached 1,012 runs without hitting a century. In 1931-32 he enjoyed remarkable success in his three innings for New South Wales, scores of 229 not out against Queensland at Brisbane and 106 and 103 not out from the Victoria bowling at Sydney giving him the phenomenal Sheffield Shield average of 438. That season, too, he averaged 33.50 in five Tests with South Africa.

Against D. R. Jardine's team in 1932-33, in what is often called "the body-line tour", when England employed fast leg-theory bowling to a packed leg-side field, McCabe distinguished himself by hitting 385 runs in the five Tests, average nearly 43. His 187 not out in the first match of the series at Sydney was a remarkable exhibition of both craftmanship and courage. He made his runs out of 278 in less than four and three-quarter hours, after his earlier colleagues failed, with twenty-five 4s among his figures. His hooking of short-pitched deliveries by H. Larwood and W. Voce, the Nottinghamshire pair, was something which will for ever hold a place in Australian cricket history. In England again in 1934, he put together eight centuries – more than any of his team-mates – including 240, the highest of his career, against Surrey at The Oval and 137 in the third Test at Old Trafford. As *Wisden* of the time said of him: "He blossomed forth as an almost completely equipped batsman of the forcing type and was probably the best exponent – Bradman himself scarcely excluded – of the art of hitting the ball tremendously hard and safely".

Next season at home he became captain of New South Wales and on tour in South Africa in 1935-36 he enjoyed more success, heading the Test batting figures with 420 runs, average 84. He hit 149 in the first Test at Durban, sharing a second-wicket partnership of 161 with W. A. Brown, and 189 not out in the second meeting with South Africa at Johannesburg, where he and J. H. Fingleton put on 177 together. At Johannesburg he showed his fast-scoring ability to the full by reaching 50 in forty-two minutes.

Perhaps McCabe's most famous innings was his 232 not out in the opening Test against England at Trent Bridge in 1938 which, scored at the rate of one a minute, prompted Sir Donald Bradman, his captain, to greet him on his return to the pavilion with the words: "If I could play an innings like that, I'd be a proud man, Stan."

S. C. Griffith, Secretary of MCC, commented upon this innings when paying a tribute to McCabe, calling it one of the best batting displays ever seen. "McCabe was a very great cricketer and a wonderful friend to all cricketers," said Mr Griffith.

Other tributes included:

Sir Robert Menzies, former Prime Minister of Australia: One of his great points was that he never bothered about averages; he enjoyed his batting. He was one of the two or three greatest batsmen I ever saw.

Sir Leonard Hutton: I knew him well. It would be hard to think of a greater Australian batsman. He had qualities that even Bradman hadn't got. I always liked to watch him bat and he was a most likeable fellow.

GLAMORGAN v NOTTINGHAMSHIRE
Played at Swansea, August 31, September 1, 2, 1968

NOTTINGHAMSHIRE WON BY 166 runs. This was the history-making match in which the incredible Garfield Sobers created a new world record by hitting six 6s in a six-ball over. Somehow one sensed that something extraordinary was going to happen when Sobers sauntered to the wicket. With over 300 runs on the board for the loss of only five wickets, he had the right sort of platform from which to launch a spectacular assault, and the manner in which he immediately settled down to score at a fast rate was ominous.

Then came the history-making over by the 23-year-old Malcolm Nash. First crouched like a black panther eager to pounce. Sobers with lightning footwork got into position for a vicious straight drive or pull. As Tony Lewis, Glamorgan's captain said afterwards, "It was not sheer slogging through strength, but scientific hitting with every movement working in harmony." Twice the ball was slashed out of the ground, and when the last six landed in the street outside it was not recovered until the next day. Then it was presented to Sobers and will have a permanent place in the Trent Bridge Cricket Museum.

All other events were overshadowed by Sobers' achievement, but the rest of the cricket was not without distinction. In the Nottinghamshire first innings Bolus hit a magnificent century in three hours, fifty minutes, including six 6s and fifteen 4s. Glamorgan could not match such boldness although Walker batted steadily for his second century of the season in two hours, forty minutes.

With a first-innings lead of 140 Nottinghamshire then lost half their wickets for 70, but again Sobers accomplished the inevitable, scoring 72 out of 94 in nine minutes under two hours. Eventually Glamorgan had to get 280 to win in four hours, but good bowling by Taylor, who made the most of a damp pitch caused by overnight rain, resulted in them being dismissed for 113.

NOTTINGHAMSHIRE

First Innings

J. B. Bolus c sub b Nash	140
R. A. White c Wheatley b B. Lewis	73
G. Frost c A. R. Lewis b Nash	50
M. J. Smedley c A. R. Lewis b Nash	27
†D. L. Murray b Nash	0
J. M. Parkin not out	15
*G. S. Sobers not out	76
S. R. Bielby (did not bat)	
B 4, l-b 7, n-b 2	13

1/126 2/258 3/289 (5 wkts dec.) 394
4/289 5/308

Second Innings

run out	3
b Cordle	1
b Nash	2
c Majid b Cordle	24
c Cordle b Shepherd	13
not out	9
b Shepherd	72
not out	13
B 1, n-b 1	2

1/2 2/7 3/7 (6 wkts dec.) 139
4/30 5/70 6/124

M. N. Taylor. D. J. Halfyard and B. Stead did not bat.

BOWLING: **First Innings**—Wheatley 5-0-22-0; Nash 21-3-100-4; Cordle 3-1-24-0; Walker 32-4-109-0; Shepherd 25-5-82-0; B. Lewis 13-1-44-1. **Second Innings**—Nash 17-4-53-1; Cordle 16-4-41-2; Shepherd 25-10-43-2.

It was at Swansea, in the dying moments of the 1968 County Championship that Gary Sobers, captaining Nottinghamshire against Glamorgan, finally achieved the feat which had eluded every batsman in history. His six sixes were struck with savage pulls and drives of glorious power. Here we see him batting against England at Edgbaston in 1973.

GLAMORGAN

First Innings

A. Jones c Murray b Taylor 25
R. Davis c Taylor b Stead 0
Majid Jahangir c Taylor b Halfyard 41
*A. R. Lewis c Bielby b Taylor 0
P. M. Walker not out 104
†E. Jones lbw b Sobers 29
A. E. Cordle lbw b Halfyard 4
M. A. Nash b Sobers 8
B. Lewis run out 38
D. J. Shepherd c Sobers b Halfyard 0
O. S. Wheatley b White 1
L-b 3, w 1 4

1/0 2/46 3/56 4/78 5/137   254
96/142 7/179 8/252 9/253

Second Innings

c Parkin b Taylor 1
b Stead 18
c Bolus b Taylor 4
c Bielby b White 52
c Sobers b White 16
c Stead b Taylor 3
c Smedley b Taylor 4
b White 5
b Taylor 4
b White 4
not out 0
L-b 2 2

1/40 2/45 3/49 4/85 5/96   113
6/100 7/100 8/105 9/113

BOWLING: **First Innings**—Sobers 20-6-63-2; Stead 9-3-27-1; Taylor 9-2-23-2; Halfyard 31-8-71-3; White 23.2-5-66-1. **Second Innings**—Stead 9-1-26-1; Taylor 16-6-47-5; Halfyard 7-1-29-0; White 8-5-9-4.

Umpires: J. G. Langridge and W. E. Phillipson.

IRELAND v WEST INDIES
Played at Sion Mills, Londonderry, July 2, 1969

IRELAND WON BY nine wickets. In some ways this one-day match provided the sensation of the 1969 season. The West Indies, with six of the team who had escaped on the previous day from defeat in the Lord's test, were skittled for 25 in this tiny Ulster town on a damp and definitely emerald green pitch. The conditions were all in favour of the bowlers, but the West Indies batsmen fell in the main to careless strokes and smart catching. Goodwin, the Irish captain, took five wickets for 6 runs and O'Riordan four for 18. Both bowled medium pace at a reasonable length and the pitch did the rest. It was not a first-class match, but Ireland's performance deserves a permanent record and therefore we give the full score.

WEST INDIES

First Innings

G. S. Camacho c Dineen b Goodwin 1
M. C. Carew c Hughes b O'Riordan 0
M. L. C. Foster run out 2
*B. F. Butcher c Duffy b O'Riordan 2
C. H. Lloyd c Waters b Goodwin 1
C. L. Walcott c Anderson b O'Riordan 6
J. N. Shepherd c Duffy b Goodwin 0
†T. M. Findlay c Waters b Goodwin 0
G. C. Shillingford not out 9
P. Roberts c Colhoun b O'Riordan 0
P. D. Blair b Goodwin 3
B 1 1

1/1 2/1 3/3 4/6 5/6   25
6/8 7/12 8/12 9/12

Second Innings

c Dineen b Goodwin 1
c Pigot b Duffy 25
c Pigot b Goodwin 0
c Waters b Duffy 50
not out 0
not out 0

L-b 2 2

1/1 2/2 3/73 4/78   (4 wkts) 78

BOWLING: **First Innings**—O'Riordan 13-8-18-4; Goodwin 12.3-8-6-5. **Second Innings**—O'Riordan 6-1-21-0; Goodwin 2-1-1-2; Hughes 7-4-10-0; Duffy 12-8-2-2; Anderson 7-1-32-0.

IRELAND

R. H. C. Waters c Findlay b Blair 2
D. M. Pigot c Camacho b Shillingford 37
M. Reith lbw b Shepherd 10
J. Harrison lbw b Shepherd 0
I. Anderson c Shepherd b Roberts 7
P. J. Dineen b Shepherd 0
A. J. O'Riordan c and b Carew 35
G. A. Duffy not out 15
L. F. Hughes c sub b Carew 13
        L-b 2, n-b 4 6

1/19 2/30 3/34 4/51   (8 wkts dec.) 125
5/55 6/69 7/103 8/125
*D. E. Goodwin and †O. D. Colhoun did not bat.

BOWLING: Blair 8–4–14–1; Shillingford 7–2–19–1; Shepherd 13–4–20–3; Roberts 16–3–43–1; Carew 3.2–0–23–2.

Umpires: M. Stott and A. Trickett.

ENGLAND v REST OF THE WORLD

FIFTH TEST MATCH
Played at The Oval, August 13, 14, 15, 17, 18, 1970

REST OF THE World won by four wickets. There were four notable individual performances in a match which brought a magnificent series to a distinguished close. The quality of the cricket was such that 53,000 spectators watched play over the five days, although the series had been settled. England's defeat meant that the team batting first lost in all five games, a unique occurrence.

The Lancashire medium-fast bowler, Lever, made an impressive début for England, taking seven wickets for 83 runs in the Rest of the World first innings. In the same innings Graeme Pollock re-established his reputation as one of the world's great batsmen with a graceful century. His partnership of 165 with Sobers was a batting spectacle which will live long in the minds of those privileged to see it.

Boycott also came back into his own with a masterly innings of 157 which gave England a chance of victory. His effort meant that the World XI needed 284 to win on a wearing pitch, an uphill task even though Wilson had to bowl with two damaged fingers on his left hand strapped together. Kanhai rose to the challenge with a dedicated 100. Lloyd hit powerfully for 68 and Sobers was the master of the bowling in the closing stages, making the final stroke of a series in which he had been the dominant figure.

Lever for Greig was one of two changes made by the England selectors, who named D'Oliveira twelfth man so that Amiss of Warwickshire could be given a chance to win a place on the Australian tour. He did not quite do enough, although fighting hard in both innings. For the World team McKenzie replaced Gibbs, whose three wickets in the first four matches had cost over 100 runs apiece.

Cowdrey atoned for his double failure at Leeds by making top score of 73 in the England first innings of 294, which began badly when Luckhurst was bowled by Procter's third ball. Once he had settled in Cowdrey looked complete master of the attack. Then he went into his shell and made only 13 in his final hour. Illingworth, with his sixth half-century of the series, and Knott added 86 for the sixth wicket before McKenzie took three wickets in eight balls.

Lever soon made his mark by dismissing Barlow and Mushtaq in his first nine overs but his effort, and everything else on the second day, was overshadowed by the artistry of Pollock and Sobers, who put on 135 in the last two hours. Pollock, with only 108 runs from

Because of the contentious political issues raised by South African cricket, the international career of Graeme Pollock was drastically curtailed. On the few occasions he was seen in the company of his international peers, he never failed to show his thoroughbred qualities, and must be rated among the best left-handed batsmen of the last fifty years. Ironically his great innings of 114 at The Oval in 1970 was made for a fiction called "The Rest of the World", a bogus Test side hastily assembled in the wake of South Africa's dismissal from respectable international company.

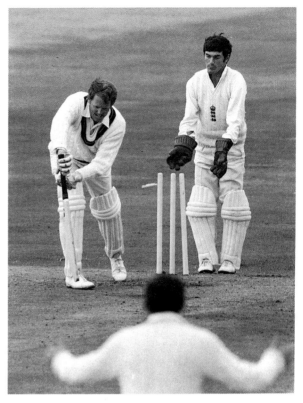

his previous six innings, made England pay dearly for a missed slip catch when he was 18. There were one 6 and sixteen 4s in his 114, which took just over two and a half hours.

On Saturday, the crowd rolled up to see Pollock and Sobers continue their assault; instead Lever took the limelight. Pollock who was restricted to 10 runs in forty-five minute was the first to fall to the Lancashire bowler who later also took the wickets of Sobers and Lloyd. His command of perfect length and direction made him a formidable opponent and only Procter of the later batsmen made progress against him.

England's arrears of 61 were cleared for the loss of Luckhurst, this time bowled first ball by Procter. Boycott set himself the task of seeing England to a match-winning score on a pitch beginning to take spin. He and Fletcher batted throughout the fourth morning and altogether added 154 for the third wicket in three and a quarter hours. When Boycott was fourth out at 289, caught off Lloyd, he had been in for six and a quarter hours and hit twenty-three 4s. This was Boycott at his best. Illingworth was dismissed first ball and the rest were swept aside by Sobers and McKenzie.

Nevertheless, the final task for the Rest of the World was formidable, especially when Barlow was bowled by Snow with six runs scored. On the final morning, Richards and Pollock were both bowled while yards down the pitch and Kanhai made some hair-raising strokes before deciding that it was possible to survive, although the ball was turning. His century in four hours was the foundation of the winning total.

Lloyd, more selective in his hitting than the South Africans, helped to wrest the advantage from the England bowlers by making 68 out of 123 put on in even time with Kanhai. With Wilson handicapped, the spinners were not up to the task and it was left to Snow to cause a late flutter by removing Lloyd, Kanhai and Mushtaq. Sobers proved immovable and his slash down to the third man boundary brought the winning runs and the crowd on to the field.

ENGLAND

First Innings
B. W. Luckhurst b Procter	0
G. Boycott c Sobers b Intikhab	24
M. C. Cowdrey c Murray b Sobers	73
K. W. R. Fletcher c Murray b McKenzie	25
D. L. Amiss b Mushtaq	24
*R. Illingworth c Barlow b Intikhab	52
†A. P. E. Knott not out	51
J. A. Snow c Barlow b McKenzie	20
C. M. Old b McKenzie	0
D. Wilson b McKenzie	0
P. Lever b Barlow	13
B 2, l-b 7, n-b 3	12

1/0 2/62 3/113 4/150 5/150 294
6/236 7/266 8/266 9/266

Second Innings
b Procter	0
c Barlow b Lloyd	157
b Intikhab	31
c Barlow b Sobers	63
c Murray b Lloyd	35
c Mushtaq b Lloyd	0
b Sobers	15
c Mushtaq b Sobers	19
b McKenzie	5
b McKenzie	1
not out	0
B 5, l-b 10, n-b 3	18

1/0 2/71 3/225 4/289 5/289 344
6/319 7/323 8/343 9/343

BOWLING: **First Innings**—Procter 20-10-22-1; McKenzie 24-7-51-4: Barlow 16.2-2-36-1; Sobers 15-5-18-1; Intikhab 44-14-92-2; Mushtaq 28-10-63-1. **Second Innings**—Procter 19-9-30-1; McKenzie 22.1-2-51-2; Barlow 16-2-42-0; Sobers 42-15-81-3; Intikhab 32-8-87-1; Mushtaq 1-0-1-0; Lloyd 18-3-34-3.

REST OF THE WORLD

First Innings
E. J. Barlow c Amiss b Lever	28
B. A. Richards b Snow	14
R. B. Kanhai c and b Wilson	13
R. G. Pollock b Lever	114
Mushtaq Mohammad b Lever	3
*G. S. Sobers b Lever	79
C. H. Lloyd c Knott b Lever	2
M. J. Procter c Boycott b Lever	51
†D. L. Murray b Snow	5
Intikhab Alam c Boycott b Lever	15
G. D. McKenzie not out	4
L-b 14, n-b 13	27

1/26 2/46 3/92 4/96 5/261 355
6/267 7/280 8/310 9/338

Second Innings
b Snow	6
b Wilson	14
c Fletcher b Snow	100
b Illingworth	28
c Fletcher b Snow	8
not out	40
c Knott b Snow	68
not out	9
B 2, l-b 8, w 1, n-b 3	14

1/7 2/41 3/92 4/215 (6 wkts) 287
5/241 6/265

BOWLING: **First Innings**—Snow 32-8-73-2; Old 21-4-57-0; Wilson 18-5-58-1; Lever 32.5-9-83-7; Illingworth 15-3-57-0. **Second Innings**—Snow 23-6-81-4; Old 7-0-22-0; Wilson 24-8-70-1; Lever 10.1-2-34-0; Illingworth 23-5-66-1.

Umpires: C. S. Elliott and A. E. Fagg.

WESTERN AUSTRALIA v SOUTH AUSTRALIA
Played at Perth, November 20, 21, 22, 23, 1970

SOUTH AUSTRALIA WON by an innings and 111 runs. The match was dominated by Richards with his great innings of 356; he was with I. M. Chappell in a second-wicket partnership for 308 runs in two hours fifty minutes. Richards missed by three runs equalling the highest score in Australian first-class cricket since the war. R. B. Simpson's 359 for New South Wales against Queensland in Brisbane in 1963–4. Richards, who hit one 6 and forty-eight 4s, batted in all for six hours and twelve minutes. Against a well-balanced attack, supported by keen fielding, he scored 325 runs on the first day, in five and a half hours; 79 before lunch, 137 from lunch to tea, and 109 from tea to "stumps". His first 100 runs came in 125 minutes, and 200 in 208 minutes and 300 in 317 minutes. He was out lbw to a full toss next morning. Irvine and Inverarity showed defiance in both innings for Western Australia. Hammond bowled effectively, taking nine for 79.

SOUTH AUSTRALIA

B. A. Richards *lbw b* Mann 356
J. J. Causby *c* Chadwick *b* Lock 38
*I. M. Chappell *st* Marsh *b* Lock 129
G. S. Chappell *c* Marsh *b* McKenzie 11
K. G. Cunningham *c* Inverarity *b* Lock 13
K. Langley *run out* 7
E. W. Freeman *c* Irvine *b* Lock 6
†R. P. Blundell *b* Mann 0
A. A. Mallett *not out* 6
T. J. Jenner *c* McKenzie *b* Mann 5
N-b 4 4

1/109 2/417 3/447   (9 wkts dec.) 575
4/551 5/553 6/563 7/563 8/564 9/575

J. R. Hammond did not bat.

BOWLING: McKenzie 19-2-101-1; Lillee 18-1-117-0; Brayshaw 12-1-69-0; Mann 20.6-1-120-3; Lock 16-1-108-4; Inverarity 8-0-56-0.

WESTERN AUSTRALIA

First Innings

D. Chadwick *c* Blundell *b* Jenner 49
C. Scarff *c* Blundell *b* Hammond 11
J. T. Irvine *b* Jenner 33
R. J. Inverarity *c* G. S. Chappell *b* Hammond 85
R. D. Meuleman *retired hurt* 28
I. J. Brayshaw *lbw b* Freeman 22
†R. W. Marsh *c* I. M. Chappell *b* Hammond 9
A. L. Mann *c* Blundell *b* Hammond 2
D. K. Lillee *c* Cunningham *b* Hammond 12
G. D. McKenzie *b* Hammond 10
*G. A. R. Lock *not out* 2
L-b 7, w 2, n-b 17 26

Second Innings

c and b Hammond 2
b Cunningham 7
c and b G. S. Chappell 57
c and b G. S. Chappell 35
absent hurt 0
c Richards *b* Mallett 13
c I. M. Chappell *b* Richards 19
c I. M. Chappell *b* Hammond 1
b Hammond 6
not out 18
c Hammond *b* Mallett 8
B 1, n-b 8 9

1/33 2/88 3/110 4/239 5/256   289
6/261 7/270 8/285 9/289

1/3 2/15 3/102 4/110 5/137   175
6/141 7/142 8/161 9/175

BOWLING: **First Innings**—Freeman 15-1-53-1; Hammond 12.3-1-54-6; G. S. Chappell 8-1-23-0; Jenner 22-4-78-2; Mallett 18-5-37-0; Cunningham 9-2-18-0. **Second Innings**—Freeman 4-0-16-0; Hammond 9-2-25-3; G. S. Chappell 12-1-41-2; Jenner 8-0-25-0; Mallett 12.5-2-43-2; Cunningham 4-0-12-1; Richards 1-0-4-1.

Umpires: W. Carter and N. Townsend.

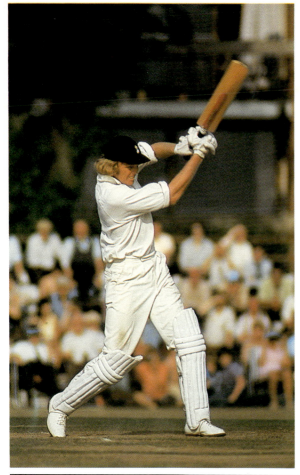

One century was never enough for Zaheer Abbas (above) and on more than one occasion he threatened to equal Arthur Fagg's record of two double centuries in the same match.

The South African, Barry Richards (left), came to Hampshire and scored many a dazzling century. In 1970-71 he spent a winter in Australia and gave further exhibitions of his apparently casual art, none more devastating than the innings he played for South Australia against Western Australia in the Sheffield Shield.

ENGLAND v PAKISTAN

FIRST TEST MATCH
Played at Birmingham, June 3, 4, 5, 7, 8, 1971

DRAWN. PAKISTAN TOOK all the honours. They had a wonderful chance of winning when rain intervened on the last day. After making 608 for seven they dismissed England for 353, enforced the follow-on and by the close of the fourth day had their opponents 184 for three in their second innings. Then came the rain. Play was not possible on the fifth day until just after 5 p.m. and then after 14.5 overs bad light sent the players off with England still 26 behind with only five wickets left.

On an easy paced pitch five centuries were made and the most remarkable was that by Zaheer Abbas, whose 274 was the highest individual score made by a Pakistan batsman against England. It fell only four short of D. C. S. Compton's 278, the highest for England against Pakistan, at Trent Bridge in 1954. Zaheer and Mushtaq Mohammad enjoyed a record second-wicket stand of 291 while Asif Iqbal with 104 not out emphasized Pakistan's immense batting strength. England would have been in a sorry state but for Knott's attacking 116 in the first innings and Luckhurst's defiant 108 not out in the second.

After returning home from Australia with the Ashes, England entered the match in understandably confident mood, Amiss of Warwickshire being the only member of the team not to have been in the tour party. Both Boycott and Snow were unfit.

Pakistan gave a first Test cap to their eighteen-year-old all-rounder, Imran Khan, because of the illness of Salim Altaf. They must have been surprised at the ease with which runs came after winning the toss. Ward's third delivery struck Aftab on the head and he had to retire to have the wound stitched. This brought in Zaheer and one soon appreciated that he was a batsmen out of the ordinary. He was particularly strong on the leg side, piercing the field with ease. Sadiq's was the only wicket England took on the first day when Pakistan finished at 270 for one, Zaheer 159; Mustaq 72. The pair scored 82 in an hour after tea.

Next morning Mushtaq was out after batting nine minutes short of six hours but Zaheer stayed for nine hours ten minutes, hitting thirty-eight 4s before a sweep at Illingworth brought his downfall. When he reached 261, Zaheer became the first batsman to complete 1,000 runs in the English season. He said afterwards that he had not felt too tired and was thinking in terms of the world Test record just before he was dismissed.

Asif Iqbal punished the dispirited bowlers on Zaheer's departure and Intikhab allowed the innings to run into the third morning when Iqbal completed his century which came in just over three hours.

England began disastrously against Asif Masood, who dismissed Edrich, Cowdrey and Amiss in his first 8.1 overs at a cost of 25 runs. A vicious break back was his most effective ball. Luckhurst fought hard and D'Oliveira hit back with 73 in two and a quarter hours but when he was out six men had gone for 148.

Knott decided to attack the spinners and succeeded brilliantly. With Lever a sturdy partner 159 were added for the seventh wicket. The England wicket-keeper raced to his century in three minutes over two hours. It included twenty-one 4s and a feast of audacious footwork. He was soon out on the Monday morning and before lunch England followed on for the first time against Pakistan.

Asif Masood, although stricken with stomach trouble and a strained thigh, again caused England to struggle, dismissing Edrich at 34, before he had to leave the field. Luckhurst and Cowdrey made a determined effort to pull the game round, but when Asif Masood came back he claimed Cowdrey with his first delivery. Amiss fell to a bouncer before the close when England were 184 for three and the new ball only nine overs away.

Then the rain came to England's aid. But Luckhurst was unbeaten at the end having completed 1,000 runs for his country in less than a year and scored a century on his first appearance against Pakistan. Asif Masood finished with nine wickets for 160 in the match and had Salim been there to give him support even the rain might not have saved England. Much of the match was played in dull, cool weather and the total attendance was no more than 25,000.

PAKISTAN

Aftab Gul b D' Oliveira 28
Sadiq Mohammad c and b Illingworth 17
Zaheer Abbas c Luckhurst b Illingworth 274
Mushtaq Mohammad c Cowdrey b Illingworth 100
Majid J. Khan c Lever b Illingworth 35
Asif Iqbal not out 104
*Intikhab Alam c Underwood b D'Oliveira 9
Imran Khan run out 5
†Wasim Bari not out 4
      B 6, l-b 14, n-b 12 32

1/68 2/359 3/441   (7 wkts dec.) 608
4/456 5/469 6/567 7/581

Asif Masood and Pervez Sajjad did not bat.

BOWLING: Ward 29-3-115-0; Lever 38-7-126-1; Shuttleworth 23-2-83-0; D'Oliveira 38-17-78-2; Underwood 41-13-102-0; Illingworth 26-5-72-3.

ENGLAND

First Innings

J. H. Edrich c Zaheer b Asif Masood	0
B. W. Luckhurst c Sadiq b Pervez	35
M. C. Cowdrey b Asif Masood	16
D. L. Amiss b Asif Masood	4
B. L. D'Oliveira c Mushtaq b Intikhab	73
*R. Illingworth b Intikhab	1
†A. P. E. Knott b Asif Masood	116
P. Lever c Pervez b Asif Masood	47
K. Shuttleworth c Imran b Pervez	21
D. L. Underwood not out	9
A. Ward c Mushtaq b Pervez	0
B 16, l-b 6, w 3, n-b 6	31

1/0 2/29 3/46 4/112 5/127 6/148   353
7/307 8/324 9/351

Second Innings

c Wasim b Asif Masood	15
not out	108
b Asif Masood	34
c Pervez b Asif Masood	22
c Mushtaq b Asif Iqbal	22
c Wasim b Asif Masood	1
not out	4
B 4, l-b 5, w 6, n-b 8	23

1/34 2/114 3/169   (5 wkts) 229
4/218 5/221

BOWLING: **First Innings**—Asif Masood 34-6-111-5; Imran 23-9-36-0; Khan 4-1-8-0; Intikhab 31-13-82-2; Pervez 15.5-6-46-3; Mushtaq 13-3-39-0. **Second Innings**—Asif Masood 23.5-7-49-4; Asif Iqbal 20-6-36-1; Imran 5-0-19-0; Intikhab 20-8-52-0; Pervez 14-4-27-0; Mushtaq 8-2-23-0.

Umpires: C. S. Elliott and T. W. Spencer.

LANCASHIRE v GLOUCESTERSHIRE
Played at Manchester, July 28, 1971

LANCASHIRE WON BY three wickets. This semi-final attracted a crowd officially returned at 23,520, with receipts of £9,738, and made Gillette Cup history by extending from 11 a.m. to 8.50 p.m., after an hour's delay through rain at lunch time. Winning the toss, Gloucestershire were given a solid start by Green and Nicholls who reached 57 before Green was run out. Nicholls played splendidly for 53 until he was second out at 87 when play reopened and afterwards Procter dominated a well-paced Gloucestershire innings by hitting one 6 and nine 4s in making 65 before being superbly caught behind the wicket.

Gloucestershire contained David Lloyd and Wood so well that Lancashire took 17 overs to raise the first 50 runs. Wood stayed and Pilling built well on a solid foundation, but Lancashire were in trouble when Mortimore dismissed Clive Lloyd and Engineer, and Davey accounted for Sullivan in a mid-innings slump. Play proceeded in gradually worsening light after 7.30 p.m. Bond and Simmons brought Lancashire back into the picture by adding 40 runs from seven overs for the seventh wicket after Bond had opted to play on in light that was now murky to say the least.

When Mortimore bowled Simmons at 203, with 27 needed from the last six overs, Hughes joined Bond and put the issue beyond all doubt with a magnificent onslaught against Mortimore. He hit the off-spinner for 24 runs, two 6s, two 4s and two 2s in the 56th over to make the scores level and amidst mounting tension and with lights on in the pavilion Bond got the winning run off the fifth ball of the 57th over. Hughes was given the man of the match award and it was well past ten o'clock before the big crowd dispersed.

Continued on P. 306

Top left: A young Mike Brearley square cuts against Yorkshire, 1965. At Cambridge between 1961–4 he achieved a record aggregate of 4,348 runs and hit ten centuries.
Above: Dennis Lillee tests out the England batting at Trent Bridge, Third Test, 1972.
Centre: Norman Gifford, Worcestershire, Warwickshire and England.
Above right: Mike Procter of Gloucestershire in characteristic delivery stride.
Far right: Zaheer Abbas batting at The Oval executes a flashing square drive.

The histrionics of the one-day game in England tended to debase the coinage of the drama, but not even the most dogged opponent of the limited-over game could have failed to be stirred by the Lancashire–Gloucestershire Gillette Cup match which ended in semi-darkness as the clocks pointed towards nine o'clock. In the fading light David Hughes, Man of the Match, hit two towering sixes and snatched an amazing victory with the lights shining brightly in the dressing-rooms.

GLOUCESTERSHIRE

R. B. Nicholls *b* Simmons	53
D. M. Green *run out*	21
R. D. V. Knight *c* Simmons *b* Hughes	31
M. J. Procter *c* Engineer *b* Lever	65
D. R. Shepherd *lbw b* Simmons	6
M. Bissex *not out*	29
*A. S. Brown *c* Engineer *b* Sullivan	6
H. Jarman *not out*	0
B 2, l-b 14, w 1, n-b 1	18

1/57 2/87 3/113 4/150   (6 wkts) 229
5/201 6/210

J. B. Mortimore, †B. J. Meyer and J. Davey did not bat.

BOWLING: Lever 12–3–40–1; Shuttleworth 12–3–33–0; Wood 12–3–39–0; Hughes 11–0–68–1; Simmons 12–3–25–2; Sullivan 1–0–6–1.

LANCASHIRE

D. Lloyd *lbw b* Brown	31
B. Wood *run out*	50
H. Pilling *b* Brown	21
C. H. Lloyd *b* Mortimore	34
J. Sullivan *b* Davey	10
†F. M. Engineer *hit wkt b* Mortimore	2
*J. D. Bond *not out*	16
J. Simmons *b* Mortimore	25
D. P. Hughes *not out*	26
B 1, l-b 13, n-b 1	15

1/61 2/105 3/136   (7 wkts, 56.5 overs) 230
4/156 5/160 6/163 7/203

P. Lever and K. Shuttleworth did not bat.

BOWLING: Procter 10.5-3-38-0; Davey 11-1-22-1; Knight 12-2-42-0; Mortimore 11-0-81-3. Brown 12-0-32-2.

Umpires: H. D. Bird and A. Jepson.

ENGLAND v AUSTRALIA

SECOND TEST MATCH
Played at Lord's, June 22, 23, 24, 26, 1972

AUSTRALIA WON BY eight wickets on the fourth day with nine and a half hours to spare. So Australia soon avenged their defeat at Manchester in a contest which will be remembered as Massie's match. The 25-year-old fast bowler from Western Australia surpassed all Australian Test bowling records by taking sixteen wickets for 137 runs; in all Tests only J. C. Laker, nineteen for 90 for England against Australia in 1956 and S. F. Barnes, seventeen for 179 for England against South Africa in 1913-14, stand above him. Moreover, Massie performed this wonderful feat on his Test début, the previous best by a bowler on his first appearance for his country being as far back as 1890 when at The Oval, Frederick Martin, a left-arm slow to medium pacer from Kent, took twelve for 102 for England against Australia on a pitch that had been saturated by rain.

Not for the first time, particularly in recent years, England were badly let down by their specialist batsmen, who failed lamentably in all respects. From the start they allowed the Australian bowlers to take the initiative and their excessive caution met with fatal results. Illingworth won the toss for the seventh consecutive time and one must admit that the hard fast pitch – it remained true to the end – was ideal for men of pace. During the first three days, too, the atmosphere was heavy and ideally suited to swing. Massie maintained excellent length and direction and his late swing either way always troubled the England batsmen. The conditions would also have suited Arnold, but England's best bowler at Manchester was suffering from hamstring trouble and on the morning of the match was replaced by Price, who proved rather disappointing. That was England's only change, whereas Australia brought in Edwards and Massie, who had recovered from a strain. Both were making their Test début and for the first time Western Australia had four representatives in the Test XI.

One must also stress the important part Lillee played in Australia's victory. Perhaps he was inspired by his six for 66 in England's second innings at Manchester. Anyhow, although this time his reward was confined to two wickets in each innings he looked a far better bowler. He had tidied his long fast approach of 22 strides, he was truly fast and he sent down far fewer loose deliveries. Massie capitalized on the hostility of his partner.

A light drizzle delayed the toss and the start for twenty-five minutes. Australia lost little time in taking the initiative, Boycott, Luckhurst and Edrich being removed for 28 runs

before any substantial resistance was offered. At times Massie bowled round the wicket, but Smith and D'Oliveira raised the score to 54 for three at lunch. Afterwards, D'Oliveira struck three fine boundaries only to be leg-before to Massie's slower ball, whereupon Greig proceeded to hit his third successive fifty for his country.

Greig and Knott enabled England to make a satisfactory recovery in their stand of 96, but immediately after tea at 147 Knott spooned Gleeson gently to mid-wicket where to everyone's amazement Francis dropped the catch. In the end both batsmen fell to casual strokes, but Illingworth and Snow played well so that at the close of a momentous and exciting first day England were 249 for seven.

Next morning the new ball was due after two overs and Massie snatched the remaining three wickets and led his team back to the pavilion. Of the 36 bowlers *Wisden* lists who have taken eight wickets in a Test innings, only A. E. Trott, for Australia against England at Adelaide in 1895 and A. L. Valentine, for West Indies against England at Manchester, 1950 had previously accomplished the performance on their Test début.

A superb century by G. S. Chappell made the second day memorable after Australia had received early shocks in the loss of Francis and Stackpole for seven runs. Ian Chappell set a noble example as captain, leading the recovery with an aggressive display. He used his favourite hook to some purpose while his brother remained strictly defensive. Ian struck one 6 near Smith before he fell to a fine running-in catch that Smith held rolling over near his ankles.

Snow, if not so fast as Lillee, bowled splendidly and soon induced a catch from Walters, but Greg Chappell, in for three hours before he hit his first boundary, now took charge, excelling with the off drive. Edwards gave valuable support, but with the light murky Illingworth brought on Gifford and then himself, tempting Edwards into indiscretion for Smith to bring off another fine running catch on the leg side. Chappell duly completed his hundred on the stroke of time and Australia wound up 71 behind with half their wickets intact.

On Saturday the gates were closed at 11.10 a.m. with 31,000 inside. Greg Chappell lasted another hour and a half, batting altogether for six and a quarter hours and in his splendid upright style hit fourteen 4s. Australia, who did not wish to face a huge target in the fourth innings, went ahead through another gallant display of powerful hitting by Marsh. He struck two 6s and six 4s in his 50, which came in seventy-five minutes and Australia gained a useful lead of 36. Snow, five for 57, alone of the England bowlers excelled.

Only the most optimistic Australian could have anticipated the success which so soon attended the efforts of Lillee and Massie. The England collapse – half the side were out for 31 – began when a fast shortish ball from Lillee lifted and Boycott, instead of dodging, preferred to let it strike his body while his bat was lifted high. It bounced off his padded front left ribs over his shoulder and dropped behind him on to the off bail. It was most unlucky for Boycott as well as England. Obviously, the Australians, having captured so valuable a wicket so cheaply, now bowled and fielded like men inspired. Luckhurst had no positive answer to Lillee's pace and soon went, to be followed by Edrich who was compelled to flick at a late outswinger (to him) that would have taken his off stump.

Again, Smith, getting right behind the ball, kept up his end, but the remainder were bemused by Massie's accuracy and late swing which meant that at the end of a miserable Saturday for England they stood only 50 runs ahead with nine wickets down.

It remained only for the weather to stay fine on Monday for Australia to gain their just reward. Gifford and Price put on 35 in the best stand of the innings but Australia needed only 81 to win and Stackpole saw them comfortably home.

With 7,000 present on the last day, the match was watched by just over 100,000 (excluding television viewers) and the receipts of £82,914 were considered to be a world record for a cricket match with the possible exception of India.   N.P.

Like a giant star nearing its end, Bob Massie shone briefly but fiercely before exploding. His 16 for 137 against England he never again remotely approached and by 1974 he had lost his place in the Western Australia XI.

ENGLAND

First Innings

G. Boycott b Massie	11
J. H. Edrich lbw b Lillee	10
B. W. Luckhurst b Lillee	1
M. J. K. Smith b Massie	34
B. L. D'Oliveira lbw b Massie	32
A. W. Greig c Marsh b Massie	54
†A. P. E. Knott c Colley b Massie	43
*R. Illingworth lbw b Massie	30
J. A. Snow b Massie	37
N. Gifford c Marsh b Massie	3
J. S. E. Price not out	4
L-b 6, w 1, n-b 6	13

1/22 2/23 3/28 4/84 5/97　　　　　　272
6/193 7/200 8/260 9/265

Second Innings

b Lillee	6
c Marsh b Massie	6
c Marsh b Lillee	4
c Edwards b Massie	30
c G. S. Chappell b Massie	3
c I. M. Chappell b Massie	3
c G. S. Chappell b Massie	12
c Stackpole b Massie	12
c Marsh b Massie	0
not out	16
c G. S. Chappell b Massie	19
W 1, n-b 4	5

1/12 2/16 3/18 4/25 5/31　　　　　116
6/52 7/74 8/74 9/81

BOWLING: **First Innings**—Lillee 28-3-90-2; Massie 32.5-7-84-8; Colley 16-2-42-0; G. S. Chappell 6-1-18-0; Gleeson 9-1-25-0. **Second Innings**—Lillee 21-6-50-2; Massie 27.2-9-53-8; Colley 7-1-8-0.

AUSTRALIA

First Innings

K. R. Stackpole c Gifford b Price	5
B. C. Francis b Snow	0
*I. M. Chappell c Smith b Snow	56
G. S. Chappell b D'Oliveira	131
K. D. Walters c Illingworth b Snow	1
R. Edwards c Smith b Illingworth	28
J. W. Gleeson c Knott b Greig	1
†R. W. Marsh c Greig b Snow	50
D. J. Colley c Greig b Price	25
R. A. L. Massie c Knott b Snow	0
D. K. Lillee not out	2
L-b 7, n-b 2	9

1/1 2/7 3/82 4/84 5/190　　　　　308
6/212 7/250 8/290 9/290

Second Innings

not out	57
c Knott b Price	9
c Luckhurst b D'Oliveira	6
not out	7
L-b 2	2

1/20 2/51　　　　(2 wkts) 81

BOWLING: **First Innings**—Snow 32-13-57-5; Price 26.1-5-87-2; Greig 29-6-74-1; D'Oliveira 17-5-48-1; Gifford 11-4-20-0; Illingworth 7-2-20-0. **Second Innings**—Snow 8-2-15-0; Price 7-0-28-1; Greig 3-0-17-0; D'Oliveira 8-3-14-1; Luckhurst 0.5-0-5-0.

Umpires: D. J. Constant and A. E. Fagg.

WEST INDIES v ENGLAND

SECOND TEST MATCH
Played at Kingston, Jamaica, February 16, 17, 19, 20, 21, 1974

DRAWN. IN THE end this became the great escape story – a match apparently lost by England but finally saved by Amiss who batted for the last nine and a half hours and scored 262 not out. Yet the achievement of Amiss, strongly and bravely supported by the tail, tended to hide the fact that this was another Test match in which England were put in jeopardy by the failure of the men in the first half of the batting order. When Denness won the toss on a pitch without pace or vice he must have been hoping for a score of around five

*The square frame and solid appearance of Dennis Amiss eloquently described the inner man. A pure distillation of bulldog spirit he averaged **46.30** in Test match cricket and no innings was more valuable than his 262 not out which saved the series for England.*

hundred. Instead, before the first day was out, England had lost five wickets for 224 and were already committed to a rearguard action.

It was a day on which the bad ball became deadly. Amiss, Hayes and Greig all hit catches off long hops from slow bowlers, Jameson went a long way down the pitch to Gibbs, hit his own ankle instead of the ball and was stumped, while Boycott, hampered for much of his innings by a pulled leg muscle, was splendidly caught by Kanhai, rolling over at short mid-off, when driving at Sobers. By the end of that opening day it was almost certain that the West Indies could not lose the match. Yet in the second half of the England innings they found resistance stiffer. Admittedly Denness, who remained the last hope of a really big score went thirty-five minutes after the start next morning for 67, but Underwood, Knott and Pocock played with such determination that the last three wickets put on 67.

Even so, 353 was a moderate score which looked somewhat less than that by the time Rowe and Fredericks had scored 206 for the first West Indies wicket. Fredericks, a left-hander who played well within limitations set by himself, was the artisan of the partnership; Rowe, who at that point had scored all his ten first-class centuries before his own Jamaican crowd, was the artist. His footwork and his balance were superb. Yet from that point of depression England's bowlers, without much success to urge them on, produced a dogged defiance that actually pinned Kallicharran, Lloyd and Sobers to defence. It was a fine performance, valuable in its context, for it erased the fear of a huge West Indian score made quickly, which would in turn have lengthened the time England would have had to survive in the second innings.

By the start of the fourth day, the West Indies were pressed into making up time. The outcome was explosive. In 58 balls Julien hit 66, adding 112 with Sobers in seventy-five minutes. Sobers, who for once in his life played the role of junior partner to whoever was at the crease with him, scored 57 and at lunch West Indies, who had added 149 in two hours off only 30 overs, declared at 583 for nine. England's bowling, so efficient the evening before, had suddenly been made to look defenceless and bewildered.

By the end of that remarkable fourth day it seemed unlikely that England could survive. With ten hours left they could only retreat and the chances of their doing so successfully were reduced dramatically when Boyce had Boycott caught off a bouncer that brushed his glove in the third over.

By the time the score was 217 – West Indies had led by 230 – five wickets had gone and Amiss had only Knott and the tailenders left for company. Among those who had fallen was Hayes, thrown out by Lloyd from cover when Amiss unaccountably challenged the man who is probably the best cover point in the world. He did the same thing later with the result that Knott also was run out (each time Lloyd scored a direct hit on the stumps). Those two errors made it even more imperative that Amiss should stay and he responded magnificently. Immediately at the start of the fifth day he had a piece of luck which almost certainly cost West Indies the match. He turned the third ball of the day firmly but straight into the hands of Sobers at backward short leg. It fell out again.

Thenceforth, England played cricket of real courage as pressure built up both on the field and in the crowd. Underwood, who had been sent in as nightwatchman, did as much as anybody to inspire it, batting on another seventy-five minutes into the last day and bravely fending off bouncers, particularly from Boyce, that became too numerous to be acceptable. Again, when Knott was quickly dismissed it seemed that England, 41 ahead with three wickets left, were doomed. Then Old, not the best player of fast bowling, withstood another barrage of bouncers to use up another hundred minutes. He and Amiss put on 72 for the eighth wicket.

Yet, such was the delicate balance of time and runs that it was not until after tea that England were finally out of danger. By then Pocock had stayed with Amiss for eighty-five minutes scoring four runs. In the end England made 432 for nine, at which point, Amiss, who had never before in his first class career scored a double century, led them off the field for the last time. His was the hero's role in a classic escape. The receipts, £36,000, were a record for Jamaica.

ENGLAND

First Innings

G. Boycott c Kanhai b Sobers 68
D. L. Amiss c Kanhai b Barrett 27
J. A. Jameson st Murray b Gibbs 23
F. C. Hayes c Boyce b Sobers 10
*M. H. Denness c Fredericks b Boyce 67
A. W. Greig c Fredericks b Barrett 45
†A. P. E. Knott c Murray b Barrett 39
C. M. Old c Murray b Julien 2
D. L. Underwood c Fredericks b Sobers 24
P. I. Pocock c Gibbs b Julien 23
R. G. D. Willis not out 6
L-b 7, n-b 12 19

1/68 2/104 3/133 4/134 5/224   353
6/278 7/286 8/322 9/333

Second Innings

c Murray b Boyce 5
not out 262
c Rowe b Barrett 38
run out 0
c Rowe b Barrett 28
b Gibbs 14
run out 6
b Barrett 19
c Murray b Sobers 12
c sub b Boyce 4
not out 3
B 10, l-b 11, w 1, n-b 19 ... 41

1/32 2/102 3/102   (9 wkts) 432
4/176 5/217 6/258
7/271 8/343 9/392

BOWLING: **First Innings**—Boyce 19-2-52-1; Julien 18-3-40-2; Sobers 33-11-65-3; Barrett 39-16-86-3; Gibbs 40-16-78-1; Fredericks 21-4-70-2; Lloyd 4-2-2-0. **Second Innings**—Julien 13-2-36-0; Boyce 21-4-70-2; Gibbs 44-15-82-1; Barrett 54-24-87-3; Sobers 34-13-73-1; Fredericks 6-1-17-0; Lloyd 3-1-5-0; Kanhai 3-1-8-0; Rowe 2-1-1-0; Kallicharran 3-0-12-0.

WEST INDIES

R. C. Fredericks b Old	94
L. G. Rowe lbw b Willis	120
A. I. Kallicharran c Denness b Old	93
C. H. Lloyd b Jameson	49
*R. B. Kanhai c Willis b Greig	39
G. S. Sobers c Willis b Greig	57
B. D. Julien c Denness b Greig	66
K. D. Boyce c Greig b Willis	8
†D. L. Murray not out	6
A. G. Barrett lbw b Willis	0
L. R. Gibbs not out	6
B 16, l-b 18, n-b 11	45

1/206 2/226 3/338   (9 wkts dec.) 583
4/401 5/439 6/551
7/563 8/567 9/574

BOWLING: Willis 24-5-97-3; Old 23-6-72-2; Pocock 57-14-152-0; Underwood 36-12-98-0; Greig 49-14-102-3; Jameson 7-2-17-1.

Umpires: D. Sang Hue and C. Jordan.

WEST INDIES v ENGLAND

FIFTH TEST MATCH
Played at Port-of-Spain, March 30, 31, April 2, 3, 4, 5, 1974

ENGLAND WON BY 26 runs with an hour to spare. The final Test was well and deservedly won by England on the strength of two outstanding personal performances – by Greig, who, bowling almost entirely in his new style as an off-spinner took thirteen wickets for 156, and by Boycott who in each innings played more convincingly than at any time since the first Test on the same ground. The toss at Port-of-Spain, where the pitch was more benevolent towards bowlers than anywhere else in the West Indies, was always important and it became more so this time with a sixth day added to the match. Denness won it and then saw the advantage dissipated as his side were bowled out for 267. Of that total Boycott, his form not right but his determination as steadfast as ever, made 99 in six hours, twenty-five minutes. He should have been run out by half the length of the pitch when he had made 9, but Kanhai, who had scrambled towards fine leg from a close-in position, threw badly to the bowler's end. Everything that happened in the rest of England's innings emphasized the importance of that miss. Only Amiss of the other batsmen made a worthwhile contribution and his 44 was the effort of a man in whom tiredness was at last beginning to show. Boycott's innings was completely defensive – he once went fifty minutes without scoring – and it ended when he was caught left-handed by Murray diving far down the leg side, still one run short of his first century on the ground where he had scored 93 in the first Test. The value of this innings was emphasized by subsequent happenings as England's last six wickets fell for 63 in ninety minutes.

The uneasiness of that position increased as the West Indies moved steadily towards that total. Fredericks and Rowe put on 110 for the first wicket and at lunch time on the third day the West Indies score stood at 208 for two, Rowe 90, Lloyd 40. Oddly, it was a position from which England began to prosper. In the space of twenty balls Greig took the wickets of Lloyd, Sobers, Kanhai and Murray for six runs so that instead of being in a commanding position when they took the lead, the West Indies had only four wickets left. The chances of that being converted into a healthy credit balance disappeared when Rowe, who had withheld his strokes to bat with the same sort of caution as Boycott, was ninth out, caught off a full toss for 123. He batted over seven hours, the West Indies totalled 305 and

Greig, in a spell of bowling that will rank among the best in Test history, took in the day eight for 33 in 19.1 overs.

Having been saved from annihilation, England batted doggedly, if not with much conviction, in their second innings. Again they dropped into danger as Amiss and Denness were dismissed for 44, but Fletcher stayed with Boycott in a stand of 101 for the third wicket before deterioration set in again. The next three wickets fell for seven runs, Julien claiming two for nine in nine overs. Boycott achieved his much wanted century after six and three-quarter hours and was then bowled by Gibbs in a manner that caused much controversy. He played forward to Gibbs and then stayed at the crease although the bail lay on the ground. Umpire Sang Hue from the bowler's end checked with his colleague at square-leg before giving him out. Apparently the ball had turned so much that his view of the stumps had been blocked by Boycott's front pad and he checked to make sure that it had hit the wicket.

Fortunately for England, Knott, who seemed to be less troubled than any batsman except Boycott, continued his successful run so that by the time he was lbw to Sobers for 44, the West Indies had been set a target of 226 to win. They started the last day 30 for none which meant that the chances of a West Indies win, an England win or a draw (the match had been constantly interrupted by rain) were all about even. Greig, significantly, had opened the England bowling with off-spinners.

Perhaps in the end the most decisive factor in the result was the tension that built up during the day. The England players withstood it better than those of West Indies, among whom some of the most experienced seemed to be the most vulnerable. The opening pair were the key players for they were the ones so clearly in form. Nothing much disturbed them until at 63 Rowe played back casually to Birkenshaw and was lbw. Two balls later Kallicharran was caught off bat and pad off Greig at first slip, thus finishing a series in which he had batted with extravagance, with a "pair". Immediately there followed an incident which may well have cost the West Indies the match.

Fredericks, who had been playing with great calmness and with an unerring judgement of stroke, played a ball from Birkenshaw past Boycott at square leg, ran a single and then surprisingly turned for a second run. Lloyd let him get as far as the middle of the pitch and then ran past him so that Fredericks watched himself being run out by several yards. In nine balls the West Indies had lost three wickets for two runs and the game had changed its complexion.

Greig again took charge for England, dismissing Kanhai and Lloyd, both of whom were clear victims of tension. Then the match swung again as Sobers, playing even in these circumstances with a charm that marked his pedigree, put on 50 for the sixth wicket with Murray, another player of good temperament. Sobers suddenly hit over a ball from Underwood and was bowled. Murray was caught driving at Greig and at 166 for eight West Indies seemed doomed.

Even then they came close to winning, for Inshan Ali, batting with a composure not apparent in some of his betters, was not dismissed until only 29 were needed and Denness in desperation had taken the new ball. Soon the innings ended and England had squared the series in a memorable match that never lacked interest and excitement even if it were sometimes short of quality.

Greig's eight wickets in an innings and thirteen wickets in the match were the best respective performances for England since Jim Laker's nine for 37 and nineteen in the match against Australia at Manchester in 1956. Greig also surpassed Trevor Bailey's seven for 34 at Kingston in 1954 as the best figures for England against West Indies.

ENGLAND

First Innings

G. Boycott c Murray b Julien 99
D. L. Amiss c Kanhai b Sobers 44
*M. H. Denness c Fredericks b Inshan 13
K. W. R. Fletcher c Kanhai b Gibbs 6
A. W. Greig lbw b Gibbs 19
F. C. Hayes c Rowe b Inshan 24
†A. P. E. Knott not out 33
J. Birkenshaw c Lloyd b Julien 8
G. G. Arnold run out 6
P. I. Pocock c Lloyd b Inshan 0
D. L. Underwood b Gibbs 4
    B 2, l-b 3, n-b 6 11

1/83 2/114 3/133 4/165 5/204   267
6/212 7/244 8/257 9/260

Second Innings

b Gibbs 112
b Lloyd 16
run out 4
b Julien 45
c Fredericks b Julien 1
lbw b Julien 0
lbw b Sobers 44
c Gibbs b Inshan 7
b Sobers 13
c Kallicharran b Boyce 5
not out 1
    L-b 4, n-b 11 15

1/39 2/44 3/145   263
4/169 5/175 6/176
7/213 8/226 9/268

BOWLING: **First Innings**—Boyce 10-3-14-0; Julien 21-8-35-2; Sobers 31-16-44-1; Gibbs 34.3-11-70-3; Inshan 35-12-86-3; Lloyd 4-2-7-0. **Second Innings**—Sobers 24.2-9-36-2; Julien 22-7-31-3; Lloyd 7-4-5-1; Gibbs 50-15-85-1; Inshan 34-12-51-1; Boyce 12-3-40-1.

WEST INDIES

First Innings

R. C. Fredericks c Fletcher b Pocock 67
L. G. Rowe c Boycott b Greig 123
A. I. Kallicharran c and b Pocock 0
C. H. Lloyd c Knott b Greig 52
G. S. Sobers c Birkenshaw b Greig 0
*R. B. Kanhai c and b Greig 2
† D. L. Murray c Pocock b Greig 2
B. D. Julien c Birkenshaw b Greig 17
K. D. Boyce c Pocock b Greig 19
Inshan Ali lbw b Greig 5
L. R. Gibbs not out 0
    B 11, l-b 4, n-b 3 18

1/110 2/122 3/224 4/224 5/226   305
6/232 7/270 8/300 9/300

Second Innings

run out 36
lbw b Birkenshaw 25
c Fletcher b Greig 0
c and b Greig 13
b Underwood 20
c Fletcher b Greig 7
c Fletcher b Greig 33
c Denness b Pocock 2
not out 34
c Underwood b Greig 15
b Arnold 1
    B 9, l-b 2, n-b 2 13

1/63 2/64 3/65 4/84 5/85   199
6/135 7/138 8/166 9/197

BOWLING: **First Innings**—Arnold 8-0-27-0; Greig 36.1-10-86-8; Pocock 31-7-86-2; Underwood 34-12-57-0; Birkenshaw 8-1-31-0. **Second Innings**—Arnold 5.3-1-13-1; Greig 33-8-70-5; Underwood 15-7-19-1; Pocock 25-7-60-1; Birkenshaw 10-1-24-1.

Umpires: D. Sang Hue and S. Ishmael.

WARWICKSHIRE v GLOUCESTERSHIRE
Played at Birmingham, July 27, 29, 1974

WARWICKSHIRE WON BY an innings and 61 runs. Jameson and Kanhai, with a brutal and ruthless assault on a weakened attack, set a new world record stand for the second wicket of 465. They came together when Abberley was dismissed by the second ball of the day and created a total of five records during their five hours, twelve minutes at the crease.

The first record to go was the county's second wicket stand of 344 by J. Devey and S. P. Kinneir in 1900. At 403 they beat Warwickshire's best for any wicket made by Kanhai and K. Ibadulla in 1968. When they reached 430 they passed the English second wicket record

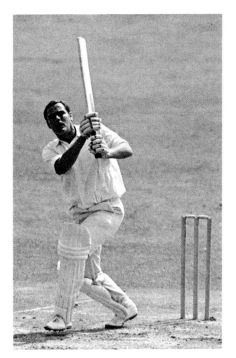 

The rapier and the bludgeon. John Jameson (above left) and Rohan Kanhai (above right) were polar opposites in batting style. The barrel-chested Jameson wielded his bat like a footpad's cudgel whilst the neat West Indian right-hander possessed a fencing master's footwork and gift of timing. Playing for Warwickshire they achieved together a world-record second-wicket stand.

established by J. G. Dewes and G. H. G. Doggart for Cambridge University in 1949 and the world second wicket record by B. B. Nimbalkar and K. V. Bhandarkar for Maharashtra against Kathiawar at Poona in 1948–49 went at 456. It was also the first occasion on which two Warwickshire players had completed double centuries in the same match.

The extraordinary partnership was not without blemish. Kanhai was dropped when 54 and both were dropped in the same over from the luckless Shackleton when they were just short of the world record. The cold statistics of the best innings of Jameson's career were one 6 and thirty-four 4s, while Kanhai hit one 6 and thirty 4s.

The Gloucestershire batsmen experienced an unhappy time. Hemmings caused a first innings collapse and when they batted a second time Willis and Blenkiron wreaked havoc.

WARWICKSHIRE

R. N. Abberley c Brown b Dixon 0
J. A. Jameson *not out* 240
R. B. Kanhai *not out* 213
    B 7, l-b 5 12

1/0   (1 wkt) 465

*M. J. K. Smith, A. I. Kallicharran, †D. L. Murray, E. E. Hemmings, W. A. Bourne. W. Blenkiron, R. G. D. Willis and D. J. Brown did not bat.

BOWLING: Dixon 17-2-91-1; Shackleton 20-2-88-0; Knight 20-2-103-0; Mortimore 31-5-87-0; Thorn 12-1-84-0.

GLOUCESTERSHIRE

First Innings
†A. W. Stovold c Murray b Willis	49
R. D. V. Knight c Jameson b Hemmings	27
A. J. Hignell c Willis b Hemmings	11
M. J. Procter c Murray b Hemmings	20
J. C. Foat c Murray b Bourne	34
M. S. T. Dunstan b Bourne	52
*A. S. Brown c and b Hemmings	4
P. L. Thorn not out	14
J. B. Mortimore c Kanhai b Hemmings	13
J. H. Shackleton b Blenkiron	2
J. H. Dixon c Kallicharran b Hemmings	7
B 4, l-b 3, n-b 3	10

1/69 2/89 3/100 4/110 5/187 243
6/198 7/202 8/229 9/236

Second Innings
b Willis	9
c Hemmings b Blenkiron	5
c Abberley b Willis	0
c Murray b Hemmings	46
b Blenkiron	7
c Bourne b Hemmings	32
b Blenkiron	40
c Murray b Willis	0
b Willis	0
b Blenkiron	11
not out	0
L-b 4, w 4, n-b 3	11

1/14 2/18 3/18 4/36 161
5/100 6/114 7/115
8/115 9/150

BOWLING: **First Innings**—Willis 13-3-40-1; Brown 11-1-44-1; Hemmings 25.5-5-87-6; Bourne 11-2-32-2; Jameson 4-0-16-0; Blenkiron 5-1-14-1. **Second Innings**—Willis 15-6-31-4; Blenkiron 9.3-4-18-4; Brown 11-4-31-0; Hemmings 19-5-45-2; Bourne 3-0-25-0.

Umpires: A. Jepson and A. G. T. Whitehead.

O'GORMAN, JOE G., who died at Weybridge on August 26, 1974, aged 84, was famous as the other half of a comedy act with brother Dave, but he always delighted in his cricket adventures with Surrey, which included batting with Jack Hobbs. This gave him as much pleasure as seeing his name in lights on Broadway. An all-rounder, he might well have made his mark in the game had he chosen. He played in three Championship matches for the county in 1927, sharing with Andy Sandham a partnership of 119 in sixty-five minutes, against Essex. O'Gorman hit 42 of those runs, with Sandham scoring altogether 230. A slow bowler, he took a wicket with his first ball in county cricket against Glamorgan at The Oval when he dismissed W. E. Bates, the opening batsman. For many years he and his brother played club cricket for Richmond for which club he took over 1,500 wickets.

AUSTRALIA v WEST INDIES

SECOND TEST MATCH
Played at Perth, December 12, 13, 14, 16, 1975

WEST INDIES WON by an innings and 87 runs. This was one of the most remarkable Test matches which can ever have been played and was a complete reversal of the First in Brisbane. The West Indies batsmen and their fast bowlers found that the fastest pitch they came across in Australia exactly suited their methods and just as everything had failed in the First Test now everything came off. The two strongest memories of the match will always be Frederick's 169 and Roberts' fast bowling, but Ian Chappell's 156 and Lloyd's 149 were scarcely less memorable. This match came as a sharp reminder that when everything is going right for them there is no side on earth which could stop the West Indies.

Walker came into the Australian side for Jenner, the leg spinner, and McCosker opened with Turner, Redpath dropping down to number five. The West Indies omitted Greenidge who had made a "pair" at Brisbane, and Inshan Ali and brought in their two all-rounders, Julien and Boyce, both of whom had been surprisingly short of form.

It looked a good toss for Australia to win, but Roberts soon sent back both openers, Julien and Boyce benefited from the pace and bounce, and Australia lost half their wickets for 189. Meanwhile, Ian Chappell, who had come in during the first over, was batting superbly. He had had just a little luck early on but was soon timing the ball beautifully as he hooked, pulled and drove. He was well supported by Gilmour later on and their stand of 88 came in only sixty-five minutes. Chappell's hundred took four and a half hours and it was one of the best innings that even he can have played, for he held the Australian batting together on his own. The next morning Holding finished off the innings in his second over with the second new ball when with the first, second and seventh balls of the over he bowled Chappell, Thomson and Mallett.

The West Indies had ninety minutes batting before lunch and, remarkably, Julien came out to open with Fredericks. Fredericks began by hooking Lillee's second ball for 6 off the edge although from then on he never made any sort of mistake. Runs came at a bewildering pace as he hooked and drove and cut at Thomson and Lillee. It was thrilling batting and the Australians could only stand and watch. Julien had a lot of luck as he flashed and missed, but when in the tenth over he fended Gilmour into the gully, 91 runs had already been scored. At lunch after only 14 overs the West Indies were an incredible 130 for one. Fredericks went on and on through the afternoon as one astonishing stroke was followed by the next. His hundred came in one hour, fifty-six minutes off 71 balls with one 6 and eighteen 4s and when soon after tea he drove at Lillee and was caught at slip he had made 169 out of 258.

Soon after that Kallicharran, who was batting well, hooked at Lillee and the ball flew off the edge and broke his nose. The Australian fielding had grown careless and before the end of the day Lloyd had been dropped twice and Murray once. The next day these two took their stand to 164 in two and a half hours. Murray's 50 had been exciting, and Lloyd produced his own special display of pyrotechnics which if not quite matching Fredericks' was very impressive. His 149 took three hours, thirty-eight minutes and he hit one 6 and twenty-two 4s. Later, Kallicharran, who continued his innings, and Boyce played some good strokes.

The West Indies had a lead of 256 and when in a wonderful spell of controlled fast bowling Roberts took four wickets before the close, the match was as good as over. Greg Chappell and Marsh continued their resistance for a while the next morning before Roberts dismissed them both and the last six wickets put on only another 65 runs. Roberts finished with seven for 54. It had been a match which had expressed vividly the full joy and exuberance of West Indies cricket and when compared to what went on before and afterwards its inconsistency as well.

AUSTRALIA

First Innings

R. B. McCosker lbw b Roberts 0
A. Turner c Gibbs b Roberts 23
I. M. Chappell b Holding 156
*G. S. Chappell c Murray b Julien 13
I. R. Redpath c Murray b Julien 33
†R. W. Marsh c Julien b Boyce .23
G. J. Gilmour c Julien b Gibbs .45
M. H. N. Walker c Richards b Holding 1
D. K. Lillee not out 12
J. R. Thomson b Holding 0
A. A. Mallett b Holding 0
 B 12, l-b 5, n-b 6 23

Second Innings

c Rowe b Roberts 13
c Murray b Roberts 0
c sub b Roberts 20
c Rowe b Roberts 43
lbw b Roberts 0
c Murray b Roberts 39
c Fredericks b Roberts 3
c sub b Julien 3
c Lloyd b Julien 4
b Julien 9
not out 18
 B 13, l-b 2, n-b 2 17

1/0 2/37 3/70 4/149 5/189   329
6/277 7/285 8/329 9/329

1/0 2/25 3/45 4/45 5/124   169
6/128 7/132 8/142 9/146

BOWLING: **First Innings**—Roberts 13-1-65-2; Boyce 12-2-53-1; Holding 18.7-1-88-4; Julien 12-0-51-2; Gibbs 14-4-49-1. **Second Innings**—Roberts 14-3-54-7; Holding 10.6-1-53-0; Julien 10.1-1-32-3; Boyce 2-0-8-0; Gibbs 3-1-3-0; Fredericks 1-0-2-0.

WEST INDIES

R. C. Fredericks c G. S. Chappell b Lillee 169
B. D. Julien c Mallett b Gilmour 25
L. G. Rowe c Marsh b Thomson 19
A. I. Kallicharran c I. M. Chappell b Walker 57
I. V. A. Richards c Gilmour b Thomson 12
*C. H. Lloyd b Gilmour 149
†D. L. Murray c Marsh b Lillee 63
M. A. Holding c Marsh b Thomson 0
K. D. Boyce not out 49
A. M. E. Roberts b Walker 0
L. R. Gibbs run out 13
 B 2, l-b 16, n-b 11 29

1/91 2/134 3/258 4/297 5/461   585
6/461 7/522 8/548 9/548

BOWLING: Lillee 20-0-123-2; Thomson 17-0-128-3; Gilmour 14-0-103-2; Walker 17-1-99-2; Mallett 26-4-103-0; I. M. Chappell 1.4-1-0-0.

Umpires: R. R. Ledwidge and M. G. O'Connell.

ENGLAND v WEST INDIES

FIFTH TEST MATCH
Played at The Oval, August 12, 13, 14, 16, 17, 1976

WEST INDIES WON by 231 runs and retained the Wisden Trophy by winning the series 3–0. The previous time England went down by a similar margin in a home series was in 1948 against Bradman's Australia side. West Indies, moreover, recorded their fifth victory in the last eight Tests in England, and many by wide margins.

This contest produced many splendid personal performances. Holding achieved two bowling records for West Indies by taking eight first innings wickets for 92 and with six for 57 on the fifth day his full analysis was fourteen for 149 – a great triumph for one of the world's fastest bowlers of all time.

After Lloyd had won the toss for the fourth time in the five Tests, Richards gave yet another glorious display with the bat. Making 291 out of 519, he hit thirty-eight 4s in a stay of eight minutes short of eight hours.

For England, Amiss made a memorable return to the Test Match scene. He looked the only class batsman in the side as he held the England first innings together by scoring 203 out of 342 before being seventh to leave, bowled behind his legs. He played nobly for five hours, twenty minutes and struck twenty-eight 4s.

While West Indies retained the eleven which won the previous Test at Headingley, England showed three changes. Amiss was preferred to Hayes, and with Snow and Ward unfit Selvey returned and Miller received his first cap after Edmonds had withdrawn from the original selection because of a sore spinning finger. Miller had an excellent match as an off-spinner and stylish bat.

Willis struck early for England when he removed Greenidge leg-before, but Richards soon took charge and with Fredericks and Rowe providing sound assistance West Indies reached 373 for three by the end of the first day. Greig caused a surprise when, after Willis had dismissed Greenidge with the last ball of his second over, he put on Underwood. A superb right hand catch by Balderstone who dived to his right at cover dismissed Fredericks and at six o'clock Knott stumped Rowe for his 220th victim in Tests against other countries and beat Godfrey Evans's record.

Richards, 200 overnight, continued his majestic exhibition and he and Lloyd put on 141 in the 32 overs England sent down on the second day before lunch, Richards getting 83 to Lloyd's 48. So Richards passed Sir Frank Worrell's 261 at Trent Bridge in 1950, the previous best for West Indies in England. One imagined that he would challenge Sir Gary Sobers' 365, the highest for all Tests, but having driven Greig high towards the Vauxhall End he went to repeat the stroke next ball only to touch it into his stumps.

During this period Greig bowled his off spin with much skill and he accounted for Lloyd at 547, but the runs still flowed until shortly before half past five, Lloyd declared, setting England the task of making 488 to prevent the follow on. West Indies' total of 687 was their highest in England, beating their 552 at Lord's three years earlier.

With the pitch slow and dusty, the West Indies decision to rely on the pacemen to the exclusion of any recognized spinner caused a good deal of comment, but Holding's speed through the air provided the answer, particularly as his side had so many runs on the board.

Amiss and Woolmer safely negotiated the 12 overs they faced at the end of the second day when some classic strokes by Amiss (22) helped the score to 34 without loss. Next morning, Holding began his devastating work by getting Woolmer leg before to a ball that kept low. Then Steele defended steadily while putting on 100 with Amiss before also being plainly leg-before. As Holding promptly removed Balderstone, England were in sore straits, but Willey resolutely kept up his end in a stand of 128 and all the while Amiss imbued confidence by the way he faced the bouncers, taking two quick steps back with a very open stance.

Greig raised hopes of a long stay with two grand cover drives off Holding, but trying again he was bowled off his pads. A disgraceful scene followed. A huge section of the crowd, mainly West Indians, swept over the ground and trampled on the pitch with the departure of the England captain. The umpires led the players off the field at about 6.10 p.m. When peace was restored Amiss and Underwood played out the last seven minutes, England's total at the week-end being 304 for five with Amiss 178.

Amiss again played well on Monday morning, but Underwood soon became another Holding victim. There was spirited late resistance by Knott and Miller but West Indies finished the half way stage with a lead of 252.

With Daniel injured and Holding needing a rest, Lloyd preferred to bat again and leave England to face the last innings. This time, the two West Indies openers enjoyed themselves at the England bowlers' expense and in two hours, twenty minutes took their unbroken partnership to 182, Greenidge hitting twelve 4s and Fredericks nine.

So Lloyd left England six hours, twenty minutes to get the runs or save the match and although Woolmer and Amiss hit freely on the fourth evening for 43, the first hour of the fifth day left England without a ghost of a chance. Half the wickets crashed for 78 and although Knott made his second fifty and Miller was again in form the West Indies sailed home with eighty minutes to spare.

The total attendance for the match was 70,000 with receipts £58,395. The full attendance for the series came to 383,000 and the gross receipts £465,000.

WEST INDIES

First Innings

R. C. Fredericks c Balderstone b Miller 71
C. G. Greenidge lbw b Willis 0
I. V. A. Richards b Greig 291
L. G. Rowe st Knott b Underwood 70
*C. H. Lloyd c Knott b Greig 84
C. L. King c Selvey b Balderstone 63
†D. L. Murray c and b Underwood 36
V. A. Holder not out 13
M. A. Holding b Underwood 32
B 1, l-b 17, n-b 9 27

1/5 2/159 3/350 4/524   (8 wkts dec.) 687
5/547 6/640 7/642 8/687

Second Innings

not out 86
not out 85

B 4, l-b 1, w 1, n-b 5 11

(no wkt dec.) 182

A. M. E. Roberts and W. W. Daniel did not bat.

BOWLING: **First Innings**—Willis 15-3-71-1; Selvey 15-0-67-0; Underwood 60.5-15-165-3; Woolmer 9-0-44-0; Miller 27-4-106-1; Balderstone 16-0-80-1; Greig 34-5-96-2; Willey 3-0-11-0; Steele 3-0-18-0. **Second Innings**—Willis 7-0-48-0; Selvey 9-1-44-0; Underwood 9-2-38-0; Woolmer 5-0-30-0; Greig 2-0-11-0.

ENGLAND

First Innings

D. L. Amiss b Holding 203
R. A. Woolmer lbw b Holding 8
D. S. Steele lbw b Holding....................44
J. C. Balderstone b Holding 0
P. Willey c Fredericks b King 33
*A. W. Greig b Holding 12
D. L. Underwood b Holding 4
†A. P. E. Knott b Holding 50
G. Miller c sub b Holder 36
M. W. W. Selvey b Holding 0
R. G. D. Willis not out........................5
B 8, l-b 11, n-b 21 40

1/47 2/147 3/151 4/279 5/303   435
6/323 7/342 8/411 9/411

Second Innings

c Greenidge b Holding 16
c Murray b Holding 30
c Murray b Holder 42
b Holding 0
c Greenidge b Holder 1
b Holding 1
c Lloyd b Roberts 2
b Holding 57
b Richards 24
not out 4
lbw b Holding 0
B 15, l-b 3, w 8 26

1/49 2/54 3/64 4/77 5/78   203
6/148 7/196 8/196 9/202

BOWLING: **First Innings**—Roberts 27-4-102-0; Holding 33-9-92-8; Holder 27.5-7-75-1; Daniel 10-1-30-0; Fredericks 11-2-36-0; Richards 14-4-30-0; King 7-3-30-1. **Second Innings**—Roberts 13-4-37-1; Holding 20.4-6-57-6; Holder 14-5-29-2; Fredericks 12-5-33-0; Richards 11-6-11-1; King 6-2-9-0; Lloyd 2-1-1-0.

Umpires: W. E. Alley and H. D. Bird.

AUSTRALIA VICTORIOUS AGAIN BY 45 RUNS

THE CENTENARY TEST MATCH

By Reg Hayter

Played at Melbourne, March 12, 13, 14, 16, 17, 1977

AN OCCASION OF warmest reunion and nostalgia, the cricket continuously compelling, a result of straining credulity. Hans Ebeling, former Australian Test bowler and the inspiration of it all, should have been christened Hans Andersen Ebeling.

From Ebeling, a vice-president of the Melbourne Cricket Club, originated the suggestion to signalise 100 years of Test Cricket by a match between England and Australia on the same ground – in 1877 the Richmond Police Paddock – on which David Gregory's team beat James Lillywhite's all-round professional England side.

The Victorian Cricket Association and the Melbourne Cricket Club co-operated to

bring this about and, with sponsorship from Qantas, TAA, Benson & Hedges and the Melbourne Hilton Hotel, a masterpiece of organisation resulted in an event which none fortunate enough to be present could forget. Unlucky were those who missed it.

Arrangements were made for the England team visiting India to extend their tour to play an official Test in the same month as the 1877 Test, and invitations to attend as guests were sent to the 244 living cricketers who had played for Australia or England in the series. All but 26 of these were able to accept for an event unique in history.

The oldest Australian Test player present was the 87-year-old Jack Ryder. Even though suffering from near blindness, the 84-year-old Percy Fender made the enervating air journey from Britain as the oldest English representative. He was accompanied by his

Derek Randall, a natural comic, inspirational fielder and tantalisingly gifted batsman enjoyed perhaps his greatest moment in this Centenary Test. His incessant chatter to himself may not have disturbed the composure of his playing partner, Michael Brearley, but succeeded in inducing a succession of bouncers from the less spiritually contemplative D. K. Lillee.

grandson, Jeremy, who became his cricketing eyes. Poor health alone prevented E. J. ("Tiger") Smith and Herbert Sutcliffe to travel and, for the same reason, Frank Woolley could not leave Canada.

Of those who went to Melbourne many told unusual stories. Colin McCool was marooned in his Queensland home by floods and had to be hauled up from his front lawn by helicopter for the airport. Jack Rutherford's train broke down and he finished the journey to the airport by taxi. Denis Compton – who else? – left his passport in a Cardiff hotel and, but for the early start to the pre-flight champagne party at London Airport which enabled a good friend to test the speed limits on the M4, would have missed the plane.

Some ex-England players – Harold Larwood, Peter Loader, Tony Lock, Barry Knight, Frank Tyson – already lived in Australia and the Australian Neil Hawke flew home from England. The gradual gathering of all at the Hilton Hotel, 200 yards across the Jolimont Park from the Melbourne Oval, brought meetings and greetings of unabated happiness. Not a hitch, not one.

Fittingly, this was also Melbourne's Mardi Gras, a week called "Moomba", the aboriginal word for "let's get together and have fun". After a champagne (much was drunk between London and Melbourne and back) breakfast and an opening ceremony in which ex-Test captains accompanied the teams on to the field, the crowd were also given the opportunity of a special welcome to all the former Test players.

Greig called correctly to Greg Chappell's spin of the specially minted gold coin and chose for England to field first. Probably he felt apprehension about his batsmen facing Lillee while moisture remained in the pitch. The resolute fast-medium bowling of Willis, Old and Lever, helped by Underwood's customary left-handed accuracy and breathtakingly supported in the field, appeared to justify Greig's decision in Australia's dismissal for 138 in front of a crowd of over 61,000.

Australia, handicapped by the early departure of McCosker, who fractured his jaw when a ball from Willis flew off his hand into his face, were always on the defensive. England's batting buckled even more swiftly against Lillee, at the zenith of his form and speed, and Walker – Australia's fielding being no way inferior to that of England.

That was the last of the bowling mastery. On the second, third and fourth days Australia increased their first innings lead of 43 so much that their declaration left England 463 to win at 40 an hour.

Marsh, who had already beaten Grout's record of 187 Test victims, added to his triumph by his first Test century against England, and Walters joyfully rode his fortune in the manner that has charmed so many cricket admirers of the cavalier approach to batsmanship. Yet the spotlight centred on the 21-year-old David Hookes who won his place on the forthcoming tour to England with an innings straight from the fount of youth. This six feet, two inches powerful left-handed batsman, who had scored five centuries in 1976–77 Sheffield Shield cricket strode to the crease with a confidence even more apparent when he struck Greig for five 4s in an over – off, pull, cover, mid-wicket, cover.

Then it was England's turn. And, in the presence of the Queen and the Duke of Edinburgh – during an interval they drove round the ground and were hugely acclaimed – royally did they apply themselves. Well as Amiss, Greig, Knott and Brearley batted, however, the innings to remember was played by Randall, a jaunty, restless, bubbling character, whose 174 took England to the doorstep of victory. The Australian spectators enjoyed his approach as much as Indian crowds had done on the tour just finished.

Once, when Lillee tested him with a bouncer, he tennis-batted it to the mid-wicket fence with a speed and power that made many a rheumy eye turn to the master of the stroke, the watching Sir Donald Bradman. Words cannot recapture the joy of that moment.

Another time, when Lillee bowled short, Randall ducked, rose, drew himself to his full five feet eight, doffed his cap and bowed politely. Then, felled by another bouncer, he gaily performed a reverse roll. This helped to maintain a friendly atmosphere in what, at all times, was a serious and fully competitive match.

The Australians responded. When Randall was 161, umpire Brooks gave him out, caught at the wicket. Immediately Marsh intimated that he had not completed the catch before dropping the ball. After consultation, the umpire called Randall back. Would that this spirit was always so! At the end of the game Randall was awarded the first prize of 1,600 dollars as the Man of the Match. To be chosen ahead of the superb Lillee, whose colleagues chaired him from the field when he finished the match with an analysis of eleven for 165, was a feat indeed.

Some time after it was over someone discovered that the result of the 226th Test between the two countries – victory by 45 runs – was identical, to the same side and to the very run, with that of the 1877 Test on the same ground. Hans "Andersen" Ebeling had even scripted the final curtain.

AUSTRALIA

First Innings

I. C. Davies lbw b Lever 5
R. B. McCosker b Willis 4
G. J. Cosier c Fletcher b Lever 10
*G. S. Chappell b Underwood 40
D. W. Hookes c Greig b Old 17
K. D. Walters c Greig b Willis 4
†R. W. Marsh c Knott b Old 28
G. J. Gilmour c Greig b Old 4
K. J. O'Keeffe c Brearley b Underwood 0
D. K. Lillee not out 10
M. H. N. Walker b Underwood 2
    B 4, l-b 2, n-b 8 14

1/11 2/13 3/23 4/45 5/51   138
6/102 7/114 8/117 9/136

Second Innings

c Knott b Greig 68
c Greig b Old 25
c Knott b Lever 4
b Old 2
c Fletcher b Underwood 56
c Knott b Greig 66
not out 110
b Lever 16
c Willis b Old 14
c Amiss b Old 25
not out 8
    L-b 10, n-b 15 25

1/33 2/40 3/53   (9 wkts dec.) 419
4/132 5/187 6/244
7/277 8/353 9/407

BOWLING: **First Innings**—Lever 12-1-36-2; Willis 8-0-32-2; Old 12-4-39-3; Underwood 11.6-2-16-3. **Second Innings**—Lever 21-1-95-2; Willis 22-0-91-0; Old 27.6-2-104-4; Greig 14-3-66-2; Underwood 12-2-38-1.

ENGLAND

First Innings

R. A. Woolmer c Chappell b Lillee 9
J. M. Brearley c Hookes b Lillee 12
D. L. Underwood c Chappell b Walker 7
D. W. Randall c Marsh b Lillee 4
D. L. Amiss c O'Keeffe b Walker 4
K. W. R. Fletcher c Marsh b Walker 4
*A. W. Greig b Walker 18
†A. P. E. Knott lbw b Lillee 15
C. M. Old c Marsh b Lillee 3
J. K. Lever c Marsh b Lillee 11
R. G. D. Willis not out 1
    B 2, l-b 2, w 1, n-b 2 7

1/19 2/30 3/34 4/40 5/40   95
6/61 7/65 8/78 9/86

Second Innings

lbw b Walker 12
lbw b Lillee 43
b Lillee 7
c Cosier b O'Keeffe 174
b Chappell 64
c Marsh b Lillee 1
c Cosier b O'Keeffe 41
lbw b Lillee 42
c Chappell b Lillee 2
lbw b O'Keeffe 4
not out 5
    B 8, l-b 4, w 3, n-b 7 22

1/28 2/113 3/279 4/290 5/346   417
6/369 7/380 8/385 9/410

BOWLING: **First Innings**—Lillee 13.3-2-26-6; Walker 15-3-54-4; O'Keeffe 1-0-4-0; Gilmour 5-3-4-0. **Second Innings**—Lillee 34.4-7-139-5; Walker 22-4-83-1; Gilmour 4-0-29-0; Chappell 16-7-29-1; O'Keeffe 33-6-108-3; Walters 3-2-7-0.

Umpires: M. G. O'Connell and T. F. Brooks.

SUSSEX v LANCASHIRE
Played at Hove, May 11, 12, 13, 1977

DRAWN, ABANDONED OWING to rain. The previous fixture, against the Australians, had been washed out after only a little play had been possible, and only four overs could be bowled in this match. John Langridge, one of the umpires, said that he had never seen the cricket square so saturated during his fifty years in the game, most of them as a Sussex player. The news concerning the Australian cricket "circus" broke during the match, and reporters switched from a wearying wait for play to start to attend a conference called by Greig.

SUSSEX
J. R. T. Barclay *not out* 6
K. C. Wessels *not out* 4
                                                            ——
                                            (no wkt) 10

R. D. V. Knight, Javed Miandad, *A. W. Greig, P. J. Graves, M. A. Buss, J. A. Snow, †A. Long, J. Spencer and C. E. Waller did not bat.

BOWLING: Lee 2-0-6-0; Ratcliffe 2-1-4-0.

LANCASHIRE
B. Wood, *D. Lloyd, H. Pilling, C. H. Lloyd, F. C. Hayes, J. Abrahams, J. Simmons, R. M. Ratcliffe, †J. Lyon, P. G. Lee and R. Arrowsmith.

Umpires: J. G. Langridge and B. J. Meyer.

Tony Greig, shortly to make the transition from England cricketer to insurance salesman tries out the briefcase for size. Greig had been an inspirational leader of England and also proved a source of inspiration for the West Indies, since for many years, following some ill-judged remarks of his concerning their fighting qualities, the West Indians never looked in danger of losing a Test to England.

GLAMORGAN v WORCESTERSHIRE
Played at Swansea, June 29, 30, July 1, 1977

DRAWN. THIS WILL go down as Turner's match. He scored 141 out of Worcestershire's total of 169. No other batsman reached double figures. In fact, the other ten batsmen contributed only 14 scoring shots between them. The next highest scorer was Gifford with 7 and he stayed with Turner for fifty minutes during which 57 were added for the ninth wicket. This not only enabled Turner to complete a century, but also saved Worcestershire from following on. The only blemish came when he was 93, Ontong missing a slip catch. A feature of Glamorgan's batting which gave them a first innings lead of 140 was an unbroken fifth wicket partnership between Llewellyn and Richards of 161. But rain on the third day denied Glamorgan the opportunity of turning their advantage into a win.

GLAMORGAN
First Innings

*A. Jones *lbw b* Gifford	48
J. A. Hopkins *lbw b* Pridgeon	28
R. C. Ontong *st* Humphries *b* Gifford	21
C. L. King *c* D'Oliveira *b* Gifford	25
M. J. Llewellyn *not out*	91
G. Richards *not out*	74
†E. W. Jones (*did not bat*)	
M. A. Nash (*did not bat*)	
A. E. Cordle (*did not bat*)	
B 4, l-b 6, n-b 12	22

Second Innings

b Holder	7
c Neale *b* D'Oliveira	45
b Cumbes	56
c D'Oliveira *b* Holder	2
b Holder	12
lbw b Cumbes	0
b Cumbes	4
not out	5
not out	4
B 5, n-b 2	7

1/57 2/98 3/117 4/148 (4 wkts) 309

1/17 2/23 3/82 4/119 (7 wkts) 142
5/124 6/132 7/137

B. J. Lloyd and A. H. Wilkins did not bat.

BOWLING: **First Innings**—Holder 19-1-54-0; Cumbes 19-3-54-0; Pridgeon 14-1-45-1; Gifford 30-8-91-3; D'Oliveira 18-8-43-0. **Second Innings**—Holder 9.3-6-48-3; Cumbes 14-4-30-3; Gifford 12-6-25-0; D'Oliveira 17-4-32-1.

WORCESTERSHIRE

G. M. Turner *not out*	141
B. J. R. Jones *lbw b* Nash	1
P. A. Neale *c* E. W. Jones *b* Wilkins	3
E. J. O. Hemsley *b* Cordle	3
B. L. D'Oliveira *c* E. W. Jones *b* Cordle	0
D. N. Patel *c* E. W. Jones *b* Nash	4
†D. J. Humphries *c* Llewellyn *b* Cordle	0
V. A. Holder *lbw b* Cordle	4
*N. Gifford *c* Llewellyn *b* Lloyd	7
J. Cumbes *lbw b* Nash	5
A. P. Pridgeon *lbw b* Cordle	0
L-b 1	1

1/18 2/35 3/68 4/71   169
5/71 6/82 7/87 8/93 9/150

BOWLING: Nash 31-14-51-3; Cordle 24-9-53-5; Wilkins 7-0-33-1: Ontong 3-0-20-0; Lloyd 3-1-11-1.

Umpires: W. E. Alley and R. Julian.

Gifted New Zealand batsmen are born to fight lonely battles. Glenn Turner was no exception. Six years before this game he had scored 223 not out for New Zealand in a total of 386 against the West Indies.

GLOUCESTERSHIRE v WORCESTERSHIRE
Played at Cheltenham, July 27, 28, 29, 1977

GLOUCESTERSHIRE WON BY an innings and 35 runs. A fine all round performance by Procter enabled Gloucestershire to win comfortably. He achieved one of his best performances of the season to take seven for 35 as Worcestershire were bundled out for 167, only Neale and Hemsley producing any substantial scores. Gloucestershire lost their first three wickets for 43 runs before solid batting by Zaheer, Hignell and Shepherd helped them to recover and a first century of the season by Procter finally saw them to a respectable total of 338. Holder took seven wickets for 117. In their second innings Worcestershire lost their first six wickets for only 40 runs, despite some stubborn batting by Ormrod. Again Procter did the damage, finishing with six for 38 for a match analysis of thirteen for 73.

WORCESTERSHIRE

First Innings

G. M. Turner c Zaheer b Procter	9
J. A. Ormrod c Stovold b Brain	19
P. A. Neale b Procter	38
E. J. O. Hemsley c Childs b Procter	56
B. L. D'Oliveira c Stovold b Procter	0
S. P. Henderson c Stovold b Procter	2
C. N. Boyns lbw b Procter	0
†D. J. Humphries lbw b Brain	12
V. A. Holder run out	8
*N. Gifford c Stovold b Procter	9
J. Cumbes not out	0
L-b 8, n-b 1	14

1/16 2/61 3/83 4/84   167
5/87 6/87 7/114 8/151 9/163

Second Innings

c Procter b Childs	16
c Hignell b Graveney	44
lbw b Procter	1
b Procter	10
c Graveney b Procter	23
b Procter	6
lbw b Procter	1
lbw b Shackleton	0
lbw b Procter	12
b Graveney	8
not out	2
B 9, n-b 4	13

1/2 2/10 3/24 4/30   136
5/31 6/40 7/104 8/114 9/131

BOWLING: **First Innings**—Brain 22-5-56-2; Procter 18.5-5-35-7; Shackleton 11-1-27-0; Graveney 8-6-10-0; Childs 13-4-25-0. **Second Innings**—Procter 20-6-38-6; Shackleton 6-1-6-1; Graveney 11.4-5-19-2; Childs 17-9-24-1; Sadiq 11-4-36-0.

GLOUCESTERSHIRE

Sadiq Mohammad c Turner b Holder	8
†A. W. Stovold c Boyns b Holder	0
Zaheer Abbas c Humphries b Holder	23
A. J. Hignell b Boyns	64
D. R. Shepherd c Humphries b Holder	38
J. H. Shackleton c Turner b Holder	0
*M. J. Procter c sub b Holder	108
P. Bainbridge c Humphries b Holder	40
D. A. Graveney b Holder	32
B. M. Brain b Cumbes	6
J. H. Childs not out	0
B 2, l-b 7, n-b 10	19

1/1 2/19 3/43 4/108   338
5/112 6/204 7/259 8/331 9/338

BOWLING: Holder 35.5-7-117-7; Cumbes 23-4-72-2; Gifford 27-9-59-0; Boyns 18-2-61-1; Hemsley 3-0-10-0.

Umpires: W. L. Budd and W. E. Phillipson.

GLOUCESTERSHIRE v SUSSEX

Played at Cheltenham, July 30, August 1, 2, 1977

GLOUCESTERSHIRE WON BY eight wickets. Everything else in this match was dwarfed by the batting of Zaheer, who set a world record when he became the first player to score a double and a single century for the third time. Remarkably his other two performances, against Kent and Surrey in 1976, finished not out like those in this game. For his 205 he batted five hours, twenty minutes, his chief hits being one 5 and twenty-two 4s and he did not offer a chance, although he lofted the ball more than usual. His 108, notable for superb cover drives, contained one 6 and seventeen 4s and came in three and a quarter hours when Gloucestershire needed 219 to win in just under four hours.

SUSSEX

First Innings

J. R. T. Barclay st Stovold b Childs	105
*P. J. Graves c Stovold b Procter	56
R. D. V. Knight b Graveney	18
Javed Miandad c Procter b Graveney	48
Imran Khan b Graveney	1
P. W. G. Parker c Zaheer b Graveney	32
M. A. Buss st Stovold b Childs	9
†A. Long *not out*	11
J. A. Snow *not out*	8
J. Spencer (*did not bat*)	
R. G. L. Cheatle (*did not bat*)	
B 4, l-b 14, w 1, n-b 2	21

Second Innings

c Bainbridge b Procter	11
b Graveney	11
c and b Graveney	21
c Stovold b Graveney	30
run out	39
c Hignell b Graveney	2
lbw b Procter	30
b Procter	20
b Childs	56
not out	9
c Shackleton b Childs	8
B 17, l-b 2, n-b 6	25

1/1 19 2/144 3/222   (7 wkts) 309
4/224 5/266 6/284 7/291

1/12 2/47 3/51 4/93 5/99   262
6/144 7/174 8/214 9/248

BOWLING: **First Innings**—Procter 25-7-51-1; Vernon 7-1-37-0; Shackleton 12-1-38-0; Childs 23-4-72-2; Graveney 33-5-90-4. **Second Innings**—Procter 29-5-91-3; Vernon 2-0-13-0; Shackleton 3-0-22-0; Childs 13.4-7-25-2; Graveney 35-10-84-4; Sadiq 1-0-2-0.

GLOUCESTERSHIRE

First Innings

Sadiq Mohammad c Barclay b Imran	0
†A. W. Stovold c and b Buss	61
Zaheer Abbas *not out*	205
A. J. Hignell c Long b Cheatle	8
*M. J. Procter b Imran	17
D. R. Shepherd c Knight b Spencer	32
P. Bainbridge c Javed b Buss	7
D. A. Graveney c Long b Snow	16
J. H. Shackleton *not out*	1
L-b 2, w 1, n-b 3	6

Second Innings

c Barclay b Javed	33
c Long b Imran	30
not out	108
not out	33
B 5, l-b 4, w 3, n-b 3	15

1/2 2/146 3/169   (7 wkts) 353
4/200 5/300 6/319 7/349

1/47 2/106   (2 wkts) 219

M. J. Vernon and J. H. Childs did not bat.

BOWLING: **First Innings**—Imran 17-5-52-2; Snow 18-3-68-1; Spencer 16-2-58-1; Buss 24-5-53-2; Cheatle 18-3-79-1; Barclay 2-1-3-0; Javed 1-0-12-0; Knight 4-0-22-0. **Second Innings**—Imran 7-3-15-1; Snow 3-0-11-0; Buss 4-0-16-0; Cheatle 18-3-71-0; Barclay 10-1-45-0; Javed 7.4-0-44-1; Long 1-0-2-0.

Umpires: W. L. Budd and D. Oslear.

RATTIGAN, SIR TERENCE MERVYN, CBE, the famous play-writer, who died in Bermuda on November 30, 1977, aged 66, was, like his father and his uncle, in the Harrow XI. He won his place in 1929 as an opening bat, but next year though he played in the XI was not in the side at Lord's. He was an elegant stroke player, but unsound.

GIMBLETT, HAROLD, who died at his home at Verwood. Dorset, on March 30, 1978, aged 63, was the most exciting English batsman of his day. Years ago, C. B. Fry wrote of MacLaren, "Like all the great batsmen, he always attacked the bowling!" If that view was once shared by the selectors, they had abandoned it by Gimblett's time. They preferred soundness and consistency. Watching our batting in Australia in 1946–47, Macartney expressed amazement that both Gimblett and Barnett had been left at home. Gimblett played in three Tests only, two against India in 1936, the first of which at Lord's he finished with a dazzling 67 not out, culminating in five consecutive boundaries, and one against the West Indies in 1939. Those of us who saw the inexpressibly feeble English batting against Ramadhin and Valentine at Lord's in 1950 shown up for what it was by the bold tail-end hitting of Wardle, longed for an hour of Gimblett, and indeed he was picked for the next Test, but was unfortunately ill and unable to play.

The start of his career was so sensational that any novelist attributing it to his hero would have discredited the book. Given a month's trial on the Somerset staff in 1935 after a number of brilliant performances in local matches, he was told before the period had expired that there was no future for him in county cricket and was sent home. Next day there was a last minute vacancy against Essex at Frome and he was recalled to fill it, mainly as a young man who could chase the ball in the field and perhaps bowl a few overs of mild medium pace. In fact, coming in to face Nichols, the England fast bowler, then at his best, with six wickets down for 107, he reached his 50 in twenty-eight minutes and his 100 in sixty-three, finally making 123 out of 175 in eighty minutes with three 6s and seventeen 4s. The innings won him the Lawrence Trophy for the fastest 100 of the season. In the next match, against Middlesex at Lord's, though lame and batting with a runner, he made 53 against Jim Smith, Robins, Peebles and Sims, three of them England bowlers. It was hardly to be expected that he could keep this up and his record at the end of the season was modest, but his second summer dispelled any notion that his early successes had been a fluke, as he scored 1,608 runs with an average of 32.81. People sometimes talk as if after this he was a disappointment. In fact his one set-back, apart from being overlooked by the selectors, was when in 1938, probably listening to the advice of grave critics, he attempted more cautious methods and his average dropped to 27. But can one call disappointing a man who between 1936 and his retirement in 1953 never failed to get his 1,000 runs, who in his career scored over 23,000, more than any other Somerset player, and fifty centuries, the highest 310 against Sussex at Eastbourne in 1948, and whose average for his career was over 36? Moreover after his first season he habitually went in first and yet he hit 265 sixes, surely a record.

Naturally, as time went on, his judgement improved with experience, he grew sounder and in particular became the master of the hook instead of its slave, though he never abandoned it, as did Hammond and Peter May. To the end, he might have said, as Frank Woolley used to, "When I am batting, I am the attack." Apart from his hook he was a fine cutter and driver, his off-drives often being played late and going past cover's left-hand, and like nearly all great attacking bats he freely employed the pull-drive, with which he was particularly severe on Mahomed Nissar at Lord's in 1936. Early in his career, on the fallacious grounds that a great games-player must be a great slip, he was put in the slips where he was only a qualified success. Elsewhere. a fine thrower and a good catch, he was far more successful and many will remember the catch at cover with which he dismissed K. H. Weekes in the Lord's Test in 1939.

For twenty years after his retirement he was coach at Millfield.

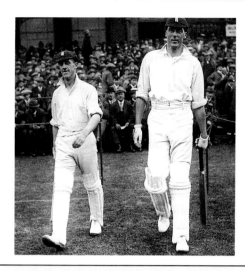

FRANK EDWARD WOOLLEY, who died in Halifax, Nova Scotia, on October 18th, 1978, aged 91, was beyond doubt one of the finest and most elegant left-handed all-rounders of all time. In a first-class career extending from 1906 to 1938 he hit 58,969 runs – a total exceeded only by Sir Jack Hobbs – including 145 centuries, to average 40.75; he took 2,068 wickets for 19.85 runs each, and he held 1,015 catches, mainly at slip, a record which remains unsurpassed.

Even more impressive than the number of runs Woolley amassed was the manner in which he made them. Standing well over six feet, he was a joy to watch. He played an eminently straight bat, employed his long reach to full advantage, and used his feet in a manner nowadays rarely seen. His timing of the ball approached perfection and he generally dealt surely with all types of bowling. Master of all the strokes, he was at his best driving, cutting, and turning the ball off his legs. He was described by Sydney Pardon as the cleanest driver since F. G. J. Ford, but he often started badly and there was something wanting in his defence. As a bowler he made good use of his height and bowled with a graceful easy swing.

As a small boy he was always to be found on the Tonbridge Cricket Ground, and his natural ability as batsman and bowler attracted so much attention that, in 1903, he was engaged to take part in the morning practice and play in a match or two in the afternoon if required. In the following year he became a regular member of the Tonbridge Ground staff, which in those days was the official Kent nursery. When given his first chance in the Kent XI in 1906, he was almost unknown to the public, and his all-round form in his third match, against Surrey at The Oval, came as nothing less than a revelation. To begin with, he took three Surrey wickets, clean bowling Hayward, Hayes, and Goatly. He then made 72, and when Surrey batted again he took five wickets for 80 runs. Finally he scored 23 not out, helping to win a wonderful game for Kent by one wicket. The match established his reputation.

When Frank Woolley announced his retirement in 1938, I spent an afternoon with him at his home in Hildenborough where he talked about "My happy cricket life". In his first season with Kent they won the County Championship for the first time and altogether between 1906 and 1913 they were top four times. Now let Woolley speak for himself as he told his story to me.

"Those were the great days when plenty of amateurs could spare time for cricket. I do not believe there are so many good players in the game now as before the [First World] War. In the old days we were probably educated in cricket in a far more serious way than now. For the purpose of giving the younger people my idea of the difference, I will put up Walter Hammond, England's captain, as an example. Before 1914 there were something like 30 players up to his standard and he would have been in the England team only if at the top of his form. I make these remarks without casting the slightest reflection on Hammond. He is a grand player and one of the greatest all-round cricketers since the War – in fact, the greatest.

"I doubt whether English cricket has really recovered from the effects of the War. You see, we missed half a generation and since then young men have found many other ways of occupying their leisure hours. Still, I believe it is only a passing phase and cricket will one day produce an abundance of great players."

Unfortunately for cricket, within a year England was plunged into another war, and in my opinion the game in this country had only just shown signs of getting on its feet again with a stream of fine young players coming through, notably in the county of Kent. But to return to the Woolley interview as he saw the game 40 years ago.

"There is little wrong with the game itself. Just a question of the way it is played. It is amazing how the public steadfastly refuse to attend the third day of a match when so often the last day produces the best and most exciting cricket.

"Touching on a personal subject I have been asked if I can explain why I was dismissed so many times in the 'nineties'. The statisticians inform me that I was out 35 times between 90 and 99 and I am also told that I am credited with 89 ducks. With regard to those 'nineties', I can honestly say that with me it was never a case of the 'nervous nineties'. Lots of times I was out through forcing the game. We were never allowed to play for averages in the Kent side or take half an hour or more to get the last ten runs under normal conditions. We always had to play the game and play for the team. It is a Kent tradition.

"As a matter of fact I consider the two finest innings I ever played were in the second Test against Australia in 1921 when I was out for 95 and 93. I don't think I ever worked harder at any match during my career to get runs as I did then, nor did I ever have to face in one game such consistently fast bowlers as the Australian pair, Gregory and McDonald. Square cuts which ordinarily would have flashed to the boundary earned only two, and I believe that those two innings would have been worth 150 apiece in a county match.

"I was not depressed when they got me out. I have always taken my dismissals as part of the game. In the first innings I was in the 'eighties' when I was joined by the last man, Jack Durston. It was my own fault completely that I lost my wicket. Mailey bowled me a full toss to the off; I walked down the pitch, stepping to the on to force the ball past extra cover, I missed it, and that fine wicket-keeper, H. Carter, eagerly accepted the opportunity to stump me. I was rather unlucky in the second innings when again I fell to Mailey. The ball stuck in his hand and dropped halfway on the leg side. I hit it pretty plumb between square leg and mid-on and just there was standing 'Stalky' Hendry. As I made the shot he jumped in the air and up went his right hand. The ball hit him, I think, on the wrist, and he lost his balance. The ball went up ten feet and as he was lying on the ground it fell in his lap and he caught it. He was the only man on the leg side and I think the shot would have carried for six. It was a marvellous catch.

"It is often argued that left-handed batsmen have an advantage compared with the right-handers. I do not agree. When the turf is worn the right-hand leg-break bowlers and left-arm slow bowlers are able to pitch the ball into the footholes of the bowlers who have operated at the other end. Right-handed batsmen can let these balls hit their pads, but the left-handers must use their bats. Perhaps the new [1937] lbw rule has not helped us there, but the amended law does not worry me, though in my opinion it has not improved the game. As for further extending the lbw rule I think it would make a farce of the game.

> "In many quarters surprise was expressed that at the age of 51 I went in number one. Until then I had never been in first regularly, though I had always preferred that place. Beginning as a bowler made Kent place me four or five in the order, and moreover the county were always rich in opening batsmen. Consequently my wish to start the innings was denied until 1938.
>
> "Because Kent have experienced their bad times against fast bowling [there were very few bouncers in those days] the cry has gone round that we cannot play the fast men, but I think if you search the records you will also find that Kent have hit a tremendous lot of runs off fast bowling. Again I must emphasise that Kent always endeavour to play sporting cricket, and trying to make runs off that type of bowling must sometimes have contributed to our downfall. It was never a policy of the Kent team that the pitch *must* be occupied all day after winning the toss.
>
> "I cannot let this opportunity pass without placing on record how much I have enjoyed my cricket with Kent. If I was a youngster starting as a batsman I think I should like to play always at The Oval, but the Kent grounds, with their natural decorations of beautiful trees, members' tents flying their own colours and bedecked with flowers, lend the right tone to cricket."
>
> After his retirement from the field, Woolley was elected a life member of MCC and Kent, and also to the county committee. He was quite active into his late 80s and in January 1971 flew to Australia to watch the last two Tests. Nine months later, in Canada, he married for a second time, his first wife having died ten years earlier. His second bride was Mrs Martha Morse, an American widow. — *Norman Preston*

ENGLAND v INDIA

FOURTH CORNHILL TEST
Played at The Oval, August 30, 31, September 1, 3, 4, 1979

DRAWN, AFTER THE most gripping closing overs in a home Test since the draw at Lord's against West Indies in 1963, a match it closely resembled as all four results were possible with three balls left. Gavaskar's inspiring and technically flawless 221 earned him the Man of the Match award and brought that rarity in recent Tests in England – a final day charged with interest. Botham played the major part in preventing an Indian victory and confirmed his status as Man of the Series. As the teams fought each other to a standstill, there were many Englishmen in the crowd who would not have displayed their customary dejection at a Test defeat.

Gavaskar's innings was the highest by an Indian against England, overtaking the unbeaten 203 by the younger Nawab of Pataudi at Delhi in 1964, and his stand of 213 with Chauhan surpassed the previous best opening partnership for his country against England – 203 by Mushtaq Ali and Merchant at Manchester in 1936. India's 429 for eight – they were set 438 in 500 minutes – was the fourth-highest score in the fourth innings of a Test. To reach their target they would have needed to set a new mark for a side batting fourth and winning, but this generation of Indian batsmen have some notable performances in that department and the job did not frighten them.

England gave first caps to Butcher and Bairstow, omitting Randall and Taylor, while Willey returned after a gap of three years for Miller. Yajurvindra Singh replaced the injured Amarnath for India.

The game, played in virtually unbroken sunshine, began prosaically as Butcher and Boycott dug in without attempting to dominate. Butcher's disappointing innings ended in the over before lunch and Kapil Dev, as at Leeds, extended the breakthrough by taking two quick wickets. He slanted one into Boycott, and three balls later made one straighten at Gower, whom he had also claimed lbw for a duck at Headingley. Willey and Gooch repaired the damage, Willey playing the strokes of the day by hooking and cover-driving with immense power. Botham achieved the 3 runs he needed to reach the landmark of 1,000 runs and 100 wickets in his 21st Test, beating the 23 Tests required by Mankad for this double. But Gooch's first Test century still eluded him; he fell in the first over of the second day.

Botham, as bowler and fielder, sent India sliding into trouble, taking two wickets and holding two catches, and India had subsided to 137 for five when bad light halted the game forty minutes early. Botham's second catch was remarkable. Bairstow could only parry the ball when Vengsarkar edged Willis. The ball struck Brearley on the boot, flew upwards, and as Bairstow came across to retrieve it, Botham grabbed it one-handed at second slip. Viswanath had played exquisitely for almost three hours. England were batting again by lunch on Saturday. The regular fall of wickets, caused by much batting below Test class from both sides, had driven the match along swifter than the normal sedate progress of a Test, and this was, of course, an important factor in allowing the marvellous finish.

Butcher was unable to improve significantly on his first innings form. Gooch drove one vast 6, but when Gower failed again, Willey and Boycott decided on rather pedestrian consolidation over the last seventy-five minutes. Later events proved their caution justified. Boycott toiled with the handicap of back trouble on the Monday in the last three hours of his seven-hour effort. Botham was run out, neglecting to ascertain Boycott's intentions as he charged up the pitch, and so England were indebted to a crisp knock from Bairstow as they moved to their declaration.

At 76 for no wicket on the fifth morning, India wanted roughly a run a minute. Their rate was never brisk – 48 in the first hour, 45 in the second, and 44 in the third. Hendrick, allowing only 11 runs in six overs, did most to peg India's progress and, in mid-afternoon, Willey conceded only 2 runs in eight grudging overs. However, Hendrick disappeared for good with shoulder trouble after his spell, and Brearley's capacity for restriction was limited.

England were despairing of wickets when, after five and a quarter hours, Chauhan edged Willis. The despair soon returned as Vengsarkar joined Gavaskar in an accelerating stand which produced 153 at better than a run a minute. Gavaskar masterminded the show, doing all the thinking and playing most of the shots. Tea came at 304 for one and, after a mere six overs between the interval and five o'clock – England ruthlessly slowed down the game – the last twenty overs began at 328 for one with 110 wanted, and India favourites.

Sunil Gavaskar nudges the ball past a diving Hendrick during the match in question. His 221 in the final innings very nearly won the game for India.

At 365 Botham uncharacteristically dropped Vengsarkar on the boundary – an error for which he swiftly compensated by transforming the match with three wickets, a catch and a run-out in the remaining twelve overs. He collected a simple catch off Vengsarkar at 366 and Willey swept aside the promoted Kapil Dev. Yashpal Sharma and Gavaskar rattled the score along to 389 when Botham returned with eight overs left. It was a gamble by Brearley, for Botham had looked innocuous during the day. But he struck with the key wicket, Gavaskar drilling a catch to mid-on shortly after England had taken a drinks break – a rare move, tactically based, with the end so near. Gavaskar's memorable innings lasted eight hours, nine minutes and he hit twenty-one 4s, most of them coming from firm clips past mid-wicket and his unexpectedly powerful cover-drive. However, his cool control of the developing crisis was missed by India as much as his runs.

Viswanath unerringly found one of the widely spaced fielders, as had Vengsarkar and Gavaskar. Then Botham firmly ended India's hopes by having Yajurvindra Singh and Yashpal Sharma lbw in successive overs and, in between, making a slick stop to run out Venkataraghavan. Botham's final four overs brought him an absolutely crucial three for seventeen. A target of 15 from the last over was too much, and the climax came with fielders encircling the bat.

ENGLAND

First Innings

G. Boycott lbw b Kapil Dev	35
A. R. Butcher c Yajurvindra b Venkataraghavan	14
G. A. Gooch c Viswanath b Ghavri	79
D. I. Gower lbw b Kapil Dev	0
P. Willey c Yajurvindra b Bedi	52
I. T. Botham st Reddy b Venkataraghavan	38
*J. M. Brearley b Ghavri	34
†D. L. Bairstow c Reddy b Kapil Dev	9
P. H. Edmonds c Kapil Dev b Venkataraghavan	16
R. G. D. Willis not out	10
M. Hendrick c Gavaskar b Bedi	0
L-b 9, w 4, n-b 5	18

1/45 2/51 3/51 4/148 5/203   305
6/245 7/272 8/275 9/304

Second Innings

b Ghavri	125
c Venkataraghavan b Ghavri	20
lbw b Kapil Dev	31
c Reddy b Bedi	7
c Reddy b Ghavri	31
run out	0
b Venkataraghavan	11
c Gavaskar b Kapil Dev	59
not out	27
L-b 14, w 2, n-b 7	23

1/43 2/107 3/125   (8 wkts dec.) 334
4/192 5/194 6/215
7/291 8/334

BOWLING: **First Innings**—Kapil Dev 32-12-83-3; Ghavri 26-8-61-2; Bedi 29.5-4-69-2; Yajurvindra 8-2-15-0; Venkataraghavan 29-9-59-3. **Second Innings**—Kapil Dev 28.5-4-89-2; Ghavri 34-11-76-3; Venkataraghavan 26-4-75-1; Bedi 26-4-67-1; Yajurvindra 2-0-4-0.

INDIA

First Innings

S. M. Gavaskar c Bairstow b Botham	13
C. P. S. Chauhan c Botham b Willis	6
D. B. Vengsarkar c Botham b Willis	0
G. R. Viswanath c Brearley b Botham	62
Yashpal Sharma lbw b Willis	27
Yajurvindra Singh not out	43
Kapil Dev b Hendrick	16
K. D. Ghavri c Bairstow b Botham	7
†B. Reddy c Bairstow b Botham	12
*S. Venkataraghavan c and b Hendrick	2
B. S. Bedi c Brearley b Hendrick	1
B 2, l-b 3, w 5, n-b 3	13

1/9 2/9 3/47 4/91 5/130   202
6/161 7/172 8/192 9/200

Second Innings

c Gower b Botham	221
c Botham b Willis	80
c Botham b Edmonds	52
c Brearley b Willey	15
lbw b Botham	19
lbw b Botham	1
c Gooch b Willey	0
not out	3
not out	5
run out	6
B 11, l-b 15, w 1	27

1/213 2/366 3/367   (8 wkts) 429
4/389 5/410 6/411 7/419 8/423

BOWLING: **First Innings**—Willis 18-2-53-3; Botham 28-7-65-4; Hendrick 22.3-7-38-3; Willey 4-1-10-0; Gooch 2-0-6-0; Edmonds 5-1-17-0. **Second Innings**—Willis 28-4-89-1; Botham 29-5-97-3; Hendrick 8-2-15-0; Edmonds 38-11-87-1; Willey 43.5-15-96-2; Gooch 2-0-9-0; Butcher 2-0-9-0.

Umpires: D. J. Constant and K. E. Palmer.

NOTES BY THE EDITOR, 1980

BOTHAM'S FASTEST TEST DOUBLE

IN THE PAST two years the Somerset all-rounder, Ian Botham, has stamped his name on the Test and county scene. Now he has reached the Test double of 1,000 runs and 100 wickets in only 21 Tests at the age of 23. It is the fastest double in Test history, for he accomplished it in two fewer matches than Vinoo Mankad, the Indian all-rounder whose Test career began late owing to World War Two. Botham captured his 100th wicket in the second Test against India at Lord's, when he had Gavaskar caught in the second innings by Brearley, and his 1,000th run came in the first innings of the fourth Test at The Oval. He required only 3 runs after his magnificent 137 at Leeds in the previous Test.

Among English cricketers, Maurice Tate previously held the record in 33 appearances. Among other great all-rounders, Sir Garfield Sobers took 48 Tests for his double. Botham is the first to admit that much of his success with the ball has been due to England's wonderful catching. Soon England will be looking for someone to succeed Mike Brearley as captain. It was significant that, on the latest tour to Australia, Botham became one of the team selectors and he might well get the England captaincy. It is argued that he lacks experience of leadership, but I remember Sir Leonard Hutton (Yorkshire) and Peter May (Surrey) playing under N. W. D. Yardley and Stuart Surridge respectively. In fact, Hutton was never officially captain of Yorkshire.

BENSON AND HEDGES WORLD SERIES CUP

AUSTRALIA v WEST INDIES
Played at Melbourne, December 9, 1979

WEST INDIES WON by 80 runs. This match will remain in the memory of a crowd of almost 40,000 and thousands of others who watched it on television for Richards's exceptional batsmanship. Given pain-killing injections to ease a back injury, and hobbling throughout his innings, he launched a furious assault on every bowler, scoring 153 not out from 131 balls with one 6 and sixteen 4s. Haynes, who played his best innings of the season, was completely overshadowed in their partnership of 205. Australia, left with a virtually impossible task, never looked likely to get on terms.

WEST INDIES

C. G. Greenidge c Marsh b Lillee 11
D. L. Haynes c Marsh b Thomson 80
I. V. A. Richards *not out* 153
A. I. Kallicharran *not out* 16
　　　　B 1, l-b 10 11

1/28 2/233　　　　　(2 wkts, 48 overs) 271

L. G. Rowe, C. L. King, *†D. L. Murray, A. M. E. Roberts, M. A. Holding, J. Garner and D. R. Parry did not bat.

BOWLING: Lillee 10-1-48-1; Hogg 10-1-50-0; Chappell 4-0-24-0; Thomson 8-0-43-1; Bright 6-0-29-0; Hookes 1-0-10-0; Border 7-0-40-0; Wiener 2-0-16-0.

AUSTRALIA

B. M. Laird b Holding	7
J. M. Wiener c and b Parry	27
A. R. Border run out	44
*G. S. Chappell c Richards b King	31
K. J. Hughes b Holding	12
D. W. Hookes c Murray b Roberts	9
†R. W. Marsh c Rowe b Roberts	13
R. J. Bright not out	19
D. K. Lillee b King	19
R. M. Hogg not out	3
B 1, l-b 6	7

1/16 2/54 3/102   (8 wkts. 48 overs) 191
4/119 5/128 6/147
7/151 8/185

J. R. Thomson did not bat.

BOWLING: Roberts 8-1-33-2; Holding 10-2-29-2; Garner 10-1-26-0; King 10-0-40-2; Parry 10-0-56-1.

Umpires: K. Carmody and R. Whitehead.

INDIA v ENGLAND

GOLDEN JUBILEE TEST
Played at Bombay, February 15, 17, 18, 19, 1980

ENGLAND WON BY ten wickets with a day to spare. With the rival sides fatigued, both mentally and physically, at the end of an arduous season, the Test match to celebrate the Golden Jubilee of the Board of Control for Cricket in India produced poor cricket. But it was redeemed by an extraordinary all-round performance by Botham, whose versatility was in full bloom. There was hardly a session on which he did not bring his influence to bear, performing the unprecedented feat of scoring a century and capturing thirteen wickets in a Test. Taylor, the England wicket-keeper, also established a new world Test record by taking ten catches in the match.

To England, after the Test series in Australia, this success, even if inspired by one man, brought welcome relief. But for India, the defeat ended an unbeaten run of fifteen Test matches, four of which they had won.

With the pitch uncharacteristically grassy, England were at no disadvantage from losing the toss; even less so as an overcast sky was a further aid to swing and cut on the opening morning. The Indians, jaded after playing sixteen tests in the past seven months, could not summon the application and discipline needed to combat these conditions and were bowled out in less than a day for 242, Botham taking six for 58 and Taylor taking seven catches. India would have fared even worse but for gallant resistance from the lower order of their batting.

Batting as indifferently as they did in Australia, England at 58 for five looked most unlikely to match India's score, let alone build on the advantage created by their bowlers. But they were only 13 runs behind when they lost their next wicket two hours twenty minutes later. Botham, batting for 206 minutes and hitting seventeen 4s, scored 114 in an innings which was responsible and yet not lacking in enterprise. His stand of 171 with Taylor was England's best-ever sixth-wicket partnership against India. Taylor remained entrenched until the third day was more than an hour old and altogether scored 43 in a stay of four and a half hours. Yet their stand could have been cut short at only 85 when umpire Hanumantha Rao upheld an appeal against Taylor for a catch behind the wicket, off Kapil Dev. Taylor hesitated and protested at the decision. Viswanath, the Indian captain, who was fielding at first slip, was as certain as the batsman that there had been no contact and persuaded the umpire to rescind his verdict.

Even on the third day there was sufficient bounce and movement off the seam to trouble the Indian batsmen. Showing little spirit, India were only 2 runs ahead with half their second-innings wickets gone, and but for an innings of 45 not out by Kapil Dev, who batted in the forthright manner of Botham, the match might not have gone into the fourth day.

The recent history of Test pitches at the Wankhede Stadium – earlier in the season both Australia and Pakistan were beaten in four days, with spinners causing the havoc – prompted England to equip themselves with two specialist spinners in Underwood and Emburey. In the event Underwood bowled only seven overs and Emburey none at all. Of the ten wickets captured by the Indians, their opening bowlers, Ghavri and Kapil Dev, took five and three wickets, respectively.

INDIA

First Innings

S. M. Gavaskar c Taylor b Botham	49
R. M. Binny run out	15
D. B. Vengsarkar c Taylor b Stevenson	34
*G. R. Viswanath b Lever	11
S. M. Patil c Taylor b Botham	30
Yashpal Sharma lbw b Botham	21
Kapil Dev c Taylor b Botham	0
†S. M. H. Kirmani not out	40
K. D. Ghavri c Taylor b Stevenson	11
S. Yadav c Taylor b Botham	8
D. R. Doshi c Taylor b Botham	6
B 5, l-b 3, n-b 9	17

1/56 2/102 3/108 4/135 5/160   242
6/160 7/181 8/197 9/223

Second Innings

c Taylor b Botham	24
lbw b Botham	0
lbw b Lever	10
c Taylor b Botham	5
lbw b Botham	0
lbw b Botham	27
(8) not out	45
(7) c Gooch b Botham	0
c Brearley b Lever	5
c Taylor b Botham	15
c and b Lever	0
B 4, l-b 8, w 1, n-b 5	18

1/4 2/22 3/31 4/31 5/56   149
6/68 7/102 8/115 9/148

BOWLING: **First Innings**—Lever 23-3-82-1; Botham 22.5-7-58-6; Stevenson 14-1-59-2; Underwood 6-1-23-0; Gooch 4-2-3-0. **Second Innings**—Lever 20.1-2-65-3; Botham 26-7-48-7; Stevenson 5-1-13-0; Underwood 1-0-5-0.

ENGLAND

First Innings

G. A. Gooch c Kirmani b Ghavri	8
G. Boycott c Kirmani b Binny	22
W. Larkins lbw b Ghavri	0
D. I. Gower lbw b Kapil Dev	16
*J. M. Brearley lbw b Kapil Dev	5
I. T. Botham lbw b Ghavri	114
†R. W. Taylor lbw b Kapil Dev	43
J. E. Emburey c Binny b Ghavri	8
J. K. Lever b Doshi	21
G. B. Stevenson not out	27
D. L. Underwood b Ghavri	1
B 8, l-b 9, n-b 14	31

1/21 2/21 3/45 4/57 5/58   296
6/229 7/245 8/262 9/283

Second Innings

not out	49
not out	43
B 3, l-b 1, n-b 2	6

(no wkt) 98

BOWLING: **First Innings**—Kapil Dev 29-8-64-3; Ghavri 20.1-5-52-5; Binny 19-3-70-1; Doshi 23-6-57-1; Yadav 6-2-22-0. **Second Innings**—Kapil Dev 8-2-21-0; Ghavri 5-0-12-0; Doshi 6-1-12-0; Yadav 6-0-31-0; Patil 3-0-8-0; Gavaskar 1-0-4-0; Viswanath 0.3-0-4-0.

Umpires: J. D. Ghosh and S. N. Hanumantha Rao.

AUSTRALIA v NEW ZEALAND

THIRD FINAL MATCH
Played at Melbourne, February 1, 1981

AUSTRALIA WON BY 6 runs. With New Zealand needing 6 runs to tie the match off the last ball, Trevor Chappell, instructed to do so by his brother and captain, Greg, bowled McKechnie an underarm ball, which caused a furore that could haunt Australian-

Greg Chappell, seen here executing a typically graceful shot could on occasion display a ruthlessness more characteristic of his elder brother. The underarm incident was an unfortunate blot on a great career which saw him exceed Bradman's total of Test runs and set a new world record of 122 Test catches.

New Zealand cricket for a long time. Earlier in the day Greg Chappell, when 52, had refused to walk when Snedden, at deep mid-wicket, claimed what appeared to be a low but fair catch off Cairns; as neither umpire was watching the incident – they said they were looking for short runs – New Zealand's impassioned appeals for a catch were in vain. After quickly losing Border, Wood and Greg Chappell added 145 for Australia's second wicket in 34 overs, Chappell again being in his best form. When he was finally out, caught by Edgar diving forward at deep mid-wicket, it was to a similar catch to that which was earlier held by Snedden and confirmed by the television replays. This time Chappell went without hesitation. Late in the innings Kent and Marsh both made useful runs. Although Wright and Edgar gave New Zealand another excellent start, putting on 85 in 24 overs, and runs continued to come at a rate which made a New Zealand victory possible, such a result always seemed just against the odds. Edgar, with a splendid hundred to his name, was not out at the end. After some good blows by Parker, Trevor Chappell came on to bowl the last over with 15 still needed and four wickets left. Hadlee straight drove the first ball for 4 and was lbw to the second. Smith then hit two 2s before being bowled, swinging at the fifth ball, leaving New Zealand with 6 to tie off the now infamous underarm delivery.

AUSTRALIA

A. R. Border c Parker b Hadlee 5
G. M. Wood b McEwan 72
*G. S. Chappell c Edgar b Snedden 90
M. F. Kent c Edgar b Snedden 33
†R. W. Marsh not out 18
K. D. Walters not out 6
    B 8, l-b 3 11

1/8 2/153 3/199 4/215   (4 wkts, 50 overs) 235

K. J. Hughes, T. M. Chappell, G. R. Beard, D. K. Lillee and M. H. N. Walker did not bat.

BOWLING: Hadlee 10-0-41-1; Snedden 10-0-52-2; Cairns 10-0-34-0; McKechnie 10-0-54-0; McEwan 7-1-31-1; Howarth 3-0-12-0.

NEW ZEALAND

J. G. Wright c Kent b G. S. Chappell 42
B. A. Edgar not out 102
*G. P. Howarth c Marsh b G. S. Chappell 18
B. L. Cairns b Beard 12
M. G. Burgess c T. M. Chappell b G. S. Chappell 2
P. E. McEwan c Wood b Beard 11
J. M. Parker c T. M. Chappell b Lillee 24
R. J. Hadlee lbw b T. M. Chappell 4
†I. D. S. Smith b T. M. Chappell 4
B. J. McKechnie not out 0
    L-b 10 10

1/85 2/117 3/136 4/139   (8 wkts, 50 overs) 229
5/172 6/221 7/225 8/229

M. C. Snedden did not bat.

BOWLING: Lillee 10-1-34-1; Walker 10-0-35-0; Beard 10-0-50-2; G. S. Chappell 10-0-43-3; T. M. Chappell 10-0-57-2.

Umpires: P. M. Cronin and D. G. Weser.

KEN BARRINGTON

There should be no need for reticence in anyone paying tribute to Ken Barrington. He died of a heart attack in his hotel room at the Holiday Inn in Barbados on March 14, 1981, the Saturday night of the Barbados Test, while serving as assistant-manager on the England tour of the West Indies. As a player, as a friend, as a businessman and latterly as a leader of England's cricketers in the field, he was a man who always did what he could and, when the chips were on the table for all to see, one who could be relied upon to give of his best, his uttermost. The world and especially the cricketing world cannot ask for more. That is why Ken Barrington, master of the malaprop, the man who slept not like a log but "like a lark", commanded such affection all over the world. His widow, Ann, accompanied him on some of his later trips, and it is good that Ann is still involved in the game through the Lord's Taverners, to whom Ken gave so much.

Yet reticence there is, and the hesitation is on his family's account in recalling the circumstances of Ken's tragically premature death at the age of 50. However, *Wisden* is a book of record, and historians sometimes find that its early pages tell the facts but less than the whole truth.

To my mind, the story of Ken's death is as heroic as so many of his innings. It came as a great shock in the spring of 1969 to learn that the chest pains which had led him to withdraw from a double-wicket competition in Melbourne had in fact been a heart attack. After due reflection, taking into account not only his family but the fact that, at 38, batting in Test matches, always Ken's particular forte, was not going to get easier, Ken Barrington retired. Immediately the cares of carrying England's rickety batting through the uncertain and far from satisfying sixties slipped off his shoulders, like some leaden cloak. As he took to the village greens of charity cricket and to the golf courses where his game was good enough to be successfully competitive – and therefore a source of pleasure to a man who hated to be beaten – Ken Barrington's step seemed lighter and his stature in cricket enhanced. His admirers, both far and near, began to realise just how much private effort had gone into coping with "chuckers" and bouncers, as well as the vagaries of form and the whims of selectors.

None the less, a heart attack is a warning, a red light that never joins with amber and turns to green. Although he had managed tours to India, Pakistan and New Zealand, and indeed had had the well-deserved honour of leading the England party at the Melbourne Centenary Test, nothing in his managerial career had tested him quite like this final West Indian ordeal. As a player he had not only plundered bowlers on the great Indian sub-continent but, the son of a soldier who might well in other times have done tours in India of a different nature, he established such a good-humoured relationship there that win or lose, come triumph or disaster, the pressures of touring were easily absorbed. In Australia, where the results mattered more, his rôle was that of coach, so that the burdens were shared first with Doug Insole and then with Alec Bedser.

He was playing that same familiar part in the West Indies. Ironically, he had not been one of the early selections, but as an old player scarred in earlier wars against Hall and Griffith, he knew better than most the perils that a new manager, Alan Smith, and an inexperienced captain, Ian Botham, were flying into as they took on the world champions with their fast bowling quartet in the increasingly stormy Caribbean. In Guyana the heavy and persistent rain meant that the practice sessions which were his charge were suspended. They had been difficult in smaller islands like Antigua and St Vincent in the early weeks of the tour. And then he had to take the team, badly defeated in the first Test and now with their morale increasingly affected by the start of the Jackman affair, as well as their collective lack of practice and form, to the one-day beating at Berbice, while Alan Smith began to play one of his best innings with the politicians. The events of those few days deeply disturbed Barrington. He was also worried about Ann's imminent arrival if the tour was to be cancelled.

But once the party arrived safely in Barbados he seemed to relax. My own last, long and treasured conversation with him was in the happy atmosphere of a Cunarder's bridge, a party in the harbour which he himself had organised. Whatever he felt, he was full of hope for the more distant future, his absolute faith in the ability of Botham and Gatting made more significant by the summer of '81. He knew there were gaps in the England side, but he was old enough in the ways of cricket to know that they are not easily filled.

It was a little thing, at least in the context of that global conversation, that piled all the pressure back on to this caring man. At fielding practice it was Barrington who hit the ball that split Gooch's hand. Gooch was due to bat that day, and in fact played better than anyone – as he told me, without too much discomfort. However, Ken took it badly, as he was bound to do, but it was the way in which he said to Bernard Thomas, "I didn't mean to hurt him", that in retrospect gave the party's medical superintendent the first indication that events were getting out of proportion, upsetting the nervous balance. It was that night, with the Barringtons ready for bed, that the attack struck Ken down. Ann Barrington summoned Bernard Thomas, who was next door, and he knew at once that the attack had been instantaneously fatal. Next morning, when the team stood in Ken's memory, there were many tears.

My own first encounter with Ken Barrington was in 1948 when I was a boy at Harrow. Tom Barling, the new school coach, brought over from The Oval, where he had not long ceased to play for Surrey, a young leg-spinner from Reading with a West Country burr in his voice. The intention was not only to give us practice against a type of bowling that Harrow were likely to meet in the match against Eton at Lord's but also to show us what a *proper* cricketer in the making looked like. We were both seventeen. From then on his career in cricket progressed with its ration of setbacks until he became a record-breaking Test batsman, proudest of all in his unique achievement of scoring a century on every Test ground in England and in every Test-playing country.

As *Wisden* is a chronicle and as this was a man who rated only the best, it is not inappropriate that the essay on him as one of the Five Cricketers of the Year in the 1960 edition should have been written by Norman Preston and the piece on his retirement by John Woodcock, Preston's successor as Editor, in the 1970 edition. It is appropriate, too, to add to those assessments of his playing ability his ever-maturing skill as a leg-spinner. No-one ever bowled more enthusiastically in the nets on tour than Barrington, and whether they realised it or not the England players who faced him were getting practice against a player who might have done the double in the 1930s, a decade less demanding at Test level than the 1960s.

It is with his career in cricket during the last ten years of his life that this eulogy is chiefly concerned. It was at Adelaide during the difficult Australian tour of 1974–75 that Barrington first began to believe that he had a contribution to make as a coach at the highest level. He was brought up in a generation which believed as an act of faith that once a cricketer had played at Test level he knew it all. How else could he have been selected? Furthermore, and this is still a more prevalent attitude than Barrington liked, a player who makes as much of a fetish about practising as Boycott is regarded as a freak. As one who had to work out his technique, to subordinate under a layer of discipline the stroke-making ability he had acquired in his early days, Barrington by the time he retired was a batsman who, if he never knew it all, was a scholar (as well as a gentleman) compared to the players he now saw trying to cope with Lillee and Thomson at their devastating best. More than once Barrington himself had had to change his approach both in style and mind, and so he was ideally suited to the task of developing younger talent and skills.

Not every captain appreciates the need for such a rôle: or knows how to put such available experience to its best use. Ironically, it was on his last tour that Barrington really came to fulfil himself in this the last, and to my mind, most difficult of his cricketing lives. By that time he had mastered the art of subordinating self and position without losing respect or the power to contribute. "He would get me a cup of tea, suggest something which I'd reject probably because I was tired, but then I'd do it and usually it worked." This was Ian Botham during his apprentice days as captain. To the generation that is coming to full maturity Ken Barrington had become as important as the maypole; something solid. He was the "Colonel" around whom a team of cricketers could revolve while playing no part in the dance himself.

Like the maypole he was, too, a source of great happiness, with that rare gift of turning events into comic sketches as they happened. The rat hunt in the Ritz at Hyderabad is now part of cricketing legend. Some wretched rodent, unaware of the niceties of protocol, had eaten the shoulder out of the manager's England blazer in its search for nesting materials. By the time the "Colonel's" army was assembled, the entire staff of the hotel and all its brushes and brooms were ready to go into action. The villain was struck but not apprehended, and after such a warning honour was seen to have been satisfied on all sides. Now that he is gone, it is possible that the rôle he created and played may be forgotten through want of a successor. But Ken gave so much to cricket in the 1970s that he had left a few campaigners for the cause for the remainder of the 1980s. Even now as Gooch starts or finishes a drive or Gatting hooks, a memory of Barrington the batsman is stirred. For a coach there is no finer memorial than that. It is the man, though, that his contemporaries will miss; and for this one, at least, the hole that he began to dig on the Sixth Form Ground at Harrow more than thirty years ago is never going to be filled.

Robin Marlar

SOMERSET v GLOUCESTERSHIRE
Played at Bath, June 13, 15, 16, 1981

DRAWN. A MATCH dominated by Zaheer's remarkable 215 not out and 150 not out was eventually saved for Somerset by a memorable rearguard action from Rose and Roebuck, both of whom had sustained severe leg injuries while fielding. Zaheer, missed when 45, hit five 6s and twenty-two 4s in the first innings and one 6 and twenty-two 4s in the second. Somerset collapsed twice before Bainbridge and Wilkins, but the follow-on was averted by a brisk innings from Botham, a sturdy effort by Marks and a lively stand of 122 between Breakwell and Garner, who hit four 6s and twelve 4s in 25 overs. Although Brain was unable to bowl, Somerset's target of 349 in 200 minutes looked an unlikely one with two batsmen injured. Again Breakwell came to the rescue and, after a dedicated hour's defence from Moseley, Rose batted through the last hour and a half, hitting nineteen 4s through the attacking field. For the last three quarters of an hour he was gamely supported by the virtually immobile Roebuck, and neither batted with a runner.

GLOUCESTERSHIRE

First Innings

B. C. Broad lbw b Botham	11
Sadiq Mohammad lbw b Botham	23
†A. W. Stovold b Moseley	40
Zaheer Abbas not out	215
A. J. Hignell run out	55
P. Bainbridge not out	3
B 1, l-b 5, w 4, n-b 4	14

1/30 2/36 3/224 4/346   (4 wkts dec.) 361

Second Innings

c and b Lloyds	37
c Denning b Marks	33
(5) run out	21
not out	150
(6) not out	40
(3) b Moseley	12
B 4, l-b 2, n-b 4	10

1/64 2/82 3/87 4/182   (4 wkts dec.) 303

S. J. Windaybank, D. A. Graveney, A. H. Wilkins, *B. M. Brain and J. H. Childs did not bat.

BOWLING: **First Innings**—Garner 26-4-81-0; Botham 25-7-99-2; Richards 7-2-26-0; Moseley 15-2-56-1; Breakwell 14-4-29-0; Marks 13-2-40-0; Lloyds 3-0-16-0. **Second Innings**—Garner 10-3-20-0; Botham 9-1-45-0; Moseley 10-2-21-1; Marks 28-4-74-1; Lloyds 14-3-64-1; Richards 13-1-53-0; Denning 1-0-16-0.

SOMERSET

First Innings

*B. C. Rose c Stovold b Wilkins	21
J. W. Lloyds c Windaybank b Bainbridge	6
I. V. A. Richards b Bainbridge	2
P. W. Denning c Hignell b Wilkins	8
I. T. Botham c Stovold b Bainbridge	41
V. J. Marks c Sadiq b Brain	49
†D. J. S. Taylor c Bainbridge b Brain	18
D. Breakwell c Childs b Graveney	58
J. Garner b Wilkins	90
H. R. Moseley not out	2
P. M. Roebuck absent injured	
B 6, l-b 9, w 2, n-b 4	21

1/27 2/29 3/42 4/51 5/106 6/163 7/164 8/286 9/316   316

Second Innings

(10) not out	85
(1) c Stovold b Bainbridge	2
c Graveney b Wilkins	37
(2) lbw b Wilkins	12
(4) b Bainbridge	1
(5) c Childs b Bainbridge	9
b Bainbridge	4
(6) lbw b Wilkins	53
(8) c Sadiq b Bainbridge	16
(9) c Graveney b Childs	10
not out	13
L-b 2, w 1	3

1/14 2/20 3/52 4/52 5/67 6/79 7/125 8/137 9/200   (9 wkts) 245

BOWLING: **First Innings**—Brain 14-2-60-2; Wilkins 24-9-50-3; Childs 19-3-83-0; Bainbridge 18-3-58-3; Broad 5-1-18-0; Graveney 6-1-26-1. **Second Innings**—Wilkins 21-3-139-3; Bainbridge 20-7-68-5; Childs 11-6-15-1; Broad 3-0-15-0; Graveney 3-1-5-0.

Umpires: B. Leadbeater and P. B. Wight.

ENGLAND v AUSTRALIA

THIRD CORNHILL TEST
Played at Leeds, July 16, 17, 18, 20, 21, 1981

ENGLAND WON BY 18 runs. A match which had initially produced all the wet and tedious traits of recent Leeds Tests finally ended in a way to stretch the bounds of logic and belief. England's victory, achieved under the gaze of a spellbound nation, was the first this century by a team following on, and only the second such result in the history of Test cricket.

The transformation occurred in less than 24 hours, after England had appeared likely to suffer their second four-day defeat of the series. Wherever one looked, there were personal dramas: Brearley, returning as captain like England's saviour: Botham, who was named

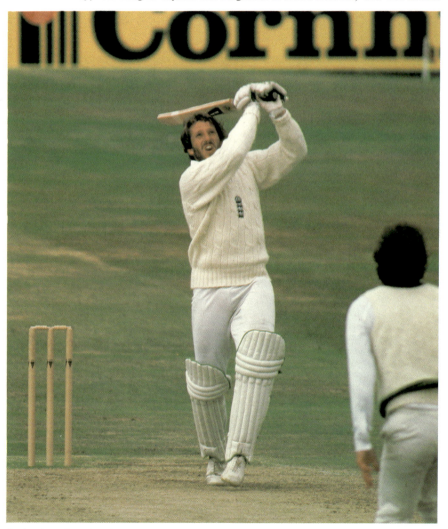

Botham's reply to the selectors. Deprived after the second Test of the England captaincy Botham countered as only he could with a brilliant and logic-defying innings.

Man of the Match, brilliant once more in his first game back in the ranks; Willis, whose career has so often heard the distant drums, producing the most staggering bowling of his life when his place again seemed threatened.

Others, too, had good reason to remember this game. It was the first time in nineteen Tests that Willey had been a member of a victorious side, there were wicket-keeping records for both Taylor (all first-class cricket) and Marsh (Tests), Dyson made his maiden century for Australia, and Lillee moved further up the list of bowling immortals. But if the statisticians revelled in such facts, they were, for most of us, submerged in the tension of a climax as near to miraculous as a Test ever can have been.

None of this had seemed remotely likely on the opening day when the familiar slate-grey clouds engulfed the chimneys which stretch away from the Kirkstall Lane End. Australia, one up in the series, were unchanged; England made two changes, Woolmer standing down for Brearley and Old returning on his home ground at the expense of Emburey. England thus went in with four seamers and only Willey to provide a measure of spin. It was a selectorial policy which caused considerable discussion. Brearley later confessed he lost sleep on the first night for fear that it had been a mistake. As things transpired, however, it was largely irrelevant.

Australia, having chosen to bat, ended the first day in fine health at 203 for three, the extra hour having reduced lost time to only fifty minutes. Dyson batted diligently for his century, playing chiefly off the back foot, and survived one chance to Botham in the gully, when 57. Chappell, who supported Dyson staunchly in a stand of 94 for the second wicket, was twice reprieved – by Gower and Botham again – so England, not for the first time this summer, suffered for their ineptitude in the field. The other talking-point of the day concerned Headingley's new electronic scoreboard, which had a mixed reception, being difficult to see from most parts of the ground when the sun began to sink.

It will come as a surprise when, in future years, people look back on a Test of such apparently outrageous drama, to know that the second day was pedestrian in the extreme. Botham, to some degree, salvaged English pride by taking five more wickets, all of them in an after-tea spell costing 35 runs, and finishing with six for 95. Naturally, the assumption was drawn that he is a more effective player without leadership duties. Despite his efforts, Australia extended their score to 401 for nine, thanks to half-centuries from Hughes and Yallop. It was another day of patchy weather and patchy cricket, completed when Gooch and Boycott saw out an over apiece from Lillee and Alderman without mishap.

At this stage, the odds seemed in favour of a draw. An England win was on offer generously, though by no means as extravagantly as 24 hours later when Ladbrokes, from their tent on the ground, posted it at 500 to 1. The reason for their estimate was a truncated day on which England were dismissed for 174 and, following on 227 behind, lost Gooch without addition. Australia's seamers had shown what could be done by bowling straighter and to a fuller length than their counterparts. Other than Botham, who opted for all-out aggression and profited by a swift 50, England at no stage commanded and were occasionally undone by deliveries performing contortions at speed. Botham fell victim to just such a ball from Lillee and the catch by Marsh was his 264th in Tests, beating Knott's record.

The third day ended with unhappy scenes similar to those seen at Lord's, when spectators hurled cushions and abuse at the umpires. On this occasion, Messrs Meyer and Evans had walked to the middle, wearing blazers, at five to six, after a lengthy stoppage for poor light. They consulted their meters and summoned the covers, abandoning play just before the hour. With cruel irony, the light improved instantly, the sun was soon breaking through and the large crowd was incited to wrathful demands for explanations as to why they were not watching the prescribed extra hour. Once more, it seems, confusion in interpretation of the playing regulations was the cause of the ill feeling: they stated only that conditions must be fit for play at the scheduled time of finish and not, as the umpires thought, that play must actually be in motion. Whether it was, in fact, fit at six o'clock is open to doubt, but the TCCB soon adjusted the ruling so that play in future Tests in the series could restart at any stage of the extra hour.

This heated diversion seemed likely to achieve nothing more than a stay of sentence for England, a view which appeared amply confirmed by late afternoon on the Monday. England were then 135 for seven, still 92 behind, and the distant objective of avoiding an innings defeat surely their only available prize. Lillee and Alderman had continued where Saturday's disturbances had forced them to leave off, and for all Boycott's skilful resistance, the cause seemed lost. Boycott, who batted three and a half hours, was sixth out to an lbw decision he seemed not to relish, and when Taylor followed quickly, the England players' decision to check out of their hotel seemed a sound move. Three hours later, the registration desks around Leeds were coping with a flood of re-bookings, Botham having destroyed the game's apparently set course with an astonishing, unbeaten 145, ably and forcefully aided by Dilley. Together they added 117 in 80 minutes for the eighth wicket, only 7 short of an England record against Australia. Both struck the ball so cleanly and vigorously that Hughes's men were temporarily in disarray; when Dilley departed after scoring 56 precious runs. Old arrived to add 67 more with Botham, who still had Willis as a partner at the close, with England 124 ahead.

Botham advanced his unforgettable innings to 149 not out before losing Willis the next morning, but Australia, needing 130, still remained clear favourites. Then, at 56 for one, Willis, having changed ends to bowl with the wind, dismissed Chappell with a rearing delivery and the staggering turnabout was under way. Willis bowled as if inspired. It is not uncommon to see him perform for England as if his very life depended on it, but this was something unique. In all, he took eight wickets for 43, the best of his career, as Australia's last nine wickets tumbled for 55 runs despite a stand of 35 in four overs between Bright and Lillee. Old bowled straight and aggressively and England rose to the need to produce an outstanding show in the field. Yet this was Willis's hour, watched or listened to by a vast invisible audience. At the end, the crowd gathered to wave their Union Jacks and chant patriotically, eight days in advance of the Royal Wedding.

Takings were £206,500 and the attendance 52,566.

AUSTRALIA

First Innings

J. Dyson b Dilley	102
G. M. Wood lbw b Botham	34
T. M. Chappell c Taylor b Willey	27
*K. J. Hughes c and b Botham	89
R. J. Bright b Dilley	7
G. N. Yallop c Taylor b Botham	58
A. R. Border lbw b Botham	8
*R. W. Marsh b Botham	28
G. F. Lawson c Taylor b Botham	13
D. K. Lillee not out	3
T. M. Alderman not out	0
B 4, l-b 13, w 3, n-b 12	32

1/55 2/149 3/196 4/220 (9 wkts dec.) 401
5/332 6/354 7/357 8/396 9/401

Second Innings

(2) c Taylor b Willis	34
(1) c Taylor b Botham	10
c Taylor b Willis	8
c Botham b Willis	0
(8) b Willis	19
(5) c Gatting b Willis	0
(6) b Old	0
(7) c Dilley b Willis	4
c Taylor b Willis	1
c Gatting b Willis	17
not out	0
L-b 3, w 1, n-b 14	18

1/13 2/56 3/58 4/58 5/65   111
6/68 7/74 8/75 9/110

BOWLING: *First Innings* – Willis 30-8-72-0; Old 43-14-91-0; Dilley 27-4-78-2; Botham 39.2-11-95-6; Willey 13-2-31-1; Boycott 3-2-2-0. *Second Innings* – Botham 7-3-14-1; Dilley 2-0-11-0; Willis 15.1-3-43-8; Old 9-1-21-1; Willey 3-1-4-0.

ENGLAND

First Innings

G. A. Gooch lbw b Alderman	2
G. Boycott b Lawson	12
*J. M. Brearley c Marsh b Alderman	10
D. I. Gower c Marsh b Lawson	24
M. W. Gatting lbw b Lillee	15
P. Willey b Lawson	8
I. T. Botham c Marsh b Lillee	50
†R. W. Taylor c Marsh b Lillee	5
G. R. Dilley c and b Lillee	13
C. M. Old c Border b Alderman	0
R. G. D. Willis not out	1
B 6, l-b 11, w 6, n-b 11	34

1/12 2/40 3/42 4/84 5/87   174
6/112 7/148 8/166 9/167

Second Innings

c Alderman b Lillee	0
lbw b Alderman	46
c Alderman b Lillee	14
c Border b Alderman	9
lbw b Alderman	1
c Dyson b Lillee	33
not out	149
c Bright b Alderman	1
b Alderman	56
b Lawson	29
c Border b Alderman	2
B 5, l-b 3, w 3, n-b 5	16

1/02/18 3/37 4/41 5/105   356
6/133 7/135 8/252 9/319

BOWLING: *First Innings* – Lillee 18.5-7-49-4; Alderman 19-4-59-3; Lawson 13-3-32-3. *Second Innings* – Lillee 25-6-94-3; Alderman 35.3-6-135-6; Lawson 23-4-96-1; Bright 4-0-15-0.

Umpires: B. J. Meyer and D. G. L. Evans.

ENGLAND v AUSTRALIA

FOURTH CORNHILL TEST
Played at Birmingham, July 30, 31, August 1, 2, 1981

ENGLAND WON BY 29 runs. A startling spell of bowling by Botham, from the Pressbox End, which brought him five wickets for 1 run in 28 deliveries, ended an extraordinary Test match at 4.30 p.m. on a glorious Sunday afternoon. And so, for a second successive Test, England contrived to win after appearing badly beaten. As at Leeds, a large crowd helped give the match an exciting and emotional finish and once again critics, commentators and writers were left looking foolish, a fact that the players of both teams were quick to point out afterwards.

For a third time in the series, after Trent Bridge and Headingley, the pitch was the centre of controversy, though when Brearley elected to bat on a fine sunny morning on what is traditionally regarded as one of the finest surfaces in England, it looked in superb condition. Hughes was reported to have said that it looked good for 800 runs. The outfield was fast and the temperature acceptable to Melbourne. Certainly no-one at Edgbaston could have dreamt that this would be the first Test since 1934, anywhere in the world, in which no batsman made a fifty.

Boycott and Brearley opened, a change in the order that had caused misgivings, and had reached 29 in forty-five minutes when Alderman's late swing defeated Boycott and then, two overs later, provoked Gower, a reluctant number three, to try, unsuccessfully, to hit over mid-on. Alderman had figures then of 7–4–4–2, and although Brearley denied himself a run for an hour, surviving a vehement appeal for a slip catch by Wood, he and Gooch saw Alderman and Lillee retire. It was Bright, making the spinner's now customary appearance just before the interval, who tempted Gooch into a rash pull that cost a third wicket at 60.

The afternoon was an English disaster. Bright, from the Pavilion End, used the rough outside the leg stump while Alderman, with Lillee in the unusual rôle of deputy, and Hogg were straight and swift from the other. By 5.30 p.m. England had been dismissed for 189, of which Brearley had made 48 in just under four hours, four boundaries off Lillee promoting his innings from one of mere resistance. Alderman had taken five for 42 before Old, from that same Pressbox End, then rattled the teaspoons in the Australian dressing-room by removing Dyson and Border, in five overs, for 19 runs by the close.

The pitch, declared England's players the following day, after they had been roasted

Terry Alderman surveys the wreckage of his stumps leaving England victorious and a scarcely credulous public to contemplate a burst of five wickets for one run by Ian Botham.

overnight by the media, was untrustworthy. It was too dry, the surface was less than firm, the occasional ball kept low, and there was turn for the spinner. Shoulder to shoulder, Australia's batsmen were later to demonstrate their solidarity with their English colleagues.

Friday was cool and grey and England did well to restrict the Australian lead to 69. Brearley was at his best, constantly varying pressure on each batsman by his bowling and fielding changes, never losing the initiative, while his men responded admirably, running out Wood and Hogg and causing enough apprehension to deter Australia from attempting up to a dozen further singles. Hughes, batting well through a stormy spell by Willis, whose five bouncers in two overs caused the umpires to confer, was unlucky to be leg-before to a low bounce. Although Brearley fell to Lillee on a gloomy evening, England had narrowed the margin to 20 runs.

Blue sky and Saturday sunshine attracted 15,000 spectators, whose holiday mood was not jollied along by Boycott, who spent three hours three minutes raising his score to 29 short of Cowdrey's Test aggregate record for an Englishman – before falling to Bright. So, too, did Gower, Gooch and Willey, and when Botham was caught behind off Lillee, England's lead was no more than 46, with four wickets standing. Fortunately for England their tail-end batsmen, urged on by the combative Gatting, batted bravely. Emburey, 37 not out, demonstrated that Bright's line allowed him to be swept profitably, while Old hit straight and hard before taking the ball to dismiss Wood in the evening haze. Yet Australia needed only another 142 to win, with two days to play. Miracles, wrote a distinguished correspondent, like lightning, do not strike twice.

Willis, bowling again as if the devil were at his heels, removed Dyson and Hughes in the first forty minutes on the fourth morning (Sunday), but Border was his resolute self and at 105 for four, with only 46 more needed, Australia seemed to have the match won. However, Border was then desperately unlucky to be caught off his gloves, a ball from Emburey suddenly lifting prodigiously. Brearley, who had ordered Willey to loosen up with the idea of using spin at both ends, in a last gamble, changed his mind and called on a reluctant Botham.

Somerset's giant bowled quicker than for some time, was straight and pitched the ball up, and one after another five Australian batsmen walked into the point of the lance. The crowd, dotted with green and gold, were beside themselves with agony and ecstasy as, only twelve days after Headingley, history amazingly repeated itself.

Botham was again named Man of the Match, though Emburey would have been the choice of many. Takings for the match amounted to £183,000 from a total attendance of 55,750.

ENGLAND

First Innings

G. Boycott c Marsh b Alderman 13
*J. M. Brearley c Border b Lillee 48
D. I. Gower c Hogg b Alderman 0
G. A. Gooch c Marsh b Bright 21
M. W. Gatting c Alderman b Lillee 21
P. Willey b Bright 16
I. T. Botham b Alderman 26
J. E. Emburey b Hogg 3
†R. W. Taylor b Alderman 0
C. M. Old not out 11
R. G. D. Willis c Marsh b Alderman 13
B 1, l-b 5, w 1, n-b 10 17

Second Innings

c Marsh b Bright 29
lbw b Lillee 13
c Border b Bright 23
b Bright 21
b Bright 39
b Bright 5
c Marsh b Lillee 3
(9) not out 37
(10) lbw b Alderman 8
(8) c Marsh b Alderman 23
c Marsh b Alderman 2
L-b 6, w 1, n-b 9 16

1/29 2/29 3/60 4/101 5/126   189   1/18 2/52 3/89 4/98 5/110   219
6/145 7/161 8/161 9/165   6/115 7/154 8/167 9/217

BOWLING: *First Innings* – Lillee 18-4-61-2; Alderman 23.1-8-42-5; Hogg 16-3-49-1; Bright 12-4-20-2. *Second Innings* – Lillee 26-9-51-2; Alderman 22-5-65-3; Hogg 10-3-19-0; Bright 34-17-68-5.

AUSTRALIA

First Innings

G. M. Wood *run out*	38
J. Dyson *b* Old	1
A. R. Border *c* Taylor *b* Old	2
R. J. Bright *lbw b* Botham	27
*K. J. Hughes *lbw b* Old	47
G. N. Yallop *b* Emburey	30
M. F. Kent *c* Willis *b* Emburey	46
†R. W. Marsh *b* Emburey	2
D. K. Lillee *b* Emburey	18
R. M. Hogg *run out*	0
T. M. Alderman *not out*	3
B 4, l-b 19, n-b 21	44

1/5 2/14 3/62 4/115 5/166   258
6/203 7/220 8/253 9/253

Second Innings

(2) *lbw b* Old	2
(1) *lbw b* Willis	13
c Gatting *b* Emburey	40
(8) *lbw b* Botham	0
(4) *c* Emburey *b* Willis	5
(5) *c* Botham *b* Emburey	30
(6) *b* Botham	10
(7) *b* Botham	4
c Taylor *b* Botham	3
not out	0
b Botham	0
B 1, l-b 2, n-b 11	14

1/2 2/19 3/29 4/87 5/105   121
6/114 7/114 8/120 9/121

BOWLING: *First Innings* – Willis 19-3-63-0; Old 21-8-44-3; Emburey 26.5-12-43-4; Botham 20-1-64-1. *Second Innings* – Willis 20-6-37-2; Old 11-4-19-1; Emburey 22-10-40-2; Botham 14-9-11-5.

Umpires: H. D. Bird and D. O. Oslear.

ENGLAND v AUSTRALIA

FIFTH CORNHILL TEST
Played at Manchester, August 13, 14, 15, 16, 17, 1981

ENGLAND WON BY 103 runs, retaining the Ashes by going three-one up in the series. Like its two predecessors, the fifth test was a game of extraordinary fluctuations and drama, made wholly unforgettable by yet another *tour de force* by Man of the Match Botham, who, with the pendulum starting to swing Australia's way in England's second innings, launched an attack on Lillee and Alderman which, for its ferocious yet effortless power and dazzling cleanness of stroke, can surely never have been bettered in a Test match, even by the legendary Jessop.

Striding in to join Tavaré in front of 20,000 spectators on the Saturday afternoon when England, 101 ahead on first innings, had surrendered the initiative so totally that in 69 overs they had collapsed to 104 for five, Botham plundered 118 in 123 minutes. His innings included six 6s – a record for Anglo-Australian Tests – and thirteen 4s, all but one of which, an inside edge that narrowly missed the off stump on its way to fine leg, exploded off as near the middle of the bat as makes no odds. Of the 102 balls he faced (86 to reach the hundred), 53 were used up in reconnaissance in his first 28 runs (70 minutes). Then Alderman and Lillee took the second new ball and Botham erupted, smashing 66 off eight overs by tea with three 6s off Lillee, all hooked, and one off Alderman, a huge pull far back in the crowd to the left of the pavilion. He completed his hundred with his fifth 6, a sweep, added the sixth with an immense and perfectly struck blow over the sight-screen, also off Bright, and was caught at the wicket a few moments later off 22-year-old Mike Whitney. The brisk left-armer, after only six first-class games (four for New South Wales, two for Gloucestershire), had been plucked out of obscurity on the eve of the match when Australia learned that neither Hogg nor Lawson was fit to play.

Unkindly, it was to the greenhorn Whitney, running back from deep mid-off, that Botham, at 32, offered the first of two chances – nearer "quarter" than "half" – a high, swirling mishit over Alderman's head. The other came at 91 when Dyson, sprinting off the third-man boundary, then sliding forward on his knees and elbows, made a heroic effort to get his hands underneath a sliced square-cut off Lillee.

Man of the match for the third time in the series at Old Trafford. Ian Botham took 3 catches, 5 wickets and scored a blistering 118 in the second innings.

Of the 149 Botham and Tavaré added for the sixth wicket – after a morning in which England had lost three for 29 off 28 overs – Tavaré's share was 28. But his seven-hour 78, embodying the third-slowest 50 in Test cricket (304 minutes) was the rock on which Knott and Emburey sustained the recovery as the last four wickets added 151.

With the pitch growing steadily easier throughout the match, the full value of Tavaré's survival was seen on the fourth and fifth days when, thanks to Yallop's artistic 114 (three hours) and a fighting 123 not out in six and threequarter hours by Border, batting with a broken finger, Australia more than once seemed to be within reach of scoring 506 to win. Border's hundred, taking 373 minutes, was the slowest by an Australian in any Test, beating by four minutes Hughes's time for his hundred against England in 1978–79.

Had Australia managed to win, it would have been in keeping with a bizarre series; but with Lillee buoyantly supporting Border for the eighth wicket, Brearley threw a smokescreen over proceedings by allowing both batsmen singles – and the Australians, suspecting some sinister motive, lost impetus and purpose. The end came with 85 minutes left for play, when Whitney was caught by Gatting at short leg.

Except that after Headingley and Edgbaston one was forewarned that the impossible was likely to become commonplace, there was no indication on the first day that the match would produce such captivating theatre. Paul Allott, who was to play a vital rôle, was one of three England changes from the fourth Test, winning his first cap on his home ground in place of the injured Old, while Tavaré came in for Willey and Knott for Taylor. Underwood, in the original twelve on the assumption that the pitch would start bone dry and later crumble, was left out in favour of a fourth seamer when moisture was found beneath the surface following a storm the week before.

It was a toss Brearley would not have minded losing. But with Australia's fourth innings collapses in mind, he chose to bat. On a slowish, seaming pitch and in often gloomy light, Lillee and Alderman, with help from Whitney, reduced England to 175 for nine by close of play, with forty minutes lost to rain. Boycott passed Colin Cowdrey's record of 7,624 runs for England, but the only innings of note was Tavaré's stoic 69 in four and three quarter hours – the first half-century in twelve Tests by an England number three.

Next morning Hughes unaccountably used Whitney as Lillee's partner rather than Alderman, his most prolific bowler, and Allott and Willis added a priceless 56. Allott, displaying a technique and calmness well above his station, mingled some good strokes through the covers with a few lucky inside edges to make 52 not out, his highest score in first-class cricket.

Wood began with three hooked 4s and a 6 off Willis and Allott, like a man working off an insult. But just as suddenly Australia were 24 for four and *en route* to their shortest innings since 1902, when Rhodes (seven for 17) and Hirst (three for 15) bundled them out for 36 in 23 overs after rain. But on this occasion they had no such excuses to fall back on; indeed, they batted with a manic desperation wholly at odds with their need to win the match. The collapse began with three fine deliveries from Willis and one from Allott in the space of seven balls, a combination of disasters to shake the most confident of side. In Willis's third over, Dyson and Yallop could not keep down rapid, rising balls, while Hughes was trapped lbw by a breakback; and the first ball of the next over, by Allott, came back to have Wood lbw. Kent counter-attacked strongly with 52 in 70 minutes, but the loss of Border, to a stupendous overhead catch by Gower at fourth slip, and Marsh, when he could not pull his bat away in time to avoid another lifting ball from Willis, wrecked Australia's chances of recovery.

Just under a day later, when England had slumped to 104 for five, Australia may have entertained the hope that their 130 would not be terminal. But then came Botham ... and it was.

Attendance was 80,000 and receipts were £295,000.

ENGLAND

First Innings

G. A. Gooch *lbw b* Lillee 10
G. Boycott *c* Marsh *b* Alderman 10
C. J. Tavaré *c* Alderman *b* Whitney 69
D. I. Gower *c* Yallop *b* Whitney 23
*J. M. Brearley *lbw b* Alderman 2
M. W. Gatting *c* Border *b* Lillee 32
I. T. Botham *c* Bright *b* Lillee 0
†A. P. E. Knott *c* Border *b* Alderman 13
J. E. Emburey *c* Border *b* Alderman 1
P. J. W. Allott *not out* 52
R. G. D. Willis *c* Hughes *b* Lillee 11
L-b 6, w 2 8

1/19 2/25 3/57 4/62 5/109   231
6/109 7/131 8/137 9/175

Second Innings

b Alderman 5
lbw b Alderman 37
c Kent *b* Alderman 78
c Bright *b* Lillee 1
(6) *c* Marsh *b* Alderman 3
(5) *lbw b* Alderman 11
c Marsh *b* Whitney 118
c Dyson *b* Lillee 59
c Kent *b* Whitney 57
c Hughes *b* Bright 14
not out 5
B 1, l-b 12, n-b 3 16

1/7 2/79 3/80 4/98 5/104   404
6/253 7/282 8/356 9/396

BOWLING: *First Innings* – Lillee 24.1-8-55-4; Alderman 29-5-88-4; Whitney 17-3-50-2; Bright 16-6-30-0. *Second Innings* – Lillee 46-13-137-2; Alderman 52-19-109-5; Whitney 27-6-74-2; Bright 26.4-12-68-1.

AUSTRALIA

First Innings

G. M. Wood *lbw b* Allott	19
J. Dyson *c* Botham *b* Willis	0
*K. J. Hughes *lbw b* Willis	4
G. N. Yallop *c* Botham *b* Willis	0
M. F. Kent *c* Knott *b* Emburey	52
A. R. Border *c* Gower *b* Botham	11
†R. W. Marsh *c* Botham *b* Willis	1
R. J. Bright *c* Knott *b* Botham	22
D. K. Lillee *c* Gooch *b* Botham	13
M. R. Whitney *b* Allott	0
T. M. Alderman *not out*	2
N-b 6	6

1/20 2/24 3/24 4/24 5/58   130
6/59 7/104 8/125 9/126

Second Innings

(2) *c* Knott *b* Allott	6
(1) *run out*	5
lbw b Botham	43
b Emburey	114
(6) *c* Brearley *b* Emburey	2
(5) *not out*	123
c Knott *b* Willis	47
c Knott *b* Willis	5
c Botham *b* Allott	28
(11) *c* Gatting *b* Willis	0
(10) *lbw b* Botham	0
L-b 9, w 2, n-b 18	29

1/7 2/24 3/119 4/198 5/206   402
6/296 7/322 8/373 9/378

BOWLING: *First Innings* – Willis 14–0–63–4; Allott 6–1–17–2; Botham 6.2–1–28–3; Emburey 4–0–16–1. *Second Innings* – Willis 30.5–2–96–3; Allott 17–3–71–2; Botham 36–16–86–2; Emburey 49–9–107–2; Gatting 3–1–13–0.

Umpires: D. J. Constant and K. E. Palmer.

NOTES BY THE EDITOR, 1982

In two unforgettable months, English cricket emerged in 1981 from a period of much gloom to a well-being that was reflected even in the enthusiasm with which ordinary men and women set about their labours. After several weeks of dreadful weather (not a single ball was bowled in any of Gloucestershire's three Championship matches in May), culminating in the loss by England of the first Test match, the sun got the better of the rain and England gained two of the more dramatic victories in the history of the game. A third, soon afterwards, meant that the Ashes were retained.

The change in England's fortunes coincided with Michael Brearley's return as captain. This not only lifted the spirits of the side, it improved its direction and freed Ian Botham of a burden which was threatening to ruin his cricket. Botham's record speaks for itself. In his twelve matches as England's captain, between June 1980 and July 1981, he scored 276 runs at an average of 13.80 (top score 57) and his 35 wickets cost 32 runs apiece. Yet by the end of last season he had made eight Test hundreds and taken five wickets in an innings seventeen times – always when without the cares of captaincy.

The seventh of these hundreds, in the third Test at Headingley, snatched victory from the jaws of defeat; the eighth won the fifth Test at Old Trafford. With some wonderful hitting Botham reached three figures in 87 balls at Headingley and in 86 at Old Trafford. At Edgbaston, between giving the Australian bowlers two such unmerciful poundings, he finished off the fourth Test by taking five wickets for 1 run when Australia needed only a handful of runs to win. Botham's catching, too, was back to its prehensile best. Small wonder that Australia's captain, Kim Hughes, said when the series was over that the difference between the two sides was represented by one man and one man only.

FINGLETON, JOHN HENRY WEBB ("JACK"), OBE died on November 22, 1981, at the Royal North Shore Hospital in Sydney. He was 73. Born at Waverley in Sydney's Eastern Suburbs, Fingleton was educated firstly by the Christian Brothers at St Francis's School, Paddington, and then at Waverley College. Leaving school at the age of fifteen, he embarked on a career as a journalist which commenced with a cadetship at the *Sydney Daily Guardian*. Later, he was to move to the *Telegraph Pictorial* where he worked for several years prior to the Second War. At the outbreak of war, he joined the Army before being seconded to the former Prime Minister, Billy Hughes, as Press Secretary. From this time onwards, he lived and worked in Canberra. Fingleton achieved no particular distinction on the cricket field while at school, but, on joining Waverley, he quickly graduated to the first eleven of a club which included Kippax, Carter, Hendry and Mailey within its ranks. A right-hand opening batsman, Fingleton was noted more for his stubborn defence than for his aggression. The one epithet unfailingly used to describe his batting was "courageous". He was also an outstandingly gifted fieldsman, whose reputation was made in the covers but who was later to win fame with Vic Richardson, and sometimes with W. A. Brown, in South Africa in 1935–36 as part of the "O'Reilly leg-trap". Neville Cardus, for whom Jack had the greatest regard, once described the Fingleton-Brown combination as "crouching low and acquisitively, each with as many arms as an Indian God".

In 1930, when 22, Fingleton won his first cap for New South Wales and within twelve months (after only five first-class matches) he was selected for Australia. In the home series against South Africa in 1931–32, he was thrice twelfth man and he eventually won his place in the side for the final Test only because Ponsford was forced out of the selected side by illness. In a game notable for its low scoring Fingleton was second top scorer with 40. In the following summer came the "Bodyline" series. Early in the season, Fingleton scored a brave century for New South Wales against the Englishmen, which was sufficient to ensure his selection for the first Test. He started the series in fine form, with scores of 26, 40 and 83, and seemed as well equipped as any to handle the novel tactics of the opposition. However, the third Test at Adelaide was a disaster for Fingleton. Australia were beaten by 338 runs, Fingleton made a "pair", and he was blamed for leaking to the newspapers details of the exchange between Woodfull and Warner which took place in the Australian dressing-room and almost led to the abandonment of the Test series. Perhaps as a repercussion, Fingleton was a surprise omission from the Australian side selected to tour England in 1934.

He was restored to the Test team for the tour of South Africa in 1935–36, a tour that was to mark the apogee of his career. Against Natal at Durban he scored 167 (the highest innings of his first-class career), during the tour he had several mammoth opening partnerships with Brown, and he concluded the series with centuries in each of the last three Test matches – 112 at Cape Town, 108 at Johannesburg and 118 in Durban. Australia won each of these games by an innings. In the following season in Australia, against an MCC side captained by G. O. Allen, he created history by scoring a fourth consecutive Test hundred at Brisbane. The achievement was later equalled by Alan Melville (whose four consecutive Test hundreds were scored between 1939 and 1947) and then surpassed by the West Indian Everton Weekes (1948–49). In the 1936–37 series, Fingleton achieved another place in the record book by sharing with Bradman, in the third Test in Melbourne, a sixth-wicket partnership of 346, a record which still stands. In 1938, Fingleton was selected in the Australian team which toured England, a Test series in which he had only moderate success. This, he was later to say, was "because I couldn't play the pull shot, I was never suited to English pitches". His Test career ended at The Oval in "Hutton's Match". For Fingleton it was a disappointing end: in the course of England's marathon innings of 903 for seven declared he sustained a leg injury which was sufficiently serious to prevent him from batting in either Australian innings.

After the Second World War Fingleton retired from first-class cricket and divided his time between Canberra, where for 34 years until his retirement in 1978 he was political correspondent for Radio Australia, and the coverage of Test matches. In Canberra he was a close friend of several Prime Ministers. Typical of these relationships was that which he enjoyed with Sir Robert Menzies, who provided him with a handsome and laudatory foreword in his book, *Masters of Cricket*. Fingleton's coverage of Tests resulted in publication of a number of books which secured for the writer a place at the forefront of Australian cricket writers. The books included *Cricket Crisis* (which involved itself principally with the Body-line series of 1932–33), *Brightly Fades the Don* (England 1948), *Brown & Company: The Tour in Australia* (Australia 1950–51), *The Ashes Crown the Year* (England 1953), *Masters of Cricket*, *Four Chukkas to Australia* (Australia 1958–59), *The Greatest Test of All* (Brisbane 1960), *Fingleton on Cricket* and *The Immortal Victor Trumper*. His final book – *Batting From Memory* – was to have been launched in Australia during the week of his death. In addition to his writing, Fingleton was a witty, good-humoured and perceptive commentator for the BBC and at various times a contributor to *The Times*, *The Sunday Times, The Observer*, and various newspapers in Australia, South Africa and elsewhere. In 1976, he was appointed OBE for services "to journalism and to cricket".

WORCESTERSHIRE v WARWICKSHIRE
Played at Worcester, May 29, 31, June 1, 1982

DRAWN. WORCESTERSHIRE 5 pts, WARWICKSHIRE 3 pts. Turner launched an amazing assault on the Warwickshire attack to complete his 100th century in first-class cricket, going on to compile a career-best 311 not out in Worcestershire's total of 501 for one declared on the opening day, His triple-hundred was a record for Worcestershire, beating Fred Bowley's 276 against Hampshire in 1914, and he became the first batsman to top 300 runs in a day in England since J. D. Robertson achieved the feat for Middlesex,

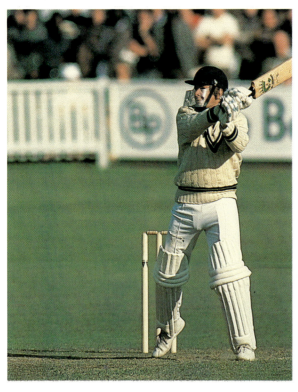

Early in his career considered something of a slouch, Glenn Turner was, by 1982, capable of the most rapid accumulation of runs. His 311 in this match made him only the second non-Englishman to score 100 first class hundreds.

against Worcestershire, in 1949. Turner reached his first 50 in 34 minutes, was 128 at lunch out of a total of 181, and in all he batted for 343 minutes, hitting two 6s and 39 4s. But Kallicharran, with a career-best 235, ensured that Warwickshire avoided the follow-on, although in their second innings, needing 289 to win in 197 minutes, they were always batting to save the game as the spinners achieved increasing turn from the wearing wicket.

WORCESTERSHIRE

First Innings

G. M. Turner *not out*	311
J. A. Ormrod *c* Cumbes *b* Lethbridge	79
D. N. Patel *not out*	88
Younis Ahmed *(did not bat)*	
*P. A. Neale *(did not bat)*	
†D. J. Humphries *(did not bat)*	
A. P. Pridgeon *(did not bat)*	
N. Gifford *(did not bat)*	
B 1, l-b 19, n-b 3	23

1/291 (1 wkt dec.) 501

Second Innings

c and b Small	32
c Humpage *b* Lethbridge	43
b Lethbridge	22
c Willis *b* Sutcliffe	10
not out	17
c and b Kallicharran	5
b Sutcliffe	12
not out	14
B 2, l-b 4, n-b 6	12

1/50 2/103 3/106 (6 wkts dec.) 167
4/124 5/129 6/152

E. J. O. Hemsley, R. K. Illingworth and S. P. Perryman did not bat.

BONUS POINTS – Worcestershire 4 (Score at 100 overs: 433–1).

BOWLING: **First Innings**—Willis 12–0–76–0; Small 7–0–54–0; Cumbes 9–0–58–0; Lethbridge 20–1–94–1; Sutcliffe 40–5–127–0; Asif Din 10–1–29–0; Lloyd 7–1–22–0; Kallicharran 7–0–18–0. **Second Innings**—Willis 5–1–17–0; Small 8–3–33–1; Lethbridge 11–5–26–2; Sutcliffe 16–3–60–2; Kallicharran 7–1–19–1.

WARWICKSHIRE

First Innings

D. L. Amiss *run out* 64
T. A. Lloyd *c* Ormrod *b* Pridgeon 0
A. I. Kallicharran *c* Perryman *b* Patel 235
†G. W. Humpage *c* Patel *b* Illingworth 15
K. D. Smith *c* Pridgeon *b* Gifford 31
Asif Din *c* Humphries *b* Illingworth 12
C. Lethbridge *c* Neale *b* Illingworth 0
G. C. Small *c* Gifford *b* Patel 0
R. G. D. Willis *c* Humphries *b* Illingworth 7
S. P. Sutcliffe *not out* 1
J. Cumbes *not out* 4
    B 2, l-b 8, n-b 1 11

Second Innings

c Humphries *b* Gifford 21
c Turner *b* Gifford 3
b Patel 35
c Patel *b* Illingworth 23
not out 62
c Turner *b* Illingworth 39
not out 2

    B 1, l-b 9, n-b 2 12

1/4 2/168 3/217 4/283   (9 wkts dec.) 380
5/326 6/346 7/347 8/364 9/372

1/31 2/35 3/81   (5 wkts) 197
4/101 5/188

Bonus points Warwickshire 3, Worcestershire 1 (Score at 100 overs 296-4).

BOWLING: **First Innings**—Pridgeon 15-2-54-1; Perryman 10-0-20-0; Gifford 41-11-100-1; Patel 40-8-110-2; Illingworth 37-9-85-4 **Second Innings**—Pridgeon 7-2-15-0; Perryman 4-1-9-0; Gifford 20-1-59-2; Patel 13-3-60-1; Illingworth 19-7-42-2.

Umpires: W. L. Budd and C. Cook.

BADER, GROUP CAPTAIN SIR DOUGLAS, CBE, DSO, DFC, the famous airman, who died on September 5, 1982, aged 72, was captain of St Edward's School, Oxford, in 1928. A good attacking bat and a useful fast-medium bowler, he later played for the RAF and in 1931 made 65, the top score, for them against the Army, a fixture which in those days had first-class status. He gained greater distinction at rugger, and at the time of the accident the following winter which cost him his legs he was in the running for an England cap.

AUSTRALIA v ENGLAND

FOURTH TEST MATCH
Played at Melbourne, December 26, 27, 28, 29, 30 1982

ENGLAND WON BY 3 runs. A magnificent Test match, to be ranked among the best ever played, produced a finish of such protracted excitement that it had the whole of Australia by the ears. Needing 292 to win, Australia were 218 for nine when Border and Thomson embarked on a last-wicket partnership of epic proportions. At close of play on the fourth day they had taken the score to 255 for nine, leaving another 37 runs to be found on the last morning for Australia, there and then, to regain the Ashes.

Although, on this last day, the match could have been over within moments, 18,000 spectators, admitted free of charge, went to the Melbourne Cricket Ground in the hope of seeing Border and Thomson achieve their improbable goal. All things considered, among them a new ball taken at 259 for nine, Thomson was rarely in trouble; Border never was. By the time Botham began the eighteenth over of the morning Australia were within 4 runs of victory. His first ball was short of a length and wide of the off stump. Thomson, sparring at it, edged a none-too-difficult catch to Tavaré, the second of Botham's two slips. Tavaré managed only to parry it, the ball bouncing away behind him but within reach of Miller, fielding at first slip, deeper than Tavaré. With a couple of quick strides Miller reached the catch and completed it, the ball still some eighteen inches off the ground.

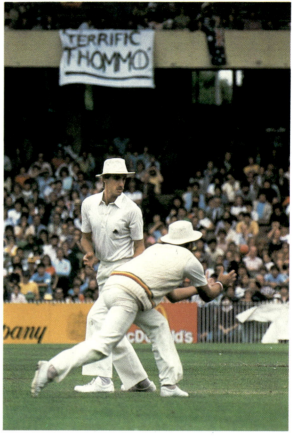

Chris Tavaré anticipating imminent egg on face is redeemed by an excellent rebound catch from Geoff Miller which won the match for England and kept the series alive. Tavaré, an excellent slip fielder and correct right-hand bat seldom produced his best for England hiding his true range of strokes behind rather too unenterprising an approach.

No-one who played in the game or watched it, or who saw it on television, or who listened to it on the radio, many of them from halfway across the world, could have been left unmoved. In terms of runs, the only closer Test match ever played was the Brisbane tie between Australia and West Indies in 1960–61. In 1902 at Old Trafford, the margin between England and Australia was also 3 runs, on that occasion in Australia's favour.

England made two changes from the side that had lost the third Test in Adelaide, one optional, the other not. Randall, having been hit in the face by a short ball from Holding during England's one-day match in Launceston, was unfit, his place being taken by Cook. Cowans was preferred to Hemmings. Australia were unchanged. For the fourth time in the series the captain winning the toss chose to field. With the match being played on a pitch that had been laid only nine months before, Chappell took a calculated gamble when he committed Australia to batting last. In the event the pitch lasted surprisingly well and was, as Chappell expected, damp enough on the first day for England to be in early trouble. When Gower was third out, immediately after lunch, they were 56 for three. The innings was saved by a brilliant fourth-wicket partnership of 161 in only 32 overs by Tavaré and Lamb.

With Cook and Fowler going in first, Tavaré was able to bat at number three, which he much prefers to opening. After his usual slow start Tavaré began to attack the bowling, especially Yardley's with unaccustomed vigour. By the time he was very well caught in the gulley, England had fairly galloped to 217. But Lamb soon followed Tavaré, a fine innings ending a little unworthily when he got himself out to Yardley, and by close of play England, having fallen right away, were all out for 284. Cook, when first out, had given

Chappell, at slip, his 111th Test catch, a new Australian record.

Each of the first three days saw one full innings completed. On the second Australia were bowled out in their first innings for 287, on the third England, in their second innings, for 294. By taking the wickets of Dyson and Chappell with successive balls in Australia's first innings. Cowans made his first impact on a match from which he was to emerge as a hero. Chappell hooked the first ball he received to deep square leg, where Lamb had just been carefully stationed. In the end Australia owed their narrow first-innings lead to Hughes's application, Hookes' good fortune laced with strokes of fine timing, and Marsh's belligerence. By now the umpiring of Rex Whitehead was becoming an irritant. On the second day, when they were in the field, and on the third, when they were batting, England were in danger of allowing it to undermine their resolve. After the match it was forgotten, all else being dwarfed by the climax, but it was undoubtedly erratic.

At 45 for three in their second innings England faced their next crisis. This time, however, after Botham had made 46 in 46 balls, their last five wickets made a vital contribution. Pringle and Taylor added 61 together, every run of some concern to Australia, faced by the prospect of batting last. Fowler, too, until hit on the foot by Thomson and forced to have a runner (the injury was to put him out of the next Test match) had played much his best innings of the tour. When Lawson found the edge of Pringle's bat Marsh claimed his 27th victim of the series, a new record for Test cricket.

Although the occasional ball was keeping very low, Australia's final target of 292, on an uncommonly fast Melbourne outfield (a prolonged and serious drought had restricted the watering of the ground), was eminently attainable. The equality of the four totals – 284, 287, 294 and 288 – tells of the unyielding nature of the match, with first one side, then the other, holding the advantage. When, as in Australia's first innings, Chappell fell cheaply to Cowans, splendidly caught low down in the covers by Gould (fielding as substitute for Fowler) off a hard slash from a short ball, England were in front, Wessels having already been bowled off his pads by Cowans. When, at 71, Dyson was beautifully caught at slip, by Tavaré off Botham, it remained that way. Hughes and Hookes then added 100, which gave Australia the initiative. Hughes's departure to a tumbling catch by Taylor off Miller, followed quickly by Hookes's, restored it to England. With Cowans, inspired by his successes over Chappell and generously encouraged by the crowd, claiming Australia's fifth (Hookes), sixth (Marsh), seventh (Yardley) and ninth (Hogg) wickets for 19 runs in seven overs, England had all but won when Thomson, his hair dyed platinum blond, joined Border.

As Thomson took root and Border switched to the attack, Willis adopted tactics which, though they brought final victory, were much criticised at the time. When Border had the strike Willis placed all his fielders in a far-flung ring, which meant that if England were to win they would almost certainly have to get Thomson out. Even for the last two overs of the fourth day, after a brief stoppage for rain, Border was allowed to bat unharassed by close fielders. It was the same next morning, even when England took the new ball.

Thus flattered, Border, whose previous fifteen Test innings brought him only 245 runs, was now at his fighting best. Thomson, growing in confidence, occasionally pierced England's off-side field, his feet spreadeagled. As Australia slowly closed the gap, every run was cheered to the echo. England, in their fielding, showed understandable signs of panic. Cowans, though he continued to bowl well, failed to find quite his best rhythm; Willis, though admirably accurate, lacked his old pace. In the end, all hope for England almost gone. Botham, their great all-rounder, produced the ball that not only won the match but revived the tour. Botham's dismissal of Thomson made him only the second Englishman, Wilfred Rhodes, being the other, to have scored 1,000 runs and taken 100 wickets against Australia.

For the first time in a Test match, Melbourne's huge video scoreboard was in operation, the screen being use to show action replays and advertisements as well as the score and other sundry details. It was, on the whole, well received, although Willis remarked after the match that there had been occasions when, needing to know the score, he found himself looking instead at a picture of a motor car or a meat pie. The first day's crowd of 64,051 might have reached 80,000 but for poor organisation. Thousands of would-be spectators turned back when they saw that it was taking up to 90 minutes to get into the ground. Even so, the total attendance, including the last day's approximate figure of 18,000 was 213,861.

ENGLAND

First Innings

G. Cook c Chappell b Thomson	10
G. Fowler c Chappell b Hogg	4
C. J. Tavaré c Yardley b Thomson	89
D. I. Gower c Marsh b Hogg	18
A. J. Lamb c Dyson b Yardley	83
I. T. Botham c Wessels b Yardley	27
G. Miller c Border b Yardley	10
D. R. Pringle c Wessels b Hogg	9
†R. W. Taylor c Marsh b Yardley	1
*R. G. D. Willis *not out*	6
N. G. Cowans c Lawson b Hogg	3
B 3, l-b 6, w 3, n-b 12	24

1/11 2/25 3/56 4/217   284
5/227 6/259 7/262 8/268 9/278

Second Innings

c Yardley b Thomson	26
b Hogg	65
b Hogg	0
c Marsh b Lawson	3
c Marsh b Hogg	26
c Chappell b Thomson	46
lbw b Lawson	14
c Marsh b Lawson	42
lbw b Thomson	37
not out	8
b Lawson	10
B 2, l-b 9, n-b 6	17

1/40 2/41 3/45 4/128   294
5/219 6/160 7/201 8/262 9/282

BOWLING: **First Innings**—Lawson 17-6-48-0; Hogg 23.3-6-69-4; Yardley 27-9-89-4; Thomson 13-2-49-2; Chappell 1-0-5-0. **Second Innings**—Lawson 21.4-6-66-4; Hogg 22-5-64-3; Yardley 15-2-67-0; Thomson 21-3-74-3; Chappell 1-0-6-0.

AUSTRALIA

First Innings

K. C. Wessels b Willis	47
J. Dyson lbw b Cowans	21
G. S. Chappell c Lamb b Cowans	0
K. J. Hughes b Willis	66
A. R. Border b Botham	2
D. W. Hookes c Taylor b Pringle	53
R. W. Marsh b Willis	53
G. F. Yardley b Miller	9
G. F. Lawson c Fowler b Miller	0
R. M. Hogg *not out*	8
J. R. Thomson b Miller	1
L-b 8, n-b 19	27

1/55 2/55 3/83 4/89   287
5/180 6/261 7/276 8/276 9/278

Second Innings

b Cowans	14
c Tavaré b Botham	31
c sub b Cowans	2
c Taylor b Miller	48
(6) *not out*	62
(5) c Willis b Cowans	68
lbw b Cowans	13
b Cowans	0
c Cowans b Pringle	7
lbw b Cowans	4
c Miller b Botham	21
B 5, l-b 9, w 1, n-b 3	18

1/37 2/39 3/71 4/171   288
5/173 6/190 7/190 8/202 9/218

BOWLING: **First Innings**—Willis 15-2-38-3; Botham 18-3-69-1; Cowans 16-0-69-2; Pringle 15-2-40-1; Miller 15-5-44-3. **Second Innings**—Willis 17-0-57-0; Botham 25.1-4-80-2; Cowans 26-6-77-6; Pringle 12-4-26-1; Miller 16-6-30-1.

Umpires: A. R. Crafter and R. V. Whitehead.

ESSEX v SURREY
Played at Chelmsford, May 28, 30, 31, 1983

DRAWN. ESSEX 7 pts, SURREY 4 pts. On the second afternoon Surrey were skittled out for the lowest score in their history, their first innings lasting a mere 14.3 overs. Phillip and Foster, making the ball swing in the humid atmosphere, were their

The free-flowing action of Norbert Phillip tormenter of Surrey as they sank to the lowest score in their history.

tormentors and only a boundary from Clark, the sole one of the innings, spared them the humiliation of recording the lowest-ever first-class score. Five wickets fell with the total on 8. The next day a fine century from Knight, well supported by Clinton, enabled Surrey to win back some self-respect. After a barren opening day because of rain, Fletcher showed that there was nothing wrong with the pitch with a century full of grace and elegance after Knight had gambled on putting the home side in to bat.

ESSEX

G. A. Gooch b Thomas 1
B. R. Hardie b Clarke 16
K. W. R. Fletcher c Lynch b Monkhouse 110
K. S. McEwan c Lynch b Knight 45
K. R. Pont b Pocock 12
N. Phillip b Pocock 8
S. Turner c and b Knight 20
R. E. East c Lynch b Clarke 19
D. E. East c Butcher b Pocock 17
N. A. Foster not out 19
D. L. Acfield run out 0
    B 4, l-b 10, n-b 6 20

1/1 2/27 3/113 4/156   287
5/179 6/222 7/238 8/252 9/276

BONUS POINTS – Essex 3, Surrey 4.

BOWLING: Clarke 20-3-58-2; Thomas 20-3-78-1; Monkhouse 13-2-49-1; Knight 17-6-33-2; Pocock 19.5-6-49-3.

SURREY

First Innings

A. R. Butcher c D. E. East b Phillip 2
G. S. Clinton c D. E. East b Foster 6
A. Needham b Foster 0
R. D. V. Knight lbw b Phillip 0
M. A. Lynch lbw b Phillip 0
C. J. Richards c Turner b Phillip 0
D. J. Thomas lbw b Foster 0
I. R. Payne b Phillip 0
G. Monkhouse lbw b Phillip 2
S. T. Clarke b Foster 4
P. I. Pocock not out 0
    B 1, l-b 8, w 2, n-b 3 14

Second Innings

c Gooch b Foster 5
not out 61
lbw b Phillip 4
not out 101

1/2 2/5 3/6 4/8 5/8 6/8 7/8 8/8 9/14   14   1/11 2/18   (2 wkts) 185

BONUS POINTS – Essex 4.

BOWLING: **First Innings**—Phillip 7.3-4-4-6; Foster 7-3-10-4. **Second Innings**—Phillip 13-2-39-1; Foster 13-2-33-1; Turner 7-3-16-0; Gooch 22-6-45-0; Acfield 17-7-23-0; R. E. East 1-0-5-0; Pont 5-1-10-0.

Umpires: W. E. Alley and J. W. Holder.

LANCASHIRE v LEICESTERSHIRE
Played at Manchester, September 10, 12, 13, 1983

DRAWN. LANCASHIRE 3 pts, LEICESTERSHIRE 5 pts. Just when the season looked to be drawing to a peaceful conclusion, a piece of history was created when O'Shaughnessy, in the last three hours of the season, equalled P. G. H. Fender's 63 year-old record of the fastest first-class century. After the first day and a half had been lost to rain Lancashire were put in to bat. Tolchard soon had his spinners operating to revive Leicestershire's flagging over-rate for the season. After taking four bowling points they needed one for batting to finish fourth in the Championship. Once this had been won Leicestershire declared, 86 behind, just before three o'clock on the last afternoon, whereupon Gower and Whitaker fed the Lancashire batsmen with long hops and full

Holder with P. G. H. Fender of the record for the fastest ever first-class century, Steve O'Shaughnessy's achievement is somewhat dimmed when one considers that for part of the time he faced the combined bowling might of David Gower and James Whitaker. Gower's first class bowling average in 1986 stood at a less than redoubtable 4 wickets at 53.5 runs each.

tosses in the hope of inducing a declaration. After a brief protest of blocking, Fowler and O'Shaughnessy hit 190 runs in the 35 minutes to tea, then took their stand to 201 in 43 minutes, the fastest first-class double-century partnership on record. O'Shaughnessy's century, in 35 minutes, included five 6s and seventeen 4s. Fowler's century, in 46 minutes, contained ten 6s and five 4s. Lancashire did not declare and the season ended in travesty.

LANCASHIRE

First Innings

G. Fowler *b Steele*	85
S. J. O'Shaughnessy *c Steele b Cook*	3
F. C. Hayes *b Clift*	11
C. H. Lloyd *c Tolchard b Clift*	24
J. Abrahams *c and b Clift*	7
D. P. Hughes *c Cook b Clift*	0
N. H. Fairbrother *c Davison b Cook*	4
J. Simmons *b Clift*	57
J. Stanworth *c Balderstone b Clift*	29
P. J. W. Allott *c and b Taylor*	4
M. Watkinson *not out*	1
B 9, l-b 1, n-b 1	11
	236

1/21 2/97 3/103 4/136
5/136 6/139 7/145 8/224 9/231

Second Innings

b Balderstone	100
st Tolchard b Balderstone	105
(4) *not out*	3
(5) *not out*	1
(3) *b Taylor*	4
W 1	1
(3 wkts)	214

1/201 2/206 3/213

BONUS POINTS – Lancashire 2, Leicestershire 4.

BOWLING: **First Innings**—Ferris 8-1-29-0; Taylor 4-0-14-1; Cook 28-10-74-3; Clift 31-5-73-5; Steele 16-3-35-1. **Second Innings**—Gower 9-0-102-0; Whitaker 8-1-87-0; Balderstone 4-0-10-2; Steele 5-2-13-0; Taylor 1.2-0-1-1.

LEICESTERSHIRE

J. C. Balderstone c O'Shaughnessy b Simmons 33
I. P. Butcher lbw b Allott 4
D. I. Gower not out 56
B. F. Davison c Lloyd b Watkinson 2
J. J. Whitaker lbw b Simmons 24
P. B. Clift not out 26
N-b 5 5

1/31 2/46 3/51 4/114   (4 wkts dec.) 150

G. J. F. Ferris, *†R. W. Tolchard, J. F. Steele, N. G. B. Cook and L. B. Taylor did not bat.

BONUS POINTS – Leicestershire 1, Lancashire 1

BOWLING: Allot 7-2-15-1; Watkinson 14-3-35-1; Simmons 15-3-51-2; Hughes 7.5-1-44-0.

Umpires: H. D. Bird and N. T. Plews.

HEADLEY, GEORGE ALPHONSO, MBE, who died in Jamaica on November 30, 1983, aged 74, was the first of the great black batsmen to emerge from the West Indies. Between the wars, when the West Indies batting was often vulnerable and impulsive, Headley's scoring feats led to his being dubbed "the black Bradman". His devoted admirers responded by calling Bradman "the white Headley" – a pardonable exaggeration. In 22 Tests, when the innings could stand or fall on his performance, Headley scored 2,190 runs, including ten centuries – eight against England – with an average of 60.83. He was the first to score a century in each innings of a Test at Lord's, in 1939, and it was a measure of his ability that from 1929 – 1939 he did not have a single bad Test series. By the start of the Second World War he had totalled 9,532 runs in first-class cricket with an average of 72.21. Afterwards, though not the power that he had been, he extended his aggregate to 9,921 runs, with 33 centuries and an average of 69.86.

Born in Panama, where his father had helped to build the Canal, Headley was taken to Jamaica at the age of ten to perfect his English – Spanish had been his first tongue – and to prepare to study dentistry in America. At school he fell in love with cricket, but he might still have been lost to the game had there not been a delay in getting his passport for the United States. While he was waiting, Headley was chosen to play against a visiting English team captained by the Hon. L. H. Tennyson.

Though not yet nineteen, he had innings of 78 in the first match and 211 in the second, and dentistry lost a student. Surprisingly he was not chosen for the 1928 tour of England immediately afterwards, but in the home series against England in 1929–30 he scored 703 runs in eight Test innings, averaging 87.80. His Scores included 21 and 176 in his first Test, 114 and 112 in the third and 223 in the fourth. In 1930–31 in Australia he scored two more Test centuries and ended the tour with 1,066 runs. Clarrie Grimmett described him as the strongest on-side player he had ever bowled against. In 1932, in a single month, he hit 344 not out (his highest-ever score), 84, 155 not out and 140 against another England side to visit Jamaica. Against sterner opposition and in more difficult conditions in England in the following year, he averaged 66 for the tour, scoring a century on his first appearance at Lord's and taking 224 not out off Somerset. In the second Test at Manchester he made 169 not out, a score he improved upon with 270 not out at Kingston in the 1934–35 series.

Headley was of medium build, compact, balanced and light on his feet. Like most great batsmen he was a superb back-foot player and seldom made a hurried shot. Sir Leonard Hutton, who saw him at his best in 1939, declares he has never seen a batsmen play the ball later. It was hard to set a field for him, such was his genius for collecting runs with his precise placement of the ball. In League cricket in England Headley also excelled. At every level of the game, in fact, he scored an avalanche of runs with a style and brilliance few of any age have matched. His contribution to the strength and power of modern West Indies teams cannot be exaggerated.

One of his sons, R. G. A., an opening batsman for Worcestershire and Derbyshire played twice for West Indies in England in 1973.

SOMERSET v WARWICKSHIRE
Played at Taunton, June 1, 3, 4, 1985

DRAWN. SOMERSET 6 pts, WARWICKSHIRE 6 pts. Toss won by Somerset. Everything was dwarfed by a magnificent 322 out of 479 by Richards, who came in when Bail had retired after a blow on the helmet and Felton was out next ball. His first 100 came from 105 balls, his second from 76, and his third in 63. In all he faced 258 deliveries in 294 minutes, and his 133 scoring strokes included eight 6s and 42 4s. Championship-best batting performances by Ferreira and Smith featured in a solid reply, but after the change bowlers had fed Somerset runs to provoke an acceptable challenge. Warwickshire displayed no interest in the final requirement of 351 in 205 minutes off a minimum of 53 overs.

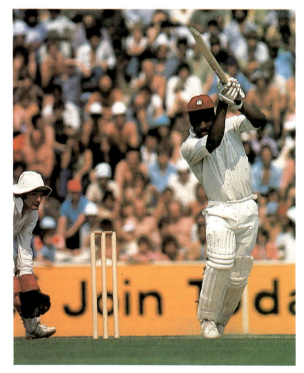

Viv Richards, pictured later the following year playing for the West Indies against England. He was brought to Somerset by a West Country bookmaker who obviously knew a good bet when he saw one. Though he was later to leave them in acrimonious circumstances his association with the county, along with Botham and Garner, brought it new life and vigour.

SOMERSET

First Innings

N. F. M. Popplewell c Tedstone b Hoffman 55
P. A. C. Bail *retired hurt* 8
N. A. Felton c Kallicharran b Small 0
I. V. A. Richards c Ferreira 322
R. L. Ollis c Hoffman b Ferreira 55
V. J. Marks c Tedstone b Gifford 65
M. R. Davis *not out* 25
M. S. Turner *not out* 17
†T. Gard *(did not bat)*
    B 1, l-b 9, w 1, n-b 8 19

1/28 2/150 3/324   (5 wkts dec.) 566
4/507 5/533

J. Garner and S. C. Booth did not bat.

P. A. C. Bail retired hurt at 28-0.

Second Innings

c Hoffman b Small 27
c Kallicharran b Small 0
(4) c Small b LLoyd 45
lbw b Wall 0
not out 66
(7) *not out* 24
(3) *run out* 47
  L-b 13, n-b 4 17

1/1 2/62 3/103   (5 wkts dec.) 226
4/105 5/175

BONUS POINTS – Somerset 4, Warwickshire 2.

BOWLING: **First Innings**—Small 16-3-70-1; Wall 18-3-72-0; Smith 11-0-73-0; Ferreira 23-0-121-2; Hoffman 14-0-85-1; Gifford 18-1-135-1. **Second Innings**—Small 8-0-31-2; Smith 9-1-43-0; Hoffman 2-0-12-0; Wall 5-2-7-1; Lloyd 16-0-64-1; Kallicharran 11.4-0-56-0.

WARWICKSHIRE

First Innings

T. A. Lloyd *lbw* b Richards 61
R. I. H. B. Dyer *lbw* b Turner 33
A. I. Kallicharran c Garner b Davis 36
D. L. Amiss c Davis b Marks 81
P. A. Smith c Turner b Marks 93
A. M. Ferreira *not out* 101
†G. A. Tedstone b Turner 22
G. C. Small c Davis b Turner 3
S. Wall *lbw* b Turner 1
D. S. Hoffman *run out* 0
*N. Gifford *not out* 0
    B 1, l-b 6, w 1, n-b 3 11

1/84 2/108 3/151 4/312 5/312   (9 wkts dec.) 443
6/399 7/419 8/431 9/431

Second Innings

c Gard b Garner 7
not out 63
c Gard b Marks 89
not out 14

  L-b 5, w 1, n-b 2 8

1/18 2/158   (2 wkts) 181

BONUS POINTS – Warwickshire 4, Somerset 2 (Score at 100 overs: 372-5).

BOWLING: **First Innings**—Garner 20-3-59-0; Davis 23.4-1-115-1; Turner 22.4-2-74-4; Richards 12-4-31-1; Marks 25-3-97-2; Booth 13-3-59-0. **Second Innings**—Garner 6-2-16-1; Davis 9-2-19-0; Marks 16-1-56-1; Turner 1-0-9-0; Booth 21-4-72-0; Bail 2-0-4-0.

Umpires: A. A. Jones and P. B. Wright.

WARWICKSHIRE v SOMERSET
Played at Edgbaston, July 24, 25, 26, 1985

DRAWN. WARWICKSHIRE 7 pts, SOMERSET 4 pts. Toss won by Somerset. Despite two quick-fire innings from Richards, the match was dominated by a performance from Botham which ranks alongside any ever seen on the ground. In 67 minutes he faced 65 deliveries and hit an unbeaten 138 out of 169 scored while he was batting. He hit twelve 6s and thirteen 4s in a whirlwind demonstration of his correct technique, which is backed by a phenomenal strength. Botham's hundred, the fastest of the season, took just 26 scoring strokes – one more than the record – and when he reached three figures off 50 deliveries, 94 runs had come in boundaries. For the home side, Dyer scored his first Championship hundred of the season on a dry pitch. That it was low of bounce and gave generous turn to the slow bowlers made the display by Botham even more remarkable.

SOMERSET

First Innings

N. F. M. Popplewell c Gifford b Hoffman	4
P. M. Roebuck c Humpage b Ferreira	40
N. A. Felton c Humpage b Hoffman	10
I. V. A. Richards c Smith b Lethbridge	65
B. C. Rose c Humpage b Ferreira	16
*I. T. Botham c Humpage b Lethbridge	5
V. J. Marks c Gifford b Ferreira	6
†T. Gard c Amiss b Ferreira	7
M. R. Davis c Humpage b Hoffman	1
S. C. Booth c Dyer b Gifford	28
C. H. Dredge not out	10
B 4, l-b 3, w 7, n-b 1	15

1/4 2/30 3/120 4/121 5/126   207
6/133 7/155 8/164 9/168

Second Innings

c Amiss b Gifford	70
c Amiss b Gifford	81
b Gifford	8
(5) c Humpage b Pierson	53
(6) run out	14
(7) not out	138
(8) not out	8
(4) c Dyer b Gifford	16
B 10, l-b 18, w 2	30

1/112 2/132 3/188 (6 wkts dec.) 418
4/213 5/249 6/345

BONUS POINTS – Somerset 2, Warwickshire 4.

BOWLING: **First Innings**—Hoffman 16-2-53-3; Smith 9-2-19-0; Ferreira 24-10-61-4; Lethbridge 19-4-62-2; Gifford 1.5-0-5-1. **Second Innings**—Hoffman 5-0-33-0; Smith 7-2-33-0; Lethbridge 4-0-17-0; Ferreira 9-4-15-0; Pierson 34-8-164-1; Gifford 42-20-128-4.

WARWICKSHIRE

First Innings

R. I. H. B. Dyer c Booth b Marks	106
G. J. Lord b Davis	9
A. I. Kallicharran c Rose b Dredge	48
D. L. Amiss c Booth b Marks	14
C. Lethbridge c Richards b Booth	47
†G. W. Humpage c and b Botham	33
P. A. Smith lbw b Botham	62
A. M. Ferreira b Botham	4
A. R. K. Pierson not out	2
*N. Gifford run out	0
D. S. Hoffman b Botham	0
B 5, l-b 4, w 4	13

1/14 2/86 3/113 4/181 5/230   338
6/332 7/336 8/338 9/338

Second Innings

c Botham b Davis	4
not out	17
not out	51
B 2	2

1/4   (1 wkt) 74

BONUS POINTS – Warwickshire 3, Somerset 2 (Score at 100 overs: 286-5).

BOWLING: **First Innings**—Botham 22-7-63-4; Davis 14-2-56-1; Dredge 11-4-21-1; Richards 8-2-26-0; Marks 40-13-91-2; Booth 23-3-72-1. **Second Innings**—Davis 3-1-3-1; Marks 12.4-5-2-0; Booth 2-0-15-0; Botham 8-1-32-0.

Umpires: J. H. Hampshire and H. J. Rhodes.

David East of Essex. His eight catches in an innings against Somerset equalled Wally Grout's world record.

SOMERSET v ESSEX
Played at Taunton, July 27, 29, 30, 1985

ESSEX WON BY seven wickets. Essex 20 pts, Somerset 4 pts. Toss won by Essex. Following an early slump by Somerset on a green pitch against Ian Pont on his Essex début, Felton and Wyatt added 92 in 30 overs. Botham, hitting four 6s and sixteen 4s, then made a remarkable 152 out of 195 in 121 balls to complete the recovery. Bad light stopped play after an over of Essex's reply and no play was possible on the Monday. Essex declared on the final morning, and after Somerset's forfeiture, Essex easily achieved the target of 296 in 90 overs, having 21 overs to spare. Garner was unable to bowl because of a knee injury. Usefully supported, Gooch carried the innings with superb batting in easy conditions, his unbeaten 173 coming off 190 balls and containing two 6s and 21 4s. East's eight catches in the Somerset innings gave him an Essex record and equalled the world record of A. W. T. Grout of Queensland in 1959–60.

SOMERSET

N. F. M. Popplewell c East b I. L. Pont	27
P. M. Roebuck c East b I. L. Pont	17
N. A. Felton c East b K. R. Pont	49
I. V. A. Richards c East b I. L. Pont	5
J. G. Wyatt c East b Pringle	50
*I. T. Botham c East b I. L. Pont	152
V. J. Marks c East b Pringle	17
†T. Gard not out	27
M. R. Davis c East b Pringle	7
C. H. Dredge b I. L. Pont	1
J. Garner not out	4
L-b 4, w 1, n-b 2	7

1/36 2/45 3/56 4/148 5/162 (9 wkts dec.) 363
6/246 7/343 8/352 9/353

BONUS POINTS – Somerset 4, Essex 4.

BOWLING: Pringle 30-2-90-3; I. L. Pont 24-2-103-5; Topley 24-3-86-0; K. R. Pont 11-0-45-1; Acfield 11-1-35-0.

Somerset forfeited their second innings.

ESSEX

First Innings

G. A. Gooch c Gard b Wyatt	19
B. R. Hardie not out	25
P. J. Prichard not out	18
K. S. McEwan (did not bat)	
D. R. Pringle (did not bat)	
L-b 4, w 2	6

1/25   (1 wkts dec.) 68

Second Innings

not out	173
b Dredge	20
b Dredge	44
lbw b Dredge	0
not out	14
L-b 11, n-b 3	14

1/84 2/165 3/165   (3 wkts) 296

*K. W. R. Fletcher, K. R. Pont, †D. E. East, T. D. Topley, D. L. Acfield and I. L. Pont did not bat.

BOWLING: **First Innings**—Garner 1-1-0-0; Wyatt 6-0-40-1; Roebuck 6-0-24-0. **Second Innings**—Botham 8-0-61-0; Davis 16-2-65-0; Dredge 22-0-82-3; Marks 18-2-48-0; Wyatt 3-0-18-0; Popplewell 2-0-11-0.

Umpires: K. J. Lyons and R. Palmer.

MOUNTAIN OF A MAN

Botham was never out of the news for long. Not since W. G. Grace can a cricketer, by his physical presence and remarkable exploits, have so caught the attention of the sporting world. Bradman's feats were, of course, more phenomenal. Sobers' more effortlessly versatile; but off the field they maintained a lower, more urbane profile than Botham. Bernard Darwin, in a vintage profile of W. G., wrote of his "schoolboy love for elementary and boisterous jokes ... his desperate and undisguised keenness, his occasional pettishness and pettiness, his endless power of recovering his spirits" – all of which could apply equally to Botham.

No-one can ever have sent the ball such huge distances as frequently as Botham did last summer. His 80 6s, most of them hit with the full face of the bat, often over extra-cover, were a record for an English first-class season. He scored at something like a run a ball for Somerset, yet still averaged 100 for them, and in the six Test matches he took 31 Australian wickets and held eight catches, some of them quite breathtaking.

Wherever he played he added substantially to the gate, and when the winter came he tested a recent operation on a knee by walking from John O'Groats to Land's End and raising over £600,000 for charity, an astonishing achievement. There was much else, not all of it quite so admirable. There are times when Botham needs to be saved from his unrestraint, as well perhaps as from those who would exploit him. Somerset, for their part, decided at the end of the season that they needed to be saved from his captaincy. To be fair to Botham, it is no easy business being a county captain while having to miss as many as ten or twelve Championship matches through playing for England. For him, no less than anyone else, England's tour of the West Indies presented a challenge – and one that he would relish. Of all the Test-playing countries, only they had not felt the full weight of his remarkable game.

WEST INDIES v ENGLAND

FIFTH TEST MATCH
Played at St. John's, Antigua, April 11, 12, 13, 15, 16, 1986

WEST INDIES WON by 240 runs. Richards's 110 not out in West Indies' second innings, the fastest Test hundred ever in terms of balls received (56 to reach three figures, 58 in all), made the final Test historic on two counts. The other was West Indies' achievement in emulating Australia, previously the only country to win all five home Tests on more than one occasion. Their previous five-love victory was over India in 1961-62, matching Australia's feats against England (1920–21) and South Africa (1931–32), the series in which Sir Donald Bradman made 806 runs in four completed innings. In addition, West Indies also won all five Tests of the 1984 series in England.

Richards's display, making him the obvious candidate for the match award, would have been staggering at any level of cricket. What made it unforgettable for the 5,000 or so lucky enough to see it was that he scored it without blemish at a time when England's sole aim was to make run-scoring as difficult as possible to delay a declaration. Botham and Emburey never had fewer than six men on the boundary and sometimes nine, yet whatever length or line they bowled, Richards had a stroke for it. His control and touch were as much features of the innings as the tremendous power of his driving. As can be calculated from the following table, he was within range of his hundred six balls before completing it (with a leg-side 4 off Botham), while from the time he reached 83 off 46 balls there had been no doubt, assuming he stayed in, that he would trim several deliveries off J. M. Gregory's previous record of 67 for Australia against South Africa at Johannesburg in 1921–22. The full innings went:

··36126141 (24 off 10)	·211·412·1 (36 off 20)	112·2111·· (45 off 30)
·1·1624441 (68 off 40)	12··664612 (96 off 50)	··21·461 (110 off 58)

Plundered in 83 minutes out of 146 while he was at the wicket, it had to be, by any yardstick, among the most wonderful innings ever played.

Though it was not until the sixth of the final twenty overs that Downton's dismissal enabled West Indies to complete their second successive "blackwash" over Gower's side, England's defeat was in one way their worst of the series. With the exception of the second Test, the pitch was the only one that did not overtly help West Indian-style fast bowling; and by winning the toss Gower gave his bowlers their best chance of exploiting any moisture beneath the surface following heavy rain the weekend before the match.

In the event, there were only two junctures when England were remotely in contention – 40 minutes before lunch on the second day when Haynes, having deservedly completed his first hundred of the series, was caught at mid-on to make West Indies 291 for six; and when Gooch and Slack opened the first innings with a partnership of 127, England's highest of the rubber.

Both positions flattered to deceive. With Gower misguidedly over-bowling Botham in the hope he would collect the extra two wickets he needed to overtake Lillee's world record

Viv Richards achieved a world record in this Test by scoring his century off only 56 balls. The record had previously belonged to J. M. Gregory playing for Australia against South Africa in the 1921–22 series. Amazingly, Richards bettered the previous mark by 11 deliveries.

of dismissals, West Indies added 183 at almost 5 an over for their four wickets (Marshall, Harper and Holding shared eight 6s). And within ten overs of Gooch's dismissal, England were 159 for four and in danger of being forced to follow on. Having taken two of the four wickets that fell on the first day – Richards was caught off a mis-hook at deep fine-leg – Botham emerged from the match with two for 225. The nearest he came to drawing level with Lillee (355) was when, with Marshall 12, Slack, diving to his left, missed a well-hit pick-up at square leg.

The game was not without its controversial moments, all of them, regrettably, centring on Richards in the field. But the first day, which was declared a public holiday and drew a full house of 10,000, established a carnival atmosphere which made the fifth Test the most enjoyable of the series. It was played in perfect weather: scorching hot but always with a sea-breeze.

Four weeks to the day after having his right thumb broken, Gatting was fit to play, while Slack and Ellison replaced Willey, who had returned to England, and Thomas. Smith's enforced withdrawal with back trouble within hours of the start gave Robinson another chance, this time at number three. Overnight there had been doubts about Gower's fitness following a blow on the right wrist, received while batting against Marshall in the previous Test, but Smith's indisposition settled the matter. West Indies were unchanged.

Haynes capped a consistent series with 131 (440 minutes, fifteen 4s) and 70; Gooch put together a pair of hard-earned 51s; Slack produced an innings of the type which should have seen him included in the original sixteen; Gower, with his captaincy possibly at stake, batted more than seven hours in the match. For once, too, there was an important contribution from a West Indian spinner, Harper striking at vital moments four times; and Emburey continued his mastery of Richardson by dismissing him for the fifth and sixth times in seven completed innings. Less encouragingly, West Indies bowled 40 no-balls which were not scored from: the most in any Test innings.

Notwithstanding his haughty treatment of the umpires in his stubborn pursuit of a ball to the liking of his bowlers, Richards, however, stood alone. For West Indian spectators, the only thing the series had lacked until the last Test was the sight of the greatest player in the world in full majestic flow. If anyone forgets that extraordinary *tour de force*, it can truthfully be said that he did not deserve to see it in the first place.

The Man of the Series award was presented to Marshall, who spearheaded West Indies' attack throughout the rubber, taking 27 wickets.

WEST INDIES

First Innings

C. G. Greenidge b Botham 14
D. L. Haynes c Gatting b Ellison 131
R. B. Richardson c Slack b Emburey 24
H. A. Gomes b Emburey 24
*I. V. A. Richards c Gooch b Botham 26
†P. J. L. Dujon b Foster 21
M. D. Marshall c Gatting b Gooch 76
R. A. Harper c Lamb b Foster 60
M. A. Holding c Gower b Ellison 73
J. Garner run out 11
B. P. Patterson not out 0
B 2, l-b 11, w 1 14

1/23 2/63 3/137 4/178 5/232   474
6/291 7/351 8/401 9/450

Second Innings

(1) run out 70
(2) c Robinson b Emburey 31
(3) not out 110
(4) not out 19
B 4, l-b 9, w 1, n-b 2 16

1/100 2/161   (2 wkts dec.) 246

BOWLING: **First Innings**—Botham 40-6-147-2; Foster 28-5-86-2; Ellison 24.3-3-114-2; Emburey 37-11-93-2; Gooch 5-2-21-1. **Second Innings**—Botham 15-0-78-0; Foster 10-0-40-0; Emburey 14-0-83-1; Ellison 4-0-32-0.

ENGLAND

First Innings

G. A. Gooch *lbw b* Holding 51
W. N. Slack *c* Greenidge *b* Patterson 52
R. T. Robinson *b* Marshall 12
D. I. Gower *c* Dujon *b* Marshall 90
A. J. Lamb *c and b* Harper 1
M. W. Gatting *c* Dujon *b* Garner 15
I. T. Botham *c* Harper *b* Garner 10
P. R. Downton *c* Holding *b* Garner 5
R. M. Ellison *c* Dujon *b* Marshall 6
J. E. Emburey *not out* 7
N. A. Foster *c* Holding *b* Garner 10
B 5, l-b 6, n-b 40 51

1/127 2/132 3/157 4/159 5/205 310
6/213 7/237 8/289 9/290

Second Innings

lbw b Holding 51
b Garner 8
run out 3
(5) *c* Dujon *b* Harper 21
(6) *b* Marshall 1
(7) *b* Holding 1
(8) *b* Harper 13
(9) *lbw b* Marshall 13
(4) *lbw b* Garner 16
c Richardson *b* Harper 0
not out 0
B 10, l-b 10, w 2, n-b 21 . . . 43

1/14 2/29 3/84 4/101 5/112 170
6/124 7/147 8/166 9/168

BOWLING: **First Innings**—Marshall 24-5-64-3; Garner 21.4-2-67-4; Patterson 14-2-49-1; Holding 20-3-71-1; Harper 26-7-45-1; Richards 2-0-3-0. **Second Innings**—Marshall 16.1-6-25-2; Garner 17-5-38-2; Patterson 15-3-29-0; Holding 16-3-45-2; Harper 12-8-10-3; Richards 3-1-3-0.

Umpires: L. H. Barker and C. E. Cumberbatch.

EDRICH, WILLIAM JOHN (BILL), DFC, who died at Chesham as the result of an accident on April 23, 1986, aged 70, was a cricketer who would have been the answer to prayer in the troubled England sides of today and especially in the West Indies in 1985–86. Endlessly cheerful, always optimistic and physically courageous, he was a splendid hitter of short-pitched fast bowling and took the blows he received as a part of the game. When he made 16 in an hour and three-quarters on a hideous wicket at Brisbane in the first innings of the first Test in 1946–47, an innings which *Wisden's* correspondent described as "one of the most skilful batting displays I have ever seen", it was reckoned that he was hit ten times by Lindwall, Miller and Toshack. So far from being demoralised by his experience, he scored in the series 462 runs with an average of 46.20, and that for a side which lost three Tests, two of them by an innings, and drew the other two. Moreover, his cricket did not end with his batting. Though he stood only 5ft 6in tall, and had a low, slinging action, he could off a run of eleven strides bowl genuinely fast for a few overs. Admittedly it was a terrible proof of the weakness of English bowling after the war that at this period he often had to open in Test matches. It is barely credible that in 1950, when his 22 wickets in the season cost him just under 50 runs each, he opened in both of West Indies' innings at Lord's. In fairness it must be added that Walcott, who made 168 not out in the second innings, was missed off him in the slips at 9. Still, in a reasonably strong side he was a valuable change as a fifth or sixth bowler, always apt to upset a good batsman by his unexpected speed. Like many natural athletes, he originally made a reputation as a tireless outfield, but he was soon found to be too valuable in the slips to spend much time elsewhere. One way and another he was always in the game, always trying his hardest.

He came of a Norfolk farming family, which sometimes produced its own XI. Three of his brothers played with some success in first-class cricket and his cousin, John, had later a distinguished Test match career. Bill Edrich first appeared for Norfolk in 1932 at the age of sixteen, and by 1936 had scored 1,886 runs for them in the Minor Counties Championship alone, not to mention an innings of 111 against the 1935 South African side. By then he had begun to qualify for Middlesex, and in

1936 he made three hundreds in first-class cricket for MCC and came second in the first-class averages with an average of 55. So it was no surprise when next year, in his first full season of first-class cricket, he scored 2,154 runs with an average of 44.87, heading the batting, and was picked for Lord Tennyson's side in India. In 1938 he stated by making 1,000 runs before the end of May, a target he achieved only with the help of an unexpectedly generous action by Bradman, who, captaining the Australians against Middlesex on May 31, made an otherwise meaningless declaration to give him a chance of getting the last 20 runs. After this feat his place in the England side was secure; so secure that he kept it right through the series even though failure followed failure and six innings produced only 67 runs. In the following winter, as a member of the side to South Africa, his ill luck pursued him, five innings bringing 21 runs. At last, in the second innings of the timeless fifth Test, when England were set 696 to win, he saved the side by batting 7 hours, 40 minutes for 219. Timeless or not, the match was abandoned when the score stood at 654 for five; the rain came down, everyone had had enough, and the Englishmen left to catch their boat.

The sequel to this innings is perhaps the strangest part of the story. There can surely be no parallel for a batsman failing in eight consecutive Tests and yet keeping his place, but one would at any rate expect that, when he had at last justified the selectors' confidence, he would have retained it. Instead, in 1939, though his average for the season was 49.68, he did not play in a Test against the West Indians, and in 1946, when Test cricket was resumed after seven years' interval, he had only one match against India and did not bat in that. Moreover he was only a late choice for the 1946–47 tour of Australia. Let anyone justify these inconsistencies who can.

During the war Edrich had joined the RAF and had a distinguished career, winning the DFC as a bomber pilot. Up to the war he had played as a professional; after it he became an amateur. Futhermore, until 1938 he had normally opened the innings. When he played his great innings in South Africa, he had been moved down the order, and in 1939 Brown and Robertson established themselves in the Middlesex side as a great opening pair. Thenceforward Edrich's normal place was first wicket. It was in Australia in 1946–47 that he showed himself indisputably a Test player. His batting in the first Test has been mentioned. In the second he scored 71 and 119 and made a gallant attempt to stave off an innings defeat. He followed this with 89 in the third Test and 60 in the fifth.

In England in 1947 came his *annus mirabilis*. Scoring in all 3,539 runs with an average of 80.43 he beat Hayward's 41-year-old aggregate of 3,518: however, Compton beat it by even more. What is not sufficiently appreciated is that, but for a strained arm, which stopped him bowling after the beginning of August, he might well have equalled J. H. Park's astonishing record of 3,000 runs and 100 wickets: Edrich had already taken 67 wickets. In 1946 he had taken 73 at 19.28. In the Tests in 1947 against South Africa he made 552 runs with an average of 110.40. At Manchester he made 191, adding 228 with Compton for the third wicket in 196 minutes. At Lord's in the previous Test, also for the third wicket, they had added 370. Edrich made 189.

In 1948, in the disastrous series against Australia, his sole notable contribution was 111 in the fourth Test at Leeds, but next year against New Zealand he averaged 54 with only one century. In 1950 he contributed a typically gallant 71 in the second innings of the first Test at Manchester, but at Lord's in the second he failed abjectly in each innings. His scores were 8 and 8: it would have been better for his reputation if he had taken two first balls. Each time he stayed long enough to make it clear that he was completely out of his depth with Ramadhin and Valentine. Nothing worse for the morale of the younger members of the side can be imagined. Inevitably he was dropped for the two remaining Tests, but for Middlesex he scored much as usual and it was a great surprise when he was omitted from the team for Australia at the end of

Above left: Clive Lloyd, West Indies v Australia at Perth 1975.
Above right: England celebrate winning the Ashes at Melbourne 1986.
Bottom left: Geoffrey Boycott batting in the Centenary Test v Australia at Lord's 1980.
Centre: Botham in full flow. Headingley 1981.
Bottom right: Viv Richards. West Indies Tour of England 1988.

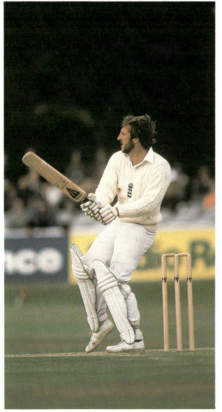

the season. The Australians themselves were astonished, and when the side proved to be incontestably the worst batting one England had ever sent out, and all the new choices were failures, there were those who thought that his courage and experience might have turned the scale in a series which was closer than the results indicated. No reasons were given at the time for his omission, but in fact an ill-advised late-night party during the first Test against West Indies, followed by his calamitous showing in the second, had convinced the selectors, and not least the captain elect, that the team would be better without him. By a generous gesture Edrich himself was at the station to see the team off and to wish them well.

Although few could have foreseen it at the time, this was the beginning of the end for Edrich. Never again was he to be the force in Tests that he had been. Recalled as Hutton's opening partner for the last three Tests against Australia in 1953, he made 64 at Leeds and was 55 not out when the Ashes were regained at The Oval after a period of eighteen years. But he did not do much in his one Test against Pakistan in 1954, and although at the end of that summer he was picked for Australia, only a fighting 88 in the second innings of the first Test showed what he could once do. That was the end of his career for England. For Middlesex he still made runs, if not on the scale of his great years. In 1951 and 1952 he shared the captaincy with Compton: this, like most such diarchies, was not a success. From 1953, he was sole captain, a position in which he certainly could not be blamed for lack of enterprise. At last in 1957, though he got his 1,000 runs, for the fifteenth time, his average dropped to 22.92 and he felt it was time to resign. Next year he played in about half the matches with only moderate results, and at the end of the season he accepted captaincy of Norfolk, for whom he continued to score runs and to take wickets with slow off-breaks until 1972.

When his first-class career ended he was 42, an age at which many great batsmen have still been batting with almost undiminished powers. However, Edrich had always relied rather on his natural gifts, his wonderful eye, his physical strength and courage than on a studiously sound technique. Granted that he was always well behind the ball when playing a fast bowler, he had a markedly right-handed grip and his best strokes were the cut, the hook and the pulled drive. His bat did not have that pendulum-like swing up and down the line which is the foundation of real soundness. Still, he had done enough for fame and had given much pleasure to many thousands of spectators.

In first-class cricket he had scored 36,965 runs, with an average of 42.39 and made 86 centuries, nine of them double-centuries: he took 479 wickets at 33.31 and held 526 catches. His highest score was 267 not out for Middlesex against Northamptonshire at Northampton in 1947. For Middlesex his figures were 25,738 runs with an average of 43.40 and 328 wickets at 30.41. and in Tests he made 2,440 runs with an average of 40, including six hundreds: he also took 41 wickets at 41.29 and held 39 catches.

AUSTRALIA v ENGLAND

FOURTH TEST MATCH
Played at Melbourne, December 26, 27, 28, 1986

ENGLAND WON BY an innings and 14 runs. A combination of excellent out-swing bowling by Small, playing in his first Test of the series, and an inept appraisal by Australia of their best means of success, effectively decided the match, and the destination of the Ashes, by tea on the first day. Australia, put in on a pitch not fully dry, were bowled out for 141 in 235 minutes, Small maintaining a high degree of accuracy to take five for 48 in 22.4 overs. A last-minute replacement for Dilley, who failed a fitness test on a jarred knee on the morning of the match, Small amply justified his preference to Foster by dismissing five of the first seven batsmen in the order. With two more wickets in the second innings, including that of Border when with Marsh the captain was showing signs of keeping Australia in the match, a valuable 21 not out at No. 11, and a good catch in the deep to finish the game, Small was a deserving winner of the Man of the Match award in only his third Test.

Well as Small bowled, however, both he and more especially Botham, for whom Whitaker made way, were helped by Australia's ill-conceived approach. Botham, bowling off the shortened run he had used three days earlier in Canberra, took five for 41, a disproportionate reward for sixteen overs at medium pace with faster variations. The loss of Boon in Small's third over did nothing for Australia's confidence. But it was hard to disassociate the way they set about their innings from a well-publicised comment by Border, in a pre-match interview, that to revive their chance of winning back the Ashes, Australia needed to play boldly.

On quite a lively pitch, with a stronger growth of grass than for some years following a transplant of couch grass from a local golf course, Kingston Heath, Australia should have been content to let runs come. Jack Lyons's last Test pitch as head curator was never a straightforward one to bat on, yielding extra and variable bounce for the faster bowlers when they bent their backs, but the home side should have known from experience that at Melbourne, with its huge, slow outfield, a first-innings total of 250 would have given them at least an even chance. Marsh, for one, looked to lose his wicket through eagerness to follow the assumed instructions of his captain. Anything but a regular player of the hook – in some 30 hours' batting against England on the tour, he had produced no more than half a dozen – he attempted to hook a rising ball from Botham which pitched well outside off stump; Richards took the first of five catches in the innings with a gymnastic upward leap.

That wicket made the score 44 for two, and when, 40 minutes later, Richards took a second fine catch to dismiss Border, diving to his left, Australia were in trouble. Against the advice of Border and R. B. Simpson, Australia's cricket manager, the selectors had omitted Ritchie, a specialist batsman, in favour of an all-rounder, thought to be Matthews, to give the side an extra option in the field. In practice, with Matthews not called upon to bowl in an England innings lasting 120 overs, the decision served only to weaken the batting. McDermott, who in effect came in for Ritchie, and Zoehrer, who reclaimed his place from Dyer, were the changes from the team that drew at Adelaide.

Jones, who hit Emburey out of the attack with two lofted leg-side fours, was the one batsman to pass 20. He batted 154 minutes, hitting one glorious on-drive off DeFreitas, before being caught at mid-off off the leading edge, attempting to tuck Small to leg. A wonderful running catch by Richards, who sprinted 30 yards to square leg to take a mis-hit hook by McDermott, hastened Australia's downfall.

It was a lamentable piece of batting which was duly reflected in a second-day attendance more than 20,000 down on the 58,203 of Boxing Day. England had set themselves to bat for two days. But a mixture of over-attacking batting, and Australia's best bowling and fielding of the series – Matthews was outstanding in the field – saw them out for 349 at stumps, despite at one time being 163 for one through a second-wicket stand of 105 by Broad and Gatting, Broad was the one batsman who played the bowling strictly on its merits, while making due allowance for the foibles of the pitch. He demonstrated the right combination of patience and sound method to produce a lengthy innings, showing the bowlers the full face of the bat and waiting for the ball to drive. His 112 took 328 minutes, came off 255 balls, and included just nine fours. Reid was again the best Australian bowler, although Sleep played a part in fanning the impatience of the batsmen by bowling most of his overs round the wicket into the rough outside leg stump.

Australia, starting their second innings on the third morning with a deficit of 208, were never on course for the score of 450 that would have made a match of it. Border's dismissal at 113 after 85 minutes' resistance, superbly caught by Emburey at third slip after driving at a wideish ball from Small, wrecked their chances. Not until Marsh was run out by Edmonds in the covers, however, did England have prospects of an innings win. Unsettled by being given the benefit of the doubt by umpire French earlier that over, when a ball from Emburey bounced from his gloves to Athey at short leg, Marsh was sent back by Waugh after embarking on a risky single and never had a hope. He had batted determinedly for 213 minutes. On his departure Australia lost their will to battle on. The last six wickets fell for 41 in 80 minutes to the spin of Emburey and Edmonds; just 40 minutes after tea the game was over, leaving the Australian Board to rue attendance figures that were 125,000 down on those of 1982-83.

Man of the Match: G. C. Small.   *Attendance:* 107,817,

Close of play: First day, England 95-1 (B. C. Broad 56*, M. W. Gatting 8*); Second day, England 349.

AUSTRALIA

First Innings

G. R. Marsh c Richards b Botham	17
D. C. Boon c Botham b Small	7
D. M. Jones c Gower b Small	59
*A. R. Border c Richards b Botham	15
S. R. Waugh c Botham b Small	10
G. R. J. Matthews c Botham b Small	14
P. R. Sleep c Richards b Small	0
†T. J. Zoehrer b Botham	5
C. J. McDermott c Richards b Botham	0
M. G. Hughes c Richards b Botham	2
B. A. Reid *not out*	2
B 1, l-b 1, w 1, n-b 7	10

1/16 (2) 2/44 (1) 3/80 (4) 4/108 (5)   141
5/118 (3) 6/118 (7) 7/129 (8)
8/133 (9) 9/137 (10) 10/141 (6)

Second Innings

(2) *run out*	60
(1) c Gatting b Small	8
c Gatting b DeFreitas	21
c Emburey b Small	34
b Edmonds	49
b Emburey	0
run out	6
c Athey b Edmonds	1
b Emburey	1
c Small b Edmonds	8
not out	0
L-b 3, w 1, n-b 2	6

1/13 (1) 2/48 (3) 3/113 (4)   194
4/153 (2) 5/153 (6) 6/175 (7)
7/180 (8) 8/185 (5)
9/189 (9) 10/194 (10)

BOWLING: **First Innings**—Small 22.4-7-48-5; DeFreitas 11-1-30-0; Emburey 4-0-16-0; Botham 16-4-41-5; Gatting 1-0-4-0. **Second Innings**—DeFreitas 12-1-44-1; Small 15-3-40-2; Botham 7-1-19-0; Edmonds 19.4-5-45-3; Emburey 20-5-43-2.

ENGLAND

B. C. Broad c Zoehrer b Hughes	112
C. W. J. Athey lbw b Reid	21
*M. W. Gatting c Hughes b Reid	40
A. J. Lamb c Zoehrer b Reid	43
D. I. Gower c Matthews b Sleep	7
I. T. Botham c Zoehrer b McDermott	29
†C. J. Richards c Marsh b Reid	3
P. A. J. DeFreitas c Matthews b McDermott	7
J. E. Emburey *c and b* McDermott	22
P. H. Edmonds lbw b McDermott	19
G. C. Small *not out*	21
B 6, l-b 7, w 1, n-b 11	25

1/58 (2) 2/163 (3) 3/198 (1)   349
4/219 (5) 5/251 (4) 6/273 (6) 7/277 (7)
8/289 (8) 9/319 (9) 10/349 (10)

BOWLING: McDermott 26.5-4-83-4; Hughes 30-3-94-1; Reid 28-5-78-4; Waugh 8-4-16-0; Sleep 28-4-65-1.

Umpires: A. R. Crafter and R. A. French.

Graham Gooch pictured during the Bicentenary Game. After a hesitant start in Test match cricket he gained a place at the very pinnacle of English batsmanship.

MCC v REST OF THE WORLD

MCC BICENTENARY MATCH
Played at Lord's, August 20, 21, 22, 24, 25, 1987

DRAWN. RAIN WASHED out the last day's play with the Rest of the World, 13 for one overnight, needing another 340 to win. It was a sad finish to a match which provided many marvellous moments while, off the field, friendships were renewed and nostalgia was indulged in as cricketers, young and old, came together to celebrate the 200th anniversary of MCC. In memory there will be cameos rather than a broad sweep of canvas, for in the modern sporting context this was a game rather than a contest. It may even have been appropriate that neither side won. In their performances and their sportsmanship, the finest players in the world had recognised that cricket should be the winner. Because of the spirit in which the match was played, MCC increased from £25,000 to £30,000 the prizemoney to be shared by the two teams in the event of a draw. The winners would have received £25,000 and the losers £12,000.

If it is futile to speculate who might have won, it is none the less fascinating to ponder. The pitch was perfect for batting, as it had been from the start. On the fourth day MCC had scored their 318 in 88 overs, indeed having to keep a tight rein on the innings at the end to stop it from bolting. And although the Rest had lost Gavaskar, bowled off stump in Marshall's first over that evening before bad light stopped play, they possessed batsmen of the calibre to challenge such a target. Moreover, Javed Miandad, troubled by a back strain, had been unable to express his unique talent in the first innings. The second would have provided an opportunity.

From the teams originally chosen, there were three changes. For MCC, M. D. Crowe and I. T. Botham were unfit and replaced by Gooch and Rice. The latter's inclusion gave the celebrations a South African presence, for no-one from that country had been invited. With so many players coming from countries hostile to the South African government, MCC had avoided possible embarrassment by restricting selection to players currently engaged in county cricket (MCC) or, not being current county cricketers, from the Test-playing countries (Rest of the World). I. V. A. Richards withdrew from the Rest XI in order to play a match for Rishton in the Lancashire League and was replaced by Vengsarkar.

The sun shone in a blue sky when Gatting won the toss with a Spade Guinea, minted in 1787, the year of the first game at Thomas Lord's original ground. And when Greenidge clipped Imran's first ball for four, it signalled the batting feast to follow. Broad, playing no stroke, missed out, but this brought in Gooch. He had had an unhappy summer. Now, although beaten early on by Imran and Walsh, he was to rediscover his form and his confidence. By lunch Greenidge had reached fifty, off 91 balls with nine fours, but in the second over of the afternoon, stepping out, he lifted Qadir over – so he must have thought – mid-on; only for Harper, 6ft 5in tall, to intercept the ball as it passed overhead.

Impressive in its casualness, the catch was nothing to his dismissal of Gooch in the evening. Gower, out of tune, had come and gone, walking without waiting, and Gooch and Gatting had added 103 when Gooch went down the wicket and drove Harper straight. In an instant Harper fielded the ball and, while Gooch was still moving forward with the momentum of his stroke, threw down the stumps, the action of taking and throwing being as one. Even Gooch was drawn to smile in admiration, and well he could afford to. His 117, from 210 balls in 4 hours 50 minutes, had taken him from a shadow into sunlight. In recent seasons he had swayed at the crease like an oak in the wind: here, he was upright and still, waiting for the ball and punching it with the authority of his best years. He hit eighteen fours and had, in addition, removed Qadir from the attack, bruising the bowler's fingers with a straight drive. It was in finishing this over that Miandad strained his back.

Gatting, in a sunhat, and Rice, helmeted, put on 201 in a partnership of contrasts. Gatting, hitting his fourth hundred in a month – two of them in Tests – was in wonderful form, especially powerful off the back foot and deft with orthodox and unorthodox sweeps. He scored 90 of the 136 runs that came on the second morning and there were 26 fours in his 179, made from 273 balls in five and a quarter hours. Rice, who was not timing the ball so well, batted with determination rather than dash, his unbeaten 59 taking 202 minutes (156 balls).

The Rest's innings began at 2.15 with a no-ball from Marshall. His first legitimate delivery, fast and low, struck Gavaskar on the pad and he was fortunate to get away with a leg-bye instead of a leg-before. Next ball, Haynes was dropped by Gatting at third slip. Almost an hour later, Rice showed how such catches can be taken, moving low to his right at first slip and grasping the ball two-handed. He took another splendid catch to dismiss Border late in the day, diving wide and low to his left at cover.

When Shastri was bowling his slow left-arm spin to Gavaskar and Vengsarkar, with the canopies of the new Mound Stand behind them, the setting could have been the subcontinent; but not when Hadlee or Marshall was bowling from the Pavilion End after tea (69 for one). For the first time in the match, a competitive edge could be felt. Hadlee to Gavaskar was a duel between two masters, the bowler probing with all his skills for an opening, the batsman correct and studious in defence, awaiting the chance to counterattack. Gavaskar won the bout. But if Hadlee's weapon was the épée, Marshall's was the sabre. From round the wicket, on so placid a pitch, he removed Vengsarkar with a ball that kicked, took the shoulder of the bat and flew to Gooch, the finer of two gullies. Border, gritty, rode the storm, and when Gavaskar reached his fifty (121 balls) with a flowing cover drive off Marshall, they had entered calmer waters. The evening was made charming by the artistry of these two small men against the spinners: driving or deflecting, the execution of their strokes was classical.

Gavaskar, when 75, had a lucky escape when the ball rolled from his pads to rest against the stumps; and next day, contemplating a suicidal second run to bring him his first hundred at Lord's, he was firmly sent back by Imran Khan. Here was a moment to savour. Earlier in the year, Imran had dismissed Gavaskar with the first ball in the Test match at Jaipur. Now he was rescuing him. The smiles on their faces were large. Next over, when Gavaskar turned Shastri backward of square, the hug of congratulation from the bowler was spontaneous. His hundred had taken Gavaskar 215 balls, and when he clipped Hadlee through mid-wicket, then rocked back and hooked him for another boundary, a second hundred looked possible. The sky was clearing after an overcast start; play began at 11.30 on Saturday after excellent work by the groundstaff had removed the effects of heavy overnight rain.

Imran was an ideal foil for the "Little Master". Once he had seen him to his hundred, he hit Emburey straight for six, reached fifty with two lovely off-side fours in an over from Hadlee, and carted Emburey high into the President's box above the Tavern concourse. When he was bowled, making room to cut, he and Gavaskar had put on 180 in 2 hours 40 minutes. Kapil Dev kept up the entertainment for twenty minutes until he was caught in front of the Pavilion.

Gavaskar now was 177, making steady and stylish progress towards a Bicentenary double-hundred. So it came as some surprise when Shastri, with a little flight and a little turn, beguiled him into a return catch. Gavaskar had batted for six and threequarter hours, faced 351 balls and hit 22 fours. He was accorded an outstanding reception – he had announced his retirement from Test cricket the previous evening – and as if the gods too were mourning his leaving, it rained during the tea interval. Play did not resume until 5.46, when Harper and Walsh, almost indistinguishable in the dark, added 30 before rain returned at six o'clock. Walsh hit a mighty six, they ran, with their giant strides, 4 to third man: and all the while lightning and thunder raged above them.

Border's declaration that evening put the onus on Gatting to set a target. It also gave Greenidge the opportunity to score the hundred he had desired on the first day. He was careful over it, batting for five hours and needing 223 balls, but Gooch (118 balls), Gower (73 balls) and Hadlee (39 balls) kept the score moving nicely. Qadir ran through his repertoire all afternoon, unchanged except to change ends; but he bowled as much to contain as to attack: a pity. By late afternoon, however, the sky was threatening rain, and soon all that had passed would be merely memories. But what memories.

Awards of £2,000 each were made to the Batsman of the Match, S. M. Gavaskar, the Bowler of the Match, M. D. Marshall, and the Fielder of the Match, C. E. B. Rice. D. C. S. Compton chose the batsman, Sir George Allen the bowler, and they consulted on the fielder – G.W.

Attendance: 80,555; *receipts:* £691,233.50.

Close of play: First day, MCC 291–4 (M. W. Gatting 68*, C. E. B. Rice 14*); Second day, Rest of the World 169–3 (S. M. Gavaskar 80*, P. J. L. Dujon 8*); Third day, Rest of the World 421–7 dec.; Fourth day, Rest of the World 13–1 (D. L. Haynes 3*, R. A. Harper 9*).

MCC

First Innings

C. G. Greenidge c Harper b Qadir	52
B. C. Broad lbw b Imran	10
G. A. Gooch run out	117
D. I. Gower c Dujon b Harper	8
*M. W. Gatting b Walsh	179
C. E. B. Rice not out	59
R. J. Hadlee (did not bat)	
R. J. Shastri (did not bat)	
J. E. Emburey (did not bat)	
B 11, l-b 15, w 1, n-b 3	30

1/21 2/96 3/151 4/254 5/455   (5 wkts dec.) 455

Second Innings

b Qadir	122
c Dujon b Kapil Dev	2
b Harper	70
c Border b Imran	40
(8) not out	4
(5) c Imran b Walsh	36
(6) not out	10
(7) c Haynes b Qadir	7
B 15, l-b 11, n-b 1	27

1/11 2/146 3/231   (6 wkts dec.) 318
4/289 5/293 6/308

M. D. Marshall and †B. N. French *did not bat.*

BOWLING: **First Innings**—Imran 25-6-97-1, Walsh 28.1-6-102-1; Kapil Dev 24-8-54-0; Qadir 16.2-7-30-1; Harper 34-5-125-1; Miandad 5.4-0-21-0. **Second Innings**—Imran 13-4-33-1; Kapil Dev 7-0-21-1; Walsh 12-3-54-1; Qadir 36-9-112-2; Harper 20-2-72-1.

REST OF THE WORLD

First Innings

S. M. Gavaskar c and b Shastri	188
D. L. Haynes c Rice b Marshall	23
D. B. Vengsarkar c Gooch b Marshall	22
*A. R. Border c Rice b Shastri	26
†P. J. L. Dujon c Gooch b Marshall	9
Imran Khan b Shastri	82
Kapil Dev c Marshall b Emburey	13
R. A. Harper not out	17
C. A. Walsh not out	21
B 3, l-b 8, w 4, n-b 5	20

1/46 2/93 3/148 4/173   (7 wkts dec.) 421
5/353 6/372 7/389

Second Innings

b Marshall	0
not out	3
(3) not out	9
L-b 1	1

1/2   (1 wkt) 13

Javed Miandad and Abdul Qadir *did not bat.*

BOWLING: **First Innings**—Marshall 20-3-53-3; Hadlee 21-2-71-0; Rice 12-1-63-0; Shastri 42-4-130-3; Emburey 29-7-93-1. **Second Innings**—Marshall 2.3-0-10-1; Hadlee 2-1-2-0.

Umpires: H. D. Bird and D. R. Shepherd.

In addition to the above players, the following reserves were selected: MCC – P. H. Edmonds, M. A. Holding and C. J. Richards; Rest of the World – J. G. Bracewell, J. Garner, D. M. Jones, Maninder Singh, J. R. Ratnayeke and B. A. Reid.

The selectors of the two squads were M. C. Cowdrey, P. B. H. May and M. W. Gatting for MCC and G. H. G. Doggart, C. H. Lloyd and A. R. Border for the Rest of the World.

THE RELIANCE WORLD CUP FINAL

AUSTRALIA v ENGLAND

Played at Calcutta, November 8, 1987

AUSTRALIA WON BY 7 runs. Toss: Australia. Batting first suited Australia; and when they took the field to defend a total of 253, it was in the knowledge that no side batting second had scored 254 to win in this World Cup. England, 135 for two after 31 overs, and with Australia beginning to show signs of disarray in the field, were then almost on target. But in a moment too crass to contemplate, Gatting handed back the initiative. To Border's first ball, bowled on the line of his leg stump, the England captain attempted to play a reverse sweep. Having in the semi-final swept the ball on to his leg stump, he now contrived to hit it on to his shoulder, whence it looped into Dyer's gloves. The Australians' joy was unconcealed.

England had conceded points from the start, an erratic opening spell from DeFreitas and Small helping Marsh and Boon post 52 in ten overs. Foster and the two spinners repaired the damage, with Foster's eight overs costing just 16 runs and bringing the wicket of Marsh in the eighteenth over. Gooch, too, was economical until coming under fire as Border and Veletta (31 balls, six fours) added 73 in the ten overs following Boon's dismissal. Boon's 75 (125 balls, seven fours) was his fifth score of 50 or more in six innings. DeFreitas, brought back to bowl the last over, went for 11 to bring to 65 the runs scored from England's last six overs.

Robinson, undone by pace to no-one's great surprise, was out first ball to McDermott's fourth. Gooch (57 balls) and Athey put on 65 in seventeen overs, Athey and Gatting (45 balls) 69 in thirteen, Athey (104 balls) and Lamb 35 in just over eight. It was Waugh whose throw ran out Athey as he went for a third run; and with England slipping farther behind the run-rate (75 from ten overs had drifted to 46 from five), he bowled Lamb (55 balls) in the 47th over. DeFreitas gave England renewed hope with 14 (464) in McDermott's penultimate over, but Waugh conceded just 2 runs, as well as having DeFreitas caught, in the 49th. That left 17 runs needed from the final over, and there was no way McDermott was going to allow that.

Attendance: 70,000 approx.

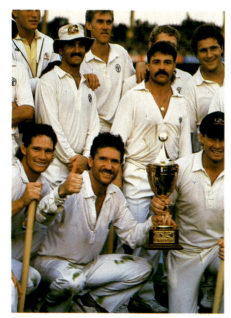

Australia, pictured (left) with the World Cup trophy. England captain Mike Gatting (above), seen batting during the game.

AUSTRALIA

D. C. Boon c Downton b Hemmings	75
G. R. Marsh b Foster	24
D. M. Jones c Athey b Hemmings	33
C. J. McDermott b Gooch	14
*A. R. Border run out	31
M. R. J. Veletta not out	45
S. R. Waugh not out	5
B 1, l-b 13, w 5, n-b 7	26

1/75 (2) **2**/151 (3) (5 wkts, 50 over) 253
3/166 (4) **4**/168 (1) **5**/241 (5)

S. P. O'Donnell, †G. C. Dyer, T. B. A. May and B. A. Reid did not bat.

BOWLING: DeFreitas 6–1–34–0; Small 6–0–33–0; Foster 10–0–38–1; Hemmings 10–1–48–2; Emburey 10–0–44–0; Gooch 8–1–42–1.

ENGLAND

G. A. Gooch lbw b O'Donnell	35
R. T. Robinson lbw b McDermott	0
C. W. J. Athey run out	58
*M. W. Gatting c Dyer b Border	41
A. J. Lamb b Waugh	45
†P. R. Downton c O'Donnell b Border	9
J. E. Emburey run out	10
P. A. J. DeFreitas c Reid b Waugh	17
N. A. Foster not out	7
G. C. Small not out	3
B 1, l-b 14, w 2, n-b 4	21

1/1 (2) **2**/66 (1) **3**/135 (4) (8 wkts, 50 overs) 246
4/170 (3) **5**/188 (6) **6**/218 (5)
7/220 (7) **8**/235 (8)

E. E. Hemmings did not bat.

BOWLING: McDermott 10–1–51–1; Reid 10–0–43–0; Waugh 9–0–37–2; O'Donnell 10–1–35–1; May 4–0–27–0; Border 7–0–38–2.

Umpires: R. B. Gupta and Mahboob Shah.

Eden Gardens, Calcutta, was the scene of the 1987 World Cup final. The locals would have preferred an India v Pakistan game but still turned up in vast numbers to prove themselves a sporting and fair-minded crowd.

CRICKET RECORDS

Sir John Berry Hobbs, Surrey and England.

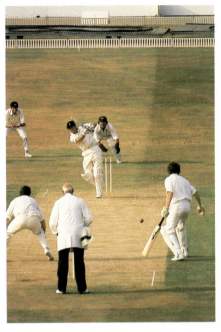

Geoffrey Boycott, Yorkshire and England.

Sir Donald Bradman, New South Wales, South Australia and Australia.

Dennis Lillee, Western Australia and Australia.

MOST HUNDREDS IN A SEASON

Eighteen: D. C. S. Compton in 1947. These included six hundreds against the South Africans in which matches his average was 84.78. His aggregate for the season was 3,816, also a record.

Sixteen: J. B. Hobbs in 1925, when aged 42, played 16 three-figure innings in first-class matches. It was during this season that he exceeded the number of hundreds obtained in first-class cricket by W. G. Grace.

Fifteen: W. R. Hammond in 1938.

Fourteen: H. Sutcliffe in 1932.

Thirteen: G. Boycott in 1971, D. G. Bradman in 1938, C. B. Fry in 1901, W. R. Hammond in 1933 and 1937, T. W. Hayward in 1906, E. H. Hendren in 1923, 1927 and 1928, C. P. Mead in 1928, and H. Sutcliffe in 1928 and 1931.

MOST HUNDREDS IN A CAREER
(100 or More)

	Hundreds Total	Hundreds Abroad	100th 100		Hundreds Total	Hundreds Abroad	100th 100
J. B. Hobbs	197	22	1923	D. G. Bradman	117	41†	1947–48
E. H. Hendren	170	19	1928–29	Zaheer Abbas	108	70†	1982–83
W. R. Hammond	167	33	1935	M. C. Cowdrey	107	27	1973
C. P. Mead	153	8	1927	A. Sandham	107	20	1935
G. Boycott	151	27	1977	T. W. Hayward	104	4	1913
H. Sutcliffe	149	14	1932	J. H. Edrich	103	13	1977
F. E. Woolley	145	10	1929	G. M. Turner	103	85†	1982
L. Hutton	129	24	1951	L. E. G. Ames	102	13	1950
W. G. Grace	126	1	1895	D. L. Amiss	102	15	1986
D. C. S. Compton	123	31	1952	E. Tyldesley	102	8	1934
T. W. Graveney	122	31	1964				

† "Abroad" for D. G. Bradman is outside Australia; for Zaheer Abbas, outside Pakistan, for G. M. Turner, outside New Zealand.

E. H. Hendren and D. G. Bradman scored their 100th hundreds in Australia, Zaheer Abbas scored his in Pakistan. Zaheer Abbas and G. Boycott did so in Test matches.

1,000 RUNS IN A SEASON MOST TIMES
(Includes Overseas Tours and Seasons)

28 times: W. G. Grace 2,000 (6); F. E. Woolley 3,000 (1), 2,000 (12).
27 times: M. C. Cowdrey 2,000 (2); C. P. Mead 3,000 (2), 2,000 (9).
26 times: G. Boycott 2,000 (3); J. B. Hobbs 3,000 (1), 2,000 (16).
25 times: E. H. Hendren 3,000 (3), 2,000 (12).
24 times: D. L. Amiss 2,000 (3); W. G. Quaife 2,000 (1); H. Sutcliffe 3,000 (3), 2,000 (12).
23 times: A. Jones.
22 times: T. W. Graveney 2,000 (7); W. R. Hammond 3,000 (3), 2,000 (9).
21 times: D. Denton 2,000 (5); J. H. Edrich 2,000 (6); W. Rhodes 2,000 (2).
20 times: D. B. Close; K. W. R. Fletcher; G. Gunn; T. W. Hayward 3,000 (2), 2,000 (8); James Langridge 2,000 (1); J. M. Parks 2,000 (3); A. Sandham 2,000 (8); M. J. K. Smith 3,000 (1), 2,000 (5); C. Washbrook 2,000 (2).
19 times: J. W. Hearne 2,000 (4); G. H. Hirst 2,000 (3); D. Kenyon 2,000 (7); E. Tyldesley 3,000 (1), 2,000 (5); J. T. Tyldesley 3,000 (1), 2,000 (4).
18 times: L. G. Berry 2,000 (1); H. T. W. Hardinge 2,000 (5); R. E. Marshall 2,000 (6); P. A. Perrin; G. M. Turner 2,000 (3); R. E. S. Wyatt 2,000 (5).
17 times: L. E. G. Ames 3,000 (1), 2,000 (5); T. E. Bailey 2,000 (1); D. Brookes 2,000 (6); D. C. S. Compton 3,000 (1), 2,000 (5); L. Hutton 3,000 (1), 2,000 (8); J. G. Langridge 2,000 (11); M. Leyland 2,000 (3); K. G. Suttle 2,000 (1), Zaheer Abbas 2,000 (2).
16 times: D. G. Bradman 2,000 (4); D. E. Davies 2,000 (1); C. G. Greenidge 2,000 (1); E. G. Hayes 2,000 (2); C. A. Milton 2,000 (1); J. O'Connor 2,000 (4); C. T. Radley; James Seymour 2,000 (1).

15 times: G. Barker; K. F. Barrington 2,000 (3); E. H. Bowley 2,000 (4); M. H. Denness; A. E. Dipper 2,000 (5); H. E. Dollery 2,000 (2); W. J. Edrich 3,000 (1), 2,000 (8); J. H. Hampshire; P. Holmes 2,000 (7); Mushtaq Mohammad; R. B. Nicholls 2,000 (1); P. H. Parfitt 2,000 (3); W. G. A. Parkhouse 2,000 (1); B. A. Richards 2,000 (1); I. V. A. Richards 2,000 (1); J. D. Robertson 2,000 (9); G. S. Sobers; M. J. Stewart 2,000 (1).

NOTES: F. E. Woolley reached 1,000 runs in 28 consecutive seasons (1907–1938). C. P. Mead did so 27 seasons in succession (1906–1936).

Outside England, 1,000 runs in a season has been reached most times by D. G. Bradman (in 12 seasons in Australia).

Three batsmen have scored 1,000 runs in a season in each of four different countries: G. S. Sobers in West Indies, England, India and Australia; M. C. Cowdrey and G. Boycott in England, South Africa, West Indies and Australia.

35,000 RUNS IN A CAREER

Dates in italics denote the first half of an overseas season; i.e. *1945* denotes the 1945–46 season.

	Career	R	I	NO	HI	100s	Avge
J. B. Hobbs	1905–34	61,237	1,315	106	316*	197	50.65
F. E. Woolley	1906–38	58,969	1,532	85	305	145	40.75
E. H. Hendren	1907–38	57,611	1,300	166	301*	170	50.80
C. P. Mead	1905–36	55,061	1,340	185	280*	153	47.67
†W. G. Grace	1865–1908	54,896	1,493	105	344	126	39.55
W. R. Hammond	1920–51	50,551	1,005	104	336*	167	56.10
H. Sutcliffe	1919–45	50,138	1,088	123	313	149	51.95
G. Boycott	1962–86	48,426	1,014	162	261*	151	56.83
T. W. Graveney	1948–71	47,793	1,223	159	258	122	44.91
T. W. Hayward	1893–1914	43,551	1,138	96	315*	104	41.79
D. L. Amiss	1960–87	43,423	1,139	126	262*	102	42.86
M. C. Cowdrey	1950–76	42,719	1,130	134	307	107	42.89
A. Sandham	1911–37	41,284	1,000	79	325	107	44.82
L. Hutton	1934–60	40,140	814	91	364	129	55.51
M. J. K. Smith	1951–75	39,832	1,091	139	204	69	41.84
W. Rhodes	1898–1930	39,802	1,528	237	267*	58	30.83
J. H. Edrich	1956–78	39,790	979	104	310*	103	45.47
R. E. S. Wyatt	1923–57	39,405	1,141	157	232	85	40.04
D. C. S. Compton	1936–64	38,942	839	88	300	123	51.85
E. Tyldesley	1909–36	38,874	961	106	256*	102	45.46
J. T. Tyldesley	1895–1923	37,897	994	62	295*	86	40.66
K. W. R. Fletcher	1962–87	37,362	1,153	167	228*	63	37.89
J. W. Hearne	1909–36	37,252	1,025	116	285*	96	40.98
L. E. G. Ames	1926–51	37,248	951	95	295	102	43.51
D. Kenyon	1946–67	37,002	1,159	59	259	74	33.63
W. J. Edrich	1934–58	36,965	964	92	267*	86	42.39
J. M. Parks	1949–76	36,673	1,227	172	205*	51	34.76
D. Denton	1894–1920	36,479	1,163	70	221	69	33.37
G. H. Hirst	1891–1929	36,323	1,215	151	341	60	34.13
A. Jones	1957–83	36,049	1,168	72	204*	56	32.89
W. G. Quaife	1894–1928	36,012	1,203	185	255*	72	35.37
R. E. Marshall	*1945*–72	35,725	1,053	59	228*	68	35.94
G. Gunn	1902–32	35,208	1,061	82	220	62	35.96

† In recent years some statisticians have removed from W. G. Grace's record a number of matches which they consider not to have been first-class. The above figures are those which became universally accepted upon appearance in W. G. Grace's obituary in the Wisden of 1916. Some works of reference give his career record as being 54,211 – 1,478 – 104 – 344 – 124 – 39.45. These figures also appeared in the 1981 edition of Wisden.

TEST BATTING – HIGHEST AVERAGES
(Qualification: 20 innings)

Avge		T	I	NO	R	HI	100s
99.94	D. G. Bradman (A) ..	52	80	10	6,996	334	29
60.97	R. G. Pollock (SA) ..	23	41	4	2,256	274	7
60.83	G. A. Headley (WI) .	22	40	4	2,190	270*	10
60.73	H. Sutcliffe (E)	54	84	9	4,555	194	16
59.23	E. Paynter (E)	20	31	5	1,540	243	4
58.67	K. F. Barrington (E) .	82	131	15	6,806	256	20
58.61	E. D. Weekes (WI) ..	48	81	5	4,455	207	15
58.45	W. R. Hammond (E)	85	140	16	7,249	336*	22
57.78	G. S. Sobers (WI) ...	93	160	21	8,032	365*	26
56.94	J. B. Hobbs (E)	61	102	7	5,410	211	15
56.68	C. L. Walcott (WI) ..	44	74	7	3,798	220	15
56.67	L. Hutton (E)	79	138	15	6,971	364	19
55.00	E. Tyldesley (E)	14	20	2	990	122	3
54.35	Javed Miandad (P) ...	86	133	18	6,251	280*	15
54.20	C. A. Davis (WI)	15	29	5	1,301	183	4
53.86	G. S. Chappell (A) ...	87	151	19	7,110	247*	24
53.81	A. D. Nourse (SA) ..	34	62	7	2,960	231	9
52.80	A. R. Border (A)	89	157	26	6,917	196	21
52.61	I. V. A. Richards (WI)	88	131	8	6,472	291	20
52.17	M. Azharuddin (I) ...	21	31	3	1,461	199	6
51.62	J. Ryder (A)	20	32	5	1,394	201*	3
51.12	S. M. Gavaskar (I) ...	125	214	16	10,122	236*	34
50.06	D. C. S. Compton (E)	78	131	15	5,807	278	17

MOST WICKETS IN A MATCH

19–90	J. C. Laker	England v Australia at Manchester	1956
17–48	C. Blythe	Kent v Northamptonshire at Northampton	1907
17–50	C. T. B. Turner	Australians v England XI at Hastings	1888
17–54	W. P. Howell	Australians v Western Province at Cape Town	1902–03
17–56	C. W. L. Parker	Gloucestershire v Essex at Gloucester	1925
17–67	A. P. Freeman	Kent v Sussex at Hove	1922
17–89	W. G. Grace	Gloucestershire v Nottinghamshire at Cheltenham .	1877
17–89	F. C. L. Matthews	Nottinghamshire v Northants at Nottingham	1923
17–91	H. Dean	Lancashire v Yorkshire at Liverpool	1913
17–91	H. Verity	Yorkshire v Essex at Leyton	1933
17–92	A. P. Freeman	Kent v Warwickshire at Folkestone	1932
17–103	W. Mycroft	Derbyshire v Hampshire at Southampton	1876
17–106	G. R. Cox	Sussex v Warwickshire at Horsham	1926
17–106	T. W. Goddard	Gloucestershire v Kent at Bristol	1939
17–119	W. Mead	Essex v Hampshire at Southampton	1895
17–137	W. Brearley	Lancashire v Somerset at Manchester	1905
17–159	S. F. Barnes	England v South Africa at Johannesburg	1913–14
17–201	G. Giffen	South Australia v Victoria at Adelaide	1885–86
17–212	J. C. Clay	Glamorgan v Worcestershire at Swansea	1937

NOTES:
H. A. Arkwright took eighteen wickets for 96 runs in a 12-a-side match for Gentlemen of MCC v Gentlemen of Kent at Canterbury in 1861.

W. Mead took seventeen wickets for 205 runs for Essex v Australians at Leyton in 1893, the year before Essex were raised to first-class status.

F. P. Fenner took seventeen wickets for Cambridge Town Club v University of Cambridge at Cambridge in 1844.

100 WICKETS IN A SEASON MOST TIMES

(Includes Overseas Tours and Seasons)

23 times: W. Rhodes 200 wkts (3).
20 times: D. Shackleton (In successive seasons – 1949 to 1968 inclusive).
17 times: A. P. Freeman 300 wkts (1), 200 wkts (7).
16 times: T. W. Goddard 200 wkts (4), C. W. L. Parker 200 wkts (5), R. T. D. Perks, F. J. Titmus.
15 times: J. T. Hearne 200 wkts (3), G. H. Hirst 200 wkts (1), A. S. Kennedy 200 wkts (1).
14 times: C. Blythe 200 wkts (1), W. E. Hollies, G. A. R. Lock 200 wkts (2), M. W. Tate 200 wkts (3), J. C White.
13 times: J. B. Statham.
12 times: J. Briggs, E. G. Dennett 200 wkts (1), C. Gladwin, D. J. Shepherd, N. I. Thomson, F. S. Trueman.
11 times: A. V. Bedser, G. Geary, S. Haigh, J. C. Laker, M. S. Nichols, A. E. Relf.
10 times: W. Attewell, W. G. Grace, R. Illingworth, H. L. Jackson, V. W. C. Jupp, G G. Macaulay 200 wkts (1), W. Mead, T. B. Mitchell, T. Richardson 200 wkts (3), J. Southerton 200 wkts (1), R. K. Tyldesley, D. L. Underwood, J. H. Wardle, T. G. Wass, D. V. P. Wright.
9 times: W. E. Astill, T. E. Bailey, W. E. Bowes, C. Cook, R. Howorth, J. Mercer, A. W. Mold 200 wkts (2), J. Newman, C. F. Root 200 wkts (1), A. Shaw 200 wkts (1), H. Verity 200 wkts (3).
8 times: T. W. Cartwright, H. Dean, J. A. Flavell, A. R. Gover 200 wkts (2), H. Larwood, G. A. Lohmann 200 wkts (3), R. Peel, J. M. Sims, F. A. Tarrant, R. Tattersall, G. J. Thompson, G. E. Tribe, A. W. Wellard, F. E. Woolley, J. A. Young.

2,000 WICKETS IN A CAREER

Dates in italics denote the first half of an overseas season; i.e. *1970* denotes the 1970-71 season.

	Career	W	R	Avge
W. Rhodes	1898–1930	4,187	69,993	16.71
A. P. Freeman	1914–36	3,776	69,577	18.42
C. W. L. Parker	1903–35	3,278	63,817	19.46
J. T. Hearne	1888–1923	3,061	54,352	17.75
T. W. Goddard	1922–52	2,979	59,116	19.84
†W. G. Grace	1865–1908	2,876	51,545	17.92
A. S. Kennedy	1907–36	2,874	61,034	21.23
D. Shackleton	1948–69	2,857	53,303	18.65
G. A. R. Lock	1946–70	2,844	54,709	19.23
F. J. Titmus	1949–82	2,830	63,313	22.37
M. W. Tate	1912–37	2,784	50,571	18.16
G. H. Hirst	1891–1929	2,739	51,282	18.72
C. Blythe	1899–1914	2,506	42,136	16.81
D. L. Underwood	1963–87	2,465	49,993	20.28
W. E. Astill	1906–39	2,431	57,783	23.76
J. C. White	1909–37	2,356	43,759	18.57
W. E. Hollies	1932–57	2,323	48,656	20.94
F. S. Trueman	1949–69	2,304	42,154	18.29
J. B. Statham	1950–68	2,260	36,995	16.36
R. T. D. Perks	1930–55	2,233	53,770	24.07
J. Briggs	1879–1900	2,221	35,430	15.95
D. J. Shepherd	1950–72	2,218	47,302	21.32
E. G. Dennett	1903–26	2,147	42,571	19.82
T. Richardson	1892–1905	2,104	38,794	18.43
T. E. Bailey	1945–67	2,082	48,170	23.13
R. Illingworth	1951–83	2,072	42,023	20.28
F. E. Woolley	1906–38	2,068	41,066	19.85
G. Geary	1912–38	2,063	41,339	20.03
D. V. P. Wright	1932–57	2,056	49,307	23.98
N. Gifford	1960–87	2,037	47,755	23.44
J. Newman	1906–30	2,032	51,111	25.15
‡A. Shaw	1864–97	2,027	24,579	12.12
S. Haigh	1895–1913	2,012	32,091	15.94

† In recent years some statisticians have removed from W. G. Grace's record a number of matches which they consider not to have been first-class. The above figures are those which became universally accepted upon appearance in W. G. Grace's obituary in the Wisden of 1916. Some works of reference gave his career record as being 2,809 – 50,999 – 18.15 (these figures also appeared in the 1981 edition of Wisden), and subsequently it has been amended to 2,808 – 50,982 – 18.15.
‡ The figures for A. Shaw exclude one wicket for which no analysis is available.

TEST MATCH BOWLING – MOST WICKETS IN A SERIES

	T	R	W	Avge		
S. F. Barnes	4	536	49	10.93	England v South Africa	1913–14
J. C. Laker	5	442	46	9.60	England v Australia	1956
C. V. Grimmett	5	642	44	14.59	Australia v South Africa	1935–36
T. M. Alderman	6	893	42	21.26	Australia v England	1981
R. M. Hogg	6	527	41	12.85	Australia v England	1978–79
Imran Khan	6	558	40	13.95	Pakistan v India	1982–83
A. V. Bedser	5	682	39	17.48	England v Australia	1953
D. K. Lillee	6	870	39	22.30	Australia v England	1981
M. W. Tate	5	881	38	23.18	England v Australia	1924–25
W. J. Whitty	5	632	37	17.08	Australia v South Africa	1910–11
H. J. Tayfield	5	636	37	17.18	South Africa v England	1956–57
A. E. E. Vogler	5	783	36	21.75	South Africa v England	1909–10
A. A. Mailey	5	946	36	26.27	Australia v England	1920–21
G. A. Lohmann	3	203	35	5.80	England v South Africa	1895–96
B. S. Chandrasekhar	5	662	35	18.91	India v England	1972–73

SEASON DOUBLES

2,000 Runs and 200 Wickets

1906	G. H. Hirst	2,385 runs and 208 wickets

3,000 Runs and 100 Wickets

1937	J. H. Parks	3,003 runs and 101 wickets

2,000 Runs and 100 Wickets

	Season	R	W		Season	R	W
W. G. Grace	1873	2,139	106	F. E. Woolley	1914	2,272	125
W. G. Grace	1876	2,622	129	J. W. Hearne	1920	2,148	142
C. L. Townsend	1899	2,440	101	V. W. C. Jupp	1921	2,169	121
G. L. Jessop	1900	2,210	104	F. E. Woolley	1921	2,101	167
G. H. Hirst	1904	2,501	132	F. E. Woolley	1922	2,022	163
G. H. Hirst	1905	2,266	110	F. E. Woolley	1923	2,091	101
W. Rhodes	1909	2,094	141	L. F. Townsend	1933	2,268	100
W. Rhodes	1911	2,261	117	D. E. Davies	1937	2,012	103
F. A. Tarrant	1911	2,030	111	James Langridge	1937	2,082	101
J. W. Hearne	1913	2,036	124	T. E Bailey	1959	2,011	100
J. W. Hearne	1914	2,116	123				

1,000 Runs and 200 Wickets

	Season	R	W		Season	R	W
A. E. Trott	1899	1,175	239	M. W. Tate	1923	1,168	219
A. E. Trott	1900	1,337	211	M. W. Tate	1924	1,419	205
A. S. Kennedy	1922	1,129	205	M. W. Tate	1925	1,290	228

1,000 Runs and 100 Wickets

Sixteen times: W. Rhodes. **Fourteen times:** G. H. Hirst.
Ten times: V. W. C. Jupp. **Nine times:** W. E. Astill.

Eight times: T. E. Bailey, W. G. Grace, M. S. Nichols, A. E. Relf, F. A. Tarrant, M. W. Tate†, F. J. Titmus, F. E. Woolley.
Seven times: G. E. Tribe.
Six times: P. G. H. Fender, R. Illingworth, James Langridge.
Five times: J. W. H. T. Douglas, J. W. Hearne, A. S. Kennedy, J. Newman.
Four times: E. G. Arnold, J. Gunn, R. Kilner, B. R. Knight.
Three times: W. W. Armstrong (Australians), L. C. Braund, G. Giffen (Australians), N. E. Haig, R. Howorth, C. B. Llewellyn, J. B. Mortimore, Ray Smith, S. G. Smith, L. F. Townsend, A. W. Wellard.

† M. W. Tate also scored 1,193 runs and took 116 wickets for MCC in first-class matches on the 1926-27 MCC tour of India and Ceylon.

NOTE:
R. J. Hadlee in 1984 was the first player to perform the feat since the reduction of County Championship matches. A complete list of those performing the feat before then will be found on p. 202 of the 1982 Wisden.

WICKET-KEEPING – MOST DISMISSALS IN A SEASON

128 (79ct, 49st)	L. E. G. Ames	Kent	1929
122 (70ct, 52st)	L. E. G. Ames	Kent	1928
110 (63ct, 47st)	H. Yarnold	Worcestershire	1949
107 (77ct, 30st)	G. Duckworth	Lancashire	1928
107 (96ct, 11st)	J. G. Binks	Yorkshire	1960
104 (40ct, 64st)	L. E. G. Ames	Kent	1932
104 (82ct, 22st)	J. T. Murray	Middlesex	1957
102 (69ct, 33st)	F. H. Huish	Kent	1913
102 (95ct, 7st)	J. T. Murray	Middlesex	1960
101 (62ct, 39st)	F. H. Huish	Kent	1911
101 (85ct, 16st)	R. Booth	Worcestershire	1960
100 (91ct, 9st)	R. Booth	Worcestershire	1964

MOST CATCHES IN A SEASON

78	W. R. Hammond	1928		65	D. W. Richardson	1961
77	M. J. Stewart	1957		64	K. F. Barrington	1957
73	P. M. Walker	1961		64	G. A. R. Lock	1957
71	P. J. Sharpe	1962		63	J. Tunnicliffe	1896
70	J. Tunnicliffe	1901		63	J. Tunnicliffe	1904
69	J. G. Langridge	1955		63	K. J. Grieves	1950
69	P. M. Walker	1960		63	C. A. Milton	1956
66	J. Tunnicliffe	1895		61	J. V. Wilson	1955
65	W. R. Hammond	1925		61	M. J. Stewart	1958
65	P. M. Walker	1959				

NOTE:
The most catches by a fielder since the reduction of County Championship matches in 1969 is 49 by C. J. Tavaré in 1979.

100 WICKETS IN A SEASON OUTSIDE ENGLAND

W		Season	Country	R	Avge
116	M. W. Tate	1926-27	India/Ceylon	1,599	13.78
107	Ijaz Faqih	1985-86	Pakistan	1,719	16.06
106	C. T. B. Turner	1887-88	Australia	1,441	13.59
106	R. Benaud	1957-58	South Africa	2,056	19.39
104	S. F. Barnes	1913-14	South Africa	1,117	10.74
103	Abdul Qadir	1982-83	Pakistan	2,367	22.98

INDEX

Page numbers in italics refer to illustrations

Abdul Qadir 382, 383
Abel, R., 29, 65, 68
Alderman, T. M. 348, 349, 352, 354
Alexander, F. C. M., 270
Alexander, R. H. I. G., 95
Allen, G. O., 156, 158
Alletson, E. B., 99; *100*, obituary 285; *285*
Alley, W. E., 279
Allott, P. J. W., 353–4
Allsopp, A., 141
Ames, L. E. G., 157, 158, 162, 178, 179, 182, 191, 206; *182*
Amiss, D. L., 302, 310, 312, 313, 320, 321; *311*
Andrews, T. J. E., 118, 119
Appleyard, R., 235
Archer, R. G., 229, 231
Armstrong, W. W., 75, 76, 83, 84, 118, 119
Arnold, E., 82
Ashes, the *11*
Ashton, H., 118
Asif Iqbal 301, 302
Asif Masood 302
Athey, C. W. J., 385
Atkinson, D., 260
Australian XI (1878) *30*
Australian XI (1964) *288*

Bader, Sir D., 359
Bailey, T. E., 207, 230, 231, 235, 238, 259, 314
Bairstow, D. L., 335
Balderstone, J. C., 320
Banerjee, S., 193; *194*
Banks, E.,
 obituary 92
Bardsley, W., 118, 199
Barnes, S. F., 59, 102, 105, 126–7, 133, 163, 249, 307; *107*
Barnes, S. G., 172, 174, 207, 211, 213; *207*
Barnett, B. A., 174
Barnett, C. J., 181, 201
Barnsley, W., 288
Barratt, E., 244
Barrington, K. F., 283, 288, 289, 290; *257*
 obituary 342–4; *342*
Bartholomew, A. C., obituary 186
Bartlett, E. L., *135*
Bates, W. E., 317
Beal, C. W., obituary 121; *120*
Beal, J., 121
Bedser, A. V., 196, 198–9, 203, 211, 212, 213, 225, 228, 275
Bedser, E. A., 223
Bellamy, B., 142
Benaud, R., 238, 251, 270
Bengough, C. W., 26–7
Bennett, N. H., 195

Benskin, W. E., 114
Bensted, E. C., 141
Berry, R., 223
Bestwick, W., 148; *121*
Bhandarkar, K. V., 316
Blackham, J. McC., 111
Blenkiron, W., 316
Blythe, C., 59, 89, 90, 181; *96*
Bodyline bowling 156, 293, 356, 357; *157*
Bolus, J. B., 294
Bond, J. D., 303
Bonnor, G. J., 140 obituary 104–5; *104*
Boon, D. C. 385
Booth, B. C., 289
Border, A. R., 351, 353, 354, 359, 361, 379, 383, 385; *385*
Bosanquet, B. J. T., 80, 82, 84; *80*
Boswell, W. G. K., 94
Botham, I. T., 278–9, 334, 335, 336, 337, 338, 344, 345, 346–7, 348, 349, 351, 352, 353, 354, 355, 359, 361, 368–9, 370, 371, 372, 373, 379; *346, 350, 353, 377*
Bowden, J. 121
Bowden-Smith, W., 27
Bowes, W. E., 153, 160, 161, 174
Bowley, E. H., 125, 357
Box, T., 19; *19*
Boyce, K. D., 318
Boycott, G., 277, 290, 297, 298, 309, 311, 313, 314, 335, 347, 348, 349, 351, 354; *376, 387*
Bradman, D. G., 60, 140–1, 147–8, 150, 158, 160, 161, 162, 171, 173, 174, 177, 183, 198, 199, 207, 211–2, 213, 257, 262, 265, 293, 324, 357, 366, 372, 375; *141, 149, 161, 163, 172, 387*
Brann, G., 71
Braund, L. C., 71, 76, 78, 79, 90
Breakwell, D., 345
Brearley, J. M., 278, 346, 347, 349, 351, 355; *304*
Briggs, J., 29; *28*
Bright, R. J., 348, 349
Broad, B. C., 379
Brooks, E. W. J., 195
Brown, G., 101, 123; *123*
Brown, J. T., 46, 65–6, 109–10, 151; *46*
Brown, S. M., 204
Brown, W. A., 160, 171–2, 174, 207, 210, 211
Bryan, G. J., 125
Buller, J. S., *257*
Burge, P. J., 289, 290
Butcher, A. R., 334, 335
Butcher, B. F., 283
Butler, S. E., 139

Cadman, S., 121
Calthorpe, F. S. G., *124*
Campbell, R. C., 159
Cardus, Sir N., 15, 58

Carlin, J., 70
Carter, H., 118
Cartwright, T. W., 288, 289
Cazenove, Canon, obituary 35
Chalk, F. G. H., 168
Chapman, A. P. F., 149, 227
Chappell, G. S., 309, 318, 341, 361; *340*
Chappell, I. M., 309, 318
Chappell, T. M., 340, 341, 347
Cheetham, A. G., 192
Chipperfield, A. G., 160
Clark, T. H., 245, 247
Clarke, S. T., 363
Clinton, G. S., 363
Close, D. B., 260, 285; *282*
Coe, S., 115
Cole, F. L., obituary 186–7
Collins, A., 68
Collins, A. E. J., obituary 108
Compton, D. C. S., 173, 182, 183, 198, 199, 201, 203, 204, 205–6, 209, 210–11, 212, 217, 219, 230, 231, 235, 259, 275, 301, 324, 375; *202, 205, 209, 214*
Constable, B., 245, 263
Constantine, L., 134; *135*
Cook G., 360
Cooper, E., 166
Cotter, A., 82, 84
Cowans, N. G., 361
Cowdrey, M. C., 197, 237, 238, 250, 259, 260, 272–3, 275, 283, 284, 297, 302, 351, 354
Craig, I. D., 251
Crapp, J. F., 164
Crawford, P., 246
Crawford, V. F. S., 68
Crawley, L. G., 153
Croome, A. C. M., 12
Crowd trouble 17, 24–5, 43, 149–50, 156, 212, 262, 275, 279, 320, 347

Dalton, E. L., 177, 178
Darling, J., 50, 76, 82, 84
Davidson, A. K., 230, 231, 270; *271*
Davies, J. G. W., 206
Dawson, O. C., 202, 203
de Courcy, J. H., 231
DeFreitas, P. A. J., 385
Denness, M. H., 311
Dennett, G., 87, 93
Denton, D., 70
Dewes, J. G., 316
Dexter, E. R., 267, 277, 283, 286, 287, 290; *267*
Dilley, G. R., 348
Dipper, A. G., 101, 127, 137
Doggart, G. H. G., 316
D'Oliveira, B. L., 302, 309
  South African Tour affair 276
Douglas, J. W. H. T., 102
Doyle, Sir A. Conan, obituary 146; *146*
Drake, E. T., *30*
Ducat, A., 132, 189; *189*

Drake, E. T., *30*
Ducat, A., 132, 189; *189*
Duckworth, G., 149
Duff, R. A., 75, 82, 84
Duleepsinhji, K. S., 142, 148, 150; *143*
Dyer, R. I. H. B., 369
Dyson, J., 347, 352, 354, 361

East, D. E., 370; *370*
Ebeling, H., 322
Eden Gardens, Calcutta *386*
Edgar, B. A., 341
Edmonds, P. H., 379, 380
Edrich, J. H., 283, 290, 309; *277*
Edrich, W. J., 176, 178, 179, 182, 191, 192, 198, 199, 201, 202, 203, 204, 206, 209, 212, 217, 226, 229, 231–2; *176, 209*
  obituary 374–5, 378
Edwards, R., 307
Eligon, D., obituary 166
Elliott, C. S., *257*
Elliott, H., 121
Emburey, J. E., 339, 351, 372, 373, 379, 380, 383
Emmett, G. M., 217–8
Emmett, T., 23
England XI (1912) *97*
England XI (1921) *119*
Eton XI (1872) *16*
Eton XI (1910) *95*
Evans, E., 23
Evans, T. G., 199, 211, 212, 230, 238, 239, 250
Everett, S. C., 141

Fagg, A., 168; *145*
Falcon, M., 118
Fargus, A. H. C., obituary 108; *108*
Farnes, K., 177, 178, 183, obituary 187–8; *187*
Faulkner, G. A., 89, 90, 118
Favell, L., 273
Fazal Mahmood 235, 262
Fender, P. G. H., 114, 117, 129, 195, 323–4, 364
Fernandes, P., 134
Ferreira, A. M., 367
Ferris, J. J., 36
Field, E., 80
Fingleton, J. H. W., 158, 171, 202
  obituary 356–7; *356*
Fishlock, L. B., 193
Fleetwood-Smith, L. O'B., 172, 174
Fletcher, K. W. R., 363
Foster, F. R., 102
Foster, N. A., 362–3, 385
Foster, R. E., 65, 66, 78–9, 89, 90, 147, 173; *62, 80*
Fowler, G., 361, 365
Fowler, R. St.L., 94, 95; *95*
Fredericks, R. C., 311, 314, 318, 320
Freeman, A. P., 125; *125, 145*
Fry, C. B., 44, 58, 63, 66, 68, 71, 72, 80, 82, 89, 101, 129; *44, 64, 68, 100*
  obituary 253–5, 256; *253*

Gainford, Lord, obituary 190
Gandar-Dower, K. C., obituary 190
Garner, J., 279, 345
Gatting, M. W., 351, 373, 382-3, 385, *385*
Gavaskar, S. M., 334, 335, 336, 382, 383; *278, 335*
Ghavri, K. D., 339
Gibb, P. A., 177, 178, 179
Gibbons, H. H., 166
Gibbs, L. R., 314
Gibson, C. H., 119
Giffen, G., 32, 37; *32, 37*
Gifford, N., 309, 327; *304*
Gilchrist, R., 259
Gilligan, A. H. H., 142
Gimblett, H., 216, obituary 331
Gladwin, C., 219
Gloucestershire XI (1877) *20*
Gloucestershire XI (1897) *34*
Goddard, J. D., 227, 260
Goddard, T. W., 180-1
Gomez, G. E., 226
Gooch, G. A., 335, 343, 347, 349, 370, 372, 373, 382, 385; *381*
Goodwin, D. E., 296
Goodwin, V., 141
Gover, A. R., 193
Gower, D. I., 349, 354, 360, 364-5, 372, 373, 382
Grace, E. M., 20, 78, 113; *31*
Grace, G. F., 105, 113
Grace, W. G., 12, 15, 20, 35-6, 58-9, 111-4, 128, 164, 190, 371; *36, 42, 49, 111*
Grace, W. G. Jnr, *36*
Graham, O. B., 95
Graveney, T. W., 235, 273
Greenidge, C. G., 320, 382, 383
Gregory, D. W., 131, 322
Gregory, J. M., 118, 119, 372
Gregory, R. J., 193, 195
Gregory, S. E., 84, 288
Greig, A. W., 309, 313, 314, 320; *326*
Grieves, K., 286
Grieveson, R. E., 177, 178-9
Griffith, C. C., 283, 284
Grimmett, C. V., 160
Grout, A. W. T., 270, 370
Gul Mahomed 193
Gunn, J., 82
Gunn, W., 66

Hadlee, R. J., 341, 383
Haig, N., 134
Haigh, S., 70; *69*
Hall, W. W., 270, 283, 284
Hallam, M. R., 286
Hammond, J. R., 300
Hammond, W. R., 60, 127, 135-6, 137, 147, 148-9, 150, 157, 158, 160, 161, 164, 171, 172, 173, 174, 176, 177, 178, 179, 181, 182, 188, 191, 192, 198, 259, 290, 333; *137, 166*

Hanif Mohammad 235, 236, 265; *266*
Hardinge, H. T. W., 125
Hardstaff, J., 164, 171, 173, 174, 198, 212; *172*
Hargreaves, T. K., obituary 244
Harper, R. A., 373, 382, 383
Harris, Lord 24, 25, 59-60, 170; *24*
Harris, C. B., 164
Harris, T. A., 202
Harvey, M., 199, 213
Harvey, R. N., 238, 251
Hassett, A. L., 174, 191, 192, 199, 212, 213, 229, 231
Hathorn, M., 90
Hawke, Lord 60, 170
Hawke, N., 324
Hayes, F. C., 312
Haynes, D. L., 337, 372, 373, 383
Hayward, T. W., 65, 66, 75, 79, 82, 83, 89, 129, 375
Headley, G. A., 226
  obituary 366-7
Headley, R. G. A., 367
Hearne, J. W., 116, 134, 272
Hedley, W. C., 56
Hemingway, G. E.,
  obituary 85
Hemmings, E. E., 316
Hemsley, E. J. O., 328
Hendren, E. H., 117, 129, 132, 134, 160, 162, 195-6; *215*, obituary 272
Hendrick, M., 335
Hewett, H. T., 43
Higgins, J. B., 137
Hill, C., 37, 50, 76, 79, 82, 84
Hillyard, J. M., 94, 95
Hilton, J., 243
Hirst, G. H., 59, 70, 75, 76, 79, 82, 89, 354; *69*
Hobbs, J. B., 59, 60, 102, 114, 128-9, 131-2, 136, 148, 149, 150, 173, 272, 317; *97, 102, 103, 116, 128, 133, 387*
Holder, V. A., 328
Holding, M. A., 318, 319, 320
Hole, G. B., 229
Hollies, W. E., 223
Holmes, E. R. T., 129, 131, 204
Holmes, P., 151, 153, 155; *151, 152, 332*
Hookes, D. W., 324, 361
Hopkins, V. J., 164
Hopley, G. W. V., 94
Hopwood, J. L., 160, 161, 166
Howell, H., *124*
Hughes, D. P., 303; *306*
Hughes, K. J., 347, 351, 353, 354, 355, 361
Hunt, G., 129
Hunte, C. C., 262, 270, 282
Hurwood, A., 141
Hutton, L., 171, 172, 173, 174, 178, 179, 182, 185, 191, 198, 199, 201, 203, 212, 223, 225, 226, 227, 229, 230, 231, 238, 262, 263, 337; *172, 184*

Ibadullah, K., 315
Iddon, J., 166
Illingworth, R., 297, 309
Imran Khan 383
Inshan Ali 314
Inverarity, R. J., 300
Iremonger, J., 70
Irvine, J. T., 300

Jackson, F. S., 76, 82, 84, 227; *42*
Jackson, G. R., 121
Jackson, P. F., 166
Jameson, J. A., 311, 315–6; *316*
Jameson, T. O., 94, 95
Jardine, D. R., 129, 132, 156, 157, 195, 196, 290
Jarvis, A. H., 37
Javed Miandad 382
Jenkins, R. O., 219, 225, 226
Jessop, G. L., 40, 59, 62, 66, 72, 75, 76, 83, 87, 93, 101, 279; *59, 62, 74, 77, 92* obituary 240–2
Johnson, I. W., 199, 207, 238, 245
Johnson, P. R., 129
Johnston, W. A., 211, 212, 213, 230, 231
Jones, A. O., 70, 82, 84
Jones, D. M., 379
Jones, S. P., 121
Julien, B. D., 311, 314, 318

Kallicharran, A. I., 314, 318, 358
Kanhai, R. B., 259, 282, 297, 298, 311, 313, 314, 315–6; *316*
Kapil Dev 334, 339, 383
Kardar, A. H., 262
Keeton, W. W., 160, 161
Kent, M. F., 341, 354
Khalid Hassan 235
Khan Mohammad 262
King, B. P., 166
King, J. B., obituary 292
Kippax, A. F., 141, 148
Kitcat, S. A. P., 26–7; *26*
Knight, A. E., 14, 63; *64*
Knight, B. R., 324
Knight, D. J., 129
Knight, R. D. V., 363
Knight, W. H., 9–10
Knott, A. P. E., 301, 302, 309, 312, 314, 320, 321, 347
Knox, N. A., 89

Laker, J. C., 185, 211, 223, 230, 231, 244–5, 248–9, 250, 251, 260, 275, 307, 314; *245, 247, 249*
Lamb, A. J., 360, 385
Lancashire XI (1881) *48*
Lancashire XI (1895) *40*
Langridge, James 216
Langridge, John 216
Larwood, H., 148, 156, 157, 158, 324; *157*

Laver, F., 82
Lawry, W. M., 288, 289
Lawson, G. F., 361
Lee, H. W., 116, 117
Leeston-Smith, F. A., obituary 78
Lever, P., 297, 298
Leyland, M., 148, 156, 157, 158, 162, 171, 172, 173, 201
Lightfoot, A., 264
Lillee, D. K., 307, 309, 318, 324, 325, 347, 348, 349, 352, 353, 354, 372; *304, 387*
Lilley, A. A., 66, 75, 76, 82
Lillywhite, Fred, 8
Lindwall, R. R., 198, 199, 211, 212, 229, 230, 231, 239, 246
Lister, W. H. L., 166
Littlejohn, E. S., 86
Livsey, W. H., 123; *123*
Llewellyn, M. J., 327
Lloyd, C. H., 279, 298, 312, 314, 318, 320; *376*
Lloyd, D., 303
Loader, P. J., 245, 324
Lock, G. A. R., 230, 231, 246, 247, 250–1, 260, 324
Lockwood, W. H., 68, 76, 110
Lohmann, G., 249
London County 58, 113
Lord, T., *52*
Lord's Cricket Ground *48-9*
Loxton, S. J., 207
Luckhurst, B. W., 298, 301, 302, 309
Lyon, B. H., 137
Lyons, J. J., 32, 140

Macartney, C. G., 118, 147
MacBryan, J. C. W., 129
McCabe, S. J., 141, 148, 161, 172, 174; *149* obituary 292–3; *292*
McCool, C. L., 324
McCosker, R. B., 324
McDermott, C. J., 385
McDonald, C. C., 244, 251
McDonald, E. A., 118
McIntyre, A. J., 204, 264
McKenzie, G. D., 288, 290, 297
McKenzie, R. T. H., 87
MacLaren, A. C., 39, 50, 58, 76, 82, 83–4, 118, 119, 174; *40, 119, 144*
Maddocks, L., 237, 238
Mailey, A. A., 119
Mankad, A. V., 259
Mankad, V. M. H., 337
Mann, F. C., 205
Manners, J. N., 94
Manning, Cardinal, obituary 33
Maqsood Ahmed 235, 236
Marks, V. J., 345
Marner, P., 286
Marsh, G. R., 379, 380, 385
Marsh, R. W., 309, 318, 324, 341, 347, 354, 361

Marshall, M. D., 373, 383
Martin, F., 307
Martin, F. R., 134
Massie, R. A. L., 307, 309; *308*
Matthews, G. R. J., 379
May, P. B. H., 229, 231, 235, 236, 237, 238, 246, 247, 250, 259, 260, 275, 337; *256*
Mead, C. P., 105, 173
Mead, W., 52
Meckiff, I., 270; *269*
Melville, A., 177, 178, 179, 201, 202, 357
Menzies, Sir R., 357
Merchant, V. M., 193, 334; *214*
Middlesex XI (1912) 97
Miller, G., 320, 321, 359; *360*
Miller, K. R., 192, 199, 207, 210, 211, 212, 213, 230, 231, 238, 244; *211*, *257*
Miller, N., 68
Minor Counties Cricket Association 159
Mitchell, B., 177, 178, 202, 203
Moberley, W. O., 20
Moore, R. H., 171
Morris, A. R., 198, 199, 229
Mortimore, J. B., 289, 303
Moseley, H. R., 345
Mounteney, A., 114
Murdoch, W., 23, 24
Murray, D. L., 313, 314, 318
Mushtaq Ali 334
Mushtaq Mohammad 301, 302

Nash, M. A., 294
Nasim-ul-Ghani 262
Nawab of Pataudi 334
Nayudu, C. S., 193, 259
Neale, W. L., 164
Neville, Lord H., 22
Newson, E. S., 178, 179
Nichols, M. S., 153
Nimbalkar, B. B., 316
Noble, M. A., 75, 76, 78, 82, 84, 227
Nourse, A. D., 177, 178, 201, 202
Nutter, A., 166

Oates, T., 148
O'Brien, T. C., 109
O'Connor, J., 153
O'Gorman, Dave, *317*
O'Gorman, J. G., obituary 317; *317*
Old, C. M., 312, 348, 350, 351
Oldfield, W. A., 156, 157
O'Neill, N. C., 270, 289
O'Reilly, W. J., 160, 172, 173, 174
"O'Reilly leg-trap" 356
O'Riordan, A. J., 296
Ormrod, J. A., 329
Oscroft, W., 17–18
O'Shaughnessy, S. J., 364, 365; *365*

Packer affair 276–7
Palairet, L. C. H., 71

Palmer, K. E., 279
Pardon, Charles F., 10, obituary 32
Pardon, Sydney 10
Park, J. H., 375
Parker, C., 93, 127, 135, 136, 137; *86*, *128*
Parker, J. M., 341
Parkhouse, W. G. A., 226
Parks, H. W., 216
Parks, J. M., 283, 290
Pataudi, Jnr., Nawab of, 334
Paynter, E., 156, 173, 177, 178, 179, 188
Pearce, T. N., 168, 207
Pease, J. A. P., 190
Peel, R., *30*
Pepper, C. G., 191, 192
Perks, R. T. D., 177, 178
Phillip, N., 362–3; *363*
Phillips, J., 258
Phillipson, W. E., 166; *166*
Pickett, H., obituary 91–2
Pilch, F., 113
Pilling, H., 303
Pinder, G., *19*
Platts, J., obituary 45
Pocock, P. I., 312
Pollock, R. G., 297–8; *298*
Ponsford, W. H., 156–7, 158, 160–1, 259, 262
Poore, R. M., 55, 56; *56* obituary 170–1; *170*
Pougher, A. D., 33
Poynton, F. J., 27
Price, C. F., 192
Price, J. S. E., 289, 309
Pringle, D. R., 361
Procter, M. J., 279, 298, 303, 328, 329; *305*
Pycroft, J., obituary 37

Quaife, B. W., 137
Quaife, W. G., 121; *121*

Rae, A. F., 225
Ramadhin, S., 184, 224, 225, 226, 259, 260, 288; *225*
Randall, D. W., 324, 325; *323*
Ranjitsinhji, K. S., 50, 60, 63, 68, 71, 142, 254–5, 258, 290; *31*
Rattigan, Sir T., obituary 330
Rayment, A. W. H., 243
Reay, G. M., 115
records 388–93
Reid, B. A., 379
Relf, A. E., 79, 105
Relf, R., 99
Rhodes, W., 52, 59, 66, 70, 75, 76, 79, 82, 84, 90, 102, 105, 173, 285, 354, 361; *53*, *69*, *102*
Rice, C. E. B., 382, 383
Rice, W. I., obituary 240
Richards, B. A., 299–300; *301*
Richards, C. J., 379
Richards, G., 327

Richards, I. V. A., 279, 320, 337, 367, 371, 372, 373; *367, 372, 377*
Richardson, P. E., 250, 280
Richardson, T., 33, 59, 68; *49*
Richardson, V. Y., 156, 157, 158
Roberts, A. M. E., 318
Roberts, H. E., 125
Robertson, J. D., 191, 192, 204, 206, 221–2; 357; *214*
Robins, R. W. V., 192, 222
Robinson, F. G., 108
Robinson, R. T., 373, 385
Roebuck, P. M., 345
Rose, B. C., 279, 345
Rowan, A. M. B., 203
Rowan, E. A., 178
Rowe, L. G., 311, 313, 314
Roy, P., 259
Rushby, T., 114, 115
Russell, S. E., 280
Rutherford, J. W., 324
Ryder, J., 118–9, 323

Saggers, R. A., 207
Salmon, G. H., 114
Sandham, A., 114, 117, 129, 132, 136, 259, 317; *197*
Sarwate, C. T., 193; *194*
Saunders, J. V., 76
Shackleton, D., 243, 282, 283–4; *242*
Shastri, R. J., 383
Shaw, A., 131, 140
Sheppard, D. S., 236, 250
Shirley, W. R., 123
Shrewsbury, A., 17–18, 70, 109
Simmons, J., 303
Simpson, R. B., 287, 288, 289, 290, 291, 299; *289*
Simpson, R. T., 219, 235
Sims, J., 222
Sinclair, J. H., 90
Sinfield, R. A., 137
Skeet, C. H. L., 117
Slack, W. N., 372, 373
Small, G. C., 378–9, 385
Small, J. A., *135*
Smith, C. Aubrey 220–1; *220*
Smith, E. J., 324
Smith, M. J. K., 309
Smith, O. G., 259, 260
Smith, P. A., 367
Smith, R., 168
Smith, T. P. B., 207
Snedden, M. C., 341
Snooke, S. J., 90
Snow, J. A., 298, 309
Sobers, G. A., 262, 263, 270, 273, 279, 282, 289, 294, 297, 298, 311, 314, 320, 337; *269, 271, 277, 294*
Solomon, J., 270
Southerton, J., 131, 140

Spofforth, F. R., 23, 111
  obituary 131; *131*
Spooner, R. T., 223
Squires, H. S., 195, 204
Stackpole, K. R., 309
Stanford, R. M., 192
Staples, A., 164
Statham, J. B., 185, 236, 237, 238, 239, 275; *282*
Steel, A. I., 95
Steele, D. S., 320
Stephenson, H. W., 243
Stephenson, J. W. A., 191, 192
Stewart, M. J., 263
Stoddart, A. E., 58, obituary 109–10; *109*
Strudwick, H., *189*
Subba Row, R., 264; *264*
Summers, G., 45
Surridge, W. S., 245, 337
Sussex XI (1909) *96*
Sutcliffe, H., 148, 149, 150, 151, 152, 153, 155, 157, 170, 324; *151, 152*

Tallon, D., 199
Tarrant, F. A., 86
Tate, M. W., 142, 148, 149, 229, 337; *256*
Tavaré, C. J., 353, 354, 359, 360, 361; *360*
Taylor, M. N., 294
Taylor, R. W., 338–9, 347, 361
Test Matches
  England v New South Wales (1879) 23–6
  England v South Africa (1889) 29
  England v South Australia (1895) 37–8
  England v Australia (1898) 50–1; *51*
  England v Australia (1902) 75–7
  England v Australia (1903) 78–80
  England v Australia (1905) 82–5
  England v South Africa (1907) 88–91
  England v Australia (1912) 102–4; *103*
  MCC v South Africa (1913) 105–6; *106*
  England v Australia (1926) *144*
  England v Australia (1930) 147–50; *147*
  England v Australia (1933) 156–9
  England v Australia (1934) 160–3
  England v Australia (1938) 171–5
  South Africa v England (1939) 176–80
  England v Australia (1947) 198–200
  England v South Africa (1947) 201–4
  England v Australia (1948) 210–3, 216; *211*
  England v West Indies (1950) 224–6
  England v Australia (1953) 227–33; *228*
  England v Pakistan (1954) 235–7
  England v Australia (1955) 237–40
  England v Australia (1956) 248–52
  England v West Indies (1957) 258–61
  West Indies v Pakistan (1958) 262–3
  Australia v West Indies (1960) 269–71; *269, 271*
  England v West Indies (1963) 281–4
  England v Australia (1964) 287–91
  England v Australia (1968) *274*

England v Rest of the World (1970) 297–9
England v Pakistan (1971) 301–3
England v Australia (1972) 307–10
West Indies v England (1974) 310–5
Australia v West Indies (1975) 318–9
England v West Indies (1976) 319–21
England v Australia (1977) 322–5
England v India (1979) 334–7
India v England (1980) 338–40
Australia v New Zealand (1981) 340–1
England v Australia (1981) 346–55
Australia v England (1982) 359–62
West Indies v England (1985) 371–4
Australia v England (1986) 378–80; *377*
Thomson, J. R., 359, 361
Thornton, C. I., 104
   obituary 139–40; *139*
Titmus, F. J., 283, 289, 290
Todd, L. J., 168
Toshack, E. R. H., 199, 207
Townsend, C. L., 35, 40, 113; *36*
Trott, A. E., 44, 59, 73, 85, 309; *73, 86*
Trueman, F. S., 185, 228–9, 275, 283; *184*
Trumble, H., 75, 76
Trumper, V. T., 75, 76, 78, 79, 82, 357
Tuckett, L., 201, 202
Tunnicliffe, J., 46, 151; *46*
Turner, G. M., 327, *328*, 357–8; *358*
Tyldesley, J. T., 59, 76, 78, 82, 84, 89, 90
Tyldesley, R., 14, 148
Tyson, F. H., 185, 237, 238, 239, 324; *237*

Ulyett, G., 17, 105
Underwood, D. L., 312, 320, 339

Valentine, A. L., 225, 226, 259, 270, 309; *256*
Valentine, B. H., 178, 179, 206
Van der Byl, P. G., 177, 178
Veivers, T. R., 288, 290–1
Veletta, M. R. J., 385
Verity, H., 153, 155, 156, 157, 158, 161, 174, 177, 178, 181, 183, 188, 259; *154, 184*
Viljoen, K. G., 177, 178, 202
Vine, J., 71, 99
Viswanath, G. R., 335, 339
Voce, W., *157*

Wainwright, E., 14–15
Walcott, C. L., 184, 226, 259, 374
Walker, H. N., *323*
Walker, P. M., 294
Walsh, C. A., 383
Walters, C. F., 160, 161
Walters, K. D., 324
Ward, A., 37, 110
Wardle, J. H., 224, 225, 233, 238; *184, 233*
Warner, P. F., 80, 117, 156; *116*
Washbrook, C., 198, 199, 201, 210, 212, 226
Waugh, S. R., 380, 385
Wazir Mohammad 262; *266*
Weekes, E. D., 184, 224–5, 357

Wells, J., obituary 98
Wensley, A. F., 142
Whitaker, J. J., 364–5
White, G. C., 89
White, J. C., 129, 177
Whitehead, H., 63; *64*
Whitney, M. R., 352, 353, 354
Wilkinson, L. L., 166
Willey, P., 320, 335, 347
Williams, F. S., 22
Williams, R. G., 192
Willis, R. G. D., 316, 347, 348, 351, 354, 361; *353*
Wilson, D., 297
Wilson, G. H. R., 27
Wilson, T. B., 94
Wisden, John 8–9, 10; *9*
Wodehouse, P. G., 54–5
Wood, A., 172, 174
Wood, B., 303
Wood, C. J. B., 63
Wood, G. M., 354
Woodfull, W. M., 148, 156, 158
Woods, S. M. J., 65, 221
Woolley, F. E., 59, 195, 272, 324; *195*
   obituary 332–4; *332*
Woolmer, R. A., 320, 321
Worrell, F. M., 184, 224, 259, 260, 270, 284, 288, 320; *282*
Wright, D. V. P., 168, 178, 179, 181, 182, 199, 201, 202, 203, 205, 206
Wright, J. G., 341
Wyatt, R. E. S., 156, 157, 160, 162
Wyld, F., 17–18
Wynyard, E. G., 55, 170

Yallop, G. N., 347, 353, 354; *353*
Yardley, N. W. D., 199, 203, 211, 337
Young, A., 129
Young, J. A., 212

Zaheer Abbas 279, 301, 302, 329, 345; *301, 305*